D1074200

War of Extermination

Studies on War and Genocide

General Editor: Omer Bartov, Rutgers University

Volume 1

The Massacre in History
Edited by Marl Levene and Penny Roberts

Volume 2

National Socialist Extermination Policies: Contemporary German Perspectives and Controversies
Edited by Ulrich Herbert

Volume 3

War of Extermination: The German Military in World War II, 1941–1944
Edited by Hannes Heer and Klaus Naumann

Volume 4

In God's Name: Genocide and Religion in the Twentieth Century
Edited by Omer Bartov and Phyllis Mack

War of Extermination

The German Military in World War II, 1941–1944

Edited by

Hannes Heer *and* Klaus Naumann

Berghahn Books

New York • Oxford

Published by

Berghahn Books

This edition is based on the original German edition, published as
Vernichtungskrieg. Verbrechen der Wehrmacht 1941 bis 1944.

Library of Congress Cataloging-in-Publication Data

War of extermination : the German military in World War II, 1941-1944 / edited by Hannes Heer and Klaus Naumann.
p. cm. -- (Studies on war and genocide ; v. 3)
Includes bibliographical references and index.
ISBN 1-57181-232-6 (alk. paper)
1. Germany--Armed Forces--History--World War, 1939-1945. 2. World War, 1939-1945--Atrocities. 3. Genocide--Germany--History--20th century. 4. World War, 1939-1945--Germany. I. Series. II. Heer, Hannes. III. Naumann, Klaus, 1939-

D757 . W2612 1999
940.54'1343 21--dc21 99-043734

British Library Cataloguing in Publication Data

A catalogue record for this book is available from the British Library.

Printed in the United States on acid-free paper.

Contents

Abbreviations

AA	Auswärtiges Amt (Foreign Office)
AK	Armeekorps (Army Corps)
AOK	Armeeoberkommando (Army High Command)
BA-K	Bundesarchiv Koblenz (Federal Archive in Koblenz)
BA-MA	Bundesarchiv-Militärarchiv Freiburg (Federal Archive, Military Section, Freiburg)
BarchP	Bundesarchiv Potsdam (Federal Archive in Potsdam)
BDC	Berlin Document Center
Berück	Befehlshaber des rückwärtigen Heeregebietes (Army Commander of the Rear Area)
Brig.	Brigade (Brigade)
BSA	Belorussian State Archive, Minsk
Btl.	Bataillon (Battalion)
Div.	Division (Division)
Div.Kdr.	Divisionskommandeur (Division Commander)
DRZW	*Das Deutsche Reich und der Zweite Weltkrieg* (The German Reich and the Second World War)
Dulag	Durchgangslager (Transit Camp)
EK	Einsatzkommando (Special Unit; a subunit of the Einsatzgruppen, the murder squads of the SS and SD)
FK	Feldkommandantur (Field Command)
FS	Funkspruch (Radio Transmission)
Geb.Div.	Gebirgs-Division (Division of Mountain Troops)
Gen.	General
Gen.d.Inf.	General der Infanterie (Infantry General)
GFC	Records of German Field Commands
GFP	Geheime Feldpolizei (Secret Field Police)
GG	Generalgouvernement (General Government; the German occupation rule of Poland)
GstA	Generalstaatsanwaltschaft, Frankfurt (Office of the

	State Attorney)
H.Dv.g.	Heeresdienstverordnung (Military Decree)
HAL	Historical Archive Latvia (Latvijas Vestures Archiv)
HGr	Heeresgruppe (Army Group)
Höh.Kdo.	Höheres Kommando (High Command)
HSSPF	Höherer SS- und Polizeiführer (Higher SS and Police Leader)
ID	Infanterie-Division (Infantry Division)
IR	Infanterie-Regiment (Infantry Regiment)
IWM	Imperial War Museum, London
IZ	Institut für Zeitgeschichte, Munich (Institute of Contemporary History, Munich)
Jg.Div.	Jäger-Division (Rifle Division)
Kav.	Kavallerie (Cavalry)
Kdo.Stab	Kommandostab (Command Staff)
Kdr.	Kommandeur (Commander)
KHA	Kriegshistorisches Archiv, Prague (Historical War Archive, Prague)
Korück	Kommandant des rückwärtigen Armeegebietes (Commander of the Army's Rear Area)
Kp.	Kompanie (Company)
KTB	Kriegstagebuch (War Diary)
MA	Militärarchiv, Podolsk (Military Archive, Podolsk)
MGFA	Militärgeschichtliches Forschungsamt (Office for the Study of Military History)
NA	National Archives, Washington D.C.
Nbg.Dok.	Nürnberger Dokument (Nuremberg Document)
NCO	Non-Commissioned Officer
NKVD	Narodnyi Kommissariat Unutrennykh Del (People's Commissariat of Internal Affairs)
NSDAP	Nationalsozialistische Deutsche Arbeiterpartei (National Socialist German Workers Party)
OB	Oberbefehlshaber (Supreme Commander)
ObdH	Oberbefehlshaber des Heeres (Supreme Commander of the Army)
Offz.	Offizier (Officer)
OFK	Oberfeldkommandeur (Supreme Field Commander)
OK	Ortskommandantur (Local Command)
OKH	Oberkommando des Heeres (High Command of the Army)
OKW	Oberkommando der Wehrmacht (Supreme Command of the Armed Forces)
OT	Organisation Todt

POW	Prisoner of War
PRO	Public Record Office, London
Pz.AOK	Panzerarmeeoberkommando (Armored Army Command)
Pz.Div.	Panzerdivision (Armored Division)
RAC	Rear Area Commands
RFSS	Reichsführer SS
Rgt.	Regiment
RKO	Reichskommissariat Ostland (Reich Commissariat of the East)
RKW	Reichskuratorium für Wirtschaftlichkeit (Reich Economics Commission)
RSHA	Reichssicherheitshauptamt (Reich Security Main Office)
SA	Sturmabteilung (Storm Troop)
SD	Sicherheitsdienst (Security Service)
Sich.Div.	Sicherungs-Division (Security Division)
Sich.Reg.	Sicherungs-Regiment (Security Regiment)
SIPO	Sicherheitspolizei (Security Police)
SK	Sonderkommando (Special Force)
SS	Schutzstaffel (Elite Guard)
Stalag	Stammlager (Base Camp)
Tgb.Nr.	Tagebuch-Nummer (Diary Number)
TMWC	Trial of Major War Criminals before the International Military Tribunal
TWC	Trial of War Criminals before the Nuremberg Military Tribunal
WBO/WR	Wehrmachtsbefehlshaber Ostland/Kommandant Weißruthenien (Commander of the Armed Forces in Ostland/White Ruthenian Commandant)
WFSt	Wehrmachtsführungsstab (Armed Forces Command Staff)
WiStabOst	Wirtschaftsstab Ost (Economic Staff East)
WVHA	Wirtschaftsverwaltungshauptamt (SS Economic Administration Main Office)
ZSA	Zentrales Staatshistorisches Archiv, Riga (Central State Historical Archive, Riga)
ZSt	Zentrale Stelle (Main Office)
ZV	Zivilverwaltung (Civil Administration)

Abbreviations for Command-Level Staffs of the Army

Ia	Führungs-Abteilung (Command Staff)
Ib	Quartiermeister-Abteilung (Quartermaster Staff)
Ic	Feindaufklärung und Abwehr; geistige Betreuung (Enemy Intelligence and Defense; Political Education)

Preface

Among the many benefits of the end of the Cold War has been the boost it has given to research on World War II and in particular on the behavior of the Wehrmacht in the occupied Eastern territories. Archives that had hitherto not even been known to exist were opened up and found to contain materials that permitted a much more careful and extensive reconstruction than had been possible before of the way the war was conducted at the grass-roots level and of the devastation the Germans unleashed on millions of innocent people.

The articles and photographs published in this volume represent a selection from this fresh research, a longer version of which—also edited by Hannes Heer and Klaus Naumann and titled *Vernichtungskrieg.*[1] *Verbrechen der Wehrmacht, 1941 bis 1944*—appeared in 1995. The photos, collected by the Red Army and held in the Russian State Archives in Moscow, had been taken from killed or captured German soldiers who had kept them as souvenirs in their wallets. A good many of them depict truly shattering and depressing scenes of summary executions and atrocities perpetrated by the Wehrmacht in the East. A much larger selection from the Moscow collection and other sources subsequently formed the basis of the Wehrmacht Exhibition, organized by the Hamburg Institute for Social Research, that first toured major German cities, causing plenty of controversy. The exhibition was prevented from coming to the United States as scheduled due to another flare-up in the controversy. The photographs and the large amounts of written documents that are now available to us raise many daunting questions about the how and why of Nazi Germany's genocidal policies in which the Wehrmacht was deeply involved. The essays in this volume make a major contribution to answering these questions.

However, apart from the historical reconstruction of what happened and why, there is also the historiographical question of why it has taken so long for the terrible truths about the warfare in the

Notes for this section begin on page xviii.

East first to come out and then to become accepted by a wider public, especially in Germany. One answer, to be sure, is that for a long time the archival base was quite slim and many materials that are cited in this volume were not yet available. At the end of the war, the Western Allies had captured tons of Nazi documents, some of which were presented at Nuremberg and other war crimes trials. They were subsequently microfilmed and could be purchased through Michigan Microfilms and other research outlets. By the mid-1960s, most of the files relating to the Wehrmacht had been returned to West Germany, first to the Militärgeschichtliches Forschungsamt (MGFA) in Freiburg whence they were later transferred to the Bundesarchiv-Militärarchiv (BA-MA), an archive specifically established to collect and recatalog Nazi documents and open them to systematic research.

But the story of these delays is no more than a partial explanation. Two much more significant reasons must be added if we want to understand why it took until the 1960s for a serious evaluation of the history of the Nazi Wehrmacht and its deeds to begin. In the absence of easily accessible documents in the early postwar period, research was initially dependent on the testimonies of individual participants. Generals and ordinary soldiers from the Eastern front who had avoided capture and long-term internment in Soviet camps came forward, privately within the family circle or publicly, to give their memories of what they had seen and experienced. Their tales were invariably escapist. They had all done no more than to fight valiantly and honorably for their country to stem the tide of Soviet communism. If there had been war crimes, they had been the work of Heinrich Himmler's SS. Many claimed that they had not even witnessed anything incriminating but had merely fought a "clean" war at the front.

The Western Allies unwittingly contributed to this interpretation when they asked former generals to talk or write about their experiences. This was the beginning of the Cold War and the military confrontation with the Soviet Union, so they were most interested in gathering information on the strategies and combat practices adopted by the Germans and Russians in their deadly struggle in the East. Rarely would interviewees be questioned more closely about war crimes, and so it was easy for them to plead ignorance.

By the 1950s and with the Cold War at its height, Allied pressure to rearm newly established West Germany reinforced the tendency to sweep the criminal aspects of Wehrmacht behavior and memory under the carpet. Realistically, the Bundeswehr could not be built up without the expertise of former Wehrmacht officers, and so the new armed forces were vitally interested and heavily involved in spinning out the early postwar narratives of a Wehrmacht that had kept away from politics and Nazi racist ideology—that had concentrated on fighting a decent war with traditional means. Memoirs like Erich von Manstein's *Lost Victories* became bestsellers.[2] Its title gave the story away: It had been Hitler's dogmatism and constant interference with the strategic plans and operational decisions of the professionals that had cost Germany its victory against Stalin. Manstein's book, like many others, was totally unreliable, and if we had in 1945 known about him and many of his comrades what we know today, there may well have been more executions for war crimes.[3]

The notion of "Lost Victories," as promoted by former Wehrmacht officers and the new Bundeswehr, was complemented by powerful popular treatments of the war. Here the novels of Hans Helmut Kirst must be mentioned in first place.[4] Turned into films, the tales about the efficient but honest German soldier were seen by millions in the 1950s. We can only guess at the readership of countless *Landserhefte*, mass circulation pulp that was also marketed as adventure stories to West German teenagers who wanted to learn what their fathers—who had returned from the war battered and destitute—had achieved in the way of heroism. They would hear similar stories at *Stammtische* in village pubs where veterans would ramble on incoherently about how they had survived the tough fight in the East, their reputations untainted by SS atrocities.[5]

Early postwar trends in historical writing, ostensibly charged with an accurate reconstruction of the past, did little to counteract these discourses about the war—discourses that were no doubt very helpful in reintegrating the déclassé and alienated veterans into West German society and in stabilizing the parliamentary system of the Federal Republic.[6] Turning defeated, traumatized, and resentful ex-soldiers—many of whom had believed in Hitler's dictatorship—into loyal supporters of the postwar order and committed citizens in the confrontation with the Soviet Bloc was regarded as a vital task by most politicians. Historians contributed to this stabilization by cutting the Third Reich out of the mainstream of modern German history.[7] They portrayed the years 1933–45 as a period in which a small band of criminals had descended upon and terrorized the country and ultimately the whole of Europe, before they were defeated and the nightmare was made to disappear.

By the late 1950s, this patently apologetic view of the Third Reich, its origins, and its crimes had begun to be challenged. But a marked feature of these revisionist analyses was that they were heavily structuralist. As was widespread practice in the historical profession around the world at the time and supported by the social sciences, scholars concentrated on the organization of the Nazi regime, its bureaucratic structures and operations. It was very much a history "from above," criticizing an older Hitler-centric view, but still dealing with large-scale party organizations, propaganda apparatuses, administrative machines, and strategic elites within the overall system. The "functionalists" began to debate with the "intentionalists." This debate was enlivened and expanded by the revival of theories of fascism—developed by Marxist scholars as well as intellectual historians like Ernst Nolte—concerning the specific nature and dynamics of European fascism.They called into question the hitherto dominant paradigm of totalitarianism that had assumed that Stalinism and Nazism were modern terroristic dictatorships that were "basically alike."[8]

It is in this larger historiographical context that military history also began to change, moving away from conventional studies of campaigns and battles toward the study of the role of the German army in the Third Reich. To be sure, the focus was still primarily on politics and the maneuverings of the officer corps both as a power factor within the Nazi dictatorship and within an economy that was geared to rapid rearmament. The other key question that came to occupy a new generation of military historians was the impact of Nazi ideology on the Wehrmacht, both before and after universal service had been reintroduced in 1935.

The MGFA in Freiburg, under the scientific directorship first of Andreas Hillgruber and later of Manfred Messerschmidt, became the most important center in the Federal Republic where fresh research was undertaken on the basis of the files just returned from the United States and Britain. Some of these efforts—particularly the very ambitious multi-volume history of the armed forces during World War II, *Das Deutsche Reich und der Zweite Weltkrieg*—turned out to be more difficult than anticipated because of the large number of contributors whose approaches could not easily be reconciled.[9] Their often differing views on various aspects of the project were exacerbated by an interest that the West German Ministry of Defense, as the funding and supervisory authority of the MGFA, took in the study. However, such problems should not detract from the merits of other studies that resulted from the rethinking of military history during the founding years of the Freiburg Institute.[10]

The first book to be mentioned in this context is Messerschmidt's *Die Wehrmacht im NS-Staat. Zeit der Indoktrination.*[11] Other studies, e.g., by Klaus-Jürgen Müller, reinforced Messerschmidt's hypothesis that, far from being apolitical, the Wehrmacht increasingly became an integral part of the Nazi regime and its ideological aims.[12] Rather than keeping apart from the regime it promoted its own indoctrination with Nazism and thus became an instrument to be used for the imperialist *Weltanschauungskriege* that Hitler relentlessly prepared and, from 1939 onward, began to wage in the East.

It is against this background that generals like Manstein issued their blatantly racist orders that so shocked people when the orders were finally unearthed and republished in the 1970s. Meanwhile, scholars like Michael Geyer, by analyzing the evolution of the German army's total war doctrine, explained how the idea of absolute and terroristic warfare had become an integral part of the officer corps' thinking and ethos.[13] The pieces of the jigsaw puzzle were falling into place.

As the results of this research were gradually emerging in the 1970s, historical writing around the world took the decisive turn into social history and the "history from below." The quest was to retrieve the everyday life experiences of ordinary people, of those who unlike the elites had hitherto remained voiceless and invisible. The task was also to study their perceptions of the world. This shift in research interests and methods sooner or later also began to influence military history, including the history of World War II. At the center of interest were now no longer the generals, but the rank and file. Although their books did not appear until the second half of the 1980s, this was the time when Omer Bartov at Oxford and Theo J. Schulte at East Anglia started their research during which they traced the experiences of individual units through the war and came up with fresh insights into the "barbarization of warfare."[14]

By the time Christian Streit published his book *Keine Kameraden*, about the mass murder of Red Army prisoners of war at the hands of the Wehrmacht, professional historians firmly accepted what Manstein and his comrades had denied and covered up, i.e., that the Wehrmacht had been deeply involved in the criminal and genocidal policies of the Nazi regime.[15] Even a scholar like Helmut Krausnick, the influential editor of *Vierteljahrshefte für Zeitgeschichte*, who in the 1960s had still resisted the emerging new picture of the Nazified army, now fell into line, publishing his *Truppe des Weltanschauungskriegs*.[16]

All this did not prevent *Keine Kameraden* from being given a very hostile reception in Bundeswehr circles and in the general public. The veterans of World War II were still in denial mode. They continued to see themselves as Kirst had portrayed them in his novels, and the uproar over *Keine Kameraden* was therefore considerable. However, critical research on the Wehrmacht had meanwhile been given collateral support from historians of the Holocaust. It is significant that this genre had begun in the 1950s in the same structuralist vein that, as we have noted, pervaded much of historical writing on modern Europe at the time. Work on the Jewish genocide was preoccupied with industrialized mass murder as an administrative phenomenon in the age of totalitarian dictatorships. Thus, Hannah Arendt in *The Origins of Totalitarianism* wrote about the lonely individual who helplessly faced anonymous bureaucracies, run by "desk murderers," mercilessly grinding their victims to dust.[17] Her *Eichmann in Jerusalem* then presented Europe's Jews as a people who had passively suffered their own slaughter.[18]

This hypothesis of hers so angered many scholars that they launched a whole host of studies that took a closer look at the Jewish response to Nazi persecution. They discovered more resistance and defiance in the face of torture and death than Arendt had ever imagined.[19] But in the course of retrieving the history of the victims at the grass-roots of Eastern European society, in the villages, towns, and ghettoes, they inevitably also came across the perpetrators and bystanders. The history of the Holocaust shifted from the bureaucratized mass murder in the camps to the everyday genocide that began in 1939 with the Nazi invasion of Poland and escalated with the attack on Russia in June 1941. These crimes took place in the forests and swamps in the rear areas of the Wehrmacht and in the administrative districts that the Germans had set up.

The research on "ordinary German soldiers" and "ordinary victims"—Jews, Slavs, and Gypsies—finally came together to produce work on the Nazi *Vernichtungskrieg*, some of which is collected in this volume. These essays raise difficult questions of how to explain that these ordinary men—often themselves family fathers carrying photos of their children in their wallets—became capable of taking infirm elderly Jews, whimpering kids, and their imploring mothers into the forests outside the hamlets of Poland, the Balkans, or the Soviet Union and shooting them one by one in the neck. Christopher Browning, Omer Bartov, and the historians represented in this volume have wrestled with this daunting question.[20] It would almost be a relief if, faced with these problems, we could accept Daniel Goldhagen's hypothesis that these ordinary men committed these atrocities because they were "ordinary Germans," driven by a deep-seated anti-Semitism and racist hatred that had a long tradition in Germany alone.[21]

Yet, Goldhagen's is probably an all too simplistic answer, judging also from the response to his *Hitler's Willing Executioners*.[22] Accordingly, the essays in this volume should be seen as a contribution to a continuing debate, not only on the character of German society and the structure of the Nazi dictatorship in the 1930s and 1940s, but also on what men (and it is primarily men) are capable of doing to fellow human beings and why.

—*Volker R. Berghahn*

Notes

1. The original German term *Vernichtungskrieg* can be translated either as "war of extermination" or as "war of annihilation." Throughout the various essays, authors often use these two translations interchangeably to refer to the same phenomenon.
2. Erich von Manstein, *Lost Victories* (Novato, CA: 1958, 1982).
3. See, e.g., Gerd Ueberschär, ed., *Hitlers militärische Elite,* 2 vols. (Darmstadt: 1998).
4. See, e.g., Hans Helmut Kirst, *Forward Gunner Asch* (Boston: 1956); idem, *What Became of Gunner Asch* (New York: 1964).
5. See, e.g., the forum on "The 'Remasculinization' of Germany in the 1950s" with contributions by Heide Fehrenbach, Robert G. Moeller, and Uta Poiger in *Signs* 24 (1998).
6. See, e.g., James M. Diehl, *Thanks of the Fatherland* (Chapel Hill: 1993); Norbert Frei, *Vergangenheitspolitik* (Munich: 1996); Frank Biess, *Protracted War: Returning POWs and the Making of East and West German Citizens, 1945–1955*, Ph.D. diss. (Brown University: 1999); Robert G. Moeller, ed., *West Germany under Construction* (Ann Arbor: 1997).
7. See, e.g., Ernst Schulin, ed., *Deutsche Geschichtswissenschaft nach dem Zweiten Weltkrieg* (Munich: 1989).
8. For a helpful summary of these debates, see Ian Kershaw, *The Nazi Dictatorship* (London: 1989). The hypothesis that modern totalitarian regimes were "basically alike" was put forward by Carl J. Friedrich and Zbiegniev Brzesinski in their *Totalitarian Dictatorship and Autocracy* (New York: 1956).
9. See Omer Bartov, "Whose History Is It, Anyway?" in this volume.
10. See, e.g., Volker Berghahn, "Das Militärgeschichtliche Forschungsamt" in *Geschichte und Gesellschaft* 14 (1989): 269–74.
11. Manfred Messerschmidt, *Die Wehrmacht im NS-Staat* (Hamburg: 1969).
12. Klaus-Jürgen Müller, *Das Herr und Hitler* (Stuttgart: 1969).
13. Michael Geyer, *Deutsche Rüstungspolitik* (Frankfurt: 1984), 98ff.
14. Omer Bartov, *The Eastern Front: German Troops and the Barbarisation of Warfare* (London, New York: 1986); Theo J. Schulte, *The German Army and*

Nazi Policies in Occupied Russia (Oxford: 1989). See also Omer Bartov, *Hitler's Army* (New York, Oxford: 1991).

15. Christian Streit, *Keine Kameraden. Die Wehrmacht und die sowjetischen Kriegsgefangenen, 1941–1945* (Stuttgart: 1978).
16. Helmut Krausnick und Hans-Heinrich Wilhelm, *Die Truppe des Weltanschauungskrieges: Die Einsatzgruppen der Sicherheitspolizei und des SD, 1938–1942* (Stuttgart: 1981).
17. Hannah Arendt, *The Origins of Totalitarianism* (New York: 1951).
18. Hannah Arendt, *Eichmann in Jerusalem* (New York: 1963).
19. See, e.g., R. Ainsztein, *Jewish Resistance in Nazi-Occupied Eastern Europe* (London: 1974); J. N. Porter, ed., *Jewish Partisans* (Washington, D.C.: 1982); I. Trunk, *Judenrat* (New York: 1972).
20. See, e.g., Christopher Browning, *Ordinary Men, Reserve Police Battalion 101 and the Final Solution in Poland* (New York 1992); Omer Bartov, *Murder in Our Midst* (New York: 1996).
21. Daniel Goldhagen, *Hitler's Willing Executioners* (New York: 1996).
22. See, e.g., Norman G. Finkelstein and Ruth Bettina Birn, *A Nation on Trial: The Goldhagen Thesis and Historical Truth* (New York: 1998).

INTRODUCTION

Hannes Heer *and* Klaus Naumann

On 26 July 1941 Franz Halder, Chief of the Army General Staff, noted in his War Diary a perplexing statement by his superior. Hitler had announced that "the Russian could not be defeated through operational successes, because he simply did not acknowledge them. Thus, he had to be broken bit by bit, in small, tactical outflanking maneuvers."[1] Was this already—one month into the campaign, and following the largest successful battles of encirclement in military history—an early admission of defeat? It did confirm that the fundamental concept of the "Barbarossa" campaign—destroying the bulk of the Red Army in the west and preventing its escape to the east—could not be realized. Hitler responded by pursuing encircling maneuvers, which pulled the German armies deeper and deeper into the Russian spaces.

By the fall of 1941 at the latest, it was clear that the second underlying assumption—that the campaign would be successfully concluded within four to five months—had been a miscalculation as well. Hitler was forced to postpone his stated objectives of conquering Moscow, Leningrad, the Donets Basin, and the Caucasian oil fields until the next year. On 7 November 1941 Halder noted that his Führer had remarked: "Beyond the Russian expanses, no plan at present." And on 19 November: "What objectives can be set for the next year must remain open."[2] It is tempting to interpret the scrapping of general operational concepts in favor of tactical maneuvers as a personal failing—Liddell Hart deems it "indecisiveness"—and the constant shifting of war aims as the consequence of planning that was faulty from the outset, which Keegan dubs "inconsistency."[3] Although an already vast body of literature continues to

Notes for this section begin on page 11.

accrete evidence in support of such a view, it commits us to a conceptual vantage point from which events that played out in the east between 1941 and 1944 can be but inadequately apprehended. It is the standpoint of the professional military elite with its concepts of strategy and tactics, defense and offense, war and peace.

Hitler thought in different terms. Consequently, he must be judged by different standards. It may well be that his "improvised war plan"[4] and disdain for operational planning does not so much evince the failure of a strategy as imply a totally different conception of how war should be waged. A surprising historical parallel confirms the validity of this supposition. Hitler's behavior during the planning and execution of the attack on the Soviet Union is reminiscent of Ludendorff's famous "breakthrough" on the Western front in the spring of 1918. When queried by a commander as to the basic idea of the planned operation, the strong man of the Oberste Heeresleitung (Supreme Command of the Army) replied: "I reject the word 'operation.' We'll tear open a hole. The rest will take care of itself."[5] Of course, this attempt to reverse the fortunes of war failed. In a subsequent evaluation of this last great offensive, General Wilhelm Groener, provisional Defense Minister of the Weimar Republic, wrote that Ludendorff lacked any strategic overview and tried instead "to achieve victory by brute force."[6]

To construe the use of force not as the option of last resort but as the conceptual starting point and guiding principle of any military action is to grasp the essential element in Ludendorff's "total war." The concept arose as the result of a double failure: the collapse of Schlieffen's grandiose plan marked the failure of both the "holistic"[7] kind of military thinking dating back to Clausewitz and the attempts of conservative politicians to wage a major war within the structures that had regulated social hierarchies and work in the nineteenth century. Unlike his predecessors, Ludendorff recognized that the requirements for waging war had changed in the twentieth century and that the most important requirement was that the boundaries separating military organization and civilian society be collapsed. From that he drew radical conclusions in that he organized military force according to the rational methods of capitalistic production, made its application dependent on the human and industrial resources at hand, and discovered the possibility of compensating for the enemy's material advantage by mobilizing combat morale.

Heightened combat morale could be achieved only by "unifying the people" and by reconsecrating the war as a struggle between antagonistic cultures and systems of values, ultimately as a decisive struggle of competing peoples for "survival."[8] Such a fusion of battlefield and home front emboldened the military to escalate the war beyond anything permissible under any international rules, for example, by waging unrestricted submarine warfare. In such a coordinate system, war was no longer the servant of politics but had subjugated politics to itself. Strategy had lost its military and instrumental character. Its function was no longer to organize battles but to guarantee "total mobilization."

Ludendorff improvised his program for effectively organizing violence and for optimally mobilizing the propensity for violence in the midst of a war. He had only two years in which to realize it. Hitler began implementing his program in peacetime, and he had six years in which to put it into effect. In doing so, he adopted—and radicalized—the central maxims of his great role model.[9]

First, he lifted war's temporal restrictions and made it permanent. This occurred not merely thanks to the then widespread view that the lost war had been but the opening round and that it was now necessary to prepare for a new war, but reflected a quite fundamental shift in thinking. Since the course of life was guided by the natural laws of the rights of the strongest and the eternal selection of the fittest, war was to be regarded both as the "highest expression of the life" of a people and as a nation's only chance for survival.

Second, Hitler did not identify the enemy based on the rivalries of the past war but in terms of an overarching antagonism reaching far back into history, which had assumed a new and hazardous urgency through the circumstances of Germany's defeat and the victory of the Russian Revolution. History's "cancerous lesion" was the Jews; its most extreme manifestation was Bolshevism. Exterminating those "world polluters" and forcefully appropriating living space in the east were necessarily the sole aims of any future appeal to arms.

Third, Hitler declared that all constraints on a war deriving from international agreements or existing morality to be null and void, hence not binding. The struggle against the racial enemy and for living space must, and might justifiably, be waged by any means—even the "most inhumane." Since such a war would serve to preserve the German people, it was a "just war."

Such were the programmatic pronouncements by which Hitler transcended Ludendorff's "total war" and formulated his concept of a war of annihilation.

This model of politics as war arose in a society, and encountered a society, that had recent experience with extreme violence. Violence had first erupted as revolution and counterrevolution, in military campaigns both within and beyond the Reich's borders. But it also continued to operate within the body politic of the Weimar Republic after things had settled down. Michael Geyer has described the way in which the experience of war was assimilated: "The dead did not rest because the living carried death around inside them."[10] The survival strategies of those who escaped the war existed as a flight into fantasies of coldness and body armor, into the daydream of the nation as—here we must supplement—a continuum supplying warmth. Helmuth Lethen has pointed out that these escape mechanisms reflected the replacement of a culture of conscience with a culture of shame. Once hitherto valid ethical norms had been rent like a garment in the craters and mass graves of the war, once the "primal man" (Freud) beneath had been exposed to view, the very concept of a self-controlling individual guided by conscience was discredited. External authorities assumed the task of regulating behavior, formulating such concepts as honor, dignity, and style as behavioral norms. Self-esteem became from then on more important than self-knowledge.[11] All these reactions to the trauma of defeat were constructions of an overtaxed ego and of a collective grown numb in its silence. The postwar period had embraced an entire generation as a kind of "self-made prison."[12] A parallel process seems to have impregnated the younger generation with similar experiential models. Economic inflation and depression were experienced—much as death or being wounded in the trenches had been—as disintegration and deformation.[13] Hitler and his movement clearly succeeded on two fronts: they helped produce the cultures of flight and blew up the "self-made prison" that underlay them. The fuse they lit could easily have been the proposition: "Overcome death by killing."[14] It was the seduction by totalitarianism of which Hannah Arendt has spoken: "The iron band of terror ... [and] the 'ice-cold reasoning' appears like a last support in a world where nobody is reliable and nothing can be relied upon." In this way those in power prepared their followers for the worst.[15]

The years 1933 to 1939 were spent pursuing National Socialism's goal of making war the project of the entire society. Because the movement had come to power not through a putsch but through a parliamentary process, civil war did not have to be fought to a bloody conclusion. On the contrary, it was possible to eliminate all opposition quasi-administratively with the aid of a hijacked bureaucracy. The chaos of international politics, which had not produced a new order but was in the process of establishing an order based on bitter rivalries and aggressive ventures,[16] could be exploited to overturn Versailles and set the stage for a revisionist settling of accounts across the board. In the early years of the regime, violence hid behind institutional and legal masks even in stripping Jews of their rights and ostracizing them. Foreign policy maneuvers were at best covert preparations for aggression. At the same time, there could be little doubt that a general orientation toward war was underway. Early on, soon after Hitler took power in January 1933, the foundation was laid for a Wehrmacht freed from numerical restrictions that would be capable of defending Germany within four years and ready to wage an offensive war four years after that.[17] At the same time—looking far ahead—moves were underway to undermine the homogeneity and independence of the professional military elite, such as dismantling the barriers separating the military from National Socialist society through restricting membership in the Wehrmacht to "Aryans" and implanting elements of charismatic leadership into a hierarchically structured organization through having the troops swear loyalty to Hitler personally.[18] Paralleling this program of institutional military readiness, a mobilization of militaristic values was taking place designed to establish the martial spirit as the primary social virtue and thus transform the national community into a military community. The essentials of these campaigns, which steadily intensified over six years, consisted in propagating the right to military preparedness, the right to exact revenge, the right to conquer living space, and the duty to sacrifice one's life for *Volk* and *Führer*. Those millions of young men who had grown up under National Socialism and who, in Hitler Youth or Naploa Schools, had been trained to kill were prepared to fight for those principles unconditionally. This was a cohort of young barbarians who merely waited for the "Führer" to call upon them.[19]

Given Hitler's self-image, the war for which he began preparing on the day he took power could only be a war of annihilation, which is to say that it would end with the extermination of "Jewish Bolshevism" and the final occupation of the agriculturally and industrially developed parts of Soviet territory. That the war would also be exploited to bring about the extermination of the Jews of Central Europe was clear, even though the methods were unclear. In that sense, it is correct to call the war in the east Hitler's "real war" and view it as breaking out in 1941.[20] The armed attacks on Poland, France, and Scandinavia served only as logistical, economic, and political preparatory steps rounding out the earlier, successful annexations that had not resulted in armed conflict.

In the so-called "criminal orders" antedating the campaign, the Wehrmacht's victims were clearly defined. Commissars were to be shot, war prisoners were deprived of their protected status under international law, the civilian population, as suspected partisans, was made subject to the terror of the occupying forces. Jews, of course, were handed over to the Einsatzgruppen (special task forces), but the Wehrmacht was informed about every stage in the extermination program and took upon itself the task of organizing its prologue. The Einsatzgruppen were expected to complete the extermination of the Jews—just as the civilian administration was to physically decimate the Slavic peoples—following the military campaign, which was expected to be brief. When that expectation proved false, the extermination program was immediately set in motion with the Wehrmacht extensively involved.[21] The upper echelons had already accepted the original definition of the Wehrmacht's mission because a broader definition of war promised a corresponding enhancement of their scope of action and prospects for success. For some, that overcame existing misgivings. The leadership corps of the Wehrmacht supported this radicalization of the program because, haunted by a "traumatic fear of Bolshevism," they either considered every means that promoted its destruction justified,[22] or they were rabid anti-Semites, whereby the older officers were driven by resentment and feelings of revenge while the younger ones were enthusiastic about Nazi ideas of breeding and selection.[23] The mentalities of a majority of the rank and file differed less and less, as the war progressed, from the contingents that operated under Himmler's command. A specific policy of intervention on the part of Hitler and his military command staff, along with the inner dynamic of the war of annihilation, had contributed to that.[24]

Upon analysis, the orders establishing the general principles for "Operation Barbarossa" are remarkable in that, throughout long passages, they are not so much military orders in the sense of directives, rules, and sanctions as primers on how to argue the case. The number of these "orders" increases as the original list of enemies expands and people are targeted for the bullet in the neck or the flamethrower who, according to traditional standards of Western morality, should have been exempted from excessive violence—the ill, the old, women, and especially children. The majority of the rank and file seems to have adopted these orders because it was only the total image of the enemy, radicalized by racist megalomania, that appeared to conform to the realities of a war that knew no restraints. Habituation, propaganda, and isolation—as Omer Bartov's studies have clearly shown—contributed their share to establish genocide definitely as an integral part of this war.[25] What began as the erosion of the culture of conscience immediately after World War I and was nurtured by the *völkisch* and racially defined ethics of National Socialism, now bears fruit. The last vestiges of civilized inhibitions and personal shame are brushed aside; an extermination morale is produced that is far more radical than Ludendorff's combat morale. Hitler not only required that in order to defeat the Soviet enemy. It was also indispensable, as he had already stated before the Russian campaign, for the next and ultimate stage in his global design—the struggle against England and the US.[26]

But there was also an inner dynamic to the war of annihilation that helped produce such a mentality and required no external intervention. By the summer of 1942 at the latest, the war in the east, which had subsisted from the very beginning only on improvised plans, was fragmenting into a multiplicity of fronts, a residue of operational movements back and forth, as well as into a stationary partisan war. The partisan war especially needs to be studied as a general phenomenon of the war of annihilation, which not only is not governed by military logic but obeys the impulses of a policy driven by instinct. The message to the unconscious that we have translated as "overcoming death through killing" now assumes concrete form. A member of the armed forces may now wage all the wars that he has always yearned to wage—against women, against Jews, against children and old men, against his own fear, and against his own conscience. They are now delivered into his power in the guise of "gunwomen," "Jewish partisans," "informants," and "the son of a bitch within" (*innerer Schweinehund*). The "you should" is now complemented by the "you may."[27]

Wolfgang Sofsky has drawn upon Elias Cannetti's concept of the pack in an effort to more precisely define war as a form of violence. A pack, as he defines it, acquires cohesiveness by persecuting an opponent, who is usually inferior. The fascination that a pack holds for its members and its exaggerated violence directed outward derive primarily from the fact that the pack has no conscience. "It liberates the individual from moral restraints. It is a social movement that makes it possible to kill without feeling guilt."[28] It experiences its greatest thrill in the excesses of the massacre. Hitler's war of annihilation knew the dynamic just described, and exploited it. The human hunts and massacres that characterized the war against partisans followed an order of battle in which, as the combat reports show, the victor was known from the outset. Converting a normal war's even odds of killing or being killed into an absolute certainty that one will only kill cancels competition as war's internal principle. It was for that reason that killing without being killed very quickly became a standard component in the training of new recruits. Before young soldiers were sent to the front, they were permitted to confront death triumphant.

Wars of annihilation tend to produce and perpetuate this asymmetry, which is intended to replace the peacemaking that follows a normal war. In reality, however, establishing this radical imbalance succeeds only occasionally. That has to do not only with the fact that the degree of violence employed radically increases enemy resistance. There is clearly inherent in the degree of violence employed a potential for self-destruction that was operative long before the Wehrmacht suffered defeat. Ernst Jünger, who visited the front in the Caucasus in late 1942 and early 1943 in order to gauge the reality of his fictional characters—soldier-workers and death-dealing machine gunners—no longer recognized his fantasies or his war. He encountered only robots and a world of indifference. "The human being feels as if he is stuck in a huge machine that permits only passive participation.... The human being has arrived at the point that Dostoyevsky described in *Crime and Punishment*. He sees his fellow human being as an insect. And he must defend himself against the insect lest he himself become enmeshed in the sphere of insects. The old, monstrous 'this is you' applies to him and his victims."[29]

* * *

When the war ended, the rear-guard actions began. The OKW (Supreme Command of the Armed Forces) had already put the word out in its last situation report of 9 May 1945: "Our unique performance at the front and at home will ultimately be appreciated in a future, just judgment of history .... Every soldier can, therefore, lay down his arms with honor and pride." The battle over memory had been joined, and it appeared to be more successful than the course of the war itself. "The greatest victory of the German army," wrote Omer Bartov, "was won on the field of politics, where it managed to return from the most murderous military action in German history all but unscathed."[30] Yet this controversy is not over, and one may doubt whether it will ever be. The Wehrmacht and memories of the war remain a subject still sensitive enough to mock any efforts to bring the matter to a close.

Memories of the war were not hushed up after 1945. Postwar trials, debates over amnesty, investigations, and controversies over the rearmament of the Federal Republic provided occasions for discussion.[31] Through the media of the postwar decades flowed an endless stream of "factual reports," illustrated novels, memoirs both serious and self-exculpatory, dramatizations in plays, war movies, and novels. The "communicative silence" regarding the past existed between the lines; it was verbose rather than mute.[32]

In order to sketch the special circumstances surrounding the "politics of memory" in Germany after 1945, a retrospective on the years following World War I is helpful.[33] Where then war experience, stylized as myth, could serve as the background of anthropological visions, as lessons in "icy" behavior and antipolitical programs, a unique set of tensions developed after 1945. Of course, the "unblemished Wehrmacht" offered a licensed reservoir of memories, which met with broad approval in the context of the German contribution to collective defense. But that collection of memories was unsuited to provide meaningful interpretations of war experiences—a qualification that requires explanation.

Meaningful interpretations of individual experiences were displaced by pride in efficiency, competence, and strength, or shifted into the private realm of past experiences of comradeship in a community of men who had shared a common fate and survived—categories that were relevant to reconstruction and the economic miracle. Neither political nor antipolitical meaning could be generated from them; the interpretive scheme accommodated itself to an apolitical habit of personalization. War memories of this kind comprised the baggage for marching back into the civilian life of postwar society, which seemed to swallow up without a trace the violence of its origins.

Of course, the important point lies in the unexpressed ambivalences still inherent in diminished memory. However accurate the apolitical self-image may be—which is denied by historians such as Omer Bartov[34]—the vagabond memory of having participated in a war of annihilation remains. Even merely doing one's job, adapting, participating, or observing—not to mention actual involvement—sufficed to keep in motion the machinery of persecution and extermination—the war within the war. Even the discourse of normalization, which war memoirs have produced in abundance, did not provide escape from the dilemma posed by the complicity that results from having been a working part (*arbeitsteiliger Täterschaft*).[35]

The extreme and abnormal circumstances of war—violence and death, injury and dying, discipline and arbitrariness, euphoria and desensitization, intense emotions and boredom, affection for one's homeland and alienation—are recalled as exceptional circumstances. And it is precisely the uniqueness of an experience far removed from the everyday that provides the key to its "normalization" in memory, a "normalization" that is all the more powerful because the norms of war do not belong to everyday experience—"it was just war." As far as German participation in, and memory of, World War II is concerned, this mechanism can only be described as a successful failure.

Certainly that peculiar, half-frightening, half-enticing extraterritoriality of the war experience existed, and continues to exist, in everyday memory. And doubtlessly the plurality of wars included in the war of annihilation favors a considerable and, taken on its own terms, legitimate range of variations in individual memories. And yet when the "German war" of the twentieth century is remembered, a deceptive gray area remains. The feeling of emptiness is fed by two sources, first, from the experience of the senselessness of the war, and second, from the annihilative quality of a war that was different from others that had preceded it. Its senselessness has been eloquently lamented; large quantities of postwar literature are devoted to this subject—to the point of sentimentality over having been deceived, misused, and victimized. The second experience, however, has remained hidden, hedged about by cover memories, anecdotes, and projections, which often make use of the old models equating partisans with bandits. As soon as this background knowledge is summoned forth, nerves lie fully exposed. Even today.[36]

In taking stock of memory gone wrong, it is proper to speak of a lack of political morality, of an unwillingness to do penance, and of rhetoric designed to close the subject. And yet this is only one side of the issue. Lamenting sins of omission must not stop with the self. A final accounting must include also those groups of the Wehrmacht's victims who, as such, have had no names—Jews and partisans, war prisoners and the wounded, members of the civilian population and hostages, women and children. They are counted among the number of victims of the war of annihilation, but as special victims of a special group of perpetrators, they are absent from our memories. This volume is an attempt to change that as well.

—*Translated by Roy Shelton*

Notes

1. Franz Halder, *Kriegstagebuch*, ed. Hans-Adolf Jacobsen, 3 vols. (Stuttgart: 1962–64), 3:123.
2. Halder, *Kriegstagebuch*, 3:283, 295.
3. Liddell Hart, *Geschichte des Zweiten Weltkrieges* (Wiesbaden: 1970), 212; John Keegan, *The Mask of Command* (New York: 1988), 264.
4. Andreas Hillgruber, *Hitlers Strategie. Politik und Kriegführung 1940–1941* (Bonn: 1993), 362.
5. Rupprecht von Bayern, *Mein Kriegstagebuch*, 3 vols. (Munich: 1929), 2:372.
6. Jehuda L. Wallach, *Das Dogma der Vernichtungsschlacht* (Frankfurt am Main: 1967), 278.
7. Michael Geyer, "German Strategy in the Age of Machine Warfare 1914–1945," in *Makers of Modern Strategy*, ed. Peter Paret (Princeton: 1986), 528.
8. Erich Ludendorff, *Der totale Krieg* (Munich: 1936), 16, 87f.
9. Quotations from Hitler's *Mein Kampf*, cit. in Hans-Adolf Jacobsen, "Krieg in Weltanschauung und Praxis des Nationalsozialismus 1919–1945," in *Beiträge zur Zeitgeschichte. Festschrift für Ludwig Jedlicka zum 60. Geburtstag*, ed. R. Neck and A. Wandruszka (St. Pölten: 1978), 238ff.
10. Michael Geyer, "Das Stigma der Gewalt. Todeserfahrungen in Deutschland 1914–1945," lecture at the Hamburger Institut für Sozialforschung on 20 September 1994.
11. Helmuth Lethen, *Verhaltenslehren der Kälte. Lebensversuche zwischen den Kriegen* (Frankfurt am Main: 1994), 26ff.
12. Modris Eksteins, *Tanz über Gräben. Die Geburt der Moderne und der Erste Weltkrieg* (Reinbek: 1990), 434.
13. Elias Cannetti, *Masse und Macht* (Frankfurt am Main: 1985), 202ff.
14. Geyer, *Stigma*.
15. Hannah Arendt, *The Origins of Totalitarianism* (London: 1951), 477f.
16. Michael Geyer, "Krieg als Gesellschaftspolitik. Anmerkungen zu neueren Arbeiten über das Dritte Reich im Zweiten Weltkrieg," *Archiv für Sozialgeschichte* 20 (1986): 562.
17. Michael Geyer, "Militär, Rüstung und Außenpolitik. Aspekte militärischer Revisionspolitik in der Zwischenkriegszeit," in *Hitler, Deutschland und die Mächte. Materialien zur Außenpolitik des Dritten Reiches*, ed. Manfred Funke (Düsseldorf: 1976), 249.
18. Klaus-Jürgen Müller, *Armee und Drittes Reich 1933–1939* (Paderborn: 1989); Manfred Messerschmidt, *Die Wehrmacht im NS-Staat* (Hamburg: 1969).
19. Christian Schneider, Cordelia Stillke, Bernd Leineweber, *Das Erbe der Napola: Versuch einer Generationengeschichte des Nationalsozialismus* (Hamburg: 1996), 53ff.
20. Hillgruber, *Hitlers Strategie,* 362.
21. On the specific evolution of extermination plans, see Christopher Browning, *The Path to Genocide* (Cambridge, Mass.: 1992), 101ff.
22. Christian Streit, "The German Army and the Policies of Genocide," in *The Policies of Genocide*, ed., Gerhard Hirschfeld (London, Boston, Sydney: 1986), 8.
23. Hannes Heer, "Bittere Pflicht," in *Die Wehrmacht im Rassenkrieg*, ed. Walter Manoschek (Vienna: 1996), 125ff.
24. Hannes Heer, *Tote Zonen: Die deutsche Wehrmacht an der Ostfront* (Hamburg: 1999), 120ff.

25. Omer Bartov, *The Eastern Front 1941–45: German Troops and the Barbarization of Warfare* (London, New York: 1986); idem, *Hitler's Army* (New York, Oxford: 1991).
26. Halder, *Kriegstagebuch*, 2:283.
27. Jan Philipp Reemtsma, "Charisma und Terror," in *Materialien* 10 (1994): 9ff.
28. Wolfgang Sofsky, "Die Meute. Zur Anthropologie der Menschenjagd," in *Neue Rundschau* 4 (1994): 15.
29. Ernst Jünger, *Kaukasische Aufzeichnungen*, vol. 2 of *Sämtliche Werke* (Stuttgart: 1979), 459f.
30. Omer Bartov, "Brutalität und Mentalität: Zum Verhalten deutscher Soldaten an der 'Ostfront,'" in *Erobern und Vernichten. Der Krieg gegen die Sowjetunion 1941–1945. Essays*, ed. Peter Jahn and Reinhard Rürup (Berlin: 1991), 183.
31. Cf. Ulrich Brochhagen, *Nach Nürnberg. Vergangenheitsbewältigung und Westintegration in der Ära Adenauer* (Hamburg: 1994); Michael Schornstheimer, *Bombenstimmung und Katzenjammer. Vergangenheitsbewältigung: Quick und Stern in den 50er Jahren* (Cologne: 1989).
32. Cf. Hermann Lübbe, "Der Nationalsozialismus im politischen Bewußtsein der Gegenwart," in *Deutschlands Weg in die Diktatur*, ed. Martin Broszat et al. (Berlin: 1983), 329ff.
33. Cf. as an introduction Gottfried Niedhart und Dieter Riesenberger, eds., *Lernen aus dem Krieg? Deutsche Nachkriegszeiten 1918 und 1945* (Munich: 1992).
34. Cf. Omer Bartov, *The Eastern Front 1941–1945*.
35. Cf. Manfred Messerschmidt, "Das Heer als Faktor arbeitsteiliger Täterschaft," in *Holocaust: Die Grenzen des Verstehens. Eine Debatte über die Besetzung der Geschichte*, ed. Hanno Loewy (Frankfurt am Main: 1992), 166ff.
36. Cf. Klaus Naumann, *Der Krieg als Text. Das Jahr 1945 im kulturellen Gedächtnis der Presse* (Hamburg: 1998).

– *Chapter 1* –

THE CONCEPT OF THE WAR OF ANNIHILATION

Clausewitz, Ludendorff, Hitler

Jan Philipp Reemtsma

But then: "there is a more than ample lack of evidence that military men can be good and reasonable citizens."

—Martina (Arno Schmidt, *Evening Edged in Gold*)

The war of annihilation is a cultural phenomenon. It does not exist merely because war exists. A war of annihilation—that is to say, a war which is waged, in the worst case, in order to exterminate or merely to decimate a population, but likewise a war aimed at exterminating the enemy population capable of bearing arms, the opposing armies, and indeed also a battle of annihilation in which the aim is not merely to defeat or beat back the opposing army but to kill the enemy in the greatest possible numbers—all these forms of the war of annihilation, however widespread they may be in geographic space and historical time, are not historical inevitabilities.

The foregoing statement implies nothing about human nature—other than humankind's historically proven capacity to fight battles of annihilation and to wage wars of annihilation. But humans have not always used that ability, any more than they have always created monotheistic religions, states, or social welfare systems. Indeed, some examples show that people cannot make use of these capabilities at will, that is, without a sometimes time-consuming learning process.

Notes for this section begin on page 33.

Asking *how* a culture has acquired the ability to wage wars of annihilation is not quite the same as asking why other cultures have not done it. Indeed, in a certain sense, the questions are opposites. If I focus my inquiry on the cultural restraints on waging wars of annihilation, then I am implying that there is inherent, either in humans or in the nature of war, a tendency to annihilate, which from time to time has been successfully foiled or at least mitigated.

Zygmunt Bauman once wrote that the only way to find out the color of the lenses through which one has grown accustomed to seeing is to take them off. We do well to liberate ourselves from the notion that waging war so that it results in the highest possible number of deaths lies in the nature of war itself. It is a sign of our culture to wage war in this way. There is no "essence of war," and even the definitions of "war," "winning a war," or "fighting a battle" cannot be formulated independent of a specific culture. Influenced by our cultural habits, however, we find it hard to identify certain conflicts as "war" and thus give them special characterizations, which usually include the words "ceremonial" or "ritualistic." Through such turns of speech, we would like to stress that such wars are not "real" wars. Even the British military historian John Keegan, who has often pointed to the ritualistic elements in modern wars, feels compelled to assure us that the ancient Egyptians—however "ceremonial" their way of waging war, as we know it, may have been for hundreds of years—must have derived their ceremonies from an original war of annihilation: "Battle was certainly not ceremonial when fought against foreigners" just as he writes of the Aztecs that we know of their way of waging war only at a specific point in time: "it tells us only about the warfare of the Aztecs at the height of their power and not how they fought when they were struggling to achieve it. The probability is that they slaughtered those who opposed them, as all conquerors have always done."[1] But as Keegan writes in another passage, "[war] is always an expression of culture, often a determinant of cultural forms, in some societies the culture itself."[2] If we want to understand our culture, we must learn to understand it as one in which the concept of annihilation has become so much a given that we imagine that it lies in the very nature of things.

We seldom succeed in removing our cultural eyeglasses and looking at received truths with new eyes. Analyzing a cultural conflict offers us a chance to do that. For our purposes, the conquest of Mexico by the Spaniards is extremely revealing and at the same time *the* example of the collision of two cultures that were completely alien to each other. Less interesting is the fact that the Aztecs had a different way of waging war from the Spaniards. What is remarkable is that they were unable to change their way of waging war when to do so was literally a question of their survival. In this inability to learn a new way of waging war lies the open secret of why a force of 500 Spaniards succeeded in defeating Aztec armies numbering in the tens of thousands—the ability of the Spaniards to wage a war of annihilation and the inability of the Aztecs to acquire this skill in time.[3] For even if John Keegan is right in supposing that the Aztecs possessed this ability when they rose to power, they did not manage to recollect it when it was no longer merely a question of retaining their power but of simply surviving. That this fact strikes us as so implausible reveals to us how very much *our* assumptions about plausibility are bound to historically contingent circumstances. Thus it is that this encounter of two cultures, so catastrophic for one of the parties, is so revealing to the descendants of the victors.

The Aztec capital, Tenochtitlan—larger and more beautiful than any Spanish city, according to the conquerors—was literally reduced to ashes in seventy-five days of battle. Estimates of Aztec losses vary from between 240,000 and 1,000,000 (Cortés' figures) men, when one includes in the count those who died of starvation in the beleaguered city; women and children are not counted in any estimates.[4] The Aztecs captured and sacrificed around seventy Spaniards.[5] If one assumes that Cortés' fighting strength, after losses in earlier battles and the addition of troops, who had deserted from the Cuban governor Velazquez, was more or less back to his original five hundred, then seventy captured amounted to one seventh of his troops. If he had experienced a kill-to-capture ratio typical of two-sided battles of annihilation—especially those waged man-to-man and house-to-house—his losses would have far exceeded the number of his troops. If the Aztecs had *wanted* to fight a battle of annihilation, they *could* have destroyed the Spaniards. The number of prisoners they succeeded in taking provides evidence of that, despite any assumed superiority of the Spaniards and despite the huge losses the Aztecs suffered for each captive they managed to extract from the slaughter alive. Without Spanish leadership, the numerous Indian auxiliary troops would have fled, and the Aztecs would have—at least this time—preserved their power and saved their lives.[6]

In Europe, as the *Iliad* teaches, the war of annihilation is an old concept. But it has by no means been the sole determinant of how wars have been fought. The dominance of the concept of the war of annihilation is an achievement of recent history. In the ancient world, the enslavement of war prisoners always came into play and provided a constant motivation to take prisoners. Hannibal's massacre of wounded and captured Romans served extraordinary ends deriving from the fact that he was fighting a war while isolated in central and southern Italy. He had no access to any slave market and no possibility of guarding thousands of prisoners while simultaneously continuing to wage war. This should not be viewed as a "logic of war" but rather as the decision to follow in part the logic of a war of annihilation.

The same is true of the English king, Henry V, whose order to kill, or at least threaten to kill, prisoners taken in the first French assault at Agincourt was refused by the aristocrats among his men, and who had to rely on archers who were not sworn to uphold any caste-based code of ethics but had been recruited from among vagabonds and drop-outs.[7] The question of how great a role so-called material interests played is quite irrelevant. The issue is not a conflict between morals and self-interest, but rather the English knights' wanting to wage a different kind of war from the kind their king wanted to wage.

> The teacher of warfare, von Clausewitz, states correctly in his work *On War* ... that war is an act of violence by which one state aims to subjugate another to its will. In considering how to achieve that goal, Clausewitz thinks only of annihilating the armed forces of the enemy through battles and engagements. That has become an indisputable principle of waging war, and observing it has been the first task of leadership in a total war. What Clausewitz says about annihilation on the battlefield will always have a profound significance. General von Schlieffen expressed that fittingly in his foreword to the 1905 edition of Clausewitz's work. I can only underscore the point.

These are Ludendorff's words in 1937,[8] at a time when the concept of the war of annihilation had reached a level of dominance that it had not had in the foregoing centuries of European history. In the following pages, we shall consider this transformation—and how Prussian and German general staffs played the role of midwife in bringing it about.

Ludendorff was not alone in naming Clausewitz as the father of the idea that the battle of annihilation was the actual essence of war, and therefore, the father of the concept of the war of annihilation—although many have denied that the attribution is accurate. Nonetheless, it can hardly be disputed that the reception of Clausewitz's book *On War* contributed greatly to the increasing ascendancy of the concept of annihilation, and it is difficult to acquit the book entirely of a degree of responsibility for the influence it exerted. Born in 1780, Clausewitz was a soldier from the time he was twelve years old. He participated in the siege of Mainz, was taken prisoner by the French at Jena and Auerstedt, became Scharnhorst's bureau chief on his release, taught at the war academy in Berlin, opposed the politics of the Prussian government, which was too pro-French for his taste, requested his discharge, and entered Russian service. At Tauroggen he served as a negotiator and actively pursued the shift in coalitions. He made propaganda for an anti-French *levée en masse*. Accepted back into Prussian service in 1814, he soon served on the general staff, became director of the Berlin war academy, was promoted to brigadier/general and appointed to the Supreme General Staff, elevated to the nobility in 1825, and died of cholera in 1831. His unfinished work *On War*, published by his widow after his death, soon became *the* classic work on military theory and finds enthusiastic readers in all political camps.

On War is an attempt to systematize the collective experience of military strategists. The book avoids casuistic argument and instead is presented, in the philosophical fashion of the time, as an attempt at a systematic theoretical treatment. Clausewitz's effort to maintain the closed form of a deductive treatise conceals, however, the fact that his thoughts—like those of any good casuist—are contradictory. Thus, Clausewitz has been the scapegoat for a variety of very different consequences that others have drawn from his work. The fault does not, however, derive primarily from a lack of clarity in Clausewitz's work; on the contrary, the fault lies in his tendency to systematize where there is nothing to be systematized.

The most significant controversy among Clausewitz's interpreters revolves around whether Clausewitz propounded the theory that the only aim of war was the complete destruction of the enemy (and that everything else represented a forced distortion of that true war aim for political reasons), or whether war as an instrument of politics has only those goals that politics prescribes. Both views can be substantiated by passages from the text. In his essay, "Instrumentelle und existentielle Auffassung des Krieges bei Carl von Clausewitz,"[9] Herfried Münkler traces this controversy among Clausewitz's interpreters to changes in Clausewitz's political thinking that caused him, in his effort to create and preserve a unified theory, to vary the emphasis placed on a particular thought, when relating it to various other thoughts. Münkler, along with Raymond Aron, assumes that a break occurred in Clausewitz's thinking around 1827—the year in which he was elevated to the nobility. They argue that prior to 1827 Clausewitz's model was the Napoleonic strategy, "the doctrine of the decisive battle aimed at the destruction of the enemy,"[10] which, after 1827, had lost its "paradigmatic status in Clausewitz's theoretical edifice." The distinction between the Napoleonic and a different strategic concept is built into the distinction between "absolute" and "real" war. The Napoleonic strategy has been assigned a philosophic value—a significance—which no longer permits it to be taken sometimes as a model and at other times not.

"We said," writes Clausewitz in the second chapter of the eighth book entitled 'Absolute War and Real War,' "in the opening chapter that the natural aim of military operations is the enemy's overthrow, and that the strict adherence to the logic of the concept can, in the last analysis, admit of no other. Since both belligerents must hold that view it would follow that military operations could not be suspended, that hostilities could not end until one or the other side were finally defeated."[11] Of course, Clausewitz goes on, one seldom or never encounters war in this pure form,

> one might wonder whether there is any truth at all in our concept of the absolute character of war were it not for the fact that with our own eyes we have seen warfare achieve this state of absolute perfection. After the brief prelude of the French Revolution, Bonaparte brought it swiftly and ruthlessly to that point. War, in his hands, was waged without respite until the enemy succumbed, and the counterblows were struck with almost equal energy. Surely it is both natural and inescapable that this phenomenon should cause us to turn again to the pure concept of war with all its rigorous implications.[12]

Yet, with all his fascination with Napoleon and the Prussification of his model to "Immer-Feste-Druff" (Keep-Banging-Away), Clausewitz knows

> that our theory, though strictly logical, would not apply to reality. We must, therefore, be prepared to develop our concept of war as it ought to be fought, not on the basis of its pure definition, but by leaving room for every sort of extraneous matter. We must allow for natural inertia, for all the friction of its parts, for all the inconsistency, imprecision, and timidity of man; and finally we must face the fact that war and its forms result from ideas, emotions and conditions prevailing at the time—and to be quite honest we must admit that this was the case even when war assumed its absolute state under Bonaparte.[13]

And yet, after the great model of the period prior to 1827 has himself sanctioned our turning away from him, we read later in the text: "Theory must concede all this; but it has the duty to give priority to the absolute form of war and to make that form a general point of reference, so that he who wants to learn from theory becomes accustomed to keeping that point *(Richtpunkt)* in view constantly, to measuring all his hopes and fears by it, and to approximating it *when he can or when he must.*"[14]

One can cogitate long and in vain over this—especially over what the metaphor "bearing point" (*Richtpunkt*) is supposed to mean. For if one employs in such an important passage an unfortunate metaphor, one contradictory in its visual reference, then the underlying thought is unclear and contradictory. It has been debated whether "absolute war" is correctly understood as a "regulative idea" in the Kantian sense (as the means to systematize disparate phenomena) or merely as a "theoretical fiction ... which war would be if it were waged outside of time and space"; and however much the quoted passage seems to favor the plausibility of the first interpretation, we must also consider Münkler's view that this quotation belongs to an older textual layer while other passages, which were composed later, support the second view.[15]

The notorious formula according to which war is the continuation of policy is a consequence of turning the theoretician's attention from "absolute" to "real" war; it is, so to speak, the attempt to bring order among all those circumstances that turn absolute war into real war, the attempt to bring rationality back from the sphere of knowledge of the absolute into the realm of war that is merely real: "War plans cover every aspect of war, and weave them all into a single operation that must have a single ultimate objective in which all particular aims are reconciled. No one starts a war—or rather, no one in his senses ought to do so—without first being clear in his mind what he intends to achieve by that war and how he intends to conduct it. The former is its political purpose; the latter is its operational objective."[16] If the purpose is no longer the annihilation of the enemy, as dictated by abstract logic that dominates reality, then destroying the enemy becomes a matter of choice for the party waging war, and at this point the *instrumentalist* definition of war as an instrument of politics comes into play.

The existential concept of war, "which construes war not as an instrument of politics but as the medium constituting or transforming a political entity,"[17] is primarily found before Clausewitz worked on *On War*, at the time of his unbroken fascination with Napoleon and his simultaneous nationalistic hatred of France, which motivated him to renounce temporarily his loyalty to the Prussian king and enter Russian service. In Tolstoy's *War and Peace*, Clausewitz strides through the pages. At this stage there is talk of the "rebirth of the people in bloody and honorable struggle"[18] and the like. As Carl Schmitt has pointed out in his *Theorie des Partisanen*,[19] the model for such talk was the Spanish guerrilla war against French occupation, a war for national independence and, incidentally, also for the reintroduction of the Inquisition; the Spanish struggle served as a model for the bands of German irregulars during the first phase of the so-called War of Liberation, but also for the Prussian government at a certain point in time—1813, one year after Tauroggen and one year before Clausewitz rejoined the Prussian army. The Prussian government ordered its subjects to wage war against the enemy with weapons of all types, "hatchets, pitchforks, scythes, and shotguns are ... expressly recommended," and there was talk of a kind of self-defense "that sanctifies all means."[20] This proclamation was soon withdrawn, but it is worth noting.

One got a grip on oneself again and was successful with declaring "a people's war." A dozen years and one ennoblement later, Clausewitz' ideal was no longer the body of a nation newly forged in the cauldron of war but the sovereign Prussian policy of the future, which ultimately had become possible not so much *in* war as *through* war and the subsequent peacemaking and diplomatic agreements—and for which war should be and remain a dispositive. This is the context in which the man who was several times a member of the general staff said that war had its own grammar but not its own logic.

In reality, this sentence is so problematic because it is usually false. In Clausewitz's work, it is false because the distinction between absolute and real war had been imported not merely into the grammar but into the logic of the chain of reasoning, and its fundamental importance was confirmed anew by every qualification. The idea becomes dominant because, as the work's fundamental metaphor, it sculpts its physiognomy. Whenever a text which aspires to be philosophical posits something essential, true, absolute, an idea, a basic principle or tendency, a foundation or a goal that is desirable even if unattainable in opposition to the merely real—then it organizes itself around this center of gravity. Moreover, there is an obvious, rationalistic misconception. In Clausewitz' work, "politics," much like "war," acquires the reality of a cardboard cutout. Since its goals (the goal of war would be clear if politics did not exist) are not subject to debate, it can be assumed that those goals would be laid out "in reality" as precisely as required by the general staff in order to work out a plan for its campaign. As a rule, such is not the case and, in particular, politics changes when peoples clash.

The first war chronicled by our culture in such a way that we are able to cite how it was experienced in texts such as this was the

Peloponnesian War. It began as an instrumental war if there ever was one. We can use it to demonstrate two points: first, how erroneous the concept of an instrumental war is, and, second, that even the concept of an instrumental war is not a genuinely modern concept and is not inextricably linked to modern rationality, but can arise in disparate cultural settings. "Around the middle of the fifth century," writes Christian Meier,

> there arose in Greece a peculiar awareness of human capabilities, a distant relative of the modern concept of progress.... It was not the awareness of a protracted historical process but of the great possibilities of taking action and producing effects—possibilities that were available primarily to professionals, a small circle of well educated men. It was realized that the *téchnai* as a whole—that capacity to develop expert, methodological solutions to various problems—had progressed very far. Artists believed that they had achieved the ultimate possibilities in their art forms. Physicians were on the verge of inventing a new science.... Thinkers were beginning to map out entire social orders on the drawing board. Sophists were claiming that they could put their pupils in a position to achieve whatever they desired in both economics and politics.... The notion arose that there was no such thing as chance; chance was merely the excuse of people who had not calculated correctly. Thus Pericles decided that it would be possible to plan an entire war between Athens and Sparta.[21]

According to Pericles' plan of war, the Athenian population should retire behind the "Long Walls," the fortifications linking Athens and the harbor at Piraeus, and avoid a battle on land. In the meantime, the Athenian fleet was supposed to ravage the Peloponnesian coast and erect strong points from which lightning raids could be launched into the interior. In Pericles' judgment the war could not be lost because Athens had what it took to win a war—a plan and money. "The war plan represented a splendid example of human calculation: Apparently anything possible might occur—and Pericles knew that a war meant vicissitudes—without the chances of success being diminished. To that extent, chance had been calculated in."[22]

Meier identifies the fundamental error in Pericles' planning. He failed to take into account that populations at war are not mathematical values that remain constant. A hundred thousand people were supposed to settle behind the "Long Walls"—both temporarily and for the duration. The great "plague" of Athens broke out and also claimed Pericles. The problems that Athens soon faced resulted, however, not in growing despair but in that increasing radicalization in thought and deed of which Thucydides gives the following testimony: "'Foolish boldness' came to be considered a 'courageous devotion to the cause;' 'watchful waiting' became 'an excuse for cowardice.' 'Prudence' was a 'mask for unmanliness,' and a 'jack of all trades was a 'master of none.' Being 'beside yourself with rage' was posited as 'part of the human condition,' and 'thinking things over' to 'be on the safe side' was 'a glib excuse for a cop-out.' The lover of violence was 'semper if,' and the man who challenged him a 'subversive.'"[23] After a certain point, that was also true of the other side: "Pericles' strategy of attrition was born in peace. It led in fact to much dissension, devastation, supply problems, and other things that might have awakened resistance to the war. As soon as war came, however, rage inevitably resulted, the will to wreak revenge—the will to win."[24] Pericles shared Clausewitz's view that war was the continuation of policy, and neither he nor Clausewitz experienced what those born after them were forced to experience—that policy would become a continuation of war.

It was not Ludendorff in his work *Total War*, but, much earlier, Alfred von Schlieffen, head of the German general staff from 1891 to 1905, who explicitly cited war as the highest goal of policy; both referred to Clausewitz. This inversion of Clausewitz's aphorism is in fact a misappropriation of Clausewitz's text, albeit one which suggests itself. Here we must surely agree with John Keegan, who not only begins his *History of Warfare* with the sentence: "War is not the continuation of policy by other means"[25] but characterizes Clausewitz's work in general by saying: "... his philosophy of warfare was a recipe for the destruction of European culture...."[26]

It is precisely in the instrumentalist concept of war that the existential concept triumphs and turns instrumentalization around. "The instrumentalist concept of war is and remains linked to an unquestionably legitimate political order; this order defines the aims that war is the means to attain. The existential concept of war is different; here, too, war is certainly a means—not a means by which to pursue preexisting aims, but rather one which produces its own aims while it is in progress."[27] Now *every* war alters the political aim in pursuit of which it is unleashed, simply because war is the means by which the aim is being pursued. Strictly speaking, that is true of all means-ends relationships, because the complex of options from which this or that political decision is selected changes once the decision has been made. Every act transforms teleologically the preceding events. What was previously the subject of free choice is later the object of explanation as to why things had to turn out as they did. In the case of war, this is true in an especially dramatic way.

In Thucydides' case, this teleological deformation led to the establishment of historiography as a science, specifically in

Thucydides' distinction between the occasion of war and the cause of war. While the conservative Aristophanes in his *Acharnians* cites the accidental and trivial nature of the occasion of war to support his polemic against democratic war policy, Thucydides, historian and admirer of Pericles, uses that triviality as a reason to look for a deeper cause.[28] The underlying true cause *(alethestáte próphasis)* of the war, according to Thucydides, was the fact that the growing power of Athens had produced rivalry on the Peloponnesian peninsula and a growing tension that had to be released. The distinction between a mere occasion and an actual cause is so familiar to us that we readily overlook the fact that it conceals a risk: "The distinction between occasion and cause has always been admired and celebrated as one of the great insights of history as a discipline. And that is justified. And yet it requires interpretation according to the individual case in order to avoid the impression that freedom of political action did not exist and that the path to war was unavoidable."[29] Thucydides, in Christian Meier's view, not only defended Pericles' war plan "in a striking way"; he also, in marked contrast to Aristophanes, "relieves the first man of Athens of responsibility for the war. For if war was unavoidable, then the only question left was when and how it would begin."[30]

Thucydides has Athenian ambassadors legitimate the city's policy in this way:

> Because of that act we were constrained from the beginning to develop the empire into what it is today, under the influence, first, of fear; then of respect; and finally of gain. It also didn't seem safe to risk relinquishing our empire when most people hated us, when some rebellious cities had already been quashed, and when you were no longer the friends you once were, but had turned querulous and suspicious.... Faced with the greatest dangers, no one can be reproached for managing their interests well.[31]

Here one sees how conveniently the distinction between occasion and cause comported with the Athenian diplomats' self-justifications. But we also see that Thucydides is well aware of the fact that it was not Athens' position of power alone that determined its war policy, but that the initial hostilities also played a role. As the war went on, the cult of feasibility was gradually supplanted by talk about the absence of freedom and the nature of man, against which man was held to be powerless.[32] The Athenian diplomats justified Athens' claim to power on the grounds that this was part of human nature and hence, not open to discussion. Since the opponent could produce the same argument, war was unavoidable because it too was part of human nature. And, in fact, an absolute war as defined by Clausewitz: "One saw every imaginable kind of death, and everything that is likely to take place in situations like this did, in fact, take place—and even more."[33]

Clausewitz's adherence to the philosophical figure of absolute war as true war in contrast to a merely real war, which is the instrument of politics, has the same effect as the insight encapsulated in academic reasoning that the danger of reversing instrumentalization can never be banished. But we do not want to give the impression that we intend to refute one mystification with another. It is not that war itself unavoidably escalates to the level of annihilation; rather it is the case that, once the notion of annihilation rules over politics and minds, it is difficult to operate below annihilation's standards. Annihilation can then become as much a cultural pattern as so-called "ritualized" wars.

Chief of the General Staff von Schlieffen, whose foreword introduced the five editions of Clausewitz's collected works that appeared between 1905 and 1915, was charged, qua position and profession, with the task of designing a war scenario for the event that Bismarck's policy of alliances failed, indeed to plan for the eventuality that it would fail in the worst way and Germany would find itself in a two-front war against France and Russia. This was a political task. Schlieffen solved the problem by designing a plan for a war of *aggression* against France and Russia that involved overwhelming France first so that Germany could then turn all its forces against Russia. In order to make the second part of the plan possible, the first part had to be realized unambiguously: "Overwhelming" France necessarily meant the annihilation of the French army. France had to be rendered completely defenseless with one blow. Schlieffen planned the war against France as a single decisive battle of annihilation, and was able to cite Clausewitz: "Whatever the final act [in defeating an enemy] may turn on in any given case, the beginning is invariably the same—the annihilation of the enemy's armed forces, which implies a major victory and their actual destruction."[34] For Schlieffen, all of Clausewitz crystallized in this one thought.

Schlieffen's historical model was Hannibal's victory at Cannae. He meant to stage the entire French campaign as a single, gigantic Cannae, embracing the entire French army in a pincer movement, then encircling and "smashing" his opponent. The Schlieffen Plan does not interest us here because it was hypertrophic and demonstratively impracticable.[35] Nor are we concerned with its political and military "side effects." (Since geography required that one half of the "pincer" run through Belgium, thus violating Belgian neutrality, Great Britain, the guarantor of Belgian neutrality, was automatically drawn in as a third opponent).[36] What interests us here is the inversion of the instrumental relationship between policy and war. The original assignment—designing military measures for a political eventuality—was certainly not inherently offensive by nature. The result was an offensive plan that *had* to be implemented before the opposition set its own offensive plans in motion—put briefly, an assault. In order for it to succeed, the military plan in turn required that politics fulfill an "assignment"—finding the appropriate time for the attack, that is, creating a political situation that would justify the offensive.[37] This inversion of the relationship between politics and war is the result of thinking which follows the "Dogma of the Battle of Annihilation," as Jehuda Wallach called his excellent study of Clausewitz and Schlieffen. Germany's First World War generals did not free themselves from this kind of thinking even when Schlieffen's war plan proved to be an illusion;[38] it culminated in the military dictatorship under Ludendorff and Hindenburg in the years 1917 and 1918.

The idea of the battle of annihilation endemic in Western culture evolved in Schlieffen's sand table (he died in 1913) into the concept of the war of annihilation because Schlieffen combined war and battle in the notion of a single, large, outflanking and encircling maneuver culminating in wholesale slaughter. When the German generals found themselves confronted with the failure of this plan, and, as a result, with trench warfare, there was no turning back to conventional forms of planning and waging war, and no serious effort on the part of politicians to take control of the war. On 21 December 1915, General Falkenhayn suggested a new strategy to Wilhelm II. It consisted not in an attempt to change from trench warfare to a strategy of movement, but rather in the attempt to combine the reality of trench warfare with the notion of the battle of annihilation. In the Schlieffen Plan, only the opposing army had been the object of "smashing," that is, partial annihilation and complete disarmament; the object of Falkenhayn's annihilation fantasies, however, was a segment of the French population—an entire generation of men capable of bearing arms. The place that Falkenhayn had selected for the successive annihilation of human beings stretching over months was Verdun.

Falkenhayn calculated correctly that France would be unable to give up Verdun. The attack on Verdun was not designed to win territory, nor was it to lead to a classical decisive battle, nor was it even supposed to succeed in the traditional sense. Because they were unaware of this further evolution of the idea of the battle of annihilation, the staff officers who had to conduct the battle were left in the dark as to its aim. "On 26 May 1916, i.e., three months after the battle of Verdun had begun, Falkenhayn said during a conference of the army chiefs of staff near Mezière: 'It was never the aim of the Army High Command to take Verdun.'"[39] "Seldom in the history of warfare has a commander of a large army been so cynically deceived."[40]

The idea of forcing French troops to fight for a place that they had to hold at all costs for reasons of national self-esteem, but against an army that they were too weak to repel, rested, in Wallach's words, on a "gruesome concept":

> If the French took up the challenge, "the French army will be bled to death." *That was an entirely new concept in the history of warfare.* Until then commanders had tried to defeat the enemy by victory in one battle or in a series of battles.... Falkenhayn deviated from this method of waging war. His theory of "bleeding to death" rested on the assumption that the aggressors would always inflict heavier losses on their opponent in a protracted struggle than they would suffer in the same period. His goal was not to pass over to mobile operations or to achieve a breakthrough in the conventional sense, but to construct a gigantic "vacuum pump" with which to suck the blood out of the French. Later Falkenhayn habitually called the battlefield of Verdun the "mill of the Meuse."[41]

The metaphors speak for themselves. As we know, Falkenhayn's calculation—which Wallach quite fittingly calls "satanic,"[42] although it was again merely an adaptation, an expansion of Schlieffen's annihilation fantasies to fit the existing military situation—was wrong. Falkenhayn expected a casualty ratio of 5:2 to France's disadvantage. The actual number killed was 362,000 on the French side, 336,000 on the German.[43] And over and above the death toll was the fact that "the two opposing armies were never the same after they had passed through the 'mill of the Meuse.'"[44] "War," Kant once quoted a Greek as saying, "is an ill in that it makes more evil people than it takes away."[45] And because he was right, we find recollections of Verdun such as the following:

> For months the battle has raged
> In a semicircle around Verdun.
> Along the entire front rages the drumbeat of artillery,
> or put better,
> it howls like a heavenly hurricane,
> in which a single strike can hardly be heard.

Those lines were written in 1924 by Rudolf Heß.[46] In prose, the thought runs: "There must be something tremendous, colossal about dying. It may be that I tremble slightly at this memory, perhaps even at the feeling of inner happiness. It seems to me that a crown of thorns has today been pressed down upon my young, passionate life." The book from which these words are cited bears the title: *Der Glaube an Deutschland. Ein Kriegserleben von Verdun bis zum Umsturz* (Faith in Germany: Experiencing the War from Verdun to the Overthrow).[47] It appeared in 1931 with a foreword by Adolf Hitler. In 1945, the author, Heinz Zöberlin, as the leader of a werewolf unit, commanded an execution squad.

After Verdun, the enemy was no longer the opposing army but the opposing *society*. This shift is manifested in the declaration of unrestricted submarine warfare, as well as the attempt to destabilize Russia by supporting the Bolsheviks. The shift was especially visible, however, in the domestic political consequences brought on by the change in military leadership beginning in October 1916. Under Ludendorff and Hindenburg, Germany was de facto transformed into a military dictatorship. Politics became the servant of war not only in fact but openly and consciously. The war increasingly became what Ludendorff would later call "total." "The Law of Emergency Service to the Fatherland," wrote *Frankfurter Zeitung* on 2 December 1916,

> which affects the economic, social, and personal circumstances of the working *Volk* like no other, and which expands the military mobilization of August 1914 to the still more impressive mobilization of an entire nation, was accepted by the Reichstag today by a vote of 235 to nineteen. By this vote, the German people confirm through the mouths of their representatives the will to victory with which they entered into the war that was forced upon them, confirms their firm resolve to convert the will to victory into fact and bring the war to a quick and happy conclusion. It cannot fail to make an impression that no one other than the trade unions stressed that it was the law's high purpose that convinced them to support it. The law is a national act that will come to fruition only when its execution makes of the common task a joy for all participants.[48]

Ludendorff commented on the law's underlying concept (he believed that the law itself did not go far enough) as follows:

> The war imposed on us the duty to summon up and put at its disposal the ultimate in human capacity. Whether that occurred in battle, behind the front, for the war economy, or in other service in the home army or for the state, did not matter. As early as September 1916, the Army Supreme Command's first appeals, calling for the selfless mustering up of human capabilities, reached the chancellor. The Supreme Command argued with increasing resolve that in war the capacity of every individual belonged to the state, that therefore every German between the

> ages of fifteen and sixty had a duty to serve the state, and that the same duty to serve should also apply to women, albeit with some restrictions. Such a duty could be discharged by military service or by labor service—in the broadest sense—at home.... Introducing compulsory work for the war effort as obligatory service had the moral significance of placing every German in the service of the fatherland in these grave times, as was the case under the ancient Germanic legal system.[49]

Ludendorff saw the relationship of the Army Supreme Command to the government as follows: "The overall balance among army, navy, and home front [was brought about] by the Army Supreme Command in cooperation with the relevant agencies at home. Only the Army Supreme Command could come close to exercising overall supervision; even the Prussian Ministry of War had insufficient and only limited knowledge of the forces confronting the enemy and the necessities of war."[50] Since the "necessities of war" related to the entire population's duty to serve, these sentences mean that the Army Supreme Command now formed a de facto government.

The mobilization of the entire population for war—"the more the army demanded, the more the home front had to give"[51]—and Ludendorff's initially successful technocratic conversion of the national economy into a total war economy was linked to the ideology of "the struggle of peoples." Early signs of enforced ideological conformity can be detected. Not only politics, not only the economy—the entire population served to continue the war by any means, and the opponent's population as such was represented as the enemy. Michael Geyer writes about the Army Supreme Command:

> On the one hand, it diversified and expanded the understanding of what constituted a decision-oriented use of force by introducing indirect means of warfare against the morale and social fabric of the Allies. On the other hand, it dissolved the instrumental nexus between means and ends that had guided "idealist" strategy and the utilitarian approach to limiting warfare in the nineteenth century. The new "strategy" expanded war beyond the confines of the military institution and provided a rationale for national mobilization. Strategy lost its instrumental character and became both an explanation and legitimation for total war. The Supreme Command ended up with reinterpreting power politics in terms of racial or *völkisch* antagonisms. War became truly total once it was seen as an ideological and cultural clash (*Kulturkrieg*) between mobilized nations whose goal was national-racial survival through the subordination of other nations.[52]

The "breakthrough in the west" that Ludendorff and Hindenburg hoped to attain by abandoning Falkenhayn's strategy of slowly bleeding the enemy dry and putting their faith in the impact of brutal attacks—"I reject the word 'operation.' We'll tear open a hole. The rest will take care of itself."[53]—failed. On 5 April 1918, Rupprecht[54] wrote: "It is striking that, in all of the directives issued by the Supreme Command, it is impossible to discern an actual aim; they are always talking only about terrain sectors to be taken; and I have the impression that the Supreme Command is living from hand to mouth, so to speak....." Rupprecht also complained that, again and again, new offensives in new directions were ordered without allowing enough time for preparation. Unjustified haste in the face of the enemy's still organized front were characteristic of each series of steps taken. Despite dwindling ammunition and an inadequate re-deployment of artillery and assault troops, the new offensives were pushed ahead with a kind of mad vigor. "One gets the impression that somebody at Supreme Headquarters has lost his mind."[55] One can, circumspectly but surely, relate this breakdown in strategic thinking, which is only not perceived when success occurs despite the breakdown,[56] to the war's having become total. Schlieffen had already collapsed the distinction between a war's purpose and a war's goal, which, according to Clausewitz, were to be clearly distinguished and which, operating as distinct factors, produced a war plan—thus justifying Wallach's view that, as strange as it might sound, "Germany entered the war in 1914 without having a comprehensive war plan."[57] Once war is construed not as a struggle between armies but between peoples, then the war is over only when the enemy people as a people has been annihilated or at least rendered defenseless. That is connected to the notion of constant warfare, which moves struggle per se to the forefront of all thinking. If battle itself is the essential reality, then strategic concepts that view battle as a means subordinate to a war plan (which implies that one can use it or *not* use it) lose all significance.

Thus, in this last phase of the war, the struggle per se, killing became—at least in tendency—an end in itself. Nevertheless, the fact that the war was being lost—and that a major reason for its being lost was that it had "become total"—could not remain hidden.

> How was it possible that the more the nation invested in the war effort the less it achieved? The Third Supreme Command found an answer in blaming workers, homosexuals, and youth, and increasingly turning its own lack of comprehension of what was happening into venomous attacks against a "Jewish conspiracy" eating away at the vitals of the German army. Radical nationalists lost interest in even the most ambitious territorial goals as the war became for them a struggle for the liberation of the German race from evil. Germany began to cross over into an apocalyptic war.[58]

Part of this war was fought in Russia after the capitulation of 1918. Marauding German troops, cut off from chains of command and operating as armed bands, waged an anti-Bolshevik and racist mini-war on into 1919. "In 1919 and 1920, they carried their militant ideology and their *völkische* practice of war back to Germany."[59] "Between 1941 and 1943, the apocalyptic vision of war became strategic reality in the East,"[60] and one can probably say that in the battles, massacres, mass murders of the "Russian campaign," Clausewitz's real and absolute wars had become one.

The concept of "total war" is a radicalization of the concept of the war of annihilation. It is a result of World War I, and not at all limited to Germany.[61] It can be regarded as an obvious consequence of the influence of advanced technology on the national economy, and that view is not entirely false. Yet it is also true that war technology would never have experienced this rapid development if there had not been a nationwide readiness to finance it. In order to appear as the natural form of warfare that it has become historically, the idea of a war of annihilation has to become sufficiently compelling to cause people to forget that it does not lie in the nature of things but is an attribute of a culture that is prepared to subordinate itself to that idea. Once it has become that persuasive, technological development can open up new possibilities. Only with the development of atomic weapons did it become possible to play strategic mental games in which annihilating the enemy's population is regarded as a preventive measure.

In Germany, however, the totalization of the concept of annihilation took on a dimension that had nothing to do with technology or economics. In World War II, Germany waged not only a war of one society against another but, by its own lights, a racial war. This racial war, which was waged in the extermination camps and battlefields on the Eastern front, was not based on the dogmas of any classical ideology. On the contrary, the articles of faith that promoted it are something like the crystallizations of diffuse resentments acquired earlier, coalescing around the idea of annihilation, which became a central obsession. It is no longer aimed at any enemy population. The enemy is something in the enemy's population, one's own population, or the population of the world, that contradicts an ideal of homogeneity, the attainment of which alone can guarantee final victory and peace.

At this point, the National Socialist state surpasses Ludendorff's military dictatorship, for the idea of an army leadership drafting an entire people into the service of war becomes obsolete at the moment total mobilization actually embraces the entire society.

Then, politics again takes over. And yet war is not converted back into an instrument, for politics and war have become one. War—the total war of annihilation—is the unmediated realization of nationalist and racist policy. "National Socialist war was a war for the sake of social reconstruction through the destruction of conquered societies."[62] Annihilation is no longer a means for winning the war, but rather war consists in annihilating entire populations—or at least in their subjugation and enslavement. Ludendorff's compulsory service is continued not only in the National Socialist labor service, but also in the extermination of concentration camp inmates and prisoners of war through overwork. "Total discretionary power over subjugated peoples was to maintain and guarantee the social life and organization of the Germans. A terrorist racism became the essence of National Socialist politics as its leaders strove toward war."[63]

Viewed from this perspective, the oft-cited example of transportation capacities needed for "rational" military purposes being made available instead for the commission of "irrational" mass crimes in the extermination camps neither loses any of its inherent horror nor gains anything that would pass for logic under normal circumstances. And yet it fits into the logic of the war of annihilation pursued to its most extreme consequences. "In total war, the focus is on the people," writes Ludendorff, invoking this idea in his 1937 book *Der totale Krieg*. "Obedience to deep racial and spiritual laws will lead to success in welding the people, the military leadership, and politics into a powerful union, which is the foundation of the people's survival."[64] This "powerful union" of the people, war, and politics marks the triumph of the ideal of the war of annihilation; it is waged both internally and externally. It is total in that it creates itself in the creation of its enemies and contains its goal within itself; and it is total also in a temporal sense—it does not end unless someone stops its executors.

In 1930, Ernst Jünger, in his gloomily effusive essay "Total Mobilization," envisions the transformation of Ludendorff's total war into Hitler's total war of annihilation:

> The German descended deep beneath the iridescent surface of conflicts ... into the realm of chaos. Although his struggle might appear pointless, "senseless" seen from this surface of the Barbusses and the Rathenaus—why should that not concern us? In the crater's depths, war has a meaning which no arithmetic can master. That meaning was intuited in the cheering of the volunteers, in which the voice of the German demon erupted, the voice in which disgust of the old values was united with the unconscious yearning for a new life ... thus it is that the result of this war for the true warriors can be nothing less than the acquisition of the

> deeper Germany. That this is indeed the case is confirmed by the restlessness that is the mark of the new race, which no ideal of this world and no image from the past can satisfy. Here a fruitful anarchy reigns, sprung from the elements of earth and fire and bearing within it the seed of a new ruling power. Here new rearmament is in the offing, which seeks to forge its arms of purer, harder ore, tested against every opponent. The German waged the war with the ambition, unworthy of him, of being a good European. But since Europe was waging war against Europe, who other than Europe could emerge the victor? And yet this Europe, whose surface then stretched over the entire planet, has worn very thin, no more than veneer; what it has won in space, it has lost in credibility. For us, partaking of Europe's values means being a reactionary, a man of yesterday, a man of the nineteenth century. For deep below the regions in which the dialectic of war aims is significant, the German encountered a more powerful force: he encountered himself. Thus for him, this war was, at the same time and above all else, a means of self-realization. And thus it is that the new rearmament, in which we have already long been involved, must be a mobilization of the German, and nothing else.[65]

Sigmund Freud, in a letter to Arnold Zweig dated 23 September 1935 expressed the same thought more succinctly:

> It is like a long-hoped-for liberation. At last the truth, the grim ultimate truth, which is nevertheless essential. You cannot understand the Germany of today if you know nothing of Verdun and what it stands for.... If I had drawn the right conclusions from Verdun, then I should have known that I could not live among these people. We all thought it was the war and not the people, but other nations went through the war as well and nevertheless behaved differently. We did not want to believe it at the time, but it was true what the others said about the *Boches*.[66]

—Translated by Roy Shelton

Notes

1. John Keegan, *A History of Warfare* (London: 1993), 132, 114.
2. Ibid., 12.
3. The usual explanations—superior Spanish arms, the cavalry, the superstitions of the Aztecs, epidemics—account for individual aspects of what occurred, not for events in their entirety. On this subject, see Jan Philipp Reemtsma, "Cortez et al.," in Reemtsma et al., *Falun. Reden und Aufsätze* (Berlin: 1992).
4. See Richard Lee Marks, *Cortés: The Great Adventurer and the Fate of Aztec Mexico* (New York: 1993), 255f.
5. Ibid., 328.
6. It is not our intention to examine the question why the Aztecs had another way of waging war, but merely to refer the reader to the extremely plausible—though, of course, not uncontroversial—thesis of the American anthropologist Marvin Harris, who sees the origins of the Aztecs' method of waging war in their cannibalism. See Marvin Harris, *Wohlgeschmack und Widerwillen. Die Rätsel der Nahrungstabus* (Stuttgart: 1990).
7. John Keegan, *Das Antlitz des Krieges* (Frankfurt am Main: 1991), 124ff. We would like to note that the pompous German title (The Countenance of War) is quite inappropriate. *Das Gesicht der Schlacht* would be correct and suitable. Originally published as *The Face of Battle* (London: 1988).
8. Erich Ludendorff, *Der totale Krieg* (Munich: 1937), 3.
9. Herfried Münkler, "Instrumentelle und existentielle Auffassung des Krieges bei Carl von Clausewitz," in Herfried Münkler, *Gewalt und Ordnung. Das Bild des Krieges im politischen Denken* (Frankfurt am Main: 1992).
10. Ibid., 95.
11. Carl von Clausewitz, *On War*, trans. Michael Howard and Peter Paret (London: 1993), 700.
12. Ibid., 701.
13. Ibid., 702.
14. Ibid.
15. Münkler, *Gewalt und Ordnung,* 97.
16. Clausewitz, *On War*, 700.
17. Münkler, *Gewalt und Ordnung,* 103.
18. Cited in Münkler, *Gewalt und Ordnung,* 106.
19. Carl Schmitt, *Theorie des Partisanen* (Berlin: 1992).
20. Ibid., 47f.
21. Christian Meier, *Athen* (Munich: 1993), 470.
22. Ibid., 529.
23. Thucydides, *The Peloponnesian War: A New Translation, Backgrounds and Contexts, Interpretations*, trans. Walter Blanco and Jennifer Tolbert Roberts (New York: 1998), 2:82, n.130.
24. Meier, *Athen*, 532.
25. Keegan, *A History of Warfare*, 3.
26. Ibid., 27.
27. Münkler, *Gewalt und Ordnung,* 108.
28. See also Herfried Münkler, "Die Weisheit der Regierenden. Varianten der Kriegsursachenanalyse," in Münkler, *Gewalt und Ordnung,* 80ff.
29. Meier, *Athen*, 523.
30. Ibid., 535.
31. Thucydides, *The Peloponnesian War,* 1:75.

32. Cf. Meier, *Athen*, 536ff.
33. Thucydides, *The Peloponnesian War*, 3:81.
34. Clausewitz, *On War*, 755.
35. See Jehuda L. Wallach, *Kriegstheorien. Ihre Entwicklung im 19. und 20. Jahrhundert* (Frankfurt am Main: 1972).
36. After a certain point in the development of tensions between Germany and Great Britain, this effect may have been welcome with a view to Kaiser Wilhelm II's naval policy. See also Robert K. Massie, *Die Schalen des Zorns. Großbritannien, Deutschland und das Heraufziehen des Ersten Weltkrieges* (Frankfurt am Main: 1993), 768ff. Originally published as *Dreadnought: Britain, Germany, and the Coming of the Great War* (New York: 1991).
37. "The outbreak of war in 1914 is history's most shocking example of political leadership's helpless dependence on the planning of military technicians. The historical guilt of Bismarck's successors lies in their permitting themselves to be drawn into this state of dependence and in regarding military planning as solely the business of military experts." Gerhard Ritter, "Der Schlieffen-Plan," cited by Wallach, *Kriegstheorien,* 59. The degree to which some minds (notably Crown Prince Wilhelm and Waldersee) were obsessed by the thought that they might miss the right moment to launch a war (it mattered not against whom—Russia today, Russia and France tomorrow, England the day after) is demonstrated by John Röhl, *Wilhelm II. Die Jugend des Kaisers* (Munich: 1993), 444ff., 452ff., 742ff.
38. Recent research suggests that there were already doubts that the Schlieffen Plan would succeed before it was attempted, and that a long war was foreseen. The question thus raised—why Schlieffen's plan was more or less followed—is easy to answer: The German General Staff had no other war plan. See Wallach, *Kriegstheorien,* 62.
39. Ibid., 258.
40. Ibid., 264.
41. Ibid., 256 (emphasis added).
42. Ibid., 268.
43. Ibid., 257.
44. Ibid., 269.
45. Immanuel Kant, in Wolfgang Schwartz, *Principles of Lawful Politics: An Annotated Translation of Immanuel Kant's* Toward Eternal Peace (Aalen: 1988), 97.
46. Rudolf Heß, "Vor Verdun!" quoted by German Werth, 1916. *Schlachtfeld Verdun. Europas Trauma* (Berlin: 1994), 146.
47. Ibid., 142.
48. Quoted in Ernst Johann, ed., *Innenansicht eines Krieges. Bilder, Briefe, Dokumente 1914–1918* (Frankfurt am Main: 1968), 219f.
49. Erich Ludendorff, *Meine Kriegserinnerungen 1914–1918* (Berlin: 1919), 258ff.
50. Ibid.
51. Ibid., 215.
52. Michael Geyer, "German Strategy in the Age of Machine Warfare, 1914–1945," in Peter Paret, ed., *Makers of Modern Strategy from Machiavelli to the Nuclear Age* (Oxford: 1991), 546.
53. Cited in Wallach, *Kriegstheorien,* 279.
54. Crown Prince Rupprecht of Bavaria, Supreme Commander of Bavarian Forces on the Western front.
55. Wallach, *Kriegstheorien*, 286.

56. It is interesting that Michael Geyer considers the Wehrmacht's Blitzkrieg strategy under Hitler as a continuation of Ludendorff's primitive strategy that relies solely on speed and brute force.
57. Wallach, *Kriegstheorien,* 296.
58. Geyer, "German Strategy," 551. Here we might point to a curious historical parallel. Two years before the Peace of Callias, which brought a brief hiatus in the Peloponnesian War, Pericles changed the laws regulating Athenian citizenship. Where previously a man was a citizen if he had an Athenian father, now Athenian citizenship required two Athenian parents. This not only had the effect of reducing the number of citizens, as Christian Meier says, but also marked a change in the legal nature of citizenship. Where hitherto the rights of a citizen had been inherited, citizenship now became an inherited characteristic of a quite different nature—it now denoted a "connection through blood." "The only possible explanation is that the Athenians feared that the citizenry was losing its homogeneity," Meier, *Athen,* 400. Even more: the Athenians were attempting to guarantee biologically, so to speak, this homogeneity. Thus it becomes apparent that the crisis of the *polis* tends to lead to a destruction of politics. The proto-racism, if we may use that term, of the Periclean law seems to anticipate the attempt to form a *Volksgemeinschaft* in order to prosecute war more relentlessly and more resolutely.
59. Geyer, "German Strategy," 553.
60. Ibid., 574. Geyer also adds an important observation. "Apocalyptic war was waged by various organizations that, for the most part, were in conflict with each other. Historians should not be deceived by their competition and strife." Geyer's analysis of how rivalries function in military leadership is also interesting (586).
61. See, for example, John Frederick Charles Fuller, *Der erste der Völkerbundskriege. Seine Zeichen und Lehren für Kommende* (Berlin: 1937). Originally published as: *The First of the League of Wars, its Lessons and Omens* (London: 1936).
62. Geyer, "German Strategy," 566.
63. Ibid., 566.
64. Ludendorff, *Der totale Krieg*, 258ff.
65. Ernst Jünger, "Die totale Mobilmachung," in Ernst Jünger, ed., *Krieg und Krieger* (Berlin: 1930), 29f.
66. Sigmund Freud to Arnold Zweig, in Ernst L. Freud, ed., *The Letters of Sigmund Freud and Arnold Zweig*, trans. Prof. and Mrs. W. D. Robson-Scott (London: 1970), 110.

– Part I –

CRIMES

– *Chapter 2* –

"Coming Along to Shoot Some Jews?"

The Destruction of the Jews in Serbia

Walter Manoschek

When German troops invaded Yugoslavia in April 1941 and subsequently subdivided the country, approximately 17,000 Jews lived in Serbia under German military rule.[1] One year later, Serbia was "free of Jews."[2]

The First Steps

Six weeks after the occupation began, the Wehrmacht commander in Serbia, General Ludwig von Schröder, ordered that Jews and Gypsies be identified, registered, and required to wear gold armbands; that they be dismissed from public offices and private businesses; that their property be "aryanized";[3] and that a program of forced labor be introduced.[4] Thus, the repressive measures of individual field and local commanders, which until then had been uncoordinated and localized, were standardized throughout the Serbian zone of occupation.[5] "The three initial steps of the extermination process were put into effect in a single day."[6] At the same time, the establishment of a Jewish ghetto in the small Serbian town of Majdanpek was under consideration.[7] Of course, this plan was never put into effect. Due to the dynamics of events in Serbia, the "phase of Polish ghettoization" was skipped and a regional model for the "solution to the Jewish and Gypsy question" was developed.

Notes for this section begin on page 52.

The military commander, in consultation with the civil and police authorities, had been involved in anti-Jewish and anti-Gypsy measures from the outset. In this initial phase, which lasted until the attack on the Soviet Union, racist norms already in effect in other occupied or conquered areas were adapted to circumstances in Serbia. No military pretext was required for that. Even before the beginning of the war of annihilation against the Soviet Union, the Wehrmacht leadership had approved National Socialist Jewish policy in principle. A staff officer in the 717th Infantry Division, stationed in the Serbian Banat, also appreciated the practical advantages of persecuting Jews: "War was raging here a few weeks ago. There are no signs of that now, because the enemy broke and ran with our tanks at his heels. And yet there really are signs in the sense that all the Jews have been rounded up, shot, or imprisoned. Whole palaces, villas stand empty in all their splendor. Our soldiers, non-coms, etc. are quite comfortable there. They are living like lords."[8]

The attack on the Soviet Union in June 1941 set the stage for a bloody policy of repression in Serbia. As early as 22 June, the chief of the military administrative staff, Staatsrat Harald Turner, ordered the arrest of all leading Communists and veterans of the Spanish Civil War. Simultaneously, Belgrade's Jewish community was required to supply forty men each day as hostages to be shot in the event of partisan attacks.[9] When Tito's armed partisans took the field in July 1941, the military commander entrusted the SD-Einsatzgruppe with responsibility for putting down the resistance: "The Einsatzgruppe of the state police under my command will, therefore, operate on its own authority when it is performing the tasks that it performs in the Reich, but the Secret Field Police (GFP) are responsible for defense matters. Thus, the Einsatzgruppe will bear primary responsibility for intensifying the struggle against Communist subversion."[10] From the outset, the partisan rebellion was answered with "hostage shootings." The military and the police pursued separate tasks. Wehrmacht units were responsible for burning whole villages after partisan attacks, arresting "suspicious persons," and handing them over to the Security Police. "Suspicious persons," Communists taken into custody, and Jewish hostages comprised the "hostage reservoir" from which Einsatzgruppe Fuchs and Police Reserve Battalion 64 selected victims for shooting in the summer of 1941.

The Wehrmacht's propaganda section was responsible for "shaping opinion." Much of its activity "was designed to support, in both word and deed, the military commander in his struggle against political subversion." The section began by "preparing to initiate a massive anti-Jewish propaganda campaign" aimed at "exposing" the Jews as the "wire-pullers" behind the Communist insurrection. To that end, "several anti-Jewish and anti-Communist posters were produced," and the Serbian press was "continuously supplied both with material designed to counter Communist propaganda and with stories about Jewish activity in the Balkans."[11] Shortly thereafter, the propaganda division in Belgrade reported to Berlin that "the military commander is moving energetically against bandits and saboteurs, as well as the people behind them. The shooting of about four dozen high-level Communists and Jews up until now has not failed to make an impression on the public."[12]

The "use of police methods" failed to prevent the rapid spread of partisan insurrection. Thus, the newly named Wehrmacht commander, General Heinrich Danckelmann, demanded of the OKW "two additional police battalions and at least 200 members of the SD."[13] The OKW rejected his demand on the grounds that the police and SD were more urgently needed for those tasks in the east; the Wehrmacht should at once take up the struggle against the partisans in their stead. "Due to growing turmoil and an increase in acts of sabotage, the Führer expects [Wehrmacht] troops to be used to restore peace and order through quick and decisive action."[14]

When the Wehrmacht was ordered to take up the struggle against partisans, there occurred a closing of ranks among the SD, the police, and Wehrmacht personnel. Each Wehrmacht battalion formed a mobile strike force of between thirty and forty men, which was supplemented by SD and police. Its tasks included "striking brutally, burning buildings or villages from which attacks on the German Wehrmacht are being launched, ruthlessly shooting the enemy in combat, hanging assassins who strike at the German Wehrmacht and its interests."[15] Mixed strike forces marked the transition from clearly delineated functions to direct cooperation between Wehrmacht and police apparatus. Mixing the personnel enabled the troops to familiarize themselves with SD and police methods and special tools for dealing with the enemy.

Wehrmacht responsibility for the struggle against partisans brought no change either in the conduct of the campaign or in the definition of enemy groups. Since engaging partisans in combat proved militarily hopeless, the "policy of hostage murder" remained the centerpiece of anti-resistance strategy, and Jews and (alleged) Communists were still the primary victims. But even accelerated shootings did not accomplish the desired goal: "Swift reprisals for acts of sabotage against the Wehrmacht, in which by the end of August around 1,000 Communists and Jews were shot or publicly hanged and the houses of bandits, even an entire village, were burned to the ground, failed to stop the steady growth of armed resistance."[16]

From Terror to Systematic Extermination

In Serbia, several stages in the process leading to extermination were passed through in rapid succession in the brief period from the spring to the summer of 1941. After Jews and Gypsies were isolated and deprived of their rights and property, a number of Communists and Jews were temporarily interned as potential "reprisal victims" at the time of the invasion of the Soviet Union, and then shot by the Einsatzgruppe and the police when the partisan insurrection broke out. This progressive escalation of the extermination process had been administered by military authorities. Murdering Jews was, in the summer of 1941, a common practice of the police and SD. Of course, up to this point, Wehrmacht troops had not been directly involved in the murder of Jews and Communists.

The shift from bloody, but unsystematic terror to a purposive policy of extermination came in September 1941 with the appointment of General Franz Böhme, a native of Austria, to the post of Plenipotentiary Commanding General in Serbia. Hitler invested Böhme with complete authority and ordered him "to restore order for the long term in the entire area by the most radical means."[17] The guidelines under which Böhme operated are found in OKW Chief Keitel's order on "combating Communist insurrection in the occupied regions," which foresaw the execution of from fifty to one hundred Communists as "reprisal for the life of a German soldier" and which was issued, not coincidentally, on the day Böhme was appointed.[18]

When General Böhme arrived in Serbia, the partisans and the national Chetnik units controlled most of the country outside the large cities. While the Wehrmacht's push on Moscow appeared irresistible, the troops in occupied Serbia found themselves, for the first time and completely unexpectedly, facing an active and well organized partisan movement that was exposing the military weaknesses of the occupiers. The four divisions stationed in the country had been formed for occupation duties and consisted of only two rather than the usual three regiments. Each division had about 6,000 men with no combat experience, whose training consisted of little more than target practice. Chief of Military Administration

Turner summarized the situation: "The troops available here were completely unsuited for fighting against the rebel elements."[19] Troop morale had been affected by numerous operational failures; the reputation and prestige of the proud Wehrmacht was being damaged in this peripheral theater of the war. Moreover, a disproportionate number of the troops consisted of Austrians,[20] in whom the region, so rich in history for Austrians, awakened inevitable memories of defeat in World War I.

From the beginning Böhme left no doubt that he meant to wage war on the civilian population. Hans Helm, deputy leader of the SD-Einsatzkommando, summarizes the mentality that was prevalent in the occupation command structure beginning in the middle of 1941: "The prevailing view was that we did not have to worry much about the population. The war in Russia would be over in a few months in any case, and later it would be a simple matter to restore order."[21]

Böhme ordered additional combat units transferred to Serbia to carry out "punitive expeditions" in areas of greatest rebel strength in order to destroy the resistance's social, logistical, and supply bases. The entire population was declared the enemy. All men were to be arrested and interned in newly constructed prisons or concentration camps; women and children were to be driven from their home localities; villages were to be burned, and livestock was to be confiscated. "By ruthless measures, we must succeed in delivering a warning that will soon be known throughout Serbia."[22]

The first task was to instill clear values in the demoralized soldiers and make them aware of the importance of their mission. Böhme issued a directive to all officers, non-commissioned officers, and units in which he urged them to wage war on the population.

> If we do not proceed with all means available and with maximum ruthlessness, our losses will rise to incalculable levels. You will be carrying out your mission in a strip of territory in which, thanks to the treachery of the Serbs, both men and women, rivers of German blood flowed in 1914. You are the avengers of those dead. We must deliver a warning that will make the greatest possible impression on the population. Anyone who shows compassion will be sinning against the lives of his comrades. He will be called to account regardless of who he is and court-martialed.[23]

Historical enmities, racial stereotypes, appeals to comradeship, and threats of court-martial were intended to stoke up the aggressiveness of the troops and lower any inhibitions about the planned mass murder of civilians.

The Liquidation of Male Jews by the Wehrmacht

On his arrival in Belgrade, Böhme was immediately informed that the Jews had already been rounded up and that now Gypsies were to be taken into custody as well.[24] Those measures had been initiated by the German ambassador in Belgrade, Felix Benzler, and his "Jewish expert," Edmund Veesenmayer, who had been flooding the foreign office in Berlin since September with telegrams demanding the "arrest and removal of at least all male Jews" and their deportation to Romania or to the east.[25]

The decision to murder rather than deport male Jews was reached in a few days. In September 1941 there was general agreement among occupation authorities that the initial objective was to get rid of at least the male Jews, one way or the other. Though the metaphors of justification varied, even in this show place of extermination they can ultimately be reduced to National Socialist racist ideology, which blamed the Jews for all difficulties and outrages—in this case, for the partisan war. Administrative chief Turner contented himself with the core element of racist argumentation in his efforts to justify getting rid of Jews and Gypsies: "It must be established as a matter of principle that Jews and Gypsies represent in a general sense an element dangerous to public order and security. It is the Jewish intelligentsia that conjured up this war and it must be exterminated."[26] The representatives of the foreign office, on the other hand, urged that Jews be deported to Romania "as the first prerequisite for the desired permanent pacification"[27] of the country, since "it turns out that Jews have been involved in numerous acts of sabotage and rebellion,"[28] and, moreover, "Jews demonstrably contribute greatly to unrest in the country."[29]

These variations of the "security" argument were linked to General Böhme's military "pacification concept." After Böhme had also urged deportation of the Jews already interned in order to make room for the planned arrest of 10,000 Serbian civilians,[30] he came to recognize in a few days the possibilities that the presence of Jews and Gypsies offered for his policy of repression: Jews and Gypsies stood available as "hostage victims." In his first "reprisal order," Böhme was already making use of the option. After twenty-one Wehrmacht soldiers were killed in a fire fight with partisans, Böhme ordered the execution of 2,100 "hostages" and specified the groups from which the victims were to be drawn: "The Chief of Military Administration is requested to select 2,100 prisoners (primarily Jews and Gypsies) in the concentration camps Šabac and Belgrade."[31] For the first time the Wehrmacht was ordered to carry out mass shootings: "The execution squads shall be provided by the 342nd Division (for concentration camp Šabac) and by Corps Intelligence Section 449 (for concentration camp Belgrade)."[32]

With this order, General Böhme introduced a new phase of Jewish extermination. The Einsatzgruppe's already common practice of murdering Jews and Communists was systematized, the ratio of executions to victims of partisan attacks was set at 100 to one, and the policy was proclaimed as a military measure to be executed by the Wehrmacht itself: "Thus there came about an odd inversion of responsibilities. In the Russian camps, the Wehrmacht had seen to the selection of victims while the Einsatzgruppen carried out the shootings. Now the troops suddenly had to do the 'dirty work.'"[33]

The extent to which racist extermination policy was part and parcel of criminal occupation practices is obvious from the fate of victims in the concentration camp at Šabac. The population of this camp consisted almost exclusively of Jews from the "Kladovo Transport," a group of more than a thousand Jews, most from Austria, who had become stranded in Yugoslavia while fleeing to Palestine at the end of 1939, and who had not the slightest connection with the partisan uprising. They were among the first to be struck by the Wehrmacht murders called "reprisals."[34]

On 10 October 1941, General Böhme issued a comprehensive extermination order. Due to "the 'Balkan mentality' and widespread Communist and allegedly nationalist rebel movements," he ordered that "all Communists, people suspected of being Communists, all Jews, [and] a given number of nationalist and democratically minded inhabitants are to be seized as hostages in swift operations. These hostages are to be told that hostages will be shot if German soldiers or ethnic Germans are attacked."[35]

The lack of ambiguity in this Wehrmacht order, which exposed all male Jews to murder, even made an impression on the Einsatzgruppe. It reported with satisfaction to Berlin: "While prior to the appointment of the Plenipotentiary Commanding General ruthless action on the part of the troops necessarily failed due to the absence of unequivocal orders, General Böhme's order that 100 Serbs are to be shot for every soldier killed, fifty for every soldier wounded, has established a clear policy."[36] Even Legation Counselor Rademacher from the Foreign Office, who had come to Belgrade with representatives of the Reichssicherheitshauptamt (Reich Security Main Office) in mid-October to discuss the "solution to the Jewish problem" on the spot, stated with satisfaction in his report: "The male Jews will be shot by the end of this week, and thus the problem raised in the embassy's report will have been solved."[37]

The executions squads were comprised mainly of soldiers from units that had suffered losses in skirmishes with partisans. The soldiers regarded mass executions of Jews and Gypsies as a legitimate tactic. Numerous eye witnesses confirm that the execution squads consisted of volunteers. When a native of Vienna, who belonged to the 521st Army Intelligence Regiment, returned from leave to Belgrade, he was greeted by his comrades with the jovial challenge: "Coming along to shoot some Jews?"[38] Two reports of the shootings of Jews and Gypsies yield insight into the soldiers' mentality. Analogous notes on massacres of other segments of the Serb population do not exist. The detailed description of the course of the operation and the description of the soldiers' emotional reactions suggest that the Wehrmacht staffs were interested in getting a precise picture of the emotional effects of the shootings on the soldiers. Both reports show that the execution squads carried out orders for the shootings of Jews and Gypsies willingly:

> Secret
> Oberleutnant Walther OU, 1 November 1941
> Chef 9./I.R. 433.
>
> Report on the shooting of Jews and Gypsies
>
> After consulting with the SS section, I collected the Jews and Gypsies from the Belgrade prison camp. The trucks of Field Command 599, which had been placed at my disposal, proved unserviceable for two reasons:
> 1. They were driven by civilians. Thus secrecy was not assured.
> 2. They had neither a roof nor a tarpaulin, which meant the city's population could see whom we had in the vehicles and where we were taking them. Some wives of the Jews had gathered in front of the camp. They howled and screamed when we drove off. The place at which the shootings took place is very favorable. It lies north of Pančevo, right on the road connecting Pančevo and Jabuka, which has an embankment that is so high that it can be climbed only with difficulty. Facing this embankment is a swamp, behind that a river. At high tide (as on 29 October) the water almost reaches the embankment. Only a few men are required to prevent the prisoners from escaping. Equally favorable is the sandy soil, which makes digging the graves easier and thus cuts down on the work time.
>
> When we arrived at a spot some 1.5 to 2 kilometers from the chosen place, the prisoners got out of the trucks and marched to the place, while the trucks were being sent back at once in order to give the civilian drivers the least possible grounds for suspicion. Then I ordered the street blocked for reasons of security and secrecy.
>
> The place of execution was secured by one light machine gun and twelve riflemen:
> 1. to prevent escape attempts by the prisoners,
> 2. to guard against possible attacks by Serbian gangs.

Digging the graves takes most of the time; the shooting itself goes quickly (100 men in forty minutes).

Luggage and valuables were collected earlier and transported in my truck for turning over to the NSV (Nationalsozialistische Volksfürsorge).

Shooting Jews is simpler than shooting Gypsies. One has to admit that the Jews die stoically, standing quietly, while the Gypsies howl, scream, and are in constant motion even when they are already standing in place to be shot. Some even jumped into the grave before the salvo and played dead.

Initially, my soldiers were not impressed. On the second day, it was becoming apparent that some did not have the nerves required for carrying out extended shootings. My personal impression is that one does not experience inhibitions during the shootings. These first manifest themselves after several days, when one thinks about things quietly in the evening.

Walther, Oberleutnant[39]

Obviously, Oberleutnant Walther was able to overcome the inhibitions that the murder of roughly 600 completely innocent human beings caused him later. When he gave a legal deposition in 1962, he did not retreat to the common formula of self-justification that he had to follow orders, but testified that he "saw a certain justification for such operations given the rage toward the partisans among us soldiers."[40] The preliminary investigation directed at Walther, who was then a major in the Bundeswehr, was stopped.

An even more unvarnished report of the shooting of several hundred Jews was prepared by the company chief of Army Intelligence Regiment 521, Walter Liepe. In structure and choice of words, it is all but identical to reports composed by Einsatzgruppen in the east, and despite the unemotional, technical command language used in military documents, it provides us with insight into the mood of Wehrmacht soldiers who were carrying out a part of the holocaust against the Jews:

Liepe, Oberleutnant and Company Chief Number 26 557	13.10.1941 Military Postal Service

Report on the Shooting of Jews of 9 and 11 October 1941.

1. Mission:
On 8 October 1941 an order was issued for the shooting of 2,200 Jews located in the camp at Belgrade.
2. Officers and Personnel:
Oberleutnant Liepe and comrades of field units 26 557, [3rd Company, II. Section/ANR 521, W.M.] and 06 175 [4th Company, II. Section/ANR 521, W. M.], of which two officers and 20 men have died, sixteen are missing in action, and three are wounded.

3. Medical Care and Supervision:
Senior Physician Dr. Gasser, Field Unit 39 107 and Medical Service Sergeant Bente of Unit 26 557.
4. Transport and Vehicles:
Transporting and guarding the prisoners was carried out by the participating units. Vehicles were provided by motor pool of the Belgrade command. The transportation of participating soldiers was by army vehicles.
5. Place of the operation:
On 9 October 1941—forest roughly 12 km northeast of Kovin. On 11 October 1941 on the street to Nisch in the vicinity of the Belgrade firing range.
6. Security and Concealment:
Carried out in close cooperation with the Security Police in Belgrade and Pančevo.
7. Filming and Photography:
Propaganda Company S.
8. Supervision:
Oberleutnant Liepe, Leutnant Viebrans, Leutnant Lüstraeten, SS Oberscharführer Enge, Security Police of Belgrade.
9. Implementation:
After the area had been thoroughly reconnoitered and prepared, the first shooting took place on 9 October 1941. The prisoners, together with their few belongings, were picked up at the camp in Belgrade at 05.30. Spades and other tools were distributed to create the impression of a work detail. Each vehicle was guarded by only three men, so that the number of guards would not awaken suspicions about the true nature of the operation.

The prisoners were transported without difficulty. The mood of the prisoners during transport and preparations was good. They were happy at being away from the camp because they were allegedly being housed there against their wishes. The prisoners were kept occupied eight kilometers from the place of execution and then taken there as needed. The site was sufficiently secured during both the preparations and the shootings. Shooting was accomplished with rifles from a distance of twelve meters. Five shooters were ordered to fire at each prisoner. In addition, two shooters stood ready to kill with a shot to the head if the physician so instructed them. Valuables and other articles were removed from the prisoners under close supervision, and later turned over to the NSV or the Security Police.

The prisoners were composed during the shooting. Two people tried to escape and were shot immediately. Some expressed their feelings by giving a last cheer for Stalin and Russia. One hundred and eighty men were shot on 9 October 1941. The shooting was over by 18.30 hours. There were no incidents that deserve noting. The units returned to their quarters well satisfied.

Due to construction work on the Danube ferry, the second round of shootings could not be carried out until 11 October 1941. Because of the construction, the next shooting had to take place in the vicinity of Belgrade. That required reconnoitering a new site and redoubled security. The next shootings occurred on 11 October 1941 near the firing

> range. It was carried out according to plan. 269 men were shot. None of the prisoners escaped at either shooting, and the troops reported no remarkable or untoward events. A squad from Major Pongruber under the command of Lieutenant Hau was brought in to strengthen security. A total of 449 men were shot on 9 and 11 October 1941 by the units designated above. Unfortunately, a third shooting by these units had to be canceled and the task passed on to Major Pongruber's unit.
>
> Liepe (in his handwriting)
> Oberleutnant and Company Chief[41]

Liepe and his execution squad performed their duties with enthusiasm. Liepe's and Walther's report make it clear that the troops did not have to be compelled to carry out General Böhme's orders to murder Jews; they wanted to do so. The mass shootings were described in letters home and documented with enclosed photographs, so that the staff section found it necessary to issue a sharply worded order concerning "violations of security in correspondence": "Reports of the military postal service reveal that members of units in Serbia discuss in detail their duties in Serbia, sometimes mentioning their own losses and German reprisals (mass executions) in letters home. Sometimes photographs are enclosed .... The troops must be reminded that henceforth such offenses will be dealt with by all available means."[42]

The Gassing of Jewish Women and Children in Sajmište

Even while Jewish men were being murdered in the fall of 1941, Administrative Chief Turner implemented the first measures aimed at interning Jewish women and children: "Imprisonment of all Jewish men in Belgrade in the camp accomplished. Preparations for a Jewish ghetto in Belgrade completed. Following completion of the liquidation of the rest of the male Jews ordered by the commander, the ghetto will contain approximately 10,000 Jewish women and children."[43]

Thus the initiative in the extermination process passed from the Wehrmacht back to the police and the SD. And yet the Wehrmacht had justified even the interning of women and children with absurd military pretexts. Counterintelligence (Ic/AO) in Saloniki—which Kurt Waldheim would join a few months later—justified dragging women and children into the Sajmište concentration camp by insisting: "All Jews and Gypsies are being transferred to a concentration camp near Semlin .... They are clearly informants for the rebels."[44]

During the winter 1941–42, approximately 7,000 Jewish women, children, and old men, as well as 500 Jewish men who had been exempted from the shootings in order to help keep order in the camp, and 292 Gypsy women and children were brought to the concentration camp at Sajmište. Their fate had already been sealed before they arrived. In early 1942, Military Administrative Chief Turner, with the support of SD headquarters in Belgrade, had requested that Berlin send in the latest technology for exterminating Jews—the gas van.[45] The gas van arrived in Belgrade at the beginning of March 1942 and was immediately put into service.[46]

While the Wehrmacht lied to the victims, pretending that they were to be put to work in order to conceal their fate from them, the head of the concentration camp, SS-Untersturmführer Herbert Andorfer from Linz, used another method to prevent unrest in the camp. He announced that the inmates were to be transferred to a better camp, even going so far as to post fabricated regulations for the new camp. Large numbers of inmates volunteered for the supposed transfer in order to escape the gruesome conditions in the Sajmište camp. Each morning, beginning in early March, two trucks drove up in front of the camp gate. "Resettlement baggage" was loaded into one; between fifty and eighty Jewish women and children got in the other.[47] Then the trucks set off toward Belgrade. After the vehicles had crossed the Save bridge, the baggage truck turned off, while the other truck made a brief stop. The two drivers, Wilhelm Götz and Erwin Meyer, got out and worked a lever that vented the exhaust into the interior of the truck. The victims were gassed during the subsequent drive through Belgrade to Jajinci (roughly fifteen kilometers to the southeast of the capital). A prison detail unloaded the dead and buried them in graves that had been dug ahead of time. By early May 1942, approximately 7,500 camp inmates had been murdered in this way. The gas van was sent to Berlin, refitted, and sent to Belorussia, where it was used to gas Jews in Minsk.

Summary

Serbia was the second country in the Nazi sphere of domination, following Estonia, that was rendered "free of Jews." The process of extermination unfolded in four successive stages. Identification, isolation, and deprivation of rights and property were followed in the spring of 1941 by the partial liquidation of male Jews by the police and SD after the partisan campaign had begun. When the struggle against partisans was taken over by the Wehrmacht and General Böhme was appointed, the Wehrmacht extended the extermination program to include all male Jews. During the murder of the males, women and children were already being interned in the Sajmište camp; they were gassed in the spring of 1942.

What is remarkable is how smoothly the extermination process operated. The effortless cooperation of all occupation authorities in the "Jewish Question"—Wehrmacht, military command, embassy, police, and Einsatzgruppe—made possible a "local final solution" that could hardly be matched for efficiency. The central role of the Wehrmacht is clear. It was involved in all phases of the extermination process: legally (spring 1941), in partnership with the SD and the police (summer 1941), by implementing the policy (fall 1941), or through the pseudo-military justification of the interning of Jewish women and children (winter 1941/42).

The racist equation of Jews and Communists did not result from tactical calculations on the part of staff officers, but reflected the attitude of the troops. Reports of shootings, letters sent home, and countless photographs prove that the mass executions of Jews, Communists, and Gypsies were unanimously regarded as "success stories" by both the officers giving the orders and the soldiers carrying them out. The outbreak of the partisan uprising made it possible for the images of the enemy that were already blended in consciousness to meld in reality—and to be converted into acts of extermination.

—Translated by Roy Shelton

Notes

1. Holm Sundhaussen, "Jugoslawien," in *Dimension des Völkermords. Die Zahl der jüdischen Opfer des Nationalsozialismus*, ed. Wolfgang Benz (Munich: 1991), 311.
2. Walter Manoschek, *"Serbien ist judenfrei!" Militärische Besatzungspolitik und Judenvernichtung in Serbien 1941/42*, vol. 38 of *Schriftenreihe des Militärgeschichtlichen Forschungsamtes Freiburg* (Munich, 2nd ed.: 1995).
3. On the economic deprivation of the Serbian Jews, see Karl-Heinz Schlarp, *Wirtschaft und Besatzung in Serbien 1941–1944. Ein Beitrag zur nationalsozialistischen Wirtschaftspolitik in Südosteuropa* (Stuttgart: 1986), 294–302.
4. The later fate of the Gypsies in Serbia paralleled that of the Jews only partially. In July 1941, for example, an exception was made for Gypsies who had been residents since 1830; the women and children were released from the camp before the gassings began. The basic reason why the Gypsies were only partially exterminated was that it was not possible to define them unequivocally by religion. The Gypsies interned in the "hostage camps" in Belgrade and Šabac were executed along with the Jews. On the extermination of the Gypsies in Yugoslavia, see Donald Kenrick and Grattan Puxon, *Sinti und Roma—die Vernichtung eines Volkes im NS-Staat* (Göttingen: 1981); Karola Fings, Cordula Lissner, and Frank Sparing, "... *einziges Land, in dem Judenfrage und Zigeunerfrage gelöst." Die Verfolgung der Roma im faschistisch besetzten Jugoslawien 1941–1945* (Cologne: n.d.); Michael Zimmermann, *Rassenutopie und Genozid. Die nationalsozialistische "Lösung der Zigeunerfrage"* (Hamburg: 1996), 248–258.
5. For example, a few days after the occupation began, the local commander of Petrovgrad decreed the wearing of the Jewish star and the moving of the roughly 2,000 members of the Jewish community into a ghetto; NOKW-Dokument 1100, 23 April 1941.
6. Raul Hilberg, *Die Vernichtung der europäischen Juden* (Frankfurt am Main: 1991), 2:727.
7. PA-AA, *Botschaft Belgrad, Judenangelegenheiten* (Belgrade Embassy, Jewish Affairs), vol. 62/2, notes on discussion of issues relating to Jews at the headquarters of the military commander on 14 May 1941.
8. Letter by Lieutenant Peter G., sent by military post, 24 May 1941, Bibliothek für Zeitgeschichte Stuttgart, Sammlung Sterz.
9. Bundesarchiv Koblenz (BA-K), 70 Jugoslawien/33, Indictment of the commandant of the Security Police SD in Belgrade, 19.
10. Bundesarchiv-Militärarchiv (BA-MA), RW 40/79, Order regarding the use of the Security Police and the SD, 17 July 1941.
11. BA-MA, RW 4/v. 231, Situation and activity report of the propaganda section, 26 May–25 June 1941.
12. BA-MA, RW 4/v. 231, Situation and activity report, 26 June–25 July 1941.
13. BA-MA, RW 40/5, 11 August 1941.
14. BA-MA, RW 40/5, KTB Ia, Head of OKW to the military commandant in Serbia, as information, 9 August 1941.
15. BA-MA, RW 40/5, Situation report of the administrative staff for the period from 21 to 31 August 1941.
16. BA-MA, RW 40/187, 5, Situation report of the administrative staff of the military commandant in Serbia, 6 October 1941.

17. Führerweisung Nr. 31a, 16.9.1941(Führer Directive, number 31a, 16 September 1941), cited in *Hitlers Weisungen für die Kriegsführung 1939–1945. Dokumente des Oberkommandos der Wehrmacht*, ed. Walter Hubatsch (Munich: 1965).
18. BA-MA, RH 26-104/ 14, Head of OKW, Keitel, 16 September 1941.
19. BA-MA, RW 40/187, Situation report of the administrative staff of the military commandant in Serbia, 6 October 1941.
20. In the 717th and 718th ID, a majority of both officers and troops were Austrians; see BA-MA, RH 26-117/3 und RH 26-718/3. Moreover, four of the seven *Landesschützbataillone* used for security and as guards had been put together in Austria; see Georg Tessin, *Verbände und Truppen der deutschen Wehrmacht und Waffen-SS im Zweiten Weltkrieg 1939–1945* (Osnabrück: 1976), 13:127–132.
21. BA-K, All. Proz. 6 (Eichmann-Prozeß), Prosecution document in the Eichmann trial, deposition transcript for Hans Helm before the military legal section of the Yugoslav army, 8 September 1946.
22. BA-MA, RH 24-18/87, Böhme's order to the 342nd ID to clean out the Save bend, 22 September 1941.
23. BA-MA, RH 24-18/87, Böhme's directive of 25 September 1941.
24. NOKW-Dokument 892, Report by Turner to Böhme, 21 September 1941.
25. PA-AA, Inland IIg, Telegrams between the Belgrade embassy and the Foreign Office in Berlin from September 1941.
26. NOKW-Dokument 802, Turner's directive to all field and district commanders of 26 October 1941.
27. PA-AA, Inland IIg, Telegram from Benzler to Ribbentrop of 28 September 1941.
28. PA-AA, Inland IIg, Telegram from Veesenmayer and Benzler to the Foreign Office of 10 September 1941.
29. PA-AA, Inland IIg, Telegram from Benzler to the Foreign Office of 12 September 1941.
30. In a personal telegram to Ribbentrop, Benzler stressed the following practical argument: "In addition, General Böhme, along with military commanders, has asked me to appeal in their name for deportation of Jews from the country as quickly as possible. Involved are mainly 8,000 male Jews who cannot possibly be housed in their own camps because the camps have to be used for approximately 20,000 Serbs from abroad," PA-AA, Inland IIg, Telegram from Benzler to Ribbentrop of 28 September 1941.
31. BA-MA, RH 24-18/213, Telephone order from Böhme to the quartermaster section, 4 October 1941.
32. Ibid.
33. Hilberg, *Vernichtung*, 2:731.
34. On the fate of the "Kladovo Transport," see Gabriele Anderl and Walter Manoschek, *Gescheiterte Flucht. Der jüdische "Kladovo-Transport" auf dem Weg nach Palästina 1939–42* (Vienna: 1993).
35. BA-MA, RH 26-104/14, Böhme's order of 10 October 1941.
36. NO-Dokument 3402, SD Incident Report USSR, number 120, 21 October 1941.
37. PA-AA, Inland IIg, Rademacher's notes on the findings of his mission to Belgrade, 7 November 1941.
38. Zentrale Stelle der Landesjustizverwaltungen Ludwigsburg (Central Office of the State Department of Justice in Ludwigsburg), 503 AR-Z 2/1966, Investigation of charges against Walter L., witness statement by Franz H. 11 May 1965.

39. BA-MA, RH 26-104/15, Activity Report of the 704th ID.
40. Landgericht Konstanz (State Court of Konstanz), AR 146/63, Interrogation of Hans-Dieter W.
41. BA-MA, RH 24-18/213.
42. BA-MA, RH 24-18/213, Order of General Chief of Staff Pemsel. Despite this order, private reporting of war-related activities continued. In December 1941 Pemsel reiterated the ban on photographs and demanded that existing photographs be turned in, including the negatives. BA-MA, RH 26-104/52, Order of 15 December 1941.
43. NO-Dokument 3404, Turner's note of 20 October 1941.
44. NOKW-Dokument 1150, Remarks regarding the trip of the deputy supreme commander to Belgrade, 5 December 1941.
45. Beginning in December 1941, a total of six gas vans were used in Riga, Chelmno, and Poltava. They supplemented the execution squads of the Einsatzgruppen.
46. On operations involving gas vans, see Christopher R. Browning, "The Final Solution in Serbia. The Semlin Judenlager: A Case Study," *Yad Vashem Studies* 15 (1983): 55–90; Menachem Shelach, "Sajmište—An Extermination Camp in Serbia," *Holocaust and Genocide Studies* 2 (1987): 243–260; Walter Manoschek, "*Serbien ist judenfrei*," 169–184.
47. Gypsy women and children had been released from the concentration camp immediately before the gas vans arrived. Only Jewish victims were gassed.

– *Chapter 3* –

KILLING FIELDS

The Wehrmacht and the Holocaust in Belorussia, 1941–42[*]

Hannes Heer

In a report on the Jewish question dated 25 January 1942 (it also noted the murder of 9,000 Jews), the *Gebietskommissar* (Regional Commissar) in Slonim, Gerhard Erren, complained that troop zeal was slackening: "For a while, the Wehrmacht was mopping up the countryside on a grand scale; but unfortunately, only in localities with fewer than 1,000 inhabitants."[1] Somewhat later, his superior, Wilhelm Kube, chief of civil administration in occupied Belorussia, exercised his own criticism of the Wehrmacht. In a letter of 31 July 1942, he wrote, "Through an ... already reported encroachment on the Rear Area, Army Group Center, our preparations for liquidating the Jews in the area around Glubokie have been interrupted. The Rear Area, Army Group Center, has, without consulting me, liquidated 10,000 Jews whose systematic extermination we had ... already planned."[2] Here we have two reports, separated by six months, one criticizing the troops for insufficient effort, the other reproaching them for taking matters into their own hands and appropriating the laurels for a large-scale massacre. But both confirm that when it came to murdering Jews, one could count on the Wehrmacht. That this held true not only for a single case or limited area—as many military historians continue to maintain—will be shown in the following essay. Scene: Belorussia, year one of the German occupation.

Notes for this section begin on page 74.

The First Blow

On 30 January 1939, Hitler had prophesied in the Berlin Reichstag that, in another world war, "the result will not be the bolshevization of the Earth and thus the victory of Jewry, but rather the annihilation of the Jewish race in Europe."[3] Two years into the war, on 30 March 1941, before the assembled commanders and chiefs of staff, he characterized the impending campaign against the Soviet Union as a "battle of two world views" intended "to annihilate the Bolshevik commissars and Communist intelligentsia."[4] None of his soon-to-be Eastern warriors would have seen such statements as contradictory. Ever since the German defeat in 1918 and the following revolutionary upheavals, Bolshevism and Jewry were familiar enemy figures, compressed in National Socialist propaganda to the handy phrase "Jewish Bolshevism."[5] This abbreviation surfaced again and again during the hectic months of preparation for the Barbarossa campaign in the spring of 1941. In a directive of 3 March to OKW (Supreme Command of the Armed Forces), Hitler demanded the removal of the "Jewish Bolshevist intelligentsia."[6] The army leadership explained in a draft order of 6 May the decision to dispense with courts-martial against civilian suspects because, as the army leadership saw it, behind every civilian lurks a potential bearer of Jewish-Bolshevist ideology.[7] The Wehrmacht propaganda department paved the way in its "Guidelines for the Conduct of the Army in Russia" for the troops to see not the various Soviet peoples, but rather the "Jewish Bolshevist rulers" and "the heavily represented Jews" as the enemy of Germany.[8]

In this way, specific groups emerged out of the mass slated for annihilation: Red Army commissars, civilian party workers, and partisans or those suspected of partisan activity. Hitler's directive had initiated a series of "criminal commands" that the troops murder such political activists. But the other group singled out for annihilation, the Jewish population, had been a clear target long before the invasion. A direct result of Hitler's 3 March 1941 directive was that Himmler was entrusted with "special tasks," the *Sonderaufgaben*, arising from the ideological character of the approaching war.[9] To carry out Hitler's charge, Sonderkommandos der Sicherheitspolizei (SIPO) were, for example, to combat "efforts that are hostile to the German state and Reich" and take "important individuals" into custody. The 26 March agreement between Quartermaster General Eduard Wagner of the OKH (High Command of the Army) and Reinhard Heydrich did not name Jews.[10] But because General Wagner, like all generals, had become well acquainted with the tasks of the special forces during the coming Polish campaign—"'*Flurbereinigung*' [clearing the field]: Jewry, intelligentsia, church authorities, aristocracy" (Heydrich)[11]—everyone involved knew that the omission had no real significance, but was rather a carefully worded response to old rivalries between the Wehrmacht and SD dating back to 1939/40.

In 1941 the Jews were in for more than a "consolidation," or *Flurbereinigung*. Along with the well-known groups of "communist instigators" and irregulars, the "Guidelines for the Conduct of the Army in Russia," released in April, expressly named Jews as an object for "ruthless and energetic" treatment.[12] Among the tasks cataloged for the SD Sonderkommandos operating in the Balkans, formulated at the same time, murdering Jews was self-evident.[13] Even if one cannot point to any specific commands dating from this period for the eastern genocide, an explicit formulation of the "Jewish Question" existed for the Wehrmacht as well, and its "solution" was part of the agenda for the approaching campaign. Documents from the period of preparation refute any less murderous interpretation. Moreover, events of the first days of the war confirm a ready and willing attitude toward the extermination of the Jews.

On 22 June 1941, a German offensive advanced into the East. A dense network of local and field commands (Ortskommandanturen, Feldkommandanturen) immediately filled any vacuum in the conquered area. These were the first institutions of German rule. Along with the administration, economic assistance, preventative measures against epidemics, and German troop provision, the tasks of the occupation also included the *Befriedung* or calming of the area under its jurisdiction. A field commander spelled out the details in a report: "a) collection of booty, in particular all small arms; b) arrest of partisans; c) securing the Jews; d) attitude of the population; e) mine fields; f) prisoners of war."[14] After the partisans, Jews figured as the second most important enemy group. To "secure" them was a normal task for the occupying troops. What this meant is disclosed in the first directives released by the commander of the Rear Area, Army Group Center. Prepared before the onset of the campaign, and with bureaucratic exactitude by army command—as almost identical commands in the Ukraine and Baltic states suggest[15]—they appeared on 7 and 13 July in Belorussia after the capital, Minsk, fell. They decreed a general registration, identification of Jews by a yellow star or patch, their resettlement into Jewish residential districts, their obligation to be available for forced labor, and the creation of Jewish councils. Jews were forbidden to greet Germans.[16]

The everyday life of hundreds of thousands of Jews changed dramatically with the appearance of German troops. A directive of the Minsk field commander, which appeared as flyer and poster on 19 July throughout the bombed city, defined the new reality: "As of this date, a Jewish residential district is created in Minsk.... The entire Jewish population must resettle immediately in the Jewish residential district.... After resettlement, the Jewish district is to be closed off by walls from the rest of the city.... It is forbidden for Jews in work columns to remain outside the residential district assigned to them.... A forced loan of 30,000 cherwonzen is imposed on the Jewish Council to carry out the administrative measures resulting from resettlement."[17] The result was a Jewish population without property or rights, subject to the whims of the German occupation forces, and whose every move was documented. In western Belorussia, the Wehrmacht ruled the ghettos for two months, until the civil administration took over the remaining work-slaves in October. In eastern Belorussia, the army rear area, a Wehrmacht regiment particularly concerned with these matters remained for almost a year, until commandos of Einsatzgruppe B had "cleared out" the last ghetto. Up to this point, Department VII of the Local and Field Commands organization kept meticulous records of developments in the "Jewish Question" under Point 5 of their regular reports.[18]

The secondary literature tends to overlook the fact that the Wehrmacht lent a hand in annihilating eastern European Jews. Granted, this early activity pales in comparison with events from the first weeks of war, and with later organized massacres carried out by then stationary Einsatzgruppen. The one or two sentences that mention the Wehrmacht usually are confined to the organizational side of Wehrmacht assistance, downplaying the overall role of the Wehrmacht in the developing Holocaust.[19] In his book about his fate as Jewish prisoner in Auschwitz, Jean Améry imprinted on readers' consciousness the notion of the "first blow." Whether delivered with a rifle butt, human fist, or whip, the first blow made the prisoner aware "that he or she is helpless—and thus already contains the seed of everything to come." The blow breaks in the victim what had been a binding, to a certain extent universal, assumption, "the certainty that the other, on the basis of written or unwritten social contracts, will not hurt me, more precisely, that he or she will respect my physical and thus also my metaphysical existence."[20] The Wehrmacht struck eastern European Jewry this "first blow." It depersonalized and degraded the individual Jew and thus transformed hundreds of thousands into "garbage" to be cleared away systematically by the Einsatzgruppen, police, and Waffen-SS. The local and field commanders knew that their measures against the Jews were mere preparations for later events. This receives occasional mention, as in a report from 5 September 1941, with its dark and unequivocal entry: "The vast majority of male Jews in the district have been shot by the police battalion. Male Jews still living in the southern area are being interned in a prison and ... utilized for forced labor of all kinds. Their later fate remains to be seen."[21]

The Einsatzgruppen in Action

In order to implement the "special tasks on behalf of the Führer," Himmler had created for the campaign in the East four Einsatzgruppen from within the Security Police (Sicherheitspolizei, SIPO) and the Security Service (Sicherheitsdienst, SD). As defined in the 26 March agreement between Heydrich and the army high command, the Einsatzgruppen performed their tasks "on their own responsibility," but were "subordinated to the armies in relation to movement, supply, and accommodation" and, in addition, had to "notify in a timely fashion" the relevant army commander about their operations.[22] As a result of these regulations army commanders on all levels were well informed about the work of the Einsatzgruppen. The War Diaries of Rear Area, Army Group Center, meticulously note the movements of the Einsatzkommandos and their positions: "Einsatzkommando 9 will be relocated to Treuburg"; or: "the representative of the chief of the SIPO and SD is moving Einsatzkommando 8 ahead for the implementation of its tasks in Bialystok"; or Police Battalions 316 and 322, assigned to Einsatzkommando 8, "will be consecutively moved forward in such a way that one battalion will be available to Feldkomandantur 549 for several more days until the tasks in Bialystok have been carried to their end."[23] These "tasks" included the two-day mass execution of 3,000 Jews in Bialystok, an action that Himmler had initiated personally.[24] In the War Diaries of the security divisions deployed in the rear area of Army Group Center, the meticulous recording of the activities of the Einsatzgruppen was repeated. On 30 June the War Diary of the 403rd Security Division noted: "Arrival of Sonderkommandos of the Security Police.—Deployment in Grodno, Lida, and Vilna."[25] On the deployment in Wilna, commander von Ditfurth remarked in his divisional report: "All the Jews are marked with badges. A great number of executions already have taken place. I have arranged with the very loyal leader of the SD, Obersturmbannführer [SS Lt. Col.] Dr. Filbert, for these executions to be carried out as far as possible inconspicuously and to remain hidden from the army troops."[26]

In the reports of the army commanders, the operations of those SS units that Himmler—via his Higher SS and Police Führer—had assigned to them also are mentioned: The 1st and 2nd SS Cavalry Regiments operated at the southern border of Rear Area, Army Group Center, in the Pripyat Marshes. Himmler had personally given them the directive: "All Jews are to be shot. Jewish women to be driven into the swamps."[27] An interim report of the commander in the Rear Area, Army Group Center, summed up: "The SS Mounted Brigade has in the main concluded its cleansing action in the area between Highway 1 and Pripyat. Non-residents as well as soldiers of the Red Army and Jewish commissars were captured by the SS and most of them shot. By appointing mayors, establishing an auxiliary police force, and suppressing the Jews, the area can be regarded as pacified."[28] A report compiled at the same time by the SS unit was phrased more unambiguously: "Jewish plunderers have been shot.... The total number of ... plunderers, etc., shot is 6,526." The result after one month: 14,178 persons murdered.[29]

In addition to knowing about the murder of the Jews, the Wehrmacht even participated in it. From Baranovichi on 24 July, Einsatzkommando 8 reported an "especially successful" cooperation with the army. Combined *Aktionen* had targeted "bolshevist agents, political commissars ... and Jewish activists.[30] On 15 August, the 221st Security Division reported that one of its units had carried out "for the final pacification of the city of Novogrudok ... in agreement with the SD a cleansing Aktion targeting the entire city."[31] The 403rd Security Division reported in early September: "Secret Field Police and SD cooperate in fighting Jewish outrages."[32] Their brotherhood-in-arms, forged already at the beginning of the campaign, was to be fostered until winter in a series of murderous Aktionen. To sum up what has been shown so far: the Wehrmacht units in occupied Belorussia knew since the beginning of the campaign from their own observations what the special tasks of the Einsatzgruppen and thus the war crimes in the East were. An information leaflet of the 339th Infantry Division brought this up under the point, "Solution of the Jewish Problem."[33]

The Troops Go "Jew-Hunting"

In one of the very few postwar trials dealing with the crimes of the Wehrmacht, the defendants were members of the 354th Infantry

Regiment, which, as part of 286th Security Division, in the second half of 1941 operated in the rear area of Army Group Center. This trial was spurred by the diary of a member of this regiment. The author, Corporal Richard Heidenreich, reported how in July 1941 his battalion had conducted shootings of Jews in Minsk. The troops then were transferred to the village of Krupka 100 kilometers away. There the battalion fulfilled tasks such as the following:

> October 5, in the evening our Second Lieutenant selected fifteen men with strong nerves.... We waited for the morning in tense expectation. We were ready at 5 o'clock prompt, and the First Lieutenant explained what we were to do. There were approximately 1,000 Jews in the village of Krupka, and these all needed to be shot today.... After our names were read out, the column marched to the nearest swamp.... A second lieutenant and a company sergeant-major were with us. Ten shots sounded, ten Jews were blown away. This went on until all were taken care of. Only a few of them kept their composure. The children clung to their mothers, women to their men.... A couple of days later a similarly large number was shot in Kholoponichi. I was involved here too.[34]

Military historians, including those most critical of German conduct, focus their efforts to describe and evaluate the Russian campaign almost exclusively on the professional elites.[35] For this reason, we need to take a closer look at the behavior of the rank and file as reflected in trial testimony such as that cited above. Even if we cannot claim to depict a representative slice of the mentalities at work, such work can help us begin to understand how willingly the troops carried out "criminal commands."

The trial against Heidenreich's former comrades confirmed his statements.[36] It became clear that actions like the one in Krupka were part of the everyday life of the unit:

> From Krupka we carried out several so-called raids, and our task (mostly at night) was namely to cordon off and comb through the surrounding localities. There the resident Jews (men, women, and children) were taken prisoner and rounded up in the village .... The usual procedure in these operations was to alternate with parts of 12 Co. After the Jews were rounded up ... a place was selected and they were shot there .... Some Russian non-Jews were also taken along to shovel over the graves. From time to time, the Russians got in exchange the Jews' remaining belongings .... Sometimes we could catch only one Jew and then we waited until we got some more people together.[37]

Similar reports from other units of Rear Area, Army Group Center, confirm this picture.[38] Above all, extensive material from the postwar trials against former regional commissars in the part of Belorussia under civil administration—in Nazi jargon "Weißruthenien"—

confirm the suspicion that these measures involved a comprehensive action of the Wehrmacht.[39] The 727th Infantry Regiment stationed in the area around Baranovichi, under the 707th Infantry Division and its divisional commander, Major General von Bechtolsheim in Minsk, participated in this action. In surveying the damning evidence, four instances stand out:

1. These "actions" were not directed at partisan activity. Jews were the target of destruction: "During the period from the beginning of August until, I think, mid-October 1941, our unit performed occupational service in Slonim and in smaller localities in the surrounding area.... During this period our company had, as far as I can recall, one skirmish with partisans."[40] "The largest group of persons shot by Schaffitz were Jews and had not the least bit to do with the fighting."[41] "It is furthermore known to me that our company had to write so-called activity reports for the battalion. For this reason, we carried out patrols in the surrounding area during which Jews were seized and shot. In the reports, this was presented as if these persons had been shot while trying to escape."[42]

2. Hunting Jews and executing them was not an accidental or spontaneous occurrence. Such operations followed an exact and predetermined system: "The company carried out smaller actions in the vicinity of Slonim. We were driven in with trucks, sometimes we also marched in.... When on such occasions we brought Jews out of buildings, we always had the directive from Glück to pretend to the Jews that they were being taken to collection or internment camps and to bring along their luggage."[43]

"Second Lieutenant Schaffitz went on patrol again and again. As a general principle he took along only volunteers.... On these so-called patrols, S. drove with his people into the surrounding area. When he returned, he then informed the 1st Secretary S. that several partisans had been shot in action. In reality, it was generally known in the company that this meant Jews who were in no way partisans."[44]

From an army-post letter of 15 October 1941 by the company commander to his brother back home: "We are now busy hunting. That's clear to several Jewish partisans a day. There are always some wild goings-on here.... We're clearing out the whole lot—just your kind of thing."[45]

3. The brutality involved is striking. The cold-bloodedness one is more accustomed to ascribing to the Einsatzgruppen and police battalions applies just as well to the common soldier: "Our returning comrades-in-arms tell us that they had to shoot several Jewish families ... from smaller villages located in the area around the convent

.... One of the company ... said, in his exact words, 'Jew brain, that tastes good.' He said they had just shot Jews, and their brains had sprayed him right in the face."[46] "I can still remember how I saw a child grabbed by the head and then shot. The child was then thrown into a hole."[47] "H. also told how children had run away during the execution, and that these children were skewered onto a bayonet and then thrown into a hole."[48] A Jewish survivor reported, "A German Wehrmacht unit stationed in Chutchin amused itself every Saturday with 'Jew games.' At random and for no reason they tortured and shot Jews."[49] "The local commander of Slonim had a clique around him with whom he went drinking and played cards. B. from South Tirol also belonged to this clique. He had told us some of what went on, like that he always had to round up Jewish girls when the local commander was drunk."[50]

4. Mercilessness and bloodthirstiness against all so-called enemies of National Socialism could not be summoned on command. Some of the troops had already had their share, but the opportunity to act out these drives —this was created by military command. A witness reported what happened before an operation in the proximity of Slonim: "A letter was read by the company commander, according to which the Jews in our area were to be liquidated."[51] Another put it more precisely: "On the basis of a standing regimental order, all Jews were to be regarded as partisans if they were encountered outside their place of residence."[52] This testimony makes it clear that the commands were not simply directives from a few fanatic company commanders—they had to be central decisions. They were found and can be traced to the headquarters of the "Kommandant in Weißruthenien," Major General von Bechtolsheim, mentioned above. On 10 September 1941, his first report conveyed the following appraisal of his area: "The Jewish population is Bolshevik and capable of any attitude hostile to Germany. In terms of how they are to be treated, there need be no guidelines."[53] Apparently, though, Bechtolsheim did issue such guidelines on 29 September, and on 4 and 10 October. In any event he referred to them in later reports: "As already ordered, the Jews must disappear from the countryside."[54] That "disappear" did not mean simply driving them out emerges clearly in a command dated 16 October making it the duty of the men of the 727th Infantry Regiment, "to make every effort to remove the Jews entirely from the villages. In case after case, it is clear that these are the sole support the partisans find in order to survive both now and through the winter. Their annihilation is therefore to be carried out in whatever manner."[55] And three days later: "The Jews ... are our mortal enemies. These enemies are, however,

no longer human beings in the sense of our European culture; rather, they are raised to be criminals from their childhood on, and are as criminally schooled beasts. Beasts must be destroyed."[56]

"Mopping up the countryside" was no simple Wehrmacht action. Apparently it resulted from consultation with the civil administration, whose head, the Reichskommissar Ostland Hinrich Lohse (who also controlled "Weißruthenien") had established "minimal measures" in his "Provisional Guidelines for the Treatment of Jews" of 18 August 1941, for when "further measures in the sense of the final solution of the Jewish question are not possible." As one of these measures he decreed, "The countryside is to be cleansed of Jews."[57]

At the end of November, the Wehrmacht discontinued this program. The situation on the front made it necessary to return to basic military tasks. Instead of killing Jews wherever and whenever they were found, the Wehrmacht was to transport them from rural areas to the nearest major ghetto. When the local commander of Slonim related the situation to the regional commissar, the response came by return mail casting light on the Wehrmacht's active role; during the first stages of building up the civil administration and stationary SD posts, the Wehrmacht had to underwrite the annihilation of the Jews. Gebietskommissar Erren wrote to Ortskommandant Glück on 4 December 1941, "Until now you have supported me in a most commendable way in solving my political and *völkisch* tasks—I could not have done it alone with my weak police forces—and I must therefore ask you ... to convince your superior officers that the German mission in the East must continue to be able to count on your powers."[58] By this point, some 20,000 Jews in his area had fallen victim to the "German mission in the East," executed by units of the "Kommandant in Weißruthenien, Major General von Bechtolsheim."[59]

The Jew *Is* the Partisan

The Wehrmachtsbefehlshaber Ostland, Lieutenant General Walter Braemer, whose duty it was to ensure "military security" in the occupied Baltic states and in the part of Belorussia under civil administration, demanded in his guidelines of 25 September 1941, that "all factors endangering peace and order be rendered harmless." His concrete terms: "Quiet and order are endangered by a) Bolshevik soldiers and agents either scattered or intentionally left behind or dropped off in forests and isolated areas (partisans);

b) communist and other radical elements; c) Jews and circles friendly to Jews."[60] The issue here is clearly the partisan danger, while Jews and those sympathetic to them appear as part of an explosive mixture. Even critical military historians have assessed formulations suggesting a natural alliance of Jew and partisan, particularly in the notorious commands of Generals von Reichenau and von Manstein, as tactical maneuvers. One argument runs that troop leaders, by using a pseudo-military explanation, wanted to prevent any resistance among their soldiers to the genocide; another contends that they did not want to jeopardize their cooperation with the SD and Waffen-SS killer commandos in "securing and calming" the occupied territories. Both interpretations, however, rest on the assumption that no commanding officer really believed his own battle cry.[61] Aside from the fact that the troops had no problem with the Holocaust, but rather, as shown, liked to take matters into their own hands, the equation Jew-Partisan took hold long before the massacres of late fall 1941 and the emerging war against the partisans. It had already surfaced in the first weeks of war and followed few if any tactical considerations.

For 8 July, the War Diary of the 221st Security Division, stationed on the western border of the Soviet Union, contained the following entry: "It is clear that everywhere where Jews live, 'mopping up the area' runs into difficulties—because the Jews support the creation of partisan groups and the disruption of the area caused by scattered Russian soldiers. Due to this finding, the evacuation of all male Jews from all villages north of Bialoviza has been ordered, effective immediately."[62] A report of 18 August by the 350st Infantry Regiment, part of the same division, displayed a similar formulation:

> In all these measures, it is finally most important to remove the influence of Jews. In some places this influence still holds sway today and has in no way been broken. These elements must be disposed of with the most radical means because, regardless of what the community inhabitants say, they are exactly those who maintain connections to the Red Army and resistance bands and give them the necessary means for acting against the German Wehrmacht.[63]

The regimental commander passed along this report with his approval to the division, adding that "the solution to the Jewish question must take more radical forms."[64] Some among the troops did of course also try to describe the actual conditions in a more realistic way, to comprehend the emerging partisan movement as a sum of scattered Red Army soldiers and Communist civilians, or to understand the flight of numerous Jews into the forests as a response to the terror of German occupation.[65] But such attempts remained exceptions, remnants of a normal perceptive ability. What prevailed was another, racist view of things: "The Jews are without exception identical with the concept of partisan."[66]

A parallel process can be established for the armed opposition. Here too the Wehrmacht leadership had painted a clear picture well before the campaign. Whereas the "Guidelines for the Conduct of the Army in Russia" voiced a rather reserved warning about the opposition's "treacherous methods of fighting" and described Asian soldiers in the Red Army as especially "inscrutable, unpredictable, underhanded, and callous,"[67] the first issue of the "Reports for the Troops" slipped out of bounds in its description of communist commissars: "It would be insulting to animals to call the features of these, largely Jewish, offspring animal-like. They are the embodiment of the infernal, a wild, personified hatred of all noble humanity. In the form of these commissars, we experience the uprising of the sub-human against noble blood."[68] Hardly had the campaign of annihilation gotten under way when reports from the front confirmed the Wehrmacht's propaganda purposes: "In the political commissar, we encounter the Asiatic depravity of the entire Red system."[69] Or: "Bolshevism has raised Russian youth not to carry on an idea, but rather to criminality. Its means of battle are aberrations of the Asiatic brain."[70] Staff officer reports of cannibalism in prisoner-of-war camps and common soldiers' collection of "Asiatic types" in their photo albums confirm that this mentality had spread, and demonstrate that the identification of Jew and partisan did not spring from military tactics, but rather from existing racism. Despite all differences, Jew and partisan both represented something alien and hostile to Germany, and their alliance was "natural" both in terms of blood and ideology.

The photographs, army-post letters, and testimony in Soviet and German courts leave no doubt that racism was a fact of everyday troop life. Similarly clear evidence does not, however, exist for the officer corps, and no quantifiable investigations on the mentality of Wehrmacht leadership are available. Lacking these, military history enlists methodologically outmoded studies on "pictures of the enemy," "pictures of Russia," "pictures of war." Despite Manfred Messerschmidt's push toward a history of Wehrmacht mentality in his standard work of 1969, *Die Wehrmacht im NS-Staat*, little has been done in this direction.[71]

The most recent attempt to develop Messerschmidt's thesis of the "partial identity of goals" is found in Bernhard Kroener's work.[72] Taking the "partial identity of experience and memory" as his point of departure, Kroener divides the officer corps into four homogenous birth-cohorts. For the mostly aristocratic members of the birth-cohort 1880–90, who experienced World War I as staff officers and represented a large portion of generals in World War II, Kroener diagnoses a broad agreement with National Socialist foreign and domestic policies in a persisting "opposition in terms of mentality."[73] The younger generation, born in the years 1890–1900, served as front-line officers in 1914–18, and in 1939 returned to the front as staff officers. This group stemmed from the bourgeoisie and "identified much more strongly than the older officer generation with social Darwinist ideas of struggle as a form of existence and with Darwin's ... principle of the survival of the fittest as postulated by National Socialism for state and personal life."[74]

These assertions need to be supplemented by more detailed work in order to obtain a complete picture of the consciousness of this era. Both groups grew up in the imperial period, that is, in a climate of overheated fantasies of world power. Their world fell apart in 1918. They interpreted military defeat and the end of the Hohenzollern state as a result of disintegration on the home front, a consequence of the "stab in the back" carried out by Jewish-Bolshevik revolutionaries against the able-bodied "Volk." The younger generation, as Kroener points out, tried to take out their revenge on the "red rabble" as Freikorps members, and to overthrow the "system" in a putsch. The older generation worked toward a revision of existing circumstances within the framework of the Reichswehr. For the commanding officer or staff officer in 1941, entrusted with "securing and calming" the occupied areas behind the front, the trauma of 1918–23 was reactivated in the immeasurable distances of the East and in face of an invisible, elusive enemy. Class-specific or ideological reservations about National Socialism, where they existed, retreated. The Jew and the partisan had taken over the role of the Spartakists, the first name of the German Communist Party, in all their insidious metamorphoses.[75] The ghettos created by the generals seemed more and more like breeding grounds for conspiracy and uprising: fleeing from the threatened massacre, the Jew transmitted the poison of disintegration into Russian villages—every woman at the market, every farmer with his horse-drawn wagon had been infected long ago, not only potential partisans. A macabre piece of evidence for this paranoia can be found in a three-day course set up by the commanding officer of the Rear Area, Army Group Center. On 24 September, the head of Einsatzgruppe B, Arthur Nebe, held the first lecture, "The Jewish Question with Special Attention to the Partisan Movement."[76] In the final exercise,

"Clearing out a Nest of Partisans," participants encountered some Jewish families instead of the partisans they had expected. They executed them on the spot.[77]

Wehrmacht Murder on a Grand Scale

As dramatic as the "partisan studies" appear, events of October and November 1941 in Belorussia provide an even clearer instance of the state of troop consciousness. The autumn months witnessed the first annihilation actions against the ghettos,[78] introduced by an undertaking of the Wehrmachtsbefehlshaber Ostland, Lieutenant General Braemer in Riga.[79] On 4 October, two companies of the 11th Police Reserve Battalion, supported by Lithuanian Schutzmannschaften, were marched into Minsk. There the commander of the battalion reported to the staff of Infantry Division 707 in order to get exact directives. In a postwar trial, one of the officers of the battalion recalled this operation under the name "*Aktion 'judenrein.'*"[80] Following some smaller killing operations against Jews in the Minsk area, inhabitants of the Smilovici ghetto—1,338 Jews—were murdered on 14 October. A similar operation in Koidanovo, with 1,000 victims, followed on 21 October. The "action" culminated in the murder of 5,900 Jews on 27 and 28 October in the Slutsk ghetto.[81] The massacres created a sensation in the leading circles of the occupation: the Slutsk regional commissar protested that the murders had been "carried out in an almost sadistic way," and his supervisor, Wilhelm Kube, passed along the protest to the Reichskommissar Ostland in Riga. As a convinced National Socialist and Gauleiter, Kube's intervention was not provoked by moral considerations, but rather, as his letter makes clear, by rivalries and a differing, "more effective," concept of occupation policy. "Without … informing me, Police Battalion 11 from Kauen, a troop under direct Wehrmacht control, took matters into their own hands and inflicted great damage to the German image."[82] With the destruction of the three ghettos, the bloody expedition had, in short, fired the starting shot for the second, and systematic, phase of the "Final Solution" in Belorussia. And Kube's civil administration saw itself outplayed in an unexpected alliance of Wehrmacht and SD.

In order to understand this surprising contribution by the Wehrmachtsbefehlshaber Ostland to genocide in "Weißruthenien," it is helpful to recapitulate briefly how the "Final Solution" developed within overall German politics.[83] In the first half of July 1941—a grandiose German victory was underway around Smolensk—Hitler had resolved to undertake a radical annihilation of the Russian Jews. While the civil administration of the "Ostland" regarded this as a long-term task and prepared a series of transitional measures against the Jews, in early August the head of Einsatzgruppe A already was pressing for full execution and promised "an almost 100 percent, immediate cleansing of Jews from the entire 'Ostland.'"[84] In the meantime, however, the National Socialist leadership had radicalized its program. In mid-September—the fall of Kiev was in sight—Himmler related Hitler's decision to make the old Reich and protectorate "Jew-free" as quickly as possible. Soon thereafter he gave more precise directions: Jews in these areas were to be transported to their destruction in the East, to Riga, Reval, and Minsk. In mid-October—as they encircled Wjasma and Bryansk, the Wehrmacht had taken more than half a million prisoners, and panic was spreading in Moscow—the first deportation train left Vienna for Lodz. On 8 November, deportations from Germany began with a transport from Hamburg. Their destination: the Minsk ghetto.

Lieutenant General Braemer, senior military official in the occupied "Ostland," was informed of the transports early on through his friends among the top SS cadres in Riga.[85] Braemer, a fanatical adherent of the "Jew-Partisan" thesis, saw in the arrival of the German Jews, who, as he protested, "are far superior in intelligence to the mass of the 'Weißruthenien' population" an imminent danger of infection.[86] Whereas he could be sure that this problem, as far as Latvia and Lithuania were concerned, was ably handled by the ambitious chief of Einsatzgruppe A, Franz Walter Stahlecker, in Minsk the office of the SIPO and SD had yet to be firmly established. In addition, in the western part of Belorussia, as opposed to the rest of the "Ostland," already in late 1941 partisan activity was beginning. Braemer's subordinate, Bechtolsheim, continuously cited this activity to justify his requests for reinforcements.[87] This problem offered an opportunity to prove in an exemplary Aktion that the Wehrmacht was up to the task of solving the "Jewish question." Apparently, Braemer coordinated his initiative also with the commander of the Rear Area, Army Group Center: On 18 October, the latter rescinded an existing ban on Wehrmacht members entering ghettos in case of "*eventuell befohlener Aktionen*"; such "possible commanded actions" commenced two days later."[88]

On 20 October, 7,000 Jews in Borisov were slaughtered with help from the Wehrmacht.[89] In November 5,000 ghetto victims followed in Bobruysk. At the same time, the head of the Rear Area, Army Group Center—by warning of armed resistance—forbade the entry of Jewish transports into the area under his command.[90] After the departure of the 11th Police Battalion, the Wehrmacht, in the form of the 727th Infantry Regiment of the 707th Infantry Division mentioned above, assumed the task of marching against ghettos in "Weißruthenien" as well. On 30 October, the 8th Company "cleansed" the ghetto of Nesvizh and murdered 4,500 Jews. On 2 November, an unknown number of Jews in Lachovici fell victim to the same unit; on 5 November, 1,000 Jews in Turec and Swierzna, and on 9 November, a national day of honor, soldiers of the 8th Company celebrated by slaughtering all 1,800 Jews in Mir.[91] In Slonim, the 6th Company actively assisted the SD and police in the murder of 9,000 Jews on 13 and 14 November, and on 8 December, the 7th Company helped murder 3,000 Jews in Novogrudok.[92]

Most of these murderous Wehrmacht operations—small raids as well as large-scale ghetto "actions"—took place before 3 December 1941. On this day, by their own decision, Panzer Groups 3 and 4 broke off their offensive operation against Moscow. The 2nd Panzer Army followed suit on 5 December. The *Blitzkrieg* had proven a failure; the Wehrmacht had come to a standstill in the East. This date is important because, for military historians such as Omer Bartov, it is said to mark a change in the leadership of the war effort, after which the troops turned into "an ideologically motivated tool of a criminal regime" and the war became "barbaric." That the "Wannsee Conference" took place at the same time is for him no accident.[93] Even though Bartov's questions and his findings on the mentality of the troops locked in static warfare in the East are important, both his postulated turning point and causal deduction are wrong.

The Wehrmacht crimes, as summarized above for a limited territory and a short time, all occurred before these critical days in late 1941 and early 1942. The first decisive measures toward genocide against the Jews did not take place in the context of defeat, but rather were planned and carried out during the period of the greatest victories. The Wehrmacht took the step from everyday persecution to all-out murder, from raids to the Holocaust, not in the winter of 1942, but in September and October of 1941. "Approximately 19,000 partisans and criminals ... the majority Jews," reported Einsatzgruppe A, were shot before December 1941 by the Wehrmacht in Belorussia.[94] A report of SD leader Burkhardt from Minsk, also dated late 1941, made it clear that no coincidence was involved. "There exist fundamental differences of opinion ... between the Wehrmacht and the Generalkommissariat, because the Wehrmacht deems solving the Jewish question absolutely necessary for reasons of general security, while the civil administration believes that a quick solution to the Jewish question is inexpedient given the economic necessities."[95] One could count on further troop engagement to take care of the Jews: within the first half of 1942, the Wehrmacht again murdered at least 20,000 in Belorussia.

Once the Red Army launched its counter-offensive and broke through the front, especially in northeastern Belorussia, the partisan was no longer simply a projection of a range of real and imagined anxieties. The partisan existed in the flesh, and began to conduct a veritable war.[96] The "solution to the Jewish question" disappeared in the convoluted depths of this new front. It is no accident that the first large undertakings against partisans in the rear area of Army Group Center were commanded by the same general who had been responsible for the "Jew-hunts" and "ghetto actions" in the part of Belorussia under civil administration, the commander of the 707th Infantry Division, Major General von Bechtolsheim. His first command, issued on 18 March 1942, relied on tried and true methods: "In the new area of military action, the troops must conduct the war against partisans and other elements hostile to Germany with all severity, as was successfully the case in 'Weißruthenien,' especially during the fall months of 1941. The corresponding directives about ruthless and rigorous actions against men, women, and children also hold for the new area of action."[97] The result showed that his men had understood. During "Operation Bamberg" from 28 March to 4 April 1942 in the southwestern part of the rear area of the Army Group, 3,500 "partisans and helpers" were shot—as daily reports show, mostly Jews. German losses—six dead and ten wounded[98]—were so obviously low that even the commander, von Schenckendorff, voiced his criticism. Nevertheless, "Bamberg" achieved what Bechtolsheim had announced before the attack: it set standards.[99] In the future, anti-partisan undertakings were prepared so as to destroy smaller ghettos in the area either at the beginning or end of the "action." "Dissolution of peripheral ghettos" read the occupation jargon.[100]

The Wehrmacht "encroachment" in the area around Glubokie cited above also proceeded according to this pattern. Georg Heuser, the area SD advisor for Jewish issues in Minsk, described the local scenario in the early summer of 1942 as follows: "operations against Jews ... were carried out mostly in connection with anti-partisan undertakings and involved units of the municipal police [Schutzpolizei], the rural constabulary [Gendarmerie], as well as the army."[101] The Wehrmacht availed itself of an SD emissary who kept the civil administration informed of plans "to cleanse of Jews the border between the Rear Area, Army Group Center, and the areas taken over by the civil administration" and reduce the partisan danger in this zone.[102] The result of the two-week action against eight ghettos: 13,000 Jews murdered and 115,247 Reichsmarks transferred to the "Jewish property" account held by the Generalkommissariat in Minsk.[103] The commanding officer of Rear Area, Army Group Center, made a note to himself on 12 June 1942—the high point of the murders—under point 36 of a discussion among high-level military officers, "The Jewish Question on a Large Scale."[104]

For a Social History of the War

The legends of a hard-fighting but honorable Wehrmacht persisted well into the postwar period. In the 1970s and 1980s, however, a critical military history took hold, above all around the Militärgeschichtliches Forschungsamt in Freiburg. This school established both the character of the "criminal commands" prepared by Wehrmacht leadership as well as the active participation of troop leaders in the "war of annihilation" in the East. Nevertheless, considerable differences emerge when one compares the results of this case study with those of the critical "Freiburg school." The present study suggests that the Freiburg group did not go far enough.

The outcome of Wehrmacht activities in Belorussia in the period from 22 June 1941, to 1 July 1942, can be summarized as follows:

1. Wehrmacht participation in the Holocaust proceeded on all levels of military command—from commanding officers in the Rear Area, Army Group Center, and the "Ostland" under civil administration to the lower-level troop leaders. There were no cases of resistance or refusal to carry out commands.
2. The "collection" and ghettoization of Jews followed a definite plan. Its timing—like later measures of physical destruction—corresponded to the stages of the "Final Solution." It proceeded in concrete consultation with the other organs of occupation.
3. The Wehrmacht's program of annihilation in Belorussia was racist in both its goals and reasoning. As the identification of Jew and partisan shows, military considerations did not compete with racism, but rather were inherent to it.

4. The mentality of the Wehrmacht leadership corresponded to troop consciousness. The personal engagement in "Jew-hunting"—whether in volunteer cooperation with the Einsatzgruppen, or as an action of the Wehrmacht itself—betrays a spontaneous accord with the murder of Jews.

It is, of course, necessary to compare the foregoing conclusions to those deriving from studies of other regions of the occupied Soviet Union; on the other hand, this case study certainly raises the question of whether one can still speak only of "anti-Jewish tendencies in the Eastern Army" (Krausnick) or of the army's "entanglement" in the process of destruction (Messerschmidt). The comment that one must "differentiate" (Förster) between the measures aimed directly at Jews and the actions taken to calm the country is questionable when one looks at the interlocking nature of all occupation-related activities in Belorussia. Finally, it does not suffice to reduce the sources of the National Socialist *Vernichtungskrieg*, its war of annihilation, to an "ideological background" (Förster); neither does this potential exhaust itself in "anti-Bolshevism" (Streit); nor is the identification of Jew and partisan only a "connection" (Hillgruber).[105] All of these formulations have the potential to diminish the events they seek to encompass. It almost seems that, as if by gentlemen's agreement, many historians observe an internalized limit: not to describe the Wehrmacht as the apparatus of a violence-oriented society nor war as its natural expression.

Michael Geyer has described the "fusion of nationalism and violence" as characteristic of German history in this century, and National Socialism as "the most successful result of this process."[106] Millions of Germans in the inter-war period did not simply select this project as political program; rather, they collectively co-produced it. The revolutionary actions and militant strikes of the Left struck a common chord (even if they understood themselves as internationalist) with the putsches and political murders of the nationalist Right—both had defined and legitimized violence as a political means. The particular contribution of the Wehrmacht to this history of violence is found in the doctrine of "total war"; there it developed a model for solving external crises and paved the way for putting it into use.

National Socialism was the vector of this potential to employ violence. By combining fantasies of annihilation with a political program and the most rabid will to power, it achieved a stunning and deadly fusion—to create the social forms for the elite terror of the Freikorps in the shape of war. To quote Geyer's formulation,

"War and violence are organized by the state, but driven by society. They live from the ... participation of society or individual social classes in war."[107] A scholarly approach that chooses not to risk this view can perceive only separate crimes and individual criminals. To speak of crimes of the Wehrmacht thus means a decision to stop writing military history, and to start writing a social history of war.

—*Translated by Carol Scherer*

Notes

*This is a revised and expanded version of the German original. Reprinted with permission from *Holocaust and Genocide Studies* 7, no. 1 (Spring 1997): 79–101.

1. Lagebericht des Gebietskommissars von Slonim an den Generalkommissar von Weißruthenien, 25.1.1942, Żentrale Stelle Ludwigsburg vol. 25, Verschiedenes, fol. 126. (Zentrale Stelle.)
2. Generalkommissar Kube an Reichskommissar Lohse, 31.7.1942, Nuremberg Document PS-3428.
3. M. Domarus, ed., *Hitler—Reden und Proklamationen*, vol. 2 (Neustadt a.d. Aisch: 1963), 1058.
4. Generaloberst Halder, *Kriegstagebuch des Oberkommandos der Wehrmacht* ed. H. A. Jacobsen, vol. 2 (Stuttgart: 1963), 336f. (KTB Halder).
5. G. Koenen, "Überprüfungen an einem Nexus: Der Bolschewismus und die deutschen Intellektuellen nach Revolution und Weltkrieg, 1917–1924," in *Tel Aviver Jahrbuch für deutsche Geschichte* (1995): 359–391.
6. P. E. Schramm, ed., *Kriegstagebuch des Oberkommandos der Wehrmacht* (*Wehrmachtsführungsstab*) *1940–1945* (Frankfurt am Main: 1963), 1:341.
7. OKH/Gen. z.b.V.b.ObdH, BundesarchivMilitärarchiv Freiburg (BA-MA) RW 4/v. 577, cited by J. Förster, "Das Unternehmen 'Barbarossa' als Eroberungs- und Vernichtungskrieg," in *Das Deutsche Reich und der Zweite Weltkrieg*, vol. 4: *Der Angriff auf die Sowjetunion* (Stuttgart: Militärgeschichtliches Forschungsamt Freiburg i. Breisgau: 1983), 428f. (*DRZW*).
8. Besondere Anordungen Nr. 1 zur Weisung Nr. 21 (Fall Barbarossa), 19.5.1941, mit Anlage 3 zu OKW/WFSt/Abt. L IV/Q, 19. Ausf., BA-MA, RW 4/v. 524, cited in G. R. Ueberschär and W. Wette, eds., *Der deutsche Überfall auf die Sowjetunion. "Unternehmen Barbarossa" 1941* (Frankfurt am Main: 1991), 258; compare also Merkblatt AOK 17, Ic/AO, 16.6.41, Dok. NOKW 1692.
9. Richtlinien auf Sondergebieten zur Weisung Nr. 21 (Fall Barbarossa) 13.3.1941, OKW/WFSt/Abt. L (IV Q), IMT, vol. 26, 53 ff., cited in: Ueberschär and Wette, *Überfall*, 247.
10. Befehl des ObdH, Generalfeldmarschall von Brauchitsch betr. Regelung des Einsatzes der Sicherheitspolizei und des SD in Verband des Heeres 28.4.1941,

OKH/Gen. St.d.H./Gen.Qu., BA-MA, RH 22/155, cited in: Ueberschär and Wette, *Überfall,* 249f.

11. Entry of 19.9.1939, KTB Halder, vol. 1:79.
12. See note 8.
13. OKH/Gen.st.d.H./Gen.Qu. Abt. Kriegsverwaltung Nr. II/0308/41 geh./vom 2.4.1941 betr. Regelung des Einsatzes der Sicherheitspolizei und des SD beim Unternehmen "Marita" und "Fünfundzwanzig," BA-MA, RH 31-I/v.23, cited in *DRZW*, 423.
14. Der Kommandant der Feldkommandantur 528 (V), Lagebericht, 5.9.1941, BA-MA, RH 26-221-21, 303.
15. M. Vestermanis, "Der lettische Anteil an der Endlösung," in U. Backes, R. Jesse, and R. Zitelmann, eds., *Schatten der Vergangenheit* (Berlin: 1990), 427ff.; Ch. Streit, *Keine Kameraden: Die Wehrmacht und die sowjetischen Kriegsgefangenen* (Stuttgart: 1978), 113f.
16. Der Befehlshaber des rückwärtigen Heeresgebietes Mitte Abt. VII/Kr.-Verw., Verwaltungs-Anordnungen Nr. 1, 7.7.1941 and Nr. 2, 13.7.1941, Belorussian State Archive (BSA) Minsk 370-1-487, 20; and 393-3-42, 1; also Streit, *Keine Kameraden,* 113.
17. Anordnung des Feldkommandanten in Minsk, 19.7.1941, BSA Minsk, collection of flyers, 110/45.
18. Situation reports of the field and local commanders of the 221. Sich. Div., BA-MA, RH 26-221-21; similar situation reports from the Rear Area, Army Group South, may be found in the former Special (Osobyi) Archive in Moscow, 1275-3-661 to 668.
19. A. Hillgruber, "Der Ostkrieg und die Judenverfolgung," in Ueberschär and Wette, *Überfall,* 192; J. Förster, "Die Sicherung des Lebensraumes," in *DRZW*, 4:1034; for more detail see R. Hilberg, *Die Vernichtung der europäischen Juden* (Frankfurt am Main: 1991), 2:366ff.
20. J. Améry, *Jenseits von Schuld und Sühne* (Stuttgart: 1980), 55f.
21. See note 14.
22. See note 10.
23. Der Befehlshaber des rückwärtigen Heeresgebietes 102, Korpsbefehl Nr. 19, 27.6.1941, BA-MA, RH 22-224, 109; ibid., Korpsbefehl Nr. 23, 2.7.1941, BA-MA, RH 22-224, 121; ibid., Korpsbefehl Nr. 26, 10.7.1941, BA-MA, RH 22-224, 141.
24. Condensed summation of charges against members of Pol. Bat. 316, 2.3.1960, Staatsanwaltschaft Bochum, 16 Js 13/59, 18f., 20ff.; KTB Pol. Bat. 322, entry of 8.7.1941, BA Koblenz, RH 20-79, 31R; and Urteil gegen U. und andere, LG Freiburg I. Br., I AK 1/63.
25. BA-MA, RH 26-403-2, 26R.
26. Bericht über die Tätigkeit des Div. Stabes in Litauen (undated), BA-MA RH 26-403-44, 6.
27. Befehl RFSS, 28.7.1941 an das SS-Kav. Regiment 2, cited in Y. Büchler "Kommandostab Reichsführer SS: Himmler's Personal Murder Brigades in 1941," in *Holocaust and Genocide Studies* 1:1 (1986): 15; Confirmation of this order in Operation Report of the SS Cavalry Regiment 2, 12.8.1941, Kriegshistorisches Archiv (KHA) Prague, box 5, folder 30, 209,
28. Befehlshaber des rückwärtigen Heeres-Gebietes Mitte, Bericht an OKH/Gen.Qu. vom 10.8.1941, BA-MA, RH 22-227, 19.
29. SS-Kav. Rgt. 2, Bericht über den Verlauf der Pripjet Aktion vom 27.7 bis 11.8.1941 vom 12.8.1941, KHA Prag, 154-24, 451.

30. Der Chef der Sicherheitspolizei und des SD, Ereignismeldung UdSSR (EM), Nr. 32, 24.7.1941.
31. Sich. Div 221/Abt. Ia an Befehlshaber des rückwärtigen Heeresgebietes Mitte, 15.8.1941, BA-MA, RH 26-221-19, 147.
32. See note 26.
33. 339. Inf.Div./Abt. Ic, Merkblatt vom 2.11.1941, BA-MA, RH 26-339-6, 4.
34. *True to Type: A Selection from Letters and Diaries of German Soldiers and Civilians Collected on the Soviet-German Front* (London: 1961), 29–32.
35. There are—with the exception of Omer Bartov's *The Eastern Front 1941–45* (London, New York: 1986)—no scholarly studies of individual units; there are no evaluations of fieldpost letters or of trials against former army soldiers. One seeks in vain a history of the mentality of the Wehrmacht. Discussion of the Holocaust always concentrates on the higher officer grades; see for example, J. Förster, *DRZW*, 4:1045, 1054; compare also H-H. Wilhelm, "Motivation und 'Kriegsbild' deutscher Generäle und Offiziere im Krieg gegen die Sowjetunion," in M. Jahn and R. Rürup, eds., *Erobern und Vernichten* (Berlin: 1991), 173ff; Hans-Erich Volkmann, ed., *Das Rußlandbild im Dritten Reich* (Cologne: 1994).
36. Strafsache gegen W. Schönemann, LG Köln 24 Ks 1/63, Sonderband K, Zeugen C., K., A., 15f., 19f, 43f.; ibid., vol. 9, Zeugen M., F., 13f., 15f; ibid., vol. 10, Zeuge N., 154f.
37. Ibid., Zeugenaussage M., 2.12.1963, 53f.
38. Units of 339th Infantry Div. undertook "Jew-hunting" *Aktionen* at the same time in the region of Orsha-Vitebsk; compare Strafsache gegen Nöll und Zimber, LG Darmstadt 2 Ks 2/54.
39. Strafsache gegen Windisch und andere, LG Mainz 3 Ks 1/67 (Windisch); Strafsache gegen Erren und andere, LG Hamburg, 147 Js 29/67 (Erren).
40. Testimony of R., Erren, 32.
41. Testimony of B. (Spruchkammerverfahren) in Windisch, 118b.
42. Testimony of H., Windisch, 1354.
43. Testimony of G., Erren, 3063f.
44. Testimony of L., Windisch, 1178.
45. Testimony of K., Windisch, 1175.
46. Testimony of R., Erren, 33.
47. Testimony of M., Erren, 1155.
48. Testimony of Sch., Windisch, 1165.
49. Testimony of Kirszenbaum, Windisch, 1381 ff.
50. Testimony of W., Erren, 3138.
51. Testimony of M., Erren, 1154.
52. Testimony of K., Windisch, 1172.
53. Der Kommandant in Weissruthenien des Wehrmachtsbefehlshabers Otsland/ Abt. Ia, Lagebericht, 10.9.1941, BSA Minsk, 651-1-1, 25.
54. Der Kommandant in Weissruthenien/Abt. Ia, Befehl Nr. 24 vom 24.11.1941, BSA Minsk 378-1-698, 32.
55. Der Kommandant in Weissruthenien/Abt. Ia (Tagesbefehl), 16.10.1941, BSA Minsk 378-1-698, 12f
56. Der Kommandant in Weißruthenien/Abt. Ia, Lagebericht, 19.10.1941, BSA Minsk 651-1-1, 14f.
57. Der Reichskommissar für das Ostland/IIa4 Vorläufige Richtlinien für die Behandlung der Juden im Gebiet des Reichskommissariats Ostland, 18.8.1941, Central State Historical Archive (ZSA) of Latvia, Riga, 1026-1-3, 143.

58. Oberleutnant Glück. Inf. Rgt. 727, An den Gebietskommissar, 4.12.1941, BSA Minsk 3500-2-38, 533; the answer, ibid., 534.
59. Bericht der Einsatzgruppe A vom Winter 1941/42, PS-2273, cited in Hilberg, *Vernichtung,* 2:317f.
60. Wehrmachtsbefehlshaber Ostland, Richtlinien für die militärische Sicherung und für die Aufrechterhaltung der Ruhe und Ordnung in Ostland, 25.9.1941, ZSA Riga, 1026-1-25, 12.
61. Ch. Streit, "Ostkrieg, Antibolschewismus und 'Endlösung,'" in *Geschichte und Gesellschaft* 2 (1991): 251f.; A. Hillgruber, "Die 'Endlösung' und das deutsche Ostimperium als Kernstück des rassenideologischen Regimes des Nationalsozialismus," in M. Funke, ed., *Hitler, Deutschland und die Mächte* (Düsseldorf: 1977), 106ff.; Hilberg *Vernichtung,* 2:315, even speaks of a "pretext."
62. 221. Sich. Div., KTB Nr. 2, Eintrag 8.7.1941, BA-MA, RH 26-221-10, 87.
63. Inf. Rgt. 350, II. Bat., An das Regiment, 18.8.1941, BA-MA, RH 26-221-21, 294ff.
64. Ibid., 295.
65. 403. Sich. Div., KTB, Eintrag 10.9.1941, BA-MA, RH 26-403-2, 69 R.; 339. Inf.Div., An den Befehlshaber rückwärtiges Heeres-Gebiet Mitte, Beurteilung der Lage, 5.11.1941, BA-MA, RH 26-339-5, 2f.
66. Kommandantur des Sicherungs-Gebietes Weissruthenien/Abt. Ic, Lagebericht, 20.2.1942, BA-MA, RH 26-707-15, 4.
67. See note 8.
68. Mitteilungen für die Truppe, hrsg. von OKW/WFSt/WPr (IIc), Nr. 116, Juni 1941.
69. Befehlshaber rückwärtiges Heeres-Gebiet Sud/Abt. Ic, Lagebericht vom 19.7.1941, BA-MA, RH 22-170.
70. 707. Inf.Div./Abt. Ic, Lagebericht für die Monate Mai und Juni 1942, 5.8.1942, BA-MA, RH 26-707-15.
71. See note 35.
72. B.R. Kroener, "Strukturelle Veränderungen in der militärischen Gesellschaft des Dritten Reiches," in M. Prinz and R. Zitelmann, eds., *Nationalsozialismus und Modernisierung* (Darmstadt: 1991), 267–96.
73. Kroener, "Veränderungen," 273.
74. Ibid., 274.
75. Leading officers, before the court of justice, pointed out this connection, as for example Jodl during the Main War Crimes Trial, cited in H. Krausnick, *Hitlers Einsatzgruppen: Die Truppen des Weltanschauungskrieges 1938–1942* (Frankfurt am Main: 1985), 104; or Wöhler in the OKW trial, cited in J. Friedrich, *Das Gesetz des Krieges, Das deutsche Heer in Rußland 1941–1945* (Munich: 1993), 632; for an overview, see M. Messerschmidt, "Harte Sühne am Judentum, Befehlslage und Wissen in der deutschen Wehrmacht," in J. Wollenberg, ed., *"Niemand war dabei und keiner hat's gewußt": Die deutsche Öffentlichkeit und die Judenverfolgung 1933–1945* (Munich: 1989), 127; Förster, *DRZW*, 4:427f.
76. Der Befehlshaber des rückwärtigen Heeres-Gebietes Mitte/Abt. Ia, Tagesordnung für den Kursus "Bekämpfung von Partisanen," 24.–26.9.1941, 23.9.1941, BA-MA, RH 22-225, 70.
77. (Befehlshaber des rückwärtigen Heeresgebietes Mitte) Ib, Aktennotiz über den Kursus, 2.10.1941, BSA Minsk 655-1-1, 279.
78. In the large ghettos of Minsk and Mogilev there had already been mass shootings by units of the police and the Einsatzgruppen, for example in Minsk on 31.8.1941 (Polizeibataillon 322, KTB, Eintragung vom 1.9.1941, BA-R20-79,

76ff.) and in September (EM Nr. 92 vom 23.9.1941, 39); and in Mogilev on 3.10.1941 (Pol.Bat. 322, KTB, Eintragung vom 3.10.1941, op. cit., 111R).

79. The marching order came from General Major of the Polizei Jedicke; see HSSPF beim Reichskommissar Ostland/BdO Ic, An den Reichskommissar für das Ostland, Betr.: Lagebericht Weißruthenien, 17.10.1941, BSA Minsk, 651-1-1, 2. Since it was a matter of military tasks, which, according to Jedicke, could also be solved "together with the Wehrmacht," the "Wehrmachtsbefehlshaber Ostland" was responsible. The request for the police units consequently could only have been issued by Generalleutnant Braemer; see Urteil in der Strafsache gegen Lechthaler und andere, 9.1.1963, LG Kassel 3a Ks 1/61, 40f.
80. Strafsache Lechthaler, Testimony of defendant P, 16.5.1960.
81. Reserve Polizeibataillon 11, Lagebericht über den Sondereinsatz in Minsk für die Zeit vom 14.–21.10.41, 21.10.1941, BSA Minsk, 651-1-1, 3–7; Kommandant in Weißruthenien/Abt. Ic, Anlage 4 zum Monatsbericht vom 11.10.–10.11.41, Minsk 10.11.41, BA-MA, RH 26-707-2, 3.
82. Der Gebietskomissar Slutsk, An den Generalkommissar in Minsk, Betr. Judenaktion, 30.10.1941, cited in: Strafsache gegen Lechthaler und andere, 60ff.; Der Generalkommisar für Weißruthenien An den Reichskommissar für das Ostland Gauleiter Hinrich Lohse, 1.11.1941, ibid., 65ff.
83. Compare C. R. Browning, "Beyond 'Intentionalism' and 'Functionalism': The Decision for the Final Solution Reconsidered," in *The Path to Genocide* (Cambridge, Mass.: 1992), 101ff.
84. Einsatzgruppe A/Stab, Betrifft: Entwurf über die Aufstellung vorläufiger Richtlinien für die Behandlung der Juden im Gebiet des Reichskommissariats Ostland, 8.8.1941, ZSA Riga, P 1026-1-3, 237ff.
85. Braemer was a high-ranking member of the SS; his friendship with the SS leadership in Riga was confirmed during the criminal prosecution of Lechthaler and others, Strafsache gegen Lechthaler und andere, 33. On the debate over transports to Riga see Hilberg, *Vernichtung,* 2:368.
86. Brief Braemers an den Reichskommissar für das Ostland, 20.11.41, cited in Strafsache gegen Lechthaler und andere, 39.
87. Strafsache gegen Lechthaler und andere, 39f.
88. Der Befehlshaber des rückwärtigen Heeresgebietes Mitte/Abt. Ic, Ic Befehle und Mitteilungen, 18.10.41, KHA Prague, box 10, folder 94, 190.
89. See Bericht des Dolmetschers der Abwehr bei der Heeresgruppe Mitte, Soennecken, 24. Oktober 1941, PS-3047; compare also Diary Entry of General Lahousen for 28.10.1941 on his trip to the front and his talk with von Gersdorff on the massacre in Borisov, NOKW-3146.
90. (Befehlshaber rückwärtigen Heeresgebietes) Ib, 12.11.41, Militärachiv Podolsk 500-12473-164.
91. Zentrale Stelle, II202 AR-Z 16/67, Abschlußbericht, 19.7.1967.
92. Strafsache gegen Stocker, Aussage R. am 28.6.1960 und F. am 16.8.1961, StA München, la Js 545/60, 42f, 163f.; StA Traunstein, Strafsache gegen Artmann, 6 Js 72/60.
93. O. Bartov, "Brutalität und Mentalität: Zum Verhalten deutscher Soldaten an der 'Ostfront,'" in Jahn and Rürup, *Erobern und Vernichten,* 187.
94. Bericht des KdS Minsk vom Winter 1941/42 (Burkhardt Bericht), in Windisch, Dokumentenband III, 215,
95. Ibid., 216f.
96. See chapter 5, "The Logic of the War of Extermination: The Wehrmacht and the Anti-Partisan War," in this volume.

97. 707. Inf. Division/Abt. Ia, Divisionsbefehl Nr. 32, 18.3.42, BA-MA, RH 26-707-5.
98. 707. Inf. Division/Abt. la, Divisionsbefehl Nr. 43, 5.4.42, BA-MA, RH 26-707-5; on the victims, primarily Jews, women, children, all the elderly, compare Ales Adamovich, Yank Bryl, and Vladimir Kolesnik, eds., *Out of the Fire* (Moscow: 1980).
99. Der kommand. General d. Sich. Truppen und Befh i. H. Gebiet Mitte KTB 2, Eintragung 7.4.1942, BA-MA, RH 22-229.
100. StA Wiesbaden, 7 Js 140/63, Aussage G. Heuser am 21.3.63.
101. Strafsache gegen Schaupeter und andere, Aussage G. Heuser am 15.11.63, StA Hannover, 2 Js 388/65, 1295.
102. Der Gebietskommissar Glebokoje, An den Generalkommissar für Weißruthenien, Betr., Judenaktion, 1.7.1942, BSA Minsk 370-1-483, 15. In this report the Wehrmacht was indeed not explicitly mentioned as the order giver and executor. In an inspection report of the Generalkommissariat one finds, however, the handwritten note: "Glebokoje: Preserve authority of the ZV [Civilian Administration]. Shooting of Jews by the Wehrmacht"; BSA Minsk. 370-1-52, 7ff.
103. Gebietskommissar Glebokoje, An den Generalkommissar für Weißruthenien, betr.: Erfassung und Verwaltung des jüdischen Vermögens, 10 July (1942), BSA Minsk 370-1-483, 29.
104. Besprechungspunkte für die Divisionsbesprechung. 12.6.1942, BA-MA, RH 22-231, 311.
105. Krausnick, *Hitlers Einsatzgruppen,* 189; Messerschmidt, "Harte Sühne am Judentum," 126; Förster, DRWZ, 4:1044; Streit, *Keine Kameraden*, 242ff; Hillgruber, "Der Ostkrieg und die Judenverfolgung," 196.
106. M. Geyer, "The Stigma of Violence: Nationalism and War in Twentieth-Century Germany," in *German Studies Review*, Special Issue on German Identity (Winter 1992): 77.
107. M. Geyer, "Krieg, Staat und Nationalismus," in J. Dülffer, B. Martin, and G. Wollstein, eds., *Deutschland in Europa: Kontinuität und Bruch. Gedenkschrift für Andreas Hillgruber* (Berlin: 1990), 259ff.

– *Chapter 4* –

Soviet Prisoners of War in the Hands of the Wehrmacht*

Christian Streit

On 26 August 1941, two months after the attack on the Soviet Union, Hellmuth James Graf von Moltke wrote to his wife: "Once more the news from the east is terrible. Clearly we are suffering very heavy losses. And yet that would be bearable if we did not bear the responsibility for hecatombs of corpses."[1]

"Hecatombs of corpses": Moltke, certainly one of the most impressive figures in the German opposition, well informed concerning events in the east due to his work in the Wehrmacht High Command (OKW), was referring neither to the Wehrmacht's losses, which were already immense, nor to the much heavier losses sustained by the Red Army. He was speaking of the thousands of Jews, prisoners of war, and civilians who in those first weeks had already fallen victim to the German policy of annihilation in the east. In contrast to the vast majority of his contemporaries, he saw very clearly what monstrous crimes were being committed in the east and to what degree the Wehrmacht was involved.

Except for the Jews, Soviet prisoners of war suffered the worst fate of all the victims of National Socialist Germany.[2] Between 22 June 1941 and the end of the war, roughly 5.7 million members of the Red Army fell into German hands. In January 1945, 930,000 were still in German camps. A million at most had been released, most of whom were the so-called "volunteers" (*Hilfswillige*) for

Notes for this section begin on page 90.

(often compulsory) auxiliary service in the Wehrmacht. Another 500,000, as estimated by the Army High Command, had either fled or been liberated. The remaining 3,300,000 (57.5 percent of the total) had perished.

The horror of the fate suffered by Soviet prisoners becomes even clearer when one considers that, of the 232,000 English and American soldiers in German hands, 8,348 (or 3.5 percent) died.[3] In the autumn of 1941 8,348 Soviet prisoners died on a single day.

A brief sketch of how mortality rates fluctuated over time reveals the monstrous degree to which half an army of prisoners numbering in the millions was killed.[4] As early as August 1941, epidemics such as dysentery and typhus were breaking out in the camps in the east—and soon spread to the territory of the Reich. When winter weather set in, the mortality rate rose sharply. By 20 October 1941, 54,000 had already died in the camps of occupied Poland. In the next ten days alone, another 45,690 deaths were recorded—almost 4,600 per day. In November the death rate reached 38 percent; in December, 46 percent. Of the 361,000 prisoners who were being held in the Government General in the fall of 1941, more than 85 percent had died by April 1942. In the camps in the rest of the German sphere of influence, prisoners were similarly decimated. In sum, by February 1942, roughly two million of the 3.3 million who had been taken prisoner in the year 1941 had died.

Members of the military indicted at Nuremberg ascribed these mass deaths to an unavoidable crisis. They claimed that they had not anticipated such masses of prisoners and that feeding them had proved impossible. This explanation, which is still touted by representatives of veterans' organizations, is untenable. The entire design of the campaign meant that large numbers of prisoners were predictable, and feeding the prisoners was not an inherently impossible task. The more fundamental cause of the mass deaths was not the number of prisoners but the war aims that were pursued in the east. Those aims were formulated and the methods by which they were to be achieved were designed with the active participation of the command staffs of the Wehrmacht.[5]

One of the most important war aims of all was seizing the USSR's food sources. Hitler and his generals regarded hunger on the "home front" during World War I as an important cause of Germany's defeat. Ruthlessly plundering the food sources in the east was supposed to make it possible to feed the German people as in peacetime and thus preserve "wartime morale." In May 1941 it was already perfectly clear to the planners in the OKW and the ministries that the result would be "without doubt the starvation of tens of millions of human beings."[6] There was agreement among military leaders that Soviet prisoners should receive "only those rations that are absolutely necessary." The result was rations far below the minimum required for survival. In 1941, for example, during westward marches often lasting for weeks, prisoners frequently received daily rations such as "20 g millet and 100 g bread without meat" or "two potatoes."[7]

By September 1941 the signs of the approaching catastrophe were already unmistakable. Documents exist showing that in a number of camps desperate prisoners were driven by hunger to eat grass, leaves, or tree bark.[8] In some camps in the east, epidemics caused by hunger were already claiming thousands of lives. On 19 October 1941 an officer on the staff of the Military Commander in the Government General noted: "OKW is aware of the fact that mass deaths among the [Soviet] war prisoners cannot be prevented because the prisoners are at the end of their strength."[9]

Nevertheless, two days later, the General Quartermaster of the army, General Eduard Wagner, ordered a drastic *reduction* in rations in the theater of army operations. The most severely affected were those already too weak to work. They were now to receive roughly 1500 calories per day, less than two thirds of the absolute minimum required to survive. Wagner was thus acceding to demands by Göring, who was intent on maintaining the nutritional standard of the German population at any price.[10]

The army leadership, in full consciousness, accepted the starvation of Soviet prisoners as a matter of fact. That much is perfectly clear from a statement made by General Quartermaster Wagner (who, incidentally, was one of the 20 July 1944 conspirators). In a conference with the chiefs of staff of the armies in the east in November 1941, when it was pointed out to him that the Soviet prisoners needed as workers were starving in the camps, Wagner stated tersely: "Non-working war prisoners ... are supposed to starve. Working prisoners may be fed from army rations in individual cases."[11]

By that point, mass deaths had already reached epidemic proportions. Now the decimation of the prisoners was accelerated by the onset of winter, against which they had virtually no protection.[12] Hardly any preparations had been made for housing them. Because the goal was to devote minimal resources to the task, commandants charged with constructing the camps received only barbed wire, kettles for cooking, chlorine, and tools. The prisoners were expected to build their own housing with the most primitive materials. Even in the Reich, housing conditions were not substantially better than in the east. There, too, up to the spring of

1942, prisoners were forced to vegetate in "Russian camps" such as Stukenbrock or Bergen-Belsen, living in holes and earthen bunkers that they had built for themselves. The files contain no indication that participating Wehrmacht authorities tried to change this policy, the consequences of which had to be clear even to someone deficient in imagination.

Tens of thousands lost their lives on the roads from the front to the camps.[13] Most prisoners who were captured in the year 1941 were moved to the west in forced marches lasting many weeks under miserable conditions over many hundreds of kilometers. Marching units of tens of thousands of Red Army men were guarded by but a few companies of German soldiers, who were forced by necessity to resort to the most brutal violence in order to drive the starving prisoners to the next poorly prepared rest area. Thousands of exhausted prisoners were shot out of hand, even in the middle of large cities such as Minsk or Smolensk. Individual troop commanders condemned the practice in orders expressing their outrage, but—like the commander of Army Group Center, Field Marshal von Bock, or the commandant of his rear area, General von Schenckendorff—did nothing to address the causes. In any case, other commanders had a different view: in Field Marshal von Reichenau's 6th Army there was a standing order "to shoot all collapsing prisoners of war."[14]

At the same time, the transport problem was exacerbated by the troops themselves. Army High Command (OKH) had ordered that as many prisoners as possible be transported by trains making their return empty or in columns of trucks so that the roads used as supply routes would not be blocked by marching prisoners. In practice transport officers typically refused to cooperate, arguing that the prisoners were infested with lice and dirtied up the vehicles. Despite the consequences both for the prisoners and for its own operations, the OKH did nothing to compel obedience to its original orders. When prisoners were moved by rail, the OKH would permit only the use of open freight cars, which caused enormous loss of life with the onset of winter. In Army Group Center's area of operations, the use of closed railway cars was not permitted until 22 November 1941, after a hard freeze lasting more than three weeks. The immediate cause for the change was that 1,000 prisoners of a transport numbering 5,000 had frozen to death. According to a report of the Reichskomissariat Ostland, "between 25 percent and 70 percent of the prisoners" who were transported by rail were dying at that time.[15]

Between October 1941 and March 1942, thousands of Soviet prisoners of war died each day in German-controlled areas. It is doubtful that dying would have achieved such a gruesome dimension if the leadership of the Wehrmacht and the army had not made it clear in its orders to the German soldiers that it attached no value to the lives of Soviet prisoners and civilians.[16] The so-called "Barbarossa Decree" limited the purview of military justice to the prosecution of criminal acts by German soldiers. The troops were to avenge every "attack" by Soviet civilians with executions. The aim was the complete subjugation of the Soviet population and the elimination of any hint of resistance. The army leadership defined as an "attack" even the distribution of leaflets or failure to obey an order issued by a German. By contrast, crimes committed against Soviet citizens by German soldiers for which the perpetrators claimed political motivation were excused in advance.

The commissar order, the second infamous order to be mentioned in this connection, required the troops to identify political commissars among the mass of prisoners, separate them out, and shoot them. Investigations have confirmed that, in contrast to what former soldiers repeatedly claimed, this order was almost universally followed in the summer and fall of 1941.[17] In May of 1942 the order was rescinded at the urging of front-line commanders because knowledge of the shootings had drastically stiffened Red Army resistance.

Army leaders did not shrink from deception and manipulation in order to overcome possible resistance to this policy on the part of the troops. When General Eugen Müller clarified the orders to representatives of the eastern armies on 11 June 1941 on behalf of the Supreme Commander of the Army, Field Marshal von Brauchitsch, he explained that in the east "a sense of justice may have to take second place to the necessities of war." What was required, he went on to say, was a "return to the old customs of warfare," and pointed out that current law regarding war had been "established only after the World War." That was simply false; for all the actions required by the orders, including the method of treating prisoners, amounted to a clear violation of principles regarding the conduct of land warfare that had been adopted in The Hague in 1907.[18] That the USSR had neither ratified the Geneva Convention on war prisoners nor recognized as binding the Hague convention was of secondary importance, because German policy also violated general provisions of international law on warfare that were universally binding.

Members of the resistance tried in vain to persuade the military leadership to change orders. As early as April 1941, following a conversation with the Generaloberst Beck, former Chief of the Army

General Staff, Ulrich von Hassell had noted: "What the documents reveal as having been communicated about orders issued to the troops and signed by Halder [Chief of the Army General Staff] regarding our conduct in Russia and the systematic perversion of military justice vis-à-vis the population [the reference is to the Barbarossa Decree] into a caricature mocking all law—is enough to make one's hair stand on end.... By yielding to Hitler's orders, Brauchitsch is sacrificing the honor of the German Army."[19]

By transmitting these orders the military leadership quite consciously lowered the threshold of inhibitions in the Wehrmacht. So also did the dissemination of Wehrmacht propaganda representing the enemy as "subhumans." All of this was an absolute prerequisite for the development of a climate characterized by a propensity for extreme violence within days after 22 June. The orders regarding the treatment of Soviet war prisoners also need to be seen in this context.[20] They reflected National Socialist ideology even more clearly than other orders. They proclaimed that the Bolshevik soldier had "lost any right to be treated as an honorable soldier." The troops were repeatedly exhorted to "strike ruthlessly" (*rücksichtsloses Durchgreifen*). General Hermann Reinecke,[21] who was generally responsible for war prisoners, declared in an order dated 8 September 1941 laying down general guidelines that weapons needed to be used liberally with these prisoners on disciplinary grounds. Anyone failing to make energetic use of weaponry in enforcing an order "will be subject to punishment.... The use of weapons against Soviet prisoners of war is, as a general rule, regarded as legal."[22]

This was clearly a license to murder, and many soldiers understood it as such.

Resistance to abandoning the traditional principle that defenseless prisoners of war were to be humanely treated and properly fed arose only in isolated instances, and only at lower levels. Protests by the army leadership or by officers leading the troops cannot be verified. One of the most significant attempts to bring about a fundamental change was undertaken by Graf von Moltke, who has already been mentioned.[23] At his urging Admiral Canaris, Chief of German Intelligence, demanded of Field Marshal Keitel, head of the OKW, that Reinecke's order of 8 September be rescinded. Keitel categorically refused: "These misgivings reflect the soldierly conception of a knightly war! At issue here is the annihilation of a world view! For that reason I approve the measures a[nd] support them."

Both Canaris's protest and Keitel's response applied to systematic murder as well. By this time Wehrmacht involvement in extermination policy went far beyond murdering commissars.[24] In the middle of July 1941, shortly after the invasion, the OKW had reached an agreement with Reinhard Heydrich that extended the commissar order. Einsatzkommandos of the Security Police (SIPO) and the Security Service (SD) were to single out for murder among the war prisoners all "politically unacceptables" in the Reich, in occupied Poland, and in the Reichskommissariats Ostland and Ukraine. With one stroke the number of victims was multiplied several times, because the victims included not merely Communist party functionaries but, along with other categories, "all Jews."

It is significant in the context of our study that the actual front, which was controlled by the OKH, was initially exempted from this regulation. On 24 July 1941, in accordance with Chief of Staff Halder's maxim that the army must "aid in the ideological struggle," General Quartermaster Wagner had ordered that the affected categories of prisoners be shot *by the troops*.[25] An exception was made only for Jews, who were to be isolated, made clearly identifiable, and recruited as forced laborers. Wagner refused to permit SS Einsatzkommandos to participate. Three months later, at the end of October 1941, it was ordered that SS Einsatzkommandos carry out the selections in the OKH region as well. Wagner's express order forbidding such SS involvement had been widely ignored. Camp commanders had, on their own authority, summoned the Kommandos to make the selections. In the rear area of Army Group South, the commander, General von Roques, had *ordered* as much on 24 August 1941. Thus, with complete disregard for the principle of obedience to higher authority, the impetus toward a more radical procedure had arisen among the troops themselves. The number of war prisoners killed as "politically unacceptable" is estimated at far more than 140,000.[26] The connection of this mass murder with the genocide of the Jews is obvious.[27]

A further connection between the Holocaust and the mass annihilation of Soviet prisoners of war also deserves brief mention: The method that made possible the assembly-line murder of millions of Jews with the poison gas Zyklon B was developed in Auschwitz while the SS was looking for a "simpler" way to murder the many hundreds of Soviet war prisoners who had been selected for execution. The infrastructure of the extermination camp at Birkenau—and of the camp at Majdanek as well—had been created for more than 100,000 Soviet prisoners of war whom the OKW had turned over to the SS to serve as slave laborers in Himmler's projected industrial empire.[28]

The fate of wounded prisoners shows that even in the measureless misery of the prison camps an intensification of horror was still possible.[29] The criminal character of the treatment of prisoners finds its most naked expression here because both the USSR and the German Reich were signatories of the Geneva convention of 1929 on the treatment of the *wounded*.[30] Thus there existed in international law a quite unequivocal and precise obligation, which was consciously ignored by the German leadership. Up until the summer of 1942, German leaders were interested in only those prisoners who could be rendered able to work cheaply and quickly. The OKH ordered that only Soviet medical supplies be used in treating the wounded. Thus only the physically robust who had been but slightly wounded were able to survive. Seriously wounded prisoners, even if they survived their wounds, had virtually no chance to survive to the end of the war. The OKW ordered in September 1942 that prisoners who were "no longer fit for service" be turned over to the Higher SS and Police Leaders, who then arranged for them to be murdered. This development was actually initiated by the leaders of the army. In an effort to preserve food supplies, beginning in the fall of 1941, the seriously wounded were expelled from the camps into the civilian population, where they could only starve. The commanders of the army were thus operating according to the National Socialist principle of euthanasia, which denied the right to live to so-called "unproductive consumers" (*unnütze Esser*).

At the end of October 1941, the German leadership made a decision that initially appeared to make possible a fundamental change in the treatment of Soviet prisoners.[31] Since the collapse of the notion of a *Blitzkrieg* made it impossible to solve the serious labor shortage in the war economy by demobilizing soldiers, large numbers of Soviet prisoners were now to be used as laborers. Even Hitler conceded that this required "appropriate nourishment." It soon turned out, however, that National Socialist leaders were not prepared to reduce the amount of food available to the German population for that purpose. The rations for prisoners were indeed increased but remained below the minimum required for survival.[32] Only at the end of October 1944, after the situation had become quite desperate, was the ration for Soviet prisoners made equal to that of German civilians. That meant that they, in the best cases, received food in the same amount but certainly not of the same quality. As far as one can tell from the sources, the often-described, watery rutabaga soup continued to be the standard fare. It should be stressed that the fact that Soviet prisoners of war were significantly more poorly nourished than the German civilian population marks an important difference in the treatment of war prisoners in Germany and in the Soviet Union. German prisoners suffered from hunger along with the Soviet population,[33] while hunger in the German population was avoided, among other things, at the expense of the Soviet prisoners.

Even so, heightened interest in the value of the prisoners as laborers at the end of 1941 had the effect of reducing mass deaths in the spring of 1942 as well as limiting the number of mass shootings.[34] But Soviet prisoners continued to be shot in significantly higher numbers and with significantly less reluctance than other allied prisoners. Soviet prisoners who escaped and were recaptured were turned over to the SD for execution as a matter of principle. Here we can also observe the corrupting influence that the treatment of Soviet prisoners exerted on the treatment of all other prisoners. In March 1944 the OKW ordered that unproductive officers and noncommissioned officers of all enemy nations who were captured after having escaped were to be turned over to the Gestapo under the code-word "Kugel"; the Gestapo would then take them to the concentration camp at Mauthausen, where they would be murdered.[35]

Beginning in the middle of 1942, a certain rethinking is detectable in the leadership of the army and among the troop leaders. Decisive was the realization that the prisoners were urgently required for the labor force and that something must be done to win sympathy among the population of the occupied regions. Instructions concerning the treatment of prisoners now stressed the need to maintain them as laborers. Orders issued repeatedly in various armies show, however, how hard it was to put the new principles into effect. As before, prisoners were mistreated or forced to work until they died of exhaustion.

The measures that German leaders were now prepared to introduce could never come close to reducing mortality among Soviet prisoners to anything like a normal level. On the contrary, it rose again beginning at the end of 1943 because more and more prisoners came down with diseases such as tuberculosis as a result of protracted privation. In April 1945 as many as 100 per day were again dying in some camps.[36]

Basic interest in the value of Soviet prisoners as a source of labor offered soldiers with humane inclinations some leverage for working toward more compassionate treatment. In the Reich itself a number of cases have been documented in which soldiers far down in the chain of command turned on entrepreneurs who exploited prisoners with excessive unscrupulousness. But these soldiers found no support at higher levels. Industrial and party leaders regarded the application of even more brutal methods as the best guarantee of increased productivity. General Reinecke helped see to it that this policy prevailed. He was one of the most fanatical National Socialists in the OKW and, from 1941 on, had steadily increased party influence on matters regarding prisoners of war.

Thus, even if it can be demonstrated that there were soldiers in the Wehrmacht who attempted to bring about a more humane treatment of Soviet war prisoners in their spheres of influence, there is no doubt that these soldiers constituted a minority who were able to have any effect only when they encountered like-minded men—and that they had little influence on the reality of war in the east. Among Wehrmacht leaders they found no support at all, among the troop leaders very little. In any case, devoted National Socialists had completely different ideas. Hitler seems to have remarked to his inner circle in 1941 that the death of Soviet prisoners was one way of achieving the desired decimation of the "Slavic masses."[37] In the initial phase of the war in the east, not only units of the Waffen-SS but also army units had, without orders and sometimes in contravention of express orders, shot Red Army men in the act of surrendering. As late as February 1945, Field Marshal Schörner, Supreme Commander of Army Group Center and one of the most fanatical Nazis in the Wehrmacht, was praising soldiers who took no prisoners.[38]

In the fall of 1941, the prevailing attitude in some prison camps—though certainly not in all—was: "The more of these prisoners die, the better for us."[39] In some regions conscious extermination had become a "self-starter" no longer requiring concrete orders. In contrast to the extermination of the Jews, however, this tendency in the treatment of war prisoners was constrained by the fact that a fundamental interest in them as a work force was being stressed. The conflict inherent in the simultaneous pursuit of exploitation and annihilation was never fully resolved. From the NSDAP came increasingly radical demands, which found support in the OKW. Extermination remained an option for the period following "final victory."

—Translated by Roy Shelton

Notes

*This essay was originally published in Walter Manoschek, ed., *Die Wehrmacht im Rassenkrieg. Der Vernichtungskrieg hinter der Front* (Vienna: 1996), 74–89.

1. Christian Streit, *Keine Kameraden. Die Wehrmacht und die sowjetischen Kriegsgefangenen,* 3rd rev. ed. (Bonn: 1991), 131.
2. On the fate of Soviet war prisoners, see Streit, *Keine Kameraden*; Alfred Streim, *Die Behandlung sowjetischer Kriegsgefangener im "Fall Barbarossa"* (Heidelberg: 1981); on the treatment of Soviet prisoners after their return to the Soviet Union, see Streit, "Zum Schicksal der sowjetischen Kriegsgefangenen in deutscher Hand," in Hans-Adolf Jacobsen, ed., *Deutsch-russische Zeitenwende. Krieg und Frieden 1941–1995* (Baden-Baden: 1995), 448–454.
3. Streit, *Keine Kameraden*, 293.
4. Cf. Streit, *Keine Kameraden*, 128–137.
5. Cf. with regard to the following, Streit, *Keine Kameraden*, 62–66; Rolf-Dieter Müller, "Von der Wirtschaftsallianz zum kolonialen Ausbeutungskrieg" in Horst Boog et al., eds., *Der Angriff auf die Sowjetunion* (= *Das Deutsche Reich und der Zweite Weltkrieg*, vol. 4) (Stuttgart: 1983), 113ff.
6. See note to document on the conference among the state secretaries of various ministries, *Nürnberger Dokumente*, 2718-PS.
7. Streit, *Keine Kameraden*, 131, 152.
8. See Streit, *Keine Kameraden*, 135; Volker Pieper and Michael Siedenhans, *Die Vergessenen von Stukenbrock. Die Geschichte des Lagers in Stukenbrock-Senne von 1941 bis zur Gegenwart* (Bielefeld: 1988), 34. Rolf Keller is currently preparing a publication on the Stalags Bergen-Belsen, Fallingbostel-Oerbke, and Wietzendorf. For the results of this research to date, see "Bergen-Belsen. Begleitheft zur Ausstellung," hg. v.d. *Niedersächsische Landeszentrale für politische Bildung* (Hanover: 1990), 14.
9. Streit, *Keine Kameraden*, 136.
10. Ibid., 141–144.
11. Ibid,, 157f.
12. Regarding the following section, see Streit, *Keine Kameraden*, 72–76, 171–177. The works by Pieper/Siedenhans and Keller mentioned in note number 8 offer further evidence.
13. Cf. Streit, *Keine Kameraden*, 162–171.
14. Ibid., 171.
15. Ibid., 165f.
16. Concerning the following, see Streit, *Keine Kameraden*, 33–61; Jürgen Förster, "Das Unternehmen 'Barbarossa' als Eroberungs- und Vernichtungskrieg," in Horst Boog et al., eds, *Der Angriff auf die Sowjetunion*, 413–447.
17. Streit, *Keine Kameraden*; Jürgen Förster, "Die Sicherung des 'Lebensraums,'" in Horst Boog et al., eds., *Der Angriff auf die Sowjetunion* (=*Das Deutsche Reich und der Zweite Weltkrieg*, vol. 4) (Stuttgart: 1983), 1030–1078.
18. Cf. Streit, *Keine Kameraden*, 43f., 231f.
19. Friedrich Freiherr Hiller von Gaertringen, ed., *Die Hassell-Tagebücher 1938–1944. Ulrich von Hassell. Aufzeichnungen vom Andern Deutschland* (Berlin: 1988), 248.
20. Concerning the following, see Streit, *Keine Kameraden*, 72–74, 180–183.
21. Reinecke was one of the most committed National Socialists among the leaders of the Wehrmacht. From the 1930s he had worked to bring about a close

alignment of the Wehrmacht and the NSDAP and allowed the party to influence the handling of prisoners of war. For his contributions he received the Golden Party Medal in 1943. In December 1943 he was named first Chief of the National Socialist Guidance Staff in the OKW, whose duties included organizing the work of National Socialist Guidance Officers in the Wehrmacht. See Streit, *Keine Kameraden.*

22. Gerd R. Ueberschär and Wolfram Wette, eds., *"Unternehmen Barbarossa." Der deutsche Überfall auf die Sowjetunion 1941* (Paderborn: 1984), 351–354.
23. Streit, *Keine Kameraden,* 231f. The memorandum by Moltke/Canaris, along with Keitel's notations, in Ueberschär and Wette, *"Unternehmen Barbarossa,"* 355.
24. For the following, see Streit, *Keine Kameraden,* 87–105; Streim, *Kriegsgefangener,* 224–244.
25. Regarding the Halder quotation, Wagner's order, and later developments, see Streit, *Keine Kameraden,* 45, 99–105.
26. Ibid., 105.
27. For a thorough analysis, see Streit, *Keine Kameraden.*
28. Ibid., 217ff.
29. Ch. Streit, "Die Behandlung der verwundeten sowjetischen Kriegsgefangenen," in Hannes Heer and Klaus Naumann, eds., *Vernichtungskrieg. Verbrechen der Wehrmacht 1941–1944* (Hamburg: 1995), 78–91.
30. Reichsgesetzblatt 1934/II, S.207ff. On the issue of obligations under international law, cf. Streit, *Keine Kameraden,* 224ff., and a more thorough treatment in Streit, "Die Behandlung der sowjetischen Kriegsgefangenen und völkerrechtliche Probleme des Krieges gegen die Sowjetunion," in Ueberschär and Wette, *"Unternehmen Barbarossa,"* 197–218.
31. Streit, *Keine Kameraden,* 191–208.
32. Ibid., 249–253.
33. Erich Maschke, "Die Verpflegung der deutschen Kriegsgefangenen im Rahmen der sowjetischen Ernährungslage," in Hedwig Fleischhacker, ed., *Die deutschen Kriegsgefangenen in der Sowjetunion* (= Zur Geschichte der deutschen Kriegsgefangenen des Zweiten Weltkriegs 3) (Munich: 1965), vii–li.
34. Streit, *Keine Kameraden,* 249–253.
35. Ibid., 257
36. Ibid., 246–249. On mortality in, for example, Stalag 326/VI K, see Volker Schockenhoff, "Wer hat schon damals genau gezählt," *Westfälische Zeitschrift* 143, 337–351. On Stalag VI A, see *Bürgerinitiative für Frieden und Abrüstung,* ed. Hemer, 16.
37. See Otto Bräutigam, *So hat es sich zugetragen* (Würzburg: 1968).
38. Streit, *Keine Kameraden,* 243f.
39. Ibid., 370f.

– *Chapter 5* –

THE LOGIC OF THE WAR OF EXTERMINATION

The Wehrmacht and the Anti-Partisan War

Hannes Heer

On the ninth day of the Minsk trial for crimes committed by the Wehrmacht, the police, and the SD, the proceedings were fairly unspectacular. The defendants who were called onto the witness stand on that day, 23 January 1946, were neither generals nor officer—they were just simple soldiers. One of them, Albert Rodenbusch, who had belonged to the 635th Training Regiment at the time of the incidents, described his participation in an anti-partisan campaign in Belorussia. It was the first time he had served on the Eastern front.

> On the evening of 29 December 1942 we started our operation in a village. There were no partisans in this village. The people from the village provided us with heated rooms and gave us food, so we were very surprised when the company commander later ordered us to burn down the village and arrest the village people. So 50 inhabitants were taken prisoner.... We then moved on to another village. It was about 10 or 11 kilometers away. On our arrival we came under fire from rifles. Our company commander ordered us to occupy the village and to shoot on sight anyone offering resistance or attempting to flee.... We shot about 70 people. Among them also women, old people and children. And then we burnt down the village. From the first village we took 14 head of cattle and from the second village 10 head of cattle. We then proceeded to the third village. We didn't come across any partisans there.

Notes for this section begin on page 120.

> But we still burnt down the village and shot around 50 people. Even women and children. And then we moved on to the fourth village and did exactly the same as we had done in the other villages. There we shot about 100 people, burnt down the village and made 80 arrests. We took them with us. After we had destroyed all these villages we moved on towards Osipovichi. On our way there we combed the woods in search of partisans.[1]

This report is remarkable in several respects. It describes a form of behavior entirely void of military logic. Irrespective of whether the population behaves hospitably, with aggressive animosity, or with neutral caution toward the occupying forces, the outcome remains the same—the village is reduced to ashes, the livestock is taken away, and the inhabitants are either shot on the spot or taken prisoner. What kind of war is it, one asks, where there is no longer any difference between friend and foe? This scheme of things evidently no longer applies. And what about the partisans, the actual reason for the operation? Maybe they represent just the convenient heading for an entirely different set of events. In any case they are mentioned only in passing at the very end, as if it all had nothing to do with them, the objects of a listless search that is ultimately called off without result. So what then is the real purpose? Rodenbusch was a recruit and this was his first operation. Did arson constitute part of the basic training? This too could be a clue—one of many. They all point to the heart of an event that has so many aspects for the very reason that it virtually embodies the quintessence of the war in the East. Evidence for this theory is based on occurrences and developments in occupied Belorussia between 1941 and 1943.

1941

The strategy of the Eastern campaign was a combination of four elements. In a surprise attack, the fully motorized armies were to penetrate deep inside the country in a spearhead movement, destroy enemy forces in huge encirclement battles and bring about the collapse of the Soviet Union's political system while it was still reeling from the shock. This plan took account of the probability that hundreds of thousands of Red Army soldiers, once overrun by the German troops, would seek refuge in the vast unoccupied areas. There was a fair chance that the dispersed militia might join up with those institutions that were still intact to form a dangerous body of potential resistance. For this reason the precautionary measure was taken of assigning three security divisions to each of the three Army groups to deal with areas behind the lines. Besides safeguarding railway lines, landing strips and communication routes,[2] their duties consisted above all of the following: 1) The "systematic purging of dispersed enemy elements"; 2) "The arrest of civilians suspected of collaborating with the enemy"; 3) "The prevention or crushing of revolts, acts of sabotage, and terrorist groups."[3] These measures, it was felt, should and could be performed with the same swiftness as the army's advance.

While the surrounding woods were being combed and the most important villages searched, posters and air-dropped leaflets ordered former Red Army militia to give themselves up to the nearest German unit, otherwise anyone who was captured would be considered a guerrilla (*Freischärler*) and consequently shot.[4] However, this order dating from mid-July appears to have had so little impact that it had to be repeated several times, and the deadline for registration was extended to 15 August and then once more to 31 August. The reason for this was the manner in which German troops dealt with dispersed enemy soldiers. "Soldiers in plain clothes (mostly recognizable by their short haircuts) are to be shot following their identification as Red Army soldiers (with the exception of deserters)."[5] Whoever was unable to prove that he was a deserter or could not think of any other excuse, was shot. As activity reports filed by the security divisions in August and September show, this applied to almost half of those taken prisoner.[6] But even those who gave themselves up usually fared no better. This is revealed in the much reiterated ban issued by the commander of the Army Group Rear area, that only those men may be shot who "are intercepted in combat, are found to be carrying weapons, or are caught plundering."[7]

There were also other obstacles hampering the swift conclusion of "pacification." The extensive task of exposing and arresting civilian suspects, so as to prevent the formation of resistance groups, meant that the original restriction of the troops' duties to safeguarding landing strips and railway lines was soon relinquished. Instead it was decreed that "every village within the area of cleansing operations and, as far as possible, every single farm is to be registered and thoroughly searched"[8] for strangers, Red Army militia, saboteurs and communists, in other words, for suspects. The Wehrmacht had turned into a police force. Surrounded on all sides by supposed enemies and without the help of interpreters or informants, it made do with collective measures of punishment. The military mind took this to mean "mass executions or the partial or total razing of villages."[9] This seems to have been the constant response to attacks upon Wehrmacht units or the discovery of the corpses of shot comrades, if no culprit could be found. In the first two months of the campaign, the commanders of the Rear Army Center and of the Army Group Rear area attempted to contain such actions by initiating investigations and issuing orders.[10] After that there were no more interventions. At first sight, this appears to stem from the fact that resistance only started taking shape behind the front lines the further the army advanced toward the East. There were reports of sabotaged telephone lines and blown-up railway tracks, raids on *kolkhoz* farms and attacks upon collaborators.[11]

The Anti-Partisan War without Partisans

However, in order to properly assess the quality of this resistance, it must be remembered that these self-assured *Blitzkrieger* were wholly unaccustomed to any resistance of this kind; hence exaggerations were not surprising. And after the war the Soviet side too portrayed the initial phase in a heroic light because the partisan struggle was expedient in promoting identification. The reality was in fact quite different.

On 3 July 1941 Stalin had delivered his famous speech on Moscow Radio in which he called for "the partisan war to be unleashed" behind the German lines and on 11 July the Central Committee issued the directive ordering the organization of this war.[12] In western Belorussia this did not immediately produce concrete results. Since this former Polish territory had only belonged to the Soviet state for two years, the Party and mass organizations were still weak and poorly established; besides, the steamrolling German invasion also increased the unlikelihood of any thoughts of resistance. In the areas to the east of Minsk however, and in particular beyond the Beresina, the situation was very different. Here there were enough weapon-trained men to make up the first "annihilation battalions" and to carry out their tasks—the destruction of strategic objects during retreat, tracking down saboteurs, and enemy reconnaissance. These forces and the "diversion groups" dropped behind the lines by Soviet aircraft—explosives experts who undertook the first assaults upon communications and supply lines—unquestionably received adequate support from loyal cadres. The annihilation battalions formed the nucleus of the first locally based partisan groups. On the way back to their units, the diversion groups came into contact with the remaining forces of the Red Army, which were also heading back toward the front and, as migrant armed groups, they played a major role in the later emergence of the partisan movement.[13]

However, in the first six months of occupation there simply was no such movement. At most—as was revealed in prisoner interrogations—it was still in the early stages of being set up, both improvised and uncoordinated. And more than anything else, it was to a large extent isolated. According to the very precise and undeniably critical reports of the Einsatzgruppen, the reaction by the majority of the population was one of friendly reticence. This attitude only vacillated when the German front operations came to a standstill—though not as a result of partisan activities. The resistance behind the lines improvised by Moscow headquarters had already failed by the autumn.[14] Tens of thousands of former Red Army soldiers had survived and were hiding out in the woods or remained undetected, having taken refuge in the villages. However, this should be interpreted neither as a result of successful Soviet propaganda, nor as an expression of patriotism. The motive for not heeding the German calls for capitulation was unpolitical and, as Wehrmacht reports made clear, sprang from a survival instinct. Most raids also followed this same logic: "The mass of partisans are convinced that, were they to be taken prisoner, they would be shot anyway."[15] Or: "Fear of execution and starvation in the prisoner camps are the reasons why they do not give themselves up."[16] And: "Only when they [the partisans—H.H.] were forced to go in search of food for their own subsistence would they risk leaving their hiding-places."[17] It was a matter of pure survival.

Such appraisals, which correctly described the character of these groups as unpolitical, were in a minority. For the Wehrmacht, the purported existence of politically motivated resistance was obviously both desirable and necessary as legitimation for their policies. Similarly, the much-reported fact that large groups of dispersed enemy soldiers were gradually moving toward the East, in other words back toward their still unoccupied homeland, was interpreted not as evidence of a retreat but as proof of the existence of a central command and a nationwide communications network.[18] Orders were tightened up accordingly, special assault groups established, training courses in anti-partisan combat carried out, and the first generalized guidelines for this type of war were formulated by the Army High Command (OKH). The terror began to escalate.[19]

Any attempt to form a picture of the extent of the German operations performed in the Army Group Rear area runs up against severe difficulties. In vain might one search for lists numbering shot victims. All one finds in the often incomplete monthly reports compiled by the commander are the numbers of prisoners taken. From July through to the end of November 1941 these add up to

45,700.[20] The term "prisoner" is misleading. The orders in fact required all prisoners to be shot after a short interrogation.[21] Those who were considered a source of more important information were handed over to the SD commandos or to the Wehrmacht's own secret police, the Army Secret Field Police (GFP). There the prisoners met with the same fate.[22]

If, as reports by the security divisions operating in the Army Group Rear area indicate, one assumes that almost two thirds of the prisoners were shot, this aforementioned list of prisoners can in fact be read as a death roll.[23] This is backed up by figures given in a commander's report from March 1942, stating that 63,257 partisans had been killed since the start of the campaign. The low number of German losses—638 killed and 1,355 wounded—illustrates that most of the "partisans" were civilians and that they had not been killed in combat.[24] Even higher figures for the short period of only two months were provided in mid-November 1941 by the Wehrmacht commander's representative in Ostland in the western region of Belorussia, an area which was under civil administration: here 10,431 of the 10,940 prisoners had been shot.[25]

The popular image of the anti-partisan war in the East is still characterized by accounts which, excepting a certain apologetic undercurrent, are actually based on the later reality of 1943/44, by which time the partisan movement had grown and posed a real threat. Such personal accounts fail to mention and indeed even conceal the events of 1941/42 and how tens of thousands of civilians were hunted, captured, and executed.[26] By contrast, the following report filed in September 1941 by an "assault group" of the 252nd Infantry Division offers a realistic picture of the bizarre situation of an anti-partisan war without partisans.[27]

After a fruitless two-day search for partisans or even traces of them, this group made up of three companies finally comes across informants. According to the regional commander of C., it appears there is extensive Communist activity in the village of M. The local village mayor confirms this, but with the reservation "that in many places in the vicinity people had turned up whose behavior bore a resemblance to partisan activity." And then finally something crops up which seems to be a concrete lead: in P. a Communist is reported to have stolen and slaughtered 30 calves and sheep, as well as being in league with partisans. So the village is surrounded and the family taken prisoner, before the denunciation is then discovered to have been an act of revenge by their neighbors. Similarly, checks on a Communist woman from the next village prove to be a false lead. And then, following so many setbacks, events take a more serious turn. The same Ortskommandant has received new information. A teacher in his area appears to have been getting food to partisans or communists hiding in the woods, and his daughter is apparently even married to the commissar of this group. And it is alleged that another Communist is maintaining contact with this teacher. Once more the village is surrounded, those under suspicion are arrested together with other members of the family who just happen to be present, and all are interrogated. "They denied everything. In their statements they all contradicted each other in every single point.... From the way he looked, the man's son-in-law gave the impression of being a commissar. They were all shot." Following this outcome, further successes seem close at hand, for a report comes in of a partisan encampment which is claimed to have served as accommodation. But the base turns out to be unoccupied and a search of the surrounding villages produces no evidence of partisans—on the contrary, the inhabitants all oppose the partisans. Obviously under pressure to act, the commando subsequently switches to carrying out police activities, doing without any additional "burdensome" measures such as interrogations. It arrests four "Communists," shoots a "former soldier," arrests "50 male suspects," and empties a Russian military hospital, from which those who "were able to march" are dispatched into captivity. When new information from the area surrounding M. is received and the squadron is deliberating how it should react, a division officer arrives, and after declaring the reconnaissance results to be "adequate and completed," orders a "concerted operation." After the unit leader fails to find a Jew and a partisan leader who have been reported to be in the neighboring village, the operation is launched—with success. "110 partisans," some still in their sleep, are taken unawares in village barns and then shot. Just before they are about to be killed, a Red Army second lieutenant and a quartermaster are discovered among them. The weapons found are a machine-gun and a mortar. Where the group has come from or where it is stationed cannot be ascertained. During the subsequent search of the surrounding woods they find absolutely no traces of partisans ("weapons, equipment, or the remains of campfires"). On the German side the casualties reported amount to two wounded military policemen.

This sortie by the Anderssen assault group is described in such detail since the account offers insight into three characteristic elements of the "anti-partisan campaign" during the first six months of occupation. 1) In their operations the role played by the security divisions was more one of a police force than of combat troops. These operations were based on information which was imprecise and arbitrary, the only reliable orientation point during action being the images of hate the occupiers had brought with them. Nonetheless, there were also instances when wrong, decisions could still be corrected. 2) The growing number of failed raids and the increased frustration saw a marked rise in the willingness to perform executions. At the outset a quasi-legal framework of interrogation and cross-questioning was still adhered to. But once the surge in violence occurred, there was no longer any time for such formal niceties. This could only climax in mass murder. 3) Following the operation, it seems that the memory of a military moral code returned and normal human behavior was resumed. This is the only possible interpretation of the subsequent attempt to disguise the mass murder of defenseless people as active combat by claiming that two enemy officers and heavy weapons had been discovered in the group.

This form of distortion is a regular feature throughout all the war journals, situation reports, and daily dispatches of this period. Other measures like the razing of villages are disguised in phrases such as: "elimination of partisan nests, partisan camps, partisan bunkers." Ultimately, the murder of women and children is only disclosed by the orders the commanders gave to their troops that they should "adhere to their task."[28]

This evidence of manipulation and falsification in the Wehrmacht's official documents adds fuel to the justified concern voiced by critical historians toward relying exclusively upon official military records when attempting a historical reconstruction of the war of extermination.[29] But this is not the point at issue in this context. Here our focus is directed more at the question why manipulation proliferated to such a degree, particularly during the first phase of the war in the East. Linked to this is the phenomenon of a totally disproportionate explosion of violence toward the civilian population. Because, contrary to claims made by revisionist, but also some critical historical studies,[30] no organized partisan resistance existed during the first six months of occupation, there must be other reasons for the "new dimension" of German measures in autumn 1941.

The Power of Orders

The radius of the violent measures had been determined prior to the campaign and was then progressively expanded once hostilities had commenced. In the general directive defining the "practice of wartime military Jurisdiction" in the "Barbarossa" area issued on 13 May 1941, the civilian population was removed from the jurisdiction of the military courts and placed under the direct control of the ranks. Should civilians act as "guerrillas" exercising violence against German soldiers or installations, or as "hostile civilians" carrying out other forms of attack, they were to be eliminated. Those localities from which attacks were started were to be treated to "collective measures of violence." Members of the Wehrmacht committing military offenses during such operations would not automatically have to reckon with prosecution. This break with all international conventions was defended on two counts: in military terms it was justified by the "expansion of the operative areas in the East," and in psychological terms it was a response to the "special nature of the enemy."[31] The "guidelines" drawn up 19 May 1941 for the troops described the Red Army soldier as "inscrutable, unpredictable, underhanded, and callous," characterized by "treacherous methods of fighting," while the civilian population was to be treated as "hostile." Beyond this, attention was drawn to the historical role played by Bolshevism and its responsibility for the collapse, revolution, and civil war in Germany in the years following 1918.[32]

In a series of meetings held in May and June, the Ic officers of the Eastern forces were introduced to this decree. The real intention underlying the separate, relatively vague guidelines was made clear: whoever "as a civilian either personally obstructs or calls for the obstruction of the German Wehrmacht" is also deemed to be a Freischärler. This broadening of enemy categories was further intensified by the fact that henceforth even the mere suspicion of such an offense could entail execution. This measure too was legitimized by evoking historical reminiscences—the reminder of Russian war atrocities in 1914—and was again backed up by global military arguments: "In certain circumstances principles of Justice must take second place behind the exigencies of war."[33]

Despite these instructions certain sections of the troops appear not to have fully grasped the intended purpose. At any rate, the Wehrmacht leadership felt obliged to further tighten the screw of terror. On 23 July 1941 Keitel issued a directive from the Führer headquarters that the occupying forces should "instill such fear as is suitable to entirely discourage any form of disobedience within the population."[34] Two days later this order was supplemented by the OKH: offering the argument "that the required ruthlessness is not being applied in all quarters," it broadened the range of measures. In cases of passive resistance or if the culprit could not be immediately seized, collective penalties were to be imposed. "Suspicious elements," the OKH order dictated, "who perhaps cannot be proved to have committed a serious offense, yet seem [!] suspicious in terms of attitude and behavior, are to be passed on to the Einsatzgruppen or the SP [SD]."[35] As the Wehrmacht leadership was fully aware, that meant certain death.

The finale of this campaign was provided by a further order from Keitel on 16 September, in which he criticized the Wehrmacht's current measures for dealing with the "insurrective movements" organized by Moscow "as inadequate," and relayed Hitler's express wish that "the most severe steps [be taken] to crush this movement in the shortest possible time." As a solemn afterthought he added: "'It should be taken into account that in the countries concerned individual human life is widely felt to be worth nothing, so a deterrent can only be achieved through unaccustomed severity."[36]

These orders were not issued in response to an objectively assessed military situation. The general decree, the "jurisdiction edict" *(Gerichtsbarkeitserlass),* had been formulated before hostilities had begun, at a time when the behavior of the enemy could only have been a subject of speculation. And, as has been shown, the more draconian commands issued in the summer and early autumn of 1941 did not arise from a dramatic change in the situation. One should not be misled by the astonishing coincidence between the timing of the most important decrees and the developments in occupied Serbia.[37] At best, the "Serbian uprising" in July and its escalation in September served as a welcome opportunity to carry out a well-planned campaign. The overall thrust becomes evident when one registers how extraordinarily little military substance is contained in these military guidelines. Instead we find argument. Its target is the individual soldier, and the constantly named theme is his motivation. Let us recapitulate: 1) On each occasion the catalogue of punishable offenses and the group of potential culprits is extended. 2) For the targeted and responsible organs of occupation this involves an enormous expansion of their executive functions. 3) This executive power means the mass murder of the civilian population; in other words, and something that is repeatedly stressed, this denotes a break with the conventions valid in the rest of the world. 4) This rupture is legitimized in a historical context by evoking the ordeal suffered at the hands of the Russians and the Bolsheviks in 1914 and 1918, in ethnic terms by the perfidious character of the enemy, and on moral grounds by the lesser value reputedly attached to human life in Eastern culture. 5) Adherence to these orders is stipulated and desired by Adolf Hitler, they are Führer commands (*Führerbefehle*).

Ian Kershaw has proposed the Weberian notion of "charismatic leadership" to characterize the Nazi system,[38] and Jan Philipp

Reemtsma has demonstrated the usefulness of this notion by applying it to the function and character of the order. As instructions for specific action, Hitler's orders are in fact rather general and vague, but as definitions of objectives they are unconditional and precise. On the one hand, this explicitness prohibits the follower from considering any other loyalties and establishes the Führer as his only authority, while on the other hand, the order's very vagueness—which requires interpretation—points to the Führer's dependence upon the interpretative ability of his follower. Thus, under National Socialism, the grammar regulating order and obedience has been extended. The imperative "you must" is now joined by the potential "you may"; the pressure of obligation is compensated for by the pleasure of permission. Only this consensus—which not existing in its own right, needs to be constantly regenerated—only the awareness of this mutual dependence—which under ideal conditions becomes a symbiosis—provides the opportunity to confirm and renew this form of rule.[39]

On the assumption that this description of the dynamics of the order in the Nazi system and the mechanisms of its impact is correct, it should be possible to make sense of the escalation of the "anti-partisan war without partisans." The avalanche of orders which descended upon the troops in summer and autumn 1941 would therefore have served the purpose of creating the right climate of inexorability and ambiguity to allow charismatic leadership to flourish. The orders set about destroying previously valid moral conventions and establishing Hitler as the single and new voice of moral authority. Thus they constantly extended the category of actual enemy groups and increased the radius of permitted punitive measures; this was the reason why, instead of employing military arguments, the complete range of historical resentments and racist prejudice was brought into play. Each order triggers action, offers the opportunity to gain new experience. With their mixture of unambiguous destructive purpose on the one hand and ambivalent choice of reasons, methods, and victims on the other, the orders in question magnified the potential for such experience. "I am supposed to wipe out the partisans, and to do this I am allowed to burn down the village. But am I then also permitted to drive women and children into the flames?"—the campaign against the partisans became an arena in which practical answers to such questions were found. And the games of manipulation and hide--and-seek encountered throughout the war journals reveal that these answers were neither arrived at immediately nor all at once. Hence, the "criminal orders" were neither propaganda, nor military commands with an "ideological background," as a certain work of critical military history would have us believe, and the terror which they unleashed was not merely and primarily intended as a measure to deter the subjugated, as military history's apologetic wing claims.[40]

What these orders prepared the ground for and subsequent actions then brought forth, was a heightened form of combat morale within the German ranks, the morale of annihilation which Hitler needed to pursue his war. When on 3 July Stalin called on his people to fight behind the German lines, the Führer was overjoyed. The pleasure at the prospect of being able to "exterminate that which opposes us" was feigned, since that was precisely the strategy that had been planned from the very outset.[41] Entirely genuine was the satisfaction at having been presented with a bundle of arguments—proof of the enemy's perfidy, justification for the necessity of their own acts of terror, confirmation of the notion that this was a mortal combat being waged between two world views. Since Hitler was indeed a master of depth psychology, he knew that the struggle for the hearts of his soldiers would be decided within the first weeks. Without a victory on this battlefield it would have been impossible to win the campaign. The mass murder behind the front in the summer of 1941 and the orders issued by Reichenau and Manstein in autumn of that year showed that Hitler had indeed won this battle.

The Jews as Demonstration Objects

Whereas in the first phase of the *Ostkrieg* there was clearly still a certain reluctance to simply slay "weaponless," capitulating Red Amy soldiers or to unquestioningly murder even women and children at mass executions, such moral barriers were absent when it came to one particular enemy group: the goal of exterminating the Jews was known and sanctioned by the Wehrmacht from the first day onwards. There was a broad consensus that Jews were agitators, saboteurs, and natural intermediaries for the partisans. Without exception, every situation report from every unit in Belorussia echoed this attitude:

> On 22 July 1941: "[In] great masses running into several thousand, Jews suspected of agitation have been shot. As a result, Jewry has been intimidated and shows willingness to work."[42]

> On 18 August: "It is ultimately of the utmost importance to eradicate the influence of the Jews and deploy the most radical measures to eliminate these elements, because they in particular ... maintain contacts with the Red Army and the bandits we are fighting."[43]

> 3 September: "Communication between the various partisan units is maintained above all by the Jews."[44]

> 10 September: "The Jewish class, which forms the largest section of the population in the towns, is the driving force behind the growing resistance movement in some areas."[45]

> 19 October: "As the spiritual leaders and supporters of Bolshevism and the Communist idea, the Jews are our mortal enemies. They are to be eliminated. Whenever and wherever reported incidents of sabotage, incitement of the population, resistance, etc. have forced us to act, Jews were found to be the masterminds and wirepullers, and in most cases they were in fact the culprits themselves."[46]

This attitude was reflected in military practice from the very first day of the war onwards. "The first large operation against Jews was carried out directly behind the borders of the *Generalgouvernement* in the large Bielovitz forest in Poland. On the grounds that the Jews were giving help to Russian soldiers hiding out in the woods and swamps, the commander of the Army Group Rear area ordered all male Jews to be evacuated from the villages and transferred to forced labor camps."[47] As can be gauged from the number of evacuees (7,800), a great many non-Jews were evidently also deported.[48] The macabre background to this measure was Göring's desire to use this area of primeval forest so abundant with game as his personal hunting grounds.[49]

The fate met by the Jews living in the Pripyat marshes was not only deportation, but also mass murder. Since the spearheads of the German armies had marched around this impassable region to the north and the south, it had been decided to clear this zone at a later date. The task was allotted to the SS-Cavalry-Brigade, which for this mission was assigned to the commander of the Army Group Rear area.[50] From 27 July onwards, the SS brigade hunted down Red Army stragglers, partisans, and "plunderers." According to a special order from Himmler, this was the term to be used to define Jews: "In most cases Jews are to be treated as plunderers. The only exceptions to this rule are particularly skilled workers, such as bakers, etc., and above all, doctors."[51] These were still needed. By contrast, women and children were to be driven into the swamps. On 18 September the commander was informed of "14,178 shot plunderers, 1,001 shot partisans, 699 shot Red Army soldiers, and 830 prisoners."[52] The role played in this by General von Bechtolsheim has been described elsewhere.[53] Bechtolsheim, holder of the highest Wehrmacht rank in the "Generalkommissariat Weissruthenien," not only led the "Jew hunt" in the flat countryside, but also carried out the first large-scale ghetto massacres.

Insight into the behavior of the troops toward the Jews is not only provided by such large-scale operations. More revealing was the day-to-day handling of the "Jewish question." Similar to the regular reports which the regional military commanders were required to file on this subject, the security divisions were also obliged to submit separate reports on the capture or shooting of Jews.[54] This process of selective awareness and treatment probably contributed more to the creation of the phantom image of the Jew than any massacre, and its daily repetition made it impossible to erase.

> 403rd Security Division, 14 July 1941: "Between 9 and 14 July interception commandos captured: a) 16 Russians, b) 66 Jews, c) 18 otherwise suspicious persons."[55]
>
> 252nd Infantry Division, 25 July: "On 24 July 7 male Jews and 1 female Jew caught tearing down official notices and constituting a public menace were shot in Hrozov."
>
> 26 July: "In Novogrodok Jews refused to take up work. The Jewish Council was again ordered to supply the required work force in spite of the Sabbath, otherwise 50 Jews would be shot. Since the work detail did not arrive by the set deadline, 50 Jews were shot. Once the execution had been carried out, the Jews began working."
>
> 16 August: "Of the 48 prisoners, 19 were Great Russians, 2 Belorussians, 13 Ukrainians, 13 Asians, and 1 was a Jew."
>
> 17 August: "Shot: 146 Jews, 1 civilian, 1 political commissar."
>
> 18 August: "Total number of prisoners 179; those shot by the SD: 107 Jews and 3 guerrillas."[56]
>
> 221st Security Division, 1 September: "In retaliation for the raid on the provisions vehicle, the 701st Guards Battalion carried out a reprisal operation in the villages of Susza, Usakino and Rasvada. 25 Jews and 9 Russian soldiers picked up near the scene of the crime were shot."
>
> 12 September: "1 Communist and 22 Jews were shot for supporting the partisans."[57]
>
> 286th Security Division, 15 September: "In a smaller operation ... 5 Jewish intermediaries of the partisan groups and 3 partisans were taken prisoner." Situation report for the period between 1 and 7 October: "In Esmon 22 Jews with proven links to the partisans were shot.... A patrol unit in Golovtchin was shot at on 4 October 1941 at 2100 hrs., presumably by a Jew. One man was wounded in the arm. Following this, 19 Jews were executed as a reprisal measure."[58]

The army's confidence in handling the Jew = partisan equation is evident. One is witness to deliberate provocations—compulsory work for Jews on a Sabbath—and then—all in strict accordance with instructions—to the subsequent execution. One learns how well the mechanism functions which makes Jews responsible for unsolved criminal attacks and uses them as hostages. The sweeping observation made by General Max von Schenckendorff, commander-in-chief of the Amy Group Rear area, concerning anti-partisan combat—it offers a "rich store of soldierly activity" for resourceful troop commanders[59]—was particularly true for the Jewish dimension of this front-line sector. Like the mobile targets on a training ground, the Jews offered the means to demonstrate and practice the art of eliminating the enemy. This was an opportunity to conjugate the entire range of comparative forms of terror, and to override—in effigy, as it were—the inhibitions of conventional morality: the blow on the head with a rifle-butt, the shot in the back or through the base of the skull, the murder of women and children, the burning down of villages, and the executions performed on the rim of open mass graves. The Jews became demonstration objects and practice fodder. When on one occasion during an anti-partisan training course in the Army Group Rear area, a planned exercise threatened to come to nothing because no partisans had been encountered, a solution was quickly found: "On the other hand, a check on the inhabitants revealed the presence of 13 male Jews, 27 female Jews and 11 Jewish children. Of these, 13 males and 19 females were executed in cooperation with the SD."[60]

1942

On 1 March 1942 the commander of the Army Group Rear Area Center presented "proposals for the liquidation of the partisans" to the Army Group and the OKW. The twelve-page document was a harsh criticism of the current policy for the occupied Eastern territories in general, and in particular of the measures employed to achieve military security in the areas behind the front line. Based on the view that the "amicability" of the Russian population offered the most effective protection against the partisan threat, the commander pointed out that neither the vanquished people's political aspirations for a free Russia, nor the social clamor for private land had as yet been met. "Until now little has been undertaken by our side to win the sympathy of the population." Given the difficult situation on the front and the growing strength of the partisans, now was the last opportunity to make concessions "of our own free will." Without a switch toward a positive population policy and the provision of additional security forces, the general concluded that it would be "impossible to actively combat the partisans."[61]

The document painted a fairly accurate picture of the mood swing within the population and of the changed "partisan situation." After one year of pitiless terror there were no longer any doubts concerning the aims of the German occupiers. In contrast to the summer and autumn of 1941, resistance now offered a greater chance of survival. This was also a result of the changes in the front situation, i.e., of the Red Army's successful winter offensive. On the one hand, the nimbus of German invincibility had been eroded and a return of the Soviet forces once again seemed conceivable. On the other hand, the imperative transferral of security forces from the hinterland to the threatened front line enhanced the combat options available to the remaining cells of resistance. A gap in the front in northwest Belorussia, which the Germans repeatedly failed to close, opened up a land corridor into the unoccupied area of the Soviet Union. The Central Committee in Moscow reacted to this situation without delay. A specially established operative group stepped up the landing of cadres behind the front and forged the isolated cells into a functioning network. This was particularly advantageous for one hitherto marginal group: those sections of front-line partisans, which had been set up by the retreating Red Army in the previous autumn. These militarily organized forces managed to re-establish contact with their headquarters and were able to receive personnel and technical reinforcements over land. In addition, the underground organizations improvised by the Party at the outset of the war had by this stage stabilized and were now beginning to provide support for existing resistance groups or to establish new ones. Altogether, by the summer of 1942 the number of partisans had mushroomed to 150,000 from 30,000 in the winter of 1941. At the same time Soviet propaganda was intensified. By January, two radio stations had started broadcasting in Belorussia.[62]

The Appetite for War

The change in policy which the Army Group Rear area commander had pleaded for, and which other Wehrmacht leaders in the rear areas had also repeatedly demanded using similar arguments, never transpired.[63] It was thwarted by the very mentality of the ranks, as was shown in the first large-scale anti-partisan operation in the Army Group Rear Area Center. Just one month after Schenckendorff's urgent request, the former commander of the civil administration region of Belorussia, General von Bechtolsheim, launched "Operation Bamberg" with about 18,000 men of his own, supported by an additional Slovak division. The preliminary orders showed who the enemy was: around 1,800 heavily armed partisans reputed to be entrenched in fortified bases, women and children acting as spies, Jews from the surrounding area who had taken refuge there, and the entire local populace, since it was generally regarded to be anti-German. Making explicit reference to the positive experience of the previous autumn—meaning the active role played by the division in the Jewish massacre—the orders called for "the most ruthless action possible to be taken against men, women and children."[64] The outcome of the week-long operation was commensurate with this demand—3,423 "partisans and helpers" were shot dead.[65] Given that the operation met with no resistance—beyond two exchanges of fire—one can imagine who the victims were: the civilian population. The report filed by one unit involved which notes that 2,000 persons were shot "during pacification maneuvers" peripheral to the fighting, is evidence of this fact,[66] as are the critical remarks later formulated by the commander, von Schenckendorff: "Among those the division reported as being partisan helpers, there appear to be many who were only very loosely connected with the partisans."[67]

In spite of this criticism, the operation did set a precedent, as we shall see. The reasons for this could probably be described as follows: 1) Such an extensive operation, coupled with its preliminary orders, the garish depiction of the enemy situation and the latest reports of atrocities, allowed each enemy group to be registered individually before they were then lumped together into one single enemy block. 2) The large number of opponents, all rated as equally dangerous, made it possible at any moment to vent fear, anger, and frustration on any one of them—preferably on the weakest group. 3) All of this became possible because one basic precondition had been fulfilled: the military buildup, the allocation of combat sectors and the tactics of encirclement—confining then clearing enemy units. This all added up to create the fiction of a war which offered maximum possibilities for killing against minimal chances of being killed. Compared to the enemy's 3,423 losses, the 707th Infantry Division suffered only 7 dead and 8 wounded.[68]

Although certainly gross, "Operation Bamberg" nonetheless represented an example of the development of the war of extermination. In July and August 1942, thirty operations were carried out against partisans in the Army Group Rear area. The German army suffered hardly any losses. Two operations in particular demonstrate this disproportion: "Operation Adler" resulted in 1,809 of the enemy shot dead, compared to 25 dead and 64 wounded on the German side,[69] while "Operation Greif" ended with 1,395 enemy losses as opposed to the Germans' 26 dead and 26 wounded.[70] The theory that the kill-or-be-killed mechanism was suspended in the "anti-partisan war" is backed up not only by the incongruity of the figures, but also by the location and the timing of the killings. According to eye-witness accounts, of the 2,000 victims killed in "Operation Bamberg," 608 were burnt to death in the *kolkhoz* building and the school in Karpilovka, 240 died in the flames at the distillery in Rudobelka, and 845 were burnt to death in the villages of Kovali and Lavstyki.[71] Mass killing thus occurred when the fighting—i.e., the hunt for partisans—was over, and in places where there were no partisans: in the villages. It was the villages which were caught in the net of the encirclement forces, even if the partisans had managed to slip through the mesh. Yet in the Wehrmacht reports nothing whatsoever is mentioned about the fate of the villages. The only exceptions to this are the reports made by a unit which normally only experienced the battlefield from above—the pilots of the Air Service Command East. In the second half of 1942 they were deployed to assist the forces of the Army Group Center and the Army Group Rear area in ground combat against the partisans. In their final report they noted that "76 partisan villages were seized and burnt down."[72]

Villages might be empty, evacuated by inhabitants who knew what was about to befall them. On certain occasions, if villagers still held some hope in life, "they placed their meager belongings in the garden so as to avoid losing everything when their houses are burnt down."[73] Other times they didn't manage to flee, or they stayed on out of misplaced belief. It might happen that they were killed individually:

> Then the order came to shoot the village inhabitants.... The Germans and Bartschke's people combed the village on their own or in groups, whereupon shooting started in various places throughout Studenka. I also walked down the street and encountered a woman carrying a child of pre-school age. I followed her into the garden and shot at her with the Nagant revolver I was carrying.... I fired one shot only and she fell down. I then shot the child. I did that because Bartschke and the German commanders had ordered all inhabitants of the village of Studenka to be shot. I believe they numbered about five hundred.[74]

But they might equally be herded together to be shot on the edge of the village or to be burnt to death in the community's largest building. According to a report by Rudolf Burchard, the second lieutenant and interpreter at the Bobruysk garrison headquarters, which described a measure carried out in July 1942, "All inhabitants were ordered to assemble and, apart from the village elder and the policemen's families, they were taken to the edge of the village and driven into the mill. The mill was then set on fire. Those attempting to flee were shot on the spot." This exercise was more like a Sunday outing, and it was not just about partisans. Lieutenant Burchard participated because he wanted to improve his food rations. Thus his report concluded: "Afterwards Müller and I drove back to Bobruysk. We took a considerable amount of provisions with us. The share I received was about two kilos of bacon and a slab of pork."[75]

Robbery, pillage, and organization are constant themes in the reports submitted by the General Commissariat at civil administration and by the commander of the Army Group Rear area. "The army holds the view that Russia equals Communism equals all state property, hence booty, hence fair game."[76] The theme of rape receives no mention unless entire units are involved.[77] This gives an indication of its prevalence on an individual level. Then there is the feeling of absolute power in deciding who will be sent into the fire and who is permitted to carry on living, and the thrill sensed watching women and prisoners who are made to cross paths mined by the partisans in order to detonate the hidden explosives: The clearing of minefields is to be performed "exclusively by clearing units composed of prisoners of war or Jews."[78] Vandalism. Pyromania. On several occasions during the summer of 1942 the commander of the Army Group Rear area called his men to order: "Take action against the soldiers' desire to see something burn." Or: "No wanton commandeering, no pillaging, no burning down of villages and shooting of women and children."[79] The anti-partisan war consisted of a multitude of wars, so once they had been let off the leash, the troops were reluctant to be harnessed again by vexed commanders—something the above-mentioned air force soldiers were quick to realize, once they became acquainted with this kind of land warfare: "Concerted large-scale operations in collaboration with the 221st Security Division did not result in enemy contact. Carrying out these operations was nonetheless of great benefit to the troops' training and contributed to the pacification and security of the population."[80]

Himmler Takes Over

A shift in occupation policy was not only hindered by the mentality within the ranks, but more importantly, the idea of a change in Eastern Front policy did not tally with the strategic concept favored by the Führer's headquarters. However, the situation in the hinterland behind the front had dramatically deteriorated during the summer months of 1942. Large partisan units, some of which were operating in unison with regular Red Army forces, had advanced to within menacing proximity of major roads and Wehrmacht bases, especially in administered middle Russia, so that for the first time they posed a serious threat to supply lines. In the civilian-administrated General Commissariat, the system of indigenous administration and agricultural levying were on the brink of collapse. The selective murder of mayors and auxiliary policemen in the area surrounding Minsk led to over half the municipalities being abandoned. In this "partisan country," Soviet rule was reinstated. A report by the Army Secret Field Police (GFP) at the end of June summed it up: "It is a widely held view that, although the Germans may control their bases, the partisans control the broad countryside."[81] The reasons for this rapidly changed situation lay in a recent development: the old scourges of a controlled economy on the land—accompanied by crippling levies—and forced labor in the towns—synonymous with being condemned to slow death by starvation—had been compounded by a new evil: deportation to Germany's forced labor camps.[82] To avoid the system of compulsory recruitment which was introduced in early 1942 and involved the Wehrmacht's participation from the outset, the population fled in large numbers into the forests. From the summer of 1942 onwards, refugees no longer hesitated before taking up active resistance.[83]

The Führer's headquarters was fully aware of the gravity of the situation. Yet the failure of the *Blitzkrieg* and the development of a second front to the rear of the Wehrmacht had done nothing to alter Hitler's basic attitude toward the Russian people: except for a small minority which served the Germans as helots, the Russians had to be obliterated. Whether their elimination was meant to be achieved through the stranglehold of terror accompanying the advance or through a systematic selection process following a lightning victory in the 1941 scenario, or whether, given the changed context of 1942, it was effected through a combination of starvation, forced labor, and bullets—the method made no difference whatsoever to the result. But something needed to be done. This was Himmler's opportunity—not in his role as the racial engineer of *Volkstum,* but as a specialist in genocide.

On 23 July OKW chief Keitel announced that the Wehrmacht leadership had requested Himmler to "set up a centralized command unit to take charge of the war against the partisans."[84] This move may have been prompted by a report by Martin Bormann's representative in the OKW on 26 May, describing a visit to the "Generalkonmmissariat Weissrussland" in which he was informed of the murder of 33 town mayors; on the other hand, the appointment might equally have been triggered by an official request submitted on 17 June by Lohse, the Reich Commissar of *Ostland*, demanding action by the OKW in response to the shooting of 27 men in a unit made up of SD personnel and indigenous auxiliary volunteers (HiWis).[85] The new command unit was only supposed to centralize and evaluate all in-coming data relevant to partisans, hence had no apparent repercussions on Wehrmacht responsibilities. Yet the directive stipulated that the army pass on all incoming information, thereby enabling Himmler's men in the occupied area to collect intelligence with complete autonomy. This suspicion was confirmed by Hitler's directive No. 46 on 18 August. In the area under military command, the Wehrmacht remained responsible for the anti-partisan campaign—on condition that, should the necessity arise, it would have to place troops at the disposal of the Higher SS and Police leadership—and the Reichsführer himself assumed responsibility in the Reich Commissariats.[86]

Himmler had grasped the initiative, and from now on his troops —the SD commandos, police regiments, and SS brigades—set the standards. This move had been in preparation for a long time: as early as 6 July 1941, Himmler's command staff drafted an initial assessment of the partisans' aims and methods of combatting them;[87] on 17 July this was followed by directives defining enemy reconnaissance and intelligence;[88] shortly afterwards, translations of the "Combat rules for partisan groups of the Red Army" were in circulation;[89] in August and September Einsatzgruppe A submitted its first comprehensive field reports[90]—it was on these reports that Himmler based his directive No. 42 on 18 November 1941.[91] This was the first well-founded appraisal of the emerging second front and a cogent attempt to establish an effective defense. The essential points made were: 1) A precondition for active anti-partisan combat is the establishment of a network of informants and constant surveillance; 2) The purpose of the campaign is not "to gain ground" by flushing out the enemy, but "the actual elimination" of the enemy.[92] Thanks to this early assessment, Himmler's Einsatzkommandos were able to take the lead ahead of all other counterintelligence and espionage services, making themselves indispensable to the Wehrmacht in the Army Group Rear area. From September 1941 onwards, they accompanied every large-scale operation.[93] This monopoly obviously gave them the power to determine the speed and the range of the anti-partisan war from early on. Starting with his very first order in this new function, Himmler made it quite clear that he had no military misconceptions about his mission. "For psychological reasons," in future the term "partisan" is always to be replaced by "bandit"; accordingly, anti-partisan operations were henceforth to be called "anti-bandit warfare" *(Bandenbekämpfung)*, and areas suspected of partisan presence referred to as "contaminated with bandit groups" *(bandenverseucht)*.[94] Anti-partisan measures mutated into vermin extermination. So it was entirely apposite for the new era that its first operation was given the code name "swamp fever." In a personally signed order, Himmler prescribed preparations for the use of "nerve gas and stun bombs."[95]

Due to start on 25 August, the operation's objective was, as Himmler put it, to "thoroughly cleanse" the General Commissariat. Yet despite the massive deployment of 6,500 men, the operation proved unsuccessful. Although the Wehrmacht garrisons at Minsk and Vilna supplied 140 trucks to transport troops across the country, partisan units could not be prevented evading larger battles in this impassable terrain.[96] Naturally, the troops did not return empty-handed: they managed to shoot 389 "bandits" and 1,274 "suspects," and had also, since it lay en route, "cleared" the Baranovichi ghetto of its 8,000 Jews. Apart from a dozen burnt-out villages, the whole area had been cleared and the population evacuated.[97]

But this didn't impress Himmler, who reacted by making further changes. The first step, on 23 October, was to appoint von dem Bach-Zelewski, the Higher SS and Police Leader for Central Russia, as "Commissioner for anti-bandit warfare."[98] Through an abundance of small-scale operations, which also extended to the Army Group Rear area, Bach-Zelewski had grasped the initiative in the anti-partisan campaign, while simultaneously demonstrating that if this type of warfare were to succeed, it had to be waged without letup.[99] The second measure concerned the transfer to Belorussia of SS-Brigadeführer von Gottberg: as head of the "combat unit Gottberg" his assignment was to ensure that this warfare was waged on a permanent basis. A former member of the Freikorps, Gottberg had gathered considerable experience; besides which, with his career as a top SS officer having been impeded for quite some time as a result of various criminal and internal party proceedings, he was also highly motivated by the desire for rehabilitation. Things worked out just as Himmler had planned. Gottberg radicalized operative conduct by declaring the entire populace to be the enemy—"bandits, a population of bandit suspects and bandit sympathizers, Jews, Gypsies, horse-riders and juveniles to be considered spies."[100] Such opponents could only be dealt with by waging war, deploying heavy weapons to hamper their retreat, by burning down their villages and systematically robbing them so as to destroy their very means of existence. Such was the outcome of Gottberg's first major operations, "Operation Nürnberg" and "Operation Hamburg," staged in November and December 1942, each of which lasted only ten days: 5,000 murdered Jews, 5,000 "eliminated bandits or suspects," 30 villages burnt down[101] and, as Bach-Zelewski radioed to Himmler, "an enormous amount of plunder, especially provisions, which as yet cannot be estimated."[102]

Taking plunder did not stem from Gottberg's own personal initiative. On 26 October 1942 Göring had issued directives for "anti-bandit warfare," especially in the Army Group Rear Area Center, in which with his own particular brand of candidness he demanded that during anti-partisan operations "all cattle stocks" be driven away and all available food provisions be requisitioned. All men and women capable of work were to be "compulsorily registered" and deported either to the Reich or to the secure territories.[103] Even the policy of declaring war on the population had been decided a long time in advance by the political and military leadership. In the "combat directive for anti-bandit warfare in the East," which the OKH had issued to the troops on 11 November 1942, "sentimental considerations" were castigated as irresponsible; captured "bandits" were to be hanged or shot, "preferably hanged," as a supplementary note stated. In reference to targeted victims a further category was added: "women too." A month later the OKW dispelled any remaining doubts concerning this directive: "against women and children every available means is to be used so long as it leads to success."[104] Thus the radicalization and extension of the campaign against the partisans can neither be attributed to the initiative of a few junior officers gone wild, nor should Himmler's assumption of the command be misinterpreted as a putsch. Both aspects were part of an overall strategy which aimed at fusing the area behind the front with the forward lines of combat to create a single battle zone, instead of selectively declaring war on the partisans within the population. In the second half of 1942 the foundations of this strategy were laid. In 1943 its results could be seen.

Clausewitz Is Wrong

The escalation which occurred in summer 1942, finding its expression in Himmler's seizure of power and the orders issued by the Reich leadership, initially had varied impact in each part of Belorussia. In the General Commissariat the Higher SS and Police Leader, flanked by his police and SS troops, had assumed complete control of all matters concerning anti-partisan warfare. The SD became solely responsible for intelligence relating to the "partisan situation" and for decisions defining "collective measures."[105] This organizational collusion made it possible to carry out the second phase of Jewish extermination (with the code name "Clearance of the border ghettos") as part of the anti-partisan campaign.[106] To this end, certain occasions required the Wehrmacht commander to make his units available, as was stipulated by the OKW directive No. 46 of 18 August 1942.

Within the Army Group Rear area the chief commander attempted, to some degree with the support of several divisional commanders, to hinder the escalation of aggression. The issues of contention were the execution of women and children, the application of collective reprisal measures, and the establishment of a death zone on either side of railway lines.[107] His adversary in this clash was von dem Bach-Zelewski, the Higher SS and Police Leader of Russia Center. First celebrated as a war hero for his reckless bravery in the euphoric summer phase of the campaign, and then, with his police and SS reserves, regarded as an indispensable helper during the 1941 winter retreat and the 1942 partisan spring, he quite suddenly appeared in a new guise to the old trooper von Schenckendorff—as a brutal and irresponsible hard-liner. But as Himmler's representative, Bach-Zelewski had been nothing else right from the start; he asserted his interests with relative ease by citing the special powers of the Reichsführer.[108] Only on the question of maintaining railway security through deforestation and evacuation of the population did the commander of the Army Group Rear area succeed in achieving a delay, by arguing that Himmler lacked the authority to issue directives for his area of command.[109] This respite lasted for no longer than one month.

On 27 August partisans attacked the small railway station of Slavnoya, killing the station-master as well as several collaborators in the village. The report submitted by this station's head office turned this incident into an event of apocalyptic proportions.[110] By the time the nature of these extraordinary exaggerations and the real facts about the incident were exposed shortly after (the station officials had been taken by surprise during a bout of drinking in the neighboring village),[111] it was already too late: in a message wired on 28 August, Hitler called for an "Immediate reprisal operation."[112] On 29 August the OKH instructed the Army Group Center to carry out Himmler's demand for a no-man's-land all along the railway lines. The dispute had been decided.[113] With his hands now tied, there was little else the commander for the Army Group Rear area could do than perform the retaliatory measure—

which meant shooting "100 male or female local residents who are either partisan supporters or Communists or members of partisans' families."[114] This action stood in stark contrast to an order he himself had recently issued not to punish the families of mere suspects.[115] Shortly afterwards, these one hundred victims were shot by a unit of the 286th Security Division.[116] None of them had been arrested in connection with the incident; 60 had been held in detention for some time by the Army Secret Field Police (GFP), while the other 40—making up the prescribed total—were taken from the reservoir of hostages held by the Higher SS and Police Leader Bach-Zelewski.[117] Hitler's original order had been far more extensive, stipulating that all the villages bordering the 150 kilometer stretch of railway line from Borisov to Orsha be burnt down. As General Richert, commander in charge of the Slavnoya hostage massacre, testified in the 1946 Minsk trial, this order had been opposed by Field Marshal von Kluge, the chief of Army Group Center.[118] But although von Kluge managed to prevent this order being carried out in August, he too was duped in October 1942. On this occasion, Göring directed his air force troops (at that time deployed in ground operations in the Army Group Rear area) to burn down any villages located in the vicinity of the sabotaged tracks.[119] Although both Schenckendorff and Kluge protested against this order, arguing that this strategy would leave Russian railway workers homeless and drive them into the arms of the partisans,[120] their intervention had no impact on the conduct of Göring's men, as can be gauged from their reports of successful punitive actions.[121]

On 18 December a remarkable meeting took place in Berlin. Representatives of the three Army Group Rear areas and of Army Groups A and B discussed the situation with emissaries of the OKW and the OKH. In their findings the army leaders were unanimous. The mood of the population had hit rock-bottom and it was felt that an improvement could only be reached by introducing a radical shift in current occupation policy: this meant granting restricted political and cultural autonomy, introducing private ownership, guaranteeing food supplies and putting an end to manhunts and deportations. As the minutes of the meeting recorded, it was predominantly the comments made by General von Schenckendorff which "made a great impression on all those present."[122] The general, as will be remembered, had already voiced the same criticism in spring, repeating it in varied forms successive dispatches. In the summer, he discovered that all his dispatches had been piling up unread in the OKH.[123] Not only did he now hope to persuade the attentive audience of his views, he also had received the assurance that these would be relayed directly to the Führer. It was his bad luck that the meeting was held in the wrong place—at the ministry for occupied Eastern territories—and that the officer reporting, Rosenberg, while gaining entry into the Führer headquarters to deliver his report, was never actually given a hearing.

On the part of the commanders this was indeed a case of veritable quixotry. In the beginning they wholeheartedly and emphatically embraced Hitler's war. There was no order to murder which they did not happily pass on, no act of atrocity they did not rigorously instruct their troops to perform. At that stage they were thrilled by the limitless terrain for war and the increased scope for action, which made victory seem inevitable. However, now that they could no longer guarantee the passage of reinforcements through to the front, nor safeguard the flow of supplies, as they were no longer able to protect their territory against partisans, and now faced the looming prospect of military failure, these generals sought political change as the only means of fulfilling the campaign's objective. But in the war Hitler was waging, such changes were not on the agenda. When by summer 1942 the cost of maintaining the *kolkhoz* economy and local government had rocketed because the partisans had been pillaging the harvest crops and murdering local mayors, Hitler renounced the system of cooperation with the cowed, yet obliging helots. From then on, the only choice available to the subjugated population was between unqualified support for the German cause and the death sentence. The permission to shoot women and children, the call for a larger number of villages to be burnt down, the order to systematically plunder, and the conversion of supply lines into corridors of death all constituted measures which would ultimately enable occupied territory to be transformed into a no-man's-land, linked up by a network of fortified villages and military strongpoints. Putting Himmler in charge of anti-partisan warfare was entirely consistent with this vision. Far from signalling a change, his appointment gave higher definition to the original idea behind this campaign. Clausewitz had been wrong: the war of extermination was structured not only by grammatical rules, but also by a particular kind of logic.[124] Whereas the grammar—as Schenckendorff and Kluge both correctly assumed—could be controlled, the logic behind the war of extermination—as Hitler knew full well—was utterly dominant and tolerated no half-measures. At the end of the second year of the war in the East this principle was nowhere so clearly in evidence as on the partisan front.

1943

During the large-scale partisan hunts of autumn and winter 1942, the troops of the Reichsführer's SS had clearly spelt out the lesson to be learned by the Wehrmacht. The enemy was not to be considered as consisting of partisan groups plus sympathizers, but instead as an entire criminal population minus the collaborators. The security divisions had no problems accommodating this approach; after one-and-a-half years of war in Russia, they were thoroughly acquainted with the enemy groups both in theory and practice. What in the campaign's early phase began as a wish concerning Red Army troops stranded behind the front and still roaming at large or in hiding, the wish that these stragglers would no longer have to be separated into distinct categories (Red Army militia, guerrillas, prisoners, deserters, men in uniform, men in civilian dress), but could instead be viewed in toto as one "organic, special entity" and then treated accordingly,[125] this wish could now be directed at the populace as a whole: 1,627 shot partisans or anyone considered to be a partisan, 2,041 persons deported to Germany as force labor, 21 villages burnt down in one single district alone. Overall, the booty amassed consisted of 9,265 head of cattle and 580 tons of foodstuffs—these statistics represent the balance of an average operation performed by an average security division—operation "Waldwinter," in January 1943.[126] Whereas Wehrmacht units had initially continued to operate on their own in the Army Group Rear area, by the middle of 1943 there was an increasing tendency to involve the SS and HSSPF units in joint major operations. This symbiosis was long overdue. None of the Wehrmacht commanders were any longer bothered by the fact that most of these operations were placed under the command of a higher SS officer—the aforementioned Brigadeführer von Gottberg. Any criticism of the fact that—as in "Operation Cottbus"—6,087 adversaries had been killed in battle and 3,709 had been "dealt with" afterwards, or that these 9,796 enemy dead compared to a mere 88 German losses, had by this point fallen silent.[127] Descriptions like the following passage from this operation's final report will probably have caused no more than a knowledgeable grin: "The mines planted along most roads and paths make the production of mine detectors a necessity. The mine detection device developed by the Dirlewanger Battalion has proven very successful."[128] The term "device" means captured civilians who were chased across minefields to detonate the explosives. For the recruits, who from autumn 1942 onwards spent the rest of their training period carrying out regular anti-partisan operations, what they witnessed there was as new and normal as anything experienced during their first maneuver.

> Let us recapitulate: "On the evening of 29 December 1942, we started our operation in a village. There were no partisans in this village.... We then moved on to another village.... We shot about 70 people. Among them also women, old people and children. And then we burnt down the village.... We then proceeded to the third village. We didn't come across any partisans there. But we still burnt down the village and shot around 50 people. Even women and children."[129]

No one questioned the military value or rationale behind such an operation. When the judge in the Minsk trial asked Lance-corporal Rodenbusch, who had given this account, "So you burnt down those villages too, even though there were no partisans there?" the accused replied "Yes, of course. That's what the company commander had ordered us to do."[130] The orders issued in early 1941, which had taken so much care to provide historical justification for the need to wipe out Jewish Bolshevism, followed by supplementary directives issued in summer and autumn which so assiduously addressed and dispelled any possible moral qualms—these orders had finally found their way down to the troops. Yet these orders, which historians would later call "criminal," had changed beyond recognition in the course of two years; they had been transformed into completely normal orders issued by some company commander or other. The shooting of women and children—that moral outpost where a number of veteran generals had fought a derisory last stand for self-esteem—had long since become an automatic reflex for their own soldiers. In the words of Rodenbusch, the recruit:

> We had just shot the four men when I saw two women and three children running away. My rifle still contained five bullets and I took one shot at each of them. All five fell over, and by the time I got to them they were already dead. I had hit four in the back and one child was shot through the neck.[131]

—Translated by Matthew Partridge

Notes

1. Court proceedings relating to the atrocities committed by German fascist insurgents in the Belorussian SSR, 15–19 January 1946 (Minsk Trial), Minsk 1947, 262–263.
2. Befehlshaber rückwärtiges Heeresgebiet Mitte (Commander of the Army Group Center Rear Area) (henceforth Berück) Korpsbefehl Nr. 31, 20.7.41, Bundesarchiv-Militärarchiv Freiburg (henceforth BA-MA), RH 22-224.
3. 102th ID/Ia Nr. 17, Divisionsbefehl 24.7.41, BA-MA RH 26-102/9.
4. Berück Korpsbefehl Nr. 26, 10.7.41, BA-MA RH 22-224; idem, Verwaltungs-Anordnungen Nr. 2, 13.7.41, Belorussian State Archive Minsk (BSA) 393-3-42; Berück 10-Tagesmeldung 10.9.41, BA-MA 22-227.
5. 56th ID Divisionsbefehl Nr. 15, Nuremberg Trial, NOKW 1458.
6. 87th ID Meldung 16.8.41, BA-MA RH 26-87/25; 339th ID Tätigkeitsbericht Ic 22.9.–22.12.41, BA-MA RH 26-339/36.
7. Berück Korpsbefehl Nr. 40, 16.8.41, BA-MA RH 22-224; similarly, in a report of Army Group South: Armeeoberkommando 6/Ia, Führungsanordnung Nr. 13, 10.7.41, BA-MA RH 20-6/755.
8. Berück Korpsbefehl Nr. 40, 16.8.41, BA-MA RH 22-224.
9. Berück Süd Befehl 23.8.41, in Case 12. Judgment pronounced against the Wehrmacht High Command on: 28.10.1948 in Nuremberg by the Military Tribunal V of the United States of America (Case 12), Berlin 1961, 233.
10. Heeresgruppe (HGr.) Mitte Bericht Ic 4.8.41 describing the mass executions in the villages of Studenka and Kostjuki performed by the 336th IR (161st ID), Military Archive (MA) Podolsk 500-12454-287; 162nd ID on a massacre performed by the 307th police unit under its command in Starobin, MA Podolsk ibid.; Berück Betr: Kollektive Gewaltmaßnahmen 12.8.41, BA-MA RH 26-221/13b.
11. Berück 10-Tagesmeldungen 10.9.41, BA-MA RH 22-227; 403rd Security Division (SichDiv) Kriegstagebuch (KTB) 3.9.41, BA-MA RH 26-403/2; 339th ID Bericht Ia 24.9.41, BA-MA RH 26-221/21; 350th IR Meldung Ia 12.10., 14.10., 18.10.41, BA-MA RH 26-221/2b; 339th ID Partisanenlage 1.12–22.12.41, BA-MA RH 26-339/10.
12. Witalij Wilenchik, *Die Partisanenbewegung in Weißrußland 1941–1944* (Wiesbaden 1984), 151ff.
13. Ibid., 155ff.
14. Armeeoberkommando 9 Bericht 2.9.41, BSA Minsk 655-1-1; cf. Ereignismeldungen UdSSR (EM) Nr. 42, 163–164; EM 73, 299; EM 90, 218; EM 92, 275; EM 123, 291; EM 144, 276. A similar assessment is also provided in the reports of the "Wehrmachtsbefehlhabers Ostland/Kommandant Weißruthenien" (WBO/WR) 11.9.–30.11.41, BA-MA RH 26-707/2; WBO/WR Lagebericht 20.9.41, Zentrales Staatliches Historisches Archiv (ZSA) Riga 70-5-37; WBO/WR Befehl Nr. 30, 18.12.41, BSA Minsk 378-1-698.
15. 339th ID Lagebericht 5.11.41, BA-MA RH 26-339/5.
16. Panzergruppe 3 Gruppenbefehl Nr. 217.9.41, Nuremberg Trial, NOKW 688.
17. Wirtschaftsinspektion Mitte, Entwicklungen und Auswirkungen der Partisanentätigkeit [probably spring 1942—H.H.] BA-MA RW 31/249.
18. WBO/WR Monatsbericht 11.10.–10.11.41, BA-MA RH 26-702/2; 339th ID (691st IR) Partisanenlage 1.12.–22.12.41, BA-MA RH 26-339/10; Wilenchik, *Partisanenbewegung*, 158.

19. Berück/Ia 10-Tagesmeldung 20.9.41, BA-MA RH 22-227; idem, Verwaltungsanordnung Nr. 9, 21.10.41, BSA Minsk 570-1-1; HGr. Mitte Ic-Anweisung 21.8.41, BSA Minsk 655-1-1; Berück/Ia Tagesordnung für den Kurs "Bekämpfung von Partisanen" 24.–26.9.41, BA-MA RH 22-225; OKH Richtlinien für die Partisanenbekämpfung 25.10.41, Nuremberg Trial, NOKW 151.
20. Berück/Ia 10-Tagesmeldungen der Monate Juli–November 41, BA-MA RH 22-227; Berück/Ia Bericht Über Monat November 9.12.41, BA-MA RH 22-225.
21. 257th ID Anweisungen 3.12.41 and guidelines of the 17th army sent on 7 December 1941 in Case 12, 173ff.
22. 286th Sich.Div./Ic Tätigkeitsbericht Ic September–Dezember 41, BA-MA RH 26-286/5; 403rd Sich.Div. Tätigkeitsbericht Ic März 42, BA-MA RH 26-403/7; 403rd Sich.Div./Ic November 41, BA-MA RH 26-403/4; 252nd ID Tagesmeldung 18.8.41, BA-MA RH 26-252/82.
23. 339th ID KTB Tätigkeitsbericht Ic 20.10.–30.11.41, BA-MA RH 26-339/36; Berück/Ia Bisheriges Gesamtergebnis der Aktion vom 10.–12.9.41, BA-MA RH 22-225; 691st IR (286th Sich.Div.) Lagebericht 1.–7.10.41, BA-MA RH 22-286/4; 403rd Sich.Div./Ia Monatsbericht Dezember 41, 4.1.42, BA-MA RH 26-403/7; 403rd Sich.Div. KTB 15.3.–20.11.41 (1.–30.10.41), BA-MA RH 26-403/2; 221st Sich.Div./Ia Tagesmeldungen 10.–15.11.41, BA-MA RH 26-221/19; 350th IR An 221st Sich.Div. 12.10.41, BA-MA RH 26-221/22b.
24. Berück/Ia Vorschläge zur Vernichtung der Partisanen im rückw. Heeresgebiet, 1.3.42, BA-MA RH 22-230.
25. WBO/WR/Ic Anlage 4 zum Monatsbericht 11. 10.–10. 11.41, BA-MA RH 22-702/15d; cf. also the summary of the adjacent Berück Nord, which between July and November 1941, in other words in only three months, took 31,525 prisoners, in Norbert Müller, ed., *Deutsche Besatzungspolitik in der UdSSR 1941–1944, Dokumente* (Cologne: 1980) 114; cf. on the issues raised by German statistics, Timothy P. Mulligan, "Reckoning the Cost of People's War: The German Experience in the Central USSR," in *Russian History* 5 (1982): 27–48.
26. Herbert Golz, "Erfahrungen aus dem Kampf gegen Banden," in *Wehrkunde,* vol. 4 (1955): 134–140; Hellmuth Kreidel, "Partisanenkampf in Mittelrußland," in *Wehrkunde,* vol. 9 (1955): 380–385.
27. Eingreifgruppe Anderssen (252nd ID) Tätigkeitsbericht 19.9.41, BA-MA RH 26-252/89.
28. Berück 10-Tagesmeldung 20.9.41 notes, for example, that during one operation "numerous officers and commissars" were eliminated. The report by the Polizei-Regiment (Pol.Reg.) responsible for the operation refers to only two officers, but mentions six shot women, Pol.Reg. Mitte Gesamtergebnis der Aktion vom 10.–12.9.41, BA-MA RH 22-225; more serious are the misrepresentations concerning the murder of 4,000 prisoners of war in Bobruysk—in the KTB of the 339th ID the fire staged by the camp's commander is represented as arson committed by the prisoners, the premeditated MG massacre is described as a measure to foil an attempted escape, cf. 339th ID Tätigkeitsbericht November 3.12.41, BA-MA RH 26-339/7; similarly the massacre of the ghettoized Jews in Borisov, 339th ID KTB 20.10.41, BA-MA RH 26-339/4; burned down villages: 339th ID Partisanenlage 1.12.–22.12.41, BA-MA RH 26-339/10; women and children: 339th ID Merkblatt 2.11.41, BA-MA RH 26-339/5.
29. Cf. Omer Bartov, "Whose History Is It, Anyway? The Wehrmacht and German Historiography," in this volume.

30. While Valdis Redelis, *Partisanenkrieg* (Heidelberg: 1958), 87ff., and Rudolf Aschenauer, *Krieg ohne Grenzen* (Leoni am Sternberger See: 1982), 129ff., both view the Wehrmacht as essentially only reacting to Soviet terror, Jürgen Förster —in his otherwise very precise essay "Die Sicherung des 'Lebensraums,'" in *Das Deutsche Reich und der Zweite Weltkrieg*, vol. 4 (1983): 1030ff.—believed a "new dimension" of the war of extermination in autumn 1941 could be discerned in the "increased incidence of well-organized, trained Soviet partisan units" (1041). In contrast, Matthew Cooper in *The Phantom War: The German Struggle against Soviet Partisans 1941–1944* (London: 1979), 17ff., confirms the total failure of the Soviet partisan offensive in autumn 1941. Wilenchik, *Partisanenbewegung,* 152ff., argues similarly. Completely irrelevant is the theory held by Erich Hesse, *Der sowjetische Partisanenkrieg 1941–1944* (Göttingen: 2nd ed. 1993), 281, that the Wehrmacht leadership did not take the partisan threat in 1941 seriously.
31. The *Gerichtsbarkeitserlaß* (practice of wartime military jurisdiction) reproduced in Gerd R. Ueberschär and Wolfram Wette, eds., *Der deutsche Überfall auf die Sowjetunion. "Unternehmen Barbarossa" 1941* (Frankfurt am Main: 1991), 252ff., 258.
32. "Richtlinien für das Verhalten der Truppe in Rußland" (guidelines), ibid., 258.
33. Report by the Panzergruppe 3 about a meeting in Warsaw on 11.6.41, in Ueberschär and Wette, *Überfall,* 283ff.
34. Case 12, 71.
35. OKH An die Befehlshaber der rückwärtigen Heeresgebiete Nord, Mitte, Süd, 25.7.41, BSA Minsk 655-1-1.
36. Cf. Ueberschär and Wette, *Überfall,* 305.
37. Cf. Walter Manoschek, "'Going to Shoot Some Jews?' The Destruction of the Jews in Serbia," in this volume.
38. Ian Kershaw, *Der NS-Staat, Geschichtsinterpretationen und Kontroversen im Überblick* (Reinbek: 1989), 208.
39. Jan Philipp Reemtsma, "Charisma und Terror," in Arbeitsstelle Fritz Bauer Institut, *Materialien* 10 (1994), 9ff.; idem, "Zur Dialektik der Zivilisation," lecture in the Hamburger Institut für Sozialforschung (October 1994), unpublished manuscript, 7ff.; Christopher Browning uses the term *symbiosis* to characterize the relationship between Hitler and Himmler in the formulation of the orders detailing the *Endlösung* (Final Solution), cf. *The Path to Genocide, Essays on Launching the Final Solution* (Cambridge: 1993), 92, 121.
40. Förster, "Sicherung," 1040, 1054; Jörg Friedrich, *Das Gesetz des Krieges, Das deutsche Heer in Rußland 1941 bis 1945, Der Prozeß gegen das Oberkommando der Wehrmacht* (Munich and Zürich: 1993), 486, 833.
41. The secret statement of intent concerning future Eastern European policy, 16.7.41, in Ueberschär and Wette, *Überfall,* 276.
42. Wirtschaftsinspektion Mitte Lagebericht 22.7.41, Strafsache Windisch, Landgericht Mainz 3 Ks 1/67, Dokumentenband IV.
43. II. IR 350, An das Regiment, 18.8.41, BA-MA RH 26-221/21.
44. SS-Kav.Brigade, Meldung über Tätigkeit 22.8.–3.9.41, BA-MA, RH 22-224.
45. WBO/WR/Ia, Lagebericht 1.9.–10.9.41, BSA Minsk 651-1-1.
46. Ibid., Lagebericht 1.10.–15.10.41, BSA Minsk 651-1-1.
47. 221st Sich.Div. KTB 8.7.41, BA-MA RH 26-221/10; Berück/Ia Meldung 9.7.41, BA-MA RH 22-227.

48. HSSPF Rußland Mitte 18.7.41, BA-MA RH 26-221/12a; HSSPF Rußland Mitte Funkspruch 2.8.41, Kriegshistorisches Archiv Prag (KHA), Prague, Box 12-File 101.
49. Berück/Ia An Sich.Div. 221 18.7.41, BA-MA RH 26-221/12a.
50. Berück Meldung an OKH 1.8.41, BA-MA RH 22-227.
51. SS-Kav. Reg. 1 Regimentsbefehl Nr. 42 of 27.7.41, MA Podolsk 500-12493-62; SS-Kav.Reg. 2 Bericht 12.8.41, KHA Prague 5-30.
52. SS-Kav.Brig. Abschlußmeldung 18.9.41, KHA Prague 24-154.
53. Cf. Hannes Heer, "Killing Fields: The Wehrmacht and the Holocaust in Belorussia, 1941–42," in this volume.
54. Cf. as examples Ortskommandantur (OK) 1/264, OK 1/827, Feldkommandantur (FK) 528, FK 551, FK 549, BA-MA RH 226-221/21.
55. 403rd Sich.Div. KTB 14.7.41, BA-MA RH 26-403/2.
56. 252nd ID Tagesmeldungen 25.7., 26.7., 16.8., 17.8., 18.8.41, BA-MA RH 26-252/82.
57. 221st Sich.Div. KTB 1.9. and 12.9.41, BA-MA RH 26-221/10.
58. 286th Sich.Div. KTB 15.9.41, BA-MA RH 26-286/2; 691st IR (286th Sich.Div.) Lagebericht 1.–7.10.41, BA-MA RH 26-286/41.
59. Berück/Ia Korpsbefehl Nr. 52 14.9.41, BA-MA RH 26-221/13.
60. Polizei-Bataillon 322 KTB 25.9.41, KHA Prague A2-1-3.
61. Berück/Ia Vorschläge zur Vernichtung der Partisanen im rückwärtigen Heeresgebiet und in den rückwärtigen Armeegebieten 1.3.41, BA-MA RH 22-230; cf. also Berück Tätigkeitsbericht Ic January 42, 4.2.41, BA-MA RH 22-243 and Berück Propagandaabteilung Stimmungsbericht 17.2.42, BA-MA RW 4/236.
62. Wilenchik, *Partisanenbewegung,* 159–178; cf. also Berück Tätigkeitsbericht Ic März 42, 10.4.42, BA-MA RH 22-243; Mulligan, 32.
63. Berück An das Oberkommando der HGr. Mitte 10.10.42, MA Podolsk 500-12454-590, containing a reference to the situation report to the OKH of June 42; Luftwaffenkommando Ost Bericht über Bandenbekämpfung 10.4.–31.12.42, 8.1.43, MA Podolsk 500-12454-598; Alexander Dallin, *Deutsche Herrschaft in Rußland 1941-1945* (Düsseldorf: 1958), 156ff.
64. 707th ID/Ia Divisionsbefehl Nr. 32, 18.3.42, BA-MA RH 26-707/5.
65. 707th ID Ic-Monatsbericht 1.3–31.3.42, 14.5.42, BA-MA RH 26-707/15.
66. 707th ID Meldungen des verstärkten slowakischen Rgt. 102, Anlage C zum Div.Bef. Nr. 43, 5.4.42, BA-MA RH 26-707/5.
67. Berück KTB 7.4.42, BA-MA RH 22-229.
68. 707th ID/Ia Divisionsbefehl Nr. 43 5.4.42, BA-MA RH 26-707/5.
69. 286th Sich.Div. "Kampfgruppe Adler," Abschlußbericht 8.8.42, BA-MA RH 26-286/12; in order to avoid being accused of executing a massacre as in "Operation Bamberg," the report filed by the 286th Sich.Div. points out that surprisingly few weapons were recovered because the partisans had thrown them all into the marshes during their escape.
70. 286th Sich.Div. "Kampfgruppe Greif," Abschlußbericht 30.8.42, BA-MA RH 26-186/12.
71. A. Adamowitsch, J. Bryl, and V. Kalesnik, eds., *Out of the Fire* (Moscow: 1980), 27ff.
72. Luftwaffenkommando Ost, Bericht über die Bandenbekämpfung 10.4–31.12.42, 8.1.43, MA Podolsk 500-12454-598.
73. 203rd Sich.Div. KTB 3.7.42, BA-MA RH 26-203/1.
74. Confession of a Belorussian member of the SS-Sonderbataillon Dirlewanger, the special unit which participated in most of the Wehrmacht's anti-partisan

operations in 1942, concerning a massacre in June in Belorussia, reproduced in Ales Adamowitsch, *Henkersknechte* (Frankfurt am Main: 1988), 168.

75. Cross-examination Burchard, 23.1.46, Minsk Trial, KGB-Archive Minsk.
76. 9. Armee, Einsatz der Wehrwirtschaftsdienste und Wehrwirtschaftslagebericht für den Bereich der 9. Armee, Bericht August 1941, BA-MA Wi I D 79, 303f.; similar: Zentrale Handelsgesellschaft Ost/Nebenstelle Slutsk, An den Hauptkommissar Paulsen in Minsk, Slutsk 5.8.42, BSA Minsk 370-1-485; Wirtschaftliche Außenstelle Smolewitschi, An den Gebietskommissar Minsk-Land, 25.3.43, BSA Minsk 339-1-321; Berück/Ia Bericht über Monat November 9.12.41, BA-MA RH 22-225; Berück Besprechungspunkte für Div.Kdr. Besprechung 9.8.42, BA-MA RH 22-233.
77. 252nd ID Merkpunkte für Kommandeur-Besprechung 14.9.41, BA-MA RH 26-252/76.
78. 403rd Sich.Div. Vorgehen bei Vorhandensein von Minen, 11.8.42, BA-MA RH 26-403/7; Cross-examination Richert 5.1.46, Minsk Trial, vol. 1, KGB archive Minsk; Nuremberg Trial, NOKW 2139.
79. Berück Besprechungspunkte für Divisions-Konnnandeur-Besprechung 12.6.42, BA-MA RH 22-23 1; Berück Besprechungspunkte für Divisions-Kdr.Besprechung 9.8.42, BA-MA RH 22-233.
80. Luftwaffenkommando Ost, cf n. 72.
81. GFP Monatsbericht 1.–30.6.42, BA-MA RW 4/237; similarly the Stimmungsberichte filed by the Propagandaabteilung Ostland from May to August 1942, BA-MA RW 4/235; reports by the agricultural branch in the Gebietskommissariat Minsk-Land, BSA Minsk 393-1-321.
82. Cf. Wilenchik, *Partisanenbewegung,* 192ff.; report by an undercover agent describing the mood in the civilian population in July 1942, BA-MA RW 4/237.
83. Cf. Rolf-Dieter Müller, "Menschenjagd. Die Rekrutierung von Zwangsarbeitern in der besetzten Sowjetunion," in Hannes Heer and Klaus Naumann, eds., *Vernichtungskrieg. Verbrechen der Wehrmacht* (Hamburg: 1995), 92–103; Propagandaabteilung Ostland, Stimmungsbericht Nr. 17, 3.5.42, BA-MA RW 4/235; Wilenchik, *Partisanenbewegung,* 220.
84. Directive of chief of OKW 23.7.42, cited in N. Müller, *Besatzungspolitik,* 129–130; on 9.7.42 at a "general meeting on partisans" in Lötzen (which included the chief of German Ordnungspolizei Kurt Daluege), Himmler informed several higher SS officers and police generals of the planned coup, cf. von dem Bach-Zelewski, Kriegstagebuch 11.7.42, BA Koblenz R 20-45b and Himmler's Kommandobefehl of 7.8.42, KHA Prague 4-17.
85. Reichsleiter Bormann's representative, Albert Hoffmann, Bericht Nr. 4, 26.5.42, Institut für Zeitgeschichte München FA 226/29, 28ff.; the permanent representative (of Reichskommissar Lohse) Betr. Partisanentätigkeit 17.6.42, BA Koblenz R6/354, 17ff.
86. Weisung Nr. 46 of the OKW 18.8.42, cit. in N. Müller, *Besatzungspolitik,* 130–131; the commander of the army rear area had already been informed on 27.7.42 of Himmler's appointment to take charge of the "Generalkommissariat Weißruthenien," Berück KTB 27.7.42, BA-MA RH 22-232.
87. Kommandostab (Kdo.Stab) RF-SS/Ia Einsatz von Truppen zur Befriedung des "rückwärtigen Heeresgebietes" und des "Gebietes der politischen Verwaltung," 6.7.41, KHA Prague 5-25.
88. Kdo.Stab RF-SS/Ic Aufklärung durch geheimen Meldedienst 17.7.41, KHA Prague 10-94.

89. (Kdo.Stab RF-SS) Richtlinien für den Einsatz der Kdo.Stab RF-SS unterstellten Verbände, 8. Folge (signed 10.9.41), KHA Prague 10-94.
90. Einsatzgruppe A Tätigkeits- und Erfahrungsbericht 17.8.41 and 29.9.41, OSOBI Moscow 500-4-93.
91. RF-SS Kommandobefehl Nr. 42, 18.11.42, KHA Prague 10-94.
92. Cf. n. 87.
93. Berück/Ia Korpsbefehl Nr. 55, 29.9.41, BA-MA RH 22-225; 339th ID Lagebericht 15.11.41, BA-MA RH 26-339/7; EM Nr. 34 of 26.7.41, EM Nr. 90 of 21.9.41; cf. on the struggle within the Wehrmacht leadership, Förster, "Sicherung," 1040–1041.
94. RF-SS Kommandobefehl Nr. 65, 13.8.42, KHA Prague 4-17.
95. RF-SS Kommandobefehl 7.8.42, KHA Prague 4-17.
96. HSSPF Ostland KTB 2.9.42, KHA Prague 19-133; the failure is frankly admitted by Jeckeln, operation commander and HSSPF Ostland, in his final report of 6.11.42, KHA Prague 19-133.
97. Abschlußbericht Jeckeln cf. n. 96; on the massacre in the Baranovichi ghetto, cf. Strafsache Heuser, Landgericht Koblenz 9 Ks 2/62, vol. 9, 1284–1285.
98. RF-SS Ernennung eines Bevollmächtigten des Reichsführers für Bandenbekämpfung, 23.10.42, KHA Prague 4-19.
99. On "Operation Albert": Der Komandierende General der Sicherungstruppen und Befehlshaber im Heeresgebiet Mitte [the new title of the former "Berück" since 1942—H.H.] Bandenbekämpfung durch den HSSPF, 4.11.42, BA-MA RH 22-235; on "Operation Nürnberg" and "Operation Karl": Kommand. Gen. d. Sich.truppen/Ia An das Okdo. HGr. Mitte 19.11.42, BA-MA RH 22-235; on "Operation Frieda": Kommand. Gen. d. Sich.truppen/Ia An das Okdo. HGr. Mitte 1.12.42, BA-MA RH 22-235.
100. 1st SS-Inf.Brigade (mot.) Angriffsbefehl Nr. 1 für das Unternehmen "Nürnberg," 20.11.42, KHA Prague 10-95.
101. On "Operation Nürnberg": Von dem Bach-Zelewski, Tagesmeldungen 27.11.42, 29.11.42, KHA Prague 10-95; Kampfgruppe von Gottberg, Tagesmeldung für den 26.11.42, in Strafsache Erren, Landgericht Hamburg 147 Js 29/67, Sonderband GG, Teil 3; on "Operation Hamburg": Kampfgruppe von Gottberg, Brief an SS-Gruppenführer von Herff, 21.12.42, in Strafsache Schultz, Landgericht Hamburg 141 Js 533/60, Ermittlungsheft 1.
102. Von dem Bach-Zelewski, Tagesmeldungen 27.11.42, 29.11.42, KHA Prague 10-95.
103. Göring's guidelines of 26.10.42, in N. Müller, *Besatzungspolitik,* 134.
104. OKH Kampfanweisung für die Bandenbekämpfung im Osten 11.11.42, in N. Müller, *Besatzungspolitik,* 136–137; OKW Bandenbekämpfung 16.12.42, ibid., 139–140.
105. Order issued by the HSSPF Ostland Pifrader 18.11.42, in *Verbrecherische Ziele—verbrecherische Mittel! Dokumente der Okkupationspolitik des faschistischen Deutschlands auf dem Territorium der UdSSR, 1941–1944* (Moscow: 1963), 149ff.
106. Testimony by Georg Heuser, the former "Jewish representative" at the KdS Minsk, on 26.8.63, in Strafsache Heuser, Landgericht Koblenz 9 Ks 2/62, Sonderband, 22.
107. Kommand. Gen. d. Sich.truppen KTB Nr. 3, Eintragungen 5.7., 7.7., 20.7., 23.7., 29.7., 3.8.42, BA-MA RH 22-232.
108. Ibid., 7.8., 10.8.42.
109. Ibid., 20.7.42.

110. Kommand. Gen. d. Sich.truppen/Ia Tagesmeldung 27.8.42, BA-MA RH 22-236.
111. Hauptbahndirektion Mitte Bericht 27.8.42, MA Podolsk 500-12454-420.
112. OKH GenStdH/OpAbt (I) 28.8.1942, BA-MA RH 19-II/153.
113. OKH GenStdH/OpAbt (I), Fernschreiben an HGr. Mitte, Eingang 29.8.42, cit. in Heinz Kühnrich, *Der Partisanenkrieg in Europa* (Berlin: 1965), 613.
114. Kommand. Gen. d. Sich.truppen, Fernschreiben an 286th Sich.Div. 29.8.42, MA Podolsk 500-12454-420.
115. Kommand. Gen. d. Sich.truppen KTB Nr. 3, Eintrag 5.7.42, BA-MA RH 22-232.
116. Kommand. Gen. d. Sich.truppen/Ia, Tagesmeldung 3.9.42, BA-MA RH 22-236.
117. Generalmajor Richert, cdr. 286th Sich.Div., cross-examination on 20 December 1945, Minsk Trial, vol. 1, KGB Archive Minsk; idem, Minsk Trial, cross-examination main proceedings on 16 January 1946, 40f.
118. Ibid.
119. Reichsmarschall des Großdeutschen Reiches/Ia/Op. 1, 16.10.42, MA Podolsk 500-12454-553.
120. Kommand. Gen. d. Sich.truppen An Obkdo. HGr. Mitte 27.10.42, BA-MA RH 22-233; Oberbefehlshaber HGr. Mitte an Reichsmarschall 29.10.42, MA Podolsk 500-12454-553.
121. From l.–15.1.43 Luftwaffe units burned down 38 villages in the Army Group Center Rear Area, twelve of these explicitly as a reaction to acts of railway sabotage, report by the Luftwaffe training and field units in the area of the Luftwaffe Command East (stamp of receipt HGr. Mitte 20.1.43) MA Podolsk 500-12454-598.
122. Meeting in the Ministry for Eastern Europe 18.12.42, BA-MA RH 22-235; Schenckendorff's extremely frank and radical polemic, in which he argues that the partisan movement was brought about by the German terror measures, can be found in a report by First Lieutenant Schlabrendorff to the HGr. Mitte of 20.12.42, MA Podolsk 12454-423-28.
123. Kommand. Gen. d. Sich.truppen KTB Nr. 3, 9.8.42, BA-MA RH 22-232.
124. Carl von Clausewitz, *Vom Kriege* (19th ed., Werner Halweg, ed., Bonn: 1980), 991. A typical example of this is an order by Dirlewanger on 15.11.43: "In doing so, anything which might offer refuge or protection is to be destroyed. The area is to be turned into a no-man's-land. All inhabitants are to be shot. Cattle, grain, and other products are to be removed." Kühnrich, *Partisanenkrieg*, 629.
125. Förster, "Sicherung," 1042.
126. Kommand. Gen. D. Sich.truppen/I1, Abschlußbericht für Unternehmen "Waldwinter" der Division Richert 31.1.43, BA-MA RH 19II/383; (286th Sich.Div.) Division Richert/Ib/Q Bericht über die Erfassung während des Unternehmens "Waldwinter" 23.12.(42)-24.1.43, BA-MA RH 26-286/13.
127. Kampfgruppe von Gottberg Gefechtsbericht 28.6.43, BA-MA RH 26-286/9.
128. Ibid.
129. Vernehmung Rodenbusch, cf. note 1.
130. Vernehmung Rodenbusch am 2.10.45, Minsker Prozeß, Bd. 21, KGB-Archiv Minsk.
131. Ibid.

Kurt Wafner, born in 1918, was from Berlin. A laboratory technician in physics, he was prevented from pursuing training as as electrical engineer by the outbreak of the war. As an anarcho-sydicalist, Wafner was an opponent of war on principle, but was unable to escape induction into the Wehrmacht. On 20 July 1941 he marched east with Landesschutzbataillon 332. The unit passed over East Prussia and Lithuania to Minsk, where it guarded prisoners of war at the main camp at Masyukovchina (Waldlager) and at the secondary camp, Pushkin Barracks. Wafner was fortunate: due to congenitally poor vision, he was assigned indoor duties—in the kitchen, the mess hall, or the uniform store. At the end of June 1943, he was discharged and sent home as unfit for service. He survived the war as an armament worker in Berlin.

Wafner did not take photographs himself but rather bought photos from his comrades or from members of other units—"usually for some tobacco." The photos survived the nights of bombing in Berlin as part of the few possessions that Wafner carried with him to the air raid shelters.

The edge of Minsk

Rubble in Minsk

Rubble in Minsk

Executed partisans in Minsk

Women of Minsk

Marketplace in Minsk

Room in the Pushkin Barracks

In front of the uniform store in the Pushkin Barracks (right: Kurt Wafner)

Prison barracks in the Waldlager

Prison barracks in the Waldlager

Guard post in Koladitsche on the rail line to Minsk

Residents of Koladitsche

Russian war prisoners on the way from the freight train station to the Pushkin Barracks camp

Transporting corpses in the Waldlager

Mass grave of Russian war prisoners

Arrival of a transport of Jews in Minsk

Jews being moved to the ghetto in Minsk

Ghetto in Minsk

Ghetto in Minsk

East gate of the Waldlager

Ukrainian guards

In front of the company kitchen in the Waldlager

The company at mealtime

Fraternizing in Minsk

Kurt Wafner

Wera

Road construction in the Waldlager

Prisoner detail in the Waldlager

War prisoners shot in the Waldlager

– *Chapter 6* –

Men of 20 July and the War in the Soviet Union*

Christian Gerlach

The literature on the "men of 20 July" contains a small deficiency: it relies almost completely on verbal statements made after the fact, memoirs, and reminiscences. When contemporary sources are drawn upon, one thing is hardly considered at all by historians—the on-going, daily work of the officers in their staffs and offices. It is almost as if they lived in a kind of never-ending leave. This oversight is astonishing because in some areas sufficient documents are available.

Up until now, the officers' opposition to Hitler has been faulted on two grounds: its members' stand on specific issues, such as the anti-Jewish policy,[1] and their ideas about Germany after Hitler's fall, because they tended to favor a monarchy, a corporate state, or other reactionary models. Examining how they actually functioned, on the other hand, enables us to criticize not what they thought or perhaps desired, but what they did or failed to do.

More than one assassination attempt against Hitler originated in the far-flung circle of officers conspiring against him. In March 1943 alone two attempts were made to blow him up. Both originated among officers of the high command or Army Group Center, "in which was concentrated the strongest opposition group that had ever existed."[2] There, Henning von Tresckow, Rudolf-Christoph Freiherr von Gersdorff—who, on 21 March 1943, meant

Notes for this section begin on page 141.

to blow himself and Hitler up while acting as a human bomb—and others had been considering assassination since 1941.

Yet, at the same time, some of the conspirators were participating in mass crimes. And really *at the same time*. For example, the picture of von Tresckow painted by his biographer Scheurig—that he went along in 1933, and even later in some ways, but then cleansed himself of guilt—is false.[3]

The findings presented below relate primarily to opposition officers from Army Group Center, which conquered Belorussia while driving toward Moscow and was responsible for Belorussia for months and for its eastern half throughout the occupation. Belorussia lost a higher percentage of its population in World War II than any other country. According to official statistics compiled in 1944 and 1945, 2.2 million civilians and prisoners of war died out of a population of 10.6 million.[4] In recent years, segments of the German public have become aware of a related phenomenon—the 600 to 5,000 (depending on how the term is interpreted) "burned-out villages" of Belorussia whose inhabitants were either shot or burned alive as part of the German anti-partisan campaign.

Knowing and Going Along

Existing treatments of the opposition group in the high command of Army Group Center[5] stress the complex structure of the conspiracy, plans to assassinate Hitler, and profound conversations over moral issues. Von Gersdorff, the counterintelligence officer (Ic/AO) of the army group, is surpassed in fame by Henning von Tresckow, its First General Staff Officer (Ia), who "emphasized ethical and moral motivations"[6] within the conspiracy by allegedly remarking with reference to the imminent putsch that it was "no longer a question of practical aims but of whether the German resistance movement, in the eyes of the world and before history, would risk taking decisive action."[7]

Reports based on the participants' memories also mention German crimes in the areas controlled by the army group, though almost exclusively the murders of Jews and the commissars (political officers) of the Red Army. Those crimes are said to have provided the impulse for active anti-Hitler involvement. The thrust of these treatments is that the high command of the army group and its officer corps prevented whatever could be prevented, such as the implementation of the order to kill commissars; but one could not prevent what one did not know about. Especially with reference to the murder of Jews, "the SS" is said to have deceived the officers by killing in secret, filing incomplete reports or none at all; if general staff officers protested, the SS threatened them.

Even the established fact that the first head of Einsatzgruppe B, the director of the Reichskriminalpolizeiamt and notorious mass murderer Arthur Nebe, had been involved in the conspiracy since as early as 1938 did little to discredit this version. Von Schlabrendorff, who sat on the Bundesverfassungsgericht from 1967 to 1975, claimed that von Tresckow and he—he was von Tresckow's ordinance officer—had convinced themselves that "under the mask of the SS leader lurked a committed anti-Nazi ..., who invented a thousand pretexts for sabotaging Hitler's murderous orders. We succeeded in saving the lives of many Russians. The Russian population often expressed their thanks to us."[8] According to von Gersdorff, von Tresckow personally brought Nebe to the army group.[9] Nothing was said about the 45,467 murder victims of Einsatzgruppe B by November 1941,[10] the point at which Nebe returned to Berlin. It was said that Nebe was filing false reports, a fact which allegedly only became known later, especially following the murder of 7,000 Jews in Borisov on 20 and 21 October, which was witnessed by members of the staff.[11]

This is, of course, nonsense. Von Gersdorff, who was in charge of information gathering, would have had to be a very bad counterintelligence officer to miss the murder of several thousand people for months on end—even if the Einsatzgruppe had not been filing regular reports and reporting to him orally from the beginning, which was clearly the case. A series of such reports, all of them sent to von Gersdorff as the staff member responsible for contact with the Einsatzgruppe, has survived, for instance for the time periods of from 23 June to 13 July 1941; from 9 to 16, from 17 to 23, from 24 to 31 August 1941; from 1 to 15, and from 16 to 30 September 1942, as well as from 15 November to 15 December 1942, along with notes relating to oral presentations from July 1941.[12] Excerpts from a report for the period from 14 to 28 July 1941 were contained in documents of Panzergruppe 3. Thus it stands to reason that the army group forwarded at least parts of the reports to the armies.[13] The reports from 1942, moreover, always went to Gersdorff in six copies. Many of the reports were initialed by von Tresckow and von Gersdorff; the report from December 1942, which gives 134,198 as the "total number of specially treated [people]," was initialed twice, on the cover sheet and on the first page. Some bear the stamp of the supreme commanders, General Field Marshals von

Bock and von Kluge, and other staff officers. The report covering the period from 9 to 16 August was submitted to Gersdorff, and a summary from mid-July was read by von Bock, von Tresckow, and von Gersdorff.[14] Such reports were, so to speak, nothing special. Einsatzgruppe D, for example, reported regularly to the Ic/AO of the 11th Army.[15]

In any event, von Tresckow and von Gersdorff were much better informed than is generally thought. In July 1941, Heydrich transmitted to them an order concerning the handling of the Polish intelligentsia in the occupied regions of the Soviet Union, which stipulated "that the purging operations are to extend primarily to Bolsheviks and Jews," while, concerning the Poles, "the decision may come down later."[16]

The opponents of the regime in the high command of Army Group Center learned much earlier, however, and in fairly full detail of the crimes being planned (not after or shortly before the war began, as the history of the resistance would have it). Already at the beginning of March 1941, more than three months before the attack on the Soviet Union, one of their number, Rittmeister Schach von Wittenau, member of the counterintelligence section and later Gersdorff's deputy, received information about the "operation of SS Einsatzkommandos behind the forward troops" and some desired improvements for which the OKW wanted to obtain Hitler's approval, for example, "that executions be carried out as far away from the troops as possible." Schach von Wittenau reported as "requests of the army group" merely the suggestion that the Secret Field Police should be strengthened and that its authority should be differentiated from that of the SD.[17]

It is also not true that the real dimensions of the crime could not be gleaned from the reports of the Einsatzgruppe (not to mention reports from other units involved in murder). How might the staff of Army Group Center have interpreted "major operation against Jews and other communist elements and looters" in Slonim, or the report: "In Minsk there is no longer a Jewish intelligentsia"?[18] In the left-hand margin of the report covering the period from 24 to 31 August, someone added a handwritten notation of the numbers of people reported killed and totaled them up: 719, and in two operations in Minsk and Zembin an indefinite "fairly large number" (the SD was actually not always *completely* candid); hence, one could calculate far more than one hundred, perhaps even several hundred dead per day. Between 20 August and 26 October 1941, the murder rate for Einsatzgruppe B averaged about 300 people daily.[19]

However, knowing is one thing; approving is another. Three days before the invasion of the Soviet Union, on 19 June 1941, Henning von Tresckow met with the chief of the command staff of the Reichsführer-SS, SS-Brigadeführer Kurt Knoblauch, on the exercise field in Arys, East Prussia. At that meeting, "the use of SS brigades and cavalry regiments was discussed."[20] A few weeks later, the units referred to—the 1st and 2nd SS Infantry Brigades and SS Cavalry Regiments 1 and 2—were already committing mass murders. Their victims for 1941 ran into the tens of thousands. They were troops supplied by Himmler to support and complement operations by the Einsatzgruppen and police battalions.

Von Tresckow and Knoblauch agreed to place the command staff and all its units under the authority of Army Group Center, specifically under Army Corps XXXXII (9th Army), not at the front, but specifically "to be used for purging and security duties."[21] In the course of this mission, the 1st SS Infantry Brigade destroyed at least one village in the area of Bialystok from which it had taken no incoming fire.[22] Army Corp XXXXII wanted to use parts of the 2nd SS Infantry Brigade to "clean *out*" Vilna on 26 June—long before any Einsatzkommandos were active there—a proposal that came to nothing due to tactical differences with Himmler.[23]

After units of the command staff had been withdrawn in order to complete their training in "pacification" matters, there developed even closer contact with the resistance fighters of Army Group Center at the end of July. Plans had been drawn up to "clean out" the Pripyat Marshes—an operation in which around 14,000 Jews were shot between 27 July and 13 August.[24] From 20 to 23 July, a delegation from the counterintelligence section of the command staff of the Reichsführer-SS traveled to Borisov for consultations with Army Group Center. In those sessions, the army group's Ic officer, Major von Gersdorff, appeared to be informed regarding the task of the SS cavalry regiments. His colleague from the command staff of the Reichsführer-SS summarized his meeting with von Gersdorff as follows: "Deployment of units of the Waffen-SS for pacification of the army's rear area is much appreciated by the army group."[25] That what was appreciated was murdering Jews is indicated, among other things, by the fact that, as early as the evening of 3 August, von Bock, supreme commander of the army group, sent the SS cavalry regiments his "special congratulations."[26] At this point, these units had not yet had the slightest contact with the enemy—that did not occur until the middle of August near the town of Turov—but had merely "liquidated 3,247 partisans and Bolshevik Jews. No losses sustained."[27]

A second example. At the end of September 1941, the commander of the rear area of Army Group Center, who was chief of security troops and military administration in the largest area under the army group's control, hosted a workshop on combating partisans in Mogilev, which was broadly attended. The speakers included Arthur Nebe, Erich von dem Bach-Zelewski, and Hermann Fegelein, the commander of the SS cavalry brigade. Nebe's subject was "the Jewish question with special emphasis on battling partisans." The cliché of the day was: "Where there is a partisan, there is a Jew, and where there is a Jew, there is a partisan."[28]

Three representatives of the army group's high command were invited to this session: "Ia or his representative," thus von Tresckow, the supply officer (Ib), Major Günther von Gericke, and Supreme Commander von Bock's adjutant, Major Carl-Hans von Hardenberg—another 20 July conspirator. Von Tresckow appears not to have attended, presumably due to his heavy workload in preparation for the offensive on Moscow, which was set for 2 October. But von Gericke wrote a brief report, primarily on two practical demonstrations that were the crowning events of the session. (He wrote not one word about the above-mentioned clichés.) On the afternoon of 25 September, the "lighting raid on a village"—the village Knyazhichi—was presented as a "police training exercise," "followed by searching the houses and interrogating the inhabitants. Police teams could have subsequently been used to seal off the village given appropriate consideration of the terrain. The searches and interrogations met with the approval of the leader of the exercise. Along with several Jews, suspicious characters from outside the village were apprehended (32 executions)." At dawn the next day, an operation was staged to clean out the village Kusikovici. "The mission was carried out effectively by a reinforced company of Security Regiment 2, which succeeded in sealing off the village and surprising and rounding up the inhabitants in a relatively short time. Interrogating the inhabitants, weeding out suspicious elements, and obtaining information about partisan troops was an excellent exercise for all participants in the course, who had had a hand in the entire operation beginning with the planning stage." Von Gersdorff initialed the report; he did not consider a marginal notation required. Along with security issues, the campaign against partisans fell into his area of responsibility at this time; had he wanted to dissent on any point for the future, even on the participation of Wehrmacht units, he could have done so with a good chance of success.[29]

Potsdam Infantry Regiment 9

The participation of some "men of the resistance" in the mass crimes committed in Belorussia was clearly not limited to knowing what was underway and openly or silently approving it.

From the first day, many German soldiers waged the war against the Soviet Union with an enormous urge to annihilate. Examples are found where not everyone would expect them, for example, in the case of the Infantry Regiment 9 from Potsdam, which the literature on the period usually tricks out with the decorative nickname "the tradition-laden," and which, due to the high percentage of nobility in its ranks and to its arrogance, was also called "Regiment Graf 9" (regiment of counts), or "von 9." More of the men who would later be involved in the 20 July conspiracy passed through this regiment than any other, and some of them were fighting in its ranks in the summer of 1941.

Infantry Regiment 9 announced on 25 June, the fourth day of the war against the Soviet Union, that the day before three Red Army soldiers had run up a white flag, and six Germans who had intended to take them prisoner had been shot from ambush. Generalmajor Hellmich, commander of the 23rd Infantry Division, immediately ordered the entire division to cease honoring the white flag. "No quarter is to be given!" On 28 June, following battles southeast of Bialystok, IR 9 reported: "No prisoners were taken!" But in place of the old excuse, the regiment cited "mutilations of fallen German soldiers."[30] On the same day, Fritz-Dietlof Graf von der Schulenburg, a member of the regiment who was later executed as a 20 July conspirator, noted in his diary: "Doubtlessly ... the danger will arise when our people start killing on their own. If we allow that, we shall have sunk to the level of the SS. Doubtlessly, the Russian does not deserve quarter due to [his] way of fighting. But they must be shot either in battle or on officers' orders. Anything else will simply loosen all restraints and make it impossible to regain control of instincts once unleashed." On the following day, he noted with satisfaction: "Only armed enemy, snipers, or prisoners offering resistance or running away may be shot. In no other cases, except on an officer's orders, who is then responsible. I am glad that the army has again clearly and decisively clarified its principles, without which things fall apart."[31] The former deputy police commissioner of Berlin and head of the administration in the area of Breslau certainly had a way with words. So let us pin things down. Soviet soldiers might be shot without cause and without offering the slightest resistance—in a disciplined manner of course, on an officer's command. Shooting Red Army men who had already been taken prisoner could have nothing at all to do with protecting German soldiers; at best, it was done out of revenge, but it was also done for the sake of killing. And the SS was having similar thoughts about the dangers of a loss of inhibitions.

Even the two most famous heroes of the resistance from Army Group Center were not uninvolved. It is true that von Gersdorff wrote a notation after returning from a tour of the front on 9 December 1941, that "the existing facts" regarding the murder of the Jews were fully known there, were a general topic of conversation, and were regarded by officers as a stain on the honor of the German army.[32] But it is also true that von Gersdorff was responsible for the units of the Secret Field Police (GFP) deployed in Army Group Center's occupation area.[33] This secret police within the Wehrmacht served first to keep an eye on German soldiers, and second, to repress the "enemy population," beginning with the prevention of resistance operations aimed at German troops. Its personnel was the same as that of the Einsatzgruppen, that is, it was dominated by members of the criminal police and the Gestapo who had been assigned to the Wehrmacht. The Secret Field Police committed mass murders to an extent that can no longer be determined with precision, primarily in the occupied Soviet regions. According to a report by the army's police chief, for example, they killed "around 21,000 persons, some in combat, some after they were interrogated, between 1 July 1942 and 31 March 1943."[34] They did not spare Army Group Center's theater of operations. The GFP killed 1,001 people in the area in October 1942 alone.[35] The monthly reports of GFP Group 723, which was active in the area, have been preserved for the period from July 1941 to September 1943. According to their incomplete numbers, by the end of 1942 they had shot at least 1,486 people, including at least 133 Jews, usually not "in combat."[36] And that was but one of several GFP groups under von Gersdorff's supervision.

It is often forgotten that German crimes, especially in occupied Soviet territory, were not at all limited to "the business with the Jews," and that Jews comprised a minority of the victims. In August 1942, Hitler's directive number 46 specified that the struggle against partisans was to have higher priority than before, and that it would, therefore, be handled by the command sections of the armies.[37] Thus, Henning von Tresckow assumed that responsibility for Army Group Center, and he continued to discharge that duty until he left in August 1943. This period was definitely not characterized by any moderation in the "struggle against bandits," which was the term used from then on, but rather by a gruesome intensification.

This intensification was the result of a new tactic introduced in the early spring of 1942 and broadly applied in the following summer. In "major operations," forces several battalions strong surrounded partisan-infested areas, "cleaned them out," and then "combed through" them in reverse direction. These tactics struck not only the partisan camps, most of which were in the forests, but also villages in the forefield that the Germans no longer fully controlled, which were burned because they, allegedly or in fact, served as supply bases for the partisans. In time, as the partisans grew stronger, these villages became the *main* targets. In some cases, the inhabitants were warned or evacuated, later to be sent to Germany as forced laborers. But often they were all either shot or burned alive in buildings suitable for that purpose.

According to an interim report on "Operation Cottbus," which was conducted in the region bordering the area under civilian control in May 1943 by combined forces of the Wehrmacht, the SS, and police troops, the Generalkommissar for Weissruthenien, Kube complained: "If only 492 rifles are taken off 4,500 enemy dead,[38] the difference shows that many peasants are among these enemy dead." In partisan units at this time, bringing along one's own rifle was a requirement for membership, and the numerical ratio of victims to rifles in such operations held fairly steady at ten to one. Kube's superior, Hinrich Lohse, Reichskommissar for Ostland, added: "What is Katyn by comparison? ... Locking men, women, and children in barns and burning the barns down does not seem to me to be a suitable method of fighting bandits *even if the aim is to exterminate the population.*"[39] The total number of victims of these operations in the occupation area of Army Group Center, with some of "Weissruthenien" included, has been estimated at no less than 250,000,[40] and was probably higher. On 6 February 1943, von Tresckow's section reported to the operations section at general staff that "for the first time, the number of bandits eliminated has exceeded 100,000" in Army Group Center's rear area.[41]

That was exactly five weeks before a bomb was placed in Hitler's airplane during his visit to Army Group Center.

This report merely adopted verbiage from the commander of the rear area, which was the typical practice. Based on the numerous documents of the army group's leadership section relating to the "struggle against bandits," most of which are housed in the military archive in Freiburg, it can be said that von Tresckow was surely not the main strategist in this campaign against the civilian population. He received reports, initialed many papers, passed reports along, and prepared some general orders. At times he shared this task with the army group's Ia/op (operations officers), Schulze-Büttger and von Voß—two more "men of the resistance." Otherwise, he left the task of initiating operations and working out plans to the commander of the rear area of the Army Group Center and the commanding officers of the rear areas of the armies (Korücks). Von Tresckow's influence on their content is seldom detectable.

And yet it would have been possible for a man in his position to exert some moderating influence. One example: During the night of 27–28 August 1942, partisans attacked the Slavnoye station on the main rail line linking Minsk and Smolensk, burned it and part of the town, and in the process killed several German soldiers. A report of the event caught Hitler's eye, and he demanded retribution without specifying what should be done. His wish was conveyed by Heusinger, the chief of the operations division in the general staff, a conspirator and later Generalinspekteur of the Bundeswehr, to von Tresckow, who passed it to the commander of the rear area of the Army Group, who passed it along to Generalmajor Richert, who commanded the 286th Security Division. Richert made a recommendation, which passed back up the same chain of command without being altered, and was then put into effect. The telegram from von Tresckow's section to Heusinger described it as follows: "A total of one hundred persons consisting of gang sympathizers (not members; C.G) and relatives of gang members from the Slavnoye region, who are suspected of having participated in or approved of the attack, are to be shot. Their houses are to be burned down. The measure is to be announced and explained on the radio."[42] Von Tresckow merely prevented the mass shooting from being carried out *before* its approval by the command.

Consequently, near the town of Krupki near Slavnoye, one hundred people, among them women, young people, children from ten to twelve years old, even nursing babies, were actually shot with machine pistols by a battalion of the 286th Security Division in the presence of—estimates vary—between 1,500 and 5,000 witnesses, who had been rounded up by force.[43] The phrase "[family] members of partisans" was unambiguous. If von Tresckow, who had advance knowledge, had wanted to prevent the murder of women and children, there is no doubt that he could have done so by replacing them with male prisoners.

At one point, von Tresckow lent a hand in designing the "struggle against gangs." On 23 June 1943, Major Georg Freiherr von Boeselager, commander of Army Group Center's cavalry regiment —also a man of the resistance—sent him a "report on the combat tactics of partisans and opportunities for reducing the risk posed by gangs," in which, after a really quite empathetic description of the combat tactics and everyday life of partisans, he proposed new measures. "It is impossible for a German soldier to distinguish between partisans and non-partisans.... The regiment's view is that the area must be subdivided into a) pacified areas, b) areas threatened by gangs, c) gang-infested areas." While normal security would suffice in areas of the first category ("only where there are German troops"), "in areas threatened by gangs, the men should be permitted to leave town and work only in groups. All males passing through such areas alone or in small groups must be shot or imprisoned at once.... The gang-infested area[44] must be swept clean of all males. Up to a specific point in time, males up to the age of 50 will be seized and turned over to the economic office as laborers. After the deadline, men in this area will be shot."

Von Tresckow was quite taken by these ideas, which were similar to models for the creation of "dead zones" that were being developed independently by several agencies. On 27 June, he personally sent copies of Boeselager's recommendations for comment to all the armies comprising Army Group Center, to the commander of the rear area, to various colleagues on the staff, to the operations section, even directly to the training section of the High Command of the Army and the Commanding Officer of the Eastern Troops (units made up of Soviet collaborators with the Germans). A copy is even to be found among the documents of the commander of the rear area for Army Group South. Von Tresckow had a summary of the predominantly positive responses prepared, and on the critical response of the 2nd Army, he noted: "1.) Of course, the 2nd Army faces special circumstances! 2.) Theoretically the unsystematic constantly shifting tactics [is] certainly the ideal, but in practice the clear demarcation of certain areas [is] often advantageous given the lackadaisical security forces. T."[45]

Von Tresckow, along with others, thus authorized a further ratcheting up of a campaign against partisans, which culminated in Himmler's order of 10 July 1943. "The Führer has decided that the gang-infested areas of the northern Ukraine and the middle region of Russia are to be cleansed of all inhabitants."[46] Initial steps in the execution of this order were taken somewhat later. Something else: During Hitler's visit to Army Group Center in March 1943, the original plan had been to shoot him and overpower his entourage. The unit assigned the latter task was none other than the cavalry regiment of Boeselager, who made these recommendations and probably had experience in this manner of "repressing gangs." At some point after 15 July 1944, the same unit set off marching for

Berlin in order to carry out the same assignment, but failed to arrive by the time set for the assassination.[47]

Peter Yorck von Wartenburg and the Policy of Pillage

In Berlin, another prominent member of the resistance contributed to the idea of creating "dead zones." Peter Yorck Graf von Wartenburg was the "heart" of the "Kreisau Circle" resistance group, a man "of exceptional modesty," whose "unqualified grounding in the Christian faith" led "to his devout recognition of eternal verities."[48] Reserve Lieutenant Peter Yorck von Wartenburg had been working since 15 June 1942 on the staff of Economic Staff East, the huge organization in charge of pillaging the occupied areas of the Soviet Union. As Deputy Group Leader I/Ia Ec(onomics), he was responsible for fiduciary issues and the "collection of all economic data."[49] In May 1943, a major conference on the partisan situation and how to combat it took place at the headquarters of the General Quartermaster of the Army, in preparation for which, on 22 May, Economic Staff East provided statistical data. With the aid of tables, diagrams, and schematic charts, the data highlighted the fact that Belorussian partisans operating from the Pripyat Marshes posed a threat to the delivery of hundreds of thousands of tons of Ukrainian grain to the Wehrmacht and to the Reich; moreover, there were 1.5 million workers in partisan areas who could not be seized. Yorck directed the preparation of these data. Indeed, Generalquartiermeister Eduard Wagner, also a resistance fighter—the man who supplied the airplane in which Stauffenberg flew from Hitler's headquarters to Berlin on 20 July 1944 after his assassination attempt[50]—had made specific suggestions as to how Yorck might "drastically express" those facts. But Yorck went even farther in transmitting his instructions.[51] In connection with the efforts of Economic Staff East and the May conference,[52] the anti-partisan operations "Weichsel" and "Seydlitz" led to a partial evacuation and extermination of the population of the Pripyat region: more than 9,000 people were killed, and at least 27,000 were expelled, most of them "seized for the work force."[53]

Yorck von Wartenburg also seems to have been a kind of multifunctionary in organizing pillage. In July 1943 he held a position in the Chief Fiduciary Office for the East (Haupttreuhandstelle Ost), which was responsible for converting non-agricultural Polish property into German holdings in the annexed regions of Poland.[54] For Fritz-Dietlof Graf von der Schulenberg, Yorck von Wartenburg was one of those men "who, because of their Christianity could not bring themselves to do the right thing," specifically to kill Hitler.[55] In other cases, his conscience permitted certain exceptions. It is all the more astonishing that Yorck, following his arrest in 1944, stated for the record that it was not just the persecution of the Jews that had especially motivated his opposition, but also "the activities that we sometimes exposed in the occupied regions."[56]

Resistance—to What?

As late as 28 June 1944, three weeks before the assassination attempt, Henning von Tresckow, in his capacity as chief of the general staff of the 2nd Army, signed an order, which read in part: "In operations against gangs, any boys and girls taken between the ages of 10 and 13 who are physically healthy, whose parents either cannot be located or who, as persons unable to work, are to be sent to the areas earmarked for remaining families (the dregs), are to be sent to the Reich." Transportation was to be provided by the labor authorities through the "OT-camp for young people in Lesin near Baranovichi."[57]

This order was issued as part of the so-called "hay operation" (*Heuaktion*; "h" for homeless [*heimatlos*], "e" for "without parents" [*elternlos*], "u" for "unhoused" [*unterkunftslos*]), in which, on the initiative of Army Group Center, from 40,000 to 50,000 "youths between ten and fourteen years of age" were to be rounded up and used as workers in the Todt organization, in the Junker factories and in German handicrafts—a major motivation being to weaken the enemy, specifically "to lower his biological vitality over time."[58] The most varied agencies, such as Army Group Center and its armies, the Board for the Four Year Plan, and the Reich Youth Leadership, cooperated in the effort. In fact, an additional 4,500 were kidnapped.[59] "Resistance"–but against what?

The question of what motivated the conspirators to want changes in the political leadership and, in part, in the political system, cannot be dealt with comprehensively here. However, their primary thrust was surely to try to preserve German interests—whatever they were thought to be—and win (or at least not lose) the war, possibly "better" than Hitler and his followers. Here are but some clues.

Legationsrat Dr. Adam von Trott zu Solz, the resistance movement's foreign policy expert with good relations to English diplomats, met on 15 July 1942 with Reichsführer-SS Heinrich Himmler.

His aim was the formation of an Indian SS Legion and the undermining of Indian troops fighting for the British in North Africa.[60] Friedrich Werner Graf von der Schulenburg, German ambassador to Moscow until 1941 and an uncle of the Schulenburg mentioned above, opposed the war against the Soviet Union. That did not prevent him from preparing propaganda in 1942 for the Foreign Office designed to destabilize certain ethnic groups in the Soviet hinterland. He suggested playing the Crimean Tartars off against the Soviet Union by giving them preferred treatment in the German agrarian reform in the occupied regions of the Soviet Union, which later actually took place.[61] Generalquartiermeister Wagner, who has already been mentioned, seriously participated in preparation for the coup only beginning in June, arguing that it would be "insupportable if Russian soldiers penetrated Reich territory. That would mean absolute ruin."[62]

It should be noted that we are not denying that the persons named in these pages worked to kill Hitler and risked their lives. Many forfeited their lives: Schulze-Büttger, the two von der Schulenbergs, Yorck von Wartenburg, von Trott zu Solz, and Nebe were executed; von Tresckow, Wagner, and von Voß committed suicide; von Gersdorff barely managed to escape prosecution (and was later cut from the Bundeswehr). Statements made here apply only to the named persons, not to other resistance fighters.

The tributes of the year 1994, the fiftieth anniversary of the attempted assassination of Hitler, demonstrated that "the 20th of July" is an affair of state significance in the Federal Republic of Germany. And the participants will continue to be honored, including all the resistance figures from Army Group Center. But everyone should know who is being honored.

—Translated by Roy Shelton

Notes

*This chapter is the revised, expanded version of an article that appeared in *Freitag* 30 (22 July 1994) under the title "Männer des Widerstands und der Massenmord." It originated as a research project, supported by the Hamburg Institute for Social Research, on German occupation policy in Belorussia.

1. See Christof Dipper, "Der deutsche Widerstand und die Juden," *Geschichte und Gesellschaft* 9 (1983): 349–380.
2. The reference is to the group of officers who opposed Hitler. Peter Hoffmann, *Widerstand—Staatsstreich—Attentat*, 3rd rev. and exp. ed. (Munich: 1979), 332.
3. See Bodo Scheurig, *Henning von Tresckow* (Frankfurt am Main, Berlin, and Vienna: 1980 [originally 1973]), 37ff.
4. These figures do not include soldiers who perished. Minsk Central State Archive, 845-1-58, 9.
5. In addition to Scheurig, the most important examples are: Fabian von Schlabrendorff, *Offiziere gegen Hitler*, ed. Walter Bußmann, based on the edition published by von Gero Schulze-Gaevernitz (Berlin: 1984 [originally 1946]); Rudolf-Christoph Freiherr von Gersdorff, *Soldat im Untergang* (Frankfurt am Main: 1977); Philipp Freiherr von Boeselager, *Der Widerstand in der Heeresgruppe Mitte* (Berlin: n.d. [1990]); cf. Hoffmann, *Widerstand*, 327–388.
6. Klaus-Jürgen Müller, *20. Juli 1944: Der Entschluß zum Staatsstreich* (Berlin: 1985), 13.
7. Von Schlabrendorff, *Offiziere*, 109.
8. Ibid., 50.
9. Von Gersdorff, *Soldat*, S. 85.
10. See Incident Report Nr. 133 (14 November 1941) of the Einsatzgruppen of the Security Police and the SD. Bundesarchiv-Militärarchiv (BA-MA) SF-01/28934, 3190.
11. See von Schlabrendorff, *Offiziere*, 50f., Von Gersdorff, *Soldat*, 97ff., Hoffmann, *Widerstand*, 334f.
12. For 1941: The Federal Commissioner of Documents of the State Security Service of the former GDR (BStU), Central Archive, ZUV 9 (legal proceeding 1 BS 13/71 of the State Attorney of Karl-Marx-Stadt against F.), 31: 3-17, 27-33, 34-44, 45-55 (reports for August, each with the notation: "for oral presentation at Army Group Center"), report notes, 20–26. These are copies of documents from an unidentified Soviet archive. For 1942: ZstA Minsk, 655-1-3, 133-203, 20-132, 4-59 (originals). A copy of the last-mentioned report is in the Federal Archive, R 70 SU/9.
13. Einsatzgruppe B II (SD): Summary report dated 29 July 1941 for the period from 14 July to 28 July 1941 (copy), BA-MA WF-03/ 5769, 175–177.
14. BStU ZA, ZUV 9, 18f.
15. See BA-MA, RH 20-11/488. My thanks to Andrej Angrick for bringing this to my attention.
16. Chief of the Sicherheitspolizei and SD, Order Nr. 2 of 1 July 1941 (copy of a copy), transmitted during July (exact day illegible) by the Administrative (*Kriegsverwaltung*) Section of the General Quartermaster of the Army. BA-MA, WF-03/9121. The heading contains von Tresckow's initials and the notation: "Forward to all Ic [officers]."

17. Conference of 6–7 March 1941, Secret Command Level Material! BA-MA WF-03/9121. The highest ranking participant was Oberst i. G. Oster, Chief of the Central Section of the OKW intelligence (Abwehr) office dealing with foreign countries, who was later executed for his involvement in the plot against Hitler. The documents show the initials of many officers from the High Command of Army Group B, among whose papers is "Overview [*Chefsachen]* Barbarossa."
18. Einsatzgruppe B, Note for Army Group Center of 22 July 1941; BStU ZA, ZUV 9, 31: 21.
19. This number can be calculated based on incident reports of the Chief of the Security Police and SD number 73 of 4 September and number 125 of 26 October 1941 (16,964 and 37,180 victims respectively). BA-MA SF-01/2893 1, 2201, and /28933, 3050.
20. RFSS Command Staff in the SS Main Office, Chief of Staff, IA, dated 19 June 1941, to Chief of SS Main Office Jüttner (copy), BA-MA SF-02/37 542.
21. War Diary of the RFSS Command Staff for 20 July 1941, in *Unsere Ehre heißt Treue* (Vienna, Frankfurt am Main, and Zürich: 1965), 9, cf. 3 and 8. Cf. the order of the General Command of XXXXII Army Corps (copy) of 20 June 1941. BA-MA SF-02/37542.
22. See the interrogation of O.S. on 23 October 1942 in an SS and Police proceedings against the battalion commander, as well as the examination of W. A. on 13 December 1967, Zentrale Stelle Ludwigsburg 202 AR-Z 1212/60, 13:3552, also 12:1828-33.
23. See General Order of XXXXII Army Corps of 26 June 1941 (copy), BA-MA SF-02/37542, and the War Diary of the RFSS Command Staff of 27 June 1941 in *Unsere Ehre heißt Treue*, 13. On 5 July a company of the 2nd SS Infantry Brigade was dispatched to Vilna "to carry out special assignments." Ibid., 16 (entry of 4 July 1941)
24. See Activity Report of the SS Cavalry Brigade for 14 August 1941, BA-MA SF-02/37575, 443, and more generally the verdict of the Braunschweig State Court 2 Ks 1/63 against Magill et al. of 20 April 1964. In *Justiz und NS-Verbrechen* (Amsterdam: 1979), 20: 23ff.
25. RFSS Command Staff, Ic Section, Activity Report Nr. 7 of 28 July 1941. BA-MA SF-02/37615.
26. In fact, this was done in a telephone conversation with the Higher SS and Police leader (HSSPF) Bach-Zelewski, who was with the SS Cavalry Regiment on 2 and 3 August. See his diary entry of 3 August 1941, as well as the entry of 2 August. BA R 20/45b, 6.
27. Daily report of HSSPF Russia-Center of 4 August 1941 to, among others, Himmler personally, relaying the status as of the evening of 3 August. BA, Zwischenarchiv Dahlwitz-Hoppegarten, ZB 6735, vol. I, 268.
28. Helmut Krausnick and Hans-Heinrich Wilhelm, *Die Truppe des Weltanschauungskrieges* (Stuttgart: 1981), 248.
29. Note on the workshop "Combating Partisans" at Command of Rear Area Center (25 and 26 September 1941). ZStA Minsk 655-1-1, 279f. Cf. Corps Order Nr. 53 of the Commander of the Rear Area Center of 16 September 1941, three drafts of the order of the day, a list of the workshop participants, and additional material: BA-MA WF-03/13302, 74–106.
30. IR 9, Section Ia, Noon Report of 25 June and Evening Report of 28 June 1941. BA-MA (BArchP) F 55447, 991 and 1040f. 23. ID, Section Ia, order of 25 June 1941. (BArchP) F 55448, 239. See also the incorrect treatment by Wolfgang

Paul, *Das Potsdamer Infanterie-Regiment 9 1918–1945*, 2nd improved ed. (Osnabrück: 1985), 175f.: It is not true that "the number of prisoners and deserters made this harsh policy impracticable." On the contrary, countermanding orders were issued on 1 July by the 4th Army (von Kluge) and the VIIth Army Corps because Soviet soldiers were resisting more bitterly and hardly any were willing to surrender. ("The Russian, as a simple-minded half-Asiatic, believes that he will be shot if he is captured.") "Necessary executions" were to be continued in secret. Nuremberg Document NOKW 2104, BA F 44993, 366, und BA-MA (BArchP) F 55447, page number illegible. Paul seems to believe that atrocities were committed only on the Soviet side.

31. Cited in Ulrich Heinemann, *Ein konservativer Rebell. Fritz-Dietlof Graf von der Schulenburg und der 20. Juli* (Berlin: 1990), 73.
32. Cited in Krausnick and Wilhelm, *Truppe*, 226. Gersdorff merely stated the fact but he withheld judgment.
33. Duty roster for the High Command of Army Group B of 20 June 1941; also duty rosters of the High Command of Army Group Center of 15 November 1942 (postwar copy). BA-MA (BArchP) F 18495, here 901, also 617.
34. Field Police Chief at the High Command of the Army, 10 April 1943, reprinted in Klaus Geßner, *Geheime Feldpolizei* (Berlin: 1986), quotation on 133; see also Geßner, "Geheime Feldpolizei—die Gestapo der Wehrmacht," in Hannes Heer and Klaus Naumann, eds., *Vernichtungskrieg. Verbrechen der Wehrmacht 1941–1945* (Frankfurt am Main: 1999), 343–358.
35. Geßner, *Feldpolizei*, 98.
36. See Bundesarchiv, Zwischenarchiv Dahlwitz-Hoppegarten ZM 868 A.4, 2-377.
37. Führer Directive Nr. 46, Guidelines for Combating more Intensely the Scourge of Gangs in the East, 18 August 1942. Reprinted in *Hitlers Weisungen für die Kriegführung 1939–1945*, ed. Walter Hubatsch (Frankfurt am Main: 1962), 201–206.
38. Apart from these "enemy dead," 5,000 other killed "suspected gang members" were reported, as was usually the case.
39. Kube on the subject of Lohse to Reichsminister for the Eastern Regions Rosenberg; Lohse to Rosenberg on 5 and 18 June 1943. In *Der Prozeß gegen die Hauptkriegsverbrecher vor dem Internationalen Militärgerichtshof* (Nuremberg: 1948) 38:371ff; emphasis added.
40. Timothy Mulligan, "Reckoning the Costs of the People's War: The German Experience in the Central USSR," *Russian History* 9 (1982): 27–48.
41. High Command of Army Group Center, Ia Nr. 1086/43 g.Kdos., 6 February 1943. Archiv des Instituts für Zeitgeschichte München (IfZ), Fb. 101/34. The signature is that of Chief of Staff of the Army Group Wöhler.
42. High Command of Army Group Center Ia, 30 August 1942 to Heusinger. See the latter's affirmative reply of 1 September 1942, in *Dokumente über die Verbrechen Adolf Heusingers* (Moscow: 1962), 193–195. In addition, transmission of recommendations of the Commander of the Rear Area of 30 August 1942 and his report on orders for carrying out the proposals to the 286th Security Division on the same day with von Tresckow's handwritten notations: "20.05 hours, return telephone call with Obstlt Boehm, not to be carried out until OKH decision received. T." BA-ZA Dahlwitz-Hoppegarten FW 490, A. 11, 2 and 6. Also, War Diary of the Commander of the Rear Area of Army Group Center of 27 and 29 August, as well as 1 September 1942. BA-MA WF-03/13352, 818ff.
43. See statement of W. A. Barantschik, in *Dokumente ... Heusingers*, 188f; interrogation of K., Pi., Pe., and M. from 1945 and 1969 (resulting from a West

German request for legal assistance). BStU, ZUV 9, 18: 5f., 21f., 82f.; and 19: 354. Also, War Diary of the Rear Commander of Army Group Center on 3 September 1942, BA-MA WF-03/13352. Note that, in contrast to the selection of victims, only men between the ages of sixteen and fifty-five were chosen as witnesses; see the statements of Pe. and Pi.

44. At this point roughly 43 percent of the operational area of Army Group Center was considered "gang-infested," about 30 percent as "threatened by gangs." *Region before and after the "Hagen" Maneuver*, BA-MA WF-03/5375, 1211f. Summary report on orders of the Ia op (von Voß) of 8 August 1943 (ibid., 1215) by "Obltn. v. Schlabrendorff."
45. BA-MA RH 19 II/172, 11 as well as 33–60, quotations on 45 and 57, also BA-MA WF-03/5367, cf. WF-03/7422, 1195–1199.
46. Copy in BA-MA RH 19 II/173, 48.
47. See Boeselager, *Der Widerstand*, 16–23.
48. *Der Kreisauer Kreis. Porträt einer Widerstandsgruppe. Begleitband zu einer Ausstellung der Stiftung Preußischer Kulturbesitz* (Berlin: 1985), 21.
49. See Economic Staff East, Staff Order Nr. 22/43, 13 July 1943, BA-MA RW 31/34; personnel list for the fourth quarter of 1942, BA-MA (BArchP) F 43386, 1121. At the end of 1943, he was promoted to Gruppenleiter: see personnel list for the period of 31 December 1943 to 1 April 1944, BA-MA (BArchP) F 43390, 474, und BA-MA RW 31/39, 154ff.
50. See Hoffmann, *Widerstand*, 486.
51. Chefgruppe La 1a 91/43 g.Kdos. of 20 May 1943 concerning a telephone conversation with Yorck on the same day, as well as a communication of the General Staff of the Army/General Quartermaster to Economic Staff East on 5 May 1943 (copy); BA-MA RW 3 1/250, 46 and 50.
52. Documents for the conference of 25 May 1943 with the report of Economic Staff East of 22 May 1943 and addenda 1-21 in Moscow Special Archive, 700-1-50, 153-197; an incomplete version is also in IfZ Fb 101/34.
53. See the final report on operations in the "Wet Triangle" on 10 June and "Seydlitz" of 30 July 1943 in the War Diary of the SS Cavalry Division, BA F 41848, 1188-90 and 1666, also the bimonthly report of the chief of units combating gangs of Reichsführer-SS of 6 August 1943; Zentrale Stelle Ludwigsburg, 202 AR-Z 52/59, Evidence Vol. 10, 99.
54. In the files of the HTO, Fiduciary Office in Kattowitz, there is a written report, dated 13 July 1943, on the conversation with the executives of the real estate companies in the Gau that took place on 7 July 1943; among those listed as present, under the heading "from the HTO," appears "Graf York von Wartenburg." Peter Yorck was Oberregierungsrat beginning in 1938 and had served from 1936 to 1942 in the department responsible for policy decisions for the Reichskommissar for Price Control. See *Der Kreisauer Kreis*, 24. In the meeting referred to here, the "York" listed among those attending expressed expert opinions with regard to price structures. BA F 72661, therein "F 16203," 103–112.
55. The statement was repeated by Marion Gräfin von Dönhoff and is quoted in Ines Reich and Kurt Finker, "Potsdam und der 20. Juli 1944," in *Brandenburg in der NS-Zeit*, ed. Dietrich Eichholtz (Berlin: 1993), 337. Similar attribution was made by Kaltenbrunner to Bormann, on 25 August 1944, in *Spiegelbild einer Verschwörung* (Stuttgart: 1961), 299–301.
56. Kaltenbrunner to Bormann, 31 July 1944, ibid., 110.

57. Army High Command 2, Nr. 4758/44 of 28 June 1944, MZAP WF-03/26818, 299. "OT" means "Organisation Todt," the official institution for construction works of military use.
58. Note of the Head of the Führungsstab Politik (in the Ostministerium)—pers. ref.—12 June 1944, quoted in Barbara Bromberger and Hans Mausbach, *Feinde des Lebens* (Cologne: 1987), 185ff.
59. Of incidental interest is the fact that Henning von Tresckow is listed in at least one of the shadow governments drawn up by the conspirators as "Head of the German Police" in the Reich Ministry of the Interior, hence as Himmler's successor. Kaltenbrunner to Bormann on 27 July 1944, in *Spiegelbild einer Verschwörung,* 61.
60. See Himmler's notation for the date 15 July 1942, Moscow Special Archive 1372-5-23, 171, and the Foreign Office's *Special Report on India*, by Dr. vom Trott zu Solz (secret) of 21 August 1942 to Himmler's personal adjutant Grothmann, BA, F 3327, 3078.
61. See note of Economic Staff East, Chefgruppe La on 23 May 1942, MZAP (BArchP) F 42749, 973f.
62. The statement was attributed to Stieff by Kaltenbrunner to Bormann on 28 July 1944; see *Spiegelbild einer Verschwörung*, 90.

– *Chapter 7* –

MILITARY VIOLENCE AND THE NATIONAL SOCIALIST CONSENSUS

*The Wehrmacht in Greece, 1941–44**

Mark Mazower

Shortly before dawn on 16 August 1943 several troop carriers drove down a dirt road south of the town of Arta in northwestern Greece. They came to a halt a short distance from the village of Komeno, which is situated in flat country near the mouth of the river Arachthos. The previous day had been an important festival in the Orthodox calendar and most of the villagers were still sleeping off the effects of the festivities. Just over one hundred Wehrmacht troops, 12th Company of the 98th Regiment of the elite First Mountain Division (henceforth 12. Co., 98 GJR, 1 Geb.Div.), climbed down from the lorries and received their operational instructions from Oberleutnant Röser, their commanding officer.

They encircled the village, and set up gun posts to cover the various paths leading from it. Two flares were then fired, giving the signal for the assault squads, armed with grenades, rifles and machine-pistols, to storm the houses. In the ensuing carnage the troops killed 317 people of all ages and both sexes out of a total population of just over six hundred. Most of those who managed to escape did so via an unguarded track which led through tall reeds to the river which they then swam across. There were no German casualties, and the medical orderlies stood idly by the lorries

Notes for this section begin on page 168.

from where they could hear the sound of gunfire and see the houses of the village go up in flames.

After several hours the shooting stopped, and while the assault groups rested under the orange trees out of the sun, ancillary troops moved in to collect the villagers' livestock, poultry, and household goods. One of these, Karl S., described many years later what he saw there: "There were bodies everywhere—in front of the houses and inside them. If I remember rightly, there was a church or a small chapel in the main square (it was one of the only buildings not to have been burned), and in front of this church lay a large heap of bodies. So far as I could see from the tangled mass of humanity there were more women and children than men there. The church door was open and there were more bodies in the church too."[1]

Karl S. gave this account in the form of an affidavit to the Austrian police in 1971 as part of a preliminary investigation (which never came to court) into the Komeno massacre. Between 1971 and 1973 West German and Austrian police traced and interviewed virtually every surviving member of 12 Co. So far as the investigators were concerned, the important point was to establish who had issued the orders for the operation. Here the responses presented a somewhat unclear picture, for though most agreed that Oberleutnant Röser (who died in 1944) had issued the instructions that morning to "shoot everyone and leave nothing standing,"[2] there was disagreement over the level of involvement of the battalion commander, K., and of Röser's second-in-command, Leutnant D., both of whom are still alive. However the reader of these statements is struck by their common reference to another matter: the effect of this massacre on the soldiers themselves.

Karl D. recalled that "within 12 Co. there was much discussion of this action. Soon all the soldiers knew about it. Few thought it right ... I myself was so sickened by the atrocities (*Grausamkeiten*) that it took me weeks to recover my peace of mind (*seelisches Gleichgewicht*)." August S.: "After the shooting it was very quiet. Most of the comrades were very depressed. Almost none of them agreed with the action.... With some exceptions all had crises of conscience (*Gewissenskonflikte*)." According to Johann E., an N.C.O. threw down his cap at the feet of Lt. Röser, saying: "Herr Oberleutnant, just remember, that's the last time I take part in something like that. That was a *Schweinerei* (disgrace) which had nothing to do with fighting a war." The same witness also claimed that during the shooting he heard men shouting: "*You* shoot! I can't. You have a machine-gun or a machine pistol, so it's simpler. I have to aim." According to Franz T., "most soldiers did not agree with this action.... Many said openly it was nothing but a *Schweinerei* to shoot unarmed civilians. Others, rather fewer, took the view that they were all a potential enemy so long as they supported the partisans against us soldiers. The argument was so heated that I might almost describe it as a mutiny *(Meuterei).*"[3]

In assessing the reliability of these statements, we should keep two considerations in mind: first, that they were offered by men who were not denying their own part in the massacre. Thus they were not designed to exculpate the speaker or anyone else. And second, that they were given independently of one another. Once we have made allowance for inaccuracies and exaggeration, they still suggest—as indeed we might expect—that the troops were not unaffected by what they had seen and done. Such an interpretation is also supported by contemporary documentary evidence. The evangelical chaplain of 1 Geb.Div. wrote explicitly in October 1943, with reference to activity over the previous three months, that "the mass killing of women and children during operations against the bands is producing a difficult inner burden on the conscience of many men." This was strong and unusual language for an official report, requiring some courage on the part of the author, especially since the general to whom it was addressed was no supporter of the church.[4]

After the massacre at Komeno, some of the troops seem to have considered moving from protest to more concrete action. "We'd had enough, we didn't want to know about the whole 'shit,'" recalled Otto G. "But in the end we lacked the courage to desert. Not a single man deserted." In the words of August S., "We fell back on the conclusion ... that we had just obeyed orders." Even so, the trust between Lt. Röser and his men had broken down, and shortly afterwards he was transferred to another unit.[5]

Taken together these pieces of evidence suggest the existence of limits to what ordinary soldiers would do with a clear conscience. Yet for all their moral revulsion, these soldiers *had* obeyed orders and—as many of the affidavits openly admit—fired on civilians. Their actions were not a spontaneous explosion of rage brought on by the tensions of a guerrilla war, nor were they carried out at gunpoint by men who stayed together only under threat of punishment and court-martial. No army, least of all the Wehrmacht, with its impressive degree of cohesion, could function through discipline alone. By what means, by appeals to what values had these soldiers been enabled to suppress their more humanitarian instincts?

This question takes us to the heart of the current debate over the role of the Wehrmacht during World War II, and the nature of the links between the armed forces and the Nazi regime. At one time it was usual to take the view that the Wehrmacht had remained immune to the Nazi virus: if the SS was, in Gerald Reitlinger's phrase, the "alibi of a nation,"[6] the German army was its "untarnished shield"[7] whose supposedly aristocratic leadership helped preserve a more high-minded conception of national duty. The 20 July plot against Hitler reinforced the notion that the Wehrmacht had been a center of resistance to the Nazi leadership, an organization which fought gallantly to keep the Russians out of Europe, but had nothing to do with the Holocaust or other unsoldierly activities.[6]

More recently this view has been shown to be deeply flawed. It has become clear that army and SS units often worked together, that at an early stage the army helped organize the mass killing of Jews in Serbia and supported the murderous activities of the Einsatzgruppen on the Eastern front. Several recent studies have revealed the extent to which political indoctrination had permeated the officer corps, and indeed become institutionalized there, and have shown how military commanders reflected Nazi ideology in their orders and actions. The conception of the war in the East as a *Vernichtungskrieg* (war of annihilation) was shared by the political and military leadership of the Reich. The 20 July plot looks rather less convincing as an argument for the military's distaste for Nazi politics when it is borne in mind that attempts to gain even minimal support among senior army officers for resistance to Hitler only succeeded after Stalingrad made some form of German defeat all but inevitable.[8]

However, in replacing the old "anti-Nazi" Wehrmacht by a newer Nazi version, recent scholarship has concentrated on relations at the élite level between the regime and the officer corps. When mentioned, the conscript soldier is typically portrayed as a passive tool in the hands of his officer. Yet it is not enough to demonstrate that the Nazi regime desired a political army—it must also be shown that it succeeded in creating one. The recent wave of work on "everyday life" in the Third Reich has underlined the need to include popular attitudes in any discussion of the way in which National Socialism maintained itself in power. Recent studies of civilian political attitudes in the Third Reich suggest a certain ambivalence toward the regime, especially once the war broke out. Both before and during the war, a variety of political attitudes emerged, ranging from "inner" (and on occasions visible) resistance to voluntary participation in processes of political denunciation.[9]

Although *Alltagsgeschichte* has left its mark on interpretations of the Third Reich, it has had only a slight impact on our understanding of the German military. Perhaps this is not surprising, since an approach which was centered around the study of social protest, which stressed resistance to authority, and whose "ethnological turn" (to cite Geoff Eley) implied "taking the subject seriously," could be adapted to the study of the German soldier only with some modification. If one did not search for areas of "resistance" among the troops, it was easy to find oneself "empathizing" with individuals who lacked the ideological palatability of the "anti-Nazi worker."[10]

The result is sometimes a rather lop-sided account of military behavior. Klausch has focused upon the story of the so-called 999 brigades, whose members included anti-Nazi political prisoners. Critical of the regime, co-operative with local resistance groups, they were hardly typical products of the Wehrmacht. At a more general level, Schulte has presented a revisionist picture of the *Landser*'s life on guard duty in occupied Russia as one of boredom and ideological apathy. German conservatives used to find sources of opposition to Hitler in the officer corps; now these younger historians, from a rather different starting-point, are looking for similar forces—ranging from inertia to active opposition—among the rank and file.[11]

The trouble with these interpretations, however, is that they emphasize sources of resistance to authority and its ideological imperatives within an army which displayed what was by any standards remarkable cohesion. Several historians have pointed to the importance of the "National Socialist consensus" within the Wehrmacht.[12] The question is: what beliefs was this consensus built around?

Addressing the same problem in the context of the Third Reich as a whole, Kershaw argued that adulation of Hitler formed "a crucial integratory force in the Nazi system of rule."[13] A similar phenomenon may have existed within the armed forces, though it is difficult to know what sort of response from the troops there was to the regime's propaganda effort. The "Hitler myth" seems to have been in decline within the Reich from late 1941 onwards. Soldiers too were becoming increasingly disaffected.[14]

A more fundamental consideration is that though Hitler may have remained popular among certain groups, notably the younger officers, the myth of the Führer did not by itself define the limits of the permissible. In the Reich itself, for example, both the euthanasia program and the wartime campaign against the Church had to be dropped by the regime in the face of popular protests.[15] Kershaw's emphasis on the "Hitler myth" stemmed from his belief that the *ideological* commitment of the German public to National

Socialism had been exaggerated. Perhaps now it is time to explore afresh the ways in which the ideological dynamism of the regime was integrated with popular modes of thought.

Looking at the way the regime gained the consent of its soldiers means taking a rather broader and more differentiated view of Nazi ideology than has been reflected in much of the debate so far. One recent work sets out to challenge the stereotype of the Wehrmacht as a "ruthless and disciplined homogeneous entity." But it does so by stressing disaffection and apathy among the troops and argues that ideology is not always "the universal determinant of behavior."[16]

Such an approach suggests that morale was lower than was generally the case and is premised on a monolithic and unrealistic conception of ideology itself. The influence of National Socialism on popular beliefs was wide-ranging and pervasive: notions of patriotism, attitudes to women, conceptions of law and military honor were all influenced by Nazi doctrine. Factors other than fanaticism may be relevant to explaining the Wehrmacht's propensity for violence against civilians, and these factors may also have stemmed, in part at least, from Nazi thinking. Between Bartov's emphasis on an existential quasi-religious commitment to the Nazi *Weltanschauung* and Mommsen's image of the *Landser* stolidly resisting the flood of propaganda aimed at him, lies a terrain of attitudes waiting to be explored.[17]

I

In June and July 1943 the troops of 1 Geb.Div. made their way into north-west Greece to secure the coastline against an anticipated Allied landing. They embarked on a series of *Säuberungen*, or "clean-up actions" against the guerrillas who threatened any Axis defense of the coast from the rear. The first large sweep, Operation "Augustus," lasted for five days, during which time German units covered several hundred miles of arid terrain, burned numerous villages and killed over one hundred "bandits." Yet few weapons were captured and the operation was judged a failure, since the guerrilla bands had simply retreated inland.[18]

It was on 12 August, during Operation "Augustus," that a German reconnaissance team drove unexpectedly into the main square at Komeno. They were the first Germans to appear there for a long time. Since 1941 the region had been controlled by Italian troops and *carabinieri*, who had displayed a tolerant attitude toward the local inhabitants. The German soldiers were no doubt surprised to find Greek guerrillas, who had stacked their guns against the village well, busy requisitioning food from the local traders. There was a moment of tension, but villagers prevailed on the two sides not to fire on one another. The frightened Germans reversed their vehicle and drove away. That night the nervous villagers slept out in the fields and only returned after they received assurances from the local Italian *commandante* in Arta that they had nothing to fear.[19]

But the Italian was wrong. Reports of the sighting reached divisional HQ and beyond, and on 14 August orders were sent to Col. Salminger, commanding 98 GJR, to prepare for a "surprise" operation against Komeno. Just a few days earlier, I Geb.Div. had received instructions from General Löhr in Salonika that *Sühnemassnahmen* (atonement measures) were to be carried out "with the most rigorous means." Under standing orders, the fact that guerrillas had been sighted there made the village and its inhabitants a potential target.[20]

The violence displayed at Komeno was not spontaneous or uncontrolled, but expressed the aims of a highly bureaucratic military structure. This could be deduced from the composition of the force that was sent to the village: some troops were detailed to carry off the booty after the operation; the canteen staff were on hand to provide the soldiers with rice pudding and fruit compote before returning to camp.[21]

Moreover, four days elapsed between the initial sighting of the guerrillas and the "surprise" attack on them. Expecting an imminent Allied landing on the Epirot coast and having failed to suppress the guerrillas who would then threaten their rear, Wehrmacht planners in Jannina and Athens may have intended the complete and unprecedented destruction of Komeno as a reminder and reassertion of German power, a dreadful warning to the region of the consequences of supporting the guerrillas. This indeed was how the massacre was interpreted by local resistance leaders.[22]

But what did the soldiers of 12 Co. think was the motive for the attack? When interviewed in the early 1970s, almost all explained that it had been a "reprisal action" (*Vergeltungsaktion*), though they disagreed about whose death they had supposedly been avenging. Most recalled the death of a senior officer who had been killed by guerrillas. They were clearly alluding to the death of their commanding officer, Col. Salminger, in a guerrilla ambush, an event which did indeed result in reprisals, but which occurred *after* Komeno on 1 October. Others remembered it differently. According to K., who as battalion commander was in a position to know, Salminger himself had delivered a fiery speech to the troops the previous evening, telling them that they were to avenge German soldiers who had been attacked at Komeno. (*We* know that no soldiers were attacked there, but the troops may not have done.) This story, that 12 Co. was avenging the deaths of other soldiers killed in the village, was repeated by a number of the men. What is striking is not the confusion and discrepancies between their accounts; it is their virtual unanimity that the slaughter in Komeno had been a form of revenge.

The vocabulary of *Vergeltungsaktionen*, *Sühnemassnahmen* and *Säuberungsunternehmen* ("reprisal actions," "atonement measures," and "clean-up operations") which resurfaces in the Ludwigsburg affidavits, will be familiar to any student of the Nazi occupation in eastern and southeastern Europe. Rather than front-line combat, it was these measures, conducted among and directed largely against civilians in the occupied territories which gave the Wehrmacht its reputation for brutality and violence.

Their origins lay in the German response to French *franc-tireurs* in 1871 and 1914. In both wars, the German army engaged in reprisals, but on a limited scale compared with what was to come. Ironically, the protests provoked on these earlier occasions caused military regulations on the shooting of civilians to be tightened up in the Reichswehr; only after 1939 was this trend reversed.[23]

The crucial period of change was the first half of 1941, which covered the invasion of Yugoslavia and Greece as well as the planning and eventual implementation of "Barbarossa," the invasion of the Soviet Union. Among the earliest examples of the new policies are the instructions issued to German troops in newly occupied Yugoslavia at the end of April 1941. Field Marshal von Weichs, who would go on to become Supreme Commander Southeast, ordered that: "If in any area an armed band appears, then even those men capable of bearing arms, who are seized because they were in proximity to the band, are to be shot to death, even if it cannot be immediately ascertained that they were connected with the band."[24]

Although von Weichs seems to have been acting here on his own initiative, similarly draconian proposals were drawn up for "Barbarossa" at OKW (the Supreme Command of the Armed Forces), which on May 13 authorized the troops assembling on the Eastern front to "liquidate" guerrillas, and ordered field commanders to seize hostages for shooting in retaliation for attacks on German personnel.[25]

Analyzing Wehrmacht behavior in Serbia in 1941, Christopher Browning has shown how even a cultivated and religious man like

Field Marshal List, who was "neither a Nazi nor a traditional Prussian officer" was prepared to insist on what his own chief of staff described as "downright violence." Browning emphasizes the variety of factors which contributed to this behavior—List's lack of political sensitivity, a concern for his own troops' welfare, indignation at the underhanded tactics of the insurgents, and fear of the damaging effects of partisan successes on the prestige of the German army itself. In the autumn of 1941, List's orders were invoked for the first time in mainland Greece by 164 Inf.Div.: it burned down several villages near Salonika and shot more than four hundred male villagers after guerrillas were reported to have rested in the vicinity.[26]

In both Serbia and Greece, the German authorities imposed a regime of terror as partisan activity increased. German occupation had led to social collapse on a scale which had no parallel in Western Europe: wholesale economic expropriation and the resulting rapid inflation caused national markets to disintegrate. This in turn led to starvation in the urban centers, strained existing state administrations to breaking-point, and eventually gave rise to alternative underground forms of social organization—in other words, movements of mass resistance.[27]

Within the occupation bureaucracies, some officials urged that the reprisal policy be toned down in the search for a political solution, which would win over local collaborators, usually on the basis of an anti-communist campaign; others demanded instead that the terror be stepped up.

Such debates occurred after the massacres at Kragujevac and Kraljevo in October 1941 when German troops, trying to fulfill their reprisal quotas, shot over 4,000 inhabitants. These included the entire Serbian work force of an airplane factory which had been taken over for the German war effort. In Greece just over two years later, there was an uproar when soldiers of the 117 Jg.Div. revenged the killing of around seventy of their number by guerrillas, by shooting seven hundred Greeks, including the entire male population of the town of Kalavryta.[28]

On both occasions the short-run outcome was that army commanders issued orders aimed at modifying existing practices. But though these may have acted as sops to those voices calling for greater sensitivity to local opinion, they had no discernible effect on military behavior. The new orders neither put an end to mass shootings, nor resulted in the punishment of officers responsible. Within months of both outrages, further massacres had occurred.[29]

To explain why the debate always ended this way, veering each time toward violence rather than negotiation, it is not enough to argue that this was simply a "normal" military response to the problems of guerrilla war. Guerrilla warfare, like war itself, is a generic category: it covers a variety of situations and possible responses. Neither in Greece, nor in the Italian zone in Yugoslavia, did Italian forces react to the guerrillas in the same way. Their military response was much softer, and local Italian commanders were more inclined to make quiet accommodations with potential resistance leaders. Indeed, Italian commanders in Epiros clashed head-on with 1 Geb.Div. over anti-guerrilla tactics, and insisted on proper treatment of the civilian population.[30]

Thus there *were* alternatives to the prevailing German policy. Even some Wehrmacht officers argued that the troops would have been more profitably deployed down in the plains to guard the harvest, starving out the guerrillas, rather than fruitlessly chasing after them into the hills.[31]

There was one reason why their voices were ignored: this was not a guerrilla war where the impetus for aggression sprang from the tensions and pressures surrounding the troops on the ground.[30] In the embryonic Nazi New Order, at least as it emerged in much of Eastern Europe, brutality was not merely condoned or tolerated, it was encouraged. Behind the *Vergeltungsaktion* and the Sühnemassnahme lay the attitudes of National Socialism, of Hitler himself.

II

In many ways Hitler was a typical ex-*Frontkämpfer*. He had won several decorations in the trenches near Ypres, and his war had been one of high risk and constant movement. Like other soldiers at the front he would have been reminded, both by his senior officers but also by the circumstances around him, of the need for "fighting spirit" and a "will to combat." In 1918 some soldiers returned home with a permanent mistrust of calls for violence; but others seemed wedded to them. Hitler came to attribute Germany's defeat to weakness of will, a flinching from the demands of war, and the result was a philosophy demanding something close to unconstrained aggression in the pursuit of military victory. "One can't fight a war with Salvation Army methods," was Hitler's response to protests over SS brutality in November 1939.[31]

A number of writers have rightly stressed the great importance Hitler attached in the run-up to "Barbarossa" to making it clear to the Wehrmacht leadership that this was to be a new kind of war, a "war of extermination" (Vernichtungskrieg). He was similarly forthright about how to deal with the guerrilla threat. In December 1942, for example, the partisan question came up in conversation between Hitler and Jodl, chief operations officer of the Wehrmacht. The Führer outlined the following scenario to illustrate how the guerrillas should be handled: "What should you do: the swine have barricaded themselves in a house in which there are also women and children. Should the soldier set fire to the house or not? If he sets fire to it, the innocent are burned. There shouldn't be any doubt about this! He must burn it down!" These were precisely the sentiments behind Röser's draconian instructions to his men outside Komeno.[34]

In an exchange which dramatized the debate described earlier, Jodl responded that a more moderate approach might avoid driving the population into the arms of the guerrillas. Hitler disagreed, and soon made his wishes known. Within two weeks, OKW had issued new anti-partisan guidelines. These directed—with the express sanction of the Führer—that: "The troops have the right and the duty to use any means in this fight, even against women and children, provided they are conducive to success.... No German participating in actions against the bands or their associates is to be held responsible for acts of violence either from a disciplinary or a judicial point of view." In the Führerstaat, there was thus a direct link between Hitler's own views and official military guidelines.[35]

These directives and operational orders contained certain recurrent motifs—*Härte, rücksichtslose Strenge* ("toughness," "ruthless severity")—which Hitler and his generals clearly saw as the virtues demanded by this sort of fighting. The German soldier, according to guidelines issued for the Balkans, needed to be "even craftier and more ruthless *(noch verschlagener und noch rücksichtsloser)*" and ready to use "all means" in the fight against a "brutal, underhanded and crafty enemy."[36]

In Greece, "toughness" seemed especially desirable, since in 1943 the gradual collapse of public order there was attributed to the Italians' lack of that virtue. At the Salzburg summit meeting in April 1943, Ribbentrop warned a senior Italian diplomat that "brutal action would have to be taken if the Greeks got above themselves. He was of the opinion that ... the Greeks should be shown in an iron manner who was master in the country."[37]

For once the foreign minister was in agreement with his military colleagues, who were alarmed at signs that the Greek contempt for the Italians was being transferred to the Germans as the mood of resistance spread. That summer in Argos, a newly arrived German soldier was beaten up in daylight by Greek civilians. The local German commander demanded a harsh response. When the

Italians who were still formally in control, showed signs of dragging their heels over the issue, he arranged for executive authority to be transferred to himself and immediately ordered the execution of three "suspected" perpetrators.[38]

Several weeks later, an intelligence officer in Athens argued that force rather than words would henceforth be required in dealing with the Greeks: "The time is past when we could rely on negotiation. The Greek is always looking for something more, using negotiations to achieve what he wants, and this makes him lose respect for German authority." A pamphlet distributed to villages in the Peloponnese warning against supporting the guerrillas put the matter more simply: "The German gun is speaking."[39]

In Greece, as on the Eastern front, this ideology of brutality was transmitted through the junior officer corps: this was, in Bartov's words, the "backbone of the German army."[40]

By their behavior junior officers were supposed to demonstrate to their men how the war should be fought, and this included an ability to be "tough" when the occasion demanded it.[41]

The regime emphasized the key role played by this stratum of the army and in return gave them virtual judicial immunity. They became, in the words of a postwar German magistrate, "masters of life and death."[42]

After one atrocity in Greece, which aroused energetic protests from the German Foreign Office at this threat to its policy of political collaboration, the regimental commander responsible was defended by his superior on the grounds that although he was a "particularly severe superior officer" who often took "draconianly harsh" measures, "he is always considerate of his men's welfare and his actions are motivated by this attitude." Another young Waffen-SS lieutenant escaped punishment for the massacre at Distomo in June 1944 because, although he "undoubtedly overstepped the bounds of the orders concerning Sühnemassnahmen," he had been motivated by the belief that "he had to set an example by which the occupying power would prove with all due severity that it knows how to counter even the most underhanded and lowest form of so-called 'warfare.'"[43]

The ideological influence of Hitler on the officer corps can be brought out through an examination of key personalities in the unit responsible for the massacre at Komeno. When 98 GJR was founded as part of the peacetime expansion of 1 Geb.Div., its first commander was Ferdinand Schörner, a man who would go on, after a rapid wartime ascent, to achieve notoriety as "the most brutal of Hitler's field marshals."[44]

A veteran of Verdun and later Freikorps Epp, Schörner was one of the few senior Wehrmacht figures for whom Hitler never lost his enthusiasm, and his links with the NSDAP were close: he was appointed the first head of the NS Führungsstab (the political indoctrination unit within the armed forces), and after he left, he continued to emphasize the importance of inculcating a National Socialist Weltanschauung in the army.

Schörner's powerful influence lingered on in 1 Geb.Div. after his departure in 1940: three years later, both the divisional commander, Walter von Stettner and the commander of 98 GJR, Josef Salminger, were men who had served under him as junior officers—the latter as head of 12 Co. itself. Both men too, in different ways, demonstrated the sorts of attitudes which helped the Wehrmacht come to terms with the Nazi regime.

General von Stettner, who came from an established military family and had fought in World War I, was a short, fussy man, whose own inferiority complex and intense ambition made him keep his personal political views to himself, and insist on unswerving obedience to Hitler's orders from his subordinates. He frowned on the role played by the divisional chaplains in the life of the 1 Geb.Div. In the guidelines he issued for operation "Augustus," he demanded that the troops retaliate against any signs or even *suspicions* of guerrilla activity by the summary shooting of suspects and the destruction of all houses in the vicinity.[45]

As a result he clashed with his immediate superior, the devoutly Catholic General Lanz, over the treatment of civilians in Epiros; according to the division's Catholic chaplain, this dispute came to take on the dimensions of an "ideological split" within the officer corps.[46]

Colonel Salminger, who cannot have been much more than thirty years old when he was killed in a guerrilla ambush several weeks after Komeno, was very different from von Stettner. Like Schörner, he was brave, impetuous, and brutal. He had joined the *Reichswehr* as an NCO, but was commissioned in 1936, and rose in remarkable fashion to take command of Schörner's own regiment. According to K., the battalion commander who served under him and was present at Komeno, Salminger saw Hitler as the savior of Germany and gave free rein to his enthusiasm. "This regiment is not just a German regiment, it is a Hitlerian regiment (*ein Hitler'sches Regiment*)," he is said to have declared in Greece to his subordinates in 98 GJR. Such sentiments raised eyebrows among more conservative officers, but did little to diminish his popularity among his men.[47]

Something of Salminger's bluntness emerges from the messages he sent to von Stettner during one of the first drives against the guerrillas in Epiros, a few weeks before Komeno, as he tried to clear the mountain road south of Jannina toward Arta. The roads were bad, the heat terrible, water was scarce; there were no interpreters and it was difficult for the troops to obtain reliable intelligence. The guerrillas avoided contact, slipping back into the hills. In frustration, Salminger radioed back to von Stettner in Jannina: "General! The way things are at present, the whole action, although carried out with the greatest efforts, is to my mind completely pointless. There is only one available option: to apprehend the entire male population. Whoever takes part in the fighting or supports the bandits ought to be shot immediately."[48]

He had been urging such a policy for some days to little avail, since the Italians, who were still nominally in control of the region, regarded it as too draconian. Venting his frustration on more "acceptable" targets, Salminger stopped a car, whose driver, though possessing a pass to travel down that road, proved suspicious on other grounds: he was "an unmistakable Jew.... That was too much for me, so I seized the *Burschen* (fellow) and his car, and have had them brought to the Division."[49]

It was still another seven months before the Jews of Jannina were to be deported to the death camps. Salminger's action—seizing the Jewish driver, but not killing him on the spot—perhaps reflected the ambiguity of Greece's intermediate position between the East, where the unfortunate man might easily have been shot straightaway, and Western Europe, where he might not have been arrested at all. On that same road, at the end of the summer, Josef Salminger would meet his own death, caught one evening in a guerrilla ambush as he drove with typical impetuosity unescorted back toward Jannina.

It was von Stettner and Salminger who set the tone for their subordinates, the all-important junior officers who came into daily contact with the rank and file. In Salminger's "Hitlerian regiment," many of them were also sympathetic to National Socialist goals: Lt. Röser, who commanded 12 Co., was described by one former soldier as a "150 percent" Nazi. Another Landser was refused promotion when Lt. D., Röser's deputy, wrote to his local party office to check on his political record, which turned out to be unsatisfactory. Major K., who knew Röser well, also characterizes him in political terms: though he was no party activist, not the sort of officer who handed over his men to the Gestapo for defeatist talk, he was a former Hitler Youth leader who brought with him many of the ideals of the Youth movement. At the beginning of the war he had volunteered for service in the Wehrmacht, where—according to K.—he proved himself to be a fine and considerate company commander, one who "was regarded by his soldiers as a comrade." Those who are tempted to attribute unit solidarity and cohesion in the Wehrmacht to coercion, surveillance, and tight discipline alone should note how important it was felt to be for junior officers to establish bonds of trust, esteem and even "love" with the men under their command. At the same time, Röser was also the man who shot the village priest at point-blank range at the entrance to Komeno, and later invited K. into the village to see "how his men had done."[50]

III

The influence of National Socialism thus revealed itself in the behavior of various officers throughout the hierarchy of 1 Geb.Div. But the sort of exposure an officer, whether regular or reserve, had to the regime and its ideology differed substantially from that of the rank and file. Salminger, for all his lower-class background, had been in the army since before 1936. Men like Lt. D. from 12 Co. (and Röser's successor as its commander), or Karl Rothfuchs, the division's intelligence officer, had begun to forge professional careers—D. as a schoolteacher, Rothfuchs as a lawyer—in the prewar Reich. They were in their mid-twenties or early thirties, familiar with the obligations and compromises necessary for advancement under National Socialism.

Conscripts, on the other hand, were younger and more poorly educated. Those in Komeno with 12 Co. were generally in their early twenties, from the villages and small market towns of Bavaria and western Austria. Most had been called up at the age of nineteen in 1941 or 1942, and had some secondary education and subsequent experience of manual or semi-skilled work. After the war they would become bakers, farmers, factory workers, and railwaymen—the archetypal "little men" as many would come to think of themselves.[51]

They lacked the commitment of a Salminger or a Röser, and it is scarcely surprising that S., one of the division's chaplains, should have noted that, as the troops were about to enter Greece, they were showing some signs of war-weariness. Growing ill-discipline, he wrote, needed to be countered by increasing their "sense of responsibility"—though they all knew "what this war is about" *(um was es in diesem Kriege geht)*. He urged junior officers to be more considerate toward their troops.[52]

Such observations point to the possibility, perhaps not of a rift between officers and men, but certainly of differences in their approach to the war. The latter did not occupy the special place in the thinking of the regime held by the officer corps, and the influence of National Socialism on them was less direct. How warmly did they respond to the notion of a *Weltanschauungskrieg*? How plausible is it to portray them either as fanatics fighting a religious war or as ideology-free "slipper soldiers"?[53]

IV

Entering Greece in the spring of 1943, officers of 117 Jg.Div. were given detailed instructions for helping their men through a "total war" in which they needed "guidance, answers and a clear message": "It is especially necessary to stiffen [the soldier's] resolve to fight and to encourage the soldierly virtues. The education of a resistance to crisis, toughness and *eine gewisse Brutalität* (a certain brutality) is absolutely necessary."[54]

But how were they to identify the enemy they were supposed to hate? What were the "soldierly virtues" and was "brutality" among them? What were the criteria for guilt and innocence in a guerrilla war? To these questions the Landser received conflicting answers.

On the one hand he was told that all civilians were to be regarded as potential enemies. "Any contact with the Greeks is forbidden. Any Greek, even when he gets on with a German, wants something from him. For each favor he wants something in return. German good-will toward the Greeks is always misplaced. 'Better shoot once too often than once too seldom.'" Such were the instructions issued to troops entering Greece for the first time in early 1943.[55]

This message was reinforced by familiar patterns of stereotyping, which overlaid the initial manifestations of Nazi philhellenism as the resistance spread. The very invisibility of the guerrilla permitted him to be demonized. Though primitive, he was supposedly all-powerful, familiar with the terrain, mobile and, through his excellent sources of information, able to anticipate any German attack. Betraying his Balkan qualities, he showed a propensity for cruelty and a tendency to "a warfare so pitiless and inhuman as to be scarcely conceivable." Occasionally he was portrayed in terms which bore more than a passing resemblance to stock anti-Semitic propaganda motifs from the Reich. Tales of the insurgents' ill-treatment of captive soldiers abounded; more than one Wehrmacht POW was to record his surprise at not being savagely put to death by his captors.[56]

For the beleaguered German soldier, practical measures reinforced this sense of constant danger. The troops were forbidden (like the Italians before them) to walk alone in the streets or to venture into the hills in less than company strength. Where permanent garrisons or sentry posts needed to be established to guard vital roads in isolated country, "strong-points" were constructed, thickly walled concrete blockhouses which expressed a more generalized fear of the outside world. The guerrillas too played on the troops' sense of isolation and vulnerability. A Greek resistance propaganda leaflet in German showed two German soldiers coming down a dark lane, with one glancing nervously over his shoulder, and a caption which read: "German soldier! Always look out. You're all alone."[57]

But if the individual soldier was supposed to stay on his guard and to be prepared to respond harshly to any attack, his own aggressive instincts were *not* to be allowed full rein. Troop commanders worried about maintaining discipline. They feared the sort of descent into anarchy which had led the territorial commander at Corinth to talk of individual soldiers' "gangster methods" against local populations, and behavior which was reminiscent of "scenes from the Wild West." Anti-partisan directives sought to distinguish between reprisals and "unjustified murder" which "of course is forbidden." Such distinctions, however, remained in permanent conflict with the endorsement of brutality. When General Löhr directed in July 1943 that "the extent of a reprisal measure is to be ordered clearly, [and] its execution must be supervised in order to prevent excesses by our own troops," he added the threat that soldiers who failed to "break up any active resistance of the population by force of arms, immediately and relentlessly" would come before a court-martial. Similarly, from Athens General Felmy warned that "infringements by the troops" such as plundering, seizing booty and acts of cruelty had to be prevented since "troop excesses have a lasting impact on discipline and inner attitudes (*innere Haltung*) and weaken the troops for future operations against worthy opponents." Yet he could not refrain from adding: "Still, in the war against the bands, weakness is as bad as excessively tough operations."[58]

Felmy's confused instructions illuminate the conflicting beliefs and values which were to be revealed at Komeno. If he was afraid of the effects of "excesses" on "inner attitudes," he feared still more being accused of weakness. And in the contrast drawn between the "bands" and future "worthy" opponents, lie the indications of a conception of soldierly honor whose dictates could not be easily satisfied in the war against the guerrillas.[59]

National Socialism had elevated the soldier to a privileged position in German society. The Landser could draw satisfaction from being part of a respected institution. He was constantly reminded that "the soldier draws his *seelische Kraft* (psychological strength) from the *ewigen soldatischen und ethischen Werten der Nation* (eternal soldierly and ethical values of the nation)."[60]

Within 1 Geb.Div., there were particular reasons for pride. The mountain life, with its associations of purity and superior endurance held great symbolic importance in National Socialist iconography.[61]

Many men in 12 Co. had been specially chosen for their Alpine skills; they had originally been drafted into the *Hochgebirgsbataillonen* (High Mountain battalions), trained beneath Hitler's eyrie at Berchtesgaden, and gone on to spearhead the German assault through the Caucasus in 1942 toward Baku. Typical of *their* conception of the war was the extraordinary episode in August 1942 when mountain troops took time off from the push southwards to plant the swastika on the summit of Mt. Elbrus—an achievement which received much excited publicity in Germany though it left Hitler himself unimpressed.

For these men war was about mastering both the elements and an enemy as technically proficient as yourself. Artillery exchanges with Red Army mountain troops in the high altitudes of the Caucasus offered challenges of fitness, skill, and perseverance which confirmed the *Gebirgstruppe's* image of themselves.[62]

The journey from the snows of Elbrus to the malarial valleys of Epiros involved more than geography: being driven in lorries at dawn out along the plain south of Arta was to be part of a less heroic enterprise.

And yet this heroized and honorable self-image—which was only an extreme form of that inculcated throughout the Wehrmacht—did not prevent the soldiers of 98 GJR from taking part in numerous reprisal actions. From the spring of 1943, 12 Co. participated in a series of anti-guerrilla sweeps that took them into Greece, through Serbia and Montenegro. At the end of July Salminger led them down the road to Arta in an initial push against the guerrillas there. All these operations produced civilian casualties. What was it about the Komeno operation that left the troops, in the words of August E., "completely demoralized"?[63]

The answer is that this was no ordinary reprisal action.

Reprisals were supposed to match terror with terror. Quotas set how many hostages or other available victims were to be shot for each assault on members of the occupation forces. On 5 December 1943, for example, men of 117 Jg.Div. took fifty hostages at the village of Andritsa in reprisal for an attack on a railway guardpost and hanged them along the track. Three days later, news that other German soldiers had been killed led 117 Jg.Division's commander to issue instructions "to kill the male population and burn villages" in the area where his men had been found dead.[64] Civilian men, particularly of an age to bear arms, were regarded as suitable targets, and formed the majority of victims. Male villagers were often killed on the spot, without interrogation or trial. It was uncommon, but by no means unheard-of, for the entire male population of a village to be shot if the quota system demanded it.

What *was* rare was for action to be taken against women or children en masse. In Serbia in the winter of 1941–42, it had been officers' reluctance to use troops to shoot Jewish women and children, after their menfolk had all been shot, which led to the first use of gas vans. On the Eastern front, some soldiers had similar qualms. In August 1941, one divisional officer was reprimanded for reminding his men that their "decent, soldierly sentiment" *(saubere soldatische Gesinnung)* precluded "force and brutality" *(Gewalt und Roheit)* being used against an unarmed population: action against women and children was no different from the cruelties practiced by their enemy.[65]

In Greece, where the racial contempt displayed by the Germans was not as strong as it was in the East, atrocities such as that at Komeno occurred seldom during the occupation. Villages German troops passed through were usually abandoned by the male population, who left their women, children, and the elderly behind—the obvious implication being that these groups were thought to be safe. One Komeno survivor recalled: "My husband at that time was sleeping in the fields. My daughter was there with him. He told her to go back to the village—he would go and hide just in case the Germans started arresting all the men. How were we to know that they would be shooting at women and children as well?" Her words echo those of Rudolf L., who took part in the massacre. Explaining the troops' subsequent disquiet, he said: "We were all clear about this, that one could not call women and children 'the enemy'; this operation was especially condemned by the soldiers because old people, women and children were shot."[66]

Conceptions of military honor and the Nazi image of woman as a passive creature of the private rather than the public sphere, together produced a reluctance to regard women as legitimate targets. Even Hitler, in the conversation with Jodl cited earlier, *assumed* that women and children were innocent; he simply insisted—as did Lt. Röser—that the Landser should not be affected by such considerations. Conversely, the idea of a woman soldier had something unnatural about it.[67]

Women resistance fighters were a monstrous phenomenon, part of a policy of *deceit*, designed deliberately to take advantage of the "humanitarian instincts" of the German soldier.[68]

We have already seen how a sense of honor was implicit in the reprisal policy. The guerrillas themselves were "unworthy" opponents, relying on stealth and surprise rather than honest open combat. The closest student of this grim subject concludes that "in ordering [reprisals], German commanders believed that they were not transgressing their soldier's code of morality, but defending it from the forces of barbarism."[69]

If so, then the reasoning which justified reprisals in response to attacks on German soldiers also precluded—or at least increased the inhibitions against—including women in the range of victims. The divisional chaplain, we should recall, had specifically alluded to the "mass killing of women and children" as reasons for the psychological problems which the troops were reporting.[70]

There was therefore a conflict between the philosophy of unconstrained violence against the "total enemy" and the belief of at least some of the troops that they were fighting in accordance with "soldierly principles."

This was closely related to another issue: the question of cruelty. Several soldiers asserted that what especially shocked them at Komeno were the signs of wanton cruelty—such as the deliberate mutilation of bodies—which they had observed. August S. "had not known till this point that there were sadists in 12 Co." He was appalled that "some soldiers made fun of the corpses and cracked jokes." When Karl D. was "sickened by the atrocities *(Grausamkeiten)*" it was not the killings themselves he was objecting to, but the manner in which they had been carried out. The attitude implicit in such comments was exemplified in a postwar decision not to prosecute an officer for the shooting of civilians because it could not be proved that he had done so "maliciously."[71]

Physical mutilation and deliberate cruelty were invariably charges Germans laid at the door of the guerrillas; they, on the other hand—or so they wanted to believe—were motivated by purely impersonal considerations. "Malice," "deceit," and a lack of self-control were incompatible with the nobility of the soldier's role.[72]

Two further considerations may also have worried the men of 12 Co. The first was that in approaching the village at dawn, on foot, and bursting into houses whose inhabitants were still asleep, they too—like the guerrillas whose tactics they despised—had used surprise and stealth against their target. This was hardly a "manly" form of warfare. The second was even more unsettling: was it true, as they had been told, that this was a guerrilla stronghold where German soldiers had been shot and killed? Observing the lack of any resistance from the inhabitants and the evident lack of weaponry in the village—confirmed in the subsequent troop report, there must have been those who, like Franz T. believed that "it had been nothing other than a "plundering expedition" *(Raubzug)* under the pretense that it was a *Vergeltungsaktion*."[73]

In these very words, however, the powerful influence of National Socialism on popular attitudes among the rank and file lies revealed. By demonstrating how much he and his fellow soldiers took to be justified, Franz T. marked the boundary of what they regarded as acceptable violence. For the men of 12 Co., the Sühnemassnahmen and Vergeltungsaktion were morally defensible categories of action and their unease after Komeno lay in the suspicion that what they had done lay outside them.

V

Ernst Fraenkel observed in 1941 that "the identification of law and morality in the Third Reich has resulted in the assimilation of morality to National Socialist law." He argued that the persistent pressure of National Socialist radicalism had pushed outward the boundaries of what would be condoned by society generally. There was no contradiction between the brutality of the Nazi regime and its reputation as the "guarantor of public decency and of law and order": on the contrary, that very image permitted its troops to justify many of their most brutal actions.[74]

Appreciating the extent to which violence had been "legalized" for the sake of the *Volksgemeinschaft* in the prewar Reich gives us a way of explaining how the troops conceived of their task against the Balkan resistance. "The National Socialist revolution," according to Hitler in a prewar speech, "provided law, jurisprudence, and the administration of law with an unambiguous basis. Their task is the maintenance and protection of the people against anti-social groups who desire to evade or who otherwise fail to fulfill all obligations required by the community."[75]

From 1941 onwards, the insurgents of the Balkans were viewed in similar terms to those earlier "anti-social groups."

The vocabulary of social deviance in the prewar Reich was now employed in a new context. A staff officer in Athens noted that the guerrillas included "numerous rootless characters who would not have found a position even under normal living conditions." From the Peloponnese, 117 Jg.Div. reported that "the bands are recruiting ... chiefly from gangsters from the large cities." Ordinary soldiers talked unselfconsciously of executing "delinquents" and "death-worthy criminals," when they were referring to the civilian victims of reprisal killings. Greek civilians were routinely reported to have been "shot in flight"—the same euphemistic formula which had become familiar in the Third Reich itself. Leutnant P., a young company commander in the Peloponnese, cynically educated his men in the correct terminology at the expense of a captured young Greek civilian: "Look, this is what you do. Give him a kick on the backside ... and now shoot him, so that he's 'shot in flight.'"[76]

The equation of insurgency with criminality received widespread acceptance in the ranks. It is no coincidence that the strongest resistance came from soldiers who had been marginal and alienated figures in the Reich itself—like men of the 999 Punishment Battalions, composed of ordinary criminals and political prisoners. Many of the 999ers who served in Greece were at least ten years older than the average conscript, and one-time socialists or communists. G., an inmate of Buchenwald from 1939 to 1943, recalled his reaction upon hearing that his unit had been assigned to Greece: "When we heard about punitive expeditions against the old men and children in the surrounding villages, where the entire male population was shot in front of the women who had been driven together with rifle butts, an enormous bitterness overwhelmed us at the thought that we too would have to take part in such operations." Prompted by such feelings, G. and several friends deserted to the guerrillas after several weeks. But while desertion plagued the 999 Battalions, it was remarkably infrequent in other Wehrmacht units. Soldiers in 12 Co., we should recall, considered deserting in the wake of Komeno, but finally turned down the idea.[77]

The Landsers of 1 Geb.Div. were neither disaffected antagonists of the regime, like the 999ers, nor Nazi fanatics. Considerations of justice, morality, and military honor mingled with widely accepted notions of racial inferiority and social deviance in their attitudes toward reprisals. "The Germans are very harsh," a Greek novelist noted in his diary on 26 September 1943, "but their harshness does not stem from hatred. It is cold and mechanical, the result of applying a given formula which aims at fulfilling a goal they believe in."[78]

If many Wehrmacht conscripts did not share the regime's belief in the transformational power of violence, its part in creating a "new man," they accepted "legal" justifications for a policy of extended brutality against the civilian populations under their control, and did so, for the most part, with few qualms about the rightness of their actions. Only occasionally, when the aggression of their officers pushed them further than they wanted to go, as at Komeno, do we see those qualms rise to the surface. The conscripts' attitude toward the war was perhaps less single-minded than that of the officer corps, and it left some space for dissent. But officers and men had enough in common to allow the Wehrmacht to maintain a remarkable degree of cohesion in a war of unparalleled brutality.

Notes

*Reprinted with permission from *Past and Present* 134 (1992): 129–158. Earlier versions of this article were read to seminars at the City University of New York and the Davis Center, Princeton University. Thanks are due to Harry Psomiades and Lawrence Stone for inviting me, and to the members of the seminars for their comments. I also want to thank David Alberman, Omer Bartov, Gary Gerstle, Felix Gilbert, Arno Mayer, Ben Mazower, Reid Mitchell, and especially Stephen Kotkin for their help and advice.

1. Zentrale Stelle für Landesjustizverwaltungen, Ludwigsburg (hereafter Z.St.), AR 1462/68, 1543–1544 (affidavit of Karl S.). In all references to this archive the name of the person whose testimony is quoted will be given in parentheses.
2. Ibid., 79 (Otto G.).
3. Ibid., 43 (Karl D.), 58–59 (Johann E.), 164–165 (August S.), 182 (Franz T.).
4. National Archives, Washington, D.C. (hereafter N.A.), Records of German Field Commands (hereafter G.F.C.) (Divisions), T-315/72/1259 (microfilm), Evang. Div. Pfarrer, 1 Geb.Div., to 1 Geb. Div/1b, "Tätigkeitsbericht für die Zeit vom 21.6–30.9.43," 20 July 1989.
5. Z.St.,AR 1462/68, 76–77 (Otto G.), 164 (August S.); ibid., 169, Landergicht München I, "Ermittlungsverfahren," 8 June 1972.
6. The phrase is from G. Reitlinger, *The SS: Alibi of a Nation* (London: 1956).
7. R. J. Evans, *In Hitler's Shadow* (London: 1989), 55–56
8. C. Browning, "Wehrmacht Reprisal Policy and the Mass Murder of Jews in Serbia," in *Militargeschichtliche Mitteilungen* xxxiii (1983): 31–49; G. Hirschfeld, ed., *The Policies of Genocide* (London: 1986); M. Messerschmidt, *Die Wehrmacht im NS–Staat: Zeit der Indoktrination* (Hamburg: 1969); O. Bartov, *The Eastern Front, 1941–1945: German Troops and the Barbarisation of Warfare* (London, New York: 1986).
9. D. Peukert, *Everyday Life in the Third Reich* (London: 1987); I. Kershaw, *The "Hitler Myth"* (Oxford: 1989); R. Mann, *Protest und Kontrolle im Dritten Reich* (Frankfurt: 1987); cf. G. Eley, "Labor History, Social History, *Alltagsgeschichte*:

Experience, Culture and the Politics of the Everyday—A New Direction for German History?" in *Jl. Mid. Hist.*, lxi (1989): 297–344; Dick Geary, "Image and Reality in Hitler's Germany," in *European Hist. Quart.*, xix (1989): 385–389; on denunciation, see R. Gellately, "The Gestapo and German Society: Political Denunciation in the Gestapo Case Files," in *Jl. Mod. Hist.*, lx (1988): 654–695; R. Gellately, *The Gestapo and German Society: Enforcing Racial Policy, 1933–1945* (Oxford: 1990).

10. See Eley, "Labor History, Social History, *Alltagsgeschichte*," 316–317, 323; Eve Rosenhaft, "History, Anthropology and the Study of Everyday Life," *Comp. Studies in Society and Hist.*, xxxix (1987): 99–105. In this respect, *Alltagsgeschichte* may be seen as a reaction to the previously dominant psychologistic model of explaining individual behavior in the Third Reich. See G. M. Gilbert, *Psychology of Dictatorship* (New York: 1950); T. W. Adorno et al., *The Authoritarian Personality* (New York: 1950). The limitations of this approach are apparent in P. H. Merkl, *Political Violence under the Swastika: 581 Early Nazis* (Princeton: 1975), 446–552 (esp. 532ff., "As the Leaders So the Men").
11. H.-P. Klausch, *Die 999er* (Frankfurt: 1986); T. J. Schulte, *The German Army and Nazi Policies in Occupied Russia* (Oxford: 1989).
12. The phrase, referring to the Werhmacht as a whole is from C. W. Sydnor, *Soldiers of Destruction: The SS Death's Head Division, 1933–1945* (Princeton: 1977), 346; Bartov, *Eastern Front,* passim; cf. M. van Creveld, *Fighting Power: German and US Army Performance, 1939–1945* (Westport: 1982).
13. Kershaw, *"Hitler Myth,"*1f.
14. Ibid., 169–227, esp. 209–210.
15. I. Kershaw, *Popular Opinion and Political Dissent in the Third Reich* (Oxford: 1983).
16. Schulte, *German Army and Nazi Policies*, 149.
17. Bartov, *Eastern Front,* passim; H. Mommsen, "Kriegserfahrungen," in U. Borsdorf and M. Janin, eds., *Über Leben im Kriege* (Reinbeck b. Hamburg: 1989), 13.
18. L. Craig, "German Defensive Policy in the Balkans, a Case Study: The Build Up in Greece, 1943," in *Balkan Studies* xxiii (1982): 403–420; J. Hondros, *Occupation and Resistance* (New York: 1983), 85–90; N.A., Rear Area Commands (hereafter R.A.C.), T-501/330/959, "Kriegstagebuch [hereafter KTB], Deutscher Generalstab b. ital. 11 A.O.K.," 5–7 August 1943; T-501/331/212-13, Deutsch. Gen. Stab. b. ital. 11 A.O.K./1a to O.B. Sudost/1a, "Tagesmeldung vom 13.8.43."
19. Interview with Alexandros Mallios, Komeno, 18 March 1988 (I am very grateful to Mr. and Mrs. Mallios for their assistance; N.A., Records of U.S. Nuremberg War Crimes Trial (hereafter War Crimes), U.S. v List et al., M-893/4/168-88, S. Pappas aff., 17 August 1947. German documents confirm both the sighting of guerrillas and the absence of shooting or casualties: N.A., G.F.C. (Div.), T-315/2305/1549, 1 Geb.Div./1c to Deutsch. Gen Stab. b. ital. 11 A.O.K., "Tagesmeldung," 12 August 1943; T-315/64/317, 1 Geb.Div., KTB, 12 August 1943.
20. Institut für Zeitgeschichte, Munich (hereafter I.Z.), Nuremberg Trials Coll., NOKW-155, 10 August 1943; a new *Führerbefehl* had been issued to the troops on 8 August 1943: N.A., G.F.C. (Div.), T-315/65/741, Deutsch. Gen. Stab. B. ital. 11 A.O.K./1a to 1 Geb.Div./1a, 8 August 1943.
21. Z.St., AR 1462/68, 53 (August E.), 105–107 (Hans K.).
22. Benaki Museum, Athens, Archive of Heraklis Petimezas, file 5, Zervas to Allied Forces H.Q./Middle East, 21 August 1943; *Apoyevmatini*, 1 August 1961

(Zervas' diary entry on Komeno). For further details of the Axis chain of command at this time, see M. Mazower, "Waldheim Goes to War," *London Rev. Books*, 26 June 1988.

23. R. C Fattig, "Reprisal: The German Army and the Execution of Hostages during the Second World War" (Univ. of California, San Diego, Ph.D. diss., 1980), ch. 1.
24. *Trial of War Criminals before the Nuremberg Military Tribunal* (hereafter *T.W.C.*), 15 vols. (Washington, D.C.: 1951–52), 11: 799.
25. A. Mayer, *Why Did the Heavens Not Darken?* (New York: 1988), 210; Browning, "Wehrmacht Reprisal Policy."
26. Browning, "Wehrmacht Reprisal Policy," 34–35; we might add a lack of training in dealing with irregular warfare: cf. the admission of one of List's subordinates in Serbia, Lt. Gen. Friedrich Stahl, that "during my thirty-eight years in a military career I was never trained in the combating of partisans ... from a military tactical point of view we were not equal to the partisan situation": N.A., T-1119/23/0227. On the massacres in Macedonia, see N.A., G.F.C. (Div.), T-315/1474/496-8, 164 ID/1a, 20 October 1941; Imperial War Museum, London (hereafter I.W.M.), box 349/FO 646, "Case VII: Hostages," Prosecution Document Book 2, NOKW-1380: 164 ID reported that it had shot 207 males aged between sixteen and sixty on 17 October, 142 on 23 October, and 67 on 25 October 1941.
27. The links between economic collapse, the delegitimation of the existing state apparatus, and resistance are illuminated by S. B. Thomadakis, "Black Markets, Inflation and Force in the Economy of Occupied Greece," in J. Iatrides, ed., *Greece in the 1940s: A Nation in Crisis* (Hanover, N.H.: 1981), 61–81; for a sociological account of the process in a similar context, see J. Gross, *Polish Society under German Occupation* (Princeton: 1979).
28. Browning, "Wehrmacht Reprisal Policy," 40–41; H. Neubacher, *Sonderauftrag Südost: 1940–1945* (Göttingen: 1956); H. Fleischer, *Im Kreuzschatten der Mächte: Griechenland, 1941–1944* (Frankfurt: 1986), 372, 547; Hondros, *Occupation and Resistance*, 153–159; H. Safrian and W. Manoschek, "Österreicher in der Wehrmacht," in E. Hanisch et al., eds., *NS-Herrschaft in Österreich* (Vienna: 1988), 331–360.
29. After Kalavryta the commander of 117 Jg. Div. himself admitted that "we are on the wrong track": N.A., G.F.C. (Div.), T-315/1300/341-4, 117 Jg. Div./Komm., "Bandenbekämpfung," 20 December 1943; for the orders issued by General Löhr (commanding officer of Army Group E, based in Salonika), see *T.W.C.*, xi, 826, 1306–1307; on subsequent atrocities and the reaction of Hermann Neubacher, the senior diplomatic representative in Greece and leading advocate of a "political" approach, see esp. *Akten zur deutschen auswärtigen Politik*, ser. E, viii (Göttingen: 1979), Nr. 27, Neubacher to Foreign Ministry (Berlin), 15 May 1944; *Trial of the Major War Criminals before the International Military Tribunal* (hereafter *T.M.W.C.*), 42 vols. (Nuremberg: 1947–49), 38:452–458.
30. N.A., G.F.C. (Div.), T-315/65/747, Gen Kdo. 26 A.K./1a to 1 Geb.Div./1a, 29 August 1943; see also R. E. Herzstein, *Waldheim: The Missing Years* (New York: 1988), 95–98; J. Steinberg, *All or Nothing: The Axis and the Holocaust, 1941–43* (London: 1990), 15–50. The most useful source for the comparative dimension is R. B. Asprey, *War in the Shadows: The Guerilla in History*, 2 vols. (New York: 1975), 1:passim.
31. I.Z.,1043/53, H.Gr. "E" 1c/AO, "Feindnachrichtenblatt (Griechische Banden), nr. 9: April/Mai 1944," 9.

32. For a typical example of such a conflict, see M. Fellman, *Inside War: The Guerilla Conflict in Missouri during the American Civil War* (New York: 1989), 112–116, 171.
33. On Hitler's World War I experiences, see J. Keegan, *The Mask of Command* (New York: 1987), 243–258; also important are E. J. Leed, *No Man's Land: Combat and Identity in World War I* (Cambridge: 1981); A. E. Ashworth, *"The Sociology of Trench Warfare, 1914–1918," in Brit. Jl. Sociol.*, xix (1968): 407–424; Merkl, *Political Violence under the Swastika*, 138–230; *Nazism: A History in Documents and Eyewitness Accounts: 1919–1945*, ed. J. Noakes and G. Pridham, 2 vols. (New York: 1988), 2: 941.
34. Hitlers *Lagebesprechungen*, ed. H. Heiber (Stuttgart: 1962), 67–68; on the clash between reformers and Hitler over the partisan question, see also T. Mulligan, *The Politics of Illusion and Empire: German Occupation Policy in the Soviet Union, 1942–1943* (New York: 1988), 139; see also Fattig, "Reprisal," 45–47; 62–68; cf H.D. Betz, *Das OKW und seine Haltung zum Landkriegsvölkerrecht* (Würzburg: 1970); on Röser's instructions, see Z.St., AR 1462/68, 163 (August S.).
35. M. Cooper, *The Nazi War Against Soviet Partisans: 1941–1944* (New York: 1979), 80–81; N.A., G.F.C. (Div.), T-315/65/741, Deutsch. Gen Stab b. ital. 11 A.O.K./1a to 1 Geb.Div./1a, 8 August 1943.
36. N.A., G.F.C. (Armies), T-312/465/8053722, Obfh. 12 Armee/1a, "Richtlinien für die Behandlung der Aufständischen in Serbien und Kroatien," 19 March 1942.
37. *Nazi Conspiracy and Aggression*, 10 vols. (Washington, D.C.: 1946), 7:D–740.
38. N.A., War Crimes, M-893/4/217, 1 Pz. Div., KTB, 23 August 1943; M-893/4/236, 68 A.K., KTB, 24 August 1943; R.A.C., T-501/331/436, 68 A.K./1c, "Lagebeurteilung," 18 July 1943.
39. N.A., R.A.C., T-501/331/442, 68 A.K./1c, "Lagebericht," 4 September 1943; War Crimes, M-893/4/222 (n.d., probably autumn 1943).
40. Bartov, *Eastern Front*, 40
41. The commander of 164 Inf. Div instructed his junior officers along these lines: N.A., G.F.C. (Div.), T-315/1474/462-6, 164 ID/1a, "Offizierbesprechung des Herrn Div.-Kommandeurs in Saloniki am 24.9.41 17.00 Uhr," 28 September 1941; cf. the instructions of the commander of 117 Jg. Div., T-315/1299 /1051-3, 117 Jg. Div./Komm., "Dienstaufsicht," 18 September 1943.
42. Z.St., AR 2056/67, 169, Landgericht München I, 1971.
43. *T.M.W.C.*, xxxviii, 425–428; Z.St., AR 12/62, vii, 314 (Werner S.), 357 (F. Husemann); Z.St., 301/J-VÜ5 (Staatsgericht Koblenz, 1 Js 3496/52); Berlin Document Center (hereafter B.D.C.), personal files of Georg Weichenrieder, Fritz Lautenbach.
44. S. J. Mitcham, *Hitler's Field Marshals and Their Battles* (London: 1989), 339–355; H. Lanz, *Gebirgsjäger* (Bad Nauheim: 1954), 304–331; E. Kernmayr, *Generalfeldmarschall Ferdinand Schörner* (Ohlendorf: 1976); Messerschmidt, *Wehrmacht im NS–Staat*, 379–382.
45. Letter to author from Herr S., 18 April 1989; N.A., G.F.C. (Div.), T-315/65/787, 1 Geb.Div./1a, 7 August 1943.
46. I.W.M., box 345/FO 646, "Case VII: Hostages," Defense Document Book 1, affidavit of G. Lipp, 12 July 1947; ibid., Defense Document Book 5, affidavit of H. Groth, 29 October 1947; letter to author from Herr S., 18 April 1989; letter to author from Herr K., 13 March 1990.
47. Letter to author from Herr K., 13 March 1990.

48. N.A., G.F.C. (Div.), T-315/65/359, G.J.R. 98/Komm., "Bericht über die Säuberung vom 22–26.7.1943."
49. Ibid., T-315/64/284, 1 Geb.Div., KTB, 18 July 1943; T-315/69/1248, Salminger to von Stettner, 24 July 1943.
50. Z.St., AR 1462/68, 57 (August E.), 130–133 (Ferdinand P.); letter to author from Herr K., 13 March 1990; on the need for the company commander to win the "love" of his subordinates through his "selflessness" and "vigorous and cheerful" bearing, see N.A., G.F.C. (Div.), T-315/2275/598-601, Sturmdivision Rhodos/1c, "Divisions-Betreuungs-Befehl Nr. 2," 15 December 1943; T-315/1299/1051-4, 117 Jg, Div./Komm., "Dienstaufsicht," 18 September 1943; B.D.C., personal file of Fritz Lautenbach.
51. See the affidavit of Otto G.: "When in my account of the reprisal action (*Vergeltungsaktion*) I make mistakes about certain important details—e.g., who was in command, who gave the orders—I hope you will bear in mind that I was just a 'little man,' then only a private, with no overview of the whole action. I was there and saw certain things which I can describe, nothing more": Z.St., 1462/68, 77.
52. N.A.,G.F.C. (Div.), T-315/64/57, Evang. Div. Pfarrer, I Geb.Div., to 1 Geb.Div./Ib, "Tätigkeitsbericht für die Zeit vom 9.4–30.6.43," 2 July 1943.
53. The idea of a religious war is in Bartov, *Eastern Front*, 104; at the opposite extreme is Schulte, *German Army and Nazi Policies,* passim.
54. N.A.,G.F.C. (Div), T-315/1299/352-9, 117 Jg. Div./1a, "Besprechung am 28/4 beim Befehlshaber Südgriechenland." The subject of military psychology in the Third Reich needs further exploration. The regime was unable to make up its mind whether brutality was desirable or not. The passage above should be contrasted with the judgment of an SS tribunal against SS Untersturmführer Max Täubner, held in May 1943, which criticized him for the "inner brutalization" (*innere Verrohung*) which had led him to acts of cruelty in the course of his duties: *"Schöne Zeiten": Judenmord aus der Sicht der Täter und Gaffer*, ed. E. Klee, W. Dreysen, and V. Reiss (Frankfurt: 1988), 189; cf. ibid., 14–15.
55. N.A., G.F.C. (Div.), T-315/1299/361, 117 Jg. Div/1a, "Besprechung am 28/4 beim Befehlshaber Südgriechenland."
56. N.A., Historical Division European command (Foreign Military Studies Branch), Record Group 338 (hereafter R.G. 338), H. Lanz, "Partisan Warfare in the Balkans," MS. P-055a, 8, 10; ibid., introduction by Hans V. Greiffenberg, 8; see also *T.W.C.*,1:890–892, 1056. On the treatment of German P.O.W.s, see I.W.M., box 343/FO 646, affidavit of Erhard Glitz, 13 October 1947, where incongruous anti-Semitic overtones are obvious; N.A., War Dept./ 7th Army Interrogation Center, R.G. 165/179, box 651, "Interrogation Report on 5 German POWs." The study of the ways in which soldiers form stereotypes of their enemy is a vast subject in itself; there was nothing unique about the Wehrmacht in this regard. See J. W. Dower, *War without Mercy: Race and Power in the Pacific War* (New York: 1986); C. Thorne, "Racial Aspects of the Far Eastern War of 1941–1945," in *Proc. Brit. Acad.* 26 (1980): 329–377.
57. Public Record Office, London (hereafter P.R.O.), War Office files, WO 204/8869, "Report by Lt.-Col. R.P. McMullen on Present Conditions in the Peloponnese," 15 February 1944; E.L.A.S. (Greek Popular Liberation Army) pamphlet from the collection of the late Arthur Wickstead (former member of the British Military Mission to Greece). I remember him with gratitude for his assistance.
58. N.A.,G.F.C (Army Groups), T-311/179/1266-8, Feldkommandantur 1042/Peloponnes, 1c, "Lagebericht," 31 December 1943; I.W.M., box 350/FO 646,

"Case VII; Hostages," Prosecution Book 12, NOKW-1079, Löhr to 1 Pz. Div/1a, 14 July 1943; Klausch, *999er*, 138–40.

59. The conflict between "traditional" and National Socialist views of the soldier emerged in the directives issued in the course of "Barbarossa." Senior Wehrmacht generals, notably von Reichenau and Manstein, had directed the troops that beyond the imperatives of *Soldatentum* and the rules of war they should regard the soldier as "the carrier of an inexorable racial conception and the avenger of all the bestialities which have been committed against Germany": C. Streit, *Keine Kameraden* (Stuttgart: 1978), 115–117.
60. N.A., G.F.C. (Div.), T-315/1474/572, 164 ID/1c, "Weltanschauliche Erziehung and geistige Betreuung," 6 November 1941.
61. On the symbolism of mountains, see George Mosse, "War and the Appropriation of Nature," in V. Berghahn and M. Kitchen, eds., *Germany in the Age of Total War* (London: 1981), 102–122; see also S. Kracauer, *From Caligari to Hitler: A Psychological History of the German Film* (Princeton: 1974, first pub. 1947), 110–112, 257–263.
62. See Kracauer's revealing remarks on the film *Berge in Flammen* (1931), whose cameraman, Sepp Allgeier, would later shoot the opening sequence in *Triumph des Willens*. *Berge in Flammen* opens with an Austrian and an Italian officer on a mountain excursion together just before the outbreak of World War I. Kracauer comments: "Friendship between soldiers of different countries in the lulls of peace does not weaken the friends' determination to fight each other in wartime; rather, it ennobles this fight, transforming it into a tragic duty, a superior sacrifice. [This] mountain climber is the type of man on whom regimes in need of war can rely": Kracauer, *From Caligari to Hitler*, 26. Similar sentiments are revealed in issues of the current ex-servicemen's journal, *Die Gebirgstruppe*.
63. N.A., War Crimes, M-893/17/669, Obfh. Südost to OKW/WFSt., 2 July 1943; NOKW-921, 1 Geb.Div., KTB, 24–26 July 1943: Z.St., AR 1462/68, 59 (August E.).
64. N.A., G.F.C. (Div.). T-315/1300/63-5, 117 Jg. Div./1a, "Tätigkeitsbericht."
65. C. Browning, *Fateful Months: Essays in the Emergence of the Final Solution* (New York: 1985); "*Schöne Zeiten*," 142, 144.
66. Interview with Eleni Pappas, Athens, 15 February 1988; Z.St., AR 2415/67, 119–120 (Rudolf L.).
67. The O.K.W. blocked suggestions that women should be brought into the armed forces with the argument that "the 'female soldier' is incompatible with our National Socialist conception of womanhood": M. Steinert, *Hitler's War and the Germans: Public Mood and Attitude during the Second World War*, ed. and trans. T. de Witt (Athens, Ohio: 1977), 280; cf. Bartov, *Eastern Front*, 126–129; J. Stephenson, *The Nazi Organization of Women* (London: 1981), esp. ch. 5.
68. I.W.M., box 352/FO 646, Prosecution Book 21, NOKW-467, SS-Pz. Gren. Rgt./Komm. to 68 A.K./Komm., "Vorgänge in Distomon am 10.6.1944," 21 July 1944; Bartov, *Eastern Front*, 126–128.
69. Fattig, "Reprisal," 221; cf. M. Walzer, *Just and Unjust Wars* (New York: 1977), 207–216
70. N.A., G.F.C. (Div.), T-315/72/1259 (see above, note 3); cf. Schulte, *German Army and Nazi Policies*, 144, 164–170.
71. Z.St., AR 1462/68, 164 (August S.), 43 (Karl D.); AR 1187/68, 21, Staatsgericht München, "Ermittlungsverfahren gegen Blume u.a.," 1972.

72. Military judges in the SS were capable of making similar, though even finer distinctions, e.g., between "sadism" and "genuine Jew-hatred" (*wirklichem Judenhass*): see "*Schöne Zeiten*," 184–191.
73. Z.St., 1462/68, 182 (Franz T.); cf. Schulte, *German Army and Nazi Policies*, 144.
74. E. Fraenkel, *The Dual State* (New York: 1941), 110–111; Kershaw has shown how an aspect of the "Hitler myth" was the belief that the Führer condoned only "lawful, rational action": I. Kershaw, "Hitler and the Germans," in R. Bessel, ed., *Life in the Third Reich* (Oxford: 1987), 51; Peukert, *Everyday Life in the Third Reich*, 197–200; also important in this connection is James J. Weingartner, "Law and Justice in the Nazi SS: The Case of Konrad Morgen," *Central European Hist.*, xvi (1983): 276–295, which notes on page 276 that "duality did not imply balance, however, for law survived largely as a discretionary tool of total power." Bessel refers to the contradiction between brutality and the image of law and order in his introduction to Bessel, ed., *Life in the Third Reich*, 19.
75. Fraenkel, *Dual State*, 108; for an account of the use made by the Wehrmacht of the concept of the *Volksgemeinschaft*, see M. Messerschmidt, "The Wehrmacht and the *Volksgemeinschaft*," *Jl. Contemporary Hist.*, xviii (1983): 719–744. Emphasizing the army's role in this task, Hitler's speech on Heroes' Memorial Day in April 1940, later distributed to the troops, ended with the reminder that "our will is the National Socialist *Volksgemeinshaft*." As Messerschmidt has shown, this concept came to provide the basis for military law, too: O. Bartov, "Indoctrination and Motivation in the Wehrmacht: The Importance of the Unquantifiable," *Jl. Strategic Studies*, ix (1986): 16–34; M. Messerschmidt, "German Military Law in the Second World War," in W. Diest, ed., *The German Military in the Age of Total War* (Leamington Spa: 1985), 325.
76. I.W.M., box 343/FO 646 Defense Document Book 2, affidavit of G. Kleykamp 25 October 1947; N.A., G.F.C. (Div.), T-315/1300/378, Kampfgruppe Glitz, "Abschlussbericht," 18 December 1943; Z.St., AR 12/62, vii, 68 (Walter V.); Col. Salminger and 98 G.J.R. reported "87 suspects shot in flight" on 4 July 1943: N.A., War Crimes, M-893/17/671. On Leutnant P., as remembered by a witness, see Z.St., AR 2056/67, 110–113 (Alois W.).
77. Wiener Lib., London, PIII, g. 470: "Interview with non-Jewish ISK member," 26 October 1955; N.A., G.F.C. (Div.), T-315/1300/260-1, Festungs-Regt.965, "Meldung vom 1. Dez. 1943"; other testimonies are to be found in R.G. 165/179, boxes 650-1; Klausch, *999er*, passim.
78. G. Theotokas, *Tetradia imerologiou (1939–1953)* (Diary Notebooks [1939–1953]) (Athens: n.d.), 443.

– *Chapter 8* –

CIVITELLA DELLA CHIANA ON 29 JUNE 1944

*The Reconstruction of a German "Measure"**

Michael Geyer

Rigorous action and rapid, draconian measures must be taken.[1]

I

When the men of Civitella at the edge of the Chiana valley and the surrounding area set out for early morning mass on the feast day of St. Peter and Paul, they did not think they would be the subject of academic discussions half a century later. This also applied to those who for some reason or another remained at home. For apart from the kind of farmer or farm hand who always find something to do when it comes to going to mass, there were also Fascists, Communists, and Jews in Civitella who would not be found in church on a Catholic feast day. That in 1944 they all lived in one village and that they all died together distinguishes the Italian situation in 1944.

Under the prevailing circumstances, it made no difference that the Civitellini had been taking precautions. Following what all sides agreed was an unwished-for incident, on 18 June, in the Dopo-Lavoro Club in Civitella in which two German soldiers were killed and a third was wounded the men of the town had hidden in

Notes for this section begin on page 208.

the woods or carried themselves very carefully. After more than a week of this and after a German unit had been through the town on 20 June the danger of German "measures" appeared to have faded. The Germans were generally known to react quickly so that one could believe Civitella had been spared. The village was, in spite of the shooting, certainly not conspicuous for its support of the partisans. In fact, one rather would want to assert the opposite—and the women of Civitella demonstrated their caution and concern and, possibly, their empathy when on 19 June they paid their respects to the dead German soldiers at the cemetery. Still, as of the evening of 29 June 1944, the men of Civitella were dead.[2]

On the morning of that day, German soldiers encircled the town as well as the surrounding villages. They searched the houses and shot many of the men on the spot, some before the eyes of their wives and children. The soldiers drove the surviving men to the church square. Meanwhile, those who were attending mass were cleared out of the church and divided by sex and age. The soldiers forced the women and children out of town in the direction of Poggiali where some of them found shelter in an orphanage. Another group fled to friends and relatives in the countryside. The men were then lined up sideways in groups of five along the city wall and shot. One young man escaped, while another survived the massacre. One German soldier may have refused to take part in the reprisal and, according to local lore, was shot as well—a fact that historians, however, doubt.[3] Following the action in Civitella, German soldiers combed through the villages of Burrone, Cornia, Gebbia, and San Pancrazio along with the surrounding farmsteads, apparently with Italian support. In San Pancrazio and Gebbia they proceeded as in Civitella. The men were separated from the women and children, led together to an area, and individually shot in the neck. Unlike in Civitella, though, the soldiers selected a small group of men and women whom they took along to Monte San Savino for interrogation with the purpose of finding out information about the partisans. In Cornia, by contrast, the action devolved into a wild slaughter, with children and women being slain along with the men. In all these villages some houses as well as outlying farmsteads were plundered and all were lit ablaze.[4] At the end of the day, there were 212 victims of the German action of which 100 were from Civitella, 67 from San Pancrazio and 45 from Cornia, according to a British inquiry undertaken immediately after the liberation of Civitella. Local recollection puts the number murdered at around 250.

II

The executions left behind deep scars in local memory. Collective remembrance began to take shape immediately after the event with an English military commission conducting comprehensive interviews to investigate the background and origins of the massacre.[5] Moreover, the surviving widows' testimonies, from Civitella, were gathered and published by the novelist Romano Bilenchi in 1946 in Florence and later in *Les Temps modernes*.[6] From the beginning, therefore, the Civitella massacre had an international and literary public. Local memory rested on a dense network of stories that found support and permanence in local memorials to the dead.[7] This stream of local accounts and memories culminated in the fiftieth anniversary of the massacre, now with increasing attention from academics focused on the event, the result being both an international conference in Arezzo as well as moving local memorials, such as the premiere of an oratorio "Voices of Memory" in the church in Civitella, performed by the local choir.[8]

While it appears that a younger generation of Civitellini is now trying to create some distance from the events and would like to lead a "normal" life uninfluenced by the terror of 29 June 1944, one cannot say that this generation has forgotten the dead. The immediate impressions of the events have begun to fade, art and history taking on a more prominent role, but the dead of Civitella and the surrounding villages retain a presence in the town and the region.

One of the sore points of local memory has been the absence of a German record of the killings. This has become a source of conflict that continues to generate controversies after fifty years. For the question remains open: How could all of this have happened? How do we account for the German action? Local tradition has it that the guilt for the massacre must lie with the partisans who through their rash action in the Dopo-Lavoro Club brought "German death" to Civitella. This version derives from easily decipherable local tensions. The old, conservative-Catholic town of Civitella—high up on a mountain, a tourist's dream—controls local memory. The new city of Civitella resting in the valley below, however, dominates the postwar everyday, with a left-wing city government holding political power both in the city and in provincial government. The old Civitella has lost much of its influence to the surrounding industrial area in the valley. It has become a community for commuters and former inhabitants who return for vacations. It has lost its position as a magnet for the peasants in the surrounding area, although it still appears to be enough of a borough to control local memory. All of that can be glossed over at ceremonial occasions, but not in an unsettled and haunted memory which intertwines the past with the present. In that context, the local geography of power sets an official, highly public and, indeed, national cult of the *Resistenza* against the memorial of the dead which sees the partisans as the instigators and the main culprits of the massacre.

Quite apart from reflecting a distinct geography of power and memory, which both links Civitella to and separates it from the province and the nation, the charges against the partisans also appear to be an attempt to bring an otherwise incomprehensible act down to the only known entity, the partisans' action as the evident cause for the reprisal. Certainly, the Germans are present as the ultimate culprits, but they remain so ghostlike and foreign, their actions so unfathomable, that they are sooner recognized as death-dealing fate than as active perpetrators. The partisans, on the other hand, are part both of the local scene and of Italy and are the lightning rod for robust political conflict. While a full reconstruction of the German action and its reason cannot heal the wounds and while it will not solve these conflicts, it can help to make sense of a deed which brutally tore apart the communities of Civitella, Burrone, Gebbia, and San Pancrazio on 29 June 1944, leaving fissures of the mind and the body that remain to this day. History can place the massacre where it belongs: into the past to be recalled and commemorated in the present.

III

The effort to reconstruct the German side of the massacre encounters enormous difficulties because crucial German documentation is missing and the perpetrators have remained silent about the massacre. The most pertinent German records do not mention by name the incident in the Dopo-Lavoro Club on 18 June. Neither do they refer to a firefight between German soldiers and partisans in nearby Montaltuzzo on 23 June, which is taken as an aggravating factor on the way to the reprisal. Nor do they register the massacre on 29 June. Consequently, we must proceed like archaeologists who gather discrete and disparate traces of the past and assemble them in order to shed light on the circumstances and background of what we otherwise can only know from a haunted memory: the shooting of the men in Civitella and environs.

A so-called partisan map [*Bandenlagekarte*] of 30 June 1944, provides the first solid piece of evidence. Found among the papers of the 76th Panzer Corps' intelligence officer, this map shows a series of incidents and acts of sabotage in the hills between the Chiana and Tiber valleys.[9] Circles mark three partisan areas on the map. The smallest circle is drawn in the environs of Gubbio, which fell into the rear area of the 51st Mountain Army Corps, the military formation neighboring the 76th Panzer Corps, both together forming the 10th Army. There the map notes a "Garibaldi Band." Historians of the Italian resistence movement know this "band" as a very sizeable and militarily organized formation, but from the vantage point of the 76th Panzer Corps it was beyond their jurisdiction—hence, of only indirect and minor concern despite the actual significance of the formation. A second and larger circle veers around Poppi to the north of Arezzo and encompasses the entire western side of the Pratomagno mountains. With "4 band camps (1,000 men), 1 general, 1 colonel," this circle is defined much more precisely—which should be no surprise, because it falls within the rear of the 76th Panzer Corps. Finally, the largest, somewhat baggy, marking turns up west of Arezzo. It reaches from the main Arezzo-Florence road in the north to the Bucine-Monte San Savino road in the south and encompasses the villages of interest to us, though they are not actually named on the map. This large area is designated as a "band area." The map refers to a "G.M. 29.6," probably a combat report from this date.[10] Further, it makes notice of *V-Lager* (supply depot?) south of the Levane. Next to Levane we find the reference "cleared 28 June." Whether or not this remark applies to the entire area within this largest circle on the map remains as unclear as the significance of the statement. In any case, the map suggests that Civitella lay on the edge of an extended partisan area which was subject to some major action on 28/29 June. Whoever drew this map suggested that this area was quite as partisan infested as the ones around Poppi and Gubbio, although it should be noted that curiously there was no indication of any particular partisan formation, known to the intelligence officer of the 76th Panzer Corps, which was operating in the area.

The second piece of evidence is the War Diary of the intelligence officer of the 10th Army which suggests that the information was pushed up the chain of command. For 27 and 28 June, the War Diary reports: "The band situation continued to aggravate, particularly in the Arezzo area where the supply routes to the front were completely blocked off. Our operations were successful."[11] While it is unclear where these operations occur, it is reasonable to think that they fit the events which culminated with the massacre in Civitella. The partisan map along with this remark may be read to suggest that Civitella fell victim to a German "operation" against partisans in a heavily partisan-infested, if not partisan-controlled area. Not least, this interpretation is independently verified through British interviews with Italian witnesses. The latter reported that on 29 June the German soldiers set out to destroy a partisan center.[12]

A more wide ranging search of documents yields further traces of the events in Civitella. A map of the High Command Southwest detailing band activity for the period from 13 June through 24 June provides a more detailed picture of partisan incidents in and around Arezzo. Particularly noteworthy are partisan attacks south of Ambra on 17 June where one soldier was wounded. For the same day, the map noted "3 soldiers dead, 1 severely wounded" south of Arezzo and a "band attack" on 22 June.[13] In spite of the discrepancies, these references fit in general the Dopo-Lavoro incident on the one hand and the events near Montaltuzzo on the other, as local memory recalls them. If these are indeed the same events, the German record predates the events by a day and counts three rather than two soldiers as dead.

What do we make of this? Before we rush to any conclusions about the two incidents, we should wonder about German record-keeping. It is strange that a record of these two incidents cannot be found in the documents of the 76th Panzer Corps or, for that matter, in the War Diary of the 10th Army, in whose territory Civitella lay. How did the information get to the High Command Southwest without leaving a trace in the records of the 10th Army or the 76th Panzer Corps?

A consideration of the disposition of the German formations helps at this point. Civitella sat right on the western border of the 10th Army's operational area, adjacent to which lay the operational areas of the 14th Army. The latter was responsible for the entire area due west of the Chiana valley to the Adriatic Sea. The border running between the two armies allowed for certain overlaps, all the more since their main lines of movement diverged from one another. While the 14th Army wheeled northwest around the Siena-Florence axis, the 10th Army oriented itself in a northeasterly direction. This suggests that the information which entered the High Command map may well have come from the 14th rather than the 10th Army. And so it is. The War Diary of the 14th Army notes the two incidents. In fact, there is a quite detailed account of the incidents which, notwithstanding the noted discrepancies, may well refer to the partisan activities in Civitella and Montaltuzzo. In addition, there is other information which sheds some light on anti-partisan activities in the area. The 14th Army War Diary notes:

> On the morning of 20 June a band attacked an automobile carrying three soldiers on the road near Fattoria Palagio (3 km 68/01); one soldier was taken prisoner and the car was stolen.
>
> An operation was led immediately by the divisional medical doctor, Dr. Hox, which pushed north of San Martino, where it engaged a band of about 200 men, which attacked with grenade launchers, submachine guns, and machine pistols. In this engagement, the Assault Unit *[Kampfgruppe]* (34 men of Hospital Detachment 4) took 38 prisoners, and achieved 25 enemy dead with only one wounded on our side. 18 bandits were condemned according to martial law and hung, 4 bandit houses were burned down. Two bandits shouted before their deaths "Viva Russia." 8 bandits had identification papers from *Organisation Todt* and the *Transportflotte* Speer.
>
> On 17 June, north of S. Ambra (12 km south of Levane) a truck with men on the Arezzo-Florence road was fired upon from houses while departing a village and 2 soldiers were surrounded by bandits in the village. An assault unit from Hospital Detachment 4 under Paymaster Sonntag freed the surrounded soldiers, left one enemy dead and took a prisoner.
>
> *In a town near Arezzo (name [of town] not confirmable) 4 soldiers were attacked in an inn on the evening of 17 June. After a firefight, 3 of our soldiers were dead and 1 severely wounded.*[14]

The latter characterizes the incident in the Dopo-Lavoro Club, if our conjecture is right. It also provides us with some clues about the German rendition of the event. For one thing, it was considered to be a very serious incident. Three soldiers dead—this is more than occurred in most anti-partisan campaigns in the area, as we saw, and it is one of the gravest incidents noted on the High Command's map. However, in contrast to Civitella's local accounts which are familiar with every detail, the German documents give an overwhelming impression of distance from the events. Even the name of the town where the fatal shooting occurred was unknown. They were only clear on one point. German soldiers were killed and wounded.

There is no German record of an initial German reaction on 20 June, but the testimony gathered by the British military commission helps at this point. Witnesses report that on the evening of 20 June approximately one platoon of German soldiers drove to Civitella and collected the residents of the city on the square in front of the church. The significance of this action remains unclear. Perhaps a reprisal measure was planned, but was called off because the majority of Civitella's men were in hiding. Also, on 20 June the main concern still lay in getting hold of the partisans—and this is the more likely interpretation. While the response was delayed, the action was meant to ferret out partisans and to intimidate sympathizers.[15] Moreover, the Civitellini made a variety of overtures to local German authorities explaining their predicament. They also knew that something serious had happened in their town. But with all the exculpations and explanations and the good services of interlocutors, the Civitellini were misled or, more likely, misled themselves into believing that the worst was over, after the soldiers had departed on 20 June.

This said, we reach a certain impasse. Other leads prove to be less fruitful. There is a great deal of confusion about which divisional units the soldiers of 20 June belonged to. In the British interviews, a 14th Division, supposedly quartered in the vicinity of Arezzo, was repeatedly mentioned; yet, while there was a 14th Army, there was no 14th division—the next closest thing being the 114th Jäger Division and that lay further east in the territory of the 51st Mountain Corps. If the unit belonged to the 14th Army, it may have been an element of the 1st Paratroop Division which was shoved into the gap between 10th Army and 14th Army. There are several references to this division in local testimony. But obviously, this is not enough to identify the unit(s) which originated the massacre on 29 June. In the first action, on 20 June, all signs point to soldiers of the 1st Paratroop Division.[16] However, it seems prudent to separate the first action on 20 June from the second one on 29 June, both in terms of perpetrators and motivations.

Following the lead of the 14th Army War Diary, we should take notice of the firefight near San Martino/Ambra for its exemplary quality in terms of anti-partisan action. It was led by a medical doctor and 34 men and a paymaster in the second instance, both commanding groups of medics. This reflects German doctrine. Anyone —whether medic, paymaster, cook, or truck driver—could be used in counterattacks. If an assault group of medics was thrown into anti-partisan warfare, as German sources state matter-of-factly, an anti-partisan commando could have been carried out by any unit in the vicinity. Therefore, it is not to be rejected out of hand that elements of the Hospital Detachment, which were committed in Ambra, on 17 June, were involved in the massacre on 29 June. At a minimum, witness statements regarding the massacre in San Pancrazio establish that a truck or trucks of a hospital unit, designated as such by the Red Cross, were involved in the operation,[17] in what capacity we do not know. All we know is that Hospital Detachment 4 had been previously used to form an assault group and, hence, is not beyond suspicion, all the more since a Red Cross truck was seen at the scene.

All of this leaves us with a somewhat mixed record. While we gathered some useful information about German actions in the area, it remains unclear, within the limits of this particular documentation, how we get from simple recognition of the event to the action taken on 29 June. In order to approach the massacre yet more closely, it is useful to step back for a second and to reflect on what has transpired so far. Three things seem noteworthy. First, if the area west and north of Civitella was really a heavily partisan-infested area, as the map of the 76th Panzer Corps suggests, one begins to wonder about German actions in the area. To be sure, the German army was, at this point, prone to take "quick and rigorous action," which is to say that elements of all kinds of units were used to form assault groups. Therefore, while I am less concerned that medics were used for rapid response, it is worth noting that, from all we can gather, these groups (including the one that appeared in Civitella on 20 June) were small, lightly armed, and without backup. This is not what one expects from an "action" in a supposedly partisan-infested area. Second, the massacre in Civitella on 29 June was evidently a delayed action rather than an immediate response by an assault group to an incident. In contrast to the counter-measure at Ambra, there was no hot pursuit of a partisan band which had killed two (and according to the German record: three) German soldiers. At the very least, this suggests that the reprisal in Civitella was planned well in advance. One does begin to wonder, if the Civitellini were not, after all, set up.

Third, the German and Italian perception and plan of action differed radically. For the Civitellini the event unfolded seamlessly starting with the initial incident in the Dopo-Lavoro Club and culminating in the massacre of 29 June. It was (and remained) embedded in a local geography of power in which the partisans were as unwelcome as the fascists and the retreating Germans were the threat to watch and, if possible, to avert. In contrast, the German side lifted the incident out of its local context and re-configured it as part of a regional assessment of the partisan situation (as it was put down in the various partisan maps). The action then taken reflected guidelines and orders that pertained to the entire Italian theater of war. What mattered is not the Italian town, but the fact that two (three) German soldiers were killed. The distance between the locals and the German soldiers was immense. Triggered by an incident instigated by a band of partisans, two incommensurate worlds clashed.

IV

The German forces had reinforced their occupation of Italy in September 1943 with a pre-emptive escalation of anti-partisan warfare.

German counter-insurgency warfare picked up on the lessons from the Balkans, Greece, and the occupied Soviet Union and put them to use, as it were, in a condensed form, while the Italian resistance scene was still evolving. The initial measures against partisans in Italy thus occurred on a plane of experiences and expectations that reached far beyond Italian conditions.[18]

Initially, the 75th (Army) Corps, responsible for coastal defense between Cecina and Genoa, carried out much of the preventive combat. This corps constituted the training ground for anti-partisan warfare in Italy. Following a key conference on the partisan situation, held in Verona on 3 April 1944, the 75th Corps undertook a series of campaigns that came straight off the drawing board.[19] Focusing on the Apennines and northern Tuscany, these operations, extending for several weeks, were implemented with overwhelming force. For every one of these actions, detailed combat reports recapitulated the German experiences and the results achieved.

The common tenor of these reports is an attitude of disparaging superiority: "Given firm, energetic leadership it is possible to successfully fight all these bands."[20] Clearly, the commanding officers had seen worse and did not consider these actions a serious test. The partisan bands were compared to robbers and highwaymen, not really serious opponents. The fight against partisans hardly compared with battle situations. The German units would be better off preparing for front-line duty, rather than going about anti-partisan warfare. German troops were too good for search operations; the latter were better left to informers and Fascist units who could do the job of ferreting out and encircling partisan areas "in order to allow the liquidation [of partisans] to be undertaken by regular troops."[21] German units were to come in for the kill. This arrogance (and the implicit division of labor between auxiliaries and regular forces) was not empty talk. The well-planned sweeps through the Apennine mountains, carried out without any apparent counter-pressure by partisans, erupted into a brutal war of annihilation, striking the civil population—men, women, and children—in a frenzy of destruction.[22]

Units of the armored paratrooper division Hermann Göring were among those who stood out for their ferocity and the insouciance of their reports—paratroopers having acquired a certain caché in the Wehrmacht for unrestrained violence.[23] Quite typically, an officer of the Hermann Göring's Reconnaissance Battalion insisted in one of the after-action reports that all civilians his unit encountered were nothing other than disguised partisans and therefore had to be "executed" and "their houses either burned down or blown up."[24]

The tone here is more important than the particulars. These units and their leaders not only fought the partisans, but rather meant to assert a pose vis-à-vis the local population—and, perhaps more importantly, in relation to other German units. The villagers of San Paolo in Alpe, Molino di Bucchio, Sorelli, Valucciole and Croce di Mari became the victims of this particular pose in one of the larger operations involving elements of the *Hermann Göring* that commenced around Monte Falterona between 13 and 17 April 1944.[25]

The peculiarity of this attitude is all the more noticeable, since there was some debate as to the effectiveness of this particular form of unrestrained violence. One of these debates was triggered by a particularly boastful report from the Monte Falterona operation which asserted:[26]

> Shaken by the operations and our energetic knuckling down [*Zupacken*], [the partisans] tried to disguise themselves as harmless civilians. Nobody wanted to have seen anything of a band. The civilians were all found guilty as co-conspirators and executed in accordance with the Führer order regarding anti-partisan warfare, their houses burned down or blown up. In many cases, undiscovered munitions exploded.

The responsible staff officers of the 75th Corps—otherwise not known for reticence—remained unconvinced, notwithstanding the confrontational reference to the Führer order (about anti-partisan warfare).[27]

They insisted that this kind of anti-partisan activism hit civilians who at best only sympathized with the partisans and, in effect, strengthened the partisan cause. Moreover, the better organized the partisans and, correspondingly, the more dangerous they were, the easier it was for them to evade German sweeps. Hence, the 75th Corps attempted to restrict the shootings, without, however, changing the practice of anti-partisan warfare very much.[28]

The same debate occurred in the 14th Army whose rear area encompassed Monte Reatini (Umbria) in March 1944, where elements of the 3rd Regiment of the Brandenburg Division operated. The Brandenburg Division originated as a formation of the military Abwehr (Armed Forces Intelligence) that specialized in partisan warfare.[29] The 14th Army's intelligence officer bluntly challenged the 3rd Regiment's reports of its successes in and around Leonessa, declaring that the regiment's extremely brutal anti-partisan measures in the area hit civilians instead of effectively fighting the bands. In that conclusion he was certainly correct. But he offered no alternative to combat partisans more effectively.[30]

In short, there was a debate within the German military staffs in Italy as to the proper and most efficient way to deal with partisans.

There was internal critique of the measures taken. One might even discern a certain tension between "regular" units and those who, like the Brandenburgers or the Hermann Göring Reconnaissance Battalion, specialized or made a name for themselves in anti-partisan warfare. But the fact is that, for one thing, there was always a mixture of units involved in any one of these search and destroy missions and, for another, there was no evident alternative presented.

The bottom line is that brutal strikes against the civilian population as a way of fighting partisans were common in Italy.[31] While I have used the record of a Corps in northern Italy, specifically designated to fight partisans, the situation in the rear of the retreating front-line units was not significantly different, as the debate about the Brandenburgers suggests. While surely not all officers and soldiers (and, hence, not all "Germans") shared in the extremism of some units, they partook in a mentality which they countenanced or, at the very least, were unable or unwilling to oppose.

The massacres of Valcasotto, Villaminozzo, Valucciole, Sant'-Anna di Stazzema, the Padule di Fucécchio, Marzabotto are some of the best-known witnesses to this mentality of punishment and deterrence. The normality of a war of annihilation against the population in all of occupied Italy was an intrinsic feature of anti-partisan warfare in 1944. In view of the bloody track of anti-partisan terror up and down the Italian peninsula, the inhabitants of Civitella were well advised when they took precautions after the attack on four German soldiers that left three of them dead. Other towns had been destroyed and their inhabitants had been killed for much less in the name of what the German side rationalized, if occasionally with some qualms, as anti-partisan warfare.

V

Compared with late 1943 and even early 1944 when German units, with unmistakable arrogance and apparently complete control of the situation, had imported a war against partisans to Italy, the situation a year later, in September and October 1944, had completely changed. In the first months of 1944 the German side still counted on a relatively stable Italian front. With the Allied advance on the Cassino Front stalled and the beachhead at Anzio sealed off for the time being, they expected to remain "master [*Herr*]" of the situation in Italy for a long time to come.[32] These expectations foundered in the early summer of 1944 and had all but collapsed in September/October. Between May and September 1944, the position of the German army in Italy deteriorated both on the front and in the rear. The German retreat turned more and more into a flight which was only temporarily slowed down. The nadir of this development occurred in the second half of June 1944 when, after a hasty retreat from Rome, High Command Southwest attempted to stabilize the front at the edge of the Tuscan foothills. The War Diary of the Wehrmacht High Command (OKW) noted that 18 June (the day of the Dopo-Lavoro Club incident in Civitella) was "so far the hardest day" in Italy.[33]

The local centers of this crisis lay in the defensive battles in the coastal plain, where the 16th SS Panzergrenadierdivision was committed, and in battles around the Trasimenian Lake. A main actor in the latter battles was the 76th Panzer Corps of the 10th Army, on whose extreme right flank (adjacent to the 1st Paratroop Division) fought the armored paratrooper division Hermann Göring, now fully committed to front line service. Previously, this division had taken part in the retreat through southern Italy, was temporarily transferred over to OKW Reserve for replenishment, and used in anti-partisan operations within the context of the 75th Army Corps, only to return once again in full strength to the front in the critical days of May/June 1944. Civitella happened to fall in this division's rear combat zone.

VI

Meanwhile, up north the Army Detachment (Armeeabteilung) *von Zangen* was formed from the remnants of the 75th Corps with the single purpose of taking over anti-partisan warfare north of the Po River. This formation was separated geographically from the unfolding events in Tuscany, but its initiatives characterize paradigmatically the reaction of military command authorities in Italy to intensifying partisan activities in the entire theater of war. This changing significance of anti-partisan warfare is attested by an entry in the daily reports of the *Wehrmachtführungsstab* back in Germany. Again, the key entry occurred on 18 June:[34]

> Band activity has … enormously intensified. Numerous destroyed bridges along the main lines of supply and attacks on our supply columns endanger supply. Attacks on an ordnance officer driving alone and destruction of communication lines affect decisively our own command and control.

The reaction to this situation by the 75th Corps was draconian. Its order No. 17 for Anti-Partisan Warfare from 29 June 1944 (the same day as the Civitella massacre), characterized the military situation in the rear as follows:[35]

> Band activity in the upper Italian area, particularly in the mountainous regions of the Apennines, sparked by proclamations from the enemy side and the advances of the enemy's offensive, increased to such a degree that [now] the systematic preparation and organizational consistency of the band war is unmistakable. Today this war is no longer a matter of isolated groups independent from one another; it has become an insurrectionary movement that is clearly led from the enemy side and exhibits a unified will to fight. This movement is organized, militarily led, and guided by principles of guerrilla war. We deal with an enemy fighting in our rear.

One day later, the Corps issued a detailed catalog of measures on the basis of order No. 17's assessment of the situation. While the task definition was not new in practice, it had so far not been put down as mandated actions. One item is particularly important in our context:[36]

> Where bands appear in larger numbers, a percentage, to be determined case by case, of the male population living in the region is to be arrested and in case of violent activity is to be shot. The inhabitants of the region are to be informed of this.
>
> If soldiers are fired upon from a village, the village is to be burnt to the ground. The culprits or ringleaders are to be publicly hung.

The order of the 75th Corps applied to northern Italy where a vicious counter-insurgency warfare ensued. But other corps and armies in the Italian theater acted similarly. The commander of the 14th Army issued his order on 3 July. The emphasis was, once again, that hard and vigorous action be taken:[37]

> I will protect every leader who in the choice and severity of the method for fighting the bands surpasses what we consider the customary measure. In these cases the old principle applies that, in asserting dominance, a mistake in the choice of the method is always better than failure to take action or negligence.

The 51st Mountain Corps, as part of the 10th Army, reported on 2 July:[38]

> Headquarters [10th Army] orders reinforced security measures to be taken for detachments sent into the rear and for the entire traffic situation; divisions are given authorization to make the civil population in individual villages responsible for security and order.

This entire series of army and corps orders dating from the second half of June and the first days of July goes back to a basic decree, "New Regulations in Anti-Partisan Warfare," which Field Marshall Albert Kesselring, the commander of the Southwest theater, issued on 17 June with amendments on 1 July and 3 July, for the entire Italian theater.[39] This decree was drawn up in consultation with the Armed Forces (OKW) Headquarters in Berlin. Hence the attention paid to the partisan situation in the Italian theater in the OKW reports. Hence also the reaction down the chain of command, some formations acting faster than others, but all of them adjusting their previous stance toward partisans to fit the Kesselring decree. The key element and the novelty of this decree and subsequent Army and Corps orders was that "for the first time the population was made responsible for the appearance [*Auftreten*] of partisans."[40]

Two points stand out as having an impact on the events in Civitella. First, the character of the Resistenza had changed as far as the German, military perception was concerned. If they had initially looked down upon the partisans as "cowardly people," they now considered them to be a significant factor in the balance of forces, an enemy in the rear.[41] The war against partisans had become an integral part and an extension of warfare at the front. While counterinsurgency had primarily been a matter of maintaining lines of communication and logistics across the Alps and the Apennines, it now became a matter of immediate and systematic concern for front line units because of their rapid, fighting retreat through what they now had to consider (or were called upon to consider in order not to be caught for negligence or for lacking initiative) enemy territory. Individual units had lashed out against civilians in the previous months. Now they were called upon to consider all civilians suspect.

Second, if the war against civilians had still been a matter of some debate in the anti-partisan campaigns during spring 1944, it became a subject of detailed orders in the second half of June 1944. The critical or, possibly, cynical voices had disappeared. While the tenor of these orders varied somewhat from unit to unit, the baseline, established by the Kesselring decree and subsequent amendments, was clear enough. In order to fight partisans, German units were to hold the civilian population responsible for any action by partisans. It was pure happenstance, but on 17 June 1944, the war against the civilian population—previously the mark of particularly tough units at the front and of search and destroy missions in the rear—became the norm in the Italian theater of war.

The events in Civitella thus unfolded at the very moment at which, as a result of the highest orders, anti-partisan warfare in the Italian theater was retooled. The new standard applied, irrespective of which unit or assault group was ordered to take action. Furthermore, it applied independent of what the Civitellini might have said or done in order to mitigate the circumstances of the 18 June incident. By the very fact of the event—and the mere appearance of partisans would have been quite enough—they had become accomplices.

VII

The War Diary of the 10th Army—briefly mentioned above in our discussion of partisan maps—casts light on how the mounting tensions worked themselves out in Tuscany. For 10 June through 13 June we find the first of a series of entries, expressing alarm about partisan activities. "Band Situation: Supported by enemy instigation, weapons drops, and cooperation with enemy paratroopers, band activity ... steadily increases. It came to repeated attacks on individual soldiers, small detachments, and in some cases on entire columns of troops." For 22 June it reads "band activity in the last days ... has quantitatively increased in the area near the front due to General [Harold] Alexander's appeal." On 25 June: "The band situation continues to grow. Attacks on single trucks, supply camps, and trains continue. The staff officer for propaganda had leaflets distributed to the population which informed it that all band activity and support is to be punished with death. The Brandenburg battalion was transferred into the Arezzo area." Finally for 27 and 28 June, it states, as mentioned above: "The band situation continued to aggravate, particularly in the Arezzo where the supply routes to the front were completely blocked off." As a monthly balance the War Diary reported summarily: "658 prisoners, 30 re-arrested, 36 bandits taken prisoner, 223 shot, 16 suspicious civilians apprehended, 3 people wandering near the front taken into custody."[42]

This is quite an impressive list of partisan incidents and activities. The War Diary linked them to an appeal of General Harold Alexander on 7 June which encouraged insurrectionary war in the rear to disrupt supply lines and indicates the draconic measures the German rear commands were taking in order to establish security of transport and communication. It seems plausible to tie this information to the events in and around Civitella—and in a general way (security of supply lines; threat of death in case of partisan activity) it fits. But massacres do not happen in general and, unfortunately, the particulars do not quite add up.

The 10th Army, while deeply concerned with partisan activities, showed little interest in the area around Civitella. The above entries in the 10th Army's War Diary referred not to the Chiana valley southwest of Arezzo, but to the Pratomagno range in the northwest. 10th Army intelligence was concerned with the main roads to Florence which led around the Pratomagno mountains. It was there, not in the hills around Civitella, that elements of the 3rd Regiment of the Brandenburg Division, which we had earlier observed operating in Umbria, now found itself engaged with the partisans.

> In the Cetica area (8 [?] km west southwest of Poppi) an 8 hour long firefight between the 2nd battalion/3rd Brandenburg Regiment and the bandits. 45 bandits shot, 1 prisoner brought in. Large amounts of weapons and munitions destroyed. 2 standards of the 22nd Garibaldi Assault Brigade captured. The village of Cetica set ablaze. Strength of the band at least 3,500 men, probably stronger. Band well trained and well led. In battle in the Schaggia valley (10km west of Poppi) another 10 bandits shot. Casualties of the 2nd Battalion/3rd Brandenburg Regiment: 2 dead, 5 wounded.[43]

In the Pratomagno, well organized partisan units and German counter-insurgency units engaged in open combat. What the partisan map of the 76th Panzer Corps indicated with smaller circles were in fact the main sites of action. Inasmuch as the 76th Panzer Corps engaged in anti-partisan measures, they were concentrated in the region north of Arezzo. Suffice it to say that a corps (as opposed to a division) commits units in order to counter a threat in the pursuit of its autonomous operations. This threat was present in the Pratomagno mountains, as far as the 76th Panzer Corps was concerned, and around Gubbio, as far as the 51st Mountain Corps was concerned. What it meant to be in a hot-spot of insurrectionary warfare, targeted by corps operations, is indicated by the combat report of the Brandenburgers which points to the systematic scorched earth tactics employed by counter-insurgency units.

But what about the third circle in the partisan map? In between Resistenza and Counter-Resistenza myths, one easily loses perspective and a sense of proportion. The fact of the matter is that, while the area around Civitella witnessed isolated attacks, sabotage, and the like, these activities were neither particularly frequent nor are there any indications that the operations of the partisans in the Chiana valley were considered to be a threat to the corps or the army. From the vantage point of the 10th Army, the incidents in Ambra, Civitella, and Montaltuzzo reflected the general state of insecurity in

June 1944, but, for better or worse, it was not one of the centers of insurrectionary war and, for that matter, of counterinsurgency.[44]

Then again, after 17 June 1944 it did not need all-out anti-partisan warfare in order to bring forth a harsh response by German units. There was another incident not unlike the one in Civitella, but with a different outcome. It occurred a few kilometers northeast of Arezzo and was even remarked upon in the daily reports of the *Wehrmachtführungsstab*.[45] Partisan units had captured the colonel responsible for transportation routes in the Pratomagno on the Anghiari-Sansepolcro road and severely wounded his driver, a sergeant, on 25 June. In the same area, but further north on the Arezzo-Poppi road, another colonel, a commander of an anti-aircraft brigade, had been previously wounded. Much as in the case of Ambra, this triggered an instant response. The Transportation Command Arezzo ordered "that the entire population of all towns along the road Anghiari-Montauti-Borgo-Agiovi [*sic*: Borgo a Giovi] plus all the villages and hamlets along the road was be taken hostage immediately.... If in the next 48 hours the colonel and the NCO are not brought back, the male population is to be shot and the villages burnt to the ground."[46] Since the German side encountered a very well organized, military resistance, negotiations ensued in which the command of the partisan detachment threatened to shoot the captured officer and the driver if retaliation took place against the villagers.[47] Meanwhile, an informer employed by the Germans reported that the colonel had not really fallen into the hands of the "Italian liberation army," but was captured by a "band chieftain named Andrea, probably of Slovenian nationality, who mostly was engaged in theft and raids in order to make a living."[48] Obviously, this could just as well have been malicious gossip, but it points to the fact that "partisans" came in different shapes and guises. In any case, the informer reported that the real partisans spared no effort to get the colonel under their control in order to free him in exchange for the release of the hostages—and apparently he was set free. The situation map of the High Command Southwest for 30 June notes: "Upon threatened reprisal measures there was an exchange of letters between the bandits and the Arezzo Transport Command. June 29: On the basis of our countermeasures, Colonel Freiherr von Gablentz was released."[49] One presumes that the hostages were also released. In any case, this potential massacre was averted.

While the events around Anghiari heighten the puzzle of what happened in Civitella, they also provide us with some new insight. First, we may note that just below the level of anti-partisan operations conducted on the corps level, there was another realm of counterinsurgency by rear area commanders and, for that matter, divisional commanders. Even in a quite notorious case like the one in Anghiari, actions were taken by lower level commands.

Second, the comparative case of a massacre averted gives us a better idea what happened and what went wrong in Civitella and environs between 17 June and 23 June. It provides us with an instructive look at the actions of the local partisans, the "Renzino" group, that cuts through layers of accusation and exculpation. The Renzino group's action began with an attempt to disarm four German soldiers in the Dopo-Lavoro Club which ended in the death of two soldiers and the wounding of a third. For all intents and purposes, this was a high-risk undertaking. More than anything, the undertaking suggests a dire lack of weapons which was a notorious problem of all partisan groups, but evidently more of a problem for the more marginal groups. Given that the initial undertaking went seriously wrong, one might well think of the Montaltuzzo incident as an attempt to undo the effects of the first one. Quite evidently, this action consisted in an attempt to take hostages in order to protect the population from retaliation for the first botched action. However, this effort also failed, leading to instant German countermeasures near Montaltuzzo which freed the hostages after a short firefight.[50]

One might further surmise that these bungled actions—especially if taken together with the incident at Ambra—created the impression that the area around Civitella was indeed becoming a partisan area—and that these actions posed a threat to the road from Monte San Savino to Buccine which paralleled the main road in the Chiana valley and was earmarked for the retreat of units of the 10th Army toward Florence.[51]

The bottom line here is simple enough, although not really flattering to the partisans. At every step the actions of the Renzino group between 17 June and 23 June went fundamentally awry—obviously not only a matter of bad luck, but also a sign of weakness. From all we can gather, they were not strong enough to exert pressure on the Germans, for example by taking hostages, but they were surely active enough to warrant attention—attention which was magnified by what the German side had come to expect as a universal partisan threat and was ordered to put down in a war against civilians.

VIII

The absence of direct German references to the massacre in Civitella and the surrounding villages remains an enigma. Still, not all is lost even in the absence of direct evidence. Military violence, even in extreme situations, proceeds within territorial jurisdictions and follows a certain logic of violence. If we can reconstruct either one or both, we can determine with some certainty what happened.

Three alternatives are worth considering. One possibility is that the military command responsible for the rear army areas put together a search and destroy commando (Jagdkommando), in which case that organization would have been Korück 594.[52] But this possibility should be ruled out because the boundaries of responsibility changed in the time between 17–18 June (Dopo-Lavoro Club attack) and the massacre on 29 June. As of 20 June, the area south of the Florence-Arezzo-Sansepolcro road, including Civitella, came to fall within the operational area of the 76th Panzer Corps. Subsequently, Korück 594 was in charge only for the area north of this road.[53] This shift in territorial authority may well have been a factor in the odd delay between the Dopo-Lavoro Club incident and the German response. The second, more remote likelihood is that elements of the 3rd Brandenburg Regiment were involved, for this regiment was "deployed, for the time being, in its current area of operation [province of Arezzo] for band warfare."[54] This is to say that, if the action in Civitella was really an anti-partisan operation, the 3rd Brandenburg Regiment was in the area. This possibility cannot be ruled out entirely, but there is every reason to believe that this anti-partisan unit operated where the 76th Panzer Corps spotted major concentrations of militarily organized partisan units: in the Pratomagno Mountains rather than in Civitella and the Chiana valley.

The main clues for the third alternative come from the testimony of witnesses.[55] Witnesses agree that the troops who murdered and pillaged in Civitella, San Pancrazio, Burrone, Gebbia, and Cornia came from Monte San Savino in the south, not from Arezzo. They explicitly refer to a villa which housed staff. At this time, the headquarters of the Hermann Göring Division moved into the vicinity of Monte San Savino. By 26 June at the latest, but in any case after the events of 18 June, Civitella came within the operational area of this division.[56] This is to say that on 29 June Civitella lay within the rear area and, hence, the command authority of the Hermann Göring Division.

Within the jurisdictional hierarchy of the division, the main responsibility for counterinsurgency—especially if it was not a Jagdkommando—lay with the Geheime Feldpolizei, the much feared and secretive German military police. Witnesses confirm that a group of about 100 men of the 3rd company of the Feldgendarmerie Abteilung

581, located at the time near Monte San Savino, under the leadership of Captain Heinz Bartz, were quartered near Civitella on the eve of 29 June.[57] Therefore, it is safe to say that the core of the troops that committed the massacre in Civitella came from the 3rd Company of the Feldgendarmerie Abteilung 581.[58]

There is other, more circumstantial evidence. We have already noted the Red Cross truck in San Pancrazio. Witnesses also claim to have seen a group of the Italian *brigate nere* (black brigade)—blackshirts with death heads symbols that were covered with camouflage paratroopers jackets—participating in the actions in San Pancrazio and Cornia.[59] These *brigate nere* were in addition to Italian informers who accompanied the German troops at every location.

There are further clues from the detritus of the operation to be taken into account. Two soldiers left their military mail addresses *(Feldpostnummern)* behind in the location near Civitella which also quartered the military police. One of them (on an envelope) traces back to the 3rd Supply Company of the Hermann Göring Division and the other (in a copy of Goethe's Faust dedicated to one of the female witnesses) to the Music Corps of the Hermann Göring Division.[60] We do not know the role of these two men. One of them may well have been a truck driver with his relative, the musician, possibly tagging along for some piece of action. They may have been the classic accomplices and bystanders. Then again, if medics can form a Jagdkommando as we have seen in Ambra, members of a supply company may well have been called upon to participate in this particular measure. A reconstruction of the various bivouacs of soldiers participating in the massacre rather suggests the latter. In any case, Goethe's Faust belongs as much to the detritus of the operation as the brass plates that identified members of the Geheime Feldpolizei.

The soldiers participating in the massacre in Civitella came from or were attached to the Hermann Göring Division. We had encountered elements of the armored paratrooper division Hermann Göring, especially the Reconnaissance Batallion together with members of an anti-aircraft detachment and miscellaneous other units, as being engaged in the counter-insurgency war of spring 1944 in the context of the 75th Corps. The division with the curious designation of a paratroop-tank division is an example of the competition over power in the Third Reich. Originally formed out of Prussian police units, this division always operated as an armored formation of the field army, but belonged to Luftwaffe jurisdiction. It was an armored division of the air force which operated within the context of the field army. Replenished in June 1943 in Sicily from the remnants of the General Göring Division which had been destroyed in Tunisia, the division had its training units, among other things, in southern France.[61] Trained in the summer and fall, these recruits were introduced into the division shortly after their basic training. They were committed to operations in April 1944 in the 75th Army Corps' anti-partisan warfare efforts. Units of the division shared partial responsibility for the already mentioned operations in Cassentino as well as in Valdarno and in particular for the massacres around Monte San Giulia (18 March), in Villaminozo (18–20 March), and Monte Falterona (13–17 March)—actions which, from the vantage point of the division, must be considered training exercises for recruits. In May 1944, the division was in its entirety transferred to the 10th Army/76th Panzer Corps, where it was thrown into the fighting retreat from Rome and then into the bloody defensive battles beween Città di Pieve, Chiusi, and the Trasimenian Lake.[62]

The Hermann Göring Division was a good example of the National Socialist army in the making.[63] Its recruiting base was national, which means that it fell back on volunteers and conscripts from National Socialist organizations. Its soldiers were decidedly young; only around 17 or 18 years of age. They received their training in occupied Europe and their baptism of fire in the partisan war. The unit was well outfitted in material terms, but suffered from an extraordinary shortage of officers and NCO's. In its commander's estimation, the lack of officers and NCO's made the unit only conditionally fit for front-line operations.[64] Built on the model of Waffen SS divisions, it was *not* an SS division.[65] The division had the emblem of the parachutists, but never really reached the elite status of the paratroopers. The same was the case in terms of armor. While the division's main disposition resembled that of a Wehrmacht tank division, it was really more of a mixed formation with substantial armored components. One cannot say that the division overall had been particularly ideologically motivated or fanatical, although its combat reports from March 1944 create this impression. It was, however, more so than comparable units from the army, a product of the National Socialist regime, raised within and stamped by a National Socialist rule in occupied Europe and aspiring to be one of the elite divisions of the new Reich.

Why do we know so little about the actions of this division and, particularly, the events on 29 June? Above all, because we actually know very little about the Hermann Göring Division. There are two reasons for this. First, the division was transferred to the Eastern front shortly after or more likely already during the massacre in Civitella.[66] It was expanded into a panzer corps and deployed at the

Weichsel River bend, where it was ground up. What remained of the Hermann Göring Panzer Corps was a Kampfgruppe within the 4th Panzer Army which was wiped out toward the end of the war.[67] The records of the division and, subsequently, the corps were destroyed. Second and, perhaps more importantly, Luftwaffe formations, such as the Hermann Göring or the 1st Paratroop Division, that were only tactically subordinated to the Army, were notoriously protective of their independence. This had repeatedly led to complaints, as, for example, when the division began to withdraw units from the front (evidently in preparation for deployment at the Eastern front). Not even Fieldmarshall Kesselring, the commander of the Italian theater and himself a Luftwaffe general, was sufficiently informed about the plans of the division.[68] Therefore, it is not surprising that the actions of this division—much as those of the neighboring 1st Paratroop Division—left only sparse traces in the records of the higher command authorities.[69] The Luftwaffe divisions acted very much on their own and kept information to themselves. From the little we know, the Geheime Feldpolizei was even more secretive.

This said, the Hermann Göring was still a division under the jurisdiction of the 76th Panzer Corps/10th Army, with the military police reporting to the division. Its deployment as well as daily actions are generally reflected in the record of these higher military commands. Therefore, the absence of any record on Civitella is still somewhat puzzling. While it is well understood that anti-partisan actions tend to find only sparse and mostly summary expression in German documents, there is usually enough of a record of such events. Anti-partisan actions which at the time were carried out in the Pratomagno Mountains and the ones in Lunigia (in the rear of the 14th Army by the 16th SS Panzergrenadierdivision "Reichsführer SS," an autonomous formation if there ever was one) have at least found operational or tactical justifications in the form of combat reports or daily action records. The language of these records is notorious for whitewashing, but anti-partisan actions at least find some resonance in the documents.[70]

IX

Witness testimony is consistent on one issue. The action of 29 June against the inhabitants of Civitella and surrounding villages was executed according to plan. It followed a clear sequence of events and a time table. It was not a spontaneous measure. The witnesses also mention other telling details. First, the German commando did not expect resistance. The advance of the soldiers, their dispersal over a wide area, and their breaking up into small groups (often two or three soldiers acting on their own), in particular in the area of San Pancrazio and Cornia, negates the supposition that they expected a confrontation with partisans. Second, contrary to 20 June (when a smaller group of soldiers rounded up the Civitellini, but left them unharmed), the partisan issue played only a minor role. In San Pancrazio, men willing to talk were taken aside. However, one of the men used this as an opportunity to flee and the others were shot.[71] Nothing similar is known from Civitella. In contrast to San Pancrazio, interrogation was not at issue. Third, at least two men in Civitella saved themselves when they vociferously protested that they had been directed to Civitella as refugees from allied bombing and, hence, were not in fact Civitellini. The German soldiers were not prepared for this contingency, but after further inquiry the two men were carried off as "prisoners" and subsequently released.[72] The men of Civitella, in other words, were deliberately and demonstratively shot because they were Civitellini.

This makes the killing of 212 mostly male inhabitants of Civitella, San Pancrazio, Cornia, Burrone, and Gebbia the classic case of a reprisal. It was a premeditated action, a demonstration. The men were shot, the houses burnt down because two German soldiers were killed and one was wounded. This is what the Civitellini expected and feared after the Dopo-Lavoro Club incident and this is what happened.

A German-Italian leaflet distributed some time between 29 June and 2 July around Anghiari spells out the logic and reason of such reprisals.[73]

> Proclamation to the Italian population:
>
> Criminal elements in civilian clothing have repeatedly shot at German soldiers in ambushes. To atone for these crimes, several villages have been burnt to the ground and a portion of the male inhabitants of these villages have been shot.
>
> Concerning these matters the German Command makes the following known:
>
> All residents of every municipality are in their entirety to be held responsible that in their municipalities no acts of sabotage or attacks be perpetrated on individual German soldiers.
>
> A person who knows of the presence of a bandit or saboteur and does not immediately report their whereabouts, becomes an accomplice and exposes himself to the danger of being called to account for the misdeeds of these criminals.
>
> Municipalities in which attacks on German soldiers or sabotage acts take place, will be burnt down and a number of its male inhabitants will be shot.

> The mayors, village elders, and priests are urged, in the interest of the security of their fellow citizens, to encourage their municipalities to remain quiet and diligent and to cooperate in the tracking down of bandits.
>
> The German Command

This particular flyer originated in the command area of the 51st Mountain Corps.[74] It resembles the content of similar leaflets and wall posters which the 14th Army distributed.[75] And undoubtedly, the 10th Army and the 76th Panzer Corps also issued such fliers, although they were extremely hard-pressed at this point by the advancing allies. The main thrust of these proclamations articulated what the people of Civitella expected and feared. The Civitellini, much as most Italians, had come to expect that whenever partisans were hunted, civilians were hit. In Italy and elsewhere the Germans struck the stationary population when combating the mobile partisans. What they did not know is that, with Kesselring's decree of 17 June, reprisals had become the order of the day.

The reprisal had the effect that Kesselring had expected when issuing the order. It left a deep and indelible mark on the survivors in Civitella and the surrounding villages and has shaped local memory. It left no trace on the German side—at least not in a collective consciousness.[76] For the German soldiers the reprisal was a day's work. We don't know very much about them. But what we do know does not make them, as a group, particularly blood-thirsty or fanatical. Contemporary witnesses refer to some individual cases of hesitation. One of the soldiers confessed that "he did not like carrying the war into civilian homes."[77] Yet on the whole, the majority was not plagued by any scruples—and whatever scruples they had, they numbed with alcohol. They did this day's business: reprisal shooting in Civitella and environs. They obviously knew what they were doing. In the evening, they were roaring drunk.

Local memory and German military history remain incommensurate. Against the significance of the event in the memory of Civitella's inhabitants, no corresponding justification, no commensurate *consciousness* of the event exists on the German side. The men of Civitella became victims of a military action that makes war murderous in the true sense of the word.

X

Reprisals are extreme measures to subdue an insurrectionary population. They are an instrument of war and occupation which the Wehrmacht used widely in Eastern and Southeastern Europe. We need not enter the debate on the Wehrmacht's war of annihilation which the frequency and systematicity of this practice has engendered.[78] But we must take a second look at the nature of reprisals in Italy at this point in time. For although the reprisal in Civitella, which initially appeared so obscure as far as the German record was concerned, now appears to be perfectly transparent, the nature of these reprisals is not quite as self-evident as it may appear. That is, we know the perpetrators and the institutional logic of the reprisal, but it is still quite difficult to fathom why the Wehrmacht in Italy turned to this particular instrument and why it made civilians stand in for partisans.

Reprisals against the civilian population are a very problematic tool of warfare. It was well understood by the German staffs that these measures tended to achieve the opposite of what they set out to do—that they increased solidarity with partisans rather than separating the population from them. All the more we might ask why it is that German authorities in Italy hit upon such a counterproductive tool at this point? What is the reason for escalating the dirty war against partisans into an outright war against civilians, if German military experience had previously led to the conclusion that these terror methods were ineffective?

The prevailing answers to these questions tend to be both too narrow and too broad. The narrow answer is to follow the German script which makes abundantly clear that such reprisals were understood as anti-partisan measures. But then one wonders why any calculating staff officer would engage in such action, if there is enough experience that suggests the opposite effect. The answer to this puzzle tends to emphasize the spill-over of the brutalizing "Russian"—and one might add the Balkan and Greek—experience into Italy.[79] If we do not want to think of "brutalization" as an act of mechanical transmission that comes with the fact that officers or units had been deployed "in the East," we should wonder what was so "Russian," "Serbian," or "Greek" about the Italian experience at this point?

With this consideration in mind, we can turn to the quote with which this essay started. The call for "rapid and draconian measures"came from an assessment of the defensive situation in Italy by the 75th Army Corps, dated 13 June.[80] This strategic analysis of the entire Italian theater of war concluded that the "band unrest" had steadily increased so that, particularly in the rear areas, "effective anti-partisan warfare is no longer possible." The reasons for this otherwise quite extreme statement were that the Italian allies, Italian command authorities, units of the police and military could no longer be trusted. Desertions showed "that in the hour of need they [the Italians] will almost always fail." Furthermore, "wide portions of the population hate the war and are of the opinion that Italy would only be reduced to a theater of war between Germany and the Anglo-Americans; they are war-weary. The German Wehrmacht no longer finds the support that it needs."[81] In short, the partisans are out of control, because the Italians at large cannot be trusted. What matters here is the perception of a near total isolation in the Italian theater. This is the prerequisite for a dirty war against partisans turning into an all-out war against civilian populations.[82] This is what was "Russian" about the Italian situation in June 1944.

The resulting violence did not follow an instrumental logic, even when and where this rationality was twisted and bent by ideology (as we saw for the months of March and April). Rather, it followed a symbolic logic. This is to say: whatever impact the campaign against civilians was thought to have on the pursuit of war and on maintaining dominance in a rapidly deteriorating military situation, it was meant, above all, to pay back. In this situation, reprisals were not or no longer supposed to subdue an insubordinate population. They were intended, to punish and, in a second instance, to deter.[83]

In June 1944 the SS and Police Leader for Middle Italy, Karl-Heinz Bürger issued the following order, which epitomizes this kind of brutalization:[84]

> In case of the slightest signs of a rebellious, anti-German [*deutschfeindlich*] activity and sentiment, and be it only in the forms of gestures (Bolshevik greetings and the like) or disparaging remarks, I expect of all German and Italian SS and police units the sharpest possible and merciless intervention.... All energetic intervention is suitable, as method of punishment and deterrence, in order to nip in the bud outrages of a greater extent.

It should be understood that this was an SS and not a Wehrmacht order—and it would be intriguing to compare the Wehrmacht and SS languages of reprisals. But the point is that the notion of punishment and deterrence is the same.

As far as the Wehrmacht is concerned, the use of words is indicative of the penal turn in warfare. At the outset, it should be noted that the German term, commonly used for reprisal, has a distinctly non-military and, in fact, religious meaning—*Sühnemaßnahme,* measure of atonement. The term is so peculiar because it invokes notions of justice, rather than asserting a purpose (such as threatening an insubordinate population), as one is led to expect from a professional military. This terminology, however, changes in 1944. The notation in the War Diary of the intelligence officer of the 14th Army on 13 June is symptomatic: "On the basis of rising band activity, in consultation with the operations officer, a *retribution order* [*Vergeltungsbefehl*] was issued."[85] Here we find a language not of sin and atonement, but of retribution and revenge. This is the language of penal warfare, if not of a blood feud or vendetta. However much the military necessity of combating partisans was at issue in the High Command's decrees and their subsequent renditions on an army and corps level (for there was a partisan problem), they all pegged violence to a penal calculus of retribution.

But retribution for what? First of all, for the shooting of two soldiers and the wounding of a third by partisans in the town of Civitella. Surely, this was the reason at hand for the reprisal in Civitella—and given the orders coming down from superior headquarters just at this moment, it was more than enough to warrant draconian action. In addition, there were the immediate circumstances of the Hermann Göring Division which was mauled, in the second half of June, by their immediate military opponent, the 6th South African Armored Division.[86] Further, there was the case of a division that, in the eyes of its commander, did not (and could not) really live up to its front-line tasks due to a lack of officers and NCOs. And, of course, there is the case of the armored air force division with the curious name, fighting side-by-side with the elite, notoriously tough, and bloody-minded 1st Paratroop Division. In late June 1944, the Hermann Göring Division was in great need of recovering composure and self-esteem. And it was a division that was not just retreating through Tuscany, but was leaving Italy.

The causes of retribution were thus very concrete and circumstantial, but they reflected in their specificity a more general assessment of the situation which was made up of a variety of elements. There was first the acute sense of isolation and betrayal: "The basic tendency of the population is to wait and see. As long as an area is occupied by the Wehrmacht, the people remain calm. But it has been repeatedly observed that they take part in action against retreating troops which expresses their true attitude."[87] Reprisals were punishment for and deterrence of disloyalty which was taken for granted.

This sense of disloyalty was aggravated by the fact that soldiers and officers clearly recognized that the Third Reich was losing the war—and that in the defense of Germany Italy was a sideshow. Retribution linked local incidents to a horizon of perception which stretched from one front to the other and back home into the Reich. The experience of helplessness in the face of overwhelming Allied power was in the first instance a local one. There was no way around the fact that the Wehrmacht in Italy had nothing to pit against the "towering superiority" of the Allies.[88] But while Italy was the place for German soldiers to fight, the *Heimat* was their true place of concern. It is back in Germany, not in Italy, that they lost their self-confidence, as the censorship officer of the 14th Army suggested:[89]

> Above all, it is recognizable from the content of the letters that the grave concerns which the letter writers, in particular the East Prussians and the Upper Silesians, had about our eastern border region exercises a significant, alarmingly depressing influence. Doubting voices increase as to whether we are in a position to withstand the enemy pressure. The wish is often pronounced to defend one's own homeland against the Russians, rather than fight here in Italy for a people that one judges in no way favorably.

This is why I think that the call for "rigorous action and rapid, draconian measures" is so telling for the nature of reprisals in Italy in June 1944. The reason is that it has nothing at all to do with Italy, but a great deal with the deteriorating fortunes of the Third Reich:[90]

> Rigorous action and rapid, draconian measures must be taken. At a time, when women and children daily fall victim to the Allied bombing terror, every consideration for the population of an occupied area is prohibited, even if the area is led by a friendly government.

This then is the reason why the men of Civitella had to die: retribution for the partisan attack in Civitella which left two soldiers dead and one wounded. Retribution for a raid that pointed to the vulnerability of soldiers in a land that had become strange and, in a wider sense, triggered images of their inability to protect their own home, women, and children. The German war against Italian partisans was so bitter in June 1944 not only because the soldiers in Italy were pressed to the limit, but because they knew that they were losing the war—and were losing it, however bloody the battles in Italy, at the Eastern front and in the air war over Germany.

The escalation of the dirty war against partisans into a war against the civilian population entails, in my view, a mostly implicit admission that the war was lost and that the partisan situation was out of control because the war was lost. This is to say that, in the first instance, reprisals were a brutal way of buying time—and in the rear of the battle zone this was a matter of days and weeks.

Civitella was liberated on 9 July. With the region being evacuated, it made no difference, if the civilians were to support the partisans in the end. As a measure of fighting partisans reprisals amounted to burning bridges. Making deals with the local populations (which is what the Civitellini had hoped for) was no longer a concern. Retribution and revenge were the aim of reprisals in June 1944.

XI

There is, however, another and yet deeper layer in this history of reprisals. It is an altogether unexpected stratum in a history of anti-partisan warfare which has pointed time and again to the harshness of the German culture of war and the readiness for retribution. These characteristics are not in doubt. However, the deepest layer in our archaeology of the event in Civitella reveals not blood-lust but a yearning for peace and for an end to the war. The people in Tuscany had this yearning in common with many German soldiers, but in a situation shaped by deep enmity and distrust even this common sentiment became a source of hate and conflict.

The German assessment of public opinion in the Arezzo area was unequivocal:[91]

> The population is of the view that through the policy of the Duce a situation was created which imposed burdens of the war on them that would have been avoided through a coalition with the Allies. The Italian people see in the German Wehrmacht only the force that contributes to the prolongation of the war. Only a very few exceptions recognize what the Duce means for Italy and what Germany means for Europe.

This report could have been written to describe the situation in Civitella: The Nazi-Fascist regime still had the support of individuals and small groups who were, however, quite isolated in the local population and generally well known. But altogether the local population distanced itself from the Fascist authorities, as well as the partisans and above all the Germans. The majority attempted to weather the storm and to take cover, while basically supporting liberation from the German occupiers. I have already expressed my doubts about the seriousness of the partisan threat in this particular region, although there was an active resistance which in memory became the Resistenza. There was, in any case, a keen awareness of the fact that the Nazi-Fascist regime was at its end and that liberation would come soon with the front advancing rapidly. A cautious readiness to support the allied progress was to all appearances more widespread among the peasants and the local underclasses than in other groups in the population.[92]

What the Civitellini could not know is that the same sentiment was found among German soldiers as well. The Mail Censorship Office of the 14th Army concluded:[93]

> The wish for a conclusion to the war moves more and more into the foreground; one finds an increasing indifference and war-weariness. In almost every letter of the examined mail, references are made to express this desire. The entire picture is one of varied morale; clearly owing to the hard battles in the East and West [Soviet Union and France] and not least due the long fighting retreat in the South, [Italy] morale must frequently be called downright depressed.

If the Army's Mail Censorship Office referred to a yearning for peace among German soldiers, this yearning was not simply a part of the usual grumbling among the soldiers. An order from the Commanding General of the 10th Army points out the seriousness of the situation in Tuscany, especially if we keep in mind that the 10th Army, in contrast to the poorly rated, neighboring 14th Army, had been repeatedly praised for its model fighting spirit.[94] On 17 June the Commanding General of the 10th Army had the following to say:[95]

> Over the course of the battles of the last days, I have had to conclude that, at certain occasions, officers and men no longer show the fighting spirit that is to be expected from German troops. I demand that all the troop commanders personally exert themselves to raise the fighting spirit among the troops and regenerate a total spirit of resistance.

There were ominous signs that German cohesion was cracking. The number of prisoners of war taken by the Allies increased in these weeks. Small troops of soldiers wandering around in the rear without apparent aim and soldiers sitting in bars and drinking were the source of repeated stern reprimands.[96] Moreover, the number of German soldiers absent without leave, although a tiny minority, rose considerably during the months of May through July 1944—in the 76th Panzer Corps from a mere 67 cases in May to 153 cases in July. Allied troops (Croatians) and Volksdeutsche (Tyrolians) were disappearing at an even faster rate, with desertion no doubt made easier by the fact that the former were Catholics and the latter spoke some Italian.[97] In any case, the impression of an elite, armored consciousness—something which the Hermann Göring Division was prone to give off—misses the mentality of German soldiers in 1944 and especially the morale of the German troops in Italy in mid-June 1944. War weariness had become a factor not to be underestimated in the experience and actions of the German side.

However, the war-weariness among German soldiers at large only reinforced the harshness of military discipline and the single-minded pursuit of violence, especially among crack units. It set in motion a spiral of self-assertion and defiance. It did so both in the interaction among Germans and in the relationship of Germans and Italians. The mix of the two elements proved to be deadly.

At stake was not merely the internal cohesion of fighting units, but the self-esteem of both the individual and the collective. War weariness undercut the very spirit of defiance which the German military leadership tried to impress, with some success, on the rank and file. If defiance was increasingly seen as the only means to counter Allied superiority, it was the panacea for the isolation in a foreign land. The more alien the country, the more overpowering the enemy, the more urgent the need for decisive action. One of the first anti-partisan decrees of the High Command Southwest states:[98]

> Energetic, decisive and rapid action is the first requirement. I will call to account weak-kneed [*schlapp*] and indecisive leaders for endangering the security of their troops and the reputation of the German Wehrmacht. In the current situation, sharp, radical action will never be grounds for punishment.

This is the moment when the pursuit of honor and self-esteem—manliness—became murderous, not simply by way of imputing motives, but quite literally so. The punishment of Italians as partisans became a measure for German defiance. As the Italians were punished, the Germans sized each other up, asking whether or not they lived up to the challenge.

For the majority of soldiers, the fact that "the Italians" did what many of them would have preferred to do themselves gave rise, not as one might expect, to empathy but further alienation which in turn reinforced prejudice. The same report of the mail censor who spoke of the growing war weariness of the German soldiers mentioned a wave of dislike, even hate of "the Italians" and of everything Italian. Thus, one soldier is quoted to have written: "Up until now they [the Italians] were lazy and uninterested, so that it took a lot of nerve to observe this slovenliness. I can only repeat again and again that I will never understand these people."[99]

Another one is quoted, suggesting the implications of the first observation: "Today is Sunday again, a day like every other [for us]; yes, one makes no difference anymore, only that the Italians dress better than they do during weekdays. I have a deep anger toward these people for whom so many dear comrades had to lose their lives."[100]

The 14th Army Censorship Office held that this attitude conformed with the basic tenor of German letters: "The letter writers concern themselves a lot with the Italian people and their position in the current events. The entire life and the wheeling and dealing among the Italians as well as the constantly growing band danger are so foreign to German nature that one encounters a growing sense of rejection [of all things Italian]."[101] Private Schulze brought this sentiment to the point: "They [the Italians] betray us all body and soul."[102]

It should be said explicitly that this kind of resentment was not the cause for the reprisal in Civitella. There are much more straightforward reasons for the massacre. But Private Schulze articulates the emotional horizon within which this massacre happened, especially if we recall that he may well have been just another war-weary foot soldier.

It belongs to the aporias of June 1944, that in the course of this month, war weariness among the Germans and the Italians alike was also the emotional horizon that exacerbated atrocity and terror. A tiny minority of German soldiers placed their trust in the Italian strangers and deserted.[103] But for the vast majority a deep chasm opened between themselves and the other. This distance was the prerequisite for fighting the civilian population of Italy in the context of an all-out war against partisans. It was the emotional horizon of a war that most everyone wanted to end then and there, but which neither the Civitellini nor ordinary German soldiers could bring to an end by their own volition or on their own terms.

This distance was perpetuated into the poswar period by the soldiers of the armored paratrooper division Hermann Göring in the massacre in Civitella. Perhaps, the chasm began to close on the occasion of the fiftieth anniversary, when the effort was made to articulate local memory and German military history as part and in the context of *una memoria Europea*.

—Translation by Jonathan Gumz

Notes

*This essay is a revised version of "'Es muß daher mit schnellen und drakonischen Maßnahmen durchgegriffen werden.' Civitella in Val di Chiana am 29. Juni 1944," in Hannes Heer and Klaus Naumann, eds. *Vernichtungskrieg: Verbrechen der Wehrmacht 1941–1944* (Hamburg: 1995). While the majority of revisions were made in 1996 for the Italian version of this essay (though not incorporated into the Italian translation), I have made some use of the newer literature on the subject. Unfortunately, the study of Carlo Gentile which will be the definite factual account of the events in Civitella is not yet available. I would like to acknowledge that a conversation with Gentile in Rome in 1997 was responsible for my moving the 3rd Company Feldgendarmerie Abteilung 581 from a footnote (where I had put the unit as a perpetrator identified by witnesses) into the text as the main, albeit not the only, culprit of the massacre in Civitella. My special thanks to Miriam Hansen for her editorial comments and suggestions under trying circumstances.

1. 75th Army Corps, Commanding General, Order from 13 June 1944, 151/44 g.kdos., Bundesarchiv-Militärarchiv, Freiburg (hereafter BA-MA), RH 24-75/22.
2. Among the older literature, see Enzo Droandi, "La guerra nell' Aretino nel Kriegstagebuch della 10ma Armata Germanica, 15 Giugno–2 Ottobre, 1944," in *La battaglia per Arezzo, 4 Giugno–2 Ottobre 1944* (Arezzo: 1984). Starting point for the scholarly concern was the conference, in Arezzo, on "In memoria: per una memoria Europea dei crimini nazisti" from 22–24 June 1994. See Leonardo Paggi, ed., *Storia e memoria di un massacro ordinario* (Rome: 1996) as well as the video, Giovanni Contini and Silvia Paggi, eds., *La memoria divisa: Civitella della Chiana 29 Giungno 1944–94* (Rome, 1996: RM170496 823), and Leonardo Paggi, ed., *La memoria del Nazismo dell'Europa di oggi* (Florence: 1997). Among the recent historiography, see Friedrich Andrae, *"Auch gegen Frauen und Kinder:" Der Krieg der deutschen Wehrmacht gegen die Zivilbevölkerung in Italien, 1943–1945* (Munich: 1995); Gerhard Schreiber, *Deutsche Kriegsverbrechen in Italien: Täter, Opfer, Strafverfolgung* (Munich: 1996); Giovanni Contini, *La memoria divisa* (Milan: 1997); Michele Battini and Paolo Pezzino, *Guerra ai civili: Occupazione tedesca e politca del massacro, Toscana 1944* (Venice: 1997); Lutz Klinkhammer, *Stragi Naziste in Italia: La guerra contro i civili, 1943–44* (Rome: 1997).
3. Christopher Browning argued during the Arezzo conference that in the context of such events Christians of all creeds almost always remember such a soldier, whose existence, however, cannot be verified. On Browning's point, see also the contribution at the same conference by Andrea Loizzo, "The Good German."
4. Contini, *La memoria divisa*, with a detailed account.
5. "Atrocities Committed by German Troops at Civitella, Cornia, and San Pancrazio Districts," 78 Section, SIB; Public Record Office (PRO), Kew, London, W 0204/11479-XC1211 (cited hereafter as PRO, name of witness, date of statement, and page number). I am indebted to Leonardo Paggi for a copy of this extensive compilation.
6. At first appearing in the journal *Società*, Spring 1946, these recollections were newly edited in a collection of essays by Romano Bilenchi. See Romano Bilenchi, *Cronache degli anni neri* (Rome: 1984). For the French edition, see "Lamento de Civitella della Chiana," *Les Temps modernes* 2/23–24 (August–September 1947). A reconsideration of this tradition can be found in Victoria de Grazia and Leonardo Paggi, "Story of an Ordinary Massacre: Civitella della Chiana,

June 29, 1944," *Cardozo Studies in Law and Literature* 3 (Fall 1991): 153–169.

7. On the politics of local memory, see Contini, *La memoria divisa,* and de Grazia and Paggi, "Story of an Ordinary Massacre."
8. Giugno 1944—Giugno 1994 Civitella ricorda con "Voci dalla Memoria," Commune di Civitella in Val di Chiana, 1994.
9. Chief of Operations (Ia),76th Panzer Corps, Intelligence (Ic), "Band Situation—30 June 1944," secret; BA-MA RH 24-76/13.
10. At Castiglion Fiorentino and Città di Castello there is a similar remark. It reads, "60–70 male prisoners, 3–4 trucks shot at, combat report 30 June."
11. 10th Army, Intelligence (Ic/AO), "Activity Report June 1944—Entry for 27–28 June," BA-MA RH 20-10/106.
12. PRO, Mario Pacienza, 16 January 1945, 389ff; PRO, Don Ermano Grifoni, 13 November 1944, 411ff; PRO, Nello Paressi, 16 January 1945, 375. Paressi claims that German troops declared, "Tomorrow morning we are going to destroy the three towns Civitella, Cornia, San Pancrazio as they are full of rebels."
13. High Command Southwest, "Daily Map on Band Activity—13–24 June 1944," BA-MA RH19X/29K-1.
14. 14th Army, Intelligence (Ic), "Daily Report from 23 June 1944," BA-MA RH20-14/106. The italics are mine.
15. PRO, Luigi Lamminoni, 29 November 1944, 40. In this case, the German soldiers declared, "By twelve o'clock tomorrow we want to know who the partisans are; if not, reprisals."
16. PRO, Luigi Lamminoni, 29 November 1944, 39ff; PRO, Guido del Bono, 18 March 1945, 72ff. One of the intriguing aspects of the event on 20 June is that the otherwise very precise descriptions of the uniform of the soldiers by witnesses (see Guido del Bono, 18 March 1945, 72f), do not mention the characteristic insignia of the unit involved in the 29 June massacre. I still think that the soldiers appearing on 20 June were from the 1st Paratroop division. The British Military Commission also came to the conclusion that the 20 June and 29 June events involved different units.
17. PRO, Ugo Casciotti, 15 January 1945, 267ff; PRO, Giulia Valenti, 2 February 1945, 270ff.
18. For two excellent studies on that point, see Claudio Pavone, *Una guerra civile: Saggio sulla moralità nella Resistenza* (Turin: 1991); Lutz Klinkhammer, *Zwischen Bündnis und Besatzung: Das nationalsozialistische Deutschland und die Republik von Salo, 1943–1945* (Tübingen: 1993).
19. "Minutes of a Conference with the Commander of the *Ordnungspolizei* in Italy, General von Kamptz, in San Martino near Verona," 3 April 1944, BA-MA RH 24-75/20. At this conference it was arranged "that, first, the bands in the Apennines are to be fought, since there already are large areas which have become completely dominated by the bands. Cleansings of this extensive area will take considerable time. It depends on the then existing band situation if further actions are to be carried out."
20. Hermann Göring Division, Reconnaissance Battalion, Operations Officer (Ia), "Combat Report on the Operations against the Bands on 18 March 1944," 19 March 1944, BA-MA RH24-75/20.
21. Hermann Göring Division, Reconnaissance Battalion, Operations Officer (Ia), "Combat Report from 22 March 1944," BA-MA RH24-75/20.

22. Enemy, most likely civilian, casualties were 670 dead and 277 taken prisoner. See 356th Division, "Combat Report on the Operations of the 356th Division in Valcasotto from 12–20 March 1944," BA-MA RH24-75/20.
23. Schreiber, *Deutsche Kriegsverbrechen*; Lutz Klinkhammer, "Der Partisanenkrieg der Wehrmacht, 1941–1944," Rolf-Dieter Müller and Hans-Erich Volkmann, eds., *Die Wehrmacht: Mythos und Realität* (Munich: 1999), 815–836. Ernst Andrae calls attention to the special roll of the "Paratroop" units (the 1st Paratroop Division and Hermann Göring Division) in the massacres in middle Italy. See Friedrich Andrae, *"Auch gegen Frauen und Kinder"* (Munich: 1995).
24. Hermann Göring Division, Reconnaissance Battalion (Ia), Rittmeister von Loeben, Report to Hermann Göring Division Headquarters, 19 March 1944, BA-MA RH24-75/20.
25. 75th Army Corps, Intelligence Officer (Ic), "Report on the Band Situation," Nr. 822/44 geh., 23 April 1944, BA-MA RH24-75/20. Taking part in this action were the Reconnaissance Battalion of the Hermann Göring Division along with the 1st and 2nd Panzer Battalions of the Hermann Göring Division's Panzer Regiment, and 2 anti-aircraft batteries from the Hermann Göring Division. The reconnaissance battalion was short one company and the Panzer battalions did not have *tanks*.
26. Hermann Göring Reconnaissance Battalion, Operations (Ia), "Combat Report from 22 March 1944," BA-MA RH24-75/20.
27. On the context, see Timm C. Richter, "Die Wehrmacht und der Partisanenkrieg in den besetzten Gebieten der Sowjetunion," in *Die Wehrmacht: Mythos und Realität*, ed. Rolf-Dieter Müller and Hans-Erich Volkmann (Munich: 1999), 837–857.
28. 14th Army Corps, Intelligence (Ic), Contribution to the Corps Order of the Day from 3 March 1944, BA-MA RH 24-75/20. The officer states, "Houses are only to be burned down when armed bandits are identified. The need to exterminate entire villages exists, therefore, only in rare cases. As experience shows, such measures have the result that the then remaining part of the population goes over to the bands."
29. During the war, the 3rd Regiment of the Brandenburg Division had operated in the rear army area of Army Group Center in Russia, in southern France, and in Italy. The elements of the 3rd Regiment that remained in Italy finally comprised the Machine Gun Battalion "Field Marshall Kesselring." See Georg Tessin, *Verbände und Truppen der deutschen Wehrmacht und Waffen SS im Zweiten Weltkrieg 1939–1945*, vol. 14 (Osnabrück: 1980), 28.
30. 14th Army, Intelligence (Ic), Nr. 1738/44 geh., 15 April 1944, BA-MA RH20-14/104. This body count is instructive in comparison to the action around Monte Falterona: 239 dead of which 1 was English and 3 were Serbs, 698 prisoners, of which 19 were English and Americans, 2 were French, 1 was Australian, and 1 was a Serb.
31. Mark Mazower, "Military Violence and National Socialist Values: The Wehrmacht in Greece, 1941–1944," *Past and Present* 134 (February 1992): 129–158.
32. Typical of this feeling of superiority is an ironically intended note from the intelligence officer of the 14th Army. "At the occasion of the 40th anniversary of the beachhead: Since the existence of the beachhead, the opponent could only take 14 km at the furthest spot in 3 months, that is a pace of 155 meters per day. With this lightning fast pace the opponent needed another 228 days in order to reach Rome, but in order to reach Florence the opponent needed much more, namely, 1,686 days. Should the opponent push its goal so far as

the Brenner Pass, it would need 3,966 days. The Anglo-Americans could therefore, after 10 years and 1 month stand at the Brenner Pass; that would be 22 May 1954. But this calculation would only be right if the Germans were not there. For in three months alone they have inflicted the following casualties on the opponent: 6,691 prisoners and 30,000 men worth of bloody casualties. In order to approach the Brenner, it would cost the Anglo-Americans 1,1480,193 men." BA-MA RH20-14/104. Sly calculating of this type also appeared to have prevailed with regard to partisans in April 1944.

33. Percy Ernst Schramm, ed., *Kriegstagebuch des Oberkommandos der Wehrmacht*, vol. 4, no. 7 (Herrsching: 1982), 523.
34. Kurt Mehner, ed., *Die geheimen Tagesberichte der deutschen Wehrmachtsführung im Zweiten Weltkrieg, 1939–1945* (Osnabrück: 1985), 10:278.
35. Army Detachment von Zangen, Operations Officer (Ia/T), Nr. 166/44g.kdos, 29 June 1944, BA-MARH24-87/37. Army Detachment von Zangen was created after the 14th Army's commenced operations at Nettuno on 17 March 1944. On 31 July expanded into a German-Italian Army "Liguria."
36. Army Detachment von Zangen, Operations Officer (Ia/T), Nr. 166/44 g.kdos, 30 June 1944, BA-MA RH24-87/37.
37. 14th Army, Commanding General, Order from 3 July 1944, Nr. 174/44g.kdos, BA-MA RH24-14/42.
38. 51st Mountain Corps-Intelligence Officer, to the 10th Army-Intelligence Officer, 2 July 1944, BA-MA RH20-10/194.
39. High Command Southwest, Order issued by Field Marshall Kesselring (Ia/T Nr. 0402/44), 17 June 1944. This decree can be found as an attachment to the War Diary of the German Plenipotentiary General in Italy. See German Plenipotentiary General in Italy, War Diary, 20 June 1944, BA-MA RH31VI/10; cited in Friedrich Andrae, *"Auch gegen Frauen und Kinder,"* 155.
40. Lutz Klinkhammer, *Zwischen Bündnis und Besatzung*, 477.
41. The quote is by Colonel Almers, commander of the 135th Fortress Brigade, in, 75th Army Corps, Commanding General, "Inspection Report of the Commanding General," 21 July 1944, BA-MA RH24-75/15.
42. 10th Army, Intelligence Officer, "June 1944 Activity Reports," BA-MA RH20-10/194. See also Ivan Tognarini, ed., *Guerra di stermino e resistanza: La provincia di Arezzo 1943–1944* (Naples: 1990), 391–402.
43. High Command Southwest, Daily Report of 29 June 1944, Teletype, BA-MA RH19X/27. See also High Command Southwest, Operations (Ia), Contribution to the War Diary of the 10th Army, 30 June 1944, BA-MA RH19X/23.
44. The maps expressly confirm this assessment. See Second Air Fleet, Intelligence, "Defense Situation April 1944," Nr. 4064/44 geh., 3 May 1944, BA-MA 24-75/22; 14th Army, Intelligence, "Band Occurrences: Additions for the Period from 9–21 June 1944 and further band reports through 28 June 1944," BA-MA RH 20-14/104; High Command Southwest, "Band Positions—June 1944," BA-MA RH19X/29k-4. Of particular interest are the so-called "dot" maps on individual partisan activities. They all point to the fact that the area southwest of Arezzo was unusually quiet. The maps can be found at BA-MA RH19X/29K1-3. Altogether, map 3 notes 236 attacks, 12 instances of plundering, 29 acts sabotage against streets, 113 acts of sabotage against trains, and 78 acts of sabotage against communication cables. These daily maps ignore many smaller acts of sabotage that were mostly cable sabotage, such as the sawing off of cable poles and disconnection of wires. These acts of sabotage can be reconstructed from morning and daily reports of the 10th Army's intelligence officer. See 10th Army, Intelligence (Ic), Morning and Daily Reports of the Intelligence Officer,

1 April–30 June 1944, BA-MA RH 2–14/106. See also the chronology of partisan actions in Ivan Tognarini, *Guerra di stermino e resistanza*, 391– 402.

45. *Wehrmachtsführungstab*, Daily Report of 30 June 1944, in Percy Schramm, ed., *Kriegstagebuch*, vol. 10, 308.
46. *Korück 594* to the *Strassenkommandantur Arezzo*, undated, RH24-76/13.
47. Partisan General Command, 28 June 1944, German translation, BA-MA RH 20-10/194.
48. Telephone message from the *Strassenkommandantur Arezzo* to *Korück 594*, 28 June 1944, BA-MA RH20-10/194
49. High Command Southwest, 24 Hour Map on Band Activity from 25–30 June 1944, BA-MA RH19X/29K-2.
50. PRO, Eduardo Succhielli, 28 March 1945, 20ff.
51. Contini, *La memoria divisa*, 149–152.
52. 10th Army, Operations Officer, Nr. 7725/44 geh., 5 June 1944, belatedly settled the establishment of Korück 594. This new institution in Italy is hardly to be compared with the old *Korücks* on the Eastern front, since its tasks had changed in the scope of the retreat. Its tasks, determined by the 10th Army in reference to Führer Order No. 5, were as follows: "In all large localities and along all major roads of retreat road, battle commandants are to be named. The battle commandants alone have the responsibility for the defense of the locality and ordered implementation of evacuations and retreating movements and for that complete dictatorial powers. They have the duty to ruthlessly employ all methods against all people in order to fulfill their tasks. Their general task is: the defense to the very end of the concerned locality. Exhausting every possibility for this, employing also the last German fighters, preventing that panics come into being." See 10th Army, Operations Officer, Teletype, geh., 6 June 1944, BA-MA RH 24-76/12. Preceding this was a teletype from the Commanding General of the 76th Panzer Corps that forbade "every voluntary movement of retreat." In the rear army areas the *Korücks* became then an organ of the *Durchhalteparole* ("stick it out" slogan). See 76th Panzer Army, Commanding General, Order of 26 May 1944, BA-MA 24 76/12. Führer Order No. 5 dated from 21 February 1944.
53. 10th Army, Operations and Quartermasters Sections (Ia/OQu/Id), Letter Book, Nr. 2284/44 g.Kdos., 20 June 1944. This order was received by 76th Panzer Corps on 23 June; it was reissued with handwritten modifications by the 10th Army as 10th Army, Operations (Ia), 660/44 g.K., 24 June 1944, BA-MA RH24-76/13.
54. 10th Army, Operations Officer, handwritten entry to Order of 24 June 1944, BA-MA RH24-76/13.
55. This source had not been available to me for the first, German version of this essay. In the meantime, Carlo Gentile's meticulous and persistent research has unearthed German records to back up the testimony given to a British commission of inquiry.
56. 76th Panzer Corps, Operations Officer, Nr. 661/44 g.Kdos., BA-MA RH24-76/13. Strictly speaking, Civitella rested on the boundary between the Hermann Göring and the 1st Paratroop Divisions, as the first appendix to this order shows. By early July, however, the 1st Paratroop Division had moved to the left flank of the Hermann Göring Division.
57. Giorgio Geri mentioned a Captain Kainz Bards (correct name is Heinz Bartz) who led the the 3rd Detachment of the Feldgendarmerie Section 581. He reported for duty in soldiers quarters with 100 men of the Hermann Göring Division near Civitella. On the latter, see PRO, Lina Gori, 4 January 1945, 368.

58. There is some question as to the soldiers involved in the massacre. Evidently, some of them wore the typical insignia of the Military Police (a small brass plate on a chain, worn around the neck, which is difficult to overlook), but the majority is simply remembered for the armband of the Hermann Göring Division.
59. On Italian participation, see PRO, Franca Cardinali, 1 January 1945, 263ff; PRO, Giulia Casciotti, 25 January 1944, 267. Another witness reported remembering that those wearing Blackshirts spoke Italian to him. See PRO, Giulia Valenti, 2 February 1945, 270.
60. We owe this information to Licia Carletti, with whom Sergeant Rolf Matthes, from Chemnitz, left his army mail address in a copy of Goethe's *Faust*, which indicates that he was member of the Hermann Göring Division's music corps. See PRO, Licia Carletti, 5 April 1945, 364. References pointing to the 3rd Supply Company of the Hermann Göring Division are found in the statements of Enrico Arriguci and Giorgio Cantucci. While sweeping up a storeroom, Cantucci found an envelope of Wilfried Matthes, whose army mail code confirms that he was from the supply company. See PRO, Enrico Arriguci, 12 April 1945, 384, and PRO, Giorgio Cantucci, 10 April 1945, 395.
61. As to these training units of the Hermann Göring Division, Madelon de Keizer mentioned at the conference in Civitella that they were responsible for a reprisal in Putten in Holland. She refers to the Reserve Regiment Hermann Göring, which in the summer of 1944 was expanded into the Fallschirm Panzer-Ersatz und Ausbildungsregiment Hermann Göring. The elements of this regiment, which remained in Holland, were put under the Wehrmacht Commander in Chief in Holland. Madelon de Keizer, "Il massacro nazista di Putten (Olanda), 1–2 ottobre 1944. Cinquant'anni di storia e memoria (1944–1994)," in Paggi, *La memoria del nazismo nell'Europa di oggi*, 113–144. See Georg Tessin, *Verbände und Truppe*, vol. 14, 119–123.
62. See the account in Klinkhammer, *Stragi naziste in Italia*.
63. Bernhard R. Kroener, "Strukturelle Veränderungen in der militärischen Gesellschaft des Dritten Reiches," in Michael Prinz and Rainer Zitelmann, *Nationalsozialismus and Modernisierung* (Darmstadt: 1991), 267–296.
64. The assessments of the division by its commander are sobering. The report on the personnel situation for March notes: "The state of training of the individual men is serviceable. The training and the ability of the young officers and NCO's is insufficient.... The lack of experienced leaders and NCO's cannot be made up for through the enthusiasm of the young volunteers. Particularly in retreats, sturdy leadership is lacking." The Report of 1 June called the morale of the troops "good," the same report from 1 July called the morale "strengthened and good." BA-MA, RL 32/37.
65. De Grazia and Paggi assume this and with that follow a widespread practice. The mentioning of the SS is a narrative element that gives the extermination action additional weight. Nevertheless, the only Waffen SS unit was committed on the Adriatic coast. In order from right to left in the combat zone of the 76th Panzer Corps there were: Hermann Göring Division, 1st Paratroop Division, the 334th Infantry Division, the 15th Panzergrenadier Division and the 305th Infantry Division.
66. On the transfer of the entire division, which was complete on 4 August, see Percy Schramm, ed., *Kriegstagebuch*, vol. 4, no. 7, 583.
67. Georg Tessin, *Verbände und Truppe*, vol. 14, 117.
68. See, among others, High Command Southwest, Teletype to the Commanders of the Hermann Göring Division and the 1st Paratroop Division, 18 June 1944,

BA-MA RH24-75/12. The teletype reads, in part, "The 10th Army receives no correct records regarding personnel and materiel strength. [However], it knows that personnel and materiel are sent to the rear, even beyond the Appenine, at an above average rate. 10th Army has no authority, given the special status of the two divisions, to find out what really happened." In his telegram the Commander in Chief of High Command Southwest, Kesselring, emphasized his standing as the "most senior Luftwaffe general" in order to "urgently implore" the divisions to provide the requisite information.

69. On the other hand, there is no indication that either of the two divisions ever suppressed information about a massacre. Quite the opposite, the combat reports from April and May 1944 suggest a certain pride.
70. Droandis' attempt to connect the action in Civitella with a note in the War Diary of the 76th Panzer Corps for 28 June 1944 remains unconvincing. The note refers to formation of new rear army area, issued on 26 June. See 76th Panzer Corps, Operations (Ia), Nr. 662/44 g.kdos., 28 June 1944, BA-MA 24-76/13.
71. PRO, Ugo Casciotti, 21 January 1945, 267 ff. Casciotti succeeded in fleeing, but the other men who had indicated a willingness to show where the partisans were apparently were shot.
72. On the refugees from Florence: PRO, Rino Cesarini, 21 November 1944, 76ff; PRO, Giovanni Binachi and his son, 15 November 1944, 80.
73. Flyer in German and Italian, 28 June 1944, BA-MA RH20-10/194.
74. Intelligence Officer of the 51st Mountain Corps to the Intelligence Officer of the 10th Army, "Band Activity from 18 June–1 July 1944," BA-MA RH24-10/194. The report notes further, "In many actions carried out by the divisions in their combat zones, a number of band groups were destroyed with heavy casualties, much captured materiel brought in, [and] a large number of German soldiers freed."
75. 14th Army, Intelligence Officer, Activity Report for the Period from 1 March–30 June 1944, Entries from 17 June and 22 June, BA-MA RH 20-14/103. The 17 June entry noted 800 wall posters and 10,000 fliers, while the entry from 22 June noted 20,000 fliers.
76. Alfred Otte, *Die weissen Spiegel: vom Regiment zum Fallschirmpanzerkorps* (Friedberg: 1982); Roger James Bender, *"Hermann Göring": From Regiment to Fallschirmpanzerkorps* (Atglen, PA: 1993 [1975]); Franz Kurowski, *Von der Polizeigruppe z.b.V. "Wecke" zum Fallschirmpanzerkorps "Hermann Göring": die Entstehung, Entwicklung und das Endschicksal der Luftwaffeneinheiten mit dem weissen Spiegel "Hermann Göring"* (Osnabrück: 1994); Franz Kurowski, *The History of the Fallschirmpanzerkorps Hermann Göring: Soldiers of the Reichsmarschall* (Winnipeg: 1995).
77. On the behavior of the German soldiers, see PRO, Giovanni Massini, 30 March 1945, 393. Massini testified to their laughter, drunkeness, and plundering. Fabio Parenti testified to dancing and drunkeness. See PRO, Fabio Parenti, 27 March 1945, 401f. According to Licia Carletti "[A German soldier] thought that war between men was unfortunately necessary, but he did not like carrying the war into civilian houses." See PRO, Licia Carletti, 18 December 1944, 362. Another soldier declared "I am only a soldier, my orders are to collect every man." See PRO, Rosa Arriguci, 26 January 1945, 327. In another instance, two soldiers let a man pass, while a third turned him back. See also de Grazia and Paggi, "Story of an Ordinary Massacre."

78. The starting point for the debate was Peter Jahn and Reinhard Rürup, eds. *Erobern und Vernichten. Der Krieg gegen die Sowjetunion 1941–1945* (Berlin: 1991). Hannes Heer and Klaus Naumann, eds. *Vernichtungskrieg: Verbrechen der Wehrmacht 1941–1944* (Hamburg: 1995). See also the various positions taken in Rolf-Dieter Müller and Hans-Erich Volkmann, eds., *Die Wehrmacht: Mythos und Realität* (Munich: 1999).
79. Klinkhammer, "Der Partisanenkrieg der Wehrmacht."
80. 75th Army Corps, Commanding General, Order from 13 June 1944, 151/44 g.kdos., BA-MA RH 24-75/22.
81. The increasing isolation of Wehrmacht units cannot be given its due in this essay. Still, it appears to me a crucial element of their self-understanding and may help to explain their withdrawal into a unit culture on the one hand and a heightened, even paranoid readiness to fight against everyone. This readiness to lash out was carried back into Germany and Austria.
82. See in this context Gerhard Schreiber, *Die italienischen Militärinternierten im deutschen Machtbereich, 1943 bis 1945: verraten, verachtet, vergessen* (Munich: 1990).
83. One of the aftereffects of the Civitella massacre was the remark of a soldier when carrying out a search of a house: "Do not attempt to escape. We are the soldiers from Civitella, and we will do the same to you." See PRO, Ubaldo Nannini, 19 March 1945, 406.
84. Higher SS and Police Leader in Middle Italy, Letter Book, Nr. 36/44, 8 June 1944, BA-MA RH24-75/22.
85. 14th Army, Intelligence (Ic), Activity Reports, 1 April–30 June 1944, BA-MA RH20-14/103 (my emphasis—MG)
86. The number of dead and wounded was very high. In the time between 21 May and 12 June, the losses of the 76th Panzer Corps amount to 1,255 dead, 2,833 wounded, and 2,235 missing and captured. Of these, 759 dead, 1,476 wounded, and 1,154 missing were from the Hermann Göring Division. See Hermann Göring Division, "Daily Personnel Losses," no date, BA-MA RH24-76/12.
87. Military Police (*GfP*) Detachment 741, Nr. 47601, "Activity Report," 515/44 geh., Appendix 1 to the Activity reports for July 1944, BA-MA RH20-10/195.
88. High Command Southwest and Commander of Army Group C, Operations (Ia), Nr. 0385/44, geh.Kdos, 16 June 1944 (copy), BA-MA RH24-76/13: "The fighting over the last weeks has shown once again that our courageous troops are far superior to the enemy infantry which outnumbers them, as long as the enemy's superior air force and heavy weaponry does not crush or smother them."
89. 14th Army, Army Mail Censorship Office, "Activity Report of the Mail Censorship Office in the 14th Army in August 1944," BA-MA RH13/48. Bernhard R. Kroener, "Strukturelle Veränderungen in der militärischen Gesellschaft des Dritten Reiches," in Michael Prinz and Rainer Zitelmann, *Nationalsozialismus and Modernisierung* (Darmstadt: 1991), 267–296.
90. 75th Army Corps, Commanding General, Order from 13 June 1944, 151/44 g.kdos., BA-MA RH 24-75/22.
91. Secret Field Police (GFP) Group 741, Field Post Number 47601, "Activity Report," 515/44 geh., Appendix 1 to the Activity Reports for July 1944, BA-MA RH20-10/195.
92. Battini and Pezzino, *Guerra ai civili*. Anna Bravo, "La resistenza civile," in Paggi, *Storia e memoria di un massacro ordinario*, 144–165.

93. 14th Army, Army Mail Censorship Office, "Activity Report of the Mail Censorship Office in the 14th Army in August 1944," BA-MA RH13/48.
94. 10th Army, Commanding General, von Vietinghoff, "Call to the Soldiers of the 10th Army, 12 June 1944," BA-MA RH26-96/13.
95. 10th Army, Operations (Ia), Nr. 2160/44 g.Kdos., 17 June 1944, BA-MA RH24-76/13.
96. 10th Army, Operations (Ia), Letter Book, 7926/44 geh., 12 June 1944, BA-MA RH24-76/12: "numerous young soldiers wander back north with some cattle without apparent control. They report destinations which are way beyond the rear areas of their unit." Two units of Military Police were ordered to the rear to prevent such practices. 76th Panzer Corps, Telegram 14 June 1944 (01:00h), BA-MA RH24-76/12
97. When one adds the *Volksdeutschen* as well as Russian and Croatian soldiers who were separately counted, the numbers lie still higher: in May, 99, in June, 289, and in July, 610 desertions. See 10th Army, Intelligence Officer, Nr. 3064/44/184 g. Kdos., 8 August 1944, BA-MA RH20-10/195.
98. High Command Southwest, Operations (Ia/T), Teletype Nr. 8684/44, BA-MA RH19X/35. It states: "In attacks, the area surrounding the guilty village is to be cordoned off, all civilians without respect to class or person found in the area are to be arrested. In particularly severe attacks immediate burning down of houses, out of which shots were fired, can also come into consideration.... The immediate punishment is more important than the quick report. All superior officers have to use the greatest severity in pursuit. As for the rest, it is made known through the local commanders that in the slightest occurrence against German troops the sharpest countermeasures are ordered. With that, every local inhabitant should be warned: *no offender or nominal follower should count on leniency*."
99. 14th Army, Army Mail Censorship Office, "Activity Report of the Mail Censorship Office in the 14th Army in August 1944," BA-MA RH13/48.
100. Ibid.
101. Ibid. See also Friedrich Andrae, "*Auch gegen Frauen und Kinder*," 158.
102. 14th Army, Army Mail Censorship Office, "Activity Report of the Mail Censorship Office in the 14th Army in September 1944," 8 October 1944, BA-MA RH13/49.
103. The Military Police counted 101 cases of desertion for May and 393 cases of desertion for June and July out of a total of 721 cases. See Secret Field Police, Group Nr. 741, Tgb. 515/44 geh., no date, BA-MA RH20-10/195.

– Part II –

FORMATIONS

– Chapter 9 –

Local Headquarters Liepaja

Two Months of German Occupation in the Summer of 1941

Margers Vestermanis

In the first weeks of the campaign against the Soviet Union, when the Wehrmacht was racing to the east, a German unit on the far left flank of Army Group North unexpectedly ground to a halt. It was the army's strongest division, Generalleutnant Herzog's[1] 291st Infantry (ID).[2] The city before which German troops encountered fierce resistance was the Latvian harbor of Liepaja, called Libau in German.

After the 291st ID had overrun Soviet border fortifications, its next objective was Riga. Then it was supposed to push past Reval (Tallin) to Leningrad. One regiment of the division—Colonel Loymeyer's[3] 505th—was supposed to swing north; by no later than 25 June 1941, it was to occupy Liepaja with its naval port, which was important for the German navy.

On 23 and 24 June, German advance units were thrown back from Liepaja both at Upper and Lower Bartau (Nica and Barta) as well as east of the city at Grobin (Grobina). Units of the 67th Soviet Infantry Division and the 12th Section of the border guards had fallen back to Liepaja. They were joined by Soviet navy combat personnel from submarines lying at anchor in the Liepaja shipyard, along with roughly a thousand workers from the Tasnare shipyard and factories who had no military training and were insufficiently armed. Altogether, this ragtag collection totaled at most 10,000

Notes for this section begin on page 234.

men. It was not an insignificant military force, even though the defenders of Liepaja had to fight in complete isolation, without supplies, without air support, and without contact with their high command.[4] The unexpectedly determined resistance forced the 291st ID to halt and call for the aid of other regiments and reinforcements. The city was now cut off from the east and the north. It was occupied on 29 June after fierce fighting resulting in heavy losses on both sides.

Occupation

The clashes over Liepaja have been extensively treated in German propaganda during the war and in postwar military histories.[5] To an even greater degree, the Soviets played up the military and political significance of the defense of Liepaja.[6] In this study, we are interested in only two incidents that occurred in the course of those clashes. One occurred on 28 June, when the northern part of the city, called New Liepaja, was already in German hands; fighting was shifting to positions along the canal that separated New Liepaja from the historical district. Old Liepaja was held by scattered groups of Red Army soldiers and armed civilians. In order to put down the last resistance, the Germans used not only artillery and bombers but also loud speakers, through which the defenders were called on to surrender. According to the unanimous statements of many contemporary witnesses, some of the enemy were promised mercy; transmissions constantly repeated in Russian and Latvian are said to have included the words: "We won't do anything to you. We're only killing Jews and Communists."

The other incident also involves a text. The orders of the day and the situation reports of Army Group North mention the participation of armed residents in the battles around Liepaja. The upper echelons of the Wehrmacht reported the situation to the Einsatzgruppe of the Security Police and SD. In doing so, they gave the SS mass-murder apparatus direct instructions to employ terror. The Bulletin of the Reichssicherheitshauptamt (RSHA), "Ereignismeldung USSR" number 12 of 4 July 1941, contains the relevant passage: "Since we were informed by Army High Command (AOK) 18 that in Liepaja civilians have been involved in fighting Germans, the part of EK [Einsatzkommando] 1a, which had already been sent there, was reinforced with part of EK 2 with orders to proceed ruthlessly."[7]

Neither the propaganda broadcast cited above nor the symbiosis between Wehrmacht and SD documented in the "Ereignismeldung

USSR" was anything unique or remarkable; both were typical of warfare in the east. For that very reason, however, they are symptomatic of the readiness of the Wehrmacht leadership at various levels to involve the army in the "ideological struggle" against Jews and Communists. The record of events in and around Liepaja during the early months of the German occupation provides abundant evidence of that.

The situation report of Army Group North for 29 June contains the notation: "291st ID currently pacifying coastal area around Liepaja and Windau."[8] In reality, the division was "pacifying" a much broader area reaching from south of Liepaja to the Lithuanian border. Only one document relating to this operation has been preserved, the Combat Report of Jagdkommando Buttkowitz covering the period from 26 June to 4 July 1941.[9] It documents a German reprisal in the Latvian village Gramsden. According to a report by Lieutenant Buttkowitz, on 30 June, the midwife (Emma Liepina) was shot for bandaging a wounded Red Army man. The wounded man was also shot. The unit also managed to take several prisoners, of whom "one with dumdum ammunition and a Jew were shot."[10] We learn of subsequent events from the memoirs of the local parish pastor. Fourteen buildings were set ablaze, including the church, the parsonage, and the organist's residence.[11] The reason for these prophylactic punishments was that scattered Red Army soldiers had opened fire on a column of trucks belonging to the Wirtschaftskommando Riga between Gramsden and the Lithuanian village of Sijupai.

More information about how the 291st ID treated prisoners of war can be gleaned from the memoirs of Gustavs Celmins,[12] one of the Latvian special officers attached to the division, which appeared in the Latvian press in 1942. The special officer describes the shooting of a captured Soviet political commissar, after the man had been interrogated at the division staff headquarters in the presence of the commander, as a routine matter. General Herzog disliked the prisoner. The general is said to have commented, "The guy has a revolting expression." "A shot out by the stone gate to the barnyard signaled an end to the matter," writes Celmins, who said that he had "thoroughly interrogated" the commissar before his execution.[13]

Photographs often make powerful statements and can save a lot of guesswork about the ideological stance of their subjects, for example, when a division commander—again Kurt Herzog—has himself and his general staff memorialized by the press on the "battlefield" before Liepaja in victorious poses with the corpses of Red Army men piled at their feet.[14]

Both the “combat report” of Jagdkommando Buttkowitz and the memoirs of the special officer have not been arbitrarily selected from a wealth of available documents in order to slander a German army unit. They are the only documents at this author’s disposal containing statements about the conduct of the 291st ID toward war prisoners. They document four shootings that in all probability were typical. In two instances, a reason for the execution was given. One of the condemned had dumdum ammunition, the other tried to hide. In the other cases, the documents’ authors did not consider it necessary to give reasons. The shooting of the political instructor could be justified based on the infamous “commissar order”; no rules on the treatment of Jews had come down “from above” by the last week of June 1941. Even so, the decision described in our first example corresponded to the conduct demanded by the Nazi regime on the basis of racist ideology, which was accepted without reservation by a considerable portion of Wehrmacht personnel. That this behavior resulted in murders committed against Jewish civilians in the early days of the Russian campaign is confirmed by testimony from the former General Staff Officer (Ia) of the 291st ID, who heard of “shootings of Jews in Krottingen by several soldiers of Artillery Regiment 291 operating without orders from the division commander.”[15] The fanatical desire to exterminate on the part of several soldiers documented in this account was no accident. Once the frontier was crossed, many members of the Wehrmacht lost their moral inhibitions. The thin veneer of civilized behavior could now be shrugged off, and the hatred of Jews that had been fanned for years could erupt in bloody excesses.

As a rule, the front-line unit that captured a town also manned the local military administration headquarters. Thus the 505th Grenadier Regiment was ordered to form a local military administration headquarters while fighting was still going on in Liepaja. Regimental Commander Colonel Lohmeyer was named local commander of Liepaja. He issued his first “Order to the Inhabitants of Liepaja” on 28 June.[16] His moment of glory did not last long, because supreme command for the operational area of coastal defense—a ten kilometer stretch along the entire coastline—had been assigned to Naval Commander “C” (Baltic Sea). He claimed unlimited power in Liepaja, which was to be exercised by his plenipotentiary as the naval defense commander and commander of the fort and local military headquarters. In this capacity, Lieutenant Captain Walter Stein took command on 29 June; he was followed after a week by Lieutenant Captain Brückner, who was in turn relieved by Captain Dr. Kawelmacher on 16 July 1941.[17] The period of "dual authority" ended when Dr. Kawelmacher took charge. The local commander of the 505th regiment announced the end of his command. Around that time, a unit of the 207th Security Division arrived in Liepaja, probably in order to establish a local headquarters of its own. But the unit was quickly withdrawn. More is not known about its activity in Liepaja.[18]

During the two weeks in which Commander Lohmeyer exercised dual authority with the commander, units of the 505th Regiment[19] and naval assault troops who had participated in taking the city were in Liepaja.[20] According to Walter Alnor, District Commissar for Courland, the garrison reached a strength of 4,000 men in mid-August and quickly grew by another 7,000.[21]

SD and police units marched into Liepaja with the 291st ID. A sub-unit (Teilkommando) of Einsatzkommando Ia, which was led by SS-Obersturmführer Fritz Reichert, appeared first on 30 June.[22] It left town moving toward Riga after the arrival of another SD-Kommando, Teilkommando Grauel of EK 2 on 5 July.[23] Even Obersturmführer Erhard Grauel was in Liepaja only until the last ten days of July. SS-Untersturmführer Wolfgang Kügler from the staff of EK 2 was ordered to replace him. Grauel brought, in addition to the SD people of his command, a part of the 3rd squad of the 1st Company of Reserve Police Battalion 9.[24] Shortly after Liepaja was taken, an additional platoon of the 1st Company of Reserve Police Battalion 22 was transferred there.[25] And on 22 July, Captain Georg Rosenstock appeared with the 2nd Company of Reserve Police Battalion 13.[26] Like the police and SS officers before him, he duly reported to the fort commandant for housing assignments and orders. All these units were given the same assignment—pacify the city.[27] The SD had already decided what pacification would entail: "Proceed ruthlessly!"[28]

Collaborators: The Lithuanian Self-Defense

When war broke out, an anti-Soviet movement of irregulars erupted throughout the Baltic. As is well known, the Baltic states had been forcibly annexed by the Soviet Union exactly one year earlier. When Soviet troops marched in, the democratic opposition, which had formed against the authoritarian regimes in the Baltic, was enthusiastic about the possibility of revolting against the conservative, ethnocratic regimes. They willfully ignored Soviet claims to power. Relatively broad circles, especially among Jews, were initially prepared to accept annexation because it created the illusion of safety and security. It was assumed that the mighty Red Army would provide protection from the terrors of a world war and a German invasion. The reality of everyday Soviet life and the dictatorship of the Communist Party in the guise of "socialism" proved a great disappointment for everyone, but did not automatically put an end to pro-Soviet sentiment on the part of the workers and left-wing intellectuals. The stubborn resistance put up by the civilian defenders of Liepaja provides eloquent testimony of that.

At the opposite, anti-Soviet, end of the spectrum stood the upper class, which had been dispossessed, stripped of power, and driven to increasingly active opposition by Soviet terror. Military intelligence agents acted as catalysts through rumor-mongering and illegal agitation. Soviet mass deportations on 14 June 1941 were decisive in provoking open resistance. Latvian military officers and *Aizsargi* (members of a paramilitary organization of the conservative and ethnocentric farmers' union) took out their hidden weapons and headed for the woods in expectation of an imminent German invasion. They had formerly been staunchly anti-German, but the Germans, the Nazis, now represented their only chance to save their necks. Military intelligence could manipulate them at will and exploited them as a "fifth column."

Fanatical Latvian nationalists regarded all Jews as supporters of the Soviet system. In effect, this was merely a pretext for giving free reign to long suppressed racial hatred—just as the Jews had been denounced for sympathizing with Germany in 1919. In the interregnum between the withdrawal of the Soviets and the German invasion, however, there were no excesses directed at Jews, as one might have expected. The armed Latvian nationalists, who called themselves *Pasaizsardziba* (Self-Defense), adopted a wait-and-see approach, and were disinclined to anticipate German instructions.

The Wehrmacht and the navy made haste to take direct control of Latvian Self-Defense, which was to act as an auxiliary police force for the Germans under the direction of the local Wehrmacht authorities. To that end, Naval Commander "C" appointed to his staff a Latvian colonel and made him responsible for building up Self-Defense in the coastal region.[29] But the 291st ID engaged in activities that were incomparably more ambitious. Division staff worked out a precise set of regulations governing the subordination of the Latvian Self-Defense to German military authorities and the kinds and numbers of their weaponry. The following entry appears in the War Diary of the 291st ID on 1 July 1941: "Order [of the division commander] to Intelligence Officer (Ic): organize Self-Defense, equip with rifles." The text of the proclamation referred to is included in the War Diary. It urges inhabitants to join Self-Defense "in order to pacify the country and cleanse it of Bolshevist terror and scattered Russian military personnel." Simultaneously, a timetable for the distribution of small arms was announced.[30] By the end of July, the German occupiers could call on more than 720 Latvian auxiliary police in the town and more than 3,485 in the Liepaja district.[31]

The local Wehrmacht and navy commands to which Latvian Self-Defense answered directly in the first weeks must have known about the thirst for revenge and the plans for exterminating Jews motivating their "activists in the first hour." A bloodbath was in the offing. It was in the hands of the occupation force to prevent it, but it did the opposite. The occupiers of Liepaja did not have to comply with orders from above, because both commands were initially provisional and thus virtually inaccessible for orders from higher levels of authority. The rapid advance and unclear situation behind the front lines produced ample opportunities for independent decision-making. The orders of the two local commanders were also not the result of careful political calculation; had that been the case, quite a few inflammatory announcements would not have been made. Obviously, these officers, like many others, were acting in accord with their own inclinations, their subjective need to subjugate the town, to "get pay back" for their unexpected losses. This attitude made a St. Bartholomew's Night in Liepaja unavoidable. The troops marching into Liepaja knew very well from the beginning that it would be the Jews who would suffer for the Communists, who were difficult to sniff out, and the defenders, who had gone underground.

The Beginning of "Pacification"

The Chief of Staff of the 291st ID, whom we have already quoted, said from the witness stand in 1969: "The attack on Liepaja was hard and bloody.... Liepaja was finally taken on 29 June.... On 29 June there were still some street battles; on 30 June, peace reigned everywhere."[32] Another witness, David Siwzon, a survivor of the Liepaja ghetto, has other memories of 29 June: "At 5 p.m. on 29 June, the first Germans appeared in the town. In Uhligstraße they seized seven Jews and twenty-two Latvians and shot them next to a bomb crater at house number 7/9. The corpses were then thrown into this pit."[33] At 9 o'clock that same evening, Germans dressed in field gray appeared at the Villa Minkowska in Wittestraße, where Walter Hahn, a Jewish emigrant from Austria, composer and the director of the Liepaja opera lived. All the tenants were hauled from their apartments and lined up in the courtyard. Among them was a dentist named Sebba, who later reported what occurred. When the Germans asked whether any of those present were emigrants from the Reich, Walter Hahn answered yes and took several steps forward. He was shot on the spot. In a show of contempt for the dead man, it was ordered that his body be buried next to the garbage cans.[34]

Who were the killers? At this early stage the witnesses were not yet attuned to specifics regarding the German military occupation troops. They could testify only that the killers had been people in field gray uniforms. It could not, therefore, have been naval assault troops, and Teilkommando Ia of the Security Police would not arrive in Liepaja until 30 June. The killers must have been Wehrmacht personnel, most likely members of the 505th Grenadier Regiment, which occupied the center of town.

On 30 June, when "peace reigned everywhere" in Liepaja, Latvian Self-Defense forces began mass arrests of all the Soviet sympathizers they could get their hands on. Of course, the local Communist leaders had either fled or perished in the battles around Liepaja; those who remained were insignificant fellow travelers. Nevertheless, within the first few days, all of the jails were crowded. The local military headquarters of the 505th Regiment was forced to build a "provisional jail" to house Red Army men and civilian defenders of the city who were delivered into their custody. For that purpose, eighteen cells were constructed in the vaulted cellars of the metallurgical works. The number of people arrested is not known. Numerals with German text scratched on the doors of the cells, by which the guards recorded the number of prisoners, offer the only clue. They suggest that it must have been several hundred. Those held in custody were then shot, one group after the other.[35]

In the meantime, German soldiers had been posted at every intersection in the city. The local commandant had ordered that all weapons be turned in to those men "by no later than 8 o'clock on 29 June." The order was rendered unenforceable by the fact that it was not publicized until 2 July, and yet anyone found possessing a weapon after 29 June was supposed to be shot on the spot. Local commandant Lohmeyer declared a state of siege in the city and placed the town under curfew from eight o'clock in the evening to five o'clock in the morning. Locking house doors was forbidden; soldiers were supposed to shoot into any undarkened windows. The tenth and last point of the order read: "Any attempt at sabotage will be punished by death." Even an attempt![36]

In the first days of the occupation, there were instances of troops plundering, and not only in Jewish dwellings. This was confirmed twenty-five years later by the former fort commander and other officers.[37]

On 2 July, the commander of the fort and of local military headquarters, Lieutenant Captain Stein, published in the local Latvian newspaper, *Kurzemes Vārds* (No. 1), an official "summons" to scattered Red Army men and the population of the city. Red Army soldiers behind the German front lines were called on to turn themselves in to German authorities within twenty-four hours. After that deadline had expired, all Red Army men taken prisoner would be shot. The civilian population was informed that "ten hostages held in German hands will be shot for every act of assault, sabotage, or plundering."

Shootings had been underway since the first day of the occupation. The commandant's pronouncements made it clear that these were not accidental, "wild" measures and that what lay ahead was the most violent terror. One is sorely tempted to attribute the order unleashing a campaign of terror to the panicky reaction of a young naval officer who, having been dispatched to Liepaja to determine whether the harbor might be serviceable, found himself unexpectedly named, first by General Herzog and then by Naval Commander "C," Admiral Clasen, fort commander in a town whose dramatic conquest he had personally experienced. "*In dubio pro reo*!" Yet in this case, and in the case of orders to commit murders yet to be mentioned, "higher authorities" seem to have played a role. The proof is that an identical appeal was issued in another harbor town, in Windau (Ventspils) by the local naval commander, Lieutenant Meitinger.[38] It is worth noting that there had been no military action of any kind in the Windau area; the town had been taken without a single loss on the German side. This circumstance justifies us in assuming that the actual authors of the orders to commit murder issued by the local naval commandants are to be found at a higher level of command, in all probability among the staff of Naval Commander "C." In any case, it can be asserted with certainty that the Supreme Naval Commander, who was present in Liepaja with his staff from 1 to 6 July, approved the actions of his administrative officers.

On 8 July, the day Lieutenant Meitinger issued the "summons" in Windau, a similar "announcement" was publicized in Liepaja: "During the past several nights, shots have been fired at German sentries. Thirty Bolshevik and Jewish hostages were shot in response. Latvian inhabitants are urged to report immediately all

Bolshevists and Jewish robbers in hiding to the Security Police. Should the attacks of the last several nights be repeated, one hundred hostages will be shot for every German soldier wounded."[39]

That was the debut of the new local commandant, Lieutenant Captain Brückner, who was relieved eight days later by Captain Dr. Kawelmacher, who did not lag far behind his predecessors. On 11 October, he announced that, recently, German sentries had repeatedly been shot at. In reprisal, he was ordering that a "certain portion of Liepaja's inhabitants, the exact number yet to be determined," would be arrested and shot.[40]

Although the fall of 1941 lies beyond the scope of this study, the orders to murder hostages cited here can only be analyzed in a broader context. Taken as a whole, they show an unmistakable similarity; the horrifying escalation in the number of "reprisal victims" is especially striking. In the fall, the town was completely "pacified," and despite the reported armed attacks, no perpetrator was ever discovered, not one German soldier wounded. In any case, the population was generally convinced that the perpetrators of the "shooting incidents" were probably the frequently drunk naval personnel in the harbor.

Given the state of mind revealed in the orders to murder hostages, it is not surprising that the local commands of the navy and the army in Liepaja worked closely with the Security Police (SIPO) and SD, carried out mass executions independently, and were especially active in persecuting and murdering Jews.

Murdering Jews

On 2 July the field commandant for Riga, Colonel Ullersperger, issued the first order that discriminated against the Jews in Latvia. Jews were forbidden to stand in line in front of stores. The practical effect was to forbid Jews to buy food.[41] Local Commandant Brückner in Liepaja outdid his superiors in Riga with his "Order for all Jews in Liepaja" of 5 July. Point one stipulated: "All Jews (men, women, children) are required, effective immediately, to affix to their clothes, over their chests, and on their backs, readily visible badges in the form of yellow pieces of cloth no smaller than ten by ten." All men between sixteen and sixty years old were to present themselves at the fire station at seven o'clock each morning "in order to perform public work." Jews could be on the streets only during a four-hour period of the day. They were strictly forbidden to use public transportation or enter parks or public baths. All transportation vehicles, radios, and typewriters were to be turned in immediately. The limited period in which Jews might be out of doors effectively banned Jews from the streets. Even so, the far-sighted commander saw himself confronted with the theoretical possibility that a German in uniform might come face to face with a Jew on the sidewalk. He therefore decreed in point six that in such a situation the Jew had to leave the sidewalk without delay.[42]

One did not have to be especially perceptive to recognize the still greater threat lurking behind this derision and ostracism. The last point, number 11, suggests as much. Anyone bold enough to violate the order would be dealt with "most harshly." What could be more horrible than civic death? Physical death!

July 4 must be regarded as the beginning of systematic mass shootings. In the afternoon, forty-seven Jews and five Latvian "Communists" were shot by Teilkommando 1a in the town park (Raipa parks). The squad's leader, SS-Obersturmführer Reichert, was merely carrying out an assignment he had received from the fort commandant.[43] Jews were brought in groups from the women's prison at 5 Tiesas Straße, which had served since 2 July as a collection point for Jews arrested and marked for shooting. Only men were arrested in Liepaja in the summer of 1941; they were simply seized when they gathered at the fire station or were beaten and driven from their dwellings. Jews who gathered at designated points to register offered additional opportunities to arrest the men and take them to the women's prison. There are innumerable, consistent statements from survivors, guards, SD-members, and people not directly involved about the inhumane conditions in the prisons. On 6 June a war correspondent assigned to a navy propaganda company spent several hours in the prison. He later testified from the witness stand that "he had asked that three or four of the doors be opened, and had seen Jews packed together in small rooms. They had been standing so close together that they could not lie down or relieve themselves."[44] A former guard stated that the Jews had quickly realized that there was only one way out of this prison—into the pit.[45]

The next mass shooting is said to have taken place on 6 July. Detailed information is lacking. On that day a direct demand that Jews be physically exterminated appeared in the newspaper *Kurzemes Vārds*, which was censored by a German Sonderführer.[46] On 7 July Teilkommando Grauel carried out the shooting of hostages demanded by the fort commandant. SS-Obersturmführer Grauel went personally to the women's prison, had the prisoners brought out, and selected every fifth man. "Only" thirty were supposed to be selected, but between a hundred and a hundred and fifty were shot. The men selected were driven into the courtyard by members of the SD and Latvian Self-Defense; from there they were transported in trucks to the shooting site.[47] Large-scale shootings followed on 8, 9, and 10 July.[48] The victims were primarily Jews. On 12 July, only Jews were shot; they were seized at the labor office when they came to register.[49] On the following day, the dismantling of Liepaja's Great Choral Synagogue began. *Kurzemes Vārds* editorialized on this act of barbarism with great enthusiasm: "Tearing down the temple deprives Jews of the possibility to gather and hammer out plans for the enslavement of Christians under the leadership of the rabbi."[50] Jews were forced to help dismantle their synagogue. Torah scrolls were thrown from desecrated synagogues into the street. As special "entertainment," these writings, held sacred in the east and west, were spread out at the fire station, and Jews were forced to march on the revered parchment by Self-Defense and SD members wielding clubs.

According to witnesses' statements, mass shootings were carried out every evening in mid-July in the dunes south of the lighthouse. Most of the victims were Jewish men. Documentation is available only for the shooting of 15 July, in a diary entry written by Karl Heinz L., a sailor on the tanker *Mittelgrund*:

> Liepaja 15 July
>
> We horse around in the water and try to score with the little Latvian chicks. But all good things must end, and we all have to be back on board at 8 o'clock. We're strolling back when, not far from the beach, we come upon a lot of people.... At first glance, it looks like a sports event. Yes, it's an event all right, even if of another type. We've come upon the place where so and so many snipers are shot every evening.... Soldiers are standing around, I guess around 600 to 800 men, satisfying their gruesome curiosity.[51]

On that evening, "only" twenty-five men are supposed to have been shot. They included no "snipers," perhaps a few "politicals"; the rest were Jews.

In the latter part of July, the SD Teilkommando, in close cooperation with the Latvian auxiliary police, planned a "major operation" aimed at exterminating most of the Jewish men in Liepaja. It began with a decree from the head of Latvian Self-Defense that, effective immediately, all civilian employers were to fire any Jews who had been assigned to them as unpaid forced laborers. Jews were ordered to gather at the fire station "to receive a special assignment."[52] The "assignment" was to arrest all Jews not employed by the German authorities immediately and chase them with hands raised through the town to the women's prison. But the number of arrests did not live up to the organizers' plans, so a regular hunt for Jewish men was arranged, first in Jewish dwellings, then among men coming home from work. Identity papers showing that the men were employed by German authorities were simply confiscated, and the victims were taken to the prison.[53] The shootings, which claimed about 500 victims, took place on 22, 23, and 24 July at the naval base.

In the last days of July, Kommando Arājs appeared in Liepaja—a unit put together by the staff of EK 2 in Riga for the specific purpose of carrying out executions under the leadership of Victor Arājs. North of Liepaja at the harbor close to Schkeden (Škēde), the Kommando shot about a hundred Jews after forcing them to dig their own graves.[54] There were more shootings with hundreds of victims at the naval base in August.[55]

The pelotons for the first shootings were provided chiefly by the Wehrmacht and the navy. An SD officer was usually in command. SD men fired into the pit to finish off survivors.[56] An amateur film taken by an orderly sergeant in mid-July shows marines acting as an execution peloton in the dunes near Liepaja.[57] Only gradually did firing squads come to be formed from police units stationed in Liepaja, especially from Reserve Police Battalion 13. Initially, the Latvian Self-Defense was only supposed to round up the victims, form convoys, set up sentry lines, and shovel sand on the corpses. But the roles in murdering were soon reassigned. From mid-July, Self-Defense members participated directly in the killings, and at summer's end the Latvian guard platoon was supplying a standing death squad, ready at all times for any assignment.

Summary

Because of the protracted struggle over the Baltic Sea islands, the coast of western Latvia remained, until the end of October 1941, a zone of military operations in which the local, fort, and naval commandant in Liepaja was provided special authority that assured him practically unlimited freedom of action. In the last stage of the conquest of the Baltic Sea islands, the fort commandant in Liepaja was also given authority to function as a Wehrmacht commander in Courland. Even so, as early as September, the military was gradually yielding its authority in civilian matters to the district commissioner. With the appointment of the SS- and Polizeistandortführer in Liepaja on 15 September, the fort commandant lost his police authority in the civilian realm.

The two-month period of unlimited military authority in Liepaja was over. In this short period, the military had demonstrated a bloodthirstiness unmatched anywhere else in the Baltic region. The fortress commandant in Liepaja was not the only officer who, on his own authority, ordered the public identification of Jews two weeks before the general order to that effect was issued. Similar orders were issued by the local commandants of Windau, Talsen, and Dünaburg, so that every subordinate in uniform could give free reign to his sadistic fantasies in selecting the sign he would require Jews to wear. Thus it was that Jews came to wear a yellow square in Liepaja, a triangle in Windau, a circle in Talsen, and a five-pointed star in Daugavpils. Liepaja's fort commandant's order of 5 July was, however, the first comprehensive anti-Jewish directive to take effect on Latvian soil, as well as the most radical during the initial phase of the persecution of the Jews. It must be noted that Liepaja was not the only town where hostages were shot. In Bauske, on 2 July, the local commandant had twenty hostages publicly shot at the Memel bridge by a peloton supplied by the local headquarters, allegedly in "reprisal" for the German soldiers who had fallen in the battles for the town.[58] But that was an isolated incident. The hostage shootings in Liepaja, on the other hand, were implemented as a system designed to motivate and justify the continued shooting of Jews. I have estimated the total number of victims in the two months of military rule in Liepaja to have been 3,000 at most, which probably included no fewer than 2,500 Jewish victims.

But it is not only the mass murders of defenseless Jews in the guise of hostage justice that qualifies those bloody events as a typical example of the crimes of the Wehrmacht. In the amateur film mentioned earlier, in the diary, and in the testimony of witnesses during the trials of Grauel and Rosenstock in the state court in Hanover, the reactions of the mass of soldiers to the mass executions carried out through the end of July in full public view have been preserved. "The shootings were crowded with gawking soldiers," one witness recalls.[59] There were always hundreds of onlookers from the army and the navy. Not only soldiers, railroad workers are also said to have been in attendance from time to time.[60]

Several witnesses claim that they did not come on their own accord but were ordered to attend the shootings by their superiors. But most of them clearly came of their own free will. "Here and there a rough laugh rings out," writes the sailor, Karl Heinz L. in his diary. "Here and there, necks crane in an effort not to miss any of this spectacle."[61] Another witness testified that some onlookers "were so crude that they sang out, 'Let him have it!'"[62] Nor did they stop at angry words. The film also shows physical violence directed at the victims. A navy man kicks a man who is being driven into the pit. The general mood, however, is probably more faithfully captured in a diary entry by Karl Heinz L: "The entire execution lasted only a few minutes. The firing squad stood around telling stories and smoking. I studied the faces of the crowd. Unfeelingness, indifference, or satisfaction are written on them." And most set out toward home "laughing and joking."[63]

It can be safely assumed that not all the "gawkers" at the shootings were committed anti-Semites and cruel sadists. It is more plausible that they played the role of onlookers at the awful spectacle because they were afraid of being branded as "unacceptable" should they refuse. There was also always the fear of being driven from the "herd," from the *Volksgemeinschaft*, the dread of being categorized as "politically incorrect" (*politischer Fehlgänger*). Yet the secret sympathizers, the malicious "gawkers," and the sadistic killers had much in common. Taken as a group, they approved the National Socialist regime of violence. From that ultimately flowed their acceptance of the extermination of the Jews as a necessary part of the "ideological war." Some did so enthusiastically, others only with hesitation and reluctance while searching for explanations and excuses for those horrible events. That did not protect them from complicity in bloody crimes, from guilt and responsibility. How deep was the abyss into which a criminal regime managed to drag an entire people? The events in Liepaja in the summer of 1941 offer a depressing example.

—Translated by Roy Shelton

Notes

1. Kurt Herzog (1889–1948), Major General, 1942 General of artillery, Commander of the XXXVIII Panzer Corps. Died in Soviet captivity.
2. The 291st Infantry Division consisted of: 504th, 505th, 506th Grenadier Regiments, AR 91, Pioneer Battalion 291, Pz. Jg. Abt. 291, AA/Füs. Btl. 291, Nachr. Abt. 291, FEB 291, Dinfü (Vers. R) 291. At the time of the battles around Liepaja, the following were also attached to the division: Landesschützen Btl., a Radf. Btl., schw. Art. Abt. rnOt 633, Mörserbattr./schw. Art. Abt. 637, Marine Art. Abt. 530, a Bttr. Eisenbahngeschütz, Kp. Heeres-Fla-Abt. 272, a Panzerzug, a Kette Heeresflieger. See Wolfgang Keilig, *Das deutsche Heer 1939–1945* (Bad Nauheim: n. d.), 2:101; W. Conze, *Die Geschichte der 291. Infanteriedivision* (Bad Nauheim: 1953), 93; W. Haupt, *Baltikum 1941* (Neckargemünd: 1963), 69.
3. Kurt Lohmeyer (1893–1942), Oberst, 1942 Brigadier General, died at the front while commanding a division.
4. W. Sawtschenko, *Sem ognennich dnjei* (Seven Blazing Days) (Riga: 1985), 50.
5. Of the flood of panegyric publications on the war, only two are cited here: K. Gloger, *Oberst Lohmeyer* (Berlin: 1942); F. Pessendorfer, *Sturm zum Finnmeer* (Riga: 1943). For the postwar period: W. Haupt, *Kurland. Die letzte Front* (Bad Nauheim: 1961); idem, *Baltikum 1941* (Neckargemünd: 1963).
6. Approximately 150 books, brochures, and major articles on the defense of Liepaja had appeared by 1979. See *Revoljuzionnaja Liepaja. Ukasatel literaturi* (Liepaia: 1979), 58–79.
7. E. Rusins, "Nevienlidziga cina" (Unequal Battle), in *Komunists* (Liepaja: 24 April 1946).
8. Cited in Haupt, *Baltikum 1941*, 69.
9. NOKW-Dokument 1170.
10. See Szymou Datner, *Presruplenija nemezko-faschistskogo wermachta w otnoschenii woennoplennich* (Crimes of the German, Fascist Wehrmacht against Prisoners of War) (Moscow: 1969), 434–444.
11. Haralds Biezais, *Saki tā, kā tas ir* (Say How It Is) (n.p.: 1986), 140.
12. Gustavs Celmins (born 1899), leader of the Latvian fascist organization "Perkonkrusts" (Cross of Thunder).
13. Gustavs Celmins, "No Memeles lidz Rigai ar vacu armiju" (From the Memel to Riga with the German Army), in *Kurzemes Vārds*, 7 June 1942.
14. *Befreiung* (Liberation), illustrated publication of the Propaganda Company of the 18th Army (n.p.: 1941), 2.
15. Witness statement of W. v. R., Office of the District Attorney at the State Court in Hanover in Criminal Proceedings against Grauel et al., 2 Ks 3/68, Protokollband II/"b":147.
16. The order could be published in the Latvian newspaper *Kurzemes Vārds* only after a long delay.
17. *Kurzemes Vārds* of 16 July 1941.
18. *Latvijas Vestures Archiv* (Latvian Historical Archive, HAL), 80/3/1, 55.
19. According to the former Ia officer of the 291st Infantry Division, the 505th Regiment left Liepaja around 1 July. District Attorney in Hanover, Criminal Proceeding against Grauel et al., Protokollband II/"b."
20. Haupt, *Baltikum 1941*, 62.
21. Situation Report of the District Commissar for Courland of 27 August 1941, HAL, 69/1a/17/B1. 106.

22. "Ereignismeldung [Incident Report] (EM) UdSSR," 6 (27 June 1941); "EM UdSSR," 9 (1 July 1941).
23. "EM UdSSR,"12 (4 July 1941). District Attorney of Hanover, Criminal Proceeding against Grauel et al., Indictment, vol. 22, 35.
24. Ibid., 55–60.
25. HAL, 83/1/22/Bi. 15; see also State Attorney of Hanover, Criminal Proceeding against Grauel et al., 72; ibid., vol. 18, 78.
26. District Attorney of Hanover, Criminal Proceeding against Grauel et al., Indictment, Bd. XXII, 24f.; District Attorney of Hanover, Criminal Proceeding again Grauel et al., verdict, vol. 30, 286f.
27. In the trial of Grauel, Rosenstock et al., the primary role of the fort commandant was regarded as definitely proven. The 2nd Company of Reserve Police Battalion 13 was assigned on the verbal order of the commander of Ordnungspolizei Ostland to Fort Commandant Kawelmacher; see District Attorney of Hanover, Criminal Proceeding against Grauel et al., vol. 30, 288.
28. "EM UdSSR," 12 (4 July 1941).
29. *Kurzemes Vārds*, 4 July 1941.
30. District Attorney of Hanover, Criminal Proceeding against Grauel et al., verdict, vol. XXX, 53; ibid., Protokollband 6 (V):83.
31. HAL, 69/ia/17/B1. 158.
32. District Attorney of Hanover, Criminal Proceeding against Grauel et al., Protokollband II/B:143.
33. HAL, 132/30/21/B1. 3. D. Siwzon's testimony is corroborated by many other witnesses. Accounts regarding the number of victims vary.
34. Ibid. Additional facts emerged in the witness statement of Kalman Linkemer on 22 October 1970; see District Attorney of Hanover, Criminal Proceeding against Grauel et al., vol. 29, 121. The murder of W. Hahn is also confirmed in *Kurzemes Vārds* of 13 August 1941, in which it was asserted that he deserved to die because he had called for the defense of the town.
35. Materials in the Museum for the History of the City of Liepaja; I. Pinksis, G. Freibergs, V. Leijins, *Revolucionara Liepaja* (Liepaja Revolutionaries) (Riga: 1955), 198.
36. *Kurzemes Vārds*, 2 July 1941.
37. District Attorney of Hanover, Criminal Proceeding against Grauel et al., Protokollbände II/B 72, 6 (V); 156.
38. *Ventas Balss*, 8 July 1941.
39. *Kurzemes Vārds*, 8 July 1941.
40. Ibid., 11 October 1941.
41. *Tevija*, 2 July 1941.
42. *Kurzemes Vārds*, 5 July 1941.
43. District Attorney of Hanover, Criminal Proceeding against Grauel et al., verdict, 30:211; ibid., Protokollband:211.
44. District Attorney of Hanover, Criminal Proceeding against Grauel et al., verdict, 30:90.
45. Ibid., 96.
46. *Kurzemes Vārds*, 6 July 1941.
47. District Attorney of Hanover, Criminal Proceeding against Grauel et al., verdict, 30:73–75, 90.
48. Ibid.
49. Ibid., 29:122.
50. *Kurzemes Vārds*, 15 July 1941.

51. Karl Heinz L.'s diary was published in Norbert Haase, ed., *"Wie eine Sportveranstaltung, wenn auch etwas anderer Art ..." Mord an den Liepajaer Juden im Sommer 1941. Aus dem Tagebuch eines Augenzeugen* (n.p.: n.d.).
52. *Kurzemes Vārds*, 15 July 1941.
53. Witness statement of Roma Isakson, District Attorney of Hanover, Criminal Proceeding against Grauel et al., Protokollband II/B:2; witness statement of David Siwzon, HAL, 132/30/29, 19; Solomon Feigerson, "Svidetelstvuju" (I Bear Witness), in *Alef* (Israel), 17 December 1989, 29–30; Aaron Vesterman, "Survival in a Liepaja bunker," in *Muted Voices: Jewish Survivors of Latvia Remember*, ed. G. Scheider (New York: 1987), 159.
54. District Attorney at the State Court in Hamburg, indictment of Viktor Arājs, 141 Js 5 34/60, 117.
55. Indictment issued by the Committee of State Security of the Latvian SSR on 28 August 1972 against R. Pavelkops et al., Criminal Proceedings, Document 11, 5.
56. District Attorney of Hanover, Criminal Proceeding against Grauel et al., Protokollband II/B:175–176; ibid., 5:68.
57. Ibid., Protokollband II/B:216.
58. HAL, 132/30/9/7; 132/26/7/9; W. Braemer. "Zum Tage der Befreiung Rigas," in *Ostland*, H. 1/1942, 7.
59. District Attorney of Hanover, Criminal Proceeding against Grauel et al., Protokollband II/B:180.
60. Ernst Klee, Willi Dreßen, Volker Rieß, eds., *"Schöne Zeiten"* (Frankfurt am Main: 1988), 124.
61. Haase, *Tagebuch*.
62. District Attorney of Hanover, Criminal Proceeding against Grauel et al., Protokollband II/B:180.
63. Haase, *Tagebuch*.

– *Chapter 10* –

ON THE WAY TO STALINGRAD

The 6th Army in 1941–42

Bernd Boll *and* Hans Safrian

Stalingrad: Golgotha of the 6th Army?

Even today, collective memory identifies the 6th Army with the battle of Stalingrad. Since 1945, no other major unit of the Wehrmacht has been a more frequent subject of publications in German-speaking countries. Yet, oddly, scholarly as well as biographical, literary, journalistic, and film treatments deal almost exclusively with the death of the 6th Army on the Volga. Exhibiting varying degrees of interest in the facts and shifting propagandistic intent, they describe an army's "self-sacrifice." Controversies have flared up primarily over whether its "ruin" was unavoidable and who should answer for it. Given the number of victims—60,000 German soldiers died in the encirclement; of the 110,000 who went into Soviet captivity, only 5000 returned after the war[1]—it seems reasonable at first glance to view things from this perspective. But closer examination reveals that tightly focusing on the topos of "victim," which has characterized discourse concerning Stalingrad until today, historically perpetuates National Socialist mythologizing.

Reinterpreting the loss of an entire army as a heroic example for the nation was consistent with the logic of an ideology that was always prepared to exploit the sacrifice of the individual for the

Notes for this section begin on page 264.

Volksgemeinschaft to rhetorical ends. The commander in chief of the 6th Army, Generaloberst Friedrich Paulus, set the tone on 29 January 1943 in his congratulatory radio message to Hitler on the tenth anniversary of the Nazis' assumption of power: "May our struggle serve as an example for this and future generations that one must never capitulate even in the most hopeless predicament. Then Germany will triumph."[2] Meanwhile, Berlin had already established the official line by which the predictable defeat on the Volga could be converted into propaganda capital to strengthen resolve both at the front and at home. "As always in world history, even this sacrifice will not have been in vain," Hitler wired Paulus in response on the following day. "Even now the entire German people cast their eyes toward this city with deep emotion. Clausewitz' dictum shall be fulfilled. Only now is the German nation beginning to grasp the seriousness of this struggle; it will make the greatest sacrifices."[3]

On the same day, Göring expressed himself in a similar fashion in the "Hall of Honor" of the Reich Ministry of Aviation in a speech to German Wehrmacht officers and enlisted men, which was broadcast to Stalingrad. "The destiny of Europe lies in our hands, along with Germany's freedom, its culture, and its future. That is the highest significance of this sacrifice, which you, my comrades, can be asked to make at any time and at any place. Each of you should be mindful of the soldiers of Stalingrad; then you will be hard as steel."[4] In the same spirit, the supreme commander of Army Group Don, Generalfeldmarschall Erich von Manstein, prepared a radio address to the 6th Army on 31 January, which could not be delivered because communications had already been cut: "Our thanks for your heroic sacrifice will be our struggle to fulfill the legacy that you have left for us."[5]

Then on 3 February, when the endless columns of survivors were marching into captivity, the Supreme Command of the Armed Forces (OKW) broadcast to the German public a "special report" containing the official interpretation of the defeat at Stalingrad and its utility for German claims to dominance. "The army's sacrifice was not in vain. Throughout many weeks, standing as a bulwark of Europe's historic mission, it broke the momentum of six Soviet armies." The myth had been born: heroic self-sacrifice for the well-being of future generations. "They died," the report went on, "that Germany might live. Their example will bear fruit to the end of time, despite all false Bolshevik propaganda."[6] The press carried the report a day later under the dramatic headline: "They died that Germany might live."[7]

With some adjustments, the myth of sacrifice survived the end of National Socialism. It is the common thread running through such best-selling fictional treatments of the subject of Stalingrad as those by Heinz G. Konsalik, Heinrich Gerlach, and Fritz Wöss,[8] which purport to portray the common soldier who had been "betrayed by a leadership devoid of conscience," and yet always "clung to the principles of comradeship and military decency."[9] Most of all, organizations of former combatants at Stalingrad in the Federal Republic of Germany and Austria—who, unlike veterans' groups from divisions, derive their sense of belonging from having taken part in the battle—cultivated the myth for decades and thus influenced public perception. Through the whole range of lessons that their spokesmen draw from their experience runs the constant attempt "to represent the deeds and sufferings of the soldiers as a meaningful sacrifice," comparable in its historical significance to the battle of Thermopylae.[10]

The theme of the "betrayed army" and its sacrifice continues to influence popularized scholarship on the subject. Typical of an image of Stalingrad still widespread today is a book by Franz Kurowski published in 1992 on the fiftieth anniversary of the battle, in which the author quotes memoirs of top officers and descriptions of personal experiences from both sides of the conflict for pages on end, while completely ignoring recent research by military historians. Kurowski goes even further than earlier versions in proclaiming the myth of sacrifice, consecrating it with quasi-religious solemnity: "Stalingrad became a symbol for the death of an entire army and the sacrificial deployment of the Luftwaffe. Stalingrad was a word that every soldier on the Eastern front could speak only with horror in his heart." A few pages earlier, Kurowski has already gone so far as to proclaim: "The city on the Volga had become the Golgotha of the 6th Army."[11]

But even liberal discourse, for which Stalingrad serves as a beacon calling for the outlawing of war and the reconciliation of erstwhile enemies, cannot escape the embrace of the myth of sacrifice. Klaus Bresser, chief editor of ZDF (Zweites Deutsches Fernsehen—a public channel), said of the television series "Der verdammte Krieg—Entscheidung Stalingrad" (The Cursed War—Decision at Stalingrad): "Stalingrad became a mass grave, became a symbol for the senseless sacrifice of war, became a synonym for sadness and suffering in the former Soviet Union and in Germany."[12] How tenaciously the mythologizing that began a half century ago blocks other interpretations is clear even in recent attempts by military historians to describe the war "from below." It is precisely this focusing of attention on the often traumatic experiences of the simple soldier that confirms the paradigm of victim rather than calling it into question.[13]

And yet the 6th Army had marched a long road on its way to Stalingrad. For one and one-half years, it had marched east through the Soviet Union as the executor of the National Socialist regime's policy of conquest and annihilation, actively participating in genocide—and not only on orders from above. It was neither accident nor unfortunate exception in January 1942 when the 75th Infantry Division (ID), then attached to the 6th Army, ordered that henceforth, in reprisal for "atrocities committed against our soldiers," all Asians, whether military or civilian, were to be shot. And it was no less routine when the chief of the general staff of Army Corps (AK) XXIX transmitted the same instruction on the following day to all divisions under his command.[14] Thus, this chapter examines the first stage in the march of the 6th Army to Stalingrad, the first half year from the beginning of "Operation Barbarossa" reaching up to the winter of 1941–42. It is at the same time a case study in waging a war of annihilation that manifested itself in the genocide of the Jews, in the struggle against real and imagined partisans, and in the starvation of the civilian population.

The "Criminal Orders" and Their Execution

Before "Operation Barbarossa" began, the Decree on Jurisdiction and the "Commissar Order" defined certain segments of the civilian population and the Red Army as enemies and ordered measures aimed at their "complete elimination." Irregulars, political commissars in the Red Army, civilian commissars who resisted the Wehrmacht or fomented resistance, along with other "hostile civilians," were to be killed at once. The troops had sweeping authority to carry out those directives in the absence of specific orders. No binding order mandated the killing of civilians who were merely suspected of committing a hostile act. In those cases, decisions regarding life and death lay in the hands of the officer nearest at hand. Killing within the framework of "collective measures" aimed at localities from which attacks were launched against German troops could only be authorized by an officer from battalion command or higher. Commissars without hostile intentions were initially supposed to be left "unmolested," with the proviso, of course, that they would later be turned over to the SD (Security Service of the SS).[15]

Thus, to be sure, restrictions on reprisals seemed to have been significantly loosened; on the other hand, they had been clearly laid out: Only instances of proven armed resistance were to be answered with shootings on the spot. The "Guidelines for the Conduct of Troops in Russia," however, were at once vaguer and more severe. While they did not name explicitly the measures to be taken, they branded additional groups as enemies and emphatically included "Bolshevik agitators, irregulars, saboteurs, Jews" among those to be "eliminated." The accompanying, vaguely formulated demand for the "complete elimination of any active or passive resistance" was a proviso designed to justify extending the definition of the enemy at any time. Armed with this carte blanche, warned for good measure about "treacherous methods of fighting" by the Red Army in general and "Asian soldiers" in particular ("inscrutable, unpredictable, underhanded, and callous")—the troops began their attack on the Soviet Union.[16]

Written "Guidelines for the Treatment of Political Commissars" were issued by the OKW on 6 June 1941 and, once amended by the Wehrmacht commander, von Brauchitsch, transmitted to the commanders of the armies and air force.[17] On 10 and 11 June 1941, intelligence (Ic) officers and military judges of the army groups, armies, and armored groups were briefed on the commissar order and the "Führer Decree," i.e., the decree regarding the exercise of military justice, by the general for special duty at the level of the Supreme Commander of the Army, Generalleutnant Müller. Among other things, Müller stressed point one of the decree, "dealing with crimes by hostile civilians," which specified that crimes by hostile civilians did not fall under military justice or a regular court-martial; on the contrary, "irregulars," were to be "eliminated without mercy" by the "troops in combat or in flight." He went on to define as irregulars "in a larger sense, agitators, people distributing leaflets, and saboteurs."[18]

When the Ic officer of AOK 6, Major Paltzo, returned from the conference with Müller to the 6th Army's main headquarters on 12 June, he explained the "Guidelines for the Treatment of Political Commissars" to the commander in chief, von Reichenau.[19] On the same day, P. reported to the chief of the general staff and the Ia (first general staff/operations) officer the "results of the conference at the headquarters of the general for special duty of the OKH regarding 'Führer decrees' [*sic*!], treatment of hostile civilians and commissars."[20] That evening the Ic officer and the chief of the general staff conferred on how to disseminate the "Guidelines for the Conduct of Troops in Russia." It was agreed that the "guidelines" should be disseminated down to the battalion level.[21] On 13 June Major Paltzo presented section Ia of the general staff with the entire complex of orders regarding "a) conduct of the troops in Russia, b) behavior regarding a hostile civilian population, c) treatment of red commissars—and notations regarding these points based on a conference with the General for special duty."[22] Responsible groups on the general staff had thus been informed of the entire range of criminal orders, partly by the High Command of the Army (OKH), partly by Major Paltzo.

AOK 6 summoned its military judges to a meeting in Zamosc on 15 June, at which the chairmen of the divisional courts were present. "The main item" on the agenda was the Decree on Jurisdiction.[23] On the following day the Decree on Jurisdiction and the guidelines for the conduct of troops in Russia were communicated to division commanders, who informed the units under their commands what the orders required of them.[24] On 16 June, the orders were passed on to all Ic officers of the army corps and divisions of the 6th Army during a conference at staff headquarters in Tarnobrzeg. The Ic/AO group had prepared for the meeting of Ic officers by putting together "points for introductory remarks by the chief of the general staff," which covered "explanation of the decrees [*sic*!] of the Führer concerning the treatment of a hostile civilian population, behavior of German soldiers toward the civilian population, the treatment of Russian commissars," and the "instructions regarding conduct of troops in Russia."[25] Following these preparations, the chief of the general staff spoke at the meeting of Ic officers about "a) conduct of troops in Russia, b) treatment of Russ[ian] civilian population, behavior of German soldiers toward population, c) treatment of [Russian] commissars."[26] A further point involved informing the Ic officers about the planned activities of SS Einsatzgruppen[27] in the areas of military operations: "Use [of] GFP [Secret Field Police] and SS Einsatzkommandos. Distinguishing the missions of the two."[28]

The commanding general of Army Corps XVII transmitted the directives to the commanders of his troops on 20 June in the vicinity of Ludvinov, and consulted—surely on the same subject—the commanders of the 56th and 62nd infantry divisions.[29] Finally, written directives from AOK 6 (still communicating under the code name "Sector Staff Staufen") concerning the competencies of the counterintelligence groups, special units of the Foreign Office, and SD-Sonderkommandos in the 6th Army's area of operations went out to the divisions bearing the date 20 July 1941.[30] Explicit orders that the subordinate units are to "assist by any means possible, as far as the combat situation permits," the Kommandos "in carrying out their important special assignments by instructing the troops, providing auxiliary personnel, sharing vehicles, and in other ways"[31] stand in contrast to the vague description of the activities planned for the Sonderkommandos.

How then were the orders actually put into effect? Shootings of captured Red Army political commissars by units of the 6th Army can be most clearly documented. As early as 23 June—"Operation Barbarossa" had begun the day before—Panzer Group I reported to the Ic of AOK 6: "In the sectors of both Army Corps XXXXVIII and III, a political commissar was captured and dealt with accordingly."[32] Army Corps XVII reported on 25 June that the 62nd ID (Infantry Division) had shot nine alleged "irregulars"—hence civilians—and that "one political commissar" had been "captured in the forest north of Sztun and dealt with according to standing orders."[33]

The Ic officer of AOK 6 made sure that the criminal orders were obeyed. On 30 June 1941, he ordered the Ic officers of the subordinate army units "re: Ic conference of 16 June 1941 in Tarnobrzeg" "to address briefly in Ic daily reports the presence of political commissars among the Red troops."[34] On 1 July, Army Corps XVII reported that the 298th ID had "dealt with" a commissar "according to the guidelines."[35] A supplementary report states: "62nd ID 5 pol[itical]-commissars, 298th ID 1 pol[itical]-commissar captured and dealt with as ordered.[36] On 2 July Army Corps XXXXIV reported that so far "1 military political commissar had been taken prisoner and been treated according to orders" and that another one had shot himself upon his capture. And Army Corps XVII informed the Ic of the 6th Army that the 62nd Infantry Division had "treated a further 9 political commissars according to the guidelines."[37]

In the following months, weeding out and shooting captured political commissars clearly became routine for the units of the 6th Army. The Ic of the 44th ID included as a rather incidental remark in his War Diary after the battle of encirclement at Kiev: "Sa[turday], 4 October 1941. No enemy contact. On-going Ic matters. Ic at garrison command post in Pirjatin for reports on partisans. Report to Army Corps LI on liquidated commissars (122 commissars)."[38]

Even more serious than putting the commissar order into practice were the consequences of the judicial decree and the "Guidelines for the Conduct of Troops," which aimed at combating imagined or real "irregulars" and "saboteurs." Here arbitrariness ran rampant. Often untested denunciations, crude suspicions, or the fact that someone was a Jew was enough to "justify" shooting, as is documented in several instances. For example, on 25 June 1941 in Ivanice, an inhabitant who was alleged to have played a leading role in the Communist Party and a Jew were shot by the 168th division as a "reprisal" for the sabotage of a cable when the real culprits went undetected.[39] At the same time, the 299th ID, especially Infantry Regiments (IR) 529 and 530, were acting with similar harshness. In Litovits, the troops shot three "irregulars" on the day of the attack; on the following day, two army commissars who had been "captured while operating as snipers" were shot.[40] Commissars fighting as partisans, Red Army men in civilian clothes, and "wives of active soldiers" seemed to be everywhere, especially "in localities occupied by Jews."[41] A few days later, IR 530 lost all restraint. After individual riflemen and small groups of armed men, both in uniform and civilian clothes, had repeatedly opened fire on the road along which the regiment was advancing, the troops stopped taking prisoners and carried out several mopping-up operations, in which "around thirty irregulars were shot." Since only two light machine guns and one machine pistol were captured, the action may well in reality have been a reprisal.[42] On 10 July, the Ic of AOK 6 reported that in Krzemieniec three "of the functionaries identified by the Ukrainian committee" had been "captured and turned over to the SD." The three alleged Communist Party functionaries were shot "along with a Jew who had warned other suspicious elements of an impending house search."[43] Army Corps XVII reported to the Ic of AOK 6 on 13 July that the 79th ID, stationed close to Tsviahel, had shot eight Jewish males, allegedly "members of the Russian secret police," "for strengthening civilian resistance in the rear area."[44] The Wehrmacht was more or less lumping Jews together with people designated as "irregulars." Thus the Ic officer of the 299th ID was able to report two days into the war: "Irregular activity is especially strong in localities occupied by Jews."[45] It is unclear whether such attitudes were chiefly a reaction to the orders, instructions, and exhortations that had recently been disseminated or whether anti-Semitism and racist views were virulent among officers and enlisted men.

As early as July 1941, the general staff of the 6th Army was issuing orders for a more vigorous response to "hostile elements in the civilian population," adopting in part measures already practiced by individual units. In the command directive of 10 July, AOK 6 considered it necessary, "in the interest of security," to take certain "measures" once a locality was captured:

> a) *soldiers dressed as civilians*, most of whom are recognizable by their short haircuts, are to be shot after it has been determined that they are Russian soldiers (exception: deserters!); b) *civilians* who prove hostile in their attitudes [*sic*!] or actions, especially by supporting the Red Army (for example, by maintaining contact with troops hiding in the forests), are to be shot as irregulars; c) *unreliable elements*, e.g., local Soviet functionaries, are to be arrested by the troops with the aid of the

> Ukrainian committees that are presently being formed in all localities. When the troops withdraw, those elements should, whenever possible, be turned over to the Field Police or the SD Einsatzkommando. If that is not possible, they may be turned over if need be to the auxiliary police established by the Ukrainian committee.[46]

And in the command directive issued on 19 July, AOK 6 ordered that collective measures be carried out in the cases of sabotage attacks when the perpetrators could not be identified. "These may consist in shooting local Jews or Russians, or in burning down Jewish or Russian homes."[47] These "measures" had to be ordered by a battalion commander or an officer of even higher rank.

Some soldiers and units overstepped the boundaries laid down in the orders and carried out executions on their own authority. The 298th Infantry Division reported to Army Corps XVII that on 3 July 1941 "two Russian prisoners were shot on the road from Klevan to Luck near a forester's station by an SS man and a member of the Wehrmacht belonging to a supply company."[48] According to the report, the prisoners had given no cause for weapons to be used: "the prisoners were not even trying to escape." Although the division took the position that a "shooting of this sort ... is in no way authorized by existing orders," the two killers were not called to account: "The SS man and the member of the Wehrmacht were instructed not to shoot prisoners on a public street and to make sure that both corpses were buried immediately. The two guards went to fetch spades in order to bury the two bodies."[49]

By the end of July, orders had repeatedly been passed down from AOK 6 to the troops for "dealing with" suspicious elements of the civilian population.[50] Neither a proven action by the victim nor a concrete suspicion was required for "punishment." Lumping scattered Red Army soldiers, civilian functionaries of the Communist Party, "unreliable elements," and Jews together with partisans meant that these groups were the first to be struck by the judicial decree and the commissar order.

"Active Support"—the 6th Army and the Murder of Jews

Sonderkommando (SK) 4a, the subunit of Einsatzgruppe C that had marched through the Ukraine behind or alongside the 6th Army, again compiled an interim statistic of mass murder at the end of October 1941: "The number of executions carried out by SK 4a has now risen to 55,432."[51] This record is followed by information that reveals something about the identities of the victims and of those aiding the SS unit: "Of the total executed by SK 4a in the second half of October, along with a relatively small number of political functionaries, active communists, saboteurs, etc., most were again Jews, and these include a large number of Jewish prisoners of war turned over by the Wehrmacht. In Borispol, at the request of the commandant of the prisoner of war camp located there, 742 Jews were shot by a platoon of SK 4a on 14 October 1941, another 357 on 16 October 1941, among them a few commissars and seventy-eight wounded Jews who were turned over by the camp doctor. At the same time, the platoon executed twenty-four partisans and Communists who had been arrested by the local commandant in Borispol. It should be noted that the efficiency with which operations in Borispol were carried out was due in no small measure to the active support of the local Wehrmacht authorities."[52]

It goes without saying that a unit of roughly seventy SS men acting alone was in no position to commit mass murder on the scale cited. The "active support" of other formations was absolutely required for that to occur. How did the cooperation between the 6th Army and the SS units operating in its area of operation develop? (Sometimes, in addition to Sonderkommando 4a, Sonderkommando 4b and Einsatzkommando 5, as well as the 1st SS Infantry Brigade, were operating in the region.) And what did that cooperation look like in practice?

SK 4a represented its first mass murders as executions of "saboteurs" and reprisal for atrocities. Wehrmacht personnel and Ukrainian nationalists actively supported those operations, for example the murder of 1,500 Jewish men in Lutsk in late July and early August 1941. Reports of "atrocious murders" had reached section Ic/AO of AOK 6 by the end of July. According to a Ic report of the evening of 1 July, 2,800 people had been murdered in Lutsk, 500 in Dubno "in Soviet prisons before the Reds pulled out." The Ic had already responded: "SS Sonderkommando and Prop.Company have been dispatched."[53] An advance unit of SK 4a had already arrived in Lutsk on 27 June and reported that it found the town in flames. "According to the [Wehrmacht] town commandant, the fire had to have been set by Jews.[54] According to tales being told by Ukrainians, "it was again mainly Jews who participated" in the arrests and killings of 2,800 Ukrainians shot in the prison. The SS Kommando immediately began a "search for the Jews and Communists responsible for the pillage and looting."[55] Ukrainians who, according to a former member of Military Administration Headquarters 579, were "lusting for blood," helped in rounding up Jews.[56] On this search, with the aid of Ukrainian "volunteers," the SS Kommando seized

300 Jews and twenty "looters." On 30 June, the victims were shot. But that was not the end of the killings.[57] With the cooperation of Wehrmacht authorities in Lutsk, posters were put up ordering all Jews able to work to report to an announced location on 2 July and to bring with them tools for digging ditches and drainage.[58] The more than 1,000 men who answered the call had to dig their own graves next to the ruins of the Lubarta castle in Lutsk; they were murdered by the SS, police, and Wehrmacht infantry—in "reprisal," as the SS Sonderkommando asserted. "Following the discovery of a total of ten corpses of members of the German Wehrmacht on 2 July, 1,160 were shot with the assistance of a police platoon and an infantry platoon."[59]

Sonderkommando 4b staged the murder of Jews in Tarnopol even more clearly as an "operation of reprisal." Bloody pogroms were incited intentionally. A report of the incident dated 11 July speaks of the execution of 127 people by SK 4b. "Additionally, in the wake of the persecutions of Jews inspired by the SK, 600 Jews liquidated."[60]

SK 4b described its procedures in even greater detail in its report of 20 July. It reported that corpses of Ukrainians murdered by the NKVD had also been found in Tarnopol, the final count "calculated at around 600," and that the bodies had shown "signs of the most heinous mutilation." "Troops passing through, who had the opportunity to see these abominations, and especially the corpses of murdered German soldiers, beat a total of roughly 600 Jews to death and set their houses ablaze."[61] How "inspiration" by the SS, rumors of atrocities, and deep-seated anti-Semitism coalesced into a readiness to exact lynch-mob justice and murder innocent people is shown in one of the few preserved letters in which a soldier reports on his participation in the murder of Jews:

> Tarnopol, 6 July 1941. Dearest Parents! I have just returned from the laying out of our comrades from the Air Force and mountain troops who were captured by the Russians. I can find no words to describe such a sight. Our comrades are bound, ears, tongues, noses, and genitals have been cut off. That was how we found them in the basement of the courthouse in Tarnopol, and we also found 2,000 Ukrainians and ethnic Germans [*Volksdeutsche*] who had been maltreated in the same way. There you have Russia and the Jews, the workers' paradise.... Revenge followed at once. Yesterday we and the SS were merciful, shooting on the spot every Jew we caught. Today is different, because another sixty comrades were found mutilated. Now the Jews are forced to carry the corpses up from the cellar and lay them out nicely. Then we show them the horrible things they have done. After they have viewed the victims, they are killed with clubs and spades. Up to now, we've launched about 1,000 Jews into the great beyond, but that is far too few for what they have done. The

> Ukrainians said that the Jews had all the important positions, and together with the Soviets, had a regular public festival while executing Germans and Ukrainians. I beg you, dear parents, to spread the word, also, father, in the local branch [of the Nazi Party]. We're going to bring photos. Then there won't be any doubt. Many greetings, your son Franzl.[62]

After units of SK 4a had carried out more shootings in July in Berdicev[63] and other towns,[64] murdering for the first time not only Jewish men but also women and children,[65] the main force came to Zhitomir, where the 6th Army's general staff had set up its headquarters. One of their first actions was to kill war prisoners and civilians turned over to the SD by the person in charge of a prison camp: "In Zhitomir, 187 Soviet Russians and Jews were shot; a number of them had been turned over by the Wehrmacht as civilian prisoners."[66]

In Zhitomir at the beginning of August, Sonderkommando 4a followed up the public hanging of two victims with a mass shooting of Jewish men. In Cernyakhov two members of the Soviet regional court, Kieper and Kogan, were apprehended and forced by members of the Sonderkommando to "confess" to having committed "atrocities."[67] Simultaneously, with the support of the town commandant, more than 400 Jewish men were arrested in a sweep in Zhitomir.

On 7 August, a car outfitted with a loudspeaker belonging to Propaganda Company 637 rode through town announcing in German and Ukrainian that a public execution was about to take place in the marketplace. Gallows had been set up, and the 400 recently arrested Jewish men had been gathered under the supervision of SS guards. Numerous members of the Wehrmacht were among the hundreds of onlookers. One soldier, who was an eyewitness to the proceedings, stated under oath: "The guards asked the people standing around whether anyone had a score to settle. More and more Ukrainians stepped forward and accused one Jew or another of some misdeed. These Jews, then in sitting position, were repeatedly hit and kicked and otherwise mistreated, mostly by the Ukrainians."[68] SS men brought Kieper and Kogan, stood them in the bed of a truck parked beneath the gallows, and put nooses around their necks. In the meantime, Kieper's and Kogan's alleged "atrocities" were announced through the loudspeaker, along with their sentences.[69] Another eyewitness asserted that the crowd cheered when the truck started up. "Festively dressed Ukrainian women lifted up their children, the soldiers who were watching roared, 'Slow, slow,' so that they could get better photographs."[70] Afterwards the SS brought the 400 men to a shooting ground outside of town. Numerous onlookers were present at these mass murders as well. One of them, a colonel on the court-martial committee, Army High Command 6, Dr. A.N., testified in the Callsen trial that several staff officers had witnessed the shootings. "I was standing with various staff members.... Colonel v. Sch. and I looked at each other without saying a word; we understood. It became clear to me that these people were Jews.... There was a long procession of Jews, and I noticed that the Jews were being exterminated. We discussed the matter, and it was mentioned that in other cases Wehrmacht personnel had taken part in the shootings. For us, on military grounds, that went against the grain. Then the army issued an order forbidding any participation by Wehrmacht personnel in executions."[71]

Einsatzgruppe C listed the public mass murders in Zhitomir as a complete success.

> Organization, both at the execution of the two Jewish murderers and at the shooting, can be called exemplary.... Our relation to the Wehrmacht is, as always, completely unstrained. Above all, Wehrmacht circles are showing a steadily growing appreciation for the tasks and the importance of police security. This was especially obvious at the executions. Moreover, the Wehrmacht itself is taking pains to support the security police in accomplishing its tasks. Thus it is that, in all the offices of the Einsatzgruppe, Wehrmacht reports are constantly coming in regarding Communist functionaries and Jews who have been arrested.[72]

The staff of the 6th Army was deeply concerned that members of the Wehrmacht had been observing and photographing executions, especially that soldiers had been participating in mass murders without orders from their superiors. It was probably feared that—as the Wehrmacht put it—the troops would run wild. Thus, on 10 August, AOK 6 issued an order with the subject line: "Executions by the SD," which was transmitted via the general staff supply and administration officer to subordinate units.[73] The order stated that in various localities in the territory of 6th Army operations "necessary executions are being carried out against criminal, Bolshevik, primarily Jewish, elements by organs of the Security Service [SD] of the Reichsführer-SS and Chief of the German Police." However, it was now becoming apparent "that off-duty soldiers have volunteered to assist in carrying out executions, have been present when such operations were underway, and have photographed them." Von Reichenau ordered: "Any participation by soldiers of the army, as onlookers or participants at executions, is forbidden unless ordered by a military superior." Moreover, Reichenau forbade photographing executions; existing photographs were to be confiscated by the disciplinary authorities. He had, however, no objection to orderly cooperation: "If the SD comes to the town commandant with a request to provide a security team to seal off from onlookers a space allotted for an execution, such a request is to be honored."[74]

This order is noteworthy in several respects. It was known at the general staff of the 6th Army that the Einsatzgruppe operating in the 6th Army's area was killing mainly Jews, and the staff acknowledged that as "necessary." It is not true, as the former colonel at the court-martial committee testified, that any participation of Wehrmacht personnel in executions was forbidden, but only participating without having been ordered to do so by a superior officer. Authorized executions—for example, shooting Jews accused of being somehow connected to "sabotage"—were not prohibited by Reichenau; on the contrary, certain auxiliary tasks, such as providing security, were expressly authorized. Institutional cooperation with the SD by the authorized sections of the army was quite welcome. Cooperation between the army's local commanders and their forces, such as the Military Police (*Feldgendarmerie*), Secret Field Police (GFP), and Ukrainian "auxiliary police"—and SD Kommandos had first developed during the early months of the occupation and was to be elaborated in the future.

One of the tasks taken over by these Wehrmacht sections was arresting, guarding, and delivering Jews to the SD. A former member of the Military Police gave unambiguous information in a hearing:

> In cooperation with the SD, to which we were not attached, we of the Military Police had to seek out Jews in their dwellings and, with the aid of interpreters, make it clear to them that they had to assemble the next day at a specific place in town, at a specific time.... We had to guard the Jews until the SD came and took custody of the Jews.... Although we always answered the Jews' questions by saying that they were going to a camp—and at first we did not know any better ourselves—the fact was that the Jews were shot at places that had been prepared outside of town. In all localities taken during the advance of the German Wehrmacht, the same game was played out again and again. We of the Military Police, aided by the Russian Hipo [the witness is presumably referring to the Ukrainian auxiliary police—B.B./HS], which belonged to us, got the Jews out of their dwellings. The SD took control of the Jews and led or drove them to the shooting sites.[75]

Another form of cooperation—often in the guise of fighting sabotage—consisted of organs of the station or military administration headquarters shooting Jews, after which the SS Sonderkommando exterminated the surviving Jewish community. For example, "In Fastov, where the town commander's Secret Field Police and a territorial defense battalion [Landesschützenbataillon] eliminated about thirty snipers and 50 Jews, peace could really be restored only after a former terrorist and all Jews between the ages of twelve and sixty, a total of 262, had been shot by SK 4a."[76]

How far the Wehrmacht's complicity with the SS had progressed is especially clear in the case of the murder of Jewish men, women, and children of Belaya Tserkov' and in the way in which objections to the murder of children were handled. In mid-August, the town commander of Belaya Tserkov' ordered the registration of Jews. The first people who reported at station headquarters were escorted by a GFP unit to a building resembling a school some distance outside of town. The GFP turned over about seventy adults to an SS officer of Sonderkommando 4a, who had them taken away and shot by members of a Waffen-SS platoon.[77] The children, whom the parents had brought along to the "registration," stayed behind in the school-like building. In the following days, military administration headquarters, station headquarters, and the SS continued to look for Jewish inhabitants of Belaya Tserkov', gradually murdering hundreds of men and women. The children of the victims were housed in the above-mentioned building. On 20 August, soldiers camped close to the building who had heard the children whimper during the night drew the attention of two chaplains to the children's misery. The chaplains, following up on the reports, approached Lieutenant Colonel Groscurth, the Ia officer of the 295th Division, which was then stationed in Belaya Tserkov'. They examined the house and discovered that ninety children ranging in age from a few months to seven years had been left in the rooms of the building, had no food, and were not being cared for. Several four-year-olds were scraping plaster from the walls and eating it. Infants were whimpering and crying. Soldiers told how, on the night before, "three trucks had been driven away with children inside."[78] When Groscurth questioned an SS-Oberscharführer who had walked over about the fate of the children, the man answered that the children's relatives had been shot and that the children "were also to be eliminated."[79] Seeking clarification, Groscurth went to the commander of military administration headquarters, who explained to him that the SS-Oberscharführer was right and that the man was carrying out "his mission ... with the knowledge of the commander of military administration headquarters." Groscurth tried to prevent the murder of the children by demanding a decision from higher authority and requested the SD to delay transporting the children. He spoke by telephone to a staff officer of Army Group South, who referred him to AOK 6. In a long-distance call with the Ic officer at AOK 6, he learned that the supreme commander's ruling could not be obtained before evening. Meanwhile, in late afternoon, a truck had been loaded with children and was standing outside the house. When the decision of the army high command to delay the operation arrived, the children were taken back inside the house and given bread and water.

That evening the staff of the 6th Army conferred on how to proceed. According to the War Diary, the counterintelligence officer, Captain Luley, spoke about the "incident SD—295th Division in Bialacerkiev,"[80] and Reichenau reached a decision, which he later recorded: "Immediately upon receiving the division's inquiry by telephone, and following a subsequent conversation with Standartenführer Blobel [leader of SK 4a—B.B./H.S], I delayed the execution because it had not been properly arranged. I ordered Blobel and the AOK representative to go to Bialacerkiev on 21 August and investigate the matter. I have decided on principle that the operation that had begun should be properly carried through."[81] Thus, the general staff and Reichenau had passed a death sentence on ninety children.

On the morning of 21 August, the Ic at AOK 6 informed Groscurth by telephone of the decision to murder the children. The War Diary states simply: "Telephone conversation with Lieutenant Colonel Groscurth, Ia of the 295th Infantry Division about shootings of Jews Bialacerkiev."[82] Before noon on that same day, a discussion took place at military administration headquarters in Belaya Tserkov', between Groscurth, the commander of military administration headquarters, Riedel, AOK 6 representative Luley, participating on behalf of the Wehrmacht, and Blobel and the leader of the unit in Belaya Tserkov' representing the SD. Groscurth faced a solid front of Wehrmacht and SS officers who wanted to silence the troublemaker. Luley and the commander of military administration headquarters characterized Groscurth's report as unwarranted interference. The commander of military administration headquarters considered "the extermination of Jewish women and children urgently required ... in whatever form it takes place."[83] As a result of Groscurth's intervention, "the elimination of the children was pointlessly delayed by twenty-four hours." Blobel endorsed Riedel's view and said that the unit that had done the sniffing around should do the shooting, and added that "officers who delay these measures should themselves take command of the [execution] squad."[84] Groscurth could only defend himself against threats aimed directly at him; he could not stop the executioners. The SD representative and the other Wehrmacht officers could quote Reichenau's instructions. On that very evening, the children were murdered; it is uncertain whether that was done by members of the Waffen SS or by Ukrainian "auxiliary police." Throughout the discussions Groscurth had the impression that "all the executions had been proposed by the commander of military administration headquarters, and that shooting the adult Jews had necessarily resulted in the "need to eliminate the children, especially the infants." "Housing the children somewhere else was declared impossible by the field commandant and the Obersturmführer, while the field commandant repeatedly asserted that this brood must be exterminated."[85]

On the day after the children were murdered in Belaya Tserkov', the counterintelligence officer gave a "report on the shooting of Jews in Bialacerkiev" at a meeting of the officers of Ic/AO group;[86] a recommendation for Captain Luley's promotion was also discussed at the same meeting. Still on 22 August, the counterintelligence officer reported to the chief of the general staff on the "incident in Bialacerkiev between 295th Div.—SD—Kdo." The result of that conversation reads: "O.B. [Supreme Commander] should settle case,"[87] which Reichenau did in the communication of 26 August 1941 cited above.

The case was settled. The children's murder had been discussed by staff officers both before and after the event. The supreme commander had made a clear decision: the 6th Army was no longer fighting merely against Jewish "commissars," "snipers," "saboteurs." Already in August 1941, the 6th Army was making itself a willing accomplice to genocide. Reichenau, like the officers and soldiers of the 6th Army, required no special order from Hitler to contribute to the mass murder of Jewish men, women, and children.

From this point on, cooperation between SS Kommandos and the 6th Army was a routine matter. When towns with sizable Jewish communities were occupied, town and city commanders conferred with the SD Einsatzkommando. Proclamations produced by the propaganda company and issued by the town commander ordered the Jewish population to gather at a certain time. SS and police escorted the victims from the collection point to the murder sites, which were located on the edge or somewhat outside of town, where they were shot by members of the Sonderkommando 4a or the Waffen-SS. The largest mass murder of this type took place in Kiev.

On 27 September 1941, the municipal commandant held a meeting "regarding counterintelligence matters in Kiev," at which Ic officers, engineer officers, members of the SD, the police, and the GFP were present.[88] According to a statement made by the former

Ic officer of Army Corps XXIX, the participants talked about "evacuating the Jews," but those present were aware that what was being planned was killing.

> As far as I can recall, nothing was said at the meeting about the Jews being evacuated in reprisal for the Russians setting off time bombs in the city. I still recall that we, as Ic officers, were promptly informed that these explosions in Kiev were to be expected. Moreover, the troops had constantly been warned before Kiev was captured of the possibility of all sorts of disruptive activities.... My impression at the time was that these were technical military operations purposely directed that had nothing to do with the Jews.[89]

Propaganda Company 637 prepared the proclamations, as can be inferred from the War Diary of the Ic/AO Group of AOK 6: "Two thousand placards proclaiming that the Jews were to assemble at a specific place were prepared in the print shop of *Ostfront*."[90] The proclamation in three languages posted by the Ukrainian auxiliary police read:

> All Jews of the city of Kiev and its environs are to appear at 8 o'clock on the morning of 29 September 1941 at the corner of Mielnikovskaja and Dokhturovskaja streets (next to the cemetery). They are to bring the following articles: papers, money, valuables, and warm clothing, underwear, etc. Any Jew who does not obey this order and is found at any other place will be shot. Citizens who enter apartments abandoned by Jews and take items for themselves will be shot.[91]

The entire Sonderkommando 4a, along with forces from the police regiment "Russia South," the battalion of the Waffen-SS on special assignment, and Reserve Police Battalion 9, were called up to assist in the massacre. In the pre-dawn of 29 September, members of the police battalions cordoned off the area surrounding the ravine Babi Yar and the streets along which the victims would pass on their way out of town. Long lines of Jewish men, women, and children came to the prescribed place. From there, the SS drove them to the Babi Yar ravine. Near the entrance to the ravine, SS men registered the victims, who were forced to give up their valuables and take off their clothes. More than 33,000 people were shot in the ravine by members of Sonderkommando 4a in the course of 29 September and the following day.[92] Immediately following the massacre on 30 September, engineers blew up the edges of the ravine in order to cover the mass grave with stones and earth.

The Sonderkommando congratulated itself for the "exceedingly skillful organization" of the massacre: "The difficulties involved in carrying out such a large operation—above all in getting the Jews together—were overcome in Kiev by posting notices ordering the Jewish population to take part in resettlement. Although only about 5,000 to 6,000 Jews were originally expected, over 30,000 Jews showed up, who, thanks to exceedingly skillful organization, continued to believe that they were to be relocated until right before they were executed."[93]

The last large city that the 6th Army conquered in the fall of 1941 was Kharkov. Here, in addition to the city's Jewish inhabitants, broad sectors of the civilian population were the victims of purposive measures by the 6th Army and the SS. Already at the end of October, the officers of the Ic/AO group at AOK 6 were conferring with the leading officers of the SS Sonderkommando concerning "deployment SD Kommando" in Kharkov.[94] At the beginning of November, concrete steps were devised in conversations at military administration headquarters:

> Cleansing operation still in progress, but work made very difficult in Kharkov because, in contrast to other towns, no records or lists were turned up. Individual informers put in place. In Kharkov, moreover, very many emigrants from all over the world. Most suspicious [are] Jews who were allowed to return as contacts or communications agents. Since Jews still mostly hidden, operations against Jews not contemplated for some time. Meantime, order to the chief rabbi of local Jews to deliver all money and foreign exchange in order to "protect" Jewish wealth.[95]

At the same time, staff officers of AOK 6 were discussing what should be done with the civilian population of Kharkov in view of the precarious food and resupply situation. While the quartermaster section wanted to evacuate the entire population of Kharkov, the Ic officer recommended selective mass murder. He rejected the idea of evacuating the entire population, writing: "From a security standpoint, the following measures are considered desirable and practicable: a) immediate arrest of all Jews, political commissars, politically suspicious persons, and all non-residents of the area.... Detention and further treatment of these elements would be the task of the SD, which is, however, too weak by itself and therefore requires the support of the troops."[96]

When explosives prepared by the Soviet military detonated in Kharkov in November 1941, mainly male Jews, along with other groups of people, were arrested and hanged as "atonement" for the bomb attacks. Seizing all the Jewish inhabitants of Kharkov was delayed, as the SS Sonderkommando explained: "As agreed to by the competent general staff and military administration headquarters, preparatory work for a larger Jewish operation will be initiated by SK 4 as soon as tasks relating to the housing of the Kommando have been accomplished."[97]

Preparations had been completed by mid-December.

> The first task was to work closely with the housing office of the city to acquire appropriate land for the evacuation of the Jews. A strip of land was chosen where the Jews could be housed in the barracks of a factory settlement. Then, on 14 December 1941, there appeared a proclamation to the Jews of Kharkov in which the Jews were ordered to go to the settlement described in the proclamation by 16 December 1941. The evacuation of the Jews proceeded smoothly, except for a few instances of looting, which occurred while the Jews were being marched to their new quarters, and which were committed almost exclusively by Ukrainians. There still exists no statistical summary regarding the Jews evacuated. The counting of the Jews is begun. Preparations for shooting the Jews are concurrently underway. Three hundred and fifty Jews who had been spreading rumors injurious to the German Wehrmacht were shot at once.[98]

The SS had assembled more than 20,000 Jewish men, women, and children in the barracks of the tractor factory outside of Kharkov. In December 1941 and January 1942, the SS shot the Jewish victims or murdered them in a gas van.

Battling "Partisans" as Part of Extermination Policy

Orders for the "safety of the troops," which AOK 6 issued on 10 July 1941, pulled civilians who, allegedly or actually, were in contact with partisans or the Red Army (including soldiers scattered behind German lines) into the undertow of an increasingly brutal implementation of the "criminal orders." They, as supporters, were to be shot, as were Red Army soldiers dressed in civilian clothes, as long as the latter were not turncoats.[99] But even regular Soviet combat groups were required to be clearly recognizable in order to be treated as prisoners of war.[100]

Irregulars, as defined in a decree of the OKH of 25 July 1941, consisted not only of Red Army personnel who failed to turn themselves in, but anyone who even attempted operations aimed at Wehrmacht "personnel or materiel" or who supported partisans in any way. Collective measures taken against the population in response to unexplained attacks required no prior notice. Anyone who appeared suspicious—not of committing specific acts but "with regard to attitude and sentiment"—fell under the auspices of the SD.[101] During August and September, instances of sabotage increased. Often the Wehrmacht apprehended small groups consisting primarily of young people who had been sent behind German lines to gather intelligence and whose interrogations suggested the existence of a spy network with its headquarters in Kiev. Between 7 and 21 August, the 168th ID arrested twenty-three people including nineteen young women; several were shot, four were sent to the prison camp in Zhitomir, and the rest were turned over to the Secret Field Police. Moreover, several partisan groups were appearing; in one instance there had been an armed clash.[102]

After a Soviet combat manual for partisans was captured, AOK 6 reacted to the new situation on 4 August by adding more groups to the list of enemies to be summarily "eliminated." A no-man's-land was to be created on every quiet front by evacuating towns and stopping all civilian traffic. Tarrying in one of those areas became prima facie evidence of guilt of spying, sabotage, or belonging to the partisans. Anyone falling under suspicion was to be shot by the Secret Field Police. Nonresidents without a legitimate reason for being in the area were to be handed over to the SD Kommandos; that applied even to "boys and young girls." All parachutists were to be "brought down" as partisans, even if they were involved in carrying out military operations.[103]

These regulations were applied somewhat later, on orders of the commander in chief of the army, von Brauchitsch, in response to a query by the 6th Army, to all Russian soldiers and combat units who, "after the actual battles have ceased," became active in the rear areas. Beginning in mid-September, all soldiers and civilians "who carry out 'guerrilla-war-like' [*volkskriegsähnliche*] missions in rear areas (blowing up bridges, attacking single vehicles or barracks, etc.)" were regarded as partisans. Whether members of the Red Army who operated behind the front during battles should be shot, von Brauchitsch left to the discretion of troop commanders "according to the tactical situation."[104]

While most reported partisan activity up to this point had involved mainly Soviet soldiers behind German lines who had merely been categorized as partisans, following the capture of Kiev on 19 September the Wehrmacht actually began encountering resistance groups, which they combated in cooperation with the SD through policing the streets, conducting raids, and carrying out mass arrests.[105]

When the advance to the east resumed, the office "Foreign Armies in the East" (Fremde Heere Ost) in the OKH requested that the divisions intensify their efforts aimed at irregulars. Even isolated towns should be "combed." "Older people who appear honorable and honest" should be viewed as suspect because they were especially well suited to serve as agents and spies for partisans.[106] Immediately, the 299th ID put together motorized "hunting squads" (Jagdkommandos) to combat partisans in the area around Romny, thus paving the way for an escalated approach.[107] In his order concerning the "Conduct of the Troops in the East," dated and distributed to the companies on 10 October 1941, the commander in chief of the 6th Army, Field Marshal Walter von Reichenau, ordered that the approach mentioned above be pursued consistently: "The struggle against the enemy behind the front is not yet being taken seriously enough. Treacherous, cruel partisans and degenerate women are still being made prisoners of war. Snipers and tramps, half in uniforms or dressed in civilian clothes, are still being treating as honorable soldiers and sent to POW camps." He demanded "draconian measures" against all civilians who failed to prevent partisan attacks: "Fear of German countermeasures must be stronger than the threat posed by wandering remnants of Bolshevik units." He made it unmistakably clear how the war was to be waged: as a war of annihilation, in order to liberate "the German people from the Asian-Jewish peril" for all times. The implementation of this order was not long in coming.

At the end of October, the 75th ID shot in an act of reprisal 230 prisoners of war from a Soviet unit that in two separate attacks had killed three soldiers of a reconnaissance unit and twenty-three members of an engineering company.[109] Then the division's Ic officer issued instructions supplementary to Reichenau's 10 October order to the army: Red Army soldiers, armed or unarmed, who did not surrender voluntarily were to be shot at once, as were all women in uniform, who could "not be regarded as members of the opposing army."[110]

Pursuant to guidelines issued by the commander in chief of the army on 25 October, Army Corps XXIX ordered its divisions to begin forming mounted hunting squads armed with machine guns, machine pistols, and hand grenades in order to prevent scattered Red Army personnel from joining forces with the newly formed partisan groups.[111] Of course, the partisan groups posed no serious threat to the Wehrmacht; they possessed strength worth noting only in the rear area around Cerkassy, west of Nikopol, and near Cernigov and Lubly. By the middle of November, they had been completely wiped out. But in the region around Sumy and Kharkov as well as in the Donets industrial basin, the commanders in the rear areas were anticipating hunger riots during the winter, unleashed by "the naked struggle for survival in a country that has largely been sucked dry."[112]

As early as the spring of 1941, the OKW and the Reich Ministry for Food and Agriculture had agreed that, in order to improve the food situation of the German population and relieve the overburdened transportation routes to the Eastern front, "Operation Barbarossa" should result in as much food as possible being shipped from the occupied areas to the Reich. The consequences—not only a drastic reduction in the Soviet population's consumption but the starvation of millions of people—had been calculated into the equation from the beginning.[113] For the troops this meant scavenging for basic food supplies while advancing, because supplies from the Reich were limited. And yet the Wehrmacht was justifying its invasion to the civilian population by claiming that it was liberating people from the "yoke of Bolshevism"; thus, in the first weeks, the "principle of strict legality" was at least verbally adhered to. In mid-July AOK 6 ordered its subordinate units to pay for confiscated food supplies—or at least issue receipts.[114] Soldiers, however, had already begun plundering on their own—a circumstance that motivated Reichenau to issue orders for the orderly execution of such "collections."[115]

At the end of September, supplies were further reduced, and frugal handling of food supplies and the "most extensive exploitation of the land" had become matters of urgency. AOK 6 instructed the troops to secure food supplies and establish caches of food for the winter.[116] By the end of October, requisitions had assumed forms that forced Army Group South to institute rigorous measures for the "maintenance of discipline." "Thefts, break-ins into trains and supply depots for food and clothing, black market operations at replacement supply depots, disobedience of orders, among other things" were being reported more and more frequently both in the army group rear area and in the army rear areas. The staff of the 62nd ID even threatened its soldiers with death for theft, break-ins, embezzlement, bribery, bartering, or any illegal acquisition of supplies.[117]

When the troops reached their winter positions, it turned out that the areas assigned to some divisions had been all but stripped of food supplies.[118] In the Belgorod region, there was livestock on hand for fourteen days, potatoes for one or two weeks, bread for six to eight weeks; there was no pork (hence no fat), beans, or fresh vegetables at all. The situation was roughly similar regarding feed for horses. The oats would last three to four weeks; feed turnips were available, but there was no straw at all.[119] In order to distribute supplies evenly among all units, the 75th ID ordered at the end of January that all unofficial requisitions be stopped and the matter of supply left in the hands of the division.[120] Since the division was unable to handle the problem, self-service continued for months. When division command became aware of more and more cases of "collection" in March 1942, especially in the area of Gotnya, Ilek, and Krasnopolye, the troops were informed that future cases would no longer be handled as simple disciplinary matters but would result in legal charges.[121]

Only crumbs remained for the indigenous population. Since plundering the Ukraine continued to be a top priority and the Wehrmacht was dependent on a work force consisting of civilians and prisoners of war, Göring came up with the notion that the workers should eat cat and horse meat. According to this extermination logic, large cities were allotted none of the food that might assure survival, smaller cities very little, peasants and workers employed by Germans a minimal supply.[122] This was a policy that the 6th Army also put into practice.[123]

Military Government Headquarters in Kharkov left supplying the inhabitants completely to the civilian authorities, who were expected to confiscate and equitably distribute all private supplies. Otherwise, they simply allowed retail trade and farmer's markets.[124] But that was quite insufficient. So as not to risk food riots, at the end of November agencies responsible for supplying the troops ordered that unusable blood, waste fat, inedible innards, and other spoiled foods be distributed to the population, while the veterinarian field hospitals should supply horses that had died; fishing in the local ponds was also permitted. On the other hand, private food supplies were to be seized and foods "whose consumption by the civilian population is not desired," such as sugar, coffee, flour, marmalade, etc., should be turned over to the Wehrmacht.[125] Even prisoners of war and civilians working for the Wehrmacht were sustained primarily on garbage in order to preserve supplies for the troops.[126]

Inevitably, December saw people dying of hunger almost daily. In January 1942 a third of the 300,000 inhabitants who were left in the city were suffering symptoms of malnutrition. Because a complete evacuation of the civilian population to the east was regarded as beyond the capacity of the troops to carry out, the military government headquarters promoted voluntary emigration by issuing passes, but the population used them primarily for foraging trips into the surrounding region,[127] which involved the risk of being shot as a tramp by Kommandos combing the area for partisans. In April 1942, the districts of Oboyan and Medevenka farther to the north were stripped completely. Until the next harvest, there was enough grain for exactly 100 grams per day per inhabitant. After army units were done plundering, there was no grain, potatoes, or livestock left, and feeding the troops was no longer possible. Nothing more could be "seized" except for milk, butter, cottage cheese, and eggs.[128]

In Kharkov, which was captured on 24 October 1941, Army Corps LV took over command of the city. AOK 6 had already demanded "unhesitating harshness" in the spirit of the army's order of 10 October: "Mainly Jews and Bolsheviks are to be brought for collective atonement. Saboteurs or persons offering armed resistance are to be publicly hanged." In order to force the population to identify buildings that had been mined, the buildings were to be occupied by hostages, primarily by Jews.[129] By the end of October, the 57th ID—whose mission included among other things securing the city—had shot civilians who had defended the city, "treated" three political commissars "in accordance with operative regulations," and publicly hanged seven saboteurs, including one woman, in order to intimidate the public.[130] When telephone lines were cut, streets blown up, and explosive devices discovered on public streets and in public places, the military commander established a check point on the road to Ogulitsy manned by locals; the men assigned to the post would forfeit their lives if sabotage was not prevented; ten local inhabitants would be shot should the men flee.[131]

During the night of 5 and 6 November, partisans killed three soldiers and five members of Organisation Todt (OT). Reichenau immediately issued yet another order, which he transmitted down to company level, in which he granted the troops a free hand in dealing with "the conscienceless, homicidal beasts." He instructed them to employ "means to exterminate these murderers that are alien to us and have never before been used by German soldiers against a hostile population," and ordered that the "harshest methods" be employed in interrogating and transporting partisans "of either sex, in uniform or civilian clothes," that all farms and villages where partisans enjoyed support be burned, that hostages be shot, that accomplices be hanged—unless the population could prove that they had suffered losses themselves in combating partisans.[132] Reichenau followed up a few days later by forbidding the population to leave the city limits at night, or, in locations occupied by German troops, even to leave one's house at night without a written permit. Violators were to be "shot ruthlessly," as indeed were the inhabitants of villages in which acts of sabotage occurred despite the presence of Ukrainian guards.[133]

Military Administration Headquarters 787 responded by establishing in Kharkov a camp for hostages in the "Hotel International" on Dzerzhinsky Square, using forces from the SD and the

Military Government Headquarters. The 68th ID was responsible for guarding the hostages. Authority to order the killing of hostages lay with the city commander, the commander of the 57th ID, Brigadier General Dostler, who was succeeded by Major General von Puttkamer on 13 December, after Kharkov was designated part of the army rear area.[134] Following a raid on 15 November, Dostler's division took 500 hostages and sent them to the "Hotel International." The first twenty of them were hanged following a bomb explosion in the office of an engineering regiment.[135] "Fifty Bolsheviks were hanged from the Main Street balcony" on 16 November in reprisal for mines having been detonated.[136] AOK 6 reported to Army Group South in early December that the troops in Kharkov had "hanged several hundred partisans and suspicious elements in the city" within six weeks.[137]

The 6th Army's goal was the "complete annihilation" of partisans. In mid-November, it ordered the 57th ID to establish under the direction of Captain Weber von Ostwalden a network for reporting partisan activity, which was directly subordinate to the army's Ic officer. All reports were forwarded to report centers in the individual sections and battalions or report offices in the Ukrainian militia in the surrounding villages, which relied in turn on a network of informants. Other organizations, such as OT, were also integrated into this comprehensive spy system.[138] The merciless pursuit of irregular Soviet combat units had long been in progress. In the zone of the 299th ID, which had been stationed in the Sumy region since 5 November, several partisan groups had been discovered in the area northwest of Byelopolye, east and north of Sudzha, and near Soldatskoye on the road to Kursk. These had been partly annihilated, partly forced out of the area.[139] Their primary objective was to impede the Wehrmacht's transport of winter supplies between Sudzha and Yunakovka.[140] The reconnaissance detachment of the 299th ID, which was securing the northern flank of Army Corps XXIX in the area of the 75th ID north of Belgorod, seized the families of partisan leaders at Mogritsa as hostages.[141]

When Army Corps XXIX ordered the formation of hunting squads on 1 November, the 299th ID detached 115 men, the 75th ID, 185 men, who in the following weeks systematically combed the area of Kharkov, Sumy, Sudzha and Belgorod.[142] The Ic officer of the 299th ID boasted at the conclusion of the operation that between 6 November and 9 December the division had "destroyed" 380 "partisans."[143] The hunting squads of the 75th ID had even fewer inhibitions about arresting and shooting civilians and Red Army men by the hundreds and burning down parts of towns or entire villages.

Infantry Detachment 202, which reported to the regiment on 22 November that it had shot seventy-six partisans and burned a village, was especially brutal.[144] When Army Corps XXIX reported on 7 December that 1,064 partisans and suspicious parties, along with 342 hostages, had been shot or hanged between 20 October and 5 December, most of that total could be credited to the 75th and 299th ID. By year's end, the total had again risen by at least fifty-six people.[145] According to the Ic officer at AOK 6, the total number of people publicly hanged and shot in the area of the 6th Army during the campaign against partisans in fall 1941 ran into the thousands.[146]

These figures are hardly compelling evidence of widespread armed resistance to the Wehrmacht, or even of widespread support for groups that were beginning to organize for armed struggle. As early as 30 November, Army Corps XXIX had stated that in its area partisan attacks had not occurred in recent weeks and that the only bomb attacks had probably been carried out with time fuses. The corps gave primary credit for that to the campaign against "tramps."[147] Another group of shooting victims was supposedly former Red Army men.[148] In its report to Army Group South, AOK 6 conceded that, in addition to partisans, the troops primarily "have eliminated the many elements moving about the country without identity papers, among whom are concealed partisan intelligence agents." In any case, the goal had been accomplished: "Acts of sabotage have since ceased."[149]

The 6th Army had assured an increase in the number of suspicious "tramps" in still another way. In early December 1941, a few days before Belgorod was occupied, the 75th ID burned three towns northeast of Rshava "in order to do away with the possibility of flanking movements being launched from them."[150] A bit later Army Corps XXIX ordered the evacuation and destruction of villages located "in the direction of the enemy" in order to secure the winter positions, along with the seizure of civilian hostages as a precaution against attacks.[151] A few days later, the 75th ID reported that the burning had begun and was being pursued "with all means."[152] In late December the division destroyed all the villages in its area that were located in front of its winter positions, thus driving the population to the east. The inhabitants of villages to the east of the Belgorod-Kursk rail line were gathered up one village at a time moving east and forced into the region thirty kilometers west of the rail line. Anyone who entered the villages after that was shot.[153]

With its indiscriminate terror against the entire civilian population, the 6th Army had passed the point of requiring a clear definition of the enemy, whatever that definition might be, long before its attack on Stalingrad. The consequences of hunger brought on by a policy of pillage, in conjunction with cold and sickness, were no longer directed against specific groups. Neither ethnic origin nor political allegiance, neither timid passivity nor active collaboration, could protect the civilian population from becoming objects of retaliation at any time, depending on the tactical situation. The entire civilian population had become a hostage of the Wehrmacht.

—*Translated by Roy Shelton*

Notes

1. Rüdiger Overmans, "Das andere Gesicht des Krieges: Leben und Sterben der 6. Armee," in Jürgen Förster, ed., *Stalingrad. Ereignis. Wirkung. Symbol*, 2nd ed. (Munich and Zürich: 1993), 419–455. The data in the literature presented here concerning the soldiers of the 6th Army who were trapped, evacuated, died, or became prisoners of war are contradictory. We accept Overman's attempt at a critical analysis while bearing in mind that even these numbers should be regarded as merely an approximation.
2. Radio message from Generaloberst Paulus to Hitler on 29 January 1943, BA-MA RL 30/5; cited in Gerd R. Ueberschär, "Stalingrad—eine Schlacht des Zweiten Weltkrieges," in *Stalingrad. Mythos und Wirklichkeit einer Schlacht*, ed. Wolfram Wette and Gerd R. Ueberschär (Frankfurt am Main: 1992), 18–42, here 36.
3. Radio message from Hitler to Generaloberst Paulus on 30 January 1943, BA-MA RL 30/5, cited in Wette and Ueberschär, *Stalingrad*, 36.
4. Cited in Rolf Günter Renner, "Hirn und Herz. Stalingrad als Gegenstand ideologischer und literarischer Diskurse," in Förster, *Stalingrad*, 472–492, here 472. See also Wolfram Wette, "Das Massensterben als 'Heldenepos'. Stalingrad in der NS-Propaganda," in Wette and Ueberschär, *Stalingrad*, 43–60, here 52f.
5. Army Group "Don" to the 6th Army, 31 January 1943; cited in Wette and Ueberschär, *Stalingrad*, 38.
6. Radio "Special Report" of the OKW on 3 February 1943, BA-MA RW 4/v140, 1–2; cited in Wette and Ueberschär, *Stalingrad*, 54.
7. Wette, "Massensterben," 46.
8. Fritz Wöss, *Hunde, wollt ihr ewig leben. Roman* (Heidelberg and Hamburg: 1958; idem, *Der Fisch beginnt am Kopf zu stinken. Roman* (Hamburg: 1960); Heinrich Gerlach, *Die verratene Armee. Ein Stalingrad-Roman* (Munich: 1957); Heinz G. Konsalik, *Der Arzt von Stalingrad. Roman* (Munich: 1956).
9. Ulrich Baron, "Stalingrad als Thema der deutschsprachigen Literatur," in Wette and Ueberschär, *Stalingrad*, 226–232, here 232. For a structural analysis of these and other literary treatments of the Stalingrad myth, see the essay by Rolf Günter Renner in Förster, *Stalingrad*, 472–492.

10. Detlef Vogel, "Die deutschen und österreichischen Stalingradbünde. Schritte vom Mythos zur Realität," in Wette and Ueberschär, *Stalingrad,* 247–253, here 248.
11. Franz Kurowski, *Stalingrad. Die Schlacht, die Hitlers Mythos zerstörte* (Bergisch Gladbach: 1992), 371, 394. The paperback version that first appeared in December 1992 was already in its second printing in February 1993.
12. Editorial by Klaus Bresser, in *Begleitheft zur fünfteiligen Dokumentation von ZDF/Ostankino, "Der verdammte Krieg—Entscheidung Stalingrad,"* by Guido Knopp, Harald Schott, and Anatolij Nikiforow, ZDF 1992, 3.
13. Thomas A. Kohut and Jürgen Reulecke, "'Sterben wie eine Ratte, die der Bauer ertappt.' Letzte Briefe aus Stalingrad," in Förster, *Stalingrad,* 456–471. See also the contributions by Martin Humburg, Wolfram Wette, Sabine Rosemarie Arnold, and Manfred Hettling as well by Nadeshda B. Krylowa, in Wette and Ueberschär, *Stalingrad,* 67–106; additional references are also found there.
14. 75th ID/Ic (Infantry Division/Intelligence Section) to all subordinate units, 6 January 1942, BA-MA RH 26-75/121; XXIX AK (Army Corps)/Ic; morning report of 7 January 1942, BA-MA 24-29/47.
15. Decree regarding administration of wartime military jurisprudence in the "Barbarossa" region and special troop assignments of 13 May 1941, amended by the commander in chief of the army, 24 May 1941; guidelines for the treatment of political commissars of 6 June 1941, amended by the commander in chief of the army on 8 June 1941; both are cited in *Der deutsche Überfall auf die Sowjetunion. "Unternehmen Barbarossa" 1941*, ed. Gerd R. Ueberschär and Wolfram Wette (Frankfurt am Main: 1991), 251–254 and 259–260.
16. Special Instruction (*Anordnungen*) No. 1 to Order (*Weisung*) No. 21 (Case "Barbarossa"), 19 May 1941 with enclosure (*Anlage*) 1: Structure and Tasks of the Economic Organization to be Deployed in "Barbarossa" Region, and enclosure 3: Guidelines for the Conduct of Troops in Russia, in Ueberschär and Wette, *Barbarossa*, 254–258.
17. On the origins of the commissar order, see Hans-Adolf Jacobsen, "Kommissarbefehl und Massenexekutionen sowjetischer Kriegsgefangener," in Hans Buchheim et al., *Anatomie des SS-Staates* (Munich: 1967), 2:143ff.; and Jürgen Förster, "Das Unternehmen 'Barbarossa' als Eroberungs- und Vernichtungskrieg," in *Das Deutsche Reich und der Zweite Weltkrieg (DRZW)*, vol. 4: *Der Angriff auf die Sowjetunion*, published by the Militärgeschichtliches Forschungsamt Freiburg i. Br. (Stuttgart: 1983), 435ff. The full text of the commissar order appears in Ueberschär and Wette, *Barbarossa*, 259f.
18. Cited in Förster, "Barbarossa," 4: 433.
19. AOK 6, Activity Report of Group IC/AO of 12 June 1941, BA-MA RH 20-6/488.
20. Ibid. Only the directive limiting military justice was issued by the Führer. As cited above, the commissar order was issued by the OKW.
21. AOK 6, Activity Report Ic/AO of 12 June 1941, BA-MA RH 20-6/488.
22. AOK 6, Presentation of the Ic (Intelligence Section) to the Ia (Operations Section) on 13 June 1941, BA-MA RH 20-6/488.
23. Section III—Court of the 57th ID, Activity Report, 1 to 30 June 1941, BA-MA RH 26-57/112.
24. 56th ID, War Diary/Ia, 16 June 1941, BA-MA RH 26-56/16(a). In 62nd ID, the meeting with the commanders took place on 18 June: Discussion list for meeting with commanders, 18 June 1941, RH 26-62/40.
25. AOK 6, Ic/A0, Ic conference, BA-MA RH 20-6/487, fol. 85.

26. AOK 6, lc/A0, Points of discussion for the Ic conference, BA-MA RH 20-6/487, fol. 86.
27. For information on the SS Einsatzgruppen in earlier campaigns and consultations between the leadership of the SS and the Wehrmacht on their use in "Operation Barbarossa," see Helmut Krausnick, *Hitlers Einsatzgruppen. Die Truppen des Weltanschauungskrieges 1938–1942* (Frankfurt am Main: 1985).
28. AOK 6, Ic/A0, Points of discussion for the Ic conference, BA-MA RH 20-6/487 fol. 86.
29. XVII AK, War Diary/Ia, Ereignisse, BA-MA RH 24-17/226.
30. Orders of Section Staff Staufen Nr. 38, 20 June 1941: BA-MA RH 24-44/39.
31. Ibid.
32. AOK 6, Ic, 23 June 1941, Report of Enemy Contact Panzer Group 1, BA-MA RH 20-6/514.
33. Ibid., 25 June 1941, Report of Enemy Contact XVII A.K.
34. AOK 6, Ic, 30 June 1941, Telex to XVII., XXIX., XXXXIV, and LV. A.K. Ic, BA-MA RH 20-6/513.
35. AOK 6, Ic, 1 July 1941, Report of Enemy Contact XVII A.K. BA-MA RH 20-6/515.
36. AOK 6, Ic, 2 July 1941, Report of Enemy Contact XXXXIV. A.K., BA-MA RH 20-6/515.
37. Ibid., 2 July 1941, Report of Enemy Contact XVII AK.
38. 44. ID, Ic, Activity Report, 21 June–31 December 41, BA-MA RH 26-44/32.
39. 168th ID, Ic, Activity Report, 25 June 1941: BA-MA RH 26-168/49.
40. 299th ID/Ic, Activity Report, 22 June 1941; IR (Infantry Regiment) 529 to 299th ID, 23 June 1941, BA-MA RH 26-299/118.
41. 299th ID/Ic, Daily Report to XXIX AK/Ic, 24 June 1941; IR 530/Ia to the 299th ID, 25 June 1941, BA-MA RH 26-299/118.
42. IR 530/Ic to the 299th ID, 28 June 1941, BA-MA RH 26-299/118.
43. AOK 6, Ic/A0, 10 July 1941, BA-MA RH 20-6/516; see also, ibid., Ic Evening Report of 10 July 1941.
44. AOK 6, Ic, 13 July 1941, Report of Enemy Contact XVII AK, BA-MA RH 20-6/517.
45. Daily Report of 299th ID/Ic to XXIX AK/Ic, 24 June 1941, BA-MA RH 26-299/118.
46. AOK 6, 10 July 1941, Ia Az. 15 Nr. 1814/41g. (Führungsanordnung [Command Directive] No. 13, point 5.) Safety of the Troops, BA-MA RH 20-6/755 (emphasis in original).
47. 62nd ID, War Diary, Ic, Entry of 21 July 1941, BA-MA RH 26-62/40.
48. NOKW 1538, cited in Krausnick, *Hitlers Einsatzgruppen,* 200.
49. Ibid.
50. A0K 6/Ia, Command Directive No. 16, 19 July 1941, BA-MA RH 26-56/ 17; 62nd ID/Ic, 21 July 1941, BA-MA RH 26-62/40; AOK 6/OQu/Qu1BAV No. 43, 29 July 1941, RH 24-17/255.
51. Ereignismeldung (Operational Situation Report) USSSR No. 132, Chief of the Security Police and the SD, 12 November 1941.
52. Ibid.
53. AOK 6, Ic, Evening Report of 1 July 1941, BA-MA RH 20-6/515.
54. Operational Situation Report 24, 16 July 1941.
55. Ibid.
56. Statement of J. Sch., Zentrale Stelle der Landesjustizverwaltungen Ludwigsburg (ZSt.), Generalstaatsanwaltschaft (GstA) Frankfurt Js 4/65, Legal proceedings

against Callsen and others, Sonderband Vernehmungen (Supplementary volume on interrogations) X. That Ukrainians in various places in Volhynia organized pogroms as soon as the Red Army withdrew, without being urged to do so by the SS or the Wehrmacht, is also described in Shmuel Spector, *The Holocaust of Volhynian Jews 1941–1944* (Jerusalem: 1990), 64ff.

57. See Operational Situation Report 24, 16 July 1941.
58. See Report A.K., ZSt. 204 AR-Z 287/59.
59. Operational Situation Report 24, 16 July 1941.
60. Operational Situation Report 19, 11 July 1941.
61. Operational Situation Report 28, 20 July 1941.
62. Letter from Tarnopol, 6 July 1941, BA-MA RW 4/v.442. The letter was confiscated by Wehrkreiskommando (Military District) XVII, Vienna, Abt. Ic/WPr. (Section Counter Intelligence/Propaganda), and sent to Wehrmacht High Command, section Wehrmacht Propaganda, under the heading "Atrocity Reports in Letters from the Field," with the explanation that the letter had been "found in duplicated form in a display window of a shop in Vienna.... Inquiries by the local counterintelligence office revealed that copies of this letter had been forwarded by a *Kreisleiter* of the NSDAP to the *Ortsgruppenleiter* of his district for propaganda purposes."
63. See Operational Situation Report 47, 9 August 1941: "In Berdichev, prior to the arrival of Einsatzkommando 5, a detachment of Einsatzkommando 4a was active. 148 Jews were executed for plundering and communist activities."
64. See Operational Situation Report 58, 20 July 1941: "Search operations by the Einsatzkommandos are continuing. Almost all villages and larger localities in the vicinity of Berdichev and Zhitomir have been dealt with methodically."
65. See the indictment in the legal proceedings again Callsen and others, Zst., GstA Frankfurt Js 24/66, 201ff.
66. Operational Situation Report 30, 22 July 1941.
67. See Operational Situation Report 58, 20 August 1941: "After exhaustive interrogation it was possible to convict Kieper and his accomplice of the mass murders of which they stood accused.... Kieper, at last compelled to confess, described his atrocities with typical Jewish cynicism."
68. ZSt., GstA Frankfurt Js 4/65, Sonderband Vernehmungen II, Aussage (Statement) of P.A.
69. See Operational Situation Report 58, 20 August 1941.
70. Witness Statement J., cited as quoted in the indictment in the legal proceeding against Callsen et al., 221.
71. ZSt., GstA Frankfurt Js 4/65, Legal proceeding against Callsen et al., Verhandlungs-Protokollband (Transcripts) VI, 20. February 1967.
72. Operational Situation Report 58, 20 August 1941.
73. Anlageband 3 zum KTB XVII A.K./Qu. (Supplementary volume to War Diary of Army High Command XVII), Order of the Army High Command 6, O.Qu./Qu. 1., A.H.Qu., 10 August 1941, Special instructions for provisions, enclosure 1, regarding executions by the SD, BA-MA RH 24-17/255.
74. Ibid.
75. ZSt., GstA Frankfurt Js 4/65, vol. V: Statement of H.Z., Field Police (Feldgendarmerie) 455.
76. Operational Situation Report 80, 11 September 1941.
77. See indictment in the legal proceeding against Callsen, 260ff.
78. Report of the Catholic division chaplain, Dr. Reuss, 29 August 1941, published in Helmuth Groscurth, *Tagebücher eines Abwehroffiziers. Mit Dokumenten*

zur Militäropposition gegen Hitler, ed. Helmut Krausnick, Harold C. Deutsch, and Hildegard von Kotze (Stuttgart: 1970), 538f.

79. Groscurth's report of 21 August 1941, *Tagebücher*, 534f.
80. Activity Report of Group Ic/AO of 20 August 1941, BA-MA RH 20-6/491; "Bialacerkiev" is the spelling of "Belaya Tserkov" adopted from the Ukrainaian.
81. Reichenau's position paper of 26 August 1941 on the report of the 295th ID on the events in Bialacerkiev, to Army Group South and the 295th ID; reprinted in Groscurth, *Tagebücher*, 541.
82. Activity Report of Group Ic/AO of 21 August 1941, BA-MA RH 20-6/491.
83. Groscurth's report of 21 August 1941, *Tagebücher,* 536.
84. Ibid.
85. Ibid., 537.
86. Enclosure to Activity Report of Group Ic/AO of 22 August 1941, officers' conference, BA-MA RH 20-6/491.
87. Activity Report of Group Ic/AO of 22 August 1941, BA-MA RH 20-6/491.
88. XXIX AK, Enclosure to War Diary/Ic, BA-MA RH 24-29/77.
89. Statement of G. Sch., ZSt., GstA Frankfurt Js 4/65, Supplementary vol. X.
90. Activity Report, Propaganda Company 637, BA-MA RH 20-6/492
91. Zst., GstA Frankfurt Js 4/65, Supplementary volume with translations from Russian, Part I.
92. See Operational Situation Report 106, 7 October 1941, which sets the numbers of victims at 33,771.
93. Operational Situation Report 128, 3 November 1941.
94. AOK 6, Ic/AO Activity Report, 26 October 1941, BA-MA RH 20-6/494.
95. 57th ID/Ib, 4 November 1941—"Conference at Kharkov Military Administration Headquarters on 4 November 1941, 09.00 hours": BA-MA RH 26-57/113.
96. Ic/A0, AOK 6 to Qu. 2 zu Hdn. Herrn Hauptmann i.G. von Bila, regarding draft of order for the evacuation of the civilian population, BA-MA RH 20-6/494.
97. Operational Situation Report 156, 16 January 1942.
98. Operational Situation Report 164, 4 February 1942.
99. AOK 6, No. 1814/41, secret, 10 July 1941—Leadership Directives No. 13, BA-MA RH 26-299/118.
100. 75th ID/Ic, Report on Enemy Activity No. 12, 18 July 1941, BA-MA RH 26-75/111.
101. Excerpts copied from the directive of the OKH regarding the treatment of enemy civilians and Russian prisoners of war, 25 July 1941, in Ueberschär and Wette, *Barbarossa,* 295f. (BA-MA RH 20-11/381).
102. 75th ID/Ic, Report on Enemy Activity No. 28, 11 August 1941, BA-MA RH 26-75/112; 75th ID/Ic, Addendum to War Diary/Ic, 14–31 August 1941, BA-MA RH 26-75/113; 168th ID/Ic, Activity Report of 20 July to 21 August 1941, BA-MA RH 26-168/40.
103. AOK 6/Ic/AO. Intelligence Section III, No. 2757/41, secret, 4 August 1941, BA-MA RH 20-6/491. Distribution included GFP Troop 560 and SD-Sonderkommando 4a.
104. 75th ID/Ic, Report on Enemy Activity No. 45, 18 September 1941, BA-MA RH 26-75/114; the division cited as its authority OKH/Gen.z.b.V.b. ObdH/Az 454 Gr. R. Wes. No. 1678/41, secret, 13 September 1941, BA-MA RH 23/295; see Jürgen Förster, "Das Unternehmen Barbarossa als Eroberungs- und Vernichtungskrieg," in Horst Boog, Jürgen Förster, Joachim Hoffmann, Ernst Klink, Rolf-Dieter Müller, and Gerd R. Ueberschär, *Der Angriff auf*

die Sowjetunion (originally published as vol. 4 of *DRZW*) (Frankfurt am Main: 1991), 1239.

105. Corps Command XXIX AK/Ic, 22. September 1941, BA-MA RH 26-299/122; XXIX AK/la, Interim Report, 23 September 1941, BA-MA RH 24-29/9; XXIX AK, Morning and Evening Report, 25 September 1941, BA-MA RH 24-29/9; 299. ID/Ic to SD Kiev, 26 September 1941, BA-MA RH 26-299/123; 299th ID, War Diary Ia, 25 and 26 September 1941, BA-MA RH 26-299/40. It is hardly credible that the bombings and incidents of arson were actually the work of the roughly 1,000 partisans whom the 6th Army assumed to be operating in the city; XXIX AK had already determined on 20 September that Kiev had been systematically vacated, that public utilities had been shut down, and that the streets and rail lines had been either destroyed or mined. XXIX AK, War Diary/Ia, 20 September 1941, BA-MA RH 24-29/9.
106. OKH/GenStdH/OQuIV/Fremde Heere Ost/IIc secret, 2 October 1941, BA-MA RH 26-299/123.
107. 299th ID, War Diary/Ia, 7 and 10 October 1941, BA-MA RH 26-299/40.
108. Order to the army of the commander in chief of the 6th Army, General Field Marshal von Reichenau, 10 October 1941; in Ueberschär and Wette, *Barbarossa*, 285.
109. 75th ID, War Diary/Ia, 27 October 1941, BA-MA RH 26-75/39; 75th ID/Ic, Morning Reports of 27, 28, and 31 October 1941; 75th ID/Ic to Infantry Regiment 202, 28 October 1941, BA-MA RH 26-75/115.
110. 75th ID/Ic, Addendum to the order of AOK 6 Ia on 10 October 1941 concerning the conduct of troops in the east, 28 October 1941, BA-MA RH 26-75/115.
111. ObdH, Guidelines for Combating Partisans, 25 October 1941, BA-MA RH 24-29/77; XXIX AK/la-Ic, 26 October 1941, BA-MA RH 26-299/124.
112. Commander of Army Group Rear Area South/la-Ic No. 2270/41, secret, 6 November 1941; Commander of Army Group Rear Area South/Ia No. 2532/41, secret, 20 November 1941, BA-MA RH 26-62/42.
113. Rolf-Dieter Müller, "Das Scheitern der wirtschaftlichen "Blitzkriegstrategie," in Militärgeschichtliches Forschungsamt Freiburg, *Reich,* 4: 1116–1226, here 1168ff.
114. AOK 6/1c AO, Instructions on the conduct of German Military Authorities in the Eastern Ukraine, 15 July 1941, BA-MA RH 26-299/119.
115. IV AK (Group Schwedler), 4 August 1941, BA-MA RH 24-4/95; AOK 6/III Az. 14n, Order to the Army of 31 July 1941, BA-MA RH 26-56/19a.
116. Commander in chief of the 6th Army, Order to the Army of 28 September 1941, BA-MA RH 24-17/262; Commissary of AOK 6, Instructions of 2 October 1941 for the Execution of Order to the Army of 28 September 1941, BA-MA RH 26-62/59; AOK 6/Ch.d.Ge.St. (Chief of the General Staff) No. 310/41 of 26 October 1941, BA-MA RH 24-17/262.
117. OKdo HGr Süd (High Command of Army Group South)/Ia-Ib No. 2987, secret, 27 October 1941, concerning the maintenance of discipline; 62. ID/IIb Nr. 1749/41, secret, 7 November 1941, BA-MA RH 26-62/42.
118. XXIX AK, War Diary/Ia, 29 October 1941, BA-MA RH 24-29/9.
119. 168th ID, War Diary/Ia, 14 November 1941, BA-MA RH 26-168/8.
120. 75th ID/Ib, 29 January 1942, BA-MA RH 26-75/170.
121. 75th ID/Ib, 1 March 1942; 75th ID, Commander to the commanders and leaders of independent units, 7 April 1942, BA-MA RH 26-75/170.
122. Müller, in *DRZW*, 4: 1186f.

123. 57th ID/Ib, report on the meeting that took place on 24 November 1941 in the Military Administration Headquarters' mess hall on feeding the civilian population of the city of Kharkov, BA-MA RH 26-57/113.
124. 57th ID/Ib, meeting in the Military Administration Headquarters in Kharkov of 4 November 1941, BA-MA RH 26-57/113.
125. 57th ID/Ib, report on the meeting that took place on 24 November 1941 in of the Military Administration Headquarters' mess hall on feeding the civilian population of the city of Kharkov, BA-MA RH 26-57/113.
126. Telex of the agricultural officer of the 57th ID, Oberleutnant Dr. Goecke, No. 159 of 9 January 1942, BA-MA RH 26-57/116; Military Administration Headquarters of Kharkov, Order of the Military Administration Headquarters No. 17, 18 December 1941, BA-MA RH 26-57/39.
127. Müller, *DRZW*, 4: 1192.
128. 57th ID, War Diary/Ib, 13 April 1942 and 15 April 1942; 57th ID/Ib to XXIX AK/IV Wi, 15 April 1942, BA-MA RH 26-57/116.
129. AOK 6/Ia/OQu, 17 October 1941 regarding Kharkov, BA-MA RH 24-17/262.
130. 57th ID/Ic, Activity Report 1 September to 31 October 1941, BA-MA RH 26-57/57.
131. Undated announcement of the military commander; 57th ID/Ib to AK LV, 4 November 1941, BA-MA RH 26-57/113.
132. Commander in chief AOK 6, Order to the Army of 9 November 1941 (Oberst-Sinz-Befehl), BA-MA RH 26-299/124.
133. Supplement to Order to the Army (Oberst Sinz) of 9 November 1941, issued on 14 November 1941, transmitted through XXIX AK/Ic, BA-MA RH 26-299/124.
134. Orders of the Military Administration Headquarters No. 4 of 11 November 1941, No. 7 of 19 November 1941, No. 8 of 22 November 1941, No. 14 of 6 December 1941, No. 16 of 6 December 1941, BA-MA RH 26-57/39.
135. 57th ID/Ic, Activity Report 1 November to 31 December 1941, BA-MA RH 26-57/58.
136. XVII AK, Addendum to War Diary for 16 November 1941, BA-MA RH 24-17/226.
137. AOK 6, War Diary/Ic, 7 December 1941, BA-MA RH 20-6/132.
138. AOK 6/Ia-Ic AO No. 2451/41, secret, 15 November 1941 regarding Combating partisans in the area of army operations, BA-MA RH 26-299/124; 57th ID/Ic, Activity Report 1 November to 31 December 1941, BA-MA RH 26-57/58.
139. 299th ID, War Diary/Ia, 5 November 1941, BA-MA RH 26-299/40; 299th ID/Ic to XXIX AK, 30 October 1941, BA-MA RH 26-299/123;XXIX AK, War Diary/Ia, 30 October 1941, BA-MA RH 24-29/9; 75th ID/Ic, Bulletin on Enemy Activity No. 52, 31 October 1941, BA-MA RH 26-75/115.
140. 299th ID, War Diary/Ia, 28 October 1941, BA-MA RH 26-299/40.
141. 299th ID, War Diary/Ia, 29 October 1941, BA-MA RH 26-299/40; 299th ID/Ic, Summary Intelligence Report of Combating Partisans, 12 December, 1941, BA-MA RH 26-299/120.
142. Post headquarters in Sumy to I./IR 530, IV./AR 175, II./AR 63, AA 175, Beob.Abt z.K., 1. January 1942; 75th ID/Ic, Activity Report 1 to 27 November 1941, BA-MA RH-75/116.
143. 299th ID/Ic, Summary Report on Combating Partisans, 12 December 1941, BA-MA RH 26-299/120.
144. 75th 1D/Ic, Activity Report 1 to 27 November 1941, BA-MA RH 26-75/116.

145. XXIX AK/Ic, Morning Report of 7 December 1941, BA-MA RH 24-29/78.
146. AOK 6, War Diary/Ic, 7 December 1941, BA-MA RH 20-6/132.
147. XXIX AK, War Diary/Ia, 30 November 1941, BA-MA RH 24-29/18.
148. 75th ID/Ic, Activity Report Ic, Situation Assessment Regarding the Enemy, 15 to 30 November 1941, BA-MA RH 26-75/117.
149. AOK 6, War Diary/Ic, 7 December 1941, BA-MA RH 20-6/132.
150. 75th ID/Ic, Evening Report of 11 December 1941, Morning Report of 20 December 1941, BA-MA RH 26-75/118.
151. XXIX AK, Order to the corps of 18 December 1941, BA-MA RH 24-29/78.
152. 75th ID, War Diary/Ia, 23 December 1941, BA-MA RH 26-75/39.
153. 75th ID/Ic No. 436/41, secret, 23 December 1941, BA-MA RH 26-75/118; XXIX AK, War Diary/Ia, 28 December, 1941, BA-MA RH 24-29/18.

– *Chapter 11* –

Incident at Baranivka

German Reprisals and the Soviet Partisan Movement in Ukraine, October–December 1941[1]

Truman Anderson

On the evening of 4 November 1941, a German army *Kübelwagen* drove into the Ukrainian village of Baranivka, a collective farm community located in the Ps'ol river valley about six kilometers due north of the district seat of Shyshaky (Poltava region). The vehicle's passengers, a colonel named Sinz, Sergeant Graf, Corporal Schneider and Lance Corporal Tischler—all from the staff of the 677th Pioneer Regiment—were en route from Graivoron in Russia to the headquarters of the 6th Army at Poltava. As it was late, they decided to seek quarters for the night in a comfortable-looking new house which stood by the road at the southern exit from the village. This turned out to be the village clinic and home of the local doctor, Ovram Martynenko and his family. Martynenko admitted the colonel and his men to his dwelling and gave them a meal and a place to sleep.

Sinz's arrival in Baranivka was observed by villagers who were in contact with a small partisan group of fourteen men led by two officials of the Shyshaky district party underground, D. D. Kornilych, second secretary of the underground *raikom* (district party committee), and K. I. Tutka, a former chairman of the raikom executive committee. According to village memory, it was a young collective farm worker named Dutsia Borodai, supervisor of the Young

---

Notes for this section begin on page 302.

Pioneer group in Baranivka, who brought word of the Germans' arrival to Kornilych and Tutka at their base in Kuibysheve, about four kilometers distant. Another, more prosaic account assigns this role to an unidentified teenage boy. In either case, the partisans were alerted and decided to take action. Later that night their detachment entered Baranivka and quietly surrounded the clinic.

At around midnight Martynenko suddenly burst into the room where his guests were sleeping and shouted, "Herr Oberst, *Partisany!*" whereupon fire erupted from all sides. Sinz and his men, literally caught with their trousers down, scrambled to save their lives. They returned the partisans' fire but quickly found themselves overwhelmed. The colonel, who was firing a sub-machine gun from the front doorway, was gravely wounded by a grenade and shouted to the others that they should make for the Kübelwagen and leave him behind. Schneider picked up Sinz's weapon and took cover behind the stove as first Tischler and then Graf were killed trying to start the vehicle. Now alone, the corporal remained concealed as the partisans attempted to enter the clinic. Confident, perhaps, that everyone inside was dead, they shined a flashlight into the room. Schneider fired at them from his hiding place and in the ensuing confusion leapt through a window. He tossed the Colonel's dispatch bag before him, cried "Don't shoot!" in Russian and bolted for the cover of some nearby bushes. The partisans shot at him but he escaped unharmed.

The partisans searched the house inside and out and recovered the dispatches. One of their number, Hryhorii Kukhar, had been mortally wounded and died within fifteen minutes.[2] The remainder of the detachment then fled the scene and returned to their camp, leaving the wrecked vehicle and the bodies of Sinz, Graf, Tischler and Martynenko behind, concealed somewhere not far from the clinic. Corp. Schneider spent the night hiding in a nearby ditch. At daybreak, he returned to the clinic to look for his boots, but found that everything had been taken. He then set off on foot for Myrhorod, with only a couple of blankets and a pair of slippers to protect him from the bitter weather. He arrived days later and reported to the local garrison commander all that had happened in Baranivka.[3]

There had been several partisan attacks in the Myrhorod area in the preceding weeks, and a regiment of the 62nd Infantry Division was already pursuing Soviet "bandits" in the vicinity. Yet none of these attacks had thus far taken the life of a German colonel. Sinz was the staff engineer officer of the 6th Army—a man probably known personally to the army commander, Field Marshal von Reichenau. The German chain of command therefore viewed the attack at Baranivka with special seriousness. Corporal Schneider's report soon traveled all the way up to the headquarters of Field Marshal Gerd von Rundstedt's Army Group South. In response, elements of the 62nd Infantry Division began a series of punitive raids and small scale anti-partisan operations that would scatter the struggling partisan groups in the Poltava region by the end of December.[4]

The existing literature on the German-Soviet war is vast. The themes of high politics, strategy, military operations, and occupation policy have all been explored to the point where a fairly stable consensus exists on the most basic interpretive issues, particularly on the formative influence of Nazi ideology over the character of the war at its highest levels.[5] There are nevertheless significant gaps in our knowledge. This is especially true of the subject of life under German occupation. We lack a feel for the small scale and routine events that represent the most basic level of interaction between German authorities and the people. Theo Schulte's case study of the rear areas of two German armies (so-called Korücke 532 and 582) stands out as an excellent example of what can be accomplished using German records.[6] But this literature remains underdeveloped, despite the opportunities which have arisen to present both the German and Soviet sides of the story in detail. Manifold new possibilities exist for this kind of history, including further studies of specific German units or jurisdictions like Schulte's Korücke, and the exciting prospect of genuinely two-sided treatments of life in a given Soviet town, city, or region under German rule.

This chapter is intended as a modest contribution to the larger picture. It concerns a particular facet of the German occupation—anti-partisan warfare—in a particular area (the Myrhorod and Shyshaky districts of the Poltava region) over a short period of time (October–December of 1941). Its main purpose is to explore the army's use of repressive violence, in the form of reprisals and hostage-taking, against the Ukrainian communities affected by partisan activity and to illustrate how this interaction was shaped by various factors. It aims, as far as possible, to explore this question at various levels of the German chain of command and to demonstrate how reprisal orders formulated at the highest echelons of the Wehrmacht were implemented by small groups of German soldiers in the Ukrainian countryside. It also describes the events surrounding the attack at Baranivka as vividly as the sources will permit, in order that we not lose sight of the powerful emotional forces at work in this complex situation. Using a variety of German and Soviet documents, combined with published sources and the records of four interviews I conducted in the spring and summer of 1997, I have been able to reconstruct the Baranivka incident and the actions that followed in some detail.

Such a methodology implies a trade-off in favor of depth, which imposes certain analytical limitations. A "microhistorical" approach to a subject like the Eastern front cannot on its own support broad generalizations about the character of the German-Soviet war. Instead, it offers the prospect of incremental progress toward deeper understanding, progress that might strengthen the current consensus view or, alternatively, point toward potential areas of revision. For this reason, a few historiographic remarks are in order.

The Wehrmacht's institutional support for the most inhumane of Hitler's goals in the occupied USSR has long since become a matter of record.[7] The senior officer corps' enthusiasm for a bitter, unrestrained war against "Jewish Bolshevism" is no longer at issue: the German military endorsed a range of brutal occupation policies that meant death for millions of Soviet civilians and prisoners of war. Less certain—and much more controversial—is the part played by the army's lower echelons in realizing the Hitler regime's "New Order" in the east. It is clear that German soldiers followed the ideologically motivated orders given to them by their superiors, even when these orders demanded the killing of women and children, but questions remain about their motivation and about the extent of their own initiative.

Evidence of brutality on the part of German soldiers has been steadily accumulating and has called into question the well-entrenched belief that the ordinary *Landser* (the German equivalent of the American term "G.I.") remained basically indifferent to National Socialism. Omer Bartov has attempted a comprehensive explanation of the behavior of German troops in a number of books and articles, including *Hitler's Army*, published in 1991.[8] In Bartov's view, the rank-and-file German soldier came to the Eastern front imbued with a racist world view and a veneration for Hitler that he had imbibed in the Hitler Youth and Nazi-controlled school system. Confronted by the appalling, anti-modern reality of the German-Soviet war, he was steeled not by "primary group cohesion" but by fanaticism, his resolve further stiffened by the Wehrmacht's increasingly murderous system of military justice. Deathly frightened of both his implacable enemy and his own officers, he found some compensation for his many sacrifices in his official license to rob and kill Soviet civilians with impunity. In Bartov's view, these factors interacted to produce widespread war crimes and a remarkable willingness to endure the hopeless struggle with the Red Army to the bitter end. Some of the historians who helped to debunk the image of a "clean" Wehrmacht in the 1970s and 1980s have reacted to Bartov's argument with reservations, arguing that the actual behavior of German troops was less consistent than such a synthesis will allow and that non-ideological factors contributed more directly to the special horrors of the German-Soviet war.[9] To a degree, the time-honored debate about "structure" and "intent" in Third Reich historiography has simply been carried over into research on the army, with some authors placing more weight on circumstance (e.g., on higher orders, the extreme pressures of combat, Soviet brutality) and others on the power of ideas (e.g., on anti-Semitic or anti-Slavic zeal). Some of the most recent work on the Wehrmacht, however, has broken new ground. In an essay on the partisan war in Belorussia published in *Vernichtungskrieg: Verbrechen der Wehrmacht 1941–1944* (the companion volume to the well-known "Wehrmacht exhibition"), Hannes Heer has explained army atrocities against civilians as resulting from a program of deliberate brutalization orchestrated by Hitler and the Wehrmacht's most senior leaders. Their objective, he argues, was to bloody the hands of ordinary German soldiers and thereby destroy the moral inhibitions that might stand in the way of a true war of annihilation. In Heer's view, the Wehrmacht exploited the soldiers' racist attitudes toward Jews in order to lead them into wider violence against the Slavic majority and prepare them (and the German people) for a future of continuous warfare. The goal, in short, was not deterrent terror or the elimination of a particular category of enemy (i.e., Jews or communists), but the creation of a truly fanatical *Kampfmoral.* Although some senior officers resisted this radicalization, Hitler's psychological project was a success: German soldiers in Belorussia quickly expanded their definition of "partisan" to include any Soviet civilian. Only in this way, Heer maintains, can we explain the virtually genocidal character of the army's treatment of civilians during the early stages of the anti-partisan effort in Belorussia, when the partisan movement was hardly worthy of the name.[10] There are echoes here of Bartov's argument, but where Bartov contends that the galvanizing effect of brutality on German morale was probably an unforeseen (though very welcome) by-product of ideological warfare, Heer sees a deliberate design.

The evidence presented in this chapter fully confirms the consensus view of the Wehrmacht's institutional affinity for the Nazi "war of *Weltanschauungen*" in the Soviet Union. This is obvious in several respects, including the army's reflexive association of Ukrainian Jews with the partisans. The Baranivka episode is also compatible with much of Bartov's argument about the motivation of junior soldiers, as there is some indication that the lower echelons of the German units described here had internalized Nazi images of the "Jewish-Bolshevik" foe. At the same time, this essay seeks to emphasize, to a greater degree than Bartov has tended to do, how vitally important the mutual escalation of violence in the partisan war proved to be to the barbarization of warfare on the Eastern front and how markedly the behavior of German units could vary in response to circumstances. The well-known strains and frustrations of guerrilla warfare, coupled with the German army's pre-Nazi tradition of extreme harshness toward civilians suspected of resistance activity, also seem to have played an important part in conditioning the reaction of the German forces.[11] This essay shares less ground with Heer's recent work. One crucial point of difference stands out. For both ideological and pragmatic reasons, the German army took a consistently softer line toward the civil population of Ukraine than it did toward the "Great Russians." This had a genuine effect on occupation policy in areas that remained under military (as opposed to Nazi political) jurisdiction. Most notably, it worked to steer reprisal violence toward enclaves of Jewish scapegoats and mitigate reprisal violence against ethnic Ukrainian communities. In contrast to the pattern of behavior that Heer describes in Belorussia, the German army in Ukraine also tended to limit its reprisals to the actual sites of partisan activity. German reprisal violence, however wanton and disproportionate, was provoked by Soviet guerrillas who enjoyed at least passive support from the area's inhabitants. The point here is not that Heer is wrong in his description of anti-partisan warfare in Belorussia, or in his interpretation of Hitler's intentions, but rather that his overarching explanation of the mechanism of German atrocities does not account well for the army's actions in its Ukrainian jurisdiction during this time. Reprisal violence, though extreme, was not simply a vehicle for the brutalization of German soldiers.

Although focused on German behavior, this chapter also sheds some light on the early history of the Soviet partisan movement. Here the historiography is less developed and, thus far, less controversial. Although several works based on newly available Soviet sources have appeared in the past few years, current historians of the partisan war are still chiefly occupied with re-examining earlier studies and establishing new directions for research. Even the best of the Western works produced before 1989 were colored by the national security agenda of the Cold War, while Soviet accounts were committed to depicting the partisans as a "nationwide" (*vsenarodnaia*) liberation movement that contributed directly to the

German defeat.[12] Again, there are limits to how far one can generalize on the basis of a single case study, but the Baranivka story confirms recent descriptions of the early days of the Soviet resistance. The amateurism of the partisans and their uncertain sense of mission were glaringly apparent in these events. More important, the Baranivka episode revealed the highly ambivalent relationship between Ukrainian rural villages and area partisans. German authorities received a good deal of accurate intelligence from informers in the villages. As the net began to close around the Myrhorod and Shyshaky partisans and German terror became more credible than that of the guerrillas, the Soviet "shadow regime" in the Poltava region collapsed. The potential significance of this observation will be discussed further in the conclusion. For now, we must turn our attention to the background of the partisan war in Ukraine.

I. German and Soviet Visions of the Partisan War

The readiness with which the Oberkommando der Wehrmacht (OKW—Supreme Command of the Armed Forces) and Oberkommando des Heeres (OKH—High Command of the Army) embraced Hitler's vision of operation Barbarossa as a merciless ideological struggle was long ago demonstrated by Christian Streit in his ground-breaking study of Germany's treatment of Soviet prisoners of war.[13] Jürgen Förster has provided a detailed explanation of how this vision was incorporated into key directives which regulated the army's conduct in the Soviet Union.[14] Here it is enough to note that the infamous *Kommissarbefehl* (commissar order), the *Gerichtsbarkeitserlaß* (military justice decree), the orders governing the jurisdiction of the SS in the operations area, and the "Guidelines for the Conduct of the Troops in Russia" created an atmosphere in which the legal and customary restraints on military violence observed by the Wehrmacht in the campaign in the west in 1940 would be relaxed or altogether abrogated.

This corpus of directives, which was passed to the units poised on the Soviet border in the weeks before the invasion and amplified by subsequent orders from their own commanders, drew particular attention to the prospect of irregular resistance from the Soviet population. The German soldier was told to expect widespread and fanatical opposition to his advance, instigated by Communist officials and Jews, and was given license to deal with it in a summary fashion. The Gerichtsbarkeitserlaß of 21 May 1941 encouraged the use of violent reprisals against civilians in cases where the actual perpetrators of anti-German activity could not be apprehended. Such reprisals have long been a favored expedient of occupying armies, but this order radically decentralized the authority to carry out such extreme measures. German troops were also told to shoot captured partisan suspects, and any commissioned officer could authorize such killings.[15] It is important to note that the Hague Rules of Land Warfare of 1907 did not prohibit the use of reprisals and also imposed very strict standards of legal conduct on guerrillas—standards that essentially prohibited covert fighting.[16] It is also true that the British, American, and French armies authorized the use of reprisals during World War II.[17] But these regulations clearly stated that reprisals could be justified only as a last resort for keeping order in occupied areas, and the German doctrine spelled out on the eve of Barbarossa was therefore distinctly severe.

Ironically, given the special place reserved for partisan warfare in the revolutionary mythography of the USSR, Soviet authorities in 1941 had no plan for the organization of partisan units in the event of war with Germany. Stalin was confident that future conflicts would be fought on enemy soil and forbade formal planning of a guerrilla movement. Although Zhukov himself had warned Stalin in January 1941 that Germany was likely to occupy Soviet territory if war came, no formal preparations were made before the Wehrmacht struck. Thus while the German military girded itself for a struggle with the Bolshevik partisan bogeyman, the Soviet Union remained unprepared to create this kind of friction in an organized way.[18] Once the invasion began, the army, the party and the NKVD (Narodnyi Kommissariat Vnutrennykh Del—People's Commissariat of Internal Affairs) struggled (often at cross purposes) to improvise an insurgency under very difficult circumstances. The result was an uncoordinated patchwork of very diverse partisan groups that had little impact on the Wehrmacht's progress.

Beyond exhorting the German soldier to act ruthlessly toward the enemy, the Wehrmacht made few serious preparations of its own for anti-partisan warfare. Just as Stalin's confidence that the Red Army would rapidly advance beyond the borders of the USSR inhibited the organization of a partisan movement, so Hitler's confidence in a quick victory, widely shared by his generals, ensured that little thought was given to the problem of pacifying occupied territory. Complete pacification and full economic mobilization of conquered space would be the task of the civil-controlled Reichskommissariats that would spring up in the wake of the army as it advanced to the east. In previous campaigns, the Wehrmacht had divided the operations area into a forward combat zone and rear areas controlled by the various army commanders (the Korücke). For Barbarossa, however, a new echelon was interposed between the Korücke and the home area in anticipation of the unprecedented depth of the Eastern front. Here "army group rear areas" (Heeresgebiete, for short) were established, one for each of the three army groups—north, center, and south. A network of area and local garrisons known respectively as Feld- and Ortskommandanturen provided a skeletal framework for military government, and the Heeresgebiet commanders had at their disposal a number of specialized guard, police, and security formations with which to maintain order and protect key lines of communication.[19] All of these forces combined, however, filled little of the vast space that yawned behind the Wehrmacht, and indigenous policemen (*Hilfspolizei* or *Miliz* to the Germans, *politsai* to the inhabitants) and village chiefs (*starosty)* appointed by the Germans or elected under their supervision were actually the most familiar representatives of German authority in the rural areas where the partisans were most active.

The vulnerability of this structure to partisan pressure is obvious, but one must remember that it was deliberate—the rear was kept weak in order to keep men available for the front during a brief campaign. In 1942, as the partisan movement took on greater coherence under the direction of P. K. Ponomarenko, First Secretary of the Belorussian Communist Party, the inadequacies of German rear area security would become more apparent. In 1941, however, the partisans proved to be only a minor problem for the Wehrmacht, particularly in Ukraine. The records of Heeresgebiet Süd—a jurisdiction which eventually included more than 100,000 square kilometers of land and at least five million people—show that partisan activity was very limited before October, and the command's reprisal violence against the Ukrainian population was correspondingly muted. Despite the encouragements to reprisal given in pre-invasion directives and an explicit Heeresgebiet order that all reprisals be reported to the commanding general as "special occurrences" *(besondere Ereignisse),* only one incident shows up in Heeresgebiet staff papers through the end of October. Significantly, this involved the execution of sixty-three Jewish men on the basis of Ukrainian denunciations.[20] Beginning in late October, the situation began to change. In the Dnipro Bend region, Heeresgebiet forces would spend many weeks destroying partisan groups at Nikopol and Novomoskovs'k. At roughly the same time, they encountered stiffening partisan activity in the Poltava district. It is to this area that we now turn our attention.

II. The German Response to Baranivka

At the beginning of October, OKH provided the Heeresgebiet with three battered front-line infantry divisions—the 24th, 62nd, and 113th—as temporary reinforcements to help deal with the massive numbers of Red Army soldiers captured during the fighting around Kiev.[21] By the end of the month their work was finished and all three were en route to their parent commands. One battalion of the 62nd Division, however, remained under Heeresgebiet control for the purpose of dealing with a mounting partisan threat in the Myrhorod area.[22] Throughout October there had been numerous attacks on German personnel and installations in and around this small provincial city, the birthplace of Gogol and home of one of the Soviet Union's most popular mineral spas. These attacks had special significance because the large Myrhorod flour mill was the main source of supply for von Reichenau's 6th Army, and the commander of the city garrison had therefore urgently requested additional troops. He also called for the use of reprisals as a means of restoring order.[23]

The attacks were the work of several different partisan organizations. The largest, though in some ways the least active, was built up in advance of the Germans' arrival by officials of the Myrhorod district party apparatus. H. O. Ivashchenko and I. S. Zorin, two secretaries of the Myrhorod *raikom*, P.S. Vovk, chairman of the raikom executive committee, and P. O. Andreev, the head of the district branch of the NKVD, were its most important leaders. This group was very typical of the partisan detachments active in this stage of the war. Its membership was an amalgam of an NKVD "destruction battalion" and party members, Komsomol members, and "non-party activists" who had been screened by the leadership and found suitable for underground work. On 14 September, the day Myrhorod was occupied by the Germans, the staff of the detachment moved to the village of Velyka Obukhivka, about 30 kilometers northeast of Myrhorod. There it divided the group into four sub-detachments with nominal strengths of roughly 110 to 120 men each. Two of these were made up predominantly of men from Myrhorod, while the other two had been raised in and around Velyka Obukhivka itself and the nearby village of Velyki Sorochyntsi. Ivashchenko became the commander of the combined detachment, which now called itself "Victory" (*Peremoha*), and Vovk served as his commissar.[24]

"Victory" was equipped only with light weapons and a small quantity of explosives, but had unusually adequate stores of food and clothing and had taken the trouble to build several different camps in the woodlands of the Ps'ol valley. Its most important bases were at Velyka Obukhivka and Sakalivka. It had also established a network of liaison agents in nearby villages, and maintained contact with surrounding district partisan groups like the one led by Kornilych and Tutka at Baranivka (Shyshaky district). For the most part, its early activities were limited to supporting the Soviet withdrawal from the district in early October and to helping pockets of Red Army stragglers (called *okruzhentsy*) get back to Russian lines once the Germans had passed through. Propaganda was another important task. The detachment had its own printing press and ample stores of paper, and it produced thousands of leaflets. The low density of German units in the area also made it possible for the detachment staff to hold public political rallies in some of the villages, an activity which the movement rightly considered vital to the survival of its underground organization: by demonstrating the continued presence of the party the detachment created the impression that Soviet authority was more real than that of the invaders.

In late October and early November, two other partisan groups arrived in the Velyka Obukhivka area and made contact with Ivashchenko's headquarters. The first to do so was a small partisan detachment under the leadership of I.I. Kopenkin, a 24-year-old party member and future Hero of the Soviet Union. This band of about seventy-five men had originally been recruited in the "Zaporizhstal'" and "Koksokhim" works in Zaporizhzhia under either Zaporizhzhia *obkom* (regional committee) or NKVD auspices. On 25 September, it slipped into German territory from Kharkiv and made its way to the Hadiach area. Like "Victory," it had been bringing okruzhentsy back to Soviet lines and had also carried out a few attacks on German targets.[25] The second group was a similarly small outfit led by D.Iu. Bezpal'ko. Bezpal'ko's band was originally part of the Komyshnia district (i.e., party) partisan movement led by F.M. Honcharenko, first secretary of the Komyshnia raikom. After German forces arrived in Komyshnia, Honcharenko left the district with part of his men and rejoined the forces of the Soviet army farther to the east. The remaining partisans broke into three subdetachments, one of them led by Bezpal'ko. In October, operating south of Komyshnia, Bezpal'ko, too, had been working to exfiltrate okruzhentsy, but despite his detachment's small size he had more frequently attacked German targets around Myrhorod than had Ivashchenko or Kopenkin. Several of the attacks mentioned in the reports of the German authorities in Myrhorod in October were almost certainly carried out by his men, who made a specialty of roadside ambushes between Myrhorod and Komyshnia (a particular source of concern to the Ortskommandant). At the end of October, Bezpal'ko began planning a joint attack on the German headquarters in Myrhorod with Ivashchenko, but this did not come off, and soon German pursuit drove him from his base near Popivka to the greater security of Velyka Obukhivka, where he arrived on 11 November.[26]

Increasing pressure from the Germans would eventually lead these three groups, together with other, fragmentary detachments from the Hadiach area, to amalgamate formally in December of 1941 under the supervision of the first secretary of the Poltava region underground, S. F. Kondratenko. At that time, Kopenkin would become the commander of the combined group and Ivashchenko his commissar. In the interim, however, coordination between the three groups was quite loose. Judging from German records, it was Bezpal'ko's numerous attacks on German personnel in mid- to late October that drew the 62nd Division to the Myrhorod area.

The 62nd was as typical of the German army's forces then deployed in Soviet Ukraine as the "Victory" detachment was of the Soviet partisan movement. It was a reserve division from Glatz in Silesia, raised in the second wave of mobilization of 1939–1940 and comprised mainly of trained reservists under thirty-five years of age.[27] The 62nd had seen combat in both the Polish and French campaigns, and, like the whole of the German infantry, had been heavily bloodied from the outset of the fighting in the Soviet Union. Shortly before being attached to the Heeresgebiet, the division had taken part in the great battle of encirclement at Kiev as part of the 6th Army. Here it distinguished itself in several days of intense combat near Borispol and suffered further heavy casualties. By the time the division was placed under Heeresgebiet control it had therefore been repeatedly mauled and on 25 September it reported a shortfall of ninety-three officers and 5,178 men from an authorized strength of 16,562 (31.8 percent).[28] Part of this deficit was made good during October and November, but bearing in mind that the casualties in the infantry companies must have been much higher than the average figure for the division as a whole, it is fair to say that when it arrived in the Myrhorod area, the 62nd was badly under-strength and exhausted, its surviving veterans traumatized by months of high-intensity warfare.

Initially, a single battalion of the division—the 3rd Battalion, 190th Infantry Regiment (hereafter III/190)—was dispatched to Myrhorod on 24 October, while the bulk of the 62nd returned to the

6th Army. On or about the 28th, this battalion arrived in the city and on that date reported killing forty-five partisans and 168 Jews. Though the records of the Heeresgebiet staff state that these Jews, described as "the Jewish population of Myrhorod," were executed "because of ties to the partisans," there is no mention of any such offense in the internal paperwork of the 62nd Division.[29] This leaves open the possibility that this accusation was an embellishment added at the Heeresgebiet level. By this stage in the war, however, such official window dressing was becoming unnecessary. The official presumption that Jews were the ultimate source of anti-German resistance had long since been internalized by the Ostheer (eastern army), and as a result army troops were routinely shooting groups of Jews discovered in their anti-partisan patrols. Jews had also become the preferred target of reprisal violence where available. The commanding general of Heeresgebiet Süd, Karl von Roques, had ordered that Jews and Russians be selected as reprisal victims in preference to ethnic Ukrainians, in order to create the impression that the German military government was being "just" *(gerecht)*.[30] The commander of the 62nd Division, Walter Keiner, had given a similar order of his own on 21 July, instructing his troops to single out Jews and Russians for reprisals. "The Ukrainian population," he added, "which sympathizes with the Germans, is to be excepted from collective punishment."[31] It is not clear whether III/190 took the initiative in killing the Jews of Myrhorod or instead acted at the request of the Ortskommandantur, but at least one of the two units had taken their commanders' guidance about Jews to heart.

In the next few days, III/190 followed Bezpal'ko's trail of ambushes north from Myrhorod to the Popivka area, clashing several times with the partisans. The battalion discovered ammunition dumps and caches of weapons and executed a number of captured "partisans" (often called "bandits" in German records) along the way: four at Popivka on 29 October, four at Komyshnia, and twenty at Zuivtsi on the 30th, and a further twenty-one at Bakumivka on 1 November.[32] It was against this backdrop of mounting activity that the killing of Sinz at Baranivka on the night of 4–5 November took place. News of the attack did not reach the Heeresgebiet until 9 November, relayed by the 62nd Division. The language used to describe the incident in the Heeresgebiet operations diary displays the Wehrmacht's powerful contempt for guerrilla warfare very distinctly: Sinz, Graf, and Tischler were said to have been "murdered in their sleep" rather than killed in action and their dispatches "stolen" instead of captured.[33] This entry also states that the "harshest of reprisals" was being initiated. That same day the Heeresgebiet directed the 62nd Division to send further details of the attack as soon as possible and to effect "deterrent punitive measures against the guilty residents." Army Group South was also notified along with the security divisions then under Heeresgebiet command.[34]

The military police group of Ortskommandantur I(V) 268 provided the 62nd Division, now reassigned to the Heeresgebiet, with a good deal of intelligence about the partisans in the Myrhorod district, some of it quite accurate. This in part reflected the partisans' failure to screen their ranks carefully for potential German sympathizers. A man named Sakalo, one of the sub-detachment commanders in "Victory," later turned out to be a German agent.[35] The chief of the Ukrainian police in Myrhorod reported on 8 November that an informant named Jakob Kons had told him of a one hundred-man partisan detachment encamped in a school in Kuibysheve (where Kornilych's small detachment had its base). Kons named Andreev and Ivashchenko as the detachment's leaders.[36] On the 9th, an informant from Sakalivka named Zhuk reported that two hundred mounted partisans had established themselves at the collective farm there, and were requisitioning cattle and sheep and detaining paroled Soviet POWs. He claimed that parolees who refused to join the group were being shot.[37] And on the 10th, another informant, Nykyfor Iver from Velyka Obukhivka, confirmed the presence of the group at Sakalivka and provided the names of eight Velyka Obukhivka residents he claimed were in league with the partisans.[38] A Soviet account published in 1988 confirms that the names he provided were in fact members of the headquarters staff of "Victory." Two of the men named, Kyrylo Drahin and Mykhailo Zabolot'ko, lived in Velyka Obukhivka in civilian guise while serving as liaison men for Ivashchenko.[39]

As the reference to the one hundred-man group at Kuibysheve suggests, the numbers of partisans given in these reports were probably exaggerated, but as other units of the 62nd Division moved into the Ps'ol valley, the Germans nevertheless developed a rough outline of the forces arrayed against them. But what about the attitude of the civil population? Would the villagers in this area cooperate with German troops or galvanize behind the partisans? This issue is best approached in two parts. First, what did the German units expect from the populace, and second, what were the actual sympathies of the villagers?[40]

The first question is the less difficult of the two. Since the beginning of Barbarossa, the Ostheer had developed an imagined hierarchy of Soviet ethnic groups in which Ukrainians occupied one of the higher stations. Poles and Russians fell well below them and were often presumed hostile, while Jews occupied the nethermost rung. There are many examples of this type of thinking to be found in the records of Heeresgebiet Süd, a fact which chiefly reflects the persistent influence of pro-Ukrainian officials from Alfred Rosenberg's *Ostministerium* on the army's view of Ukraine. Captain Hans Koch, a strong supporter of Wehrmacht cooperation with the Ukrainian nationalist movement, served as Rosenberg's liaison officer with Army Group South and was for a time seconded to the staff of Heeresgebiet Süd.[41] Von Roques himself had instructed his troops at the beginning of the campaign to regard Ukraine as the "*Lebensraum* of a friendly people." Obviously, the key members of the Nazi hierarchy (Hitler, Göring, Erich Koch) did not share this view, and as a result the army often had precious little latitude in its treatment of Ukrainian civilians, particularly where economic questions were concerned. Nevertheless, it was a matter of official policy in Heeresgebiet Süd that Ukrainians were basically pro-German in their orientation and, accordingly, many privileges were granted to them. They were, for example, allowed to keep their radio receivers and could fraternize with German soldiers (at a time when relations with Poles were forbidden).[42] Most important, as already noted above, they were officially exempted from German reprisals by both the Heeresgebiet and the 62nd Division. That this paternalistic attitude was itself tinged with racial arrogance is clear, but as Colonel von Krosigk, the Heeresgebiet chief of staff would later note, there was to be no "negro treatment" *(Negerstandpunkt)* of Ukrainians.[43]

The 62nd Division had not been involved in sustained anti-partisan warfare prior to its assignment to Heeresgebiet Süd, thus the earlier history of the division's operations in the Soviet Union tells us little about the mind-set of the soldiers.[44] The shootings by III/190 at Myrhorod suggest that the men of at least this battalion were willing to follow orders to kill Jews preferentially in reprisals, yet the same unit had also killed twenty-one Ukrainians at Bakumivka on 1 November. As we shall see below, at least some of the division's officers would come to recognize the difficult position of the Ukrainian villagers who were trying to steer a course between the German Scylla and the partisan Charybdis, but we can only speculate as to the preconceptions held by the majority. Even the intelligence available to the 62nd Division was ambiguous with respect to the attitude of the civil populace. On the one hand, Ukrainian informants had stated that networks of Soviet agents existed in at least some villages. On the other, the very fact that there were informants who were willing to cooperate with German intelligence implied that the inhabitants of the area were not uniformly pro-Soviet in disposition. Furthermore, the content of the reports provided by informants revealed an element of duress in the people's cooperation with the partisans. A given German officer could have interpreted this information either way.

Assessing actual Ukrainian inclinations and behavior is more difficult. The persistence of the Heeresgebiet's official sympathy for ethnic Ukrainians (which lasted until the Wehrmacht's retreat in late 1943) indicates that the German view of Ukrainian *Deutschfreundlichkeit* had some basis in fact, and indeed there is tangible evidence that this was so. The most important measure of public attitudes—the low level of partisan activity—had certainly buttressed the Germans' assumptions about the agreeable posture of the majority of Ukrainians in the early months of the war. However, the reality of public opinion was doubtless much more complex than it appeared to German officials, for every town and village contained people who had suffered under Soviet rule and people who had benefitted from it. In the Myrhorod and Shyshaky areas, a key geographic cleavage also came into play. In western Ukraine (the area most hostile to Soviet rule in the first place), the German advance had come on like a flash flood, leaving Soviet authorities little time to organize. In central and eastern Ukraine the situation was different. Here the party apparatus had had time to prepare for the occupation and to build an underground structure. In Shyshaky, for example, the people had been living under a state of martial law for months. Workers in the collectives had toiled day and night to bring in the harvest before the Germans arrived. Citizens from all over the district had been mobilized for military construction projects, like the building of a new aerodrome at Myrhorod. When they were not working, the people had been summoned to political meetings where Soviet officials kept them abreast of the war news and preached to them about their duty to the socialist motherland. One account of the Shyshaky underground's activities in this period claims that 490 such meetings had been held in the district by the time the German occupation began in October.[45] The featured speakers at these gatherings were often people like Tutka who went on to hold posts in the underground. Thus in psychological as well as practical terms, the ground for resistance was much better prepared in this area than was typical of the lands to the west. Once the occupation began, the paucity of German troops coupled with the continued presence of the familiar officials who were now leading the partisan detachments prevented wholesale collaboration with the invaders and mitigated against the outward expression of pro-German sympathies.

The balance between all of these factors was first put to the test on the evening of 9 November, when III/190 arrived in the Baranivka area to investigate the killing of Sinz. The German account of what happened is terse. At Baranivka itself, the 11th Company of III/190 recovered the bodies of Sinz, Graf, Tischler and "the Russian doctor," along with the wreck of the Kübelwagen. Efforts to find the responsible persons and recover the missing dispatches proved unsuccessful, therefore the company shot ten hostages and burned the village, noting that many hidden stores of ammunition and grenades exploded in the flames. That same day the 9th and 12th companies of the battalion also claimed to have shot eleven "bandits" in nearby Iares'ky, and forty-five "partisans and their middlemen" in Sorochyntsi, where three persons were also hanged.[46] The surviving Soviet accounts, published and archival, have nothing to say about these killings in Iares'ki and Sorochyntsi, but do offer some detailed information about Baranivka. Though these sources contain discrepancies, especially regarding the exact sequence of events, when checked against German records and the interviews mentioned above, they nevertheless afford us a fairly consistent description of what a German reprisal was like.[47]

When the German troops arrived in Baranivka, they encircled the village, rounded up everyone they could find and brought them together near the clinic. There the villagers were interrogated as a group by an officer allegedly named "Hoffmann" or "Hochmann," alternately identified in Soviet accounts as a "Gestapo" official from Myrhorod or the Gebietskommissar.[48] Despite his repeated threats to shoot hostages and burn the village, no one would identify the partisans responsible for the attack. The Germans brought the crowd to the edge of a pit which lay just a few meters from the clinic. As the Germans threatened to begin shooting people, an unidentified man blurted out that he knew something. He led some of the soldiers to the home of Nadia Moroz, the mother of one of the men in Kornilych's detachment. The Germans shot this woman and set her home on fire. Apparently while this was going on, Lesia Vil'khovyk, a teacher from the village school, pleaded that the Germans should release the children. The German officer in charge agreed and released both the children and the women. But the denunciation of Nadia Moroz was not enough to satisfy him, and it was at this point that the executions began. Ten men were separated from the rest. One of them was Petro Orel. His son Ivan, then thirteen years old, recalled the death of his father and the other hostages in an account published in 1988:

> Then they chased away the children and women, but the men stayed behind. Father tore his hand from mine—it was cold and slightly trembling.... I, my sister and mother hid in our house and rushed to the windows: the crowd, the Germans—directly before us. I saw the Germans walking about near an unfinished cellar, leading five men there ... and right there they just shot them straight in the face. Again they led five men to the pit, among them father, my uncle, my brother Ivan Khorolets'—he (just) past seventeen years of age. I could see my father resist, but they hit him on his back between the shoulders. From fear I did not hear them shoot, but I saw how father staggered on the edge of the grave a long, long time, and I cried out, "Now we will never have our father again!" Mother lay fainted below the window.[49]

After the shootings, the Germans threw the body of Nadia Moroz into the pit, and the violence ended there for the night. The remaining men were held under guard in the town meeting hall but were released the following morning. The Germans then burned the village. According to the Soviet sources, at least some of the Germans remained for several days and relentlessly destroyed the entire community—more than 550 buildings in all—including its livestock and food stores. Only a handful of houses—those with flame retardant, tiled roofs—remained. Hanna Kryvoshyi, a Baranivka resident interviewed in 1997, states that this was actually not the case, and that the Germans deliberately let some of the buildings stand, explaining that they did so to provide shelter for the children during the coming winter. Kryvoshyi and Mariia Malosh, also interviewed in 1997, further agree that some Germans gave villagers time to remove their personal belongings from their homes before they set the roofs on fire.[50] Both women also expressed the view that the partisans were to blame for the reprisal.

In moral terms, this reprisal was an outrage, as is any arbitrary act of violent collective punishment, and one shudders to think of the suffering endured by the villagers in the coming winter, even if some homes were allowed to stand. It is a fact, however, that by the standards of German practice during World War II, Baranivka was a very restrained reprisal. The testimony of Kryvoshyi and Malosh, combined with the low death toll exacted by the Germans (which both German and Soviet records confirm) make it necessary to concede, however reluctantly, some element of moderation in the behavior of III/190 at Baranivka. Indeed, this reprisal approached the criteria for legality established by the American Military Tribunal at Nuremberg in the "Hostage Trial" of 1946, in that the Germans attempted to find the responsible persons before shooting hostages, and kept the number of executions in rough proportion to the gravity of the partisans' provocation.[51] One can only speculate as to the motives for this restraint: certainly the contrast with the battalion's mass execution of Jews at Myrhorod only a few days earlier is striking, and some of the other shootings of partisan suspects by the battalion already mentioned above claimed larger numbers of victims.

The events at Baranivka prompted a spate of orders about the use of reprisals from the interested German commanders. On 9 November, Field Marshal von Reichenau demanded an intensification of reprisal violence to ensure that the inhabitants remained more fearful of German punishment than they were of the partisans. He also demanded an end to the sort of carelessness that had cost Sinz and his men their lives. The commanding general of the LI (51st) Corps (to which the 62nd Division normally belonged) issued an amplifying order on the 12th.[52] Most interesting, however, is the guidance put forward by the new commander of the 62nd Division, Major General Friedrich. His instructions, dated 11 November, contained elements of restraint and political sophistication that distinguished it sharply from the other orders cited thus far. Friedrich understood the importance of gaining the cooperation of the villagers and insisted that hostage-taking was much more sensible than reprisals carried out after the fact. "Were the troops to simply shoot a number of uninvolved residents by way of a reprisal and then simply withdraw," he reasoned, "the residents' interest in finding the bandits would be reduced if not to say completely extinguished, and the danger of further support for the bandits increased."[53] His instructions also lacked any mention of ethnic categories. Whatever inclinations toward restraint Friedrich might have had, however, were soon frustrated by the savage behavior of his men in Velyka Obukhivka.

Velyka Obukhivka was, as German intelligence had noted, the actual seat of the area's partisan movement. It was there that Ivashchenko had his headquarters and "Victory's" operations in the vicinity were centered on the village. Kopenkin's group and (later) Bezpal'ko's were likewise based nearby. Prior to the arrival of 62nd Division troops, the partisans came and went quite openly. On 8 October, for example, Ivashchenko, accompanied by his propaganda chief, Lahoda (who was born in Velyka Obukhivka), had held a meeting in the Velyka Obukhivka village school to commemorate the twenty-fourth anniversary of the Bolshevik seizure of power. This was reportedly attended by more than two hundred persons. After the meeting, Ivashchenko demonstrated his ongoing authority over the district by executing eight residents accused of stealing collective farm property.[54]

As with Baranivka, the German account of what took place in Velyka Obukhivka is brief. On 12 November the 12th Company of III/190 marched to Velyka Obukhivka. As the point of the formation approached the southern edge of the village it came under fire from partisans concealed on a windmill hillock to the west. In the fire fight which followed, the company forced the Soviets (variously estimated at 100 to 160 strong) into an adjacent swamp, where, according to the company commander's optimistic report, the majority were killed.[55]

The 12th Company reported three men killed and five wounded, with two of the wounded seriously injured. No body count of the partisans was provided in the battalion's report to the division, but the killing in Velyka Obukhivka did not end with the flight of the partisans. Angered by the villagers' failure to give warning of the ambush, the German unit conducted a reprisal on the spot. In his report the company commander blandly explained that "Since the populace kept secret the presence of the partisans, the village was burned down and the populace wiped out (shot)." He did not report the number of victims. Though this massacre contradicted the division commander's new instructions regarding reprisals (which the company probably had not yet received), there is no record of any inquiry or remonstrance concerning the incident in divisional documents. There is also no evidence that the company commander had requested prior authorization for the reprisal from his battalion commander as required by standing orders.

Most Soviet accounts of the fire fight contradict both each other and the German record in several particulars.[56] Overall, the most credible is a 1944 statement made by an Velyka Obukhivka resident named Oleksandra Otryshko, whose husband was one of Ivashchenko's partisans.[57] According to her, a German column that included horsemen met Mykhailo Zabolot'ko on the road on the outskirts of the village. Asked whether there were any partisans in Velyka Obukhivka, Zabolot'ko replied that there were none, though he knew that Ivashchenko's and Kopenkin's groups were waiting in ambush just a few meters away. The Germans then blundered into the trap. According to Otryshko, four men and twenty-nine horses were killed and the Germans were forced to withdraw. They then counterattacked and drove the partisans to abandon their position and flee to the safety of the forest.[58]

Soviet documents provide a horrifying picture of what took place once the partisans withdrew. They confirm what the language of the German report implies, namely that this reprisal was nothing less than an attempt to exterminate everyone in the village. One wonders whether Ivashchenko, whose detachment included many men with family in Velyka Obukhivka, had given any thought to what might happen if his group ambushed a German infantry company on the outskirts of the village, for it seems that no effort had been made to encourage the villagers to flee for the safety of the surrounding forests. Perhaps the partisans assumed that a reprisal was in the offing and hoped to prevent it. In any case, according to Otryshko, the Germans immediately sought out and killed Zabolot'ko. Distillation of the statements made by other survivors suggests that they then deployed around the outskirts of the village and began setting the houses on fire, working their way toward the center of town and literally killing every man, woman, and child they could find. They shot people outside their homes as they attempted to flee from burning buildings or drove them into their houses and burned them alive. Small groups of people were able to slip through the cordon, but many were trapped and ruthlessly slaughtered.

Vasyl' Tkachenko, a survivor of the massacre, was thirteen years old in 1941. As the fires set by the Germans began to spread, he and nineteen other residents, unsure of what to do or where to flee, gathered at the home of a man named Hnyda. While the group stood there, two German soldiers approached and ordered them into Hnyda's house:

> We entered and the German shut the door after us. Then he started pouring some kind of liquid on the walls outside, maybe gasoline. It should be said that at that time the houses were covered not with slate as nowadays but with thatch. So a house burned quickly and fire spread in an instant.... The old man (i.e., Hnyda), just like everybody else in those times, had cabbage in the inner porch stored for the winter. The old man gathered cabbage and brought it to us.... The old man told everybody to breathe through the cabbage. If it had not been for the old man, the smoke would have choked us. And when the cabbage did not help any more, for it had got poisoned by the smoke, the old man said, "Let's break the window and get out, otherwise we will die." We did so. Everything was burning around. Cracking, roaring.[59]

The Germans had moved on from this quarter of the village and Hnyda managed to lead the group—which included a young mother and her two-week-old baby—to the safety of a nearby ravine, and thence to Lysivka, about seven kilometers distant.

Other residents managed to survive by hiding in the defensive trench which had been dug around the village.[60] The Bezpal'ko detachment, having fled their base near Popivka, happened to arrive in Velyka Obukhivka just as the German reprisal was in progress. Though they sent scouts to the village to find out what was happening (two of whom never returned), they made no effort to interfere or assist the residents.[61] Neither did Ivashchenko or Kopenkin. The massacre therefore continued until the Germans' wrath was spent and the village largely destroyed. According to Vasyl' Tkachenko, the Germans let stand only a few buildings in the center of the village in order to have quarters for themselves during the next few days. Soviet estimates of the total number of deaths vary from two hundred to five hundred persons. Between two hundred and three hundred persons killed is an acceptable estimate.[62]

The contrast between the methodical and limited killing carried out by the 11th Company of III/190 at Baranivka and the wholesale massacre of the aged, of women, and of innocent children at Velyka Obukhivka is striking. It is probably best explained by the ambush: the soldiers of the 12th Company were enraged by their losses and, if Otryshko's recollection is accurate, by Zabolot'ko's trick as well. The residents of the village were obviously aware of the presence of the partisans and had failed to give warning. Combined with the intelligence available to the 62nd Division, which identified Velyka Obukhivka as a partisan base, this set the stage for a horrible killing. Other factors, such as differing attitudes of the company commanders responsible for each incident, may also have played a role.

While the operations of III/190 in the Baranivka-Velyka Obukhivka area were in progress, other elements of the 62nd Division arrived in the Ps'ol valley and joined the battle against the partisans. The remainder of the 190th Regiment, along with one battalion from the division's 164th Regiment (II/164) patrolled actively in the area over the next several weeks. The activities of II/164 are the most noteworthy, for they produced numerous hostage-takings and executions of partisans and were particularly well documented in a series of reports written by the battalion commander, Lt. Col. Faasch. In the interests of brevity, they will only be summarized here, but for much of this period II/164 reported some type of small-scale shooting on a nearly daily basis.[63]

The battalion's movements centered on the area between Hadiach and Liuten'ka (Hadiach district), a large village situated about 10 kilometers northeast of Velyka Obukhivka, but at times carried it as far south as Sorochyntsi. Essentially, the unit moved from town to town, interrogating villagers as it went and shooting people denounced by their neighbors as partisans or their supporters. Sometimes Faasch would gather all the villagers together for an assembly, where he promised German protection from the partisans and asked the people for help. He apparently had little trouble getting information, but when he did he took hostages as suggested by Friedrich in the division order of 10 November. The battalion seized small groups of hostages, for example, in Mlyny on 11 November, in Birky on the 16th, and in Vel'bivka on the 23rd. Over time Faasch noted increased willingness on the part of area residents to cooperate voluntarily. This was probably due to several factors. First, Faasch was by all appearances a very able officer who understood the dilemma of the pro-German segments of the area's population. In his reports to his regimental commander, he emphasized the vulnerability of potential collaborators to partisan reprisals owing to the lack of any German garrison in the vicinity. Infrequent German patrols were simply not credible protection, and some villages had yet to see any German troops at all. Faasch went so far as to leave one of his own companies in Liuten'ka continually, and made the habit of returning to given villages time and again. This created the impression in the minds of many people that the Germans were in the area to stay, and made them less fearful of the partisans. Second, none of the partisan groups at large in the Ps'ol valley openly challenged the Germans after the Velyka Obukhivka reprisal, indeed they avoided direct confrontations until 27 November, when Ivashchenko, Kopenkin and Bezpal'ko joined forces to attack part of Faasch's 7th Company in Liuten'ka. Though all three detachments were still in the area while II/164 carried out these patrols, they made themselves scarce and were often just one step ahead of the Germans. Thus, for a time at least, the Germans dominated the scene. Third, it is reasonable to assume that the killings at Baranivka and Velyka Obukhivka were by now well known throughout the area, and were having the desired repressive effect. Lt. Gen. Erich Friderici, who had replaced von Roques in late October, had issued a proclamation to the inhabitants of his jurisdiction on 18 November that described the reprisal at Baranivka and warned that similar measures would follow future partisan attacks.[64] Even if this notice had not yet been widely circulated in the villages, survivors of the killings in both towns had doubtless spread the word to the neighboring communities where they sought refuge after the destruction of their homes. Kovalivka, for example, where Faasch claimed that the residents willingly identified seven partisans to him without any threat of reprisal on his part, is only about eight kilometers from Baranivka. For all of these reasons, it seems likely that the Soviet underground's hold on the area residents was being broken.

Despite this cooperation, Faasch was unable to strike the partisans directly.[65] According to the Bezpal'ko report, the partisans usually received warning of the Germans' approach.[66] This is not to say that they were not hard-pressed. At this time of year the temperature had already dropped well below freezing, and with harsher winter weather looming, the destruction of their forest bases and stores of food and clothing posed a real threat to the partisans' survival. II/164 found several of these camps during its sweeps through the woods. On at least two occasions, the battalion was led to the camps by an informer, while on the 27th Faasch's men captured a cache of partisan documents which revealed the location of two other bunker complexes near Birky and Zuivtsi.[67] The shootings carried out in the villages likewise had a cumulative effect. Between 10 and 24 November, the battalion claimed to have shot 105 persons as partisans.[68] Given the relatively good organization of the local partisans, it seems possible that many of those killed were connected to the partisans in some way, though there is no way to be sure, and there is a strong probability that Ukrainian denunciations were serving personal rather than political purposes. At least one killing was strictly racial in motive: on 23 November, a patrol from the 7th Company, II/164 shot a group of twenty-three Jews in the village of Iuriv'ka, about seven kilometers northeast of Liuten'ka.

The German report on this incident says only that twenty-three Jews were shot, and offers no pretext for the killing. A resident of Iuriv'ka who claimed to have witnessed this execution as an eleven-year-old girl said in an interview with the author that these Jews were refugees from somewhere to the west. They had fled before the German advance and gone to the local collective farm seeking help. The council agreed and had given them jobs on the farm and a house in Iuriv'ka. When the patrol from the 7th Company arrived on the 23rd, they asked a man who lived in Iuriv'ka whether there were any Jews in the village, and he told them about the refugees. The Germans ordered them from their home and shot them all—men, women, and children.[69] By all appearances this was, like the massacre of Jews in Myrhorod, a clear-cut instance of racial murder. As with the Myrhorod killing, this execution was reported up the chain of command in a very routine fashion and there is no evidence of disapproval in either the Heeresgebiet or 62nd Division records.[70]

At the same time that these Jews were put to death, the struggle between II/164 and the area partisans came to a head. In a separate incident on the 23rd, part of the battalion returned to Vel'bivka, where twenty-three "bandits" were betrayed to the Germans by informants. Efforts to arrest these people were only partially successful—most managed to flee along with their families. This prompted the hostage-taking in Vel'bivka mentioned above. Faasch ordered fourteen persons held and declared that one would be shot each day until the remaining suspects were in German hands. The outcome of this is not certain, though "several" hostages were reportedly released the next day when eight "bandits" were captured and shot by the battalion.[71] In the days which followed, two partisans from Mlyny came forward and offered to lead the Germans to a partisan base in the forest near their village in exchange for amnesty, but before this bore fruit the partisans struck the remaining platoon from 7th Company at Liuten'ka in the early morning hours of the 27th.

The raid on Liuten'ka produced few casualties on either side.[72] Having concentrated themselves for an attack, however, the partisans became more vulnerable to a riposte. On the 27th and 28th, II/164 reported killing fifty-seven partisans in and around Liuten'ka—a substantial number.[73] None of the surviving Soviet records corroborates these losses, but the Bezpal'ko report does indicate that several of the various subdetachments now active in the area were driven from their bases near Liuten'ka at this time and sought refuge in Kopenkin's camp, which had not yet been discovered by the Germans. On 1 December, elements of II/164 chased the bulk of the combined Ivashchenko and Bezpal'ko groups from their base in the forest northeast of Sakalivka, capturing a few weapons and ammunition. They then entered Sakalivka and burned the village to the ground. No explanation for this exists in 62nd Division records, although the division intelligence section also noted that thirty "bandits" were shot at the same time.[74]

The burning of Sakalivka marked the end of the 62nd Division's role in the Heeresgebiet's struggle with the partisans of the Myrhorod and Shyshaky districts. The scattered elements of the division were ordered to march to Poltava, where they returned to the operational control of the 6th Army on 21 December. Replacement brigade 202 assumed the 62nd's security duties, and continued to hunt down the now unified partisans of the Poltava region. The records of this brigade did not survive the war, and Heeresgebiet documents offer little detailed information on what took place in the months that followed (the Soviet counteroffensive in December and January brought an abrupt end to meticulous record keeping by the operations section). Soviet accounts, however, make it clear that the situation for the area's partisans became more desperate in the months which followed, despite the diversion of the Heeresgebiet's better units to front-line duty. After weeks of heavy fighting, the combined partisan formation led by Kopenkin made the decision to try to break through to Soviet lines. Several attempts met with failure, and the unit split into two parts. One of them, under Kopenkin, finally succeeded in breaking through. Kopenkin himself continued fighting as a partisan and was killed while on a raid in March 1942. The other, smaller group, led by Ivashchenko, returned to bases originally used by the Hadiach partisan organization. German pressure in this area proved unrelenting, and short of supplies, with their numbers dwindling, the band began to fall apart. Some members of the detachment felt that a breakout to the Bryansk forest was their only hope of survival, but Ivashchenko resisted this suggestion, arguing that it was their duty to remain in their own district and carry on the fight there. The group took the decision to return to the Velyka Obukhivka area. By the time it got there in February 1942, all that remained of "Victory" was twenty-four men, including Ivashchenko, Vovk, Zorin, and Andreev—the original leadership from Myrhorod. Because their bases had been destroyed in the fighting with the 62nd Division, this displacement offered little improvement in their situation. Reading between the lines of the Soviet accounts, it seems that it was now difficult for the badly weakened detachment to get help from the villages, where pro-German police detachments were now increasingly common and food increasingly scarce. With their bases destroyed and their supplies exhausted, the leadership decided to disband the detachment and go underground. According to one report, almost all of the surviving members were betrayed to the Germans and put to death in the months that followed. Ivashchenko, however, managed to survive. In early 1942 he set off again for the Hadiach area with his orderly and a female nurse, and continued his underground work until 1943, when a small band under his leadership linked up with forces of the Red Army.

The smaller Shyshaky group under Kornilych and Tutka suffered a similar fate. Hounded by the police and frequently betrayed by informants, they too faded away. Kornilych died of illness during the winter, while Tutka supposedly took his own life after weeks on the run.[75]

The 62nd Division spent the winter in defensive fighting near Poltava. The following summer it participated in the drive to the Volga. Though it did not end up in the Stalingrad pocket, it was nevertheless virtually wiped out in November of 1942 while fighting as a part of the Italian 8th Army in the Don Bend. As for the villagers of the Myrhorod and Shyshaky districts, they faced nearly two more years of life under German occupation.

III. Conclusions

Richard Evans once suggested that the weakness of "micro-history" may lie in the essentially trivial nature of the events which it describes.[76] This is an interesting comment, coming from a historian whose work has been so marvelously enriched by including humanizing details from the lives of ordinary people, but his caution is an important one. The Baranivka episode is an inherently interesting and moving story, and arguably possesses intrinsic value for merely illustrating events from the partisan war with an unusual degree of detail. More important, however, is the manner in which the story might affect prevailing interpretations of this crucial facet of the German-Soviet war.

Ideally, any discussion of the behavior of the Wehrmacht on the Eastern front should include some reflections on the general brutalization of soldiers that occurs in modern warfare and on the Prusso-German army's historic proclivity for harsh suppression of irregular resistance. Both of these contexts are all too often overlooked in the Eastern front literature, yet are unquestionably relevant to the debate. Unfortunately, there is little scope for this type of background information in this essay either, and we can only note in passing that violent reprisals are a characteristic feature of guerrilla wars and that the German army had an institutional history of quick recourse to reprisals long before Hitler came along. We must concentrate instead on two more immediate issues: the deliberate relaxation of restraints on military violence which attended the German onslaught in the Soviet Union, and the Wehrmacht's developing view of Ukraine during the first six months of the campaign.

There is little reason to doubt that the severity of the Heeresgebiet's response to the Baranivka attack reflects the license granted by the Gerichtsbarkeitserlaß and the many exhortations toward harshness that went with it. Without these inducements, Heeresgebiet troops might have arrested and interned partisan "suspects" instead of executing them on the spot solely on the basis of denunciations. The use of summary courts-martial to try captured partisans might also have reduced the number of killings. The fact remains, however, that the ideological content of the "criminal orders" was sufficiently focused on the "Jewish-Bolshevik" *Feindbegriff* to allow room for the pro-Ukrainian bias preached by Rosenberg's lieutenants to take root in parts of Army Group South and especially among the commanders and staff of Heeresgebiet Süd. The Heeresgebiet's response to the upsurge in resistance activity around Myrhorod in October and November of 1941 should therefore be viewed as an attempt to reconcile the command's official paternalism toward ethnic Ukrainians with its desire to crush a mounting partisan movement that was known to have the local cooperation of the inhabitants.

At the beginning of the operations, the official line on Ukrainians was preserved. The initial killing in Myrhorod was wholly in keeping with von Roques' reprisal order of 16 August (and the 62nd Division's own order of 21 July) exempting Ukrainians from collective punishment: forty-five persons suspected of being partisans were killed alongside the city's Jewish population. The same can be said of the killings of partisan suspects in the Popivka area that immediately followed, for no one in the Heeresgebiet chain of command had ever suggested that ethnic Ukrainian *partisans* should be spared (unless they were deserting). The death of Colonel Sinz, however, provoked an explicit call for reprisals against "responsible residents" of the Baranivka area, and opened the door to hostage-takings and reprisals with ethnic Ukrainian victims. These remained comparatively restrained at first. At Baranivka, the soldiers of III/190 shot ten hostages and one "suspect" (Nadia Moroz) and destroyed most of the village after failing to identify the partisans themselves. That same day, they also shot a large number of suspected partisans (forty-five) at Iares'ky and Sorochyntsi. But the revenge/reprisal massacre at Velyka Obukhivka followed. As argued above, this terrible killing should probably be interpreted as a violent reaction to the ambush—the first time that units from the 62nd Division had suffered casualties of their own during their hunt for the partisans. This is not to say that this reaction was not conditioned by other factors, including the knowledge that Velyka Obukhivka was indeed an important partisan base, rather that the ambush served as a catalyst to wholly indiscriminate violence from a unit which had been through many weeks of terrible combat. Judging from General Friedrich's reasoned statement about reprisals, the Velyka Obukhivka killing perhaps would not have been sanctioned in advance, but it was not criticized after the fact, either. After Velyka Obukhivka was destroyed, II/164 became the most active unit in the area. Led by Lt. Col. Faasch, who was himself persuaded of the need to gain the cooperation of the populace, the battalion moved back and forth through the partisans' area of operations, killing persons denounced as partisans by their fellow villagers. Although these killings cumulatively rivaled the reprisals at Myrhorod and Velyka Obukhivka in scale, the officers responsible for them apparently saw no contradiction between killing "communists" and protecting the ethnic Ukrainian majority as a whole. Faasch's patrols were in effect an ad hoc attempt to purge the area of its pro-Soviet element, and thus did not depart in spirit from the Heeresgebiet's pro-Ukrainian policy. That Faasch's troops also carried out a massacre of non-combatant Jews at Iuriv'ka underscores the degree to which a restrained attitude toward Ukrainians coexisted with a reflexive willingness to kill Jews.

This pattern of events conforms well with the consensus historiography on the Wehrmacht's institutional sympathy for National Socialist ideology and also with many of Omer Bartov's findings concerning the behavior and mentality of ordinary German soldiers. It is less congruent with Hannes Heer's more recent research. If there was, as Heer suggests, a grand design at the highest levels of the Reich leadership to radicalize the army through mass killings of Soviet civilians (Slavs as well as Jews), then it was substantially inhibited by Heeresgebiet Süd's policy of preferential treatment of ethnic Ukrainians—a policy that OKH also endorsed. Although the Heeresgebiet commanders cooperated extensively with the SS Einsatzgruppen at large within their jurisdiction, they consistently drew a line between Soviet Jews and the Ukrainian majority. If violence to Soviet Jews was ultimately intended to inspire mass killings of Slavs by army soldiers, then this effort failed in Heeresgebiet Süd. Even in 1942, when a serious partisan threat arose on the northern border of the jurisdiction, reprisal violence followed genuine partisan activity and did not approach the quasi-genocidal scale of anti-partisan operations in the rear area of Army Group Center described by Heer.

The analysis presented here also offers us an important look at the Soviet partisan movement's chaotic early days, and confirms above all else the impression of amateurism one receives from the more candid published Soviet sources and the most recent research. The blending of party and NKVD elements in the "Victory" detachment shows how the institutional rivalry which dogged the partisan effort as a whole was sometimes resolved fairly effectively at the local level. The sources brought to light in this essay likewise illustrate the manner in which this particular detachment struggled to develop its own sense of mission over time, moving from organizational or "infrastructure" work like propaganda and agitation to direct attacks on German security forces. Thus as a case study of the partisan movement in 1941, it has some value. The most interesting information, however, concerns the relationship between the partisans and the villagers in the Myrhorod and Shyshaky districts. There is no way to establish scientifically where the population of this area stood with respect to the Soviet regime and its underground representatives in the early winter of 1941: we are left to make our "best guess" on the basis of the available source material. Though Heeresgebiet records often directly address the issue of popular opinion in occupied territory, there is little of this type of material available that specifically refers to the Myrhorod and Shyshaky areas at this stage of the war. German documents—mainly in the form of intelligence reports on partisan activity cited above—tell us only that (1) some villages like Sakalivka and Velyka Obukhivka served as important bases for the partisans, (2) that some members of the civil population were agents of the partisans and supported them actively, (3) that there was some element of duress in the partisans' control over the villages, and (4) that some villagers felt estranged from Soviet authority and were willing to cooperate with German forces (increasingly so over time). Through a different filter, Soviet documents support the same basic conclusions, leaving us with a mixed impression. The most helpful evidence is arguably that provided by the author's recent interviews. Admittedly, great care is required in evaluating the statements made in these conversations, given the passage of so many years and the extremely small number of individuals involved. Just the same, it is worth mentioning that three of the interview subjects expressed genuine ambivalence about the partisans. Kryvoshyi and Malosh, who witnessed the Baranivka reprisal, both blamed the partisans for provoking the Germans. Tkachenko (Velyka Obukhivka) voiced a certain scorn for the partisans' achievements, and pointed out that Lysivka, a few kilometers to the north, was untouched by the Germans because the people there offered no resistance. This type of comment could never, for obvious reasons, have become part of the Soviet document record, and the interviewing of elderly subjects remains the only means we have of recovering these opinions.

Taking all of the evidence presented here into account, the following overall conclusion seems tenable: the attitude of the civil populace in this area is probably best described as docile and malleable. With the exception of the partisans themselves and small numbers of pro-Soviet and pro-German activists who were willing to risk death in order to serve their respective causes, most people seem to have been willing to obey whichever antagonist appeared most credible at a given time. This is borne out by the narrative of events. Before the arrival of the 62nd Division, the "Victory" detachment received all the support it required from the inhabitants and lived an essentially open existence. After the arrival of the division in the area, the villagers remained willing to support the partisans initially, as the refusal of the residents of Baranivka to provide information about the death of Sinz suggests. Once word of the reprisals and shootings of partisans began to spread, the villagers seemed to be more willing to cooperate with the Germans, particularly since Faasch's battalion remained active in the area for a matter of weeks. After the partisans had been weakened by their struggle with the 62nd Division, their popular support diminished further. The Soviet account of the demise of the "Victory" detachment shows that even after the departure of the Heeresgebiet's best troops for front line duty during the Soviet winter counteroffensive, the remaining Germans and their Ukrainian policemen were able to break up the detachment and effectively eliminate the group which chose to remain behind under Ivashchenko, this despite the counteroffensive's probable corrosive effect on perceptions of German "invincibility." This leads, perhaps, to a tentative conclusion about the importance of Soviet ideology in shaping the attitudes and behavior of the Ukrainian civil population: the pragmatic, day-to-day calculus of personal survival played a much more important role than did either pro-German sentiment (rooted in Ukrainian regional hostility to the Soviet regime) or Soviet patriotism.

Notes

1. Reprinted with permission from *The Journal of Modern History* 71, no. 3 (September 1999). Copyright © 1999 by The University of Chicago. All rights reserved. I am deeply indebted to many friends and colleagues for their assistance with this essay. Prof. Jeffrey Burds of Northeastern University provided invaluable help in organizing my two visits to Ukraine. Dr. Diana Kurdiumova of the Academy of Sciences of Ukraine was indispensable to me during my archival research and visits to the villages of the Poltava region. For their careful reading of drafts of this chapter, I am especially grateful to my colleagues MacGregor Knox, Robert Boyce, David Stevenson, Mia Rodriguez-Salgado, and Umberto-Igor Stramignoni of the London School of Economics, and to my friend and mentor Professor Michael Geyer of the University of Chicago. I would also like to extend my thanks to the anonymous readers of the *Journal of Modern History* whose incisive criticism did much to improve my initial submission. For research funding, I am indebted to the Andrew W. Mellon Foundation, the German Academic Exchange Service, and the Nuffield Foundation for their generous support.
2. Throughout this text, I have transliterated Ukrainian and Russian words in accordance with the Library of Congress system, using the respective conventions for each language (e.g., "geroi" from Russian but "Hryhorii" from

Ukrainian). Where place names are concerned, I have used Ukrainian variants in the body of my essay in preference to the Russian equivalents usually found in German sources ("Kharkiv" instead of "Kharkov"). I have made isolated exceptions for a few well-known English variants like "Kiev" (Kyiv). In document references, I have kept the original form of place names (e.g., "Myrhorod" in Ukrainian-language documents but "Mirgorod" in Russian and German sources).

3. There are several sources which describe the attack on Col. Sinz (usually spelled incorrectly as "Zins" in Heeresgebiet records) and his party. The most important is a detailed statement made by Corporal Schneider after his arrival in Myrhorod. See (Abschrift) Ortskommandantur Mirgorod Gendarmeriegruppe, 8. November 1941, BA-MA (Bundesarchiv-Militärarchiv) RH26-62/41. Soviet sources are more numerous but also more problematic, in that most of them were written at least two years after the event and tend to contradict each other in some respects, particularly on the role played by Dutsia Borodai, who was later killed by German authorities for her connections with the underground and is today remembered in Baranivka as a Soviet martyr. An undated statement made by the Baranivka village council (probably written in 1944) gives the wrong date for the attack and states that the fire fight at the clinic lasted more than three hours: Kharakteristika Baranovskogo S-soveta s. 1941 r. po 1944 r, DAPO (Derzhavnyi arkhiv Poltavs'koi oblasti, Poltava) 1876/8/108. A retrospective series of documents prepared by the Shyshaky district party committee of the Communist Party Ukraine contains several relevant reports. The most detailed was written by a member of the partisan group led by Tutka who actually participated in the attack. It gives the date of the incident as 5–6 November, and, as mentioned above, states that an unidentified teenage boy rather than Borodai had brought word of Sinz's arrival to the group at Kuibysheve. It also contradicts Schneider's account by stating that the Germans were the first to open fire, and adds that Sinz and his men killed Martynenko as the partisans were attacking the clinic. This same document contains another description of the attack written by an unknown author, which claims that Martynenko was shot by the Germans as he opened a window to let the partisans in. See Shishatskii raion kompartii Ukrainy, khronologicheskaia zapiska raionnoi komissii ... DAPO 105/1/358. Another account prepared by the Shyshaky raikom, openly propagandistic in tone, mentions the attack only briefly: Shishatski Raikom Kompartii Ukrainy, Pokazanie ob' iasnitl'nye zapiski i drugie dokumenty ... DAPO 105/1/357. There are two published accounts available, both of them fairly recent, which develop the Borodai story in detail: L. N. Horlach et al., eds., *Dzvony pam'yati: Kniha pro tragediiu mist i sil Poltavshchyny, Kharkivshchyny, Voroshilovhradshchyny ta Donechchyny, spliundrovanykh fashistami u roky viiny* (Kiev: 1988), 25–36; O. F. Fedorov and V. A. Maniak, *Vinok bezsmertia: Kniga-memorial* (Kiev: 1987), 331–337. Neither of these books provides footnotes, and most of the information is apparently derived from conversations with elderly witnesses. While the involvement of Borodai in the attack on Sinz cannot be completely discounted, it is nevertheless interesting that the archival sources make no mention of it. Overall, Schneider's account of these events is the least suspect, and where conflicts exist between Soviet sources and Schneider's report, I have given greater weight to the latter.

4. For messages which spread word of the attack throughout the German chain of command, see Rückw. Heeresgebiet Süd KTB (Ia), 411109 entry, U.S. National Archives—Captured German Documents Microfilmed at Alexandria

(hereafter USNA) T-501/4; Fernschreiben 62nd ID Ia/Ic an Befh. rückw. H.Geb. Süd Ia/Ic 9.11.41, USNA T-501/6; (Fernschreiben) Befh. r. H.G. Süd Ia an 62nd ID 9.11.41, 22:25, USNA T-501/6; (Fernschreiben) Bfh. rückw. H. Geb. Süd an Heeresgruppe Süd 9.11.41, 22:40, USNA T-501/6; (Fernschreiben) Bfh. rückw. H.Geb. Süd Ia an Sich.Div. 213, Sich.Div. 444, Ers. Brig. 202, Rum. VI A.K. 9.11.41, 23:00, USNA T501/6.

5. One can gain some idea of just how vast the literature is from *Hitler's War in the East 1941–1945: A Critical Assessment* by Rolf-Dieter Müller and Gerd Ueberschär (New York: 1997). This provides an excellent overview of current historiography and five thematically organized bibliographies. It is the emphasis on the ideological character of the war in the east which sets more recent research apart from the early postwar historiography. Of particular importance is the degree to which these newer works assign responsibility for Nazi crimes in the east very broadly, especially to the army. Among the more important titles are: Horst Boog et al., *Der Angriff auf die Sowjetunion* (Stuttgart: 1983), vol. 4 of the Militärgeschichtliches Forschungsamt's official history, *Das Deutsche Reich und der Zweite Weltkrieg* (hereafter *DRZW*); Omer Bartov, *Hitler's Army* (New York, Oxford: 1991); Ernst Klee and Willi Dreßen, *Gott mit Uns. Der deutsche Vernichtungskrieg im Osten 1939–1945* (Frankfurt am Main: 1989); Timothy Mulligan, *The Politics of Illusion and Empire: German Occupation Policy in the Soviet Union, 1941–1943* (New York: 1988); Theo Schulte, *The German Army and Nazi Politics in Occupied Russia* (Oxford: 1989); Christian Streit, *Keine Kameraden. Die Wehrmacht und die sowjetischen Kriegsgefangenen 1941–1945* (Stuttgart: 1978); Bernd Wegner, ed., *Zwei Wege nach Moskau* (Munich: 1991); Hannes Heer and Klaus Naumann, eds., *Vernichtungskrieg. Verbrechen der Wehrmacht 1941–1944* (Hamburg: 1995); Helmut Krausnick and H. Wilhelm, *Die Truppe des Weltanschauungkrieges. Die Einsatzgruppen der Sicherheitspolizei und des Sicherheitsdienstes 1938–1942* (Stuttgart: 1981). Some of the earlier works on the German occupation retain much of their usefulness, though one must be aware of the degree to which they overlook the complicity of the army in the extermination of the Jews of the Soviet Union, the plunder of the occupied areas, the mass murder of Soviet prisoners of war, and the general maltreatment of the Soviet civil population: Alexander Dallin, *German Rule in Russia 1941–1945* (London: 1957); Gerald Reitlinger, *The House Built on Sand: The Conflicts of German Policy in Russia* (London: 1960); John Armstrong, ed., *Soviet Partisans in World War Two* (Madison: 1964). The Soviet historiography of the occupation is also enormous. Despite their obvious ideological prejudices, many of these works are useful, particularly those dealing with specific regions (*oblasts*). Care must be taken, however, to check the factual content against German records or unpublished Soviet documents, for distortions and omissions have been discovered in this literature in the past: *Istoriia Velikoi Otechestvennoi voiny Sovetskogo Soiuza, 1941–1945* (Moscow: 1960–64); *Nemetsko-Fashistskii okkupationnyi rezhim, 1941–1944* (Moscow: 1965); P. N. Iemets' and O. P. Samoilenko, *Poltavshchina v roky Velykoi Vitryznianoi viiny* (Kharkiv: 1965). In the 1980s, a number of document collections appeared, e.g., D. F. Grigorovich et al., eds., *Sovetskaia Ukraina v gody Velikoi Otechestvennoi Voiny 1941–1945* (Kiev: 1985); *Sumskaia Oblast' v period Velikoi Otechestvennoi Voiny 1941–1945* (Kiev: 1988). For Soviet works on the partisan movement, see note 12. Ukrainian émigré historians have also produced a large corpus of work on the German occupation, much of it colored by a Ukrainian nationalist perspective: Yuri Boshyk, ed., *Ukraine during World War II: History and Its Aftermath* (Edmonton: 1986); Ihor Kamenetsky, *Hitler's Occupation*

of Ukraine, 1941–1944: A Study of Totalitarian Imperialism (Marquette: WI, 1956); Roman Illnytzhyj, *Deutschland und die Ukraine, 1934–1945; Tatsachen europäischer Ostpolitik* (Munich: 1955). For an outstanding bibliography on the German occupation of Ukraine, see Karel C. Berkhoff, "Ukraine under Nazi Rule (1941–1944): Sources and Finding Aids" in *Jahrbücher für die Geschichte Osteuropas*, no. 45 (1997).

6. Schulte, *German Army*.
7. For an insightful review of the development of this theme in the literature, see Schulte, *German Army*, 1–27.
8. Bartov, *Hitler's Army*. For examples of earlier works criticized by Bartov, see Hans Mommsen, "Kriegserfahrungen," in *Über Leben im Krieg*, ed. by Ulrich Borsdorf and Mathilde Jamin (Reinbeck: 1989); Andreas Hillgruber, *Zweierlei Untergang: Die Zerschlagung des Deutschen Reiches und das Ende des Europäischen Judentums* (Berlin: 1986); E. A. Shils and M. Janowitz, "Cohesion and Disintegration in the Wehrmacht in World War II," *Public Opinion Quarterly* 12 (1948): 208–315.
9. See, e.g., Hannes Heer's interview with Christian Streit, Manfred Messerschmidt, and Jürgen Förster in *Mittelweg 36* (June–July 1994): 41–51; Theo Schulte, "Korück 582," in Heer and Naumann, *Vernichtungskrieg*, 323–342.
10. Hannes Heer, "Die Logik des Vernichtungskrieges: Wehrmacht und Partisanenkampf," in Heer and Naumann, *Vernichtungskrieg*, 104–156. See chapter 5 in this volume.
11. German reprisals in the Franco-Prussian and First World Wars are dealt with in the following works: Michael Howard, *The Franco-Prussian War* (London: 1961); Richard Fattig, "Reprisal: The German Army and the Execution of Hostages during the Second World War" (Ph.D. diss., University of California, San Diego: 1980); Geoffrey Best, *Humanity in Warfare* (New York: 1980); Peter Schöller, *Der Fall Löwen und das Weißbuch* (Cologne: 1958); Heinrich Schütze, *Die Repressalie unter besonderer Berücksichtigung der Kriegsverbrechenprozesse* (Bonn: 1950); John Horne and Alan Kramer, "German 'Atrocities' and Franco-German Opinion, 1914: The Evidence of German Soldiers' Diaries," *Journal of Modern History* 66 (1994): 1–33.
12. For an excellent example of recent research, see Kenneth Slepyan, *The People's Avengers: Soviet Partisans, Stalinist Society and the Politics of Resistance, 1941–1944* (Ph.D. diss., the University of Michigan: 1994). This very interesting dissertation deals with the partisan movement within the context of Soviet political culture and is a very helpful guide to the most recent research. See also Leonid Grenkevich, *The Soviet Partisan Movement, 1941–1944* (London: 1999); Armstrong, *Soviet Partisans*; Edgar Howell, *The Soviet Partisan Movement, 1941–1944* (Washington, D.C.: 1956); *Sovetskie partizany: iz istorii partizanskogo dvizheniia v gody Velikoi Otechestvennoi voiny* (Moscow: 1963); *Partiinoe podpol'e: Deiatel'nost podpol'nykh partiinykh organov i organizatsii na Okkupirovannoi sovetskoi territorii v gody Velikoi Otechestvennoi voiny* (Moscow: 1983); *Voina v tylu vraga: o nekotorykh problemakh istorii sovetskogo dvizheniia v gody Velikoi Otechestvennoi voiny* (Moscow: 1974); P. K. Ponomarenko, *Vsenarodnaia bor'ba v tylu nemetsko-fashistskikh zakhvatchikov* (Moscow: 1986); A. Fedorov, *Podpol'nyi obkom deistvuet* (Moscow: 1949); *Istoriia Velikoi Otechestvennoi voiny Sovetskogo Soiuza 1941–1945* (Moscow: 1965); A. S. Zalesskii, *V partizanskikh kraiakh i zonakh. Patrioticheskii podvig Sovetskogo krestianstva v tylu vraga, 1941–1944* (Moscow: 1962). For a particularly useful overview of Soviet historiography on the Ukrainian

partisan movement in particular, see V. I. Klokov, *Vsenarodnaia bor'ba v tylu nemetsko-fashistskikh okkupantov na Ukraine 1941–1944* (Kiev: 1978).

13. Streit, *Keine Kameraden.*
14. Jürgen Förster, "Das Unternehmen 'Barbarossa' als Eroberungs- und Vernichtungskrieg" in *DRZW* (note 4 above), 4:413–50.
15. For the original orders and amendments by OKW and OKH, see the appendix to G. R. Ueberschär and W. Wette, eds., *Der deutsche Überfall auf die Sowjetunion "Unternehmen Barbarossa" 1941* (Frankfurt am Main: 1991). For amplification from field commanders issued during the early stages of Barbarossa, see, for example, the orders given by Reichenau, Manstein, and Hoth cited in Krausnick and Wilhelm (note 4 above), 258–261, and the numerous orders from the army, corps, and division levels cited in Jürgen Förster, "Das Unternehmen Barbarossa," in *DRZW* (note 4 above), 4:525–540. For commentary on the entire complex of orders, see Jürgen Förster, "Das Unternehmen Barbarossa," in *DRZW* 4:421–439; Streit, *Keine Kameraden*, 40–68.
16. The restrictions which the Hague Rules imposed on irregulars are found in articles I and II of part IV. See Leon Friedman, ed., *The Law of War: A Documentary History* (New York: 1972), 1:308–323.
17. British *Manual of Military Law, 1929*, Amendments (no. 12), ch. 14, "The Laws and Usages of War": U.S. *Basic Field Manual FM27–10, Rules of Land Warfare* (Washington, D.C.: 1940); Zentrale Stelle für Landesjustizverwaltungen in Ludwigsburg, *Geisel und Partisanentötungen im Zweiten Weltkrieg. Hinweise zur rechtlichen Beurteilung* (Ludwigsburg: 1968), 17.
18. Slepyan, *People's Avengers*, 28–36.
19. For general information on German organization of occupied territory, see Rolf-Dieter Müller, "Von der Wirtschaftsallianz zum kolonialen Ausbeutungskrieg," in *DRZW* (note 4 above) 4:98–190; Jürgen Förster, "Das Unternehmen 'Barbarossa' als Eroberungs- und Vernichtungskrieg" and "Die Sicherung des 'Lebensraumes,'" also in *DRZW* 4:413–450. Also Schulte, *German Army*, chs. 3 and 4.
20. Sich.Div. 454 Kriegstagebuch (hereafter abbr. KTB) Ia, entry of 31.8.41, BA-MA RH26-454/2.
21. Unless otherwise noted, basic chronological details of German operations have been established on the basis of the KTB of the Heeresgebiet operations staff (section Ia). See USNA T501/4.
22. 62nd ID KTB (Ia) 24.10.41 entry, BA-MA RH26-62/39.
23. Ortskommandantur II/933 Mirgorod ?.10.41 (date thus given on original) Br.B.Nr. 843/41 Betr. Erfahrungsbericht an Sich.Div. 213 Abt. Ia, BA-MA RH26-62/56.
24. The Central Staff of the partisan movement eventually compiled detailed records of the composition and activities of the many detachments, large and small, which were active in 1942 and 1943. Unfortunately, there is little archival material of this kind for the detachments that did not survive the first winter of the war. There are a few sources available which retrospectively describe the origins of the Myrhorod district partisan movement. See Prilozhenie k protokolu n37 Otchet ob antifashistskom podpol'e i partisanskoi dvizhenii na territorii Poltavskoi oblasti v period Velikoi Otechestvennoi Voiny 1941–1943 g., DAPO 15/1/2016; Sekretar' Poltavskogo obkomu KP/b/U po propagande i agitatsii, Mirgorodskii RKKP/b/U vysylaem listovki vypushchennye partizanami v period nemetskoi okkupatsii Mirgorodskogo raiona, 24.7.46, DAPO 105/1/265. This lengthy report contains several sections of interest,

including one entitled "Rasskaz zheny partizana OTRISHKO Al-ry Savovny" and an untitled narrative of the history of the Ivashchenko group written by an official named Z. I. Kazrasik and dated 13 November 1944; Poltavskii oblastnoi sovet deputatov trudiashchikhsia g. Poltava, otchet o deiatel'nosti podpol'nykh organizatsii KP(b)U i o partizanskoi oblasti v period vremennoi nemetsko-fashistkoi okkupatsii, sent. 1941–sent. 1943 gg., DAPO 4085/4/5. For a published account apparently based upon these sources, see Iemets' and Samoilenko, *Poltavshchina*, 28–35.

25. Despite the fact that Kopenkin became a hero of the Soviet Union, information about the origins of his detachment is scant. The most authoritative documents point to NKVD sponsorship of the group, while others indicate party affiliation. See Dokladnaia zapiska Narkomata Vnutrennikh Del Ukr. SSR Tsentral'nomu Komitetu KP(b)U o boevoi deiatel'nosti ob"edinennogo partizanskogo otriada pod komandovaniem I. I. Kopenkina v sentiabre 1941–ianvare 1942 gg., published as document no. 308 in Grigorovich et al., *Sovetskaia Ukraina*; Iz otcheta Poltavskogo obkoma Kompartii Ukrainy o boevoi deiatel'nosti podpol'nogo obkoma i partizanskikh formirovanii v sentiabre 1941–aprele 1942 gg., document no. 368 in *Sovetskaia Ukraina*; Prilozhenie k protokolu n37 Otchet ob antifashistskom podpol'e i partizanskom dvizhenii na territorii Poltavskoi oblasti v period Velikoi Otechestvennoi Voiny 1941–1943 g., DAPO 15/1/2016. Kopenkin's short biography in *Geroi Sovetskogo Soiuza* (Moscow: 1987–88) offers little information.
26. The most useful document on the activities of the Bezpal'ko detachment is a lengthy handwritten account, dated 26 February 1942, written by a soldier who joined Bezpal'ko's group in September 1941 after it rescued his unit from German encirclement. Labeled "top secret," it bears the simple heading "doklad" and a marginal note stating that it should be added to the files of the detachment commanded by Kopenkin: TsDAHO (Tsentral'nyi derzhavnyi arkhiv hromads'kykh ob'iednan') 62/4/34 (hereafter, this document will be referred to as the "Bezpal'ko report"). See also Iemets' and Samoilenko, *Poltavshchina*.
27. Georg Tessin, *Verbände und Truppen der deutschen Wehrmacht und Waffen-SS im Zweiten Weltkrieg 1939–1945* (Osnabrück: 1977), 5:246–248; Samuel Mitcham, *Hitler's Legions* (New York: 1985), 85–86. Bernhard Kroener, "Die personellen Ressourcen des Dritten Reiches im Spannungsfeld zwischen Wehrmacht, Bürokratie und Kriegswirtschaft 1939–1942" in B. Kroener et al., *Organisation und Mobilizierung des deutschen Machtbereichs: Halbband I—Kriegsverwaltung, Wirtschaft und personelle Ressourcen 1939–1941*, vol. 5 of *DRZW* (Stuttgart: 1988), 710. The divisional history produced by the 62nd Division's veterans group after the war contains much useful information, but the straightforward operational narrative omits any discussion of sensitive or potentially incriminating subjects, including the anti-partisan operations dealt with in this chapter: Kameradenhilfswerk der ehemaligen 62. Division, *Die 62. Infanterie-Division 1938–1944. Die 62. Volks-Grenadier-Division 1944–1945* (Fulda: 1968).
28. 62nd ID (Verlust-) Meldung vom 5.10.41., Stichtag der Meldung 25.9.41., USNA T-315/1028.
29. Rückw. H.Geb. Süd KTB Ia entry of 3.11.41, USNA T-501/4. The number of Jews killed here does not agree with internal reports of the 62nd Infantry Division, which noted 140 "partisans and Jews" shot in one place and simply, "140 partisans shot" in another. See also 62nd ID KTB Ia entry 28.10.41 BA-MA RH26-62/39; Tätigkeitsberichte (Abt. Ia 62nd ID) für die Zeit vom

26.10.41–14.11.41, BA-MA RH26-62/41; Tagesmeldung der Abt. Ic (62nd ID) 28.10.41 in Tätigkeitsbericht Abt. Ic der 62nd ID 22.6.41–31.12.41, BA-MA RH26-62/82. A list of persons shot by the Germans in Myrhorod prepared by a special commission investigating German depredations in the Poltava region shows 126 persons as having been shot on 28 October 1941. Most of those listed have common Jewish surnames, but are otherwise not identifiable as Jews. See Zaiavleniia, spisok i akty na grazhdan, rasstrelennykh nemetsko-fashistskimi okkupantami po g. Mirgorodu, Poltavskoi oblasti, DAPO 3388/1/1624.

30. (Abschrift) Rückw. Heeresgebiet Süd Abt. VII Nr. 103/41 16.8.41 Anordnung Abt. VII, Nr. 7, BA-MA Allierte Prozeße Nr. 9, NOKW-1691.
31. 62nd ID Abt. Ia/Ic 21.7.41, BA-MA RH26-62/40.
32. 62nd ID KTB (Ia) entries from 29 October to 1 November 1941, BA-MA RH26-62/39. According to the Bezpal'ko report, the "partisans" shot at Bakumivka included women, old men, and numerous children. This report also claims that the Germans burned six houses. See Bezpal'ko report, TsDAHO 62/4/34.
33. Rückw. Heeresgebiet Süd KTB (Ia), entry of 9 November 1941, USNA T-501/4.
34. (Fernschreiben) Bfh. rückw. H. Geb. Süd an Heeresgruppe Süd 9.11.41 22:40, USNA T-501/6. (Fernschreiben) Bfh. rückw. H.Geb. Süd Ia an Sich.Div. 213, Sich.Div. 444, Ers. Brig. 202, Rum. VI A.K. 9.11.41 23:00, USNA T501/6.
35. This was, according to Soviet histories of the partisan movement, a common problem for the insurgency at this stage of the war. See, for example, A. Fedorov, *Podpol'nyi obkom*. Fedorov also drew attention to this problem in the early history of the partisan movement in a very candid report he submitted to the Central Committee of the Communist Party of Ukraine (TsKKP/b/U) on 12 March 1943. See Dokladnaia zapiska o partizanskom dvizhenii ... TsDAHO, 1/22/7. For the reference to the betrayal by Sakalo, see Prilozhenie k protokolu n37 otchet ob antifashistskom podpol'e i partizanskom dvizhenii na territorii Poltavskoi oblasti v period Velikoi Otechestvennoi Voiny 1941–1943 g., DAPO 15/1/2016.
36. (Abschrift) Ortskommandantur I(V) 268 Feldgendarmeriegruppe Feldpostnummer 46852 Tgb.Nr. 2, 8.11.41, RH26-62/41.
37. (Abschrift) Ortskommandantur I(V) 268 Feldgendarmeriegruppe Feldpostnummer 46852 Tgb.Nr. 3, 9.11.41, RH26-62/41. Soviet records provide no confirmation of the killing of paroled POWs by partisans in Sakalivka. However, in an interview with the author in 1997, Vasyl' Tkachenko, a wartime resident of Velyka Obukhivka, claimed that the Kopenkin partisan group shot straggling Red Army soldiers in Velyka Obukhivka who would not join the partisans. Interview with Vasyl' Danylovych Tkachenko, 18 April 1997.
38. (Abschrift) Ortskommandantur I(V) 268 Feldgendarmeriegruppe Feldpostnummer 46852 Tgb.Nr. 3, 9.11.41, RH26-62/41.
39. Fedorov and Maniak, *Vinok bezsmertia*, 337–338.
40. The existing literature on Ukrainian collaboration with German authorities deals mainly with the cooperation between nationalist groups like the Organization of Ukrainian Nationalist (Orhanizatsiia ukrains'kykh nationalistiv; OUN) and the German military, or with indigenous military formations in German service, such as the Ukrainian formations of the Waffen-SS. See, for example, John Armstrong, *Ukrainian Nationalism 1939–1945* (New York: 1945); Peter J. Potichnyj, "Ukrainians in World War II Military Formations: An Overview" in Boshyk, *Ukraine during World War II*, 61–66. The behavior of

small communities remains largely unexplored. For an overview of the literature on Ukrainian collaboration, see Ryszard Torzecki, "Die Rolle der Zusammenarbeit mit der deutschen Besatzungsmacht in der Ukraine für deren Okkupationspolitik 1941 bis 1944," in Deutsches Bundesarchiv, *Europa unterm Hakenkreuz: Okkupation und Kollaboration 1938–1945* (Berlin: 1994).

41. Koch temporarily joined the Heeresgebiet staff after the Bandera faction of OUN's ill-fated proclamation of an independent Ukraine in L'viv on 30 June. See Heeresgebiet Süd KTB (Ia), USNA T-501/4; Kommandeur-Besprechung vom 20.6.41, BA-MA RH26-454/6a-b; Bfh. rückw. H.Geb. 103 Abt. Ic 968/41 geh., 11.7.41, Besondere Anordnungen für die Behandlung der ukrainischen Frage, USNA T-501/5; (Abschrift) Rückw. Heeresgebiet Süd Abt. VII, Nr. 103/41, 16.8.41 Anordnung Abt. VII Nr. 7, BA-MA Allierte Prozeße Nr. 9, NOKW-1691; Sich.Div. 454 Abt. Ia/Ic Nr. -, 2.8.41 Anlage 2, "Russische Kriegsgefangene," BA-MA RH26-62-454/6a-b; A.O.K. 6 O Qu./Qu.2, 12.8.41 betr. Entlassung von Kriegsgefangenen, BA-MA RH26-62 454/6a-b.
42. Sich.Div. 454 Abt. Ia, Anlage zum Divisionsbefehl Nr. 59 8.9.41, Merkblatt über Sofortaufgaben der Ortskommandanturen, BA-MA RH26-62-454/6a-b.
43. Dienstreise zu OKH 25.11.41, USNA T-501/6. Von Krosigk's notes read as follows in the original German: "Nicht Negerstandpunkt, sondern vernünftige Behandlung nach Richtlinien Reichsminister Rosenberg."
44. The 62nd ID KTB (Ia) mentions that the division shot eight persons as partisans (usually described as *Freischärler*) between 22 June and 27 October. It also states that elements of the division were attacked by partisans on at least two occasions. Interestingly, despite the fact that the responsible persons were not apprehended in these cases, no reprisals followed. See KTB entries for 14.8.41 and 18.8.41, BA-MA RH26-62/40.
45. Shishaki Raikom Kompartii Ukrainy, Pokazanie ob'yasnitel'nie zapiski i drugie dokumenty ... DAPO 105/1/357.
46. (Abschrift) Fernspruch von I.R. 190 an 62. I.D., Meldung betr. Baranowka 12.11.41, 20,20 Uhr, BA-MA RH26-62/41; Fernspruch von Lt. Schönfeld/ Gefr. Pressler betr. Strafaktion Oberst Sins [*sic*], 13.11.41 20,00, BA-MA RH26-62/56.
47. Two archival sources mention the killings briefly: Shishatskii Raikom Kompartii Ukrainy, Pokazanie ob"iaasnitel'nye zapiski i drugie dokumenty ... DAPO 105/1/357; Kharakteristika Baranovskogo s. soveta g. 1941 po 1944 g. DAPO 1876/8/108. The most detailed descriptions can be found in Fedorov and Maniak, *Vinok bezsmertia*, 329ff. This source is somewhat unsatisfactory, in that few of the sources used by the authors are given in footnotes. It is impossible to determine, for example, when the many interviews with surviving witnesses featured in the book were conducted. Nevertheless, much of the information presented in this book is consistent with the German record and with the information provided by witnesses interviewed by the author in Baranivka in 1997. Much the same can be said of Horlach et al., *Dzvony pam'yati*, which also discusses Baranivka, 28–33, and refers to some of the same witnesses mentioned in *Vinok bezsmertia*. See also Interview with Mariia Ivanovna Malosh, 18 April 1997; Interview with Hanna Fedorivna Kryvoshyi, 18 April 1997.
48. Fedorov and Maniak, *Vinok bezsmertia*, 329ff. The presence of this German named "Hoffmann" or "Hochmann" cannot be explained from 62nd Division records. This book suggests that he was an official of the German administration who remained in the area throughout the occupation. It is possible that he was an officer of the Myrhorod or Shyshaky Ortskommandanturen, for these

garrisons were usually left in place when the Reichskommissariat Ukraine assumed control of a given area from the Heeresgebiet. *Gebietskommissar* was a title used exclusively by German civil administration in occupied areas. Many Soviet sources, archival and published, popular and scholarly, display a very poor understanding of the structure of German military government, and are apt to use terms like "Gestapo" very loosely to describe any unit of military police.

49. Ibid., 335.
50. Interview with Mariia Ivanovna Malosh, 18 April 1997; Interview with Hanna Fedorivna Kryvoshyi, 18 April 1997.
51. Extrapolating from the general principles of the law of war and the norms that they discerned in various national military regulations, the members of the "Hostage Case" tribunal established a series of criteria for the legality of hostage-taking and reprisals that did little to restrict the occupying army's freedom of action. Reprisals against civilians were not formally prohibited under international law until the Geneva Convention of 1949. See *Trials of War Criminals before the Nuremberg Military Tribunal* (Washington, D.C.: 1950), 11:1230–1317.
52. Von Reichenau demanded the public hanging of all captured partisans of either sex and ordered that suspect "partisan" villages would be exempted from reprisal only when there was concrete evidence that the inhabitants had offered resistance to the insurgents. See Der Oberbefehlshaber der 6. Armee, Armeebefehl 9. November 1941, BA-MA RH26-299/124; Generalkommando LI A.K. Abt. Ic Nr. 2677/41 geh., Anlage Nr. 464 zum KTB der Abt. Ic, 12.11.1941, BA-MA RH24-51/57.
53. 62nd ID Abt. Ia/Ic Nr. 1784/41 geh. betr. Befriedung, Sühnemaßnahmen, 11.11.41, BA-MA RH26-62/41.
54. There are numerous references to this meeting in the archival sources. See Rasskaz zheny partizana OTRISHKO Al-ry Savovny in Sekretar' Poltavskogo obkomu KP/b/U po propagande i agitatsii, Mirgorodskii RKKP/b/U vysylaem listovki vypushchennye partizanami v period nemetskoi okkupatsii Mirgorodskogo raiona, 24.7.46, DAPO 105/1/265; Poltavskii oblastnoi sovet deputatov trudiashchikhsia g. Poltava, otchet o deiatel'nosti podpol'nykh organizatsii KP(b)U i o partizanskoi oblasti v period vremennoi nemetsko-fashistkoi okkupatsii, sent. 1941–sent. 1943 gg., DAPO 4085/4/5; Prilozhenie k protokolu n37 Otchet ob antifashistskom podpol'e i partizanskom dvizhenii na territorii Poltavskoi oblasti v period Velikoi Otechestvennoi Voiny 1941–1943 g., DAPO 15/1/2016. There is an odd reference to this meeting among the early records of the Poltava oblast underground in the TsDAHO—a one-page document, undated, which states that the rally took place, that two hundred people attended, and that a farm worker by the name of Korniienko displayed portraits of Lenin and Stalin, while another named Honcharenko brought out a Soviet flag: TsDAHO 1/22/19 (document headed "Poltavskaia oblast'"). See also document no. 87, "Z postanovi Biuro Poltavs'kogo obkomu ..." in *Poltavshchina v gody Velikoi Otechestvennoi Voiny* (Kharkov: 1965), 101; Interview with Vasyl' Danylovych Tkachenko, 18 April 1997.
55. Fernspruch von Lt. Schönfeld/Gefr. Presser 13.11.41 20:00 Betr. Strafaktion Oberst Sins [*sic*], BA-MA RH26-62/56.
56. Compare, e.g., an NKVD account, obviously written to play up the role of Kopenkin, with the Bezpal'ko report: Dokladnaia zapiska Narkomata Vnutrennikh Del Ukr. SSR Tsentral'nomu Komitetu KP(b)U o boevoi deiatel'nosti ob"edinennogo partizanskogo otriada pod komandovaniem I.I. Kopenkina v

sentiabre 1941–ianvare 1942 gg., published as document no. 308 in Grigorovich et al., *Sovetskaia Ukraina*; Bezpal'ko report, TsDAHO 62/4/34.

57. Otryshko, too, gives the date incorrectly as 12 December 1941. Otherwise, hers is a very sober description of events. Rasskaz zheny partizana OTRISHKO Al-ry Savovny (included in) Sekretar' Poltavskogo obkomu KP/b/U po propagande i agitatsii, Mirgorodskii RKKP/b/U vysylaem listovki vypushchennye partizanami v period nemetskoi okkupatsii Mirgorodskogo raiona, 24.7.46, DAPO 105/1/265.
58. There are several other accounts of the Velyka Obukhivka killings. A report written by the village council in May 1944 says that three Germans and twenty-seven horses were killed. See Akt No. 1, 25 Maia 1944 goda DAPO 3388/1/1627. T. Strokach, head of the staff of the Ukrainian partisan movement, described the initial fire fight in similar terms in a book published after the war: T. A. Strokach, *Nash pozyvnyi—svoboda* (Kiev: 1979), 71. A postwar account of the activities of the Myrhorod district partisan detachments (cited above) notes "several" German dead and "up to twenty" horses killed. See Poltavskii oblastnoi sovet deputatov trudiashchikhshia g. Poltava, otchet o deiatel'nosti podpol'nykh organizatsii KP(b)U i o partizanskoi oblasti v period vremennoi nemetsko-fashistkoi okkupatsii, sent. 1941–sent. 1943 gg., DAPO 4085/4/5.
59. Interview with Vasyl' Danylovych Tkachenko, 18 April 1997.
60. Horlach et al., *Dzvony pam'yati*, 48. DAPO 3388/1/1627 contains dozens of short statements made by Velyka Obukhivka residents recounting the deaths of family members during the German reprisal. Many are worded in roughly the same way, indicating that they were probably dictated by a local official or written in accordance with some sort of an example provided to the villagers. There is some variation, however, in the descriptions of the manner of death, etc. It seems probable that these statements were submitted in order to secure some kind of compensation.
61. Bezpal'ko report, TsDAHO 62/4/34.
62. There are numerous estimates of the Velyka Obukhivka death toll in Soviet records. One of several available overviews of the activities of the Myrhorod and Shyshaky district partisan detachments states that 312 persons were shot, and a further 10 burned alive: Poltavskii oblastnoi sovet deputatov trudiashchikhshia g. Poltava, otchet o deiatel'nosti podpol'nykh organizatsii KP(b)U i o partizanskoi oblasti v period vremennoi nemetsko-fashistkoi okkupatsii, sent. 1941–sent. 1943 gg., DAPO 4085/4/5 The Bezpal'ko report estimates that 500 persons were shot: Bezpal'ko report, TsDAHO 62/4/34. Iemets' and Samoilenko claim that "more than 160" persons were killed (*Poltavshchina*, 37). A short report on the cumulative loss of lives and property in Velyka Obukhivka for the duration of the occupation, prepared by the Velyka Obukhivka village council and dated 14 October 1944 states that 315 persons were shot by the Germans; Khronologicheskaia (next word illegible) V.-Obukhovenogo S.Sovet ... DAPO 1876/8/91. Oleksandra Otryshko gave a figure of 270: Rasskaz zheny partizana OTRISHKO Al-ry Savovny in Sekretar' Poltavskogo obkomu KP/b/U po propagande i agitatsii, Mirgorodskii RKKP/b/U vysylaem listovki vypushchennye partizanami v period nemetskoi okkupatsii Mirgorodskogo raiona, 24.7.46, DAPO 105/1/265 *Vinok bezsmertia* puts the figure at 200 (p. 340). Vasyl' Tkachenko stated that 273 persons were killed: Interview with Vasyl' Danylovych Tkachenko, 18 April 1997.

63. This narrative of II/164's operations in the area is taken from Faasch's detailed after-action report to IR 164. (Abschrift) II. IR 164 Abt. Ia, 12.11.41 Betr. Säuberungsaktion, BA-MA RH22/179.
64. Bfh.rückw.H.Geb.Süd Abt. VII/503/41., 18.11.41 Anordnung Nr. 28, USNA T-501/6. Von Roques was sent home on medical leave on 27 October. Rückw. H.Geb. Süd KTB (Ia) entry of 27.10.41, USNA T-501/4.
65. Strangely, one of the most impressive direct successes against partisans by elements of the 62nd Division took place on 11 November, when the engineer battalion (Pionier Abt. 162) carried out a patrol of an area including the villages of Lushnyky, Khaleptsi, Biivtsi, and Ienkivtsi (all Lubny district). The battalion captured a very large number of weapons: 1 light machine gun, 1 machine pistol, 82 rifles, 3 mines, 40 explosive devices, 4 hand grenades, 150 molotov cocktails, and 18,850 rounds of small arms ammunition. Surprisingly, twenty-eight "bandits" were reported "brought in," and rather than being executed were delivered to the POW camp at Khorol. There are two possible explanations for this variation in division practice. These partisans may have surrendered voluntarily (i.e., not as a result of combat), and were thus granted the amnesty commonly extended to partisan deserters. Alternatively, the battalion commander may simply have declined to shoot men he personally considered deserving of lawful combatant status, in violation of standing orders regarding partisans. 62nd ID Tätigkeitsberichte für die Zeit vom 26.10.–14.11.41, BA-MA RH26-62/41.
66. Bezpal'ko report, TsDAHO 62/4/34.
67. Bezpal'ko report, TsDAHO 62/4/34.
68. This figure is derived from several daily reports (*Tagesmeldungen*) from the 164th IR to the 62nd ID headquarters. See Tagesmeldung, 10.11.41– 24.11.41, RH26-62/56. See also 62nd ID Abt. Ic 24.11.41 Tagesmeldung, BA-MA RH26-62/82.
69. Interview with Polina Oleksiivna Stepa, 11 August 1997.
70. 62nd ID Ia/Ic 24.11.41 Tagesmeldung an Bfh. rückw. H. Geb. Süd Ia/Ic, BA-MA RH26-62/60. 62nd ID KTB Ia 23.11.41 entry, BA-MA RH26-62/39. IR 164 Tagesmeldung 24.11.41, BA-MA RH26-62/56. (Fernschreiben) Bfh. rückw. H. Geb. Süd Ia an Heeresgruppe Süd Ia/Ib 25.11.41, USNA T-501/6.
71. 62nd ID KTB (Ia), 23.11.41 entry, BA-MA RH26-62/39. sIR 164 Tagesmeldung 25.11.41, BA-MA RH26-62/56.
72. Nibelungen (IR 164) Nachtrag zur Tagesmeldung 27.11., BA-MA RH26-62/56. Bezpal'ko report, TsDAHO 62/4/34; Narodnyi Komissariat Vnutrennikh Del Ukrainskoi SSR, Narodnyi list na komandira partizanskogo otriada— Bezpal'ko, Dmitriia Efimovicha, opisanie sovershennogo podviga, TsDAHO 62/4/34; Dokladnaia zapiska Narkomata Vnutrennikh Del Ukr. SSR Tsentral'nomu Komitetu KP(b)U o boevoi deiatel'nosti ob"edinennogo partizanskogo otriada pod komandovaniem I.I. Kopenkina v sentiabre 1941—ianvare 1942 gg., published as document no. 308 in Grigorovich et al., *Sovetskaia Ukraina*.
73. I.R. 164 Tagesmeldung 28.11.41, BA-MA RH26-62/56.
74. 62nd ID KTB Ia entry 1.12.41, BA-MA RH26-62/39; Tagesmeldung Abt. Ic. (62nd ID) 1.12.41, BA-MA RH26-62/82. The Bezpal'ko document mentioned above offers a possible explanation by claiming that the Germans were ambushed with some losses during this operation, and that seventy persons were shot in Sakalivka itself as an act of reprisal. 62nd Division records do not reflect any such losses, but it is also possible that the Germans were simply retaliating

for the failure of the inhabitants to betray the location of this camp during their earlier patrols in the vicinity.

75. For information on the collapse of the Myrhorod and Shyshaky district partisans, see Poltavskii oblastnoi sovet deputatov trudiashchikhsia g. Poltava, otchet o deiatel'nosti podpol'nykh organizatsii KP(b)U i o partizanskoi oblasti v period vremennoi nemetsko-fashistkoi okkupatsii, sent. 1941–sent. 1943 gg., DAPO 4085/4/5; Prilozhenie k protokolu n37 Otchet ob antifashistskom podpol'e i partisanskoi dvizhenii na territorii Poltavskoi oblasti v period Velikoi Otechestvennoi Voiny 1941–1943 g., DAPO 15/1/2016; Bezpal'ko report, TsDAHO 62/4/34; Iemets' and Samoilenko, *Poltavshchina,* 41–42.
76. Richard Evans, "The Catholic Community and the Prussian State" in Richard Evans, *Rereading German History 1800–1996* (London: 1997), 91.

Eighteen pictures, nine of which are reproduced here, turned up in the pack of non-commissioned officer Fritz Lawen. Lawen, who belonged to the 12th Company of the 679th Regiment, was taken prisoner by the Soviets in the summer of 1944. The photographs were turned over to the "Special Commission" on 8 July 1944. They were discovered in the Moscow State Archives.

Female guerrillas

Female guerrillas

They were unwilling to work for Germany.

They were unwilling to work for Germany.

They were unwilling to work for Germany.

Hunger hurts.

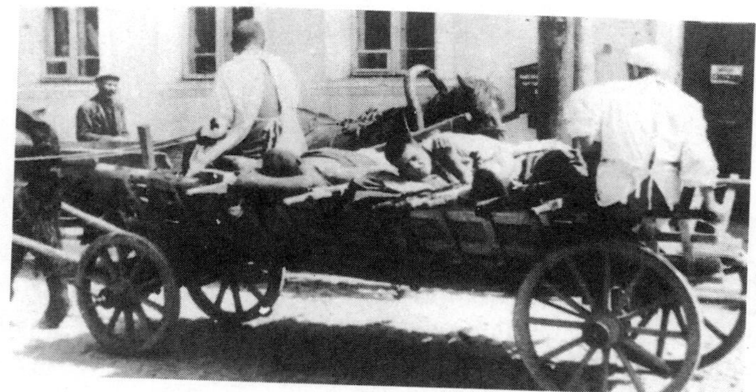
Tired brothers

– *Chapter 12* –

KORÜCK 582[1]

Theo J. Schulte

In the late 1980s, I published a study in English of German army rear area policy in the occupied Soviet Union.[2] Essentially, the work was in sympathy with fashionable research that sought to demythologize the "white shield" image of the Wehrmacht by demonstrating its close involvement in Nazi war crimes. I was aware of the reluctance of German public opinion to recognize *die verdrängte Last von 1941* (repressed burden of 1941)and had no wish to associate myself in any way with the neo-apologist factions within the Historikerstreit (particularly the ill-judged attempts at empathy in the work of Andreas Hillgruber).[3] All the same, the archival material demonstrated that historical reality was much more complex than some ultra-critical studies of the Wehrmacht suggested.

Some half-a-decade later (1994), particularly in view of the opportunities that have been offered by the discovery of Nazi documents in dusty archives from Moscow to Prague, various monographs and edited collections have established the case that the Wehrmacht's rear units, like the field police, were deeply involved in the atrocities in the East. The *Alltagsgeschichte* (daily-life history) has discovered a host of sources that make clear the fact that common soldiers as well as the higher ranks of the Wehrmacht took part in those brutalities.[4]

To hold out against this trend (with recent work arguing that even much of the most damning critical literature often uses semantics to obscure the integral relationship between the Wehrmacht and

Notes for this section begin on page 325.

National Socialism) may seem a foolhardy task.[5] Nonetheless, I believe that my basic premise is sound. If the Wehrmacht as an organizational unit has been accused of many crimes in the Soviet Union, that does not mean that every German soldier was a criminal or was guilty of the crimes that were committed in the name of the regime. Whether the Wehrmacht *in its entirety* became an ideological army, and to what extent it was involved in the crimes against humanity, remains an unresolved question. And an understandable uncertainty remains as far as personal motivation is concerned.

Korück 582

A study of a single military unit, such as Korück 582, offers the opportunity to explore some of the most contentious aspects of the debate. Provided a sense of balance is maintained, history should be concerned as much with "exceptions to the rule" as it is with the "norm." While it is illegitimate to make inferences about individual motivation or behavior from mass data, this does not preclude historians from contrasting the behavior of an individual or group with the collective behavior of large numbers of people considered as a whole. Total condemnation of the Wehrmacht is no more an aid to understanding this dark chapter in German history than is total exoneration.[6]

It is important to make the point that Korück 582 was a *rear* area, not a front-line formation. Despite the suggestion that the Wehrmacht was a single and consistent entity in terms of its military capacity and commitment to Nazism, the armed forces of the Third Reich did not constitute a homogeneous whole. A tenth of the German population served in the Wehrmacht at one time or another, and the three million men who made up the Eastern army were a mirror image of a broad range of German society. Those deployed on rear area duties in units such as Korück 582 probably reflected a wider range of social and occupational backgrounds, age groups, abilities, and, perhaps, attitudes than did many of the front line combat units.[7]

Korück 582 covered the hinterland of the 9th Army (AOK 9), one of the corps operating in the forward positions of Army Group Center, in the area around Wjasma some eighteen months after the invasion of Russia. Much of the evidence from the files of Korück 582 supports the assertion that brutal policies were in evidence from the very start during the period of success and euphoria immediately following the invasion, and not a crisis response to military setbacks in the winter of 1941/42. The daunting tasks which faced the rear area units and the hardships which they endured from relatively *early* on in the Eastern campaign should not, however, be completely neglected.

Korück 582 at its greatest extent covered an area of some 27,000 sq. kms. The military government was responsible not only for the main towns but also for over 1,500 villages and numerous hamlets and collective farms. Vast tracts of the territory were under direct German army control in name only. Partisan groups soon came to control over 45 percent of the hinterland and Soviet authority never completely vanished.[8] The problems associated with occupying an area of such physical size were accentuated by climactic factors, the varying nature of the terrain, and the underdeveloped state of the economy and infrastructure. Life was made even more intolerable for Korück soldiers by the absence of any sort of sophisticated transport network. This was not the stereotypical world of German armor and rapid movement, but one reliant on a few vulnerable railway lines and simple horse-drawn vehicles *(Panjewagen)*. Problems were exacerbated by the large numbers of troops in transit through Korück 582 to the front. Often there were simply too many for the roads to take, and the rear area found itself under immense strain to provide shelter, food, and fuel supplies. As early as August 1941, reports from Witebsk of looting by troops suggested that this was in part a strategy to overcome food shortages. By October, similar arguments were heard when heating fuel was difficult to obtain.[9]

The essentially backward and hostile nature of much of the rural environment did have a marked impact on the Korück forces, and served to reinforce the xenophobia and contempt for the Russian population that the Nazi planners had been so eager to cultivate before 1941. At the same time, the military leadership advanced a view of Russia as a constantly growing Asian monster threatening Occidental culture by a relentless drive toward the West.[10] In such a context, rear area commanders were of the strong opinion that their available forces were seriously under-strength. At the start of the campaign, AOK 9 had a shortfall of some 15,000 men, while in Korück 582 itself only 1,700 men were deployed. There were frequent complaints about the dearth of suitably trained personnel at all levels, and the officer corps was characterized at best as superannuated and at worst as incompetent. Professional serving officers were few in number, many commanders having been civilians drafted into uniform because they had administrative talents. Trained specialists with knowledge of the Russian language and conditions in the Soviet Union were almost unknown.[11]

Reports from staff officers made frequent references to the high average age of security units in the Korück. They were of the generation of the 1890s and a marked distinction could be drawn with the front-line units, where the average age of junior battlefield officers was seldom more than thirty years.[12] Landesschützbataillon 738 was fairly typical. The officer corps was made up of men between forty and fifty years of age. The average age of the junior officers was just short of forty years and the Battalion commander himself was nearly sixty years old. The men were badly trained, particularly in large-scale anti-partisan skills, and there was a high instance of physical disabilities. The overall situation was compounded by the incidence of diseases such as malaria, paratyphoid fever, dysentery, typhoid fever, and cholera.[13]

There was a grim irony in this. Many officers and men had been assigned to the Korück because duties were initially seen as administrative rather than combat-oriented. In reality, a posting to the hinterland was often akin to front-line active service. Equivalent units were often responsible for guarding lines of communication and supply equivalent to the distance from Hamburg to Vienna, yet only 300 of the troops in Korück 582 were deemed fit for full-time mobile anti-partisan roles. Feelings of isolation and danger were particularly pronounced amongst the tiny static German army units whose task it was to man the remote outposts.[14]

Acknowledgment of the conditions under which the Korück operated should not, of course, obscure the degree to which National Socialist ideology laid down the basic ground rules for various aspects of military occupation policy.

The Treatment of Soviet Prisoners of War

The Wehrmacht's brutal treatment of Soviet POWs has been well documented elsewhere.[15] The files of Korück 582 demonstrate how this monstrous whole was formed from smaller, but equally grotesque parts.

Red Army political officers were subject to summary execution (as demanded by the *Kommissarbefehl*) at the point of capture or in the camps following the screening of inmates. This was not an isolated policy confined to the Nazi special agencies such as the SD Einsatzgruppen. Korück units implemented the order from its inception in August 1941, and executions continued on a regular basis until August of the following year (1942), after the date when the order had supposedly been officially suspended.[16]

Russian prisoners who escaped immediate execution often perished in transit on the long and arduous marches to the rear. So many corpses were lying in and around the town of Wjasma in November 1941 that Korück 582 expressed serious concern that this would give succor to enemy propaganda. The most sinister dimension was that many prisoners had not died of hunger and exhaustion but at the hands of the German guard troops who summarily executed "stragglers." The brutality of the ordinary German soldiers was determined in large part by military directives passed on by the Korück, which emphasized the worthlessness of the captives and the need to respond to even minor acts of defiance, let alone escape attempts, with the utmost brutality.[17]

This said, as with so much of military policy, actual practice was often complex, not to say ambivalent and contradictory. At the same time as many troops were complying with higher command's draconian orders, Korück 582 warned its men that charges would be brought against those who used sticks to beat Russian POWs, while those who were executing prisoners would be more severely punished. Military court records for the Korück covering the first year of the war, it must be said, give no indication that any soldiers were ever charged. This is hardly surprising as the very same orders demanding proper treatment of the prisoners also warned of the dangers of too lenient an approach and the repercussions of allowing anyone to escape.[18]

Whether or not such calls for restraint had any effect, a grim fate awaited those prisoners who did reach the camps. When Korück 582 took over Armee-Gefangenensammelstelle (A.-Gef.Sa.St.) 7 in Rshew from AOK 9 at the end of November 1941, rations for the prisoners were at starvation levels. Inmates had defoliated the barbed wire enclosure, trees had been stripped of both leaves and bark, and the men were eating grass and nettles. As many as 450 prisoners at a time were crammed into unheated single-story huts, which measured no more than 12 meters by 24. Disease was rife because of malnutrition, lack of basic hygiene (there were two latrines for 11,000 prisoners), and exposure to the elements. Cases of cannibalism among the distraught inmates were not unknown.[19] Some Korück officials were often more concerned about the dietary well-being of the German perimeter guard dogs, who received fifty times the rations of the captive Russians.[20]

Again, there are exceptions to the rule. It should be recognized that much of the historical evidence used to demonstrate the degradation, abuse, and squalor is often drawn from reports by the few Korück and POW camp commanders who made strenuous efforts to improve the lot of the inmates, and entered into copious correspondence with higher authorities requesting increased resources.[21] In A.-Gef.Sa.St. 8, for example, the commander had gloves made out of old coats and clogs from waste timber (the Russian prisoners' leather boots having been confiscated by the Wehrmacht). Pressure was applied to the local population to supply food to the camp in order to dispense warm soup with horsemeat and bread three times a day. German guard units were prohibited from carrying clubs, and front-line army units were forbidden to commandeer work details unless they fed the prisoners. Similarly, when Dulag 240 came under the control of the Korück in December 1941, the new commander, a man in his seventies, organized extensive improvements. An abandoned flour mill was revived and was soon producing two tons of rye per day. Diesel was obtained for an old saw mill in order to resume plank production, which allowed barracks to be built with cavity walls filled with sawdust and woodchip insulation.[22]

The Korück's parent military command was also inclined to take positive steps. In December 1941, AOK 9 recommended that if POWs were to be fully utilized as auxiliary labor, it was essential to win over the inmates by improvements in rations and by good treatment. Pragmatism with racial overtones was clearly the motive here. Particular stress was placed on the need to avoid the use of elements described as "Asiatic subhumans," while confidence was expressed that increased contact with POW labor would not "contaminate" German soldiers, who enjoyed an "innate sense of superiority."[23]

Isolated schemes by a few energetic Korück officers to alleviate conditions were, in the final analysis, of no relevance to the vast majority of prisoners of war. In most of the camps thousands died each day of slow starvation or of disease and cold.[24] This said, the understandable focus on the grim totality has rather neglected even to consider whether such non-conformist behavior might offer insights into the way in which the dominant system as a whole functioned. No easy task, it must be admitted, particularly if one regards the ideological dimension as an immovable element in the equation. Even in camps in Korück 582 where improvements were made, inmates who were identified as special category prisoners (particularly commissars and Jews) were regularly executed under the catchall provisions of anti-partisan measures. Comparisons between A.-Gef.Sa.St. 7 and 8 (which were relatively small installations) are instructive. Camp 7 had general death rates over a three-month period that were sometimes less than 1 percent of those in Camp 8. The number of prisoners shot as "partisans" (some 75 individuals) was, however, still over 50 percent of the total for the first camp. Even this point gives rise to further ambivalence, since both camp commanders stressed on official typed pro forma returns (sometimes in manuscript for added emphasis) that the actual executions had been carried out not by the Korück troops but by units of the SD.[25]

The Extermination of Local Jews

The perverse influence of National Socialist value systems within the Wehrmacht could be regarded as more unequivocally evident in the Korück's role in the eradication of the area's Jewish population. Many were eliminated on the pretext that they were in some way or other associated with the partisans. Orders issued by Korück 582 as early as August 1941 made much of the supposed danger posed by the Jewish population and emphasized Nazi thinking on the integral link between Judaism and Bolshevism.[26] Ortskommandantur I/593 had managed to "remove" the entire Jewish population of its district by the second week in July 1941 and was using the former synagogue as its administrative offices.[27] Other local command records for September and October 1941 list frequent instances in which Jews had been executed as reprisal measures for attacks on German units, even when the only link was that they happened to live in the areas where the attacks had taken place.[28] Later reports in November 1941 from Kalinin (which at that time reported to Korück 582) noted the general elimination of "unreliable elements" including Jews by the 703rd Geheime Feldpolizei unit and a detachment of the SD. Assistance in the eradication process, which also extended to the inmates of local mental asylums, had been provided by an indigenous civilian auxiliary police unit.[29]

Unfortunately, in comparison with other rear area units, the files of Korück 582 do not contain detailed numerical information on the implementation of anti-Jewish policy in the opening months of the campaign. Reports from Korück 553 (Army Group South), for example, give details of over 20,000 Jews killed during this period.[30] The dangers of extrapolation excepted, it can be supposed that an extensive purge had also taken place in Korück 582 since few references exist in its files to individuals or groups of Jews after the winter of 1941/42. Material for this later period is not completely absent. Reports from Dulag 230 (Simez) in July 1942 noted that Jews (and Red Army Commissars) were still being handed over to the Geheime Feldpolizei.[31]

The continued survival of some Jews in Korück 582 does oblige us to consider whether the logical consequence of regarding Jews as partisans or partisan sympathizers was always immediate eradication. Administrative orders relating to various local commands in Korück 582 from July 1941 to as late as January 1942, while stressing the security threat posed by Jewish women and children as well as men, were advocating registration and ghettoization to facilitate the creation of Jewish forced labor units.[32]

Conjecture on this point should not detract from the fact that Korück 582 files never contain any suggestion that Wehrmacht officers saw Jews in anything other than absolute, categorical terms. Instances in which the unit actively resisted the killing of Jews are not to be found, for whatever reason, in the records of the Korück. The Korück was prepared to do the preparatory work and round up Jews, as well as Red Army Commissars and other "special category" prisoners. And it was prepared to carry out executions. At best, the rear area command was inclined to leave the most unsavory tasks to the SS and SD. The Korück preferred to hand Jews over to the SD in the knowledge that the army could thus distance itself from the actual eradication measures. In the POW camps under the Korück's control, in particular, the entire handover went smoothly, provided the necessary paperwork was in order. Dealings between the officers of the Korück and officials of the SD were invariably described in highly favorable terms.[33]

Collective Punishments (*Kollektive Gewaltmaßnahmen*)

On a wider front, collective "punishments" by security units of the Korück resulted in the wholesale and indiscriminate destruction of numerous peasant communities. The marked discrepancy between abnormally high "partisan" losses and abnormally low German losses indicates the sheer scale of the summary executions of civilians casually designated as "partisans" or seized as hostages. Such numerical distortions cannot adequately be explained by appeals to security needs or the exigencies of war, and it is noticeable that many actions were joint ventures of the Korück with special units of the SS.[34]

The reports from just one small local command (OKII/930) for the period 18 July to 31 December 1941 give a sense of the scale of killings across the entire Korück. Some 627 "partisans" had been shot for the loss of only two members of the German forces. This "success" rate was attributed, in part, to the efficacy of measures that made no pretense of maintaining "decent and soldier-like values." Only one episode prompted an isolated complaint from a junior officer that executions had been carried out in an unsavory manner. The shooting had degenerated into a mix of bloodbath and black farce, with the officer in charge clearly aware of the disquiet of the German troops involved, whom he cautioned to silence. High level investigations—which went beyond the Korück and involved AOK 9—came to the conclusion that matters had been clumsily handled, not that the action was unjustified. Military commanders were mainly concerned that the pretense of legality should be maintained and that all such actions should be conducted in a disciplined fashion.[35]

Contradictions and paradoxes again emerge. Later on in the war, German troops in a neighboring Korück expressed misgivings that collective "punishments" were both unsound and unnecessarily brutal, an attitude that higher command attempted to suppress by repeating arguments on security considerations, interspersed with rather more oblique references to racial menace.[36] Meanwhile, some officers in Korück 582 urged restraint, not in response to expressions of disquiet, but rather in order to curb overenthusiastic units that were engaging in the wholesale murder of men, women, and children. As the war continued a paradox emerged, with troops instructed to spare no effort to ensure rear area security yet at the same time cautioned as to the counterproductive nature of wanton and cruel destruction.[37]

Such inconsistencies between official policy and the measures undertaken by the troops on the ground toward the civilian population had, in any case, been evident from the very start of the war. Despite orders from the highest authorities, who were intent on pursuing a mass starvation policy, Korück 582's units at Witebsk in August 1941 established bread distribution centers and communal kitchens to provide hot meals for the homeless. German troops were also issuing milk to infants and small children. AOK 9 did not appear unsympathetic, but the Korück preempted criticism from higher authority by arguing that a decision had been made to avoid hunger riots which would have driven the locals into the hands of the partisans.[38]

On the Mentality of the Wehrmacht

Humanitarian acts, especially when they involved entire army corps, were clearly the exception as the scale of suffering on the part of the civilian population in the occupied areas demonstrates. Critical literature has, however, tended to dismiss such evidence too readily as merely apocryphal, and in doing so has left open questions about why such recorded instances were both isolated and short lived.

Some of the earliest work on rear area occupation policy suggested that reservations about overt political warfare emanated largely from relatively older officers of the sort found in Korück 582. Whether a "residual" officer class existed within the Third Reich, with a value system derived from perhaps even the Imperial era, remains very much part of the debate on the Wehrmacht and criminality.[39] As the files of various Korücks indicate, while the organizational structure of military government left much to the discretion of individual commanders, only a select few took advantage of their relative autonomy in order to modify otherwise harsh policy.

What was striking in the files of Korücks such as 582 was an often bizarre juxtaposition of material. Detailed criticism of the "shameful" and dishonorable behavior of German troops is be found alongside directives urging increased coercion in pursuit of elusive military goals—goals that were often clearly ideologically determined. Even if elements within the Korück officer corps had reservations about the often brutal way the war was conducted, they were, as frequent references to anti-Bolshevism demonstrate, prepared to abandon principles for the higher purpose of what they regarded as a crusade[40]

And what of the rank and file, the ordinary soldiers in the Korück who were directly responsible for the implementation of policy at the grass roots? Some of the above insights into their motives and behavior support recent anti-apologist literature which paints a grim picture of the overwhelming majority of German troops as Nazi fanatics who saw themselves engaged in some form of religious war. At best, it is argued, even when the troops did not actually engage directly in war crimes, they were morally indifferent to the suffering of the inhabitants of the occupied areas, particularly of the Jews. The sordid and lurid subject matter of their letters home and the photographs they took suggest that the rank and file might even have seen aspects of the war as a bizarre form of "tourism."[41]

Attempts to explain such behavior suggest that the breakdown of conventional rules of warfare in these "lawless territories" and the introduction of new racial/ideological guidelines were used as a pretext to demonstrate to the troops that brutality was not only permissible but a requirement of the war. The quasi-legal directives (particularly the military justice decree and the "Guidelines for the Conduct of Troops in Russia"), which abrogated traditional norms of conduct in war, had just such a purpose. As the case study of one particular execution in Korück 582 demonstrates, commanders were always at pains to stage executions in an organized and disciplined fashion. However weak and flimsy this legal fiction was, its significance for the removal of inhibitions on the part of the ordinary soldiers should not be underestimated. [42]

Yet, although the files of Korück 582 contain material in support of this depressing picture of collective involvement on the part of ordinary troops in the crimes perpetrated in the East, the same records offer other perspectives on the daily-life history of the war. Official ideology was often filtered and sometimes diluted by the inertia of army life and the boredom of occupation duty. Korück 582 reports on troop morale present a picture in which soldiers shunned official propaganda, preferring instead to retreat into the escapist world of popular light entertainment, films, and theater. A great deal of life in the rear area appeared surprisingly—perhaps disturbingly—normal.[43] To advance this view is not to present a "monolithic and unrealistic conception of ideology," nor is it to deny the dangers of historicizing the Third Reich. National Socialism clearly sought to influence popular notions of patriotism and conceptions of law, justice, and military honor in the most subtle fashion. But the actual extent to which the regime succeeded in instilling its value system remains a vast and complex subject in which there are no obvious or simple explanations.[44] A useful comparison could be drawn with a recent study of a rear area police battalion, the members of which had much in common with the men of Korück 582 in terms of their age profile and backgrounds. Even for the men of this police unit, whose war crimes are a matter of legal record, participation was not a matter of special selection, indoctrination, or ideological motivation. Rather, dogged conformity within the small unit, deference to authority, and careerism among the younger men exerted tremendous pressures on behavior and set the moral norms.[45]

Within the army proper it is often claimed that Nazi idealism maintained a resolute fighting spirit among the rank and file to the bitter end, and that this underpinned a willingness to engage in the most brutal acts. Morale in rear area units such as Korück 582 was, however, certainly well below the level suggested by such stereotypical literature on the Wehrmacht. In part this can be attributed to the fact that these units were "atypical" in that they represented those elements of the German male population who would not under ideal conditions have been deployed for active military service. The resentments and anxieties of such men may well have expressed itself in brutality toward others. But lethargy and strategies for survival, which included self-mutilation, desertion, feigned displays of incompetence, and various attempts to sit out the war, also featured.[46] Military courts in Korück 582 employed draconian punishments to maintain discipline and conformism, but even in this area there are variations from the norm which suggest that sentencing policy was not always determined by ideological thinking.[47]

Of course, as even critical literature has noted, what emerges from a study of the files of Korück 582 is not a clear dichotomy between fanatics fighting a religious war, and ideology-free, bored, and apathetic soldiers, but a continuum. Much more case study work is called for, particularly that which critically evaluates the *range* of responses to the war, particularly those that suggest differences of approach between the officers and men. Studies of nonconformism warrant particular attention, for the benefits of exploring "exceptions which prove the rule" should not be underestimated.[48]

At the same time, if units such as Korück 582 were especially representative of a broad cross-section of male German society, the debate needs to go beyond even the complex issue of the extent to which Nazi ideology alone shaped behavior. Due regard needs to be given to the insights that are offered into the impact of long-term trends in popular attitudes.[49] After all, for many of the relatively older Korück soldiers, the war in the East was a stage on which they gave expression to values instilled in the earlier, formative years of their lives.

Finally, recognition should be made of the intrinsic problems in any attempt to re-create the mental world of the Third Reich. War crimes trials indicate that many who participated in the war in the East regarded it as a different time and place, and the political vocabulary and values of the present are often inadequate in attempting to explain the situation in which they had found themselves. Some fifty years after the end of the war, despite the necessary impulse that drives historical research, there is substance to Alexander Kluge's assertion that "there is not a single human being in Germany who feels, sees, or thinks like any of the participants did in 1942."[50]

Notes

1. Korück: Kommandant des rückwärtigen Armeegebietes. Each army rear unit was identified by a number, hence Korück 582. The term referred to both the unit and its commanding office.
2. Theo J. Schulte, *The German Army and Nazi Policies in Occupied Russia* (Oxford: 1989); idem, "Die Wehrmacht und die nationalsozialistische Besatzungspolitik in der Sowjetunion," in *Unternehmen Barbarossa. Zum*

historischen Ort der deutschen-sowjetischen Beziehungen von 1933 bis Herbst 1941, ed. Roland G. Foerster (Munich: 1993), 163-176. Note: The main files on Korück 582 are to be found in the Bundesarchiv-Militärarchiv (Freiburg im Brsg.) under classmark RH23/202–270. More extensive references, drawn from this archive, on the main topics discussed in this article are to be found in the footnotes of my 1989 monograph.

3. Wolfram Wette, "Erobern, zerstören, auslöschen. Die verdrängte Last von 1941. Der Rußlandfeldzug war ein Raub- und Vernichtungskrieg von Anfang an," in *Die Zeit*, 28 November 1987, 48. Andreas Hillgruber, *Zweierlei Untergang. Die Zerschlagung des Deutschen Reiches und das Ende des europäischen Judentums* (Berlin: 1986). Hans-Ulrich Wehler, *Entsorgung der deutschen Geschichte?* (Munich: 1988), 46. Omer Bartov, "Historians on the Eastern Front," *Tel Aviver Jahrbuch für deutsche Geschichte* 16 (1987): 325–345.
4. "Auswahlbibliographie zum Thema Wehrmachtsverbrechen," in *Mittelweg 36* (June–July 1994): 52–56. *The Final Solution: Origins and Implementation*, ed. David Cesarani (London: 1994). *Operation Barbarossa: The German Attack on the Soviet Union, June 22, 1941* (College of the Humanities, Utah University: 1992). *The Shoah and the War*, ed. Asher Cohen (New York: 1992). *Die Deutschen und die Judenverfolgung im Dritten Reich*, ed. Ursula Büttner (Hamburg: 1992). Ronald Headland, *Messages of Murder: A Study of the Reports of the Einsatzgruppen of the Security Police and the Security Services, 1941–43* (Rutherford, N.J: 1992).
5. Hannes Heer, "Killing Fields: The Wehrmacht and the Holocaust in Belorussia, 1941–42" in this volume. For an example of material that inclines toward the apologetic, see Jörg Friedrich, *Das Gesetz des Krieges. Das deutsche Heer in Rußland 1941–1945* (Munich: 1993).
6. For the original phrase, see Jürgen Förster, "The Relation between Operation Barbarossa as a War of Extermination and the Final Solution," in Cesarani, *Final Solution*, 97.
7. Omer Bartov, *Hitler's Army* (London, New York: 1986). Mark Mazower, "Military Violence and National Socialist Values: The Wehrmacht in Greece 1941–44," in this volume.
8. Korück 582, 10 Januar 1942, BA-MA RH23/244/3. *Soviet Partisans in World War II*, ed. John Armstrong (Madison: 1964), 39.
9. Korück 582 (Ortskommandantur I/532) Bericht 396/8, 22.08.1941, BA-MA RH23/230, Korück 582 (Ortskommandantur I/593) Befehl 20.10.1941, BA-MA RH23/223.
10. *Das Rußlandbild im Dritten Reich*, ed. von Heinz-Erich Volkman (Cologne: 1994). Bianka Pietrow-Enker, "Die Sowjetunion in der Propaganda des Dritten Reiches. Das Beispiel der Wochenschau," *MGM* 46 (2/1989): 79–120. Schulte, *German Army*, 168. Omer Bartov, "Operation Barbarossa and the Origins of the Final Solution," in Cesarani, *Final Solution*, 122–124.
11. Korück 582, Qu/Ic 22.09.1941 BA-MA RH23/277. Werner Haupt, *Heeresgruppe Mitte: 1941–1945* (Dorheim: 1968), 70.
12. Bartov, *Hitler's Army*, 48ff.
13. K582 Qu/Ic 22.09.1941, BA/MA RH23/277. K582 Anlagen zum KTB, 04.06.1942, BA-MA RH23/24.
14. Korück 532, Halbjahresbericht, 11.11.1942, BA-MA TH23/26. Korück 582 (OK I/532) 23.10.1941, BA-MA RH23/223. Gustav Höhne, *Haunted Forests, Guides to Foreign Military Studies* (CO37) (Washington, D.C.: 1953). Armstrong, *Soviet Partisans*, 221ff.

15. Christian Streit, *Keine Kameraden. Die Wehrmacht und die sowjetischen Kriegsgefangenen 1941–1945* (Bonn: 1991)
16. Korück 582 (OKI/593) Befehl Nr. 11, "Behandlung politscher Kommissare" 20.08.1941, BA-MA RH23/223. Korück 582 (OK I/593 Demidow) Tgb. 1580/41, 28.09.1941. Wach.Batl. 721 (Cholm) an Korück 582,19.08.1942, BA-MA RH23/247. Jürgen Förster, "Die Sicherung des 'Lebensraumes," in *Das Deutsche Reich und der Zweite Weltkrieg*, vol. 4: *Der Angriff auf die Sowjetunion*, ed. MGFA (Militärgeschichtliches Forschungsamt) (Stuttgart: 1983), 1068.
17. Korück 582, OK I/593, 6.8.1941 u. 10.11.1941, BA-MA: RH23/223.
18. Korück 582 (OK I/593) Befehl 6, 6.08.1941, BA-MA: RH23/223. Tätigkeitsbericht des Gerichts des Korück 582: Oktober 1940–Dezember 1942, BA-MA: RH23/261 u. 265.
19. Korück 582, Bericht über die Dienstreise vom 6. und 7.8.1941, BA-MA: RH23/225. A.Gef.Sa.St.7 (Korück 582), BA-MA: RH23/223ff.
20. Korück 582, Besondere Anordnungen 67, 20.10.1942, BA-MA: RH23/267.
21. Korück 582, Bericht über die Dienstreise vom 6. und 7.8.1941, BA-MA: RH23/225.
22. Korück 582 (A.Gef.Sa.St.8) 31.12.1941, BA-MA: RH23/223. Dulag 240 (Korück 582), Besichtigung in Rshew, 17–20.12.1942, BA-MA: RH23/233 u. 238.
23. AOK 9, Ia Nr. 4400/41, Vermehrte Heranziehung von Kriegsgefangenen für Zwecke der Wehrmacht, 1.12.1941, BA-MA: RH23/219.
24. For example, Dulag 220 (Gomel) Korück 532, "Der Kommunist is kein Kamerad," in *Der Spiegel* (6/1978), 90.
25. Korück 582, Bezug: AOK 9, 26.11.1941, Abgänge von Kreigsgefangenen, BA-MA: RH 23/22.
26. Korück 582, Befehl 5, 4.08.1941, BA-MA: RH23/223.
27. Korück 582 (OKI/593), 12.07.1941, BA-MA: RH23/224.
28. Korück 582, Feldgend.Abt.Mot 696, Br.B.Nr. 41/41, 17.09.1941, BA-MA: RH23/227. Korück 582 (Wach.Batl. 721) Schireewitschi, 12.09.1941, BA-MA: RH23/227. Korück 582 (OKII/930) Ljubawitschi, 28.09.1941, BA-MA: RH23/223.
29. Korück 582 (OKI/302 Kalinin), 24.11.1941, BA-MA: RH23/223.
30. Korück 553, August 1941–Sommer 1942, BA-MA: RH22/202.
31. Korück 582 (Dulag 230), 23.07.1942, BA-MA: RH23/247.
32. Korück 582 (OKII/930) Partisanenbekämpfung, 1.01.1942, BA-MA: RH23/237.
33. Wachbatl. 720 and Korück 582, Betr. Kgf.Lager Wel. Luki, 5.10.1941, BA-MA: RH23/222. Korück 582, Abgänge von Kriegsgefangenen, 23.11.1941, BA-MA: RH23/222. Korück 582 (Dulag 230), 23.06.1942, BA-MA: RH23/247.
34. Korück 582 (AOK 9), Nr 4109/41, 10.10.1941, BA-MA: RH23/219. Korück 582, 29/41, 14.09.1941, BA-MA: RH23/219.
35. Korück 582 (3 Radf. Wach.Batl.50), 24.09.1941, BA: MA: RH23/228. Schulte, *German Army*, 135–137. Dokumente, 335–344.
36. Korück 532, 24.9.1942, BA-MA: RH23/26. Korück 582, Stimmung der Truppe, 10.06.1942, BA-MA: RH23/244.
37. Korück 582, Br.B.Nr. 286/42, Behandlung der russischen Bevölkerung, 28.04.1942, BA-MA: RH23/29.
38. Korück 582 (OKI/532) Tgb. Nr 396/8 dated 22.08.1941, RH23/230.
39. Alexander Dallin, *German Rule in Russia, 1941–1945: A Study in Occupation Policy* (London: 1981 [1957]), 507–508. Bernhard Kroener, ed., *Organisation*

und Mobilisierung des deutschen Machtbereichs. Teilband 1: *Kriegsverwaltung, Wirtschaft und personelle Resourcen 1939–1941* (Stuttgart: 1988), 738ff.

40. Korück 582 (OKI/624), Tätigkeitsbericht, 4.06.1942, BA-MA: RH23/247.
41. Omer Bartov, "Brutalität und Mentalität: zum Verhalten deutscher Soldaten an der Ostfront," in *Erobern und Vernichten,* ed. Peter Jahn and Reinhard Rürup (Berlin: 1991); Ernst Klee, Willi Dreßen, and Volker Rieß, *Schöne Zeiten: Judenmord aus der Sicht der Täter und Gaffer* (Frankfurt am Main: 1988), 105ff.
42. The most important documents were published in *Der deutsche Überfall auf die Sowjetunion. "Unternehmen Barbarossa" 1941*, ed. Gerd R. Ueberschär and Wolfram Wette (Frankfurt am Main: 1991). Gerhard Weinberg, *A World at War: A Global History of World War II* (Cambridge: 1994), 302ff.
43. Schulte, *German Army*, 253-276.
44. Tim Mason, *Social Policy in the Third Reich: The Working Class and the "National Community"* (Oxford: 1993), 335ff.
45. Christopher Browning, *Ordinary Men: Reserve Police Battalion 101 and the Final Solution in Poland* (New York: 1992). Cf. Konrad Kwiet, "From the Diary of a Killing Unit," in *Why Germany?* ed. John Milfull (Oxford: 1992).
46. An der Befehlshaber im Heeresgebiete Mitte, Bericht über die Bahnsicherung, 2.11.1942–31.12.1942, BA-MA: RH22/233.
47. Korück 582 (OK I/593) Befehl 6, 6.08.1941, BA-MA: RH23/223. Tätigkeitsbericht des Gerichts des Korück 582: Oktober 1940–Dezember 1942, BA-MA: RH23/261 u. 265.
48. See Mazower, "Military Violence," in this volume; idem, *Inside Hitler's Greece: The Experience of Occupation 1941–44* (Yale: 1993); Hans J. Schröder, *Die gestohlenen Jahre: Erzählgeschichten und Geschichtserzählung im Interview. Der Zweite Weltkrieg aus der Sicht ehemaliger Mannschaftssoldaten* (Tübingen: 1992); Manfred Messerschmidt, "June 1941: Seen through German Memoirs and Diaries," in *Operation Barbarossa* (Utah: 1992); Karsten Bredemeier, *Kriegsdienstverweigerung im Dritten Reich: Ausgewählte Beispiele* (Baden: 1991); *Verräter oder Vorbilder? Deserteure und ungehorsame Soldaten im Nationalsozialismus. Mit Dokumentationen* (Bremen: 1990); David Kitterman, "Those Who Said 'No!': Germans Who Refused to Execute Civilians during World War II," in *German Studies Review* (1988): 241–254; H.-P. Klausch, *Die 999er* (Frankfurt am Main: 1986).
49. *Nationalsozialismu und Modernisierung*, ed. Michael Prinz and Reinhard Zitelman (Frankfurt am Main: 1991); Alf Lüdtke, "Wo blieb die rote Glut? Arbeitererfahrungen und deutscher Faschismus," in *Alltagsgeschichte. Zur Rekonstruktion historischer Erfahrungen und Lebensweisen*, ed. Alf Lüdtke (Frankfurt am Main: 1989); Omer Bartov, "Extremfälle der Normalität und die Normalität des Aussergewöhnlichen: Deutsche Soldaten an der Ostfront," in *Über Leben im Krieg. Kriegserfahrungen in einer Industrieregion 1939–1945*, ed. Ulrich Borsdorf and Mathilde Jamin (Hamburg: 1989); Hans-Dieter Schäfer, *Das gespaltene Bewußtsein. Deutsche Kultur und Lebenswirk-lichkeit 1933–45* (Munich: 1981).
50. For a fuller discussion on the way war crimes trials in the 1980s and 1990s influenced our perceptions of the Third Reich, see Theo J. Schulte, *War Crimes in Nazi Europe and War Crimes Trials* (forthcoming).

– *Chapter 13* –

How Amorality Became Normality

Reflections on the Mentality of German Soldiers on the Eastern Front

Hannes Heer

Backed by overwhelming evidence, historical research has proved that the Wehrmacht participated in and shared responsibility for the Nazi genocide. It has not yet been able to answer the question of how millions of "completely normal German men" could become perpetrators, helpers, and witnesses. No history of Wehrmacht mentality has yet been written—be it of the high command or the generals, the officer corps or the troops. What we have are the first, and certainly quite remarkable, endeavors. For example, in his book *Die Wehrmacht im NS-Staat* (The Wehrmacht in the Nazi State), Manfred Messerschmidt has demonstrated how from 1933 onwards the military leadership systematically shaped the Wehrmacht as an institution into the "second column" of the Nazi system, forming it into a compliant tool of Nazi extermination policy. Taking a view from the bottom end based on three divisions stationed on the Eastern front, Omer Bartov has examined the reality of this extermination policy in penetrating detail.[1] By analyzing the calculated interplay of military situation and propaganda, his study manages to overcome the static focus restricted to ideological issues proposed by Messerschmidt and his school. There remain, however, several points for objection: by ascribing the war after 1942 to the condition of an overall "demodernization," he overlooks the

---

Notes for this section begin on page 342.

numerous wars which took place within the one Eastern War. By attributing the "barbarization" of the troops to their desperate situation, he fails to mention the deliberately planned and implemented erosion of morality during their advance, and while he ascribes the "distortion of reality" to indoctrination, he underestimates the soldiers' own capacity for moral assessment rooted in the prewar period and the prevailing military situation.

I therefore propose an approach which is oriented toward three categories:

1. Disposition—taken as the entirety of the formative influences and interpretational patterns previously internalized by the soldiers;
2. Situation—viewed as the sum of the various determinants resulting from military phase, operational area, issued orders and function;
3. Legitimation—defined as the interpretation of events based on personal experience (and in most cases backed up by propaganda) which, contrary to all logic, persistently made the war appear just and necessary.

It is my contention that during the first phase of the war when the army was on the advance and scoring victories, the political and military leadership succeeded in inculcating amorality as a normal condition. This basic mindset, in which the individual soldier was immersed like a protective shield, was reinforced in the course of the war by being supplemented with further attitudes (such as those analyzed by Omer Bartov).

To quote from the diary of Private Werner Bergholz:

> The war with Russia. 31/6/41. When ... we passed through Rovno all the shops were raided and everybody took whatever he could lay his hands on.... 2/7. At night two of our sentries were shot. A hundred men were put up against the wall for this. It must have been Jews.

And the diary of Senior Private Richter:

> 1/7/1941. We shot 60 prisoners at headquarters.... 7/7. Matula and I rummaged around a bit in our quarter. We acquired some booty: 25 eggs and a sack of sugar.... 19/7. Uto captured an irregular in the woods and hanged him.

From the diary of Captain Reich:

> 2/7/1941. Jews shot. 3/7. We leave. 22 Russian soldiers, some of them wounded, shot in a peasant farmyard. Fruitful valley. Windmills....

> 6/7. Rest at a Ukrainian cottage. Air attack.... 7/7. Bombers. 9/7. Commissar executed by machine-gun squad. 10/7. Departure north by train.... 13/7. German airman killed; 50 Jews shot.[2]

Take the following entry by Private Heinz Belling:

> 25/7. Gave "coup de grâce" to wounded Russians in the roadside ditch, prisoners are not to be taken. 2/8. Partisans have destroyed the railway line; all inhabitants were lined up against the wall, their fate is certain.[3]

The diary of Sergeant Friedrich Fiedler states:

> 7/8/1941. We march ... from Shitomir to Korostichev and lie down there in the school where 72 shot Jews lie buried in the garden.... 17/8. Semionovka: There seem to be no Jews here or only a few.... 22/9. The sugar factory in Grigorovka serves as a prisoner camp. At night about 900 Russian deserters arrived, guarded by 1 sergeant and 6 men, who were driven across the Dnieper by starvation.... About 35 pol[itical] commissars and functionaries are sorted out from the prisoners and "physically liquidated...." 17/10. In Mirgorod: in the evening we get commissary vodka which *Kamerad* Habich has brought with him, and he tells the following story he experienced on his return from Lubny. With the headline "modern resettlement" ... 1,600 Jewish men, women and children are divided into groups of sixty and using clubs are herded into a sandpit. Clothes, furs and jewellery are collected in sacks, and with bare backs they are made to lie down in rows, two SS men shoot each one in head with a machine gun. The next victims have to lie on top of the corpses and are physically exterminated in the same way. When the first shots are fired everyone starts screaming in fear and tries to get away, but the guards' clubs are faster and no one escapes. By the afternoon at around 3 o'clock the entire Jewish population of Lubny has been resettled in heaven. For my comrades this heroic act "calls for a drink," merry songs are struck up. *Kamerad* J. pitches in with the freedom song "The Jews are travelling along and away, travelling over the Red Sea, the waves crash down, the world is left in peace," and I quietly go to bed, teased by some for my soppy sentimentality.[4]

I. Shock and Re-normalization

If, as Clausewitz claims, war is "an act of violence" which persists "ruthlessly and without regard to loss of blood" until the aim of "forcing the enemy to carry out our will" has been achieved,[5] then the transition from civil life into this aggregate condition represents for all participants a reversal of the hitherto prevailing system of values and codes of behavior which surely must effect at least a temporary loss of orientation, confusion, and fear. So what then would be the reaction of soldiers on entering a war which—as indeed was the case in the "war of *Weltanschauung*" and the "war of extermination" between 1941 and 1944—not only revoked the rules of civil society, but repudiated even the hitherto accepted codex of war?

Thus the tale told by the letters written by the majority of soldiers who invaded the Soviet Union in summer 1941 is one of shock. There is talk of experience having turned them "into a different person," of a process of "inner change" having occurred, of being forced to "completely readjust," and also of having to "throw overboard several principles held in the past."[6] A minority of the men experienced this "adjustment" as a harrowing process of "split consciousness" which ended either in their resigned withdrawal into a world of subjective privacy—"One loses interest in anything that extends beyond one's own little self"—or in a defiant emigration into "the silent nobility of solitude."[7] Alternately, as in the case of Sergeant Fiedler, this process leads to an indulgence in the luxury of "soppy sentimentality." But most soldiers managed to adapt effortlessly to the shock: they became "hard," "indifferent," and "heartless,"[8] as the afore-quoted diary entries by the soldiers Bergholz, Richter, Reich, and Belling demonstrate. One letter from the front describes this "adjustment" and the "inner change" in the following terms: "It's like growing a shell around you that's almost impenetrable. But what happens inside this shell? You become part of a mass, a component of a relentless whole which sucks you up and squeezes you into a mould. You become gross and insensible. You cease to be yourself."[9] What this sentence describes is fraught with consequences. If someone ceases to be himself, he severs his own history and relinquishes his moral principles; he ceases to see with his own eyes and is no longer capable of absorbing fresh experiences into his identity. "I have forgotten myself," is how someone else describes this process in another letter.[10] And a third soldier writing home to his wife says: "One has to be ruthless and unmerciful. Don't you have the impression that it's not me but a different person who is speaking to you?"[11] The results of such self-denial are manipulability and a dependence upon the collective and its standpoints. These were provided in the form of basic orders and daily propaganda.

Hitler had planned the war against the Soviet Union, long in advance, as a campaign beyond the norms of international law. In order to camouflage this scenario, the enemy itself was accused of breaking international law: Stalin was alleged to have made preparations for an attack which the German Reich had just managed to forestall, and due to its national character and political mentality, the Soviet military leadership had put itself beyond all military conventions. Since "in the fight against Bolshevism ... it is unlikely that the enemy's behavior will follow the principles of humanity or international law," the German command—so the argument ran—had no choice but to react with the same methods so as to avoid being put at a disadvantage.[12] Repeatedly invoking the stereotypically bigoted foe-image of "perfidiousness, hatred, cruelty," the primary orders drawn up prior to the invasion accordingly instructed that political commissars be immediately "eliminated," that Soviet prisoners of war be treated as "criminals," that the civilian population generally be regarded as "partisan suspects," and therefore that the instruction and execution of coercive measures be put under the direct responsibility of the combat troops and not of the cumbersome military courts.[13]

Both assertions—that this was a "defensive war" and that the enemy was "brutish"—were adopted by the troops and assimilated into their own argumentation. The fact that neither Hitler's basic desire for peace, nor his proclaimed reluctance at having to wage war on two fronts were seriously doubted, was the outcome of his skillful political maneuvers in the prewar years which represented him as a "chancellor of peace" assailed by a world of enemies.[14] In the eyes of the ordinary soldier still further proof that the Russians had been preparing an invasion was provided by the enemy's military conduct, in other words, by its determined and brutal resistance. "Although I have always been fairly skeptical and critical about pronouncements made by the government, I must now unreservedly state the truth about statements concerning the combat zone. While on our side you wouldn't find a single wire barrier, anti-tank obstacle, or minor field fortification, you saw masses of them on Russian territory."[15] Or: "The German people has a gigantic obligation toward our Führer, because if these brutes, who are our enemies, had got to Germany this would have produced the greatest slaughter the world had ever witnessed."[16]

In *Mein Kampf* Hitler had analyzed the crucial role played by English atrocity propaganda in deciding the outcome of World War I. By demonizing the Germans in advance as "Huns," it allowed English soldiers to view anything done by the Germans as proof of the notorious "brutality of the barbarian foe."[17] Correspondingly, the Supreme Command (OKW/OKH) inundated the German army with a veritable flood of pamphlets describing the "brutish enemy" and the "Russian *Untermensch* [sub-human]." This too was accepted by the soldiers because it evidently coincided with their own experience of an alien and threatening world. "The conditions here are antediluvian. Our propaganda certainly didn't overdo it, maybe even understated things."[18] Or: "The crudeness repeatedly shown by the Russian can only be explained by their indoctrination. These are people who would need a long and thorough education to ever become human beings."[19] Or: "Prisoners often come toward us, alone or in crowds, apathetic, bestial and tattered—but often perfidious too."[20] Or: "Recently things have been totally crazy. You are not fighting against men, but against animals.... All the prisoners I encounter are killed, there's no two ways about it. This has been our motto in the infantry for some time now."[21]

These quotes are evidence of a recovery from the shock and of an acceptance of the crime. For most men this re-normalization offered relief since it enabled them to attune to the demands of war without being plagued by worry and self-reproach.

II. The Implantation of the Holocaust into the War: The Militarization of the "Jewish Question"

We have not yet spoken about the Jews and their fate at the hands of the Wehrmacht. In his brilliant study "The Germans and the Final Solution," David Bankier has shown how, from 1941 onwards, at a time when the deportation trains were being filled and dispatched to the extermination camps, the majority of Germans at home in the *Heimat* escaped into a mental warp of not-seeing and not-wanting-to-see.[22] Such evasion was denied to soldiers on the Eastern front. They drove Jews into ghettos, cordoned off the mass graves where Jews were shot by the SD and the police, and executed hundreds of thousands of them of their own volition. What made it possible, this transition from anti-Semitic resentment to actual violence against Jews, this transition from hating to murdering the Jews?

It began with the definition of the enemy written into the "Guidelines for the Conduct of the Army in Russia" issued on 19 May 1941, which instructed each soldier that, besides "Bolshevist agitators, irregulars, saboteurs," "the Jews" are also be viewed and treated as the enemy.[23] After the border was crossed on 22 June, "the Jews" were held responsible for every act of sabotage and for every enemy action. When it came to the retaliatory shooting of hostages, the troops were under orders to execute Jews if the culprits could not be found.[24] As "agents of the Bolshevist system" they were also given the blame for murders of ethnic Germans and political detainees, particularly in the Ukraine and in the Baltic region, which were committed by the retreating NKVD. An extract from an army chaplain's letter from the front to his wife:

> It wasn't long before they got their come-uppance. The Jews who were the wire-pullers behind the whole thing were killed where they were found. Of course, as usual the worst ones were not caught, they all escaped to safety in Russia. Whatever remained was sometimes just done away with using a shovel.... Putting someone up against a wall, everyone could agree on that, but not just killing in a disorderly way.[25]

It was only a small step from the "Jew as a wire-puller" to the "Jew as partisan." This job was undertaken by the divisional situation reports which became the instrument for a systematic campaign. The following passages have been selected from reports during the first weeks and months: "It is clear that everywhere Jews live, 'mopping up the area' runs into difficulties—because the Jews support the creation of partisan groups and the disruption of the area caused by scattered Russian soldiers. Due to this finding, the evacuation of all male Jews from all villages north of Bialoviza has been ordered, effective immediately."[26] Or: "In all these measures it is finally most important to remove the influence of the Jews.... These elements must be disposed of with the most radical means, because ... they are exactly those who maintain connections to the Red Army and the resistance groups...." In the margin the regiment commander had noted: "The solution to the Jewish question must take more radical forms."[27] Or: "The Jewish population is Bolshevik and capable of any attitude hostile to Germany. In terms of how they are treated, there need be no guidelines." And: "In case after case, it is clear these are the sole support the partisans find in order to survive both now and through the winter. Their annihilation is therefore to be carried out in whatever manner."[28] By autumn 1941, the prevailing watchword all along the front was: "The Jews are without exception identical with the concept of partisan."[29]

The stigmatization of the Jew as a partisan and the wire-puller of resistance signalled the transfiguration of the Jews as political opponents into the declared military enemy. Officially, Himmler's Einsatzgruppen were responsible for political enemies, but the military opponent in fact fell in the domain of the Wehrmacht. This had consequences which went far beyond the brotherhood in arms shared by the SD and the army; this ever-changing and extended notion of the enemy called for a new definition of the soldier's duties. In his notorious order of 10 October 1941 (which Hitler instructed to be distributed all along the Eastern front, leading to a series of similar orders from Field-Marshals Manstein and Hoth), the commander of the 6th Army, General Field-Marshal von Reichenau phrased this new status in terse language: "The soldier in the East is not only a fighter by the rules of war, but also the carrier of an inexorable *völkisch* idea and the avenger of all bestialities inflicted on the Germans or related races."[30] It was no longer merely about the "Jewish question" or "the Jews." Each individual Jew in the occupied territories was identified as the enemy and had to be eradicated. It was first Hitler in his annual speech to his old comrades *(alte Kampfgefährten)* in Munich on 8 November and then, one week later, Goebbels, who gave final shape to this position. In an article published through his mouthpiece, the magazine *Das Reich,* on 16 November 1941, which was discussed along the entire Eastern front, Goebbels used illustrations from the realm of pathology to describe the danger represented by each individual, and however amiable-seeming, Jew—and, in the style of a hygienic prevention campaign, he announced their impending eradication. The article, bearing the headline "It's the Jew's fault," concluded with ten key points. They stated: "The Jews are our ruin. They plotted and then brought about this war.... This plan must be thwarted." And then: "Every German soldier who falls in this war must be answered for by the Jews. They have him on their conscience and so they will be made to pay for it."[31] This was tantamount to enjoining each soldier to identify the murder of Jews with military duty. The timing of this radicalization was anything but accidental. The beacon which was lit in the gorge of Babi Yar on 29 and 30 September 1941 marked the first wave of ghetto massacres. At the same time, the Wehrmacht started its operation "Typhoon," an assault on Moscow as the final attempt to mount a decisive *Blitzkrieg* in the hope of winning the war.

An argument still prevalent among German historians is that the orders issued by Reichenau and the other generals were pure propaganda, that no one actually believed them.[32] Nonetheless, these orders were carried out: whether out of racist delusion, or because it was believed that this was the only means of achieving victory; whether in revenge for dead comrades, or in anger that—contrary to all promises—fighting was still going on in Russia and no end of the war was in sight. Stephen Fritz's book *Frontsoldaten—The German soldier in World War II* provides a wealth of evidence for such motives.[33]

Things didn't stop at the stigmatization of the Jews as militarily threatening "partisans." When the murder operations in the ghettos got underway (in most cases assisted by the Wehrmacht), these massacres were justified with the argument that the ghetto Jews were "*unnütze Esser*," worthless mouths to feed. Hence they would only place a burden on the already over-stretched supplies of the troops. The selections carried out at the ghetto gates were based on the logic of "fit for work—not fit for work." Jews who were deigned not able to work placed strain on the German war campaign, so they were consigned to the bullets or the gas lorry. The recollections of a former Wehrmacht soldier reveal that the blurring of moral categories had been successful and military operations could no longer be distinguished from genocidal actions: "Even those incidents which in fact clearly indicated the genocidal nature of this 'war' were interpreted by me (and probably by most soldiers at the front) as part of the general, if not 'normal' process of war, and as military operations."[34]

This confusion which, within a short time caused most soldiers to lose all sense of moral orientation, was not only a result of the war situation and individual or collective interpretation. It had already started in the prewar period and belonged to most soldiers' basic frame of mind. Let me describe it in a brief digression with one example—violence and the willingness to violence—that might explain what I define as "disposition."

The core of Hitler's program—as can be read in *Mein Kampf*—was focused on war. Given that the laws of nature dictated the course of history according to the right of the strongest and eternal selection of the best, war then offered the "highest expression of life" for any race and the nation's only chance of survival. Due to a historical antagonism, the enemy had long been made out: the Jews, as the "cancerous ulcer" of history, and Bolshevism, as the most extreme embodiment of this evil. The only conceivable aim of some future call to arms would be the annihilation of these "universal contaminators" and the forcible annexation of *Lebensraum* in the East. For the purposes of such a war, any boundaries anchored in international agreements or prevailing moral consensus would no longer be binding. The future war, so Hitler argued, is a "just war," so consequently it would be permissible to wage it with all means—even "the most inhumane."[35]

National Socialism used the period between 1933 and 1939 to entrench war as an overriding social project. German society physically experienced this process as a gigantic mobilization aimed at establishing the military spirit as an essential virtue, thus creating a shift from civilian society to military community. This was brought about by reversing various important advances which had been made toward a modern civic culture. Their own mortal fear had made it easier for citizens to accept the state's monopoly of violence and to relinquish the ideals of heroic resistance in favor of the middle-class "spirit of cowardice." Instead of this, National Socialism preached the end of all fear and the return to bravery and death.[36] This risk was rewarded with the promise of total power over all enemies of National Socialism. As an explosive means of forging collective identity, violence played an important role in the period which had seen the constitution of nation states in Europe and had thereafter been regimented within rituals and symbols into a "culture of violence."[37] It was now removed from these shackles and established as an intoxicating "cult of violence."[38] This cult was founded on the ruins of pity and empathy. The curricula practiced in the *Napola* (national political education schools) and the educational targets of the quasi-medieval *Ordensburgen*, the war games drilled by the Hitlerjugend and the endurance training performed in the elite SS-Junkerschulen, all reveal the face of this new category of barbarian warrior. There was no opposition to be feared from any socially accepted sense of justice when National Socialism finally denied the authority of the law which was founded in natural law or religious tradition, and in the place of this authority interpreted laws or rights as direct (and thus permanently changing) concepts derived from the concepts of "movement" and "racial community."[39] This destruction of human rights coupled with the conscious awareness of these rights corresponded to the substitution of the "culture of guilt"—based on personal responsibility—with the "culture of shame," which was bound by collective values and watched over by the collective. These observations are not the result of thorough research, but indicate where such research could begin.

III. The Moralization of Crime

"We were ... indeed ... for a time the masters of the world and everything was done our way ... we always had right of way, we always had priority ... everything had to make way for us, and if a town was in the way, a building was in the way, or a forest, then these things had to get out of our way too...."[40] This self-glorifying image of a German Wehrmacht hurtling forwards evoked by a veteran soldier who was still enrapt with fascination years after the war, collapsed in December 1941 on the outskirts of Moscow. In the following weeks the mightiest military power the world had ever seen appeared simply to dissolve in a series of crumbling fronts, mass-retreating armies and panic-stricken commanders. The best soldiers in the world who in a triple jump of attack, battles of encirclement, and victory had managed to conquer half of Europe, were now forced to erect entrenchments, take evasive action, dig in, and flee. Army post letters paint a plain picture of the situation. But even in the chaos of the retreat there emerged a new myth. To have survived against such pitiless natural conditions and against an enemy which ruthlessly sacrificed masses of its own men, revealed the qualities of "sacrifice" and "quiet heroism."[41] What this suggested in outline—the transformation of the victoriously advancing invader into an imperturbable and enduring defender—was rounded off into a finished and conclusive picture by the Nazi leaders. On 30 January 1942 Hitler presented a first accounting of the previous weeks in a speech in the Berlin *Sportpalast*: "Any weakling can handle victories. But only the mighty can endure the blows of fortune! Providence will give the ultimate and highest prize only to those who are capable of dealing with the blows of fortune."[42] And Goebbels outspokenly edified the winter crisis as a "great test of character." Just as the soldier on the Eastern front had shown a "heart of bronze" and "true virility," the whole nation had also undergone a "great transformation." Instead of "bringing [the war] to an end as soon as possible" and at whatever cost, everyone "wants it to be continued until full victory is secured."[43]

Sentences such as these, long before Stalingrad, point to a new type of hero. The soldier on the Eastern front now displayed a new character trait hitherto unknown in the intoxication and arrogance of Blitzkrieg warfare: the silent and reliable performance of duty. "At first we acted out of conviction, later we acted out of duty"—this wartime caesura was described thus by two former soldiers, completely independently of one another, in a film interview in 1995.[44] The notion of duty which consciously evoked the front-line fighter myth of World War I, aroused in contemporaries a whole range of connotations which stretched back to a time long before National Socialism and had the power to mobilize greater loyalty than party political programs and propaganda could muster. One veteran Wehrmacht soldier characterized it with the idea of "soldierliness" (*das Soldatische*), and described his fascination thus:

> Well, for me, being a soldierly person means encountering another man with a clean and decent attitude, it means representing viewpoints which conform with universal moral laws. But soldierliness also means showing ... courage ..., not in the sense that you are brave if you kill your enemy before he kills you, but as a strong inner conviction

> towards problems you encounter in private and personal life.... I was ... more inclined to say, alright, it's not to your taste what they are expecting of you,... but if from the point of view of the state and our philosophy this is required, well for God's sake, you'll have to do your duty, you must summon up the necessary understanding to say that this just has to be done. Fulfilling your duty is very close to the spirit of sacrifice.... There were things where you simply accepted that you have to participate, because the whole thing, the collective purpose, just requires you to do it.[45]

A moral codex and the collective purpose, performance of one's duty and the readiness to make sacrifices, this constituted the catechism German soldiers carried in their kit bags from 1942 onwards. Again and again this is referred back to by the "decent" men, those who showed insight and expressed remorse after the war. We have Klaus von Bismarck (the former president of Federal Germany's Goethe Institute and a regimental aide in wartime), who beneath the snow next to the runway discovers the piled-up corpses of shot prisoners of war. When the General Field-Marshal responds to his outraged report with a gesture of disapproval, he is forced to decide whether he should accept the crime or tender his resignation. He took, as he sees it, a third course: "I couldn't just abandon my regiment; to desert my men would have meant assuming guilt. So I decided ... to try and keep my entrusted regiment's conscience as blameless as possible."[46] Peter Bamm, a captain in the medical corps in the southern sector of the Eastern front, behaved similarly. In his postwar bestseller called *The Invisible Flag*, he reports how, when confronted with the monstrous crimes against Ukrainian Jews, for example, he and his comrades opted against resistance in favor of the daily self-sacrificing performance of duty in the hospital: "By helping those in suffering, countless acts of heroism have been carried out. Thousands have given their lives in doing this."[47] These justifications were all honorable. The men who chose to look after their regiment, fulfill their duty as a doctor, follow the military oath, or safeguard the people and the fatherland also seemed to be choosing moral principles. The fatal mistake though, was that these principles were derivative, secondary virtues. As Hannah Arendt pointed out, "because they had lost all sense of higher moral values" their decency was morally worthless.[48]

But even the most infamous murderers who admitted nothing and witnessed nothing, pleaded that they had only been doing their duty. In the evidence he gave in the Jerusalem trial Eichmann said "he was doing his duty ... he didn't just obey orders, he also abided by the law." In other words, his behavior followed the categorical imperative outlined in Kant's "idea of duty."[49] That might sound cynical, but he did it in all honesty—besides, he was also backed by a certain philosophical tradition. Kant's attempt to stress the unconditionality of the ethical dictate by formulating the categorical imperative lured him toward empty formalism. Instead of representing the awareness of a particular moral issue or principle, conscience for him represented "that consciousness which bears duty unto itself." Hegel's attempt to fill this gap by embracing family, society, and state in his definition of "true conscience" was countermanded by Nietzsche. He severed the link between conscience and universal and natural laws, redefining it in terms of its correspondence to life—with all life's creative and destructive energies. Nietzsche postulated a notion of the human subject who is "fortified by wars and victories, for whom conquest, adventure, danger, pain have even become a need." Man thus conceived is 'beyond good and evil' in moral terms.[50]

This is the person we encounter in the millions under National Socialism, be it in the extermination camps, beside the dug-out mass graves behind the front, in the prisoner-of-war camps, in the "partisan operations," or on death marches. Men with a "trans-moral conscience," as Paul Tillich termed it. In their minds misdeeds figure as a good deeds, and criminal behavior becomes the enactment of the moral code.[51] This is possible only under certain conditions: by conquering one's "weaker self" in favor of demands externally dictated "by the state or philosophy [Weltanschauung]," by setting aside the wishes formed in one's "private and personal life" in favor of "the greater entity," in other words of the Wehrmacht, Germany, or simply "der Führer."

The former soldiers Bismarck and Bamm described how they were faced with the temptation to put up resistance against barbarity, to call a halt, or to disobey it. Instead they chose duty. Hannah Arendt's dictum that in the Third Reich "evil [had] lost the attribute which makes it recognizable for most people—it no longer appeared to them as a temptation" relates to this choice. People were only brought into temptation by goodness, by moral probity. "But," she continues, "they had, God knows, learned to control their inclinations and to resist temptation."[52] Which is why, in the belief they were acting morally, the soldiers of the German Wehrmacht murdered so well and in such numbers, and why, even up to the present, they neither wish nor are able to remember any crime.

—Translated by Matthew Partridge

Notes

1. Manfred Messerschmidt, *Die Wehrmacht im NS-Staat. Zeit der Indoktrination* (Hamburg: 1969); Omer Bartov, *The Eastern Front, 1941–1945: German Troops and the Barbarisation of Warfare* (London, New York: 1985).
2. *True to Type. A Selection of Letters and Diaries of German Soldiers and Civilians, Collected on the Soviet-German Front,* Hutchinson (London, New York, Melbourne, Sidney), 11, 19, 22, 23.
3. From the collection of the author.
4. From the collection of the author.
5. Carl von Clausewitz, *Vom Kriege* (Berlin and Leipzig: 1915), 3ff.
6. Joachim Dollwet, "Menschen im Krieg, Bejahung—und Widerstand? Eindrücke und Auszüge aus der Sammlung von Feldpostbriefen des Zweiten Weltkrieges im Landeshauptarchiv Koblenz," in *Jahrbuch für westdeutsche Landesgeschichte* 13 (Koblenz: 1987): 299 (letter of 29/7/1941).
7. Lothar Steinbach, *Ein Volk, ein Reich, ein Glaube? Ehemalige Nationalsozialisten und Zeitzeugen berichten über ihr Leben im Dritten Reich* (Berlin, Bonn: 1983), 204–205; Edwin Grützner's notes, in Rolf-Dieter Müller, ed., *Die deutsche Wirtschaftspolitik in den besetzten sowjetischen Gebieten 1941–1943. Der Abschlussbericht des Wirtschaftsstabes Ost und Aufzeichnungen eines Angehörigen des Wirtschaftskommandos Kiew* (Boppard am Rhein: 1991), 615 (entry of 13/11/1941); Siegbert Stehmann, *Die Bitternis verschweigen wir. Feldpostbriefe 1940–1945* (Hanover: 1992), 219 (letter of 29/7/1942), 154 (letter of 26/12/1941).
8. Dollwet,"Menschen," 299 (letter of 26/6/1941) and 299 (letter of 19/7/1941).
9. Birke Mersmann, "*Was bleibt vom Heldentum?" Weiterleben nach dem Krieg* (Berlin: 1995), 34 (father's letter in spring 1942).
10. Stehmann, *Bitternis,* 152 (letter of 27/12/1941).
11. Karl Fuchs (letter of 28/6/1941) in Richardson and Horst Fuchs, eds./trans., *Sieg Heil! War Letters of Tank Gunner Karl Fuchs, 1937–1941* (Hamden, Conn.: 1987), 116.
12. *Richtlinien für die Behandlung politischer Kommissare* (Guidelines for the treatment of political commissars) (6/6/1941), cited in Gerd R. Ueberschär and Wolfram Wette, *Der Deutsche Überfall auf die Sowjetunion, "Unternehmen Barbarossa" 1941* (Frankfurt am Main: 1991), 259.
13. Ibid., 260; *Anordnungen über die Behandlung sowjetischer Kriegsgefangener in allen Kriegsgefangenenlagern* (Instructions for the treatment of Soviet POWs in all POW camps) (8/9/1941), cited in Ueberschär and Wette, *Überfall*, 297; *Erlass über die Ausübung der Kriegsgerichtsbarkeit im Gebiet "Barbarossa" und über besondere Massnahmen der Truppe* (Law concerning the practice of military law in the "Barbarossa" area and about special army operations) (13/5/1941), cited in Ueberschär and Wette, *Überfall*, 252.
14. Wolfram Wette, "Ideologien, Propaganda und Innenpolitik als Voraussetzung der Kriegspolitik des Dritten Reiches," in *Das Deutsche Reich im Zweiten Weltkrieg* 1 (Stuttgart: 1979), 128ff.
15. Dollwet, "Menschen," 298 (letter of 26/6/41).
16. Ortwin Buchbender and Reinhold Sterz, ed., *Das andere Gesicht des Krieges. Deutsche Feldpostbriefe 1939–1945* (Munich: 1983), 74 (letter of 10/7/1941).
17. Adolf Hitler, *Mein Kampf* (Munich: 1941), 199.
18. Buchbender and Sterz, *Gesicht*, 79 (letter of 22/8/1941).
19. Ibid., 76 (letter of 1/8/1941).

20. Ibid., 84 (letter of 15/10/1941).
21. Rolf Demeter, letter to Ursula Bischof of 28/7/1941, Staatsarchiv Bremen, 7, 10GG-383.
22. David Bankier, *Die öffentliche Meinung im Hitler-Staat. Die "Endlösung" und die Deutschen. Eine Berichtigung* (Berlin: 1995), 177ff.
23. *Richtlinien für das Verhalten der Truppe in Russland* (Guidelines for the army behavior in Russia) (19/5/1941), cited in Ueberschär and Wette, *Überfall*, 258.
24. OKH (GenStdH/H Wes.Abt. Abw.) Az.Abw., III. Nr. 2111/41 of 12/7/1941, BA-MA RH 27-7/156; AOK 17, Gruppe Ic/AO Br. B. Nr. 2784/41 of 30/7/1941, BA-MA, Alliierte Prozesse 9, NOKW 1693; similarly the command given by AOK 6 on 19/7/1941, 62. ID KTB Ic/Eintragung (entry) of 21/7/1941, BA-MA RH 26-62/40; Berück Süd Abt. VII/Nr. 103/41 of 16/8/1941, BA-MA RH 22/6; AOK 2 Ic/AO Nr. 1388/41 of 17/7/1941 BA-MA RH 20-2/1090.
25. Steinbach, *Ein Volk, ein Reich, ein Glaube?* 221.
26. 221st Sich.Div., KTB Nr. 2, Eintrag (entry) 8/7/1941, BA-MA, RH 26-221/10, 87.
27. IR 350, II. Bat., An das Regiment, 18/8/1941, BA-MA, RH 26-221/21, 294ff.
28. Der Kommandant in Weissruthenien (Belorussia) des Wehrmachtbefehlshabers Ostland/Abt. Ia, Lagebericht (field report), 10/9/1941, BSA Minsk, 651-1-1, 25; Der Kommandant in Weissruthenien/Abt. Ia, Befehl (order) Nr. 24 of 24/11/1941, BSA Minsk 378-1-698, 32; Der Kommandant in Weissruthenien/Abt. Ia (Tagesbefehl), 16/10/1941, BSA Minsk 378-1-698, 12–13.
29. Kommandantur des Sicherungs-Gebietes Weissruthenien/Abt. Ic, Lagebericht (field report), 20/2/1942, BA-MA, RH 26-707/15, 4.
30. Armeebefehl des Oberbefehlshabers der 6. Armee, Generalfeldmarschall von Reichenau, dated 10/10/1941, cited in Ueberschär and Wette, *Überfall*, 285.
31. Joseph Goebbels, "Die Juden sind schuld," in *Das eherne Herz. Reden und Aufsätze aus den Jahren 1941/42* (Munich: 1943), 85ff.
32. Jörg Friedrich, *Das Gesetz des Krieges. Das deutsche Heer in Rußland 1941 bis 1945. Der Prozeß gegen das Oberkommando der Wehrmacht* (Munich, Zürich: 1993), 424ff.
33. Stephen Fritz, *Frontsoldaten. Der erzählte Krieg* (Berlin: 1998).
34. Martin Schröler, *Held oder Mörder. Bilanz eines Soldaten Adolf Hitlers* (Wuppertal: 1991), 76.
35. H.-A. Jacobsen, "*Krieg in Weltanschauung und Praxis des Nationalsozialismus 1919–1945*," in *Beiträge zur Zeitgeschichte. Festschrift für Ludwig Jedlicka zum 60. Geburtstag*, ed. R. Neck and A. Wandruszka (St. Pölten: 1978), 238ff.
36. B. Guggenberger, "Der erste der letzten Kriege? Nachdenken zum Golfkrieg," in *Universitas* (1991/6), 559; E. Jünger, *Über den Schmerz* (1934), in *Sämtliche Werke* (complete works), vol. 7 (Stuttgart, 1980).
37. R. Kössler and T. Schiel, "Nationalstaaten und Grundlagen ethnischer Identität," in R. Kössler and T. Schiel, eds., *Nationalstaat und Ethnizität* (Frankfurt am Main: 1994), 17ff.
38. Th. Scheffler, "Ethnizität und Gewalt im Vorderen und Mittleren Orient," in Th. Scheffler, ed., *Ethnizität und Gewalt* (Hamburg: 1991), 21.
39. Hannah Arendt, *Elemente und Ursprünge totalitärer Herrschaft* (Frankfurt am Main: 1955), 675ff.
40. Mersmann, *Heldentum*, 250.
41. Buchbender and Sterz, *Gesicht*, 90 (letter of 7/12/1941), 94 (letter of 25/2/1942).
42. Max Domarus, *Hitler. Reden und Proklamationen 1932–1945* (Würzburg: 1993), 2:1826, 1831.

43. Goebbels, "Wanderung der Seelen," in *Das eherne Herz*, 191–192 and "Neue Perspektiven," ibid., 252.
44. *Jenseits des Krieges,* a film by Ruth Beckermann, 1986.
45. Steinbach, *Ein Volk, ein Reich, ein Glaube?* 31–32.
46. Unpublished manuscript of the speech by K. von Bismarck on 5/3/1995.
47. Peter Bamm, *Die unsichtbare Flagge* (Munich: 1989), 76.
48. Hannah Arendt, *Eichmann in Jerusalem* (Leipzig: 1990), 366.
49. Ibid., 173ff.
50. Paul Tillich, "Das transmoralische Gewissen," in Heinz-Horst Schrey, ed., *Glaube und Handeln. Grundprobleme evangelischer Ethik* (Bremen: 1956), 284.
51. Ibid., 284.
52. Arendt, *Eichmann*, 189.

– *Chapter 14* –

Emptying the Gaze

Framing Violence through the Viewfinder

Bernd Hüppauf

I

World War II and its extermination programs are among the well-researched periods of German history. However, a suspicion that we still know very little of what is really worth knowing about this period is wide spread. Recent controversies including the *Historikerstreit* have intensified rather than alleviated this discontent. They made no significant contribution to our understanding of the endemic violence of the National Socialist system nor of the nature of violence in general. On the contrary, a continued fixation on questions of guilt is making it difficult for new and more productive questions to be raised. Public tribunals do not create the conditions necessary for impartial inquiry. The cruel nature of the Nazi system has been documented in great detail. The relationship between violence, destruction, and the NS society needs to be conceptualized within a framework not encumbered with questions of guilt. The predominance of moral issues more often than not has led to burying a concern for understanding under rituals of passing judgment. The following essay will make an attempt to address one specific aspect of the mass murders behind the Eastern front. It is concerned with questions related to the self of soldiers and civilians prepared to take snapshots of the shooting sites. Questions will be raised as to their *perspective*. Is it possible to understand the gaze

Notes for this section begin on page 374.

of photographers of mass killings? And what impact may their documentary images have had on public and private memory? What made a soldier lift his camera, look through the viewfinder, and determine the best angle for shooting a photo of innocent women and children being shot and buried in a mass grave? It is difficult to know why soldiers would have taken such photos in breach of an official order not to take photos of the execution of civilians. The very existence of these photos needs explanation and cannot be accepted merely as an extreme chapter in the history of photography.

Film and photography are among the new fields that are contributing to changing views of history. In as much as they are no longer perceived as illustrations of a history based upon written sources but as a new province of historical knowledge they require careful theoretical reflection. For the time being, this reflection could benefit also from more speculative attempts at employing theoretical knowledge and interpretive practices from the emerging field of visual culture.[1] Theories of perception and visuality have hardly made an inroad into discourse on the Holocaust and the photo history of the Third Reich's violent practices. Photographs and films have been read as illustrations and visual evidence for shocking practices of violence and the collapse of morality and civilization emphasized by a history of the Third Reich based upon written source materials. Their relevance for the construction of a memory on the part of both Jews and Germans has only cursorily been touched upon. Primarily it has been an approach to images read as documentary evidence and a focus on ideological or moral issues that has prevented questions from being raised concerning the structure of pictorial representation, the constitution of the gaze, and mental processes of image building. Issues of subjectivity and the prerequisites for a theoretically informed approach to the extermination program are only now beginning to be explored. The tacit assumption that a pictorial history of violence is necessarily derivative needs to be challenged. A history of perception and pictorial constructions of violence needs to be liberated from the dominance of the word. This, in turn, could lead to the liberation from the rituals of confessions of guilt. Explorations of the "visual culture" have the potential to make a substantial contribution to the understanding of the emergence of the violence of the war of extermination. *Framing* through viewfinders and *attitudes* toward reality are closely related or—as Gertrud Koch's playful and suggestive book title *Die Einstellung ist die Einstellung* suggests—may even be identical. The common question "What is an image?" needs to be changed to "What do we do when we perceive?" Perceiving through a viewfinder and cinematographic techniques would then have to be interpreted as a contribution to the construction of a visual history of the violence of the Third Reich.

As far as the construction of a pictorial history of the war of extermination is concerned, it is mandatory not to facilitate but rather to render more difficult the reading of its photographs. They are customarily read for content and as illustrations of the well-known story of the immoral and barbaric ideology of the Nazi system. But such foregone conclusions render the reading of images sterile. As long as the answer to the question as to what they *show* is known in advance, they will remain silent. Repeated confirmation, through images, of the knowledge that an inhumane ideology will produce inhumane actions represented in inhumane pictures offers little insight. The questions as to what these images show, what they meant for the photographers and what they mean for us are answered neither by varied references to the murderous ideas of Nazi-racism nor by reference to the pathological psyche of actors. Only focusing on the concreteness of details and the iconography of the pictures will make "visible" what can be seen in the photos and break the blockade of silence. A reading of pictures as pictures can subvert the blinding effect, which is to the same extent a result of *knowing* in advance as of the reduction of the visual to mere illustrating documents. Instead of locating an image within a *known* category (such as genocide or eliminationist mentality) or ideological framework and thus separating it from other *images*, the viewing of photos within a field of visuality would enable the viewer to create a distance from the knowledge of the NS society that is so common, and to move between different signifying systems by redefining his/her positionality. Viewing an image not as a document of an event but as an element in a visual intertexture provides a technique of consuming its pseudo-familiarity by refusing the comforting lure of immediate understanding through the projection of meaning. Unlearning the seeing of the familiar and replacing understanding and empathy with the victim with an interest in the photographer's ways of seeing is a prerequisite for a photo-history beyond a history of mere illustrations. The empty ritual of repeating moral condemnation will only be avoided in as far as the homogenizing concept of a photo-history of the Third Reich as a mirror image of Nazi ideology and practices is dissolved and replaced with perspectives capable of reflecting upon differences and specificities in the pictorial self-representation of perpetrators, photographers, and the time. The social production of attitudes and habits, visually represented in images must be made problematic. In photos of the extermination program, established relations between visual signs and identity are broken. We are familiar with nakedness, hair, gestures, facial expressions, cloths, heaps of soil, tools, etc. as signs of a world we know, and recognizing them in these images leads us to reactions of projection or emotional repulsion. But what these images require is the effort to defamiliarize our gaze in order to be able to read them as signs of a foreign world. Empathy as a practice of reading images by transferring the self into others and identifying structures of one's own world with those in the image is misleading. On the other hand, it would be futile to try to perceive these photographs through the eyes of those pictured, and an understanding is precluded by disregarding the gap that separates our own world from that represented in these photos. A focus on the foreignness of these images and corresponding mental structures that constituted the gaze through the viewfinder is needed in order to do away with closure and the resulting from knowledge derived from interpretations of written documents. This could also spell the end of a pictorial memory that separates this past from our own present. A view guided by empathy places the viewer in an emotionally and morally privileged position which inevitably leads to seeing images of exclusiveness and uniqueness. The paradoxical effect of empathy is the separation of our own world from that shown in the images.

The first documentary photographs and films of the mass murder of six million Jews that came to public attention were taken by soldiers and professional photographers of the Allied forces when the concentration and extermination camps were liberated. Images of corpses piled high, walking skeletons, dying survivors, captured guards and the sites of torture, death, and cremation shocked the world—to the degree, that is, to which photographs still had the power to shock. In the U.S. and British zones of occupation, Germans who lived close to camp sites were made to view and sometimes bury corpses, while others were shown films and photographs documenting the atrocities. Among the various reasons for the program "to view the atrocities,"[2] it may be assumed, was the educational desire to replace the collective pictorial memory of the previous heroic twelve years with a new imagery, an imagery constructed with the help of photographic documentation. The aim was to diffuse the grandiose images of Nazi Party rallies, the autobahns, and urban architecture, organized leisure, and advanced war technology, which the National Socialist system had so successfully deployed as its vision of the present and the future. Memories of grandeur were supposed to give way to images that represented the past as a criminal and barbaric time and would lead to moral condemnation. In their efforts to document this program, American soldiers took photos of various Germans in front of such photos. More often than not these viewers, mostly women, older men, and children, were shown with stern or emotionless faces often trying to avoid looking at the photos, their eyes cast down or turned away. There is a remarkable contrast between those Germans who turn their faces away, because they do not wish to confront these images, and others who have been characterized precisely by their pathologic compulsion to look at scenes of torture and murder.[3] We know of men who took photos of the war of extermination in defiance of an official ban and often persisted in retaining them, even in circumstances that, after 1945, turned them into incriminating evidence against their owners. An extremely strong emotional attachment seems to have emanated from these images, tying their owners to them for long periods of time. For many years, these private photos were all but forgotten and the main focus was on "official" visual documents from Allied sources and German offices and archives. Among these, a limited number of photographs have been continuously reproduced in illustrated history books on the Holocaust, in textbooks for schools and universities, exhibition catalogues, tour guides, and similar publications. They continue to be shown either for educational purposes or as visual evidence in support of written texts, although they have by now become metonymical and lost their visual power. They no longer produce the urge to look away. It is intriguing to ask in what ways these photos contributed to the creation of memory and in what way memory is affected by the fading of their shocking visual content.

In conjunction with the publication of collections of photos documenting the extermination program, first attempts at writing a photo-history have been made. In an essay of 1983, Dieter Reifarth and Viktoria Schmidt-Linsenhoff argue that it is no longer sufficient to use photographs merely as evidence that the Nazi terror really existed. Rather, the interpretation of photographs should aim at better understanding what made this terror possible. It is their stated objective to read photos as the "documents of a history of mentalities of fascism" which, by transcending political and economic explanations, aims at "raising the blockade of reason in the face of the incomprehensible."[4] By focusing on specific aspects of the construction of the gaze and the iconography of photos, their own essay makes a remarkable contribution toward this end. However, they too feel compelled to resort to explanations in terms of psychoanalysis and refer to the semantics of pathological deviance. Perverted desires and the pleasures of sadism, they claim, can be detected as the driving forces in the psychology of perpetrators and photographers.[5]

Many attempts at using photographs, including those of amateur photographers, as a source for telling the story of the extermination of Jews were based on the assumption that the story to be told was one of National Socialist ideology turned into images. The precondition for the possibility of telling the story of the extermination program of the Third Reich, Schönberner writes, is the "most horrifying: it is the murderers themselves who took their photographs in the act of murdering."[6] This reading of the photos is motivated by moral outrage. But is one justified in simply assuming the identity of killer and photographer? Is the gaze through the viewfinder necessarily identical with that through the gunsight followed by pulling the trigger? And is this gaze always the same product of the ideologically impregnated mind and anti-Semitism, ready to kill? Can that which is "most horrifying" in these photographs really be understood as the documentation of an ideological relationship that defines "the actors in the role of heroes and their helpless victims as sub-human *(Untermenschen)*"?[7] Certainly, the importance of ideological indoctrination and the resulting delusions that prepared soldiers for acts of violence cannot be underestimated. However, an identification of the actors' gaze at the victim with the rhetoric of militaristic heroism and racism of the National Socialist ideology precludes one from asking questions concerning the nature of this gaze.[8] We always already *know*. It is the assumption of an ideological and homogenous consciousness which leads Schönberner to the speculation that photographers must have "spent a lot of time trying to photograph their objects in unfavorable situations. They trusted primitive psychology suggesting that fearful, tired people easily appear repulsive to a superficial viewer. But they also deliberately searched for physiognomies which in their own view were particularly unsympathetic and came close to the caricature of the Jews that had been created by anti-Semitic National Socialist propaganda."[9] While these observations fit the photography of propaganda movies and publicly distributed photographs, the consciously produced images of propaganda should not be hastily identified with the world in the minds of men and women.[10] While the officially propagated image of the Jew will have had considerable impact on directing the perception of both professional and amateur photographers, the majority of photos, including most of Schönberner's own knowledgeable and sensitive selection, do not give credence to his statement. The racist concept of "the Jew," "the Slav," disseminated in propaganda literature and referred to by Höß, Himmler, Eicke, or the SS-man Max Täubner,[11] should not too readily be equated with the images in the minds of onlookers, civilian or in uniform, or of pressured men in police units. What bystanders and photographers saw or, more rarely, expressed in words did not necessarily correspond to racist ideology. A search for the *evil physiognomy* corresponds to the actions of "willing executioners." However, the reduction of perception to a rational or ideological choice has only a very limited power of explanation. It is well known that images of "the enemy" in propaganda films based on carefully calculated choices of negative stereotypes more often than not failed to produce the desired response. An assumed correspondence between Nazi ideology and the images perceived by common soldiers is a misleading over-simplification. Moreover, it is predicated on an identity specific to the time and therefore makes a great deal of the problem disappear, because the threat would, thus, cease to exist with the end of the perverse ideology.

In a more recent collection of documents, edited by Klee, Dressen, and Riese under the sarcastic title "*The Good Old Days*," the question is explicitly raised: How is one to imagine people prepared to practice murder as their day-to-day trade (*Handwerk*)? (The German word *Handwerk* is particularly fitting, but untranslatable.) The same question can be asked in relation to the photographers of the deadly "trade." Some observations and biographical details of the perpetrators referred to in the volume by Klee, Dressen, and Riese openly contradict the *Herrenrasse*-ideology that provides the framework for comments on and interpretations of the reproduced photos. In contradistinction to the editors' assumption, the empirical facts of biographies and accounts of actions do not respond to questions concerning the subjectivity of those who "produced" extermination in a war of extermination. Nor will the abstract idea of an ideology provide an answer that goes beyond the tautology of naming the actors in a war of extermination "born" or "educated" exterminators.[12] There were and still are many "ordinary men" with the ideology of a master race in Germany and elsewhere, without their ideology having turned them into mass murderers. The reported utterance of a "Major German," responsible for a "hospital" in which prisoners of war were tortured to death, "I am responsible to no-one for your lives...."[13] shockingly condenses the absolute power of one individual over the lives of all those at his mercy in a system of complete ethical nihilism. However, abhorrence of this system must not be allowed to carry the analysis away into generalizing the attitude practiced by "Major German." As long as ideology, interpreted as a closed system of beliefs, is seen as providing the answer, this level of abstraction will preclude concrete questions from arising.

A completely different approach is adopted in Claude Lanzmann's film "Shoah." This film uses no documentary footage and is exclusively based on interviews with survivors, perpetrators, and bystanders. In her interpretation, Shoshana Felman calls film the "art par excellence which, like the courtroom ..., calls upon *witnessing* by *seeing*."[14] She goes on to ask what it means to be an eyewitness if testimony is not identical with "the observing, recording, and remembering of an event, but a unique and irreplaceable *position* with respect to what is witnessed?" The definition of such a "position" is indeed the main issue in the relationship between images and memory, images and history. "The specialness of testimony proceeds from the witness's irreplaceable performance of the act of seeing—from the witness's seeing with his/her own eyes."[15] The effect of the specific "positions" that eyewitnesses have occupied is not simply a diversity of points of view but an "incommensurability of different topographical and cognitive positions" or, as Felman calls it, "different performances of the act of seeing."[16] As Lanzmann's film demonstrates, this act of seeing is a highly complex operation interlaced with language, psychological mechanisms, and modes of representation. As a result, the photographers of the war of extermination fit neither the category of perpetrators nor that of bystanders. Occupied with technical and aesthetic aspects of shooting photos, they are distanced from the events. They are further removed than mere eyewitnesses. At the same time, their very presence at the site of shooting made them deeply implicated in the crimes. Their photos are not only documents of events that have happened in a certain place, at a certain time but also bear witness to ways of seeing. These ways of seeing appear foreign or even inaccessible to us, yet may be more closely related to "ordinary" positions and perspectives of the present than the iconographic content of their photos seems to suggest.

An epistemology that will appropriately reflect the anthropological dimension both in terms of images and subjectivity has not yet been developed. It will require a new concern with the individual, not defined, however, in terms of old concepts of subjectivity or ideology, and with perception and images, not defined, however, as mirroring social and political reality. It will have to be based upon new theories of images and image building, consciousness, and the nonrational.[17] A theoretical clarification of key concepts in these areas is of an importance equal to the former theoretical concern with "structure," "function," or "institution." The epistemological framework of a history concerned with perception, representation, memory, and the social construction of reality needs to take into account recent theories of consciousness and the non-rational. So far, it has been psychoanalysis to which historians have made reference. An oversimplified psychoanalysis has, above all other theories of the subject, provided a language for addressing the problematic mediation between the individual and the cultural practices which create complex social structures. While Lacan's linguistic reading of Freud has revitalized psychoanalysis and made it fashionable, a growing dissatisfaction with the scholasticism and unproductive semantic games of this approach coincides with a return of experimental psychology after the end of behaviorism and also with the emergence of new disciplines in the field of cognition and theories of perception and visual culture. Skepticism in relation to psychoanalysis can provide no justification, however, for failing to theorize the concept of subjectivity central to a history concerned with mentalities. Under the circumstances, substituting a homogenized construction of the anti-Semitic, brutalized, or ideologically indoctrinated actor—equipped with a gun or a camera—for a theoretically reflected concept of subjectivity will inevitably lead to sterile repetition of the same well-known knowledge. It is based upon an uncoupling of history from theory. A recreation of abstract frameworks such as racist ideologies will necessarily lead to a closure of the horizon within which a pictorial history is being constituted. For its epistemological reconstitution, anthropology and ethnology, as well as new disciplines such as cognitive science, experimental psychology, and theories of visuality ought to become constitutive.

The legitimate request to acknowledge guilt will escape ritualization only to the degree to which the categories used for observation and narration avoid empathy thereby leaving room for keeping moral judgment suspended. The emerging story will itself be subject to changes over time. But only by linking it to the changes of experienced time and space will a ritualistic emptiness be avoided. Such emptiness could be considered the moral complement of the amoral perspective of the photographers. The price to be paid is the end of a notion of the autonomy of the independent subject. There is no memory of the authentic image. This change of focus requires a methodological step toward a precarious close-up. It is the isolation of the subject which I would like to address in further detail, an isolation resulting from a destruction of intertextuality and the complementary processes of an abstraction of the gaze.[18]

The following essay will be restricted to a single issue within this field, namely that of the relationship between photographic representations of violence in the National Socialist extermination program and the subjects behind the viewfinder. The few interviews available and sparse verbal accounts of photographers concerning a definition of their "craft" and of themselves will provide no more than a springboard for reflections on aspects of a photo-history of the National Socialist terror system.

II

There is, literally, no pictorial tradition for the photography of the war of extermination on and behind the Eastern front. The Holocaust, it has been argued, is unique. Its photography denotes something new in terms of iconography and positionality. Until the nineteenth century, images of cruelties, atrocities, or disfiguration of the human body were embedded in wider contexts of myths, religious systems, or philosophical ideas. They were "meaningful" within established visual and ideological codes. There is a long European tradition of representing violence in the arts. However, representations of the dead, decaying, or mutilated body remained, until the first half of this century, part of shared narrations that created *meaning*, based upon Christianity or secular ideals such as justice, honor, glory, heroism, or the nation, that transcended the materiality of the corpse and the mere factuality of death. Powerful images of the tortured and mutilated body in Goya's "Los Desastres de la Guerra" (1810–20), his "Executions of May 3, 1808," and various sketches are among the early examples of this tradition in the modern arts that links pain and agony to ideals and makes them *comprehensible*. Despite a strong modernist tendency to uncouple aestheticized images of death and killing from moral discourse, pictorial representations of death continued to be integrated into a pictorial horizon and dominated by a philosophical tradition that can be traced back to Platonism. That tradition was centered around the idealist conception of the body as the destructible appearance of the eternal *eidos*. Even representations of the experience of the absurd, characteristic of World War I, were still related to a search for meaning and integrated in a metaphysical framework.

Photographs of dead bodies, including those of soldiers killed on battlefields prior to World War I, are rare and even during that war strict censorship prohibited the publication of such photographs save for few exceptions that could be used for the creation of meaning or propaganda. The first battlefields represented through the modern medium of photography were those of the Crimean War and the American Civil War. It is characteristic of the relationship between word and image in the middle of the nineteenth century that during the Crimean War the written word, in particular journalistic accounts in London newspapers, were considered more powerful and emotionally moving and had greater political impact on decisions about the continuation of the British involvement in the war than photographs.[19] Pictorial conventions of representing a battlefield were so strong that, in contrast to the "graphic" verbal representations of the horror of the battlefield and the extremely poor conditions at this distant front, photography created picturesque, rather than brutal or repulsive, images. Their "peacefulness" failed to convey a sense of the cruelty of a war at the threshold of modern warfare. At the same time, their picturesque character was a first step in the direction of abstraction.[20] The emptying of the moralizing and heroicizing gaze can be traced back to the photos of this war. While the photographs of the Crimean War aestheticized destruction and death on the battlefield, the photography of the American Civil War, while glorifying death by producing images of martyrs for freedom and equality, at the same time enforced the tendency toward emptying the gaze. It created the image of a nation at the threshold of modernity, entering into a future of the grand project of rationalization and abstraction.[21]

Photos taken by ordinary soldiers after 1916 represent a further step in the process of abstraction. They give expression to a new unconnectedness between the soldiers' bodies and the vast and empty space of the front. Photos are now dominated by a sense of structural disproportion between the individual and the destruction apparatus amassed in the zone of absolute danger.[22] Images speak the language of isolation and the bodies of the soldiers are often hardly visible in the overwhelming and empty landscape of destruction. Shortly after the end of the war, a number of photo albums were published which captured the emptiness and lack of orientation, in terms of both spatial and mental orientation, in a space which was emptied of all traditional characteristics of a landscape, and to which human senses no longer related. Sensuous perception was increasingly replaced with techniques designed to receive and quickly process visual and audible signals.

World War I gave rise to interpretations of technology not as a tool that offers the options of rejecting it or applying it in order to achieve certain ends, but as *techne*, as the mediation between humankind and the world to which there is no alternative and from which there is no escape.[23] Technology was no longer perceived as an object but a condition of existence. In Walter Benjamin's interpretation, images of the technological world, including, in particular, the modern battlefield perceived as a space for an unrestrained fusion of human action and technology, are celebrations of a new poverty of experience resulting from emptying the gaze of inherited cultural structures of perception. Technology is perceived as being inextricably implicated in the modern condition's destruction of the history of the gaze and in replacing it with a non-striated openness. A photograph then is "outside the zone of sensibility. A telescopic character is attached to it; one notices very clearly that the event is seen by a non-sensitive and in-vulnerable eye. It captures the flying bullet as well as the human being at the moment when he is torn to pieces by an explosion. And this has become our characteristic way of seeing; photography is nothing else but an instrument of this, our own character."[24]

Jünger makes his observations about the changing gaze with his typical attitude toward the new technology, namely a cool enthusiasm for the modern. The cool and disengaged relationship of the eye to the object of perception is an imitation of the camera's lens, not in terms of an act of will, but, as Jünger sees it, as an implication of a changed anthropological constellation. The human eye and the camera's lens are, in his view, elements of a relationship of interdependence from which there is no escape into a world free from technology, camera lenses, photographs, and unlimited reproduction. Indeed, after the gaze had fallen upon the first photograph, it was no longer possible to visualize and remember a world before that moment.[25] Jünger makes no attempt to systematize his insights into the new ways of seeing and reproducing which inevitably lead to a new position within reality. However, in his essays and contributions to collections of photographs devoted to the modern world,[26] he frequently refers to the consequences and implications this new condition has for the end of history and for remembering the past in entirely new ways. He argues consistently that modern imagery and the gaze are changing simultaneously and are increasingly ruled by emotionlessness, non-morality, repetitiveness, a preoccupation with the surface, and a fixation on the unique moment that is increasingly losing its shock character. The process of perception which, Jünger writes, is never innocuous or innocent, changes as a result of the emptying of the gaze under the conditions of the technological age. Photography both contributes and gives expression to a specifically new, that is, "cruel" *(grausam)*, way of seeing. The new gaze is driven, he observed in 1934, by a "curious" desire to change the character of living processes to that of a specimen.[27] He uses the word "Präparat," which could also refer to a prepared slide for microscopy or the work of a taxidermist. Jünger did not make his observations in isolation. Experimental psychology and philosophical anthropology provided categories for a systematic dealing with the same phenomena. Helmuth Plessner's "aesthesiology of the senses" prepared the ground for a theory of perception in which his observations in relation to the constitution of the field of vision were particularly pertinent for the entire complex addressed in Ernst Jünger's and Walter Benjamin's rudimentary media theory. Contemporaneous theories about a combination of the tactile and the visual resulting from an eye-hand interplay during the early phase of the genesis of perception led to the construction of the intervening gaze,[28] that was approached in terms of an anthropology of the senses but with no concern for the ethics of perception.

III

The collapse of a horizon of meaning for agony and death in photos of the extermination program signifies a fundamental rupture. However, these images can also be linked to a specific aspect of the development of visuality, namely abstraction. While the emergence of abstraction in images of war and violence can be traced back to the late nineteenth century, photographs of the extermination program on the Eastern front after 1941 can be read in terms of a further radicalization of these changes that effected the gaze, imagery, and ultimately, memory. Photographs no longer hid death nor was it shown as linked to transcendence. Traces of either a hidden ideal image of humanity or enthusiasm for the advance of a functional world of technology were now erased from the images. Their raw factuality and brutal nakedness were the product of a disengaged gaze and an abstraction emptied of all ethical content.

The order to shoot defenseless civilians, it has been reported, at first met with disbelief and rejection of the idea. "Policemen, not experienced with this type of work, real family men among them," a report from Poland in November 1939 says, "came close to a nervous breakdown when they realized that women and children ..." had to be shot.[29] But they obeyed and shot them. In an official photographer's report about the brutal massacres of Lithuanian Jews in Kowno in June 1941, a degree of surprise can still be sensed. He refers to the local population cheering.[30] Murderers, bloody iron bars and clubs in their hands, stated their motivation was revenge for injustices they claimed to have experienced themselves or had been told about by others. Others spoke of anti-bolshevist reactions. Sadism and emotional anti-Semitism were obviously driving forces behind such pogroms under the German military regime in the area. In his report, the photographer registers no protest and shows no sign of resistance, but neither does he express belief in the racist doctrines of the Nazi regime. Other comments demonstrate similar reactions of a weakly articulated distance and irresolute forms of repulsion. Comments made by two truck drivers and an accountant who became witnesses of mass executions in Paneriai demonstrate this very mixture of disbelief, repulsion, and feelings of discomfort, combined with curiosity.[31] They had their cameras ready and took photographs of the killing scene.

Photos and descriptions inform us about groups of soldiers positioned at the edge of the killing sites, often in elevated positions that provided an unrestrained field of vision, positions traditionally reserved for high ranking officers and associated with the "privileges" of power. The elevated position distanced from the actual shooting and put the soldier in a position of command. It created the *officer's perspective* in traditional wars associated with spatial separation. From their privileged position they watched for an hour or more and sometimes took photographs. Their position in the space of the killing as well as the arrangement in groups are of importance for defining their perspective. Peer pressure was undoubtedly important in this group constellation. The importance of pressure and seductions and also the wish to belong to a group should not be underestimated as motivations on the part of those who, as it was called in the code of the time, carried out their duty. The fear of being considered weak or cowardly or unworthy of the uniform are mentioned as reasons for watching and for shooting. Occasionally, policemen or soldiers were transferred for their "softness." Not everyone was keen to join the ranks of the killers; not everyone who became a perpetrator felt he had become a hero. Even under the impact of continuous racist brainwashing, alcohol was an important means for subduing emotions and weakening feelings of repulsion. There are reports of psychosomatic reactions (motor disorders, allergies, rashes, etc.). Under the circumstances, psychological ambivalence or emotional distance were difficult to express orally or put on paper, not only because of external and open pressures, but also because a code for such emotions was hardly available to the plumbers, painters, electricians, or policemen in these battalions. Thus, all the more care is needed in reading of the non-linguistic traces they left behind. The relationship of the photographers to their photos—and their "motifs"—is much more complex and ambiguous than that of murderous and one-dimensional ideologues to their victims.[32]

It has been argued that these photos were the object of a gaze driven by lust and a compulsion to watch pain and agony.[33] This reading of these photos as the realization of sadism and voyeurism operates within a reductionist framework, reducing them to documents of individual pathologies and perversion. This reading takes photos at face value and offers little insight in problems of a photo-history. Within the framework of psychoanalysis, these photos have been interpreted in terms of their fetish character. It is then the denial of the other as Jewishness that would make the believer in the cult of Aryan domination and the militaristic male adore, as his fetish, images of the extermination of the other.[34] While this interpretation takes care not to reduce the questions raised by these photos to the level of banalities of individual perversion, it presupposes the blood brotherhood of believers in racist and militaristic ideology as the subjects of the photo-history of violence and extermination. With the end of this ideology, the fetish would also disappear.

Photo albums, even more than individual photos, demonstrate that the wish to *document*, rather than to become a "hero" or a pathological sadism and a perverse desire to participate, through the camera, in the extermination program, was a more common motivation for taking photographs of scenes of violence and death. Lifting the camera, looking for an appropriate angle, setting the shutter speed, determining the distance, etc., kept eyes and minds occupied with the technical aspects of documenting. But what is meant by documentation when it was obvious that the photos later would be seen only by the photographer himself and a very narrow circle of those who could be trusted and from which even close relatives had to be excluded. It was rare, as the trial of SS-man Täubner demonstrates, to show such photos to others, as this could have had legal consequences. Their children later observed with amazement their fathers' silence in relation to their activities in the war. This silence corresponded to the hiding of photos, often even from close friends.[35] As a result of a policy of censorship during the Third Reich, these photos, from the moment the release button had been pressed were private memories; and even later after they had left the darkroom and become "real," they remained part of a small world of a secret imagery, not intended to be shown publicly or even to friends and relatives. And as a result of internalized censorship, they were often hidden even from the eyes of their producers, put out of sight in attics or deep drawers but not thrown away. These documenting images did not escape, to use a paradoxical phrase, the strategies of invisibility, carefully designed and applied by the organizers of the extermination. However, as far as the individual photographer was concerned, they were a product of fear, fear of loss through time. Documentation was, it is reasonable to conjecture, not a function of communication with others, but the result of a remarkable solipsism. As far as these photos are documents, they can be read as documents of the *fleeting self* behind the viewfinder representative of the fleeting self damaged by life under violent modernist conditions.

Experience teaches that memory is fleeting and unreliable. Literature of World War I was deeply concerned with the unreliability of the memory of even powerful images of battle and destruction. Over time, images stored in one's memory tend to change and fade and, with their sharpness, they lose not only their contours but also their "truth-value." This, rather than the lust of sadism on the part of pathological individuals, can be considered a more common motivation for taking photos and the inability to turn away the spellbound eye. These photos speak of a fascination with "reality." The desire to capture the "incredible" atrocities through fixed images, once and forever, sprang from the fear of losing control over one's own memory. The fear of being let down by one's own memory and of having no recourse to a stable and reliable source of imagery is complementary to the hope of securing, through the documentary quality of the photograph, an authority that will secure a position of mastery over memory in the future. With a loss of grasp of images once perceived, a piece of oneself will be lost. It is the belief in the magical qualities of the image, in contrast to its linguistic dimension, which is entrusted with the expectation of avoiding this apprehended loss. It is, paradoxically, this wish to make the self master over time and memory that turned images into a fetish which ruled over its producers. This fear turned the eyewitness into an accomplice.

This combination of fear and hope is the origin of a "neutralization" of perspective. Critical accounts of the history of the Third Reich customarily castigate the amorality and absence of resistance to the criminal political system. This absence can also be observed in the photo-history of the period. The photographic gaze was not, or only in rare exceptional circumstances, governed by motives of compassion, protest, or resistance against injustices, cruelties, and state-sanctioned crimes. In this context, the observation seems appropriate that pictures themselves do not and cannot convey moral positions. Photographs need a verbal context in order to make visible a certain attitude and value judgment in relation to their objects of representation. Photos taken in the camps or near the mass graves in eastern forests will become meaningful only in specific contexts created for seeing them. The justified critique of a lack of moral position and the absence of a will to resist the crimes of a criminal state can be extended to the photo-history of the Third Reich. However, this approach is in danger of turning into ritual unless it is prepared to take into account the conditions of photography as a medium and specific genre of visual representation. Photos do not resist and they are also little understood as actors or agents in criminal acts. Moral indifference of photographic images has to be seen in the context of the genre and its specific history from the Crimean War onwards. To ignore the specific modern space created by technology, perception, and representation, in favor of a moral and political interpretation of these photos, will remove them from time and subject them to an essentialist perspective. In order to make the social amorality of pictures visible, they need to be moved into the concrete contexts of their production and reception. Those contexts, however, were and are being destroyed in part by the photographic process itself.

Photographs of the war of extermination[36] were taken from a perspective of de-subjectivization. They presuppose an eye no longer clearly connected to the self of the photographer, but in search of a gaze that comes from a timeless and spaceless nowhere. Kant's idea of perceiving art through an attitude of pure disinterest, but now without "pleasure," seems to come to an unstable life in this gaze through the camera's viewfinder. This gaze from nowhere can possibly be understood as one last step in the process of rationalizing the gaze that Panofsky traced back to the invention of central perspective in the early modern period. Qualities that, for the mythical eye, are attached to distinguished sites and sacred or damned places evaporate before the gaze trained in rational seeing and find nothing to hold on to in a homogenized space of geometrical lines.

This abstraction can also be seen as the reversal of the inner eye's gaze upon the utopian space of a literary and philosophical tradition. The spaces of utopias were built upon political and moral positions and a spatial concretization of the imagined good society. Looking onto this imagined site of the future, the self of the early modern period, ruled by trust in the historical process and the just power of reason, created an imagined striated space well prepared for the projection of ideals among which it moved with ease. The gaze from the modern nowhere, however, is predicated upon a weak and emptied self that perceives of itself within an equally emptied space around it and is driven by fear. From the early theories of abstraction onward, it has been argued that it was anxiety and a fundamental experience of loss which led away from mimetic practices and created the opposition to empathy.[37] The desire to secure, under the condition of modernity, a precarious identity gave rise to abstraction and the emergence of a gaze from nowhere. Photography is employed as a means to this end and can be read as a symptom of the dialectics of anxiety and aggression, weakness and violence. Before incredible cruelties, the emptied gaze from nowhere assumes power, not over the actions in front of the eye, but over the threatened identity of the "I" behind the camera. As long as a reality which threatens the self by bursting open every horizon of experience and expectation and by contradicting all ideals of ethics and images of humankind—as long as that reality can be subjected to the organizing and framing gaze from behind the disinterested technical apparatus, the "I" can harbor the illusion of being present, yet not being involved and remaining free from moral responsibility. By emptying the gaze, the "I" can nurture the hope of maintaining, now and over time, its coherence. In all future situations of doubt it will be possible to refer back to the fixed image and the power of the photographic process that produced it, framed, of an unequivocal spatial order and unquestionable perspective and, at the same time, emptied of values significant for the space of morality. The trigger of the camera is being pressed in the expectation that the view on the mechanically produced simulacrum will later produce a security of knowing, free from the whims of subjectivism and in accordance with the ideal of a rationalized gaze. The aim was to be able to see *what really happened*, reducing human beings to *things* and *movements* in space, again and again. This return of a belief in the power of abstraction, characteristic of primitive art, and now defined in terms of modern technology's capacity to document, is driven by a weak self with no confidence left in its power over time and space and in need of orientation and cohesion.

In these photographs we perceive again the radical disconnection of bodies and space that first appeared in World War I photography. These bodies are shown as not belonging. The stabilization of subjectivity through acts of separating the space of the camera and a space of objects in front of it seemed to be supported by the documenting process of photography. Images taken from the perspective of nowhere are an expression of the hope of duplicating, with the camera, a reality from which the photographer is distanced by a clear line of separation and upon which his camera can therefore impose its own order. It is the emptied, abstracted space that first appeared in images of the front after 1916 that now recurs, creating conditions that turn bodies into helpless objects. The position of the photographer leads to the illusion that the self behind the viewfinder is outside and therefore in control of this space. He wishes not to belong and trusts that the camera will position him opposite this world. The desire to maintain a space for the self that remains unaffected by the documented horrors creates the necessity of emptying the gaze by desensitizing and de-corporealizing it. Pain and agony, which are corporeal experiences, are being relegated to a space on the other side of the binary divide and subjected to a gaze that, through abstraction, creates the distance necessary for maintaining a position of dominance over a threatening reality. The space representing the self is signified by photos of soldiers in clean uniforms, in front of buildings or in streets, at ease yet in well-ordered lines, displaying a composure of body and determination of mind, expressed through the eyes. Firing squads are arranged in clear lines and the perverse legality of actions is visualized through the discipline and order in which the soldiers' bodies appear in the spatial constellations. Soldiers in these photographs represent military discipline in well-ordered arrangements of straight lines, architecture, machines, and other solid structures of the given system and in stark visual contrast to the contourless gray of open landscapes or the dirt of freshly dug up trenches, and the masses of bodies, their contours often blurred.

The combination of fear and hope, together with the construction of the self through gaining power over memory, creates an empty gaze, morally indifferent to the objects represented. It is not the nature or the needs of the "motif," but the desires of an emptied subjectivity that direct the view through the viewfinder and later toward the developed photo. The photographer's position in relation to his object is always one of power and privilege. In the case of the photographer of violence in the extermination program, this power was limitless. The photographers themselves seem to have had no sense of this position. Their photos show no signs of shame or anxiety, and written sources do not speak of inhibitions. This absence is indicative. The inhibition to represent human beings in images has its roots in the magical thought that the image will contain or even take away "something" of the represented person. In the eyes of these photographers, the bodies in front of the lens are stripped of all qualities. They are not perceived within a "human space" and therefore not as human beings, but as objects and soulless things. These photographers seem to have lost a sense of the social aspect of the shared space that goes beyond its spatiality. As a consequence, they have no sensitivity concerning the ties which seeing another person necessarily always creates, even when the photographer's gaze is not returned by the "motif." The eye behind the viewfinder hardens in analogy to the camera lens.[38] There are a number of photos of naked bodies at the edges of pits moments before their deaths and a photo from Auschwitz shows naked women being herded down a "road" between the huts.[39] Among the issues raised by such photos, the one concerning the person behind the camera is particularly alarming. In the face of ultimate degradation, who could lift a camera? The moral question is at the same time an aesthetic one: what is it that these photographers saw? And what is the technique of seeing that enabled them to turn this event in the life of human beings into a scene fit for photography? Their ways of seeing must have broken with previous ways of perception, embedded in morally defined subjectivity, and transformed the eye into a neutral instrument for registering movements. This can be interpreted as an extension of the perspective of early war photography exemplified in the aesthetisizing, through abstraction, of images of destruction in the Crimean War. The camera seems to have been the adequate machine for the emptying of the gaze and it is tempting to speculate about the optical qualities of the small viewfinder of the cameras of the time as a prerequisite for this transformation. Photography, even as a tourist's mechanized form of taking snapshots, seems to retain rudimentary elements of making visual experiences. The world is perceived as segments of framed pictures and the gaze is directed by the question as to how it will later look as a framed small print. Reality changes in the act of perception through the eye of a photographer and becomes, through selecting and framing, a part of the imagined world of the self. Any experience of reality and emotions seems to be excluded by the photography of massacres. It has been claimed that sadism and a pleasure in seeing others suffer was the driving motivation. While sadism cannot be dismissed as a motivation, many of these photos are hardly suitable for creating perverse pleasures. They are the result not of the evil eye, nor of the understanding or affectionate eye of a participant observer, but of an emptied gaze of absolute disengagement. These photographers must have been unaffected by the age-old assumption that every gaze will be returned and convinced themselves that they would never be struck by the gaze of their objects.

Photographers participated in the creation of spaces of destruction by developing a technique of total control through a one-way gaze that could never be responded to because it defined the other as no longer a part of a shared space and the self as being in total control over space and time. Such a sense of absolute power spells death to the object and, in the way Ernst Jünger spoke of, turns living processes into a specimen or a slide preparation, thereby relegating it to a space outside one's life. These photos provide no justification for the concept of the uniqueness of the Holocaust or of anti-Semitism as the mental condition behind the extermination of the European Jewry. We are confronted with the same gaze in photos of Jewish, Russian, Greek, and other "groups" of victims. It is the atmosphere of shouting, hectic activity, distorted body movements, corporeal signs of ultimate degradation, gestures of force and hysteria together with the all pervasive emptiness of a gaze from nowhere that is the common denominator of this photography. Despite the specificities shared by sites like Auschwitz, Treblinka, Sobibor, and other camps, there is no separate visual space for the extermination of Jews. The visual representations of violence and extermination create a space of destruction without discriminating between groups or individuals. Their iconography is one of contempt for life displaying no shades and no distinguishing lines.

A misunderstanding of the ambivalent character of photography was at the center of this change of perception. The demand for control over time and memory led to an unchecked trust in the extra-linguistic dimension of photography. Recent structuralist and semiological theories of photography have spurned iconographic interpretations of images, emphasizing exclusively the linguistic character of visual representations. Following the 'linguistic turn' in social and cultural theories, the photograph was defined as a codified representation that could be completely decodified, no residue remaining. It seems to me that, in contradistinction to this dominant position, photographic representations of violence since World War I[40] and, in particular, images of unlimited violence to the human body during and ever since World War II, defy this claim. The medium of photography, possibly more than other more traditional media, escapes the thesis of an entirely linguistic structure pertaining to all media. It retains an element of the pictorial that cannot be translated into words and is closely related to the "silence" that is frequently asked for or considered an inevitable consequence of unspeakable horror. In his theory of perception, Rudolf Arnheim struggled with the possibilities of thinking in pictures and the concept of intuition. Freed from the harmonizing assumptions of gestaltpsychology, his theory of visual perception as "pattern perception" may well provide a key for the understanding of photographic images without reducing them to coded linguistic messages. He makes the claim that "imagery can fulfill its unique function ... only if it goes beyond a set of standardized symbols."[41] He interprets the photograph as the presence of reality, "whose irrational, incompletely defined aspects challenge the image-maker's desire for visually articulate form." It is this irrational quality of the optical material that, according to Arnheim, exerts its influence not when the viewer recognizes the documentary quality of an image, "but is actually more manifest in highly abstract photographs in which objects have been reduced to pure shapes."[42]

Photographs are made with the knowledge that they are the products of a process that combines the mechanics of a machine and chemical reactions and, until recently, there was a clear line dividing an authentic from a manipulated or falsified picture. This relationship between analogous pictorial documentation and an interpretive reading of the represented objects delineates the new, technical medium from the traditional media. Technology led to a return of the magic promise of an unmediated access to nature.[43] Even the master-mind of a semiological approach to photography, Roland Barthes, retains traces of a non-semiological interpretation of photography. He writes of a paradox of photography resulting from the co-existence of two conflicting messages, one without a code and another one with a code that is its "art" or "rhetoric" or "script." He goes on to argue that the codified message in photography, its constructed "rhetoric," may be secondary to its uncodified message.[44] In his view, the two dimensions of photography always seem to be subjected to a hierarchy. In his earlier work, the uncodified, iconic character of the photograph seems to be secondary to its being codified, whereas his last book, *Camera lucida*, seems to reverse the hierarchy by collecting observations which place emphasis on the pictorial analogy of photography.[45]

The question concerning the subject equipped and emotionally ready to record massacres seems to lead in a different direction. These photographers used their cameras in an attempt to produce images with the power of recording and demonstrating without language interfering in this self-sufficient act. Their image of the image was one beyond a need for language and the time dimension associated with narration. The "artlessness" of these crude photos is significant and goes beyond that of most amateur photography. The photographs demonstrate an unusual degree of documentary neutrality and a magical belief in the directness of representation.

In an early essay, Barthes invoked the term "mythical" for this type of photo, displaying a belief in the pure denotative status of the picture. This belief in the possibility of a perfect mechanical-chemical analog is associated with an ethical paradox. He who strives to be "neutral" or "objective," Barthes remarks, "aims at copying reality painstakingly exact as if the analogy was a power resisting the introduction of values."[46] However, Barthes argues, as a result of the dualistic character of its visual structure that makes it equally connotative and denotative, photos are simultaneously objective and charged with values. Ignoring the dualistic character of images and understanding them exclusively as analogs should not be interpreted as just an attempt to mysticize the image. Instead, it is a constitutive element in this century's revolt against the logos, against the rationality of a modern culture built upon an unrestricted exchange of goods and symbols. The belief in the authority of unequivocal pictures, to which memory can always return, because its reality remains present all the time and without communication, appeals to the ultimate power of eternal presence, in contrast to the fleeting insecurities of language and time. The motto of extermination photography could read: Against communication! It defines the photograph *as nature* in which the triangular relationship of photography is suspended and time is arrested. As a result, the photographic image would exist prior to linguistic constructions and give rise to the hope of creating a memory removed from historical time. In it, the moment of shooting the picture becomes eternal by being turned into nature.

Photos of the extermination are rarely embedded in texts and their originators' comments are laconic and short: "wonderful times" *(schöne Zeiten)*.[47] This too represents a deviation from the modern tendency of the signifier dominating the signified, a tendency particularly noticeable in the unlimited multiplication of images in photojournalism and the modern media. The belief in an extra-linguistic power of the image extends into recent interviews with those who took photographs at the time. Apart from meager technical comments about the when, where, and how, they have nothing to say about their photos. These pictures have, in contrast to a common view, no propaganda value. They do not participate in the ideological suasions propagating war and violence, and a racist message is also not their most prominent feature. Jews, Poles, and other Slavs, partisans, and all sorts of suspicious elements are represented. The photos show no explicit or hidden trace of resistance against the violence represented. But the fact that these representations of violence are themselves of a violent nature is due not to an ideological choice on the part of the photographers (there is no question that photographs of racism and sadism openly propagating violence also exist, but they are of no concern to this essay), but rather to the disengaged gaze. These images are the product of a process of de-corporealizing the gaze rather than a deliberate choice of perspective or arrangement of motifs. The web of connections that make the world outside the frame interfere with that inside the individual picture vanishes. The frame becomes an absolute line of segregation and the image is not dissimilar to a preparation to be studied under a microscope. These photographs bar the gaze from perceiving one image as a metamorphosis of others, from "seeing" an intertexture. They isolate the objects of representation by breaking their conjunctions to a point where the gaze begins to see objects within the picture frame not seen before, arrangements of objects unknown and things instead of human bodies. The severing of bonds which the gaze is educated to perceive without ever being aware of their presence, prevents the new gaze from adding to the image that which is absent from it and which links it to human experience or ideals. Emptying the gaze is identical with emptying the image. Nakedness is nakedness and bodies are bodies, nothing else.[48] The view from a non-striated nowhere prevents a relation toward the object in front of the lens and can therefore be one of emotionless violence.

IV

Little detailed information is available about the later fate of photos taken by German soldiers on the Eastern front, how frequently they were sent or taken home, how common it was to collect them in photo albums, in what kind of order these albums were commonly arranged, how frequently and by whom such albums were viewed. There is no base for the assumption that they were commonly passed around and contributed to the creation of heroes.[49] It seems doubtful that pictures of murderous violence were shown outside a small circle of callous Nazi believers. Their idea of a hero faded away quickly and, in spite of some alarming aspects of postwar German collective memory, it made no significant contribution to the image of the war.

Postwar history turned into an illusion any expectation on the part of war photographers of using their photographs as a window that could, at any time and in an act of will, be opened to provide a view onto an arrested moment of the past. This illusion can be interpreted in terms of a significant misconception of power. Photos of the extermination were based on the idea of power and powerlessness as absolute oppositions, removed from linguistic coding and communication. The world of these photos is silent in a way that differs fundamentally from the silence characteristic of most pictures. A dialogue between the persons depicted in these photos and the person looking at them is impossible and this impossibility was anticipated in the mind of the photographer at the time of pressing the release button. The violence and terror of the modern battlefield served as a model for one's own power. It is known from numerous sources that modern technology, the plane, tank, machine-gun, produced dreams of omnipotence matched by equally strong images of absolute helplessness vis-á-vis the power of the *materiel.* Fantasies of an unlimited power of those in command of the technology of destruction were complemented by the powerlessness of the victims, also intensified to the level of the absolute. This military and political definition of power turned into a personal attitude. Its consequences can be traced in the pictures taken at the extermination sites. They result from a misguided view of the nature of what photographers do with their cameras. The power of the camera over its objects is that of a triangular relationship that implicates the "I" behind the camera and the person in front of it, as well as the eyes that will, with the distance of time, look at the photo. The power of the photographing master finds its limit in the photographed slave, to vary Hegel, and, in addition, a third point of reference, the later viewer distanced by time and space, needs to be included. However, the claim to absolute power over life and death which was a driving force behind the terror system, also affected the attitudes of those involved in it, changing to an ever-increasing degree their view of time, space, and the other.

The photographer's gaze of abstraction was believed to be linked to no identified place. It was supposed to originate from nowhere and it corresponded to the expectation of a complementary gaze later to be directed onto the framed picture. However, an attempt to look at photos from a perspective of diffused indifference has to struggle with the necessarily linguistic nature of reading an image. The double nature of pictures requires a verbal representation of their visual representations and this process brings to bear all the problems of translation as an interpretive technique that is always predicated on time and changing contexts. The two meanings of the verb "remember" are never clearly separated. To remember as a subjective act (I remember a certain event) and to remember, in terms of an inter-subjective and communicative process, in the sense of making somebody else remember, i.e., to use language in order to make another person recollect the event, interrelate and collapse into one. Taking a photo with the intention of documenting through an image is based on the desire to create an identity of the object and its representation which can be brought to life every time the photo is looked at. While it is obvious that others will not necessarily be able to "see" this identity and therefore their question, "What is this?" is to be expected, it is less obvious that this question is also being asked by the person who took the photograph. Over time, facts tend to be forgotten. The memory of place, time, and details of situations fades away, creating uncertainty and the question: "What is it that I photographed at the time?" Further: over time, one's own intention becomes blurred and may no longer be accessible leading to the question: "What was it that I wished to photograph at the time?" Any attempt to "see again" what a photo represents is inextricably intertwined with the biographical moment of the subject's present. This translation from one time into another time and from one medium into another medium through a dialogue or inner monologue will inevitably destabilize the pictorial contents of memory. As time passes, the documentary qualities of pictures are reduced and looking at them with hindsight inevitably turns them into memories interlaced with a network of fantasies, images, imagined and remembered, wishful thinking, and projections. The "texture of memory," to use the term James Young introduced in his discussion of Holocaust memorials,[50] reconstitutes every detail of the photo. Even the most basic material details of the image can be "seen" only within the horizon of the lived present, which gives rise to the question directed at an image—which I know was taken by me: "What do I see?" Looking at a photo with hindsight will necessarily create a tension between the present gaze and the past gaze of which the "I" has only an increasingly vague memory. It is this tension that subverts precisely the stabilization of identity hoped for in the moment of taking the picture. The nakedness of the photographed *objects* is no longer the same nakedness, and the bodies perceived at the time of taking the photos are no longer the same bodies, because the process of remembering inevitably impregnates facticity with the interpretive and imaginative. In visualizing nakedness and spaces, bodies, and movements by looking at a picture, the brute iconic facts are inextricably intertwined with the changing self. The domination of the facticity of the photos is not identical with the expected mastery of the memory but, on the contrary, cannot prevent the implication of the self through an integration of images into the flow of time filled with linguistic discourse. Irrespective of moral attitudes toward their contents, the photos contribute to the creation of a memory in which time is not arrested, but transforms images of the past into images of the present.

It is precisely this evaporation of the solid picture into elements of fluid stories that must be dreaded by the documentary mind. Belief in pure documentation, signified by the raw qualities of the pictures, promised to save memories from the impact of time, which leads to the transformation of the iconic content into a language for the future. However, with time, moving from one signifying system to another one becomes inevitable. At the time of taking the photo, the photographer could know nothing about that future save that (even under the assumption of a fascist victory) it would not be the present language of war and extermination. The photographers were fearful of time which, after the end of the *period of action* and the return of a *period of interpretation* would inevitably subject stable contours to a process of dissolution. The emptied gaze from the wordless nowhere was supposed to shield against these effects of time. Against it, emphasis on the absolute power of the iconic dimension seemed to offer protection on which the inflexible construction of the self was dependent. The gaze on the photos, therefore, had to imitate the gaze through the viewfinder. Time has to be removed from it so that it can acquire qualities of primitive and unchanging space captured by the inanimate nature of the lens. However, photography's consumption of time is only partial, since the one dimension of the photograph cannot be had without the other being activated. The tension between the two dimensions of the image is repeated as a conflict between two mutually exclusive views of photographs. To the extent to which images of terror and extermination are the product of the emptied gaze of the photographer, they require an equally emptied gaze for viewing them, unaffected by language and time. The conjunction of the (e)motionlessness of a fixed iconography and the space of an inanimate view is irreconcilably opposed to a reading of the images in a language of the world outside the space of terror and the extermination. Attempts to block the integration of such images into the flow of time require a denial of reality, e.g., the primitive obstinacy of ideological self-delusion or denial of events, or the less threatening but wide-spread strategies of rejection, or subtle techniques of manipulating remembrance and forgetting.[51]

One striking example of the collision of these different ways of dealing with photographs would be juridical discourse. In the courtroom, photos that represent this specific gaze and expectation of an onlooker's perspective are turned into evidence by implementing them in the linguistic contexts of reconstructing murder and other crimes in the code of a time removed from that in which the photos originated. There can be no doubt regarding the justification of this practice for legal purposes. Murder must be called murder and prosecuted regardless of time. However, apart from the pragmatic requirements of the system of justice, there is a problem of the hermeneutics of interpreting photos by translating their iconic content into a code that was absent from the image in the viewfinder at the time when the shutter opened. Based upon assumptions concerning cultural invariabilities, this approach is always fraught with the danger of erasing time from memory defining it in terms of unchanging space. In so far as time is being arrested in the reading of a photo as legal evidence, it is not dissimilar to the mode of seeing envisaged by amateur photographers who took the photos. The decisive difference being the point in time that determines the grammar of the gaze and, by implication, the moral system of evaluation. In both cases, it can be argued, the reading of the images will make no contribution to memory, which is inextricably linked to time. The pain and agony of the victims become visible as soon as these pictures are read within narratives which do not erase time, but rather construct time as memory. The need to integrate the pictures into codes of the present in order to create a memory, points to the limits of mere reproduction. To "show" pictures will not transcend the speechlessness significant of most pictures of the extermination. But another question seems even more pressing. Under the conditions of the electronic age, is it still possible to experience time as memory? Has the power and pervasiveness of the world of images grown to the extent that it simply absorbs any image of the past, robbing it of its own language?

Looking at photos inevitably implicates the perceiving eye and therefore has its effects on the gaze of perpetrators and photographers as well. Despite all strategies of rejection and denial, the gaze of the past cannot be retained unaffected. The desire to produce justification is itself already a factor of change.[52] In the process of changing the perspective, the images of massacres themselves are a contributing force. Despite the isolation of the killing sites, in the east and behind barbed wire, and despite all attempts to reduce their visual representation to bare physical nature, an impact of these images on the construction of the space of the self was inevitable. Even the brutal act of separation produced at the same time a situation of complicity, tearing down the invisible walls of separation. The photographers who were spatially distanced from the killing, hidden behind their cameras, produced a world of signs shared by actors and victims. In contrast to their intentions, their images of murder and violence contribute to constituting a reality in which it is not possible to associate images of violence with the other while the "I" continues to identity with absolute power on the other side of the dividing line. A desired separation between a world of objects in front of the lens—identified with a space of death, filth, and pain—and the space of the self—offering the freedom to look away or take photos and create an order in one's own image—is continuously subverted by the images themselves.[53] Their iconic content, changing under the changed conditions of the time after Auschwitz, inevitably contributed to reshaping the space of the self. Their mere presence leads to disintegrating the construction of a motionless stare and destabilizing the "I" hiding behind it. The maintenance of a dividing line between the self and the images of a past which, with every glimpse, is turned into present images, would require a time machine capable of producing the motionlessness of an antiquarian mind that substitutes for memory a walled-in space outside of time. As Michael Geyer and Miriam Hansen observe, a "German memory" cannot be considered separate from "Jewish memory." "One memory will be implicated in the other's story, as long as there is a German and a Jewish identity, and as long as both sides are able to tell their stories...."[54]

In opposition to this inevitable implication, techniques of radical exclusion are indeed practiced in the perception of pictures representing the war of extermination. The producers of amateur films in *Mein Krieg* comment on their own films as if they were documents of an ethnological expedition of the past made by others. In their commentary they do not participate in the world of this distant space of a past that is allegedly not theirs. In a more radical withdrawal of memory from the self, the authenticity of the very films and photos that were made with the aim of pure documentation is being denied. The rhetorical strategy of the "Auschwitz lie" is not only a politically motivated falsification, but the paradoxical consequence of the desire to seal off, against the impact of time and language, a mentality, removed from time and language, that gave rise to the emptied gaze from nowhere. Under the conditions of the world after the war, a separation of these spaces is no longer a question of the mode of representation, but creates the necessity of denying the images.[55] The denial of the authenticity of signs is the consequence of a development in which the construction of a self based upon strategies of segregation can no longer be maintained through exclusive modes of image formation, but only through radical negation of the sign as the signifier of a "lost" world. Photography appeared to be the ideal medium for the construction of a world of visual signs perceived from the perspective of a de-corporealized gaze that registers without seeing. As soon as this expectation turned out to be an illusion, strategies needed to be developed that offered protection against the unexpected impact of the images. The "I" of the inanimate gaze had to be rescued from the consequences of its own actions. This required a closing of the eyes.

Notes

1. A thoughtful example is Gertrud Koch, *Die Einstellung ist die Einstellung. Visuelle Konstruktion des Judentums* (Frankfurt: 1991). "Einstellung" is the German word for both attitude and film shot.
2. Dagmar Barnouw, "Konfrontation mit dem Grauen. Alliierte Schuldpolitik 1945," in *Merkur* 554 (May 1995): 390–401, puts emphasis on questions of guilt and the victors forcing the vanquished to acknowledge it.
3. Klaus Theweleit, *Männerphantasien*, vol. 2 (Frankfurt: 1978).
4. Dieter Reifarth and Viktoria Schmidt-Linsenhoff, "Die Kamera der Täter," in *Vernichtungskrieg. Verbrechen der Wehrmacht, 1941–1944,* ed. Hannes Heer and Klaus Naumann (Hamburg: 1995), 475–503, 477.
5. Ibid., 499–502.
6. Gerhard Schönberner, *Der gelbe Stern. Die Judenvernichtung in Europa* (Frankfurt: 1991 [1st ed. Munich 1960]), 7 and 9.
7. Schönberner, *Der gelbe Stern,* 10.
8. In an essay concerned with the attitudes of common soldiers in Greece, which appears in this volume (Chapter 7), Mark Mazower pursues this very question. He quotes responses from soldiers after a massacre in 1943, when soldiers carried out the orders to kill the entire population of a small village in retaliation for partisan activities. Although in this and other instances the orders to shoot civilians were carried out, the emotional effects seem to have been devastating and some soldiers' protest fell little short of mutiny. See also Mark Mazower, "Militärische Gewalt und national-sozialistische Werte," in Heer and Naumann, *Vernichtungskrieg*, 157–190.
9. Schönberner, *Der gelbe Stern,* 10f.
10. See, however, Gertrud Koch's short essay on the subject with the aim of closing the gap between the originators of propaganda and those manipulated: "Täuschung und Evidenz in gestellten Fotos aus dem Getto von Lodz," in Koch, *Die Einstellung ist die Einstellung*, 170–184.
11. Ernst Klee, Willi Dressen, and Volker Riese, eds., *"Schöne Zeiten." Judenmord aus der Sicht der Täter und Gaffer* (Frankfurt: 1989), 202.
12. A fine example of an analysis of emotional ambivalences and twisted motivations behind a massacre is provided by Michael Geyer in this volume (Chapter 8). See also "'Es muß daher mit schnellen und drakonischen Maßnahmen durchgegriffen werden.' Civitella in Val di Chiana am 29. Juni 1944" in Herr and Naumann, *Vernichtungskrieg*, 208–238.

13. Ernst Klee and Willi Dressen, *"Gott mit uns." Der deutsche Vernichtungskrieg im Osten 1939–1945* (Frankfurt: 1989), 140.
14. Shoshana Felman, "Film as Witness: Claude Lanzmann's *Shoah*," in Geoffrey Hartman, ed., *Holocaust Remembrance: The Shapes of Memory* (Cambridge, Mass.: 1994), 90–103, 98, 92.
15. Shoshana Felman, "Film as Witness," 92.
16. Ibid., 93.
17. Rudolf Arnheim's theory of perception and imagery, based upon gestalt-psychology, had a considerable impact on the debate in the U.S. and made the position of the pictorialists popular. Based on research in brain physiology and related disciplines, the pictorialists' views have enjoyed a growing strength during recent years, and, more than once, they claimed to have finally resolved the problem that has been at the center of philosophical reflection ever since Plato. Rudolf Arnheim, *Art and Visual Perception: A Psychology of the Creative Eye* (Berkeley and Los Angeles: 1954); Stephen M. Kosslyn, *Image and Brain: The Resolution of the Imagery Debate* (Cambridge, Mass., London: 1994). To mention two more examples of the ongoing debate: W. J. T. Mitchell, *Iconology: Image, Text, Ideology* (Chicago, London: 1986); Rosalind Krauss, *The Optical Unconscious* (Cambridge, Mass.: 1993).
18. Taking an unequivocal stand on the question of guilt is a necessary prerequisite for approaching the perspective of those implicated in the extermination program.
19. Lawrence James, *1854–1856. Crimea: The War with Russia from Contemporary Photographs* (New York: 1981).
20. Bernd Hüppauf, "The Emergence of Modern War Imagery in Early Photography" in *History and Memory* 5, no. 1 (1993): 130–151.
21. Alan Trachtenberg, "Albums of War: On Reading Civil War Photographs," in *Representations* 9 (1989), associates the Civil War with the emerging industrialization.
22. "Todeszone" is the term used by Ernst Jünger and other observers of the new tendencies. See Cornelia Vismann, "Starting from Scratch: Concepts of Order in 'No Man's Land,'" in Bernd Hüppauf, ed., *War, Violence and the Modern Condition* (Berlin, New York: 1997), 46–64.
23. Heidegger's concept of technology ("Die Frage nach der Technik," 1953) benefited from his reading of Jünger's *Der Arbeiter.* See Günter Figal, "Über die Linie und über 'Die Linie,'" in Hans-Harald Müller and Harro Segeberg, eds., *Ernst Jünger im 20. Jahrhundert* (Munich: 1995), 181–197.
24. Ernst Jünger, "Über den Schmerz" in *Essays I, Werke* vol. 5 (Stuttgart: 1963), 149–198; 188.
25. Ernst Jünger, *Der Arbeiter. Herrschaft und Gestalt* (Stuttgart: 1982), 129.
26. He was the editor of photographic collections devoted to the war (*Krieg und Krieger* [Berlin: 1930]; *Das Antlitz des Weltkrieges. Fronterlebnisse deutscher Soldaten* [Berlin: 1930]; *Luftfahrt ist not!* [1931]) and was involved in the edition of a new type of "picture book" for adults that tried to capture not the essence but the physiognomy of the time: Ferdinand Bucholz, ed., *Der gefährliche Augenblick. Eine Sammlung von Bildern und Berichten* (Berlin: 1931); Edmund Schultz, ed., *Die veränderte Welt. Eine Bilderfibel unserer Zeit* (Breslau: 1933).
27. Ernst Jünger, "Über den Schmerz": "Es wohnt uns ein seltsames und schwer zu beschreibendes Bestreben inne, dem lebendigen Vorgang den Charakter des Präparats zu verleihen." (189).
28. Helmuth Plessner, *Anthropologie der Sinne* (Frankfurt: 1980).

29. *Sittengeschichte des Zweiten Weltkriegs*, ed. Dr. Andreas Gaspar et al. (Hanau), 200.
30. Klee et al.,*"Schöne Zeiten,"* 31f.
31. Ibid., 38–45.
32. Goldhagen offers no interpretation of the revolting statements he quotes. But can they be taken at face value?
33. Reifarth and Schmidt-Linsenhoff, "Die Kamera der Täter": "Diese Fotografien dokumentieren ... Schaulust und Schauzwang der Täter als weitverbreitete psychische Disposition" (p. 499).
34. Klaus Theweleit, *Männerphantasien,* 2:341.
35. While the amateur cameramen during the interviews in *Mein Krieg* show clear signs of pride in their cameras and small archives, they also make it obvious that the films had not been watched for a long time. *Mein Krieg*, a documentary film by Harriet Eder and Thomas Kufus (1990); a short comment on this extraordinary document is provided by Omer Bartov in *The American Historical Review* 97, no. 4 (October 1992): 1155–1157.
36. For historical documents, see Gerd R. Ueberschär und Wolfram Wette, eds., *Der deutsche Überfall auf die Sowjetunion. Unternehmen Barbarossa 1941* (Frankfurt: 1991).
37. This is Wilhelm Worringer's argument in *Abstraktion und Einfühlung* (Munich: 1911). Fusing Worringer's view with Nietzsche's critique, Horkheimer and Adorno (*Dialektik der Aufklärung*, 1947) place emphasis on abstraction's power of domination over nature and the self. Yet another concept of abstraction is at the center of gestaltpsychology and recent theories of perception and visual thinking. A clarification of the concept is necessary but beyond the scope of this essay.
38. This was one of Ernst Jünger's constantly recurring observations of changes induced by technical "aids" for observation during World War I.
39. Examples are: Schönberner, *Der gelbe Stern,* 125–137; Gaspar et al., *Sittengeschichte des Zweiten Weltkrieges,* 205, 635, 645.
40. See Bernd Hüppauf, "Kriegsfotografie," in Wolfgang Michalka, ed., *Der Erste Weltkrieg. Wirkung, Wahrnehmung, Analyse* (Munich: 1994), 875–909.
41. Rudolf Arnheim, "On the Nature of Photography," in R. A., *New Essays on the Psychology of Art* (Berkeley: 1986), 102–114, 111f.
42. Arnheim, "Photography," 112.
43. For a challenging discussion of the tensions between the linguistic dimension of images (*Versprachlichung*) and their mimetic character as developed by Adorno and other theoreticians of Critical Theory, see Koch, *Die Einstellung ist die Einstellung*, esp. 24–52.
44. Roland Barthes, "The Photographic Message," in R. B., *Image, Music, Text* (New York: 1977), 15–31; 19.
45. Roland Barthes, *Camera Lucida* (New York: 1981).
46. Barthes, "Photographic Message," 20.
47. See also the captions of individual photos and albums reproduced in this volume.
48. "Hell" and "inferno" are terms often used in reference to the extermination camps (Steiner, Weiss, and others). This is problematic since, in religious and literary traditions, they are closely linked to "heaven" and a concept of justice. By uncoupling them from the idea of transcendence, they lose their meaning. Over Auschwitz there was, however, only a sky, and when it darkened, it was the result of smoke from cremating dead bodies.
49. Schönberner, *Der gelbe Stern*, 10.

50. James E. Young, *The Texture of Memory: Holocaust Memorials and Meaning* (New Haven and London: 1993). Young's "hope to reinvigorate otherwise amnesiac stone settings with a record of their own lives in the public mind" (ix) is an aim diametrically opposed to the expectation embodied in the amateur photos.
51. See Heinz Pust, "Als Kriegsgefangener in der Sowjetunion," in Wolfgang Benz and Angelika Schardt, eds., *Kriegsgefangenschaft* (Munich: 1960); Wolfgang Benz, "The Persecution and Extermination of the Jews in the German Consciousness," in John Milfull, ed., *Why Germany? National Socialist Anti-Semitism and the European Context* (Providence, Oxford: 1993), 91–104.
52. Missing photos and erased captions in albums offer themselves for careful interpretation beyond the mere wish to destroy legal evidence.
53. The inanimate eye of the perpetrator had its complement in the emotional emptiness which, in order to be able to survive, prisoners of the camps developed. In Claude Lanzmann's *Shoah*, Abraham Bomba, a Treblinka survivor who had "worked" at the gas chamber, says that "it was very hard to feel anything, because working there day and night between dead people, between bodies, your feeling disappeared, you were dead. You had no feeling at all." (Claude Lanzmann, *Shoah: An Oral History of the Holocaust. The Complete Text of the Film* [New York: 1985], 116).
54. Michael Geyer and Miriam Hansen, "German-Jewish Memory and National Consciousness," in Geoffrey Hartman, ed., *Holocaust Remembrance: The Shapes of Memory* (Oxford: 1994), 175–190. Nadine Fresco appropriately observes that denying the Holocaust requires a continuous and obsessive involvement in the history of the destruction of the European Jewry. "Indeed, their radical denial forces them, paradoxically, to return constantly to the fact of genocide as an intolerable but inevitable reference point." Nadine Fresco, "Negating the Dead," in Hartman, *Holocaust Remembrance*, 190.
55. An early example is Udo Walendy, *Bild-"Dokumente" für die Geschichtsschreibung?* (Vlotho: 1973). The "Auschwitz-lie" industry offers a wide field for psychoanalytic activities. On the topic of denial, see Pierre Vidal-Nanquet, *Assassins of Memory. Essays on the Denial of the Holocaust* (New York: 1992 [first published Paris 1987]); and, with a very different approach, Brigitte Bailer-Galanda, Wolfgang Benz, and Wolfgang Neugebauer, eds., *Die Auschwitzleugner. "Revisionistische" Geschichtslüge und historische Wahrheit* (Berlin: 1996).

– Part III –

AFTERMATH

– *Chapter 15* –

FORWARD DEFENSE

The "Memorandum of the Generals" for the Nuremberg Court

Manfred Messerschmidt

One might expect that a memorandum[1] from Field Marshal Walther von Brauchitsch, the last Supreme Commander of the Army before Hitler himself took over the post, dated 19 November 1945 and drafted jointly with several generals in order to "give testimony on behalf of the entire German army" to the International Court in Nuremberg, would represent an important document for contemporary history. The five generals wanted to provide the Allies with "as clear a picture in this area as is possible" and discharge a responsibility to the former soldiers of the German army. Because of the posts they held, they were undoubtedly in a position to make important statements on military and military-political questions. They included Field Marshal Erich von Manstein, Supreme Commander of Army Group South until March 1944, Generaloberst Franz Halder, Chief of the General Staff of the Army until September 1942, General Walter Warlimont, Deputy Chief of the Wehrmacht Command Staff until September 1944, and General Siegfried Westphal, Chief of the General Staff of the Supreme Commander in the West until 7 May 1945.

According to their own statement, these men did not feel themselves obligated to oppose Hitler. Their credo was allegedly to "stay completely away from politics"—an assertion that provokes a

Notes for this section begin on page 396.

question mark in Halder's case since he belonged to the military opposition along with Oster, Canaris, Beck, and others up until the fall of 1939. One should, therefore, make note of the statement at the end of the memorandum aimed at the men of 20 July 1944: "It could not be a task of leading officers to break the army's back. Anyone who sets out to change his country's government is responsible for providing a new and better government, a new leader."[2] Having said that, the authors saw as their most important task to demonstrate that the army had been against the party and the SS, had disapproved of almost all of Hitler's important decisions, and had opposed the commission of war crimes. The explanation was composed from memory and without documents. Nevertheless, the assurance is given that each assertion could be sworn to under oath by at least one of the men signing the memorandum.[3]

From a practical point of view, the memorandum is a statement for the defense. The Allies would hardly expect to be provided with confessions or even self-criticism. But they must have found the paltry "factual content" remarkable. Its accuracy could easily be tested against the mountains of documents they possessed. Today's historian is in a similar situation. Reading the generals' memorandum is much like looking through the posthumous papers of the former general of panzer troops, Hans Röttiger, who served as Chief of the General Staff of the 4th Army and 4th Panzer Army on the Eastern front in 1942 and 1943. This general, the first Chief of Staff of the Army of the Bundeswehr, also wrote an explanation for his attorney in November 1945. In it, he wrote that he came to realize "that the struggle against bandits that we were waging had as its ultimate aim the exploitation of the military for the purpose of ruthlessly exterminating Jewry and other unwanted elements."[4] Probably after subsequent consultation with his attorney, Röttiger withdrew the paper, replacing it on 8 December 1945 with a different explanation. And in July 1946, he testified under oath that primarily leaders or agents had been captured in the struggle against bandits—mostly Jews—who, as the "chief ringleaders" in whipping up the population, were turned over to the SD, which should not be regarded as an unusual step. How they were treated by the SD "was not known to us."[5] So this was a "laundered version" for legal purposes.

The Prehistory of the War

The generals' memorandum also raises suspicions of laundered memory. Questionable actions by military agencies and commanders are not discussed. Actions taken in violation of international law are either not treated, minimized, or blamed on others. Events in Brauchitsch's and Halder's areas of competence are not mentioned. Even the prelude to the war is slanted. Actions taken against the leadership of the SA on 30 June 1934 are said to have taken the army by surprise. In fact, the army leadership gave broad support to the SS and even prepared troops to intervene.[6] It is also not true that the army defended Jewish soldiers. The first draft of the Reichswehr minister's regulation expelling Jewish soldiers originated in the army's personnel office and was already in the office of the Wehrmacht on 19 March 1934. Since the "Law for the Restructuring of the Professional Bureaucracy" offered no justification for dismissing Jewish soldiers, the personnel office recommended dismissing them without further ado on the grounds that they did not meet qualification requirements. It was argued that soldiers who did not meet the terms of the law "cannot be allowed to stay in the army."[7]

The Supreme Commander of the Army (ObdH), Generaloberst von Fritsch, was an outspoken anti-Semite. In November 1924, he hoped that von Seeckt would make himself dictator and talked of "Ebert, pacifists, Jews, democrats, black-red-gold," and the French, who wanted to destroy Germany.[8] And even after his dismissal as ObdH, he expressed the view that the struggle against the Jews was the most difficult still to be fought.[9] In a directive of 21 December 1934, he informed army officers that it "goes without saying that an officer seeks a wife only in the Aryan strata of the *Volk*.[10]

On the conduct of the army leadership in the National Socialist state, its attitudes toward National Socialism and Hitler, basically the only explanations given are designed to signal ignorance of domestic politics and misgivings about foreign policy matters. There is not one word about the proofs of ideological commitment that were an important side effect of massive rearmament. Hitler's program, it is stressed, promised peace at home and abroad. There is not one word about the violent methods that brought about this so-called domestic peace. The generals claim to have had hardly any knowledge of the concentration camps. The army generals and the officer corps felt comfortable in the Führerstaat without democrats and socialists. In a directive dated 25 April 1936, Fritsch expressed his expectation that especially officers "will act in accordance with the views of the 3rd Reich, even when such views have not been laid down in legal requirements, decrees, or military orders."[11] Brauchitsch, ObdH from February 1938, was eager to draw the army, Hitler, and National Socialism closer together. As early as December

1938, he stressed in a directive on training the officer corps: "Wehrmacht and National Socialism are from the same intellectual roots. They will accomplish great things for the nation if they follow the example and the teachings of the Führer, who embodies in his person the genuine soldier and National Socialist."[12]

The memorandum employs a transparent method to relieve army leadership of responsibility for preparing for and waging war. Was the army in fact opposed to withdrawal from the League of Nations? There was certainly a desire to get rid of the restrictions on armaments imposed by the treaty of Versailles. It is not true that plans for an army with twenty-one divisions were developed only after 1933. The Reichswehr's second armament program had envisioned that earlier. When the adoption of the MacDonald Plan began to appear likely at the disarmament conference in Geneva, the German military clearly did not want to sign on. Its strategy was calculated to gain the freedom to arm. The only way out was to withdraw from the disarmament conference, and as soon as that occurred, withdrawal from the League of Nations was a given.

Was it true that the army leadership merely wanted to develop a defensive army? Brauchitsch and Halder surely knew better. As early as 1935, Germany had shifted from the defensive strategy of the second armament program of 1932 to the concept of "offensive defense." The main point was "strengthening the army's offensive strength." Chief of Staff Beck was one of the strongest proponents of this concept. In addition to the three projected panzer divisions, one plan foresaw the formation of forty-eight panzer brigades and four light divisions by 1939.[13] These formations were to be capable of far-ranging operations. In June 1936, the army general staff was assuming that an army of 2.68 million men would be mobilized in 1937–38. In 1940, total army personnel would number 3.6 million. In 1939, the army was to have 102 divisions, which was more than in 1914. By 1 October 1939, this huge instrument was supposed to be ready to go into action. Its only conceivable purpose was an aggressive war, especially since no external threat existed. A rearmament program of that sort necessarily put extreme pressures on economic resources. Thus, General Fromm, Chief of the General Army Office (Allgemeines Heeresamt), advised the supreme commander of the army when submitting the rearmament plan on 1 August 1936 that "following the period of buildup, either the Wehrmacht must be used soon or the situation must be mitigated by a reduction in the level of war preparation required."[14] Generaloberst Fritsch, who is characterized so positively in the generals' memorandum, did not allow Fromm's words to upset him, but presented the plan to Blomberg with the remark: "According to the Führer, a powerful army is to be created in the shortest possible time."[15] Beck, of course, remained skeptical. In mid-1937, he informed Blomberg that the army would not be ready in the winter of 1938/1939.[16] His opposition to a premature move against Czechoslovakia reflected his concerns about a war for which the Wehrmacht would be unprepared. Thus, in his "Observations on Germany's Current Military Situation," dated 5 May 1938,[17] he was still proceeding on the assumption that the army would not be ready for war in the immediate future. He also believed that the idea of a surprise attack on Czechoslovakia with a motorized army was an illusion. But Beck's reservations were rendered obsolete by the very rearmament that he himself had championed. The war games of the general staff in 1938 showed that rapid success against Czechoslovakia was possible. Beck stood alone with his misgivings.

In order to skirt the facts, the "Memorandum of the Generals" operates on the assumption that "in the years 1937 and 1938, the possibility of France and Czechoslovakia attacking Germany became more significant."[18] That was ostensibly why offensive operations were considered, especially since tours by members of the general staff were supposed to have shown that Germany could not successfully win such a contest while on the defensive. One must wonder whom Brauchitsch, Halder, and Manstein thought they could convince with this far-fetched version of events. Hitler had spoken unequivocally to Wehrmacht leaders in November 1937 about wars of aggression waged for the purpose of winning living space. The December 1937 revision of the plan of operations against Czechoslovakia ("Case Green") was not aimed at countering a Czech intention to attack Germany by shifting to an offensive posture, but rather comported with the military and political plans that Hitler had expressed in November. Jodl and Beck were involved in developing the new version of "Case Green." Now the thinking was: "When Germany has reached its full war-waging capacity in all areas, then the military preconditions will exist for a war of aggression against Czechoslovakia, hence for solving Germany's space problem through victory should a major power move against us."[19] Beck seems to have assumed that such a formulation would gain him time because, of course, Germany's full war-waging capacity had not, in his view, been attained by any means. But the formulation also makes it clear that the military leaders were not thinking of a preventive war but of a war of conquest. Moreover, the reservation concerning Germany's readiness for war was undermined by another view, which held that, even without complete war-readiness, a war against Czechoslovakia could still be managed even if the Soviet Union should ally itself with Czechoslovakia. Hitler could not ask for more. Even the underestimation of the Red Army fit in with his ideas.

And how did the army leadership and the generals view the situation in 1939? In November 1945, the generals wrote that the general impression had been that Hitler "was not yet seriously considering" a war of aggression.[20] The directive "Case White" on 3 April 1939 and the general directive issued on that same day by the OKW, which set 1 September as the deadline for achieving war-readiness against Poland,[21] were the most important instructions that the high command of the Wehrmacht received from Hitler and the OKW. Hitler had ordered the ObdH on 25 March to take up the "Polish question,"[22] and he had made no secret about how he meant the issue to be dealt with: Poland was to be defeated in such a way that it would not need to be considered as a political factor for decades. According to the generals' memorandum, the military preparations being set in motion, albeit secretly, were intended merely to bring increased political pressure to bear. Brauchitsch was probably glad that he was writing the memorandum without relying on documents. One wonders whether he recalled the guidelines he issued to the "commanders" on 2 August 1939, the twenty-fifth anniversary of the outbreak of World War I, which were supposed to "provide a unified theme" for the officers in addressing their soldiers. There one reads that envy, resentment, and hatred were once again being aimed at Germany; forces aiming at encircling Germany were back at work. But this time Germany was strong and unyielding, and the Führer had built up Germany's strength and won friends and allies for the Reich.[23]

So we are offered help in understanding 2 August 1939. Once more, others were to blame. Subsequent passages refine the prelude to the war: Hitler, it is said, had not yet reached a decision to attack when he addressed the upper echelons of command on 22 August 1939. He withdrew the order for invasion of 25 August. Then Poland mobilized on 30 August. Only after that, on 31 August, was the order issued to invade on 1 September.[24] Once more, it was all merely a response to the actions of others. But, in fact, Hitler made it clear that he wanted war. Granted, he had certain doubts about the attitudes of the Western powers. But he played them down for his generals: The road lay open for the soldiers, he said. His only fear was that "at the very last moment, some son of a bitch" would confront him with a "proposed compromise." The war, Hitler said, must be waged brutally. "Close your heart to pity."[25] Some generals, for example, Sodenstern, Witzleben, Rundstedt, and even Reichenau, doubted that Poland was really isolated and foresaw that the Western powers would intervene. Rundstedt is reported to have said to his chief of staff, "This man wants war."[26] He meant a major war.

Early Origin of the Thesis of Preventive War

If one compares this version of events immediately prior to the attack on Poland with the version of events leading up to the attack on the Soviet Union, it then becomes clear that history is being concocted in order to promote one thesis: The army was surprised by practically everything. And so the story goes as follows: Hitler seems to have conceived the idea in July 1940 "that Russia might enter the war, and that he should preempt such an attack with a German offensive."[27] Here one sees the birth of the thesis of preventive war for the use of postwar society. Its champions in the 1980s—Topitsch, Suvorov, Hoffmann—thus had nothing new to offer. But which of the five generals could have made this statement under oath? According to Brauchitsch, at least one of them was supposed to be able to do that. Certainly, that could not be Warlimont, who in his memoirs recounted remarks made by Jodl, Wehrmacht chief of staff, to the officers of Abteilung L (Landesverteidigung) (Section I [Defense of the Homeland]) on 29 July 1940.[28] Jodl was passing along remarks by Hitler, who had decided "to rid the world of the danger of Bolshevism 'once and for all' by launching a surprise attack on Soviet Russia at the earliest possible moment, that is, in May 1941." In response to skeptical questions from his listeners, Jodl clarified Hitler's—and probably his own—view by saying that the settling of accounts with Bolshevism was, after all, unavoidable, and that this campaign was better waged at the height of German military might "rather than having to call the German people to arms once more in the next few years." Moreover, by the fall, the Luftwaffe would again be fully engaged against England.

Such was the view of the OKW. And the army again had not the slightest inkling of such intentions? Only in August, according to the generals' memorandum, did an order regarding "Buildup East" come from OKW, which ordered a buildup in the occupied areas of Poland—rail lines, highways, air fields, housing for troops. Hitler is not supposed to have discussed the military-geographic and operative bases for conducting an offensive in Russia with the ObdH and Halder until December 1940, ordering that all preparations be completed by 15 May 1941. This decision, according to the five generals, was "not at all welcome" in the OKH.[29] But would Brauchitsch and Halder have sworn to that under oath? That would have required an enormous lapse of memory. Hitler instructed the ObdH to address the "Russian problem" in a conversation on 21 July 1940—more than a week before Jodl's remarks to the command staff.[30] Halder mentioned this conversation in his War Diary. On 3 July, without having been ordered to do so, he had already instructed the chief of the operations section, Oberst i.G. von Greiffenberg, to investigate "how a military blow against Russia might be carried out in order to force recognition of Germany's dominant role in Europe."[31] On 21 July, as Halder noted, Brauchitsch was ready to present the results to Hitler.[32] Hitler's order of 21 July was immediately executed in the OKH. Halder ordered Generalmajor Marcks, the chief of staff of the 18th Army, which had already been transferred to Poland, to prepare a comprehensive study of the operation. In the OKH there were concerns about Germany's losing the military initiative while waiting for favorable opportunities to land in England ("Sea Lion"). The decisive conversation between Hitler and the top-level military occurred at Obersalzberg on 31 July. Halder noted Hitler's comment to the effect that England's last hope would be erased if Russia were crushed. "The faster we smash Russia, the better."[33] The purpose of the war was to destroy Russia's ability to survive. Hitler's decision was firm. The OKW and OKH were informed. Preparations were underway. Brauchitsch, Halder, and Warlimont had both first- and second-hand information. How did suppressing the more important facts of the prelude to the attack on the USSR represent, in the generals' view, "discharging a responsibility" to the soldiers of the German army? Falsifying history and a clean conscience are not a rare combination, but seldom do they exhibit themselves so unscrupulously.

For its adherents, the thesis of a preventive war implies primarily the army's innocence. The generals' memorandum also provides supporting arguments: The reconfiguration of Russian forces is said to have presented "increasingly the image of forces forming up for an attack"; the majority of Russian tank units were located near the frontier.[34] This statement is related to the period shortly before the German attack on 22 June. It intentionally ignores the fact that the massive German deployment was no longer a secret to the Soviet general staff. It also fails to consider the fact that Germany had meant to attack since July, 1940. Beyond that, the statement is false. The situation report of "Foreign Armies (East)" of 20 May 1941[35] concluded that a "preventive offensive" by the Red

Army was unlikely. The leadership was reminded of the internal weakness of the Red Army and of its low level of training. And there was also the matter of the shift to other training methods, which "provides no suitable basis for an attack, but rather a moment of weakness." Even in the view of the German general staff, a very improbable Soviet attack would have been a preventive measure in the face of the German deployment. The Soviet redeployment was judged to be defensive. "Foreign Armies (East)" recognized that the Red Army's tank units were located 140 to 500 kilometers beyond the frontier—in Vilnius, Baranovichi, Prokurov, Pskov, and South Bessarabia. Moreover, many divisions were pinned down on the Finnish border and in the Caucasus, hence not available to defend against a German attack. And after the attack had begun, that view was confirmed by stunning successes all along the line. The Red Army put up strong resistance in the south, but had to call tanks in from Zhitomir.[36] The chief of "Foreign Armies (East)" declared on 25 June, as General Heusinger reports,[37] that the regrouping of the Red Army had occurred due to concern about German intentions—but also with a view to a possible offensive. Halder replied that he agreed, but the time for an offensive was still open. This estimate gauged the strategic thinking of the Red Army more or less correctly. Part of that thinking was the principle that any attack should be answered with a counterattack as quickly as possible. The Wehrmacht went to war convinced of its own superiority. Its plans foresaw victory in a few weeks.

Criminal Orders

Having examined the preventive war argument, the reader may well be eager to learn what arguments are presented on the subjects of criminal orders, the partisan wars, the treatment of hostages, and the extermination of Jews. OKW and OKH documents on the issue of the "commissar order" and the "Judicial Decree Barbarossa" prove conclusively that drafts of these orders were prepared by these organs' legal sections—more precisely, in Halder's, Müller's, Jodl's, and Warlimont's areas of responsibility. The starting point was Hitler's address to his closest military advisers on 3 March 1941. Until that time, no discussion of the ideological exigencies in the war now being planned had taken place. Hitler explained how the war of annihilation was to be waged. The generals did not object. On that same day, 3 March 1941, instructions incorporating Hitler's demands went to Section L (Warlimont) of the Wehrmacht's command staff; these provided the basis for the "Guidelines in Special Areas to Instruction No. 21 (Case Barbarossa)." Jodl's directive referred to the deployment of organs of the Reichsführer-SS in the theater of operations deriving from the "need to neutralize at once leading Bolsheviks and commissars."[38] Military courts were not to be involved in these issues. By 5 March, Warlimont was ready to send the draft to the OKH for its reaction. Soon discussions were underway between Heydrich and General Quartermaster Wagner regarding the deployment of SS units. Cooperation between OKW and OKH went smoothly. During a situation conference on 17 March, Hitler declared in the presence of Halder, Wagner, and Heusinger: "The intelligentsia established by Stalin must be exterminated. The leadership machinery of the Russian Empire must be smashed. The most brutal violence is to be used in the Great Russian Empire."[39] When Hitler explained his intentions on 30 March to the larger circle of commanders selected for "Barbarossa" and upper-level staff officers, the leadership of the OKW and OKH were already playing the role of accomplices with knowledge of the early drafts.

The generals' memorandum begins its narrative with this date of 30 March. The generals allege that "all leaders of the army present" were outraged by Hitler's ideas. They say that, when several turned to the ObdH, Brauchitsch said that the army would never issue such an order.[40] But what did the army—meaning the OKH—really do? It was not even responsible for *issuing* the commissar order and judiciary decree. That was the business of the OKW. But the OKH had worked on the early drafts of the order. And in questions of international law relating to war, the head of the OKH legal section, General Eugen Müller, was subordinate to the chief of the general staff—Halder. On 6 March 1941, the OKH drafts of the judicial decree and the commissar order arrived in OKW/L. The draft commissar order was even more far-reaching than the recommendation of Section L (Warlimont),[41] for it generally envisioned "eliminating political authorities and leaders (commissars)" because they had "demonstrated clearly through their agitation and intelligence work their rejection of all European culture, civilization, legal principles, and order."[42] Halder took note of the draft and approved it. On the subject of the "Judicial Decree Barbarossa," the generals' memorandum refers to an order of the ObdH stating "that no measure may be carried out that would contradict German ideas of discipline."[43] The document in question is Brauchitsch's so-called discipline decree of 24 May 1941, which sought to prevent "the demoralization of the troops." Soldiers were not to indulge in arbitrary excesses aimed at inhabitants but were to continue to follow the orders of their superiors. The background of this order, which basically decreed only the obvious, was the following passage of the judicial decree of 13 May: "There shall be no automatic prosecution for acts committed by members of the Wehrmacht and follow-up forces against the civilian population, even if the action is also a military crime or offense."[44]

The background included as well the draft reply to the judicial decree prepared at the beginning of May by the ObdH General z.b.V at the headquarter of the ObdH,[45] which contained the following passages: "Punishable actions committed by army personnel arising from rage at atrocities or subversive activities by the supporters of the Jewish-Bolshevist system shall not be prosecuted as long as intervention in an individual case is not required in order to maintain discipline."

The generals' memorandum attempts to minimize the army leadership's complicity, which is perceptible even in the verbiage, by pointing out their desire to determine "specifically the attitude of the OKW." But the OKW was highly satisfied. Warlimont noted in the margin of the OKH recommendation: "Goes farther than WR [Wehrmachtsrechtsabteilung (Wehrmacht Legal Section)]."[46] The responsibility for this fateful draft lies with General Müller and his immediate superior in legal matters, Chief of Staff Halder. One wonders whether Warlimont and Halder invented the version of events recounted in the memorandum. Swearing to it under oath would have presented problems to men who remained faithful to their oath to Hitler to the very end. What attitude, what "outrage" at Hitler's ideas were to be found among the responsible parties in the legal section of the OKH can be gleaned from statements by General z.b.V./ObdH Müller and the director of the legal group under General z.b.V./ObdH, Oberstkriegsgerichtsrat Lattmann. Müller explained to intelligence officers (Ic) and army judges in Warsaw on 11 June 1941 that concern for justice had to take a back seat to the exigencies of war. "One of the two enemies must be left lying in the dust. Exponents of the enemy's views are not to be protected but eliminated."[47] One thing is clear: the so-called discipline decree of the ObdH embodied voluntary conformity to the ideological tasks. The ObdH had already used this method in Poland. Commanders at the front had reported on SS methods of purging. The commander in the east, Generaloberst Blaskowitz, in his notes of 6 February 1940 written in preparation for the visit of the ObdH in Spala, made reference to hideous incidents and crimes. Butchery is mentioned, along with remarks of

General Ulex, who had spoken of "a situation staining the honor of the entire German people."[48] Brauchitsch relieved himself of responsibility by issuing on 7 February 1940 the order "Army and SS." In it, discipline and acquiescence in political goals in the east in the light of the killing operations were combined into a code of conduct.[49] The extermination program "Tannenberg"—isolation and extermination of intelligentsia and Jews, internment, ghettoization—was carried out in full view of the army. On 13 March 1940, Himmler spoke to the generals in Koblenz on SS activities in Poland. Oberquartiermeister General von Tippelskirch informed Himmler in his invitation to the SS chief on behalf of the ObdH that it was not the harshness employed in Poland that concerned the army, but "the danger that the people participating will be turned into brutes."[50] The General Quartermaster had already passed the word to AOK 4 on 11 September 1939 "that the organs of the Reichsführer-SS are not to be interfered with."[51]

The Army Leadership and the War of Annihilation

It was this program that Brauchitsch sought to carry out against the Soviet Union. The army actively participated in extermination operations; the relevant literature provides a wealth of evidence to support that claim based on Wehrmacht documents. Discussions that the Generalquartermaster, General Wagner, held with SD Chief Heydrich on the army's cooperation with the Einsatzgruppen lay squarely within Halder's area of responsibility. Those discussions led to Brauchitsch's order of 28 April 1941 "Regulating Deployment of Security Police and SD in Cooperation with the Army."[52] Army Supreme Commander Hoepner, commander of Panzer Group 4, signed an order at the beginning of May for the imminent "conduct of battle"[53] in which he said, "every action in war must, in conception and execution, be guided by the iron resolve to annihilate the enemy mercilessly and completely. Above all, there shall be no mercy for the upholders of the Russian Bolshevik system." One of the five men who signed the memorandum, Generalfeldmarschall von Manstein, Supreme Commander of the 11th Army in 1941, issued an order[54] on 20 November 1941 in which he demanded: "The soldier must understand the need to take harsh reprisals on Jewry, the intellectual support of Bolshevik terror." Just how much understanding was forthcoming is broadly documented.[55] The names Babi Yar, Zhitomir, and Belaya Tserkov are emblematic of the participation of the military authorities in the extermination process. The general staff knew too much to have any doubts about the political extermination process. One should recall, among other events, the conversation of 25 August 1941 in the offices of the General Quartermaster of the OKH. There, in the presence of the leader of War Administration in the office of the general quartermaster, Major von Altenstadt, HSSPF SS-Obergruppenführer Jeckeln was said to have expressed his hope of liquidating by 1 September the approximately 11,000 Jews who had been driven into the "Reichskommissariat Ukraine."[56] The shootings of Jews rounded up at Kamenec-Podolski began on 26 August. On 29 August, Jeckeln reported the liquidation of "around 20,000."[57] The generals' memorandum seeks to hush all this up by claiming that the SD commandos were not permitted to inform the army about its "purely political tasks."[58] In point of fact, a direct line runs from Brauchitsch's "Army and SS" order of 7 February 1940 to its active support of SS operations. Manstein's and Reichenau's order was quite compatible with the political course of Hitler and Himmler.

The description of the attitude of the OKW toward the promulgation of the "commando order" of 18 October 1942, which had to do with the treatment of members of Allied commando operations, is no more accurate than the assertion that the commissar order was not carried out. In the Wehrmacht report of 7 October 1942, an amendment originating with Hitler[59] indicated that in the future "terrorist and sabotage troops" were to be slain without mercy "in combat." At this point, the OKH began to consider drafts of the order. Of course, it is to be assumed that Jodl and Warlimont would have preferred to avoid issuing an order that would result in a grave violation of international law regarding allied soldiers, but ultimately they submitted drafts. Which of them did that is in dispute; they blame each other. Jodl gave the order to Warlimont, who passed it on to Section Qu of the Wehrmacht Command Staff. Even Warlimont proceeded on the assumption that no prisoners were to be taken on principle. If commandos were temporarily captured, they were to be turned over to the SD following interrogation. Drawing distinctions between legal combatants and others was not contemplated, although Canaris had demanded precisely that. Warlimont rejected his idea because it would have contradicted the announcement over the radio. On 15 October 1942, his draft stated that illegal activity was to be assumed on the part of all sabotage troops, regardless of whether they were soldiers or what uniform they were wearing, so long as they carried out attacks or acts of violence, thus "in the judgment of the troops" placing themselves outside the law and conventions of war. They were to be killed "without mercy" down to the last man: no prisoners, no legalities. Even that did not satisfy Hitler. In a draft dated 17 October, qualifications regarding the methods of combat to be designated as commando operations were completely disregarded. It was expressly stated that commandos were to be killed even if they were trying to surrender. This amendment probably originated with Keitel. Hitler was glad to adopt an argument of the Wehrmacht legal staff to the effect that commandos who offered to surrender on completion of their mission "are thus abusing the Geneva Accords in the worst way." Hence, even a unit of regular soldiers involved in "sabotage or terror" was not to be treated according to the rules of the Geneva Convention, "rather it is to be wiped out completely, in all circumstances." The draft of 17 October became the model for the order issued on 18 October.[60]

Partisan Warfare

The authors of the memorandum committed another suppression of facts on the subject of the "war against partisans and bandits." Their conclusion: Bandit operations were characterized by special cruelty; Hitler's order regarding hostages was uniformly disobeyed. The OKW insisted on case-by-case investigation; the investigations usually led to no action being taken. From time to time, it was admitted, army units went into action under the command of SS officers.[61]

In contrast, the language of facts: An order issued by the OKH/GenStdH/Gen Qu/Abt: Kriegsverwaltung for the campaign in Yugoslavia on 2 April 1941 concerning the deployment of the Security Police and the SD already anticipated regulations corresponding to those promulgated for "Barbarossa." Halder and Generalquartiermeister Wagner amended the draft on 26 March so that Jews and Communists were regarded as special enemies.[62] On 28 September 1941, the OKW ordered that in the future, in addition to Jews and Communists, nationalists and bourgeois democrats should be seized as hostages.[63] Even earlier, on 4 September, Field Marshal List, acting in his capacity as Wehrmacht Commander Southeast, instructed the military commander of Serbia, General Danckelmann, to undertake at once ruthless actions against rebels (hangings, burning villages, increased seizure of hostages, internment of family members in concentration camps).[64]

On 16 September, the infamous OKW order was issued that ordered the shooting of fifty to one hundred hostages for every

German wounded or killed.[65] In contrast to assertions in the memorandum, there were no drawn-out judicial investigations. Following the Topola attack on a German unit, the "reprisal quota" was rigorously applied. In response to the deaths of twenty-one German soldiers, 2,100 prisoners, chiefly Jews and Communists selected from the Sabor and Belgrade concentration camps, were liquidated.[66] On 4 October, List ordered that partisans captured in combat be executed immediately and that anyone caught in a zone of operation and identified as a partisan be liquidated. The 717th ID shot more than 7,000 inhabitants in massacres in Kraljevo and Kragujevac in October 1941. In order to attain the "quota" for ten dead and twenty-six wounded, young people were dragged out of schools in Kragujevac. The 1st Battalion of Infantry Regiment 724 reported in October 1941: "21 October. 7 AM. the selection and shooting of those arrested begins. That completes the action. In all, 2,300 Serbs of various ages were shot."[67]

Despite these flagrant violations of international law, the OKW demanded even more brutal methods. On 7 February 1942, Wehrmacht Commander Southeast was in possession of a telegram saying that the punitive expeditions did not yet guarantee that no new uprisings would occur in the spring: "The rebels' losses are small, as is the number of those liquidated. The number of those taken prisoner is far too high."[68] The commander in Serbia, General Bader, responded on 13 February 1942 by reporting: "In the period of 1 September 1941 to 12 February 1942, the enemy suffered the following losses: a) killed and executed: 7,756; b) shot as reprisals following combat engagements: 20,149 persons."[69]

This practice continued and was even applied in Greece, although the "quotas" were not fully achieved, and army troops were not commanded by SS officers.

A wealth of material is available on operations in the Soviet Union. Especially noteworthy are the methods of the Security Divisions operating in the rear areas. The numbers make it clear that it makes no sense to talk about judicial investigations. For example:

- 285th Security Division from 22 June to 1 December 1941: 1,500 killed in combat or subsequently shot as partisans; German losses seven dead and eleven wounded.
- 707th Infantry Division within one month in White Russia: 10,431 of 10,940 prisoners shot. German losses two dead and five wounded.[70]

The generals' memorandum is important above all because leading Wehrmacht officers were reporting on their own areas of responsibility. It is, therefore, one of the most important documents in the history of the minimization of the role of the OKW and the OKH in World War II. Not one of the authors accepted responsibility for his actions or his failure to act. And yet they claimed to be fulfilling an obligation to the soldiers of the German army and combined their pleas with criticism of the military resistance to Hitler. The Bundeswehr has yet to speak to the issue of how these arguments comport with its traditions.

—*Translated by Roy Shelton*

Notes

1. Staatsarchiv Nürnberg, PS 3798, cited here as "Memorandum."
2. Memorandum, 69.
3. Introduction to Memorandum.
4. Röttiger posthumous papers, Bundesarchiv-Militärarchiv Freiburg (BA-MA), N 422/11, 3, Explanation of 28 November 1945; see Manfred Messerschmidt, "Das Heer als Faktor der arbeitsteiligen Täterschaft," in *Holocaust: Die Grenzen des Verstehens. Eine Debatte über die Besetzung der Geschichte*, ed. Hanno Loewy (Reinbek: 1992), 166–190, here 167f.
5. Röttiger postumous papers.
6. Klaus-Jürgen Müller, "Reichswehr und 'Röhm-Affäre.' Aus den Akten des Wehrkreiskommandos (Bayer.) VII in *Militärgeschichtliche Mitteilungen* (MGM) 1/1968, 107–144.
7. For more, see Manfred Messerschmidt, *Die Wehrmacht im NS-Staat. Zeit der Indoktrination* (Hamburg: 1969), 40–46. Because of the clause exempting soldiers who had served in the front lines ("Frontkämpfer-Klausel"), only seventy soldiers were affected initially.
8. Letter of 16 November 1924 to Joachim von Stülpnagel, BA-MA, H 08-5/20. On Fritsch's political views, see Klaus-Jürgen Müller, *Das Heer und Hitler. Armee und nationalsozialistisches Regime 1933–1940* (Stuttgart: 1969), 25, 41, 43, 163f.
9. The text of the letter appears in the documentation to Nicholas Reynolds, "Der Fritsch-Brief vom 11. Dezember 1939," *Vierteljahreshefte für Zeitgeschichte* (1980): 358ff., here 370.
10. The directive is reproduced in Manfred Messerschmidt and Ursula von Gersdorff, *Offiziere im Bild von Dokumenten aus drei Jahrhunderten* (Stuttgart: 1964), 259f., document no. 100.
11. Messerschmidt, *Wehrmacht im NS-Staat*, 82.

12. Messerschmidt and von Gersdorff, *Offiziere,* 274, document no. 107.
13. Memorandum of 20 December 1935 on increasing the army's offensive capability, BA-MA, II H 662. Cf. Klaus-Jürgen Müller, *General Ludwig Beck. Studien und Dokumente zur politisch-militärischen Vorstellungswelt und Tätigkeit des Generalstabschefs des deutschen Heeres 1933–1938* (Boppard: 1980), 469–477, document no. 37, and Manfred Messerschmidt, "The Political and Strategic Significance of Advances in Armament Technology: Developments in Germany and the 'Strategy of Blitzkrieg,'" in *The Quest for Stability: Problems of West European Security 1918–1957,* ed. R. Ahmann, A. M. Birke, and M. Howard (London: 1993), 249–261, here 251.
14. Allgemeines Heeresamt (AHA) No. 1780/36 of 1 August 1936, BA-MA, RH 15/70.
15. Communication of the Supreme Commander of the Army of 12 October 1936, BA-MA, RH 15/70.
16. OKH on 14 December 1937, BA-MA, III H 98/2.
17. Beck's posthumous papers, BA-MA, N 28/3.
18. Memorandum, 20a.
19. IMT, 34:745fl, document 175-C and *Akten zur deutschen auswärtigen Politik 1918–1945* (ADAP), Series D, vol. 7, Appendix III, 547ff.
20. Memorandum, 21.
21. ADAP, D, vol. 6, Addendum (*Anlage*) II. Hitler's deadline was transmitted in an OKW-WFA communication.
22. Ibid., no. 99.
23. Addendum to communication OKH/AHA of 24. July 1939. A copy is found in BA-MA, WK XII/15 C., reproduced in M. Messerschmidt, *Wehrmacht im NS-Staat,* 237.
24. Memorandum, 26.
25. Unsigned notes on Hitler's address of 22 August 1939, in ADAP, D, vol. 7, nos. 192 and 193.
26. Müller, *Heer und Hitler,* 411.
27. Memorandum, 35.
28. Walter Warlimont, *Im Hauptquartier der deutschen Wehrmacht 1939–1945. Grundlagen—Formen—Gestalten* (Frankfurt am Main: 1964), 126f.
29. Memorandum, 36.
30. Franz Halder, *Kriegstagebuch. Tägliche Aufzeichnungen des Chefs des Generalstabes des Heeres 1939–1942,* published by the Arbeitskreis für Wehrforschung, vol. 2, *Von der geplanten Landung in England bis zum Beginn des Ostfeldzuges (1.7.1940–21.6.1941)* (Stuttgart: 1963), entry for 22 July 1940, 32.
31. Ibid., entry for 3 July 1940, 6.
32. See Jürgen Förster, "Hitlers Entscheidung für den Krieg gegen die Sowjetunion," in *Das Deutsche Reich und der Zweite Weltkrieg,* vol. 4, *Der Angriff auf die Sowjetunion* (Stuttgart: 1983), 10 (*DRZW* IV).
33. Halder, *Kriegstagebuch,* entry for 31 July 1940, 2:49.
34. Memorandum, 37.
35. BA-MA, RH 2/2591.
36. OKW-KTB (War Diary), sub-volume 2, 417–420.
37. Adolf Heusinger, *Befehl im Widerstreit. Schicksalsstunden der deutschen Armee 1923–1945* (Tübingen: 1950), 130. On German estimates of the Red Army before and after 22 June 1941, see Manfred Messerschmidt, "June 1941 seen through German Memoirs and Diaries, in: Operation Barbarossa. The German Attack on the Soviet Union, June 22, 1941," in: *Soviet Union—*

Union Sovietique, vol. 18, nos. 1–3, published by The College of Humanities, University of Utah.

38. Warlimont, *Im Hauptquartier*, 168.
39. Halder, *Kriegstagebuch*, entry for 17 March 1941, 2:20.
40. Memorandum, 41.
41. For more, see Messerschmidt, *Wehrmacht im NS-Staat*, 402ff.
42. Heinrich Uhlig, "Der verbrecherische Befehl. Eine Diskussion und ihre historisch-dokumentarischen Grundlagen," in vol. 2 of *Vollmacht des Gewissens*, published by Europäische Publikation e.V. (Frankfurt am Main: 1965), 287–410, here 355ff. (= document PS-1971).
43. Memorandum, 41.
44. Reprinted in Gerd R. Ueberschär and Wolfram Wette, *Der deutsche Überfall auf die Sowjetunion. "Unternehmen Barbarossa" 1941* (Frankfurt am Main: 1991), 252f.
45. Uhlig, "Der verbrecherische Befehl," 386f., document 23.
46. Wehrmacht Legal Section, No. 32/41 gKdos. Executive matter, 9 May 1941, BA-MA, RW 4/v. 577; also Jürgen Förster, "Das Unternehmen 'Barbarossa' als Eroberungs- und Vernichtungskrieg," in *DRZW* IV, 429.
47. Panzer Group 3/Ic, Activity Report No. 2, 1 January to 11 August 1941, BA-MA, Panzer AOK 3, 29f., reprinted in Hans-Adolf Jacobsen, "Kommissarbefehl," in *Anatomie des SS-Staates* (Olten and Freiburg: 1965), 2:192. Similar statements by Lattmann, quoted in a letter by one of the participants to the author dated 20 July 1970.
48. See Messerschmidt, *Wehrmacht im NS-Staat*, 390ff.
49. "Heer und SS," NOKW-I799. See also Manfred Messerschmidt, "Völkerrecht und 'Kriegsnotwendigkeit' in der deutschen militärischen Tradition seit den Einigungskriegen," *German Studies Review* 6 (1983): 237–269, here 25ff.
50. Klaus-Jürgen Müller, "Zur Vorgeschichte und Inhalt der Rede Himmlers vor der höheren Generalität am 13. März 1940 in Koblenz," *Vierteljahrshefte für Zeitgeschichte* 18 (1970): 120, here 112; on this speech, see Messerschmidt, *Wehrmacht im NS-Staat*, 393.
51. BA-MA, W 6969/5.
52. Reprinted in Ueberschär and Wette, *Deutscher Überfall*, 249f.
53. Excerpted in ibid., 251.
54. Ibid., 289f.
55. See, among others, Förster, "Das Unternehmen 'Barbarossa,'" and Helmut Krausnick and Hans-Heinrich Wilhelm, *Die Truppe des Weltanschauungskrieges. Die Einsatzgruppen der Sicherheitspolizei und des SD 1938–1942* (Stuttgart: 1981); Christian Streit, *Keine Kameraden. Die Wehrmacht und die sowjetischen Kriegsgefangenen 1941–1945* (Stuttgart: 1978); Messerschmidt, "Das Heer als Faktor," 166–190.
56. Verbatim notes on the meeting of 27 August 1941; Nürnberger Dokument PS-197.
57. Krausnick and Wilhelm, *Truppe des Weltanschauungskrieges*, 250.
58. Memorandum, 45.
59. Nürnberger Dokument PS-1266.
60. See a more detailed discussion in Manfred Messerschmidt, "Kommandobefehl und NS-Völkerrechtsdenken," *Revue de droit pénal militaire et de droit de la guerre*, XI-1 (1972): 110–132.
61. Memorandum, 56f.
62. See Förster, "Hitlers Entscheidung," 22f., Manfred Messerschmidt, "Rassistische Motivationen bei der Bekämpfung des Widerstandes in Serbien?" in

Faschismus und Rassismus. Kontroversen um Ideologie und Opfer (Berlin: 1992), 317–341, here 322f.

63. BA-MA, 17729/8, Enclosure (Anlage) 28; Nürnberger Dokument NOKW 458
64. BA-MA, 14749/5, Enclosure 58; cf. *The Waldheim Report. Submitted February 8, 1988 to Federal Chancellor Dr. Franz Vranitzky by the International Commission of Historians* (Copenhagen: 1993).
65. BA-MA, 17729/9, Enclosure 48.
66. BA-MA, 17729/8, Enclosure 48.
67. Report on the deployment of Infantry Regiment I/724, 17–25 October 1941, BA-MA, RH 26-104. On the entire question, see Walter Manoschek, *Serbien ist judenfrei. Militärische Besatzungspolitik und Judenvernichtung in Serbien 1941/42* (Munich: 1993).
68. BA-MA, RW 40/26, 75.
69. Plenipotentiary Commanding General in Serbia, Ia, No. 108/42 to WB Southeast, 13 February 1942, BA-MA, RW 40/26.
70. Förster, "Die Sicherung des Lebensraums," in *DRZW*, 4:1054ff.

– *Chapter 16* –

WHOSE HISTORY IS IT, ANYWAY?

The Wehrmacht and German Historiography

Omer Bartov

Particularly since the end of World War II, military history has acquired the reputation of being a somewhat dubious undertaking, and those who practice it have not infrequently been dismissed as second-rate scholars concerned more with tales of heroic battles than with serious historical research. This bias can be traced back both to general postwar trends in public taste and sensibilities, and to more specific developments in the historical profession. It is, however, also closely related to the self-imposed limits and focuses of inquiry evident in the research and writing by military historians themselves, quite apart from the inherent characteristics and available topics of investigation in a sub-discipline devoted to the study of war. To be sure, popular military histories, battle accounts, biographies of great warlords, picture books on tanks and airplanes, and so forth, retain an immense public appeal, and often reach best-seller dimensions (a phenomenon which in turn makes scholars of history all the more suspicious of this genre). But by and large, within the scholarly community, military history has a bad name. This is true in most Western countries; and yet, distinctions should and can be made. While in Britain and the United States (and to a lesser extent also in France), war and the military are (or are at least perceived as being) far from the most

Notes for this section begin on page 414.

crucial element in these nations' own history, in Germany the relationship between war and society, as well as between soldiers and politics, has been accepted as a main factor in German history throughout the modern era. Conversely, while British and especially American scholars have begun to transform traditional military history into a wholly new and fascinating area of research, not least due to the increasing interest in war and violence shown by non-military historians, in Germany military history has by and large remained at the hands of the traditionalists. To be sure, German military historians have raised some contentious political issues, and have courageously brought the military institution under a searing critique. But both in terms of their methodology, and in terms of their openness to new developments in historical scholarship, they have made little progress. Moreover, even in confronting sensitive political, ideological, and conceptual issues, they have shied away from drawing more radical conclusions from their own findings, and have failed seriously to address some of the most difficult and potentially explosive questions, such as the mental make-up of the soldiers and the involvement of the army in the Holocaust.

The following essay will therefore concentrate on several aspects of military history writing in the Federal Republic of Germany since 1945, while keeping in mind some of its common characteristics with, and differences from, the historiography of war in other nations. In writing on this issue, I will attempt to take up the position of the insider as outsider, as one who belongs to the group (whether that of military historians, German historians, or historians in general), and yet is also out of it (being neither a "pure" military historian, nor a German, nor exclusively a German historian). This potentially fruitful vantage point entails, of course, the possibility of shirking one's own responsibility for the group or for one's activities within it. At the same time, however, it is far from an untypical position for historians, especially military historians, to take, not least due to the low esteem in which this branch of the profession is currently held. Hence while I will subject German military history writing to a general critique (noting both merits and limitations), I will admit right at the outset that I see myself too as subjected to this critique and criticism, and not "outside" or "beyond" it. Nevertheless, I do view this specific group of historians and their writings largely as an outsider, as, indeed, I believe I am also seen by its members. Hence I can exercise empathy without being tied down by group loyalty.

I

Before turning to the German scene, let me begin with a few words on the general context. As noted above, since 1945 military history in most Western countries has been on the defensive. While heroic war films and popular histories have always found a ready audience, professional historians tended to shy away from this field. This was both because of the general abhorrence of war following the terrible destruction of World War II, and to a growing extent due to the fact that a younger generation of historians who had not served in the military and had not experienced war at close quarters felt estranged from anything related to soldiering and the military establishment. Moreover, military history came to be associated with the official, commissioned histories of World War I, in which particular national and political biases were emphasized at the cost of a more detached, scholarly view of events, thereby exposing the more lamentable aspects of the state's ability to mobilize the intellectual community to its service.

This does not mean, of course, that no one wrote military history, but rather, that the field was left open either to historians more interested in the purely military, operational, tactical, and technological aspects of war, or to scholars who focused on strategy, politics, economics, and international relations. Consequently, military history tended to become isolated, divorced from new approaches to historical investigation and writing in the rest of the profession. Thus, while social, intellectual, and cultural historians avoided themes related to war, military historians stuck to the most conventional methodologies and closed themselves off from their colleagues' innovative ideas and concepts.

This must be seen as a lamentable process, since it both impoverished the field of military history and deprived history writing in general of a deeper understanding of the impact of war and the military on modern society. After all, in the past historians had recognized that war was an immensely important element in human civilization, and its study had indeed exercised some of the very best scholarly, intellectual, and philosophical minds.[1] Neglect of this aspect of human history did not, of course, diminish the role of war itself in our own time, but simply left us with only limited tools to analyze it. And while serious scholars pursued other avenues in the past, those who resisted this trend either felt obliged to apologize for not joining the multitude or reacted by willfully ignoring their colleagues' contributions to historical research. Institutionally, this meant that while the best minds often chose not to study war and the military, those who did could only find positions in military colleges and research institutes. This in turn diminished the reputation of military history even further, and often did indeed also narrow the horizons of such historians or put them under institutional pressures which prevented them from expanding their historical perceptions and trying out more innovative approaches. In this manner, whatever their personal political and professional biases might have been, military historians became increasingly conservative in their approach to the writing of history and, by extension often also in their views of human society and politics in general.

This should not be seen as an obvious, self-evident development. Before World War II, military historians had at times been highly original in their analyses of the past and radical in their politics. To mention just one case from German historiography, the revolutionary theses of the young historian Eckart Kehr in the 1930s, which were rediscovered and expanded during the 1960s and 1970s, were based on a close and highly sophisticated analysis of the construction of the Imperial Navy and its political, economic, and social context.[2] Yet it took close to two decades after the end of World War II before new (or renewed) approaches to the study of war and the military began changing the convention, and even then their impact has remained limited. Ironically, the same country which had produced the first modern military historian, Hans Delbrück, in the first two decades of this century, has been especially tardy in rejuvenating this sub-discipline.[3]

In Britain, and even more so in America, the last two to three decades have seen great changes in the study of war. Examples of new approaches to this field have interestingly not come necessarily from military historians, indeed, have sometimes not come from historians at all. Thus Paul Fussell's highly influential *The Great War and Modern Memory* was written by a professor of English, as was Samuel Hynes's *A War Imagined*; nor were Modris Eksteins' *Rites of Spring* or Robert Wohl's *The Generation of 1914* written by military historians, while William McNeill's *The Pursuit of Power* is also anything but a traditional military history, encompassing as it does several continents and thousands of years of human civilization.[4] As John Chambers and, in a more qualified manner, also Peter Paret have argued, there is room to speak today of a "new" military history, though I would agree that it is still both young and limited, and suffers from severe intellectual, institutional, and theoretical limitations that will take many years to overcome.[5] In fact, it would seem that only a new *cultural* military history, even more ambitious than that previously undertaken, will stand a chance of establishing itself as an intellectually vigorous, analytically and methodologically innovative, and academically respectable sub-discipline.

In Germany, however, even these early beginnings seem to be still a matter for the future. Excepting such fascinating works as Klaus Theweleit's *Männerphantasien* (which is neither by a military historian nor directly on the military, and yet can serve as a uniquely instructive model for military historians concerned with the mentality and psychology of their protagonists),[6] much of current German military history seems to plod along conventional, traditional methodological and analytical lines, unimpressed either by influences from abroad or by its own much more illustrious past. This condition needs to be further examined, not least because both the *study* of military history, as well as the *actual* military institution, let alone the phenomenon of war itself, have had such a tremendous impact on German history.

II

For the first two decades or so after the collapse of the Third Reich, German military history consisted in large part of either very technical, tactically, or strategically oriented works, or of a large host of memoirs, chronicles, and battle accounts by former members of the Wehrmacht.[7] This literature was often useful as far as the documentary and personal material it provided was concerned, although on the analytical level it often suffered from severe handicaps traceable back to strong apologetic tendencies and endemic, occasionally quite explicit prejudices carried over from the war itself. As for the historical method applied, the scholarly components of this large body of literature were crafted in a highly traditional, conservative mould, accepting the implicit assumption that the past as it had "really" happened could be reconstructed simply by reference to official documents, while the array of personal accounts seemed to imply that their writers' participation in the events they recounted was sufficient proof for the veracity of their accounts. What most of these works had in common was that they by and large accepted, confirmed, and recapitulated the official Wehrmacht view of the war, notwithstanding the fact that both the Wehrmacht and the regime it had served no longer existed. As such, this was quite a remarkable phenomenon, and one which must have had at least something to do with the great reluctance of either participants in the war or those writing about it (often the same people) to subject both their own experiences and the national experience as a whole to a fundamental critique (quite apart from reflecting the extent to which many of these men had internalized the National Socialist perception of the war without even being aware of having done so). Hence the legend of the army's aloofness from the regime, the soldiers' professionalism, "correctness," and devotion (to the Fatherland, not the Führer), the generals' abhorrence of and opposition to the crimes of the SS, their rigidly upright conduct and their strict adherence to moral codes and soldierly standards, was perpetuated and largely accepted also by many sectors of the non-German public and not a few military historians, especially in Britain and the United States,[8] all this notwithstanding the fact that as early as the Nuremberg trials the army (or at least its top echelons) was shown to have been both deeply implicated in the crimes committed by the Nazi regime, and strongly committed to the "cause" it had espoused.[9]

This situation changed significantly during the 1960s and 1970s. With the publication of several important studies on the Wehrmacht, its relationship with the Nazi regime, its educational policies, and its involvement in National Socialist crimes, the traditionally apologetic view was substantially revised, and the focus shifted from tactics and strategy to politics and complicity.[10] To be sure, much as these studies have contributed to our knowledge of the army's collaboration with the regime, they were neither forerunners in this field nor ever totally relinquished both previous traits, namely the fascination with military operations and the ambivalence regarding the army's criminal actions. Indeed, these works, innovative as far as German scholarship was concerned, had been preceded by earlier studies by British and American scholars which, though often less well documented, had already presented the main arguments on the role of the German military in politics as well as in the implementation of National Socialist criminal policies.[11] In fact, these German studies were notable for their general reluctance to acknowledge the contribution of non-German scholars to the debate. What is more, they manifested a strong predilection to avoid issues still deemed sensitive by the German scholarly establishment, the media, the political community, and the public at large. This tendency, on which I will have more to say below, can still be seen in present-day Germany.

A second important area, separate from and yet closely related to the first, in which German scholarship on the Wehrmacht has shown only slight progress and has hardly even begun the process of integration into the larger field of historical studies, is that of the range of military historians' scholarly and intellectual preoccupations and the resulting narrow and constricting methodology they apply to their sources. Over the last couple of decades we have seen social and cultural history move to the forefront of historical writing, as a result of which the official documents traditionally viewed as the primary sources of history have been subjected to much closer textual analysis and scrutiny, and have been supplemented, if not replaced, by other, more varied and far less conclusive types of evidence.[12] "Objective" historical facts are now viewed as suspect by many historians; instead they seek to uncover the conscious or unconscious motivations of those who had manufactured the evidence at our disposal, and concern themselves as much with perceptions of reality among their protagonists as with what that reality "really" was. In this context, German military historians appear at times like a throwback to another period, clinging to their documents with the tenacity of a retreating army aware of the catastrophe that awaits it at the end of the road. Instead of trying to learn from other German, and especially foreign scholars, about new concepts and approaches to historical studies, many of these scholars have increasingly insulated themselves from such influences and have reacted by ever more detailed expositions of facts and numbers, documents and maps, to the point that even the powerful analytical potential of this kind of approach has gradually become submerged in a morass of printed sources with few interpretative remarks. In a way, the text has become so similar to the documents on which it is based, that it has lost much of its effectiveness, and can itself serve only as a source, rather than as an interpretation.

III

In order to demonstrate the problems noted above more specifically, let me turn to the single most important and comprehensive work of West German military history since the collapse of Hitler's regime, the multi-volumed series *Das Deutsche Reich und der Zweite Weltkrieg* (*DRZW*), of which up to now six volumes have appeared covering approximately the period between 1939–43 (with some omissions to be treated in the forthcoming six volumes).[13]

In one sense, this vast collection, encompassing at present well over 5,000 tightly printed pages and projected to reach at least double that number by the time it is completed, makes the claim of being an authoritative study of Nazi Germany (a term judiciously avoided in the title) in World War II by its sheer weight—physical, scholarly, and thematic. In another sense, these volumes imply that history, at least the writing of *this* history, "belongs" to the group of scholars who have been composing these volumes since the 1970s in the Militärgeschichtliches Forschungsamt (MGFA) in Freiburg. Moreover, since the MGFA is (or rather was; as I write it is in the process of being moved to Potsdam) located right next to the Bundesarchiv-Militärarchiv (BA-MA), where the largest collection of German military documents is kept, this series of volumes also asserts the authority of being the official interpretation of the Truth, at least so long as we accept that this elusive entity can in fact be found in, or reconstructed from, the documents of the Wehrmacht. This physical proximity to the primary sources thus creates what I would consider the illusion that the members of the MGFA are merely giving "objective" history a voice, and are indeed uniquely situated to do what any other historian, who is neither part of the group nor maintains the same intimate relationship with the documents (and the bureaucrats who control them—and provide the MGFA with free access to them), is by definition barred from achieving.

The *DRZW* is a remarkable accomplishment. It has been recognized as such not merely by the narrower circles of scholars interested in military history, but also beyond, both in Germany and abroad. Indeed, Oxford University Press has now undertaken the mammoth task of translating the series into English and has just begun publishing these volumes in England and the United States. The series is extraordinary not only due to the immense amount of material covered by the members of the MGFA, but also because it indeed provides a highly informed, and yet critical view of wartime Germany, and manages to demolish many of the conventions hitherto staunchly held by German (as well as some non-German) historians. Especially the chapters on the military, economic and propagandistic preparation of Germany for war in the first volume, as well as on the ideological roots, military and economic planning for, and initial phases of Germany's war of destruction against the Soviet Union, namely "Operation Barbarossa," in the fourth volume, have had a major impact on all subsequent work concerned with these events.

Furthermore, the *DRZW* is a landmark publication in that, despite the fact that it was produced by members of an official institute with close ties to the German military and Ministry of the Interior, its authors have maintained a high degree of academic independence and have insisted on their right to be critical of formerly accepted and far more convenient "truths." Hence this quasi-official publication has managed to retain a high scholarly standard, a rather rare, if not unique, phenomenon where national histories of war produced by official institutions are concerned. This was not achieved without much wrangling, conflict, and some compromises, the signs of which can be detected in many of these volumes, both in the somewhat uneven quality of the contributions and in the stark contradictions between the arguments (and, ironically, "truth" claims) made by the different historians writing for the very same volume. But by and large, and within the parameters of what it had set out to do, up to now this has been a most successful historiographical venture.

What the future holds for this series is far less clear. Now that the MGFA is moving to Potsdam, against the wishes of many of its members, it may be safely assumed that those in charge of the Institute will also try to bring about a major shift in the focus of its publications and the general control over the research and writing undertaken by its members. This will obviously take time, but as members of the old group drift out to other academic posts or to retirement, one may expect that their replacements will not be given the same academic freedom enjoyed by the present team. This may mean that the prospective volumes of the series will assume a somewhat different, and much less critical, if more uniform character, depriving them thereby of much of their previous merit, rooted precisely in that precarious balance between official sanction and support, on the one hand, and commitment to criticism and scholarship, on the other. Moreover, one should not overlook the obvious fact that relocating to Potsdam perforce evokes certain associations with Prussian traditions which were not known for their tendency to criticize the military establishment. However, rather than discussing an as yet unknown future, let us instead concentrate on what the MGFA has already produced, or rather, on those issues with which the series has failed to come to grips.

For, much as there is a great deal to admire in the *DRZW*, there is also much to criticize; and although we may lament its anticipated transformation in the future, we must also emphasize the limits of its achievement, precisely because it seems that there is little chance that these limits will be surpassed in the near future.

Precisely because, as I have already noted, the *DRZW* implicitly claims the status of a definitive work, it is necessary to point out its shortcomings in three major areas. This is especially pertinent since it is here that the series reflects, rather than resolves, a general problem in military history writing (and in some respects also in other sub-disciplines of history) in Germany. These areas include:

(a) A conservative methodology, based on the assumption that a rigorous and faithful analysis of official archival documentation would suffice to reconstruct past events; that the veracity of this reconstruction would be "self-evident"; and that therefore there is no need for any further explanation, verification, or theoretical justification of this reconstruction of the past. This methodology, I would argue, fails to confront some of the most intriguing, as well as crucial questions of history in general, and of the period and events discussed in the *DRZW*, in particular.

(b) An almost complete disregard of social and cultural history and all that they might bring to such an undertaking, presumably derived from the assumption that they belong to a wholly different, and therefore irrelevant, group of sub-disciplines, which cannot effectively be applied to military history. This intentionally rigid definition of the MGFA's disciplinary location within the historical profession greatly impoverishes the scope of the undertaking and bars its scholars from raising a host of both fascinating and central questions related to their work.

(c) An almost complete absence of any discussion of the Holocaust, supposedly on the assumption that it is not directly related to the theme of Germany in World War II. Quite apart from being a false assumption, which most studies of the Holocaust have had no difficulty in dismissing,[14] this glaring absence sheds a disturbing light on the whole enterprise, raises questions regarding the pressures which might have led to this exclusion, or, perhaps even more troubling, regarding the views held by this group of historians on the connection between the Holocaust, the war, and the "German" Reich. In other words, the inevitable question here would be, to whom does the history of the Holocaust belong? In this context it should be added that, judging by the plan of the rest of the series as issued by the MGFA, we should not expect that the "Final Solution" will be addressed in any of the future volumes, at least not as a major concern that merits a separate volume or at least a substantial contribution. Hence the conclusion that the MGFA views the Holocaust as only marginally relevant to the German military history of the war.

If we restate now the question implied by the title of this essay, we can say that according to the *DRZW*, the military history of Germany in World War II belongs to military historians (the MGFA); these military historians have little or nothing to do with any other kinds of historians and history writing, and therefore neither does the military history of Germany; and this same history has little to do with the genocidal policies of the Nazi regime, at least as far as the "Final Solution of the Jewish Question" is concerned. That history, it appears, belongs to someone else (historians of the Holocaust? Jewish historians? non-German historians?).[15]

IV

Now let me briefly point out in what way a greater openness to outside influences, both of other sub-disciplines of history and of other social sciences, both from within Germany and especially from abroad, may contribute to enhancing the importance and deepening the insights of German military history, if only by enabling it to come to grips with some of the most troubling, and most profound questions of war in the modern era.

First, a less rigidly Rankean approach to history, that is, a greater distance from, and a more critical attitude toward archival sources, along with a higher degree of skepticism regarding the objective truth value of both official documents *and* one's own reconstruction of events based on such documents, would add a new dimension to such studies, if only by opening up a whole series of questions generally ignored by such works as the *DRZW*. The five-thousands pages of this study have, after all, merely given us a *version* of Germany's history in World War II, a version culled largely from the documents found in the BA-MA. This is neither the Truth, nor the whole Truth, nor nothing but the Truth. Not only has this history given us only a partial view of the events, it has also given us much which is merely conjecture, interpretation, and reconstruction on the basis of partial, indeed biased information; which is the case of *any* history. Nor is this a question of space, because neither five, nor ten, nor twenty-thousand pages on any given historical period or geographic location would ever suffice. Total history is, at best, an ideal type, not an achievable goal; definitive histories, if there is such a thing, are time and place bound. And precisely because of this limitation, it might be better to deal in less detail with some aspects of the war, and devote more attention to others.

What, then, are these other aspects which have been neglected? Let us ask, for instance, about the mentality of the soldiers who took part in this war. The volumes in front of us tell us a great deal about their conscription, equipment, losses, the orders they carried out, the defeats they sustained. But as far as their mentality is concerned, we do not proceed much farther than some vague generalities. If any individual is discussed in greater detail, it is invariably a general, or a politician. The rank and file get about as much mention as they do in any traditional military history written since Caesar and Tacitus. Nor is this an impossible task; indeed, some such studies have been written, mainly by non-German scholars, although they receive scant or no mention in the mammoth academic apparatus of the *DRZW*.[16] It is not for lack of material or even lack of interest. It simply does not fit into the historical-conceptual framework of these volumes. This makes for a gaping hole in this vast venture, since the result is very much a history from above, written, as it were, from the green-tables of the staff officers and generals, not from the view of the men who did the fighting.

Second, this Rankean mixture of history from above and rigid adherence to what are, after all, highly suspect documents, is closely associated with the scant regard given to social and cultural history. It is, one must say, a great pity that such a fine group of historians, working for a considerable period of time on the war, has made such a meager contribution to the social and cultural history of the Wehrmacht, a subject already recognized as one of major importance quite a few years ago. We still know precious little about the social composition of the Wehrmacht and the relationship between the background of the soldiers and their conduct during the war; nor do we know much about the effect which the troops' experience in the war had on their postwar social status, political affiliations, or self-perception. Similarly, we still know very little about the existence and nature of a "front culture," relations between the soldiers within their units and between subordinates and superiors, political convictions and resistance, as well as contacts between the front and the rear, soldiers' patterns of marriage and divorce, rape and prostitution, fraternization and brutality vis-à-vis occupied populations. All of these issues have not been addressed to a sufficient degree, and if they were, then not by the members of the MGFA. One also wonders whether at some later stage the series will address the issue of women in the war. A social, as well as a cultural history of the German army in World War II, a history which can not be based merely on the files of the BA-MA, nor can employ only Rankean methodology, is still waiting to be written.[17]

Third is the most obvious, and most striking absence in the *DRZW*, namely, the Holocaust. This lacuna is, moreover, related on at least two levels to the previous problems mentioned. For on the one hand, the relationship between the Wehrmacht and the Holocaust can in fact be quite well documented by means of the archival holdings in the BA-MA; that is, it can be confronted with the traditional methodology employed by the members of the MGFA. On the other hand, the reluctance of the *DRZW* to deal with the mentality of the soldiers (which cannot be easily penetrated merely with archival sources and traditional methodology) may well be rooted in a more or less conscious awareness of the potential political repercussions of such an investigation. Indeed, the conclusions which might be drawn from a frank and rigorous inquiry into the mental make-up of German troops during the Nazi regime could well prove to be as unsettling and politically uncomfortable as those one might expect from an additional volume devoted solely to the question of the Wehrmacht's role in the "Final Solution" (no such volume is planned). Namely, the realization that the young men of the Wehrmacht, who later became the founding generation of the new German Federal Republic, were deeply involved in the ideological assumptions and political actions of the Nazi regime. That is, not only that the lower ranks of the Wehrmacht were a crucial component of the realization of the "Final Solution," but that this mass complicity, precisely because it involved many hundreds of thousands, nay, millions of soldiers, was perforce reflected in attitudes (whether openly expressed or, more often, powerfully suppressed) among the young generation of the FRG, that very generation which soon emerged as the political, economic, and intellectual elite of West German democracy.

V

All this is not intended simply to criticize the *DRZW* which, as already noted, remains an admirable accomplishment. It is to say, however, that had this series sacrificed some of its detailed analyses in favor of a deeper examination of the soldiers' mentality, and had it devoted more attention to the connection between the war and the Holocaust, it would have greatly enhanced its historical value, quite apart from rendering a crucial educational and political service. For in Germany, memory still exercises a great deal of influence on people's attitudes, and history is still a major player on the political scene. And since war, ideology, and genocide have had such a prominent role in Germany's recent past, one would do much better to confront them head on than to sweep their nastier aspects under the carpet by retreating into the old defensive line of professional compartmentalization or invoking dusty arguments on the alleged function of the historian as a detached, objective "Wissenschaftler."

Hence I would like to end with a plea to young German scholars concerned with their nation's military history to go back to the example of some of their great predecessors of the interwar period and before; to approach their field with an open mind to developments in the historical profession at large, as well as in other social sciences, in Germany and especially abroad; to resist the debilitating, servile attachment to documents as the sole source of historical research, and to enhance their critical, literary, and political sensibilities; to realize that more (documents, footnotes, pages) is not always better, and that adherence to well-tried methods, though perhaps politically safe (both vis-à-vis the historical guild and on the national scene), does not necessarily bring one closer to the truth nor make for a clearer understanding of the past; and, finally, that while there is these days growing pressure in Germany to look back at past events with pride, there is still a great deal of room for explaining why such major portions of that past are so utterly shameful.

If German military historians wish to carve for themselves a significant and influential niche in the scholarly debate on the past, they can no longer afford to ignore the excellent work being done by their German and foreign colleagues. Whether this is in the area of oral or social history, whether it concerns eclectic works of great originality or major contributions to the cultural history of war, general works on the experience of whole societies in total war, or analyses of memory, commemoration, gender, and faith, and much, much more, there is now a vast array of scholarship that must inform any serious work on modern war.[18]

To be sure, this is not simply a German problem. In many other nations military history has been marginalized or has managed to marginalize itself. But I believe that in Germany, both due to the importance of the subject and because of certain institutional constraints and political sensibilities, the problem is even more urgent, and the present limitations and deficiencies are more visible. It is therefore, I would argue, high time for a new military history to emerge from Germany.

Notes

1. See, e.g., Azar Gat, *The Origins of Military Thought: From the Enlightenment to Clausewitz* (Oxford: 1989); Peter Paret, ed., *Makers of Modern Strategy: From Machiavelli to the Nuclear Age* (Princeton: 1986); and idem, *Understanding War: Essays on Clausewitz and the History of Military Power* (Princeton: 1992).
2. Eckart Kehr, *Battleship Building and Party Politics in Germany, 1894–1902* (Chicago: 1975); idem, *Economic Interest, Militarism and Foreign Policy* (Berkeley: 1977).
3. Hans Delbrück, *History of the Art of War,* 4 vols., trans. W. J. Renfroe, Jr., 2nd ed. (Lincoln and London: 1990 [*Geschichte der Kriegskunst im Rahmen der politischen Geschichte, 1900–1919*]).
4. Paul Fussell, *The Great War and Modern Memory* (New York: 1975); Samuel Hynes, *A War Imagined: The First World War and English Culture* (New York: 1991); Modris Eksteins, *Rites of Spring: The Great War and the Birth of the Modern Age*, 2nd ed. (New York: 1990); Robert Wohl, *The Generation of 1914* (Cambridge, Mass.: 1979); William H. McNeill, *The Pursuit of Power: Technology, Armed Force, and Society since A.D. 1000* (Oxford: 1983). See also the fascinating study, Norman F. Dixon, *On the Psychology of Military Incompetence* (London: 1976).
5. John Whiteclay Chambers II, "The New Military History: Myth and Reality," in *The Journal of Military History* 55 (July 1991): 395–406; Peter Paret, "The History of War and the New Military History," in his *Understanding War*, 209–226. See also: John Lynn, "Clio in Arms: The Role of the Military Variable in Shaping History," *Journal of Military History* 55 (January 1991): 83–95. Chambers cites many examples in his article. Some of the best works available now include: Geoffrey Parker, *The Military Revolution: Military Innovation and the Rise of the West, 1500–1800* (Cambridge, New York: 1988); John A. Lynn, ed., *Tools of War: Instruments, Ideas, and Institutions of Warfare, 1445–1871* (Urbana, Chicago: 1990); David Kaiser, *Politics and War: European Conflict from Philip II to Hitler* (Cambridge, Mass.: 1990); Brian M. Downing, *The Military Revolution and Political Change: Origins of Democracy and Autocracy in Early Modern Europe* (Princeton: 1992); David Ralston, *Importing the European Army: The Introduction of European Military Techniques and Institutions into the Extra-European World, 1600–1914* (Chicago: 1990); and related to that the superb study by Michael Adas, *Machines as the Measure of Men: Science, Technology, and Ideologies of Western Dominance* (Ithaca, London: 1989).
6. Klaus Theweleit, *Männerphantasien*, 2 vols. (Basel, Frankfurt am Main: 1977–78).
7. For some examples of the memoir literature, see Omer Bartov, *The Eastern Front: German Troops and the Barbarisation of Warfare* (London: 1985), 164, note 1; for chronicles of formations, see ibid., note 2. For examples of the technical approach, see Rudolf Absolon, *Wehrgesetz und Wehrdienst, 1935–45* (Boppard am Rhein: 1960); idem, *Die Personelle Ergänzung der Wehrmacht im Frieden und im Kriege* (Bundesarchiv-Zentralnachweisstelle, 1972); Georg Tessin, *Formationsgeschichte der Wehrmacht 1933–1939: Stäbe und Truppenteile des Heeres und der Luftwaffe* (Boppard am Rhein: 1959); Hans Meier-Welcker, *Untersuchungen zur Geschichte des Offizierkorps: Anciennität und Beförderung nach Leistung* (Stuttgart: 1962).

8. A good example is Basil H. Liddell Hart, *The German Generals Talk*, 2nd ed. (New York: 1979 [1948]).
9. See most recently Telford Taylor, *The Anatomy of the Nuremberg Trials* (Boston, New York: 1992).
10. The most important works are: Hans-Adolf Jacobsen, "Kommissarbefehl und Massenexekutionen sowjetischer Kriegsgefangener," in Hans Buchheim et al., *Anatomie des SS-Staates* (Olten: 1965) II: 161–279; Manfred Messerschmidt, *Die Wehrmacht im NS-Staat: Zeit der Indoktrination* (Hamburg: 1969); Klaus-Jürgen Müller, *Das Heer und Hitler* (Stuttgart: 1969), and idem, *Armee, Politik und Gesellschaft in Deutschland, 1933–45* (Paderborn: 1979); Christian Streit, *Keine Kameraden. Die Wehrmacht und die sowjetischen Kriegsgefangenen 1941–1945* (Stuttgart: 1978); Helmut Krausnick and Hans-Heinrich Wilhelm, *Die Truppe des Weltanschauungskrieges: Die Einsatzgruppen der Sicherheitspolizei und des SD 1938–1942* (Stuttgart: 1981); Gerd R. Ueberschär and Wolfram Wette, eds., *"Unternehmen Barbarossa": Der deutsche Überfall auf die Sowjetunion 1941* (Paderborn: 1984).
11. See, most notably, John Wheeler-Bennett, *The Nemesis of Power: The German Army in Politics 1918–1945*, 2nd ed. (London: 1980 [1953]); Gordon A. Craig, *The Politics of the Prussian Army 1640–1945*, 2nd ed. (London: 1978 [1955]); Alexander Dallin, *German Rule in Russia 1941–1945: A Study of Occupation Policies*, 2nd ed. (London: 1981 [1957]); F. L. Carsten, *The Reichswehr and Politics 1918–1933*, 2nd ed. (Berkeley and London: 1973 [1966]).
12. A sense of these developments can be gleaned from, e.g., Georg G. Iggers, *New Directions in European Historiography*, rev. ed. (Hanover, N.H.: 1984); Lynn Hunt, ed., *The New Cultural History* (Berkeley, London: 1989); Peter Burke, *History and Social Theory* (Ithaca, N.Y.: 1992); idem, *New Perspectives on Historical Writing* (University Park, Penn.: 1992).
13. *Das Deutsche Reich und der Zweite Weltkrieg*, herausgegeben vom Militärgeschichtlichen Forschungsamt. I: Wilhelm Deist, Manfred Messerschmidt, Hans-Erich Volkmann, and Wolfram Wette, *Ursachen und Voraussetzungen der deutschen Kriegspolitik* (Stuttgart: 1979); II: Klaus A. Maier, Horst Rohde, Bernd Stegemann, and Hans Umbreit, *Die Errichtung der Hegemonie auf dem europäischen Kontinent* (Stuttgart: 1979); III: Gerhard Schreiber, Bernd Stegemann, and Detlef Vogel, *Der Mittelmeerraum und Südeuropa: Von der "non belligeranza" Italiens bis zum Kriegseintritt der Vereinigten Staaten* (Stuttgart: 1984); IV: Horst Boog, Jürgen Förster, Joachim Hoffmann, Ernst Klink, Rolf-Dieter Müller, and Gerd R. Ueberschär, *Der Angriff auf die Sowjetunion* (Stuttgart: 1983); V/1: Bernhard R. Kroener, Rolf-Dieter Müller, and Hans Umbreit, *Organisation und Mobilisierung des deutschen Machtbereichs: Kriegsverwaltung, Wirtschaft und personelle Ressourcen 1939–1941* (Stuttgart: 1988); VI: Horst Boog, Werner Rahn, Reinhard Stumpf, and Bernd Wegner, *Der Globale Krieg: Die Ausweitung zum Weltkrieg und der Wechsel der Initiative 1941–1943* (Stuttgart: 1990). Planned volumes (working titles): V/2: *Organisation und Mobilisierung des deutschen Machtbereichs: Kriegsverwaltung, Wirtschaft und personelle Ressourcen 1942–1944/45*; VII: *Das Deutsche Reich in der Defensive: Der Krieg im Westen, im Mittelmeerraum und in Ostasien 1943–1944/45*; VIII: *Das Deutsche Reich in der Defensive: Der Krieg im Osten und Südosten 1943–1944/45*; IX/1: *Staat und Gesellschaft im Kriege: Innenpolitik und "Volksgemeinschaft" 1939–1944/45*; IX/2: *Staat und Gesellschaft im Kriege: Das militärische Instrument*; X: *Das Ende des Dritten Reiches*.
14. See, most recently, David Cesarani, ed., *The Final Solution: Origins and Implementation* (London, New York: 1994); Hannes Heer, "Killing Fields: The

Wehrmacht and the Holocaust in Belorussia, 1941–42," in this volume. See also, e.g., Christopher Browning, "Wehrmacht Reprisal Policy and the Murder of the Male Jews in Serbia," in Browning, *Fateful Months: Essays on the Emergence of the Final Solution* (New York, London: 1985), 39–56.

15. On this question, see Martin Broszat and Saul Friedländer, "A Controversy about the Historicization of National Socialism," in Peter Baldwin, ed., *Reworking the Past: Hitler, the Holocaust, and the Historians' Debate* (Boston: 1990), 102–134. Also see Ian Kershaw, *The Nazi Dictatorship: Problems and Perspectives of Interpretation*, 3rd ed. (London, New York: 1993), 80–107, 180–217.
16. See, e.g., Omer Bartov, *Hitler's Army: Soldiers, Nazis, and War in the Third Reich* (New York, Oxford: 1991); Theo Schulte, *The German Army and Nazi Policies in Occupied Russia* (Oxford, New York: 1989).
17. Some of these issues have been addressed by other historians but these do not receive any attention in the *DRZW*. See, e.g., Franz Seidler, *Prostitution, Homosexualität, Selbstverstümmelung: Probleme der deutschen Sanitätsführung 1939–1945* (Neckargemünd: 1977); Claudia Koonz, *Mothers in the Fatherland: Women, the Family and Nazi Politics* (New York: 1987); Renate Bridenthal, Atina Grossmann, and Marion Kaplan, eds., *When Biology Became Destiny: Women in Weimar and Nazi Germany* (New York: 1984); Jill Stephenson, "'Emancipation' and Its Problems: War and Society in Württemberg 1939–45," *European History Quarterly* 17 (1987): 345–365; and idem, Women in Nazi Society (London: 1975); Margot Schmidt, "Krieg der Männer—Chance der Frauen? Der Einzug von Frauen in die Büros der Thyssen AG," and Anne-Katrin Einfeldt, "Auskommen—Durchkommen—Weiterkommen: Weibliche Arbeitserfahrungen in der Bergarbeiterkolonie," both in Lutz Niethammer, ed., *"Die Jahre weiss man nicht, wo man die heute hinsetzen soll": Faschismuserfahrungen im Ruhrgebiet*, vol. 1 (Berlin, Bonn: 1983), 133–162, and 267–296, respectively.
18. Apart from works cited above, see also, e.g., Jay M. Winter, *The Great War and the British People* (Cambridge, Mass.: 1986); Jean-Jacques Becker, *1914: Comment les français sont entrés dans la guerre* (Paris: 1977); and idem, *Les français dans la grande-guerre* (Paris: 1983); Henry Rousso, *Le syndrome de Vichy: de 1944 à nos jours*, 2nd ed. (Paris: 1990); George L. Mosse, *Fallen Soldiers: Reshaping the Memory of the World Wars* (New York, Oxford: 1990); Pierre Nora, ed., *Les Lieux de mémoire*. Part 1: *La République* (1 vol., 1984); Part 2: *La Nation* (3 vols., 1986); Part 3: *Les Frances* (3 vols., 1992); Margaret Randolph Higonnet, Jane Jenson, Sonya Michel, and Margaret Collins Weitz, eds., *Behind the Lines: Gender and the Two World Wars* (New Haven, London: 1987); Annette Becker, *La guerre et la foi: De la mort à la mémoire, 1914–1930* (Paris: 1994).

– *Chapter 17* –

THE "UNBLEMISHED" WEHRMACHT

The Social History of a Myth

Klaus Naumann

The debate over the postwar perception of the German Wehrmacht's role in the Third Reich and especially in the war of extermination presently faces two problems. First of all, there is a fundamental objection to the notion that there is such a thing as a myth of the "unblemished" Wehrmacht. Proponents of that argument can point to scholarly works that have been appearing since the beginning of the 1980s. Studies by Manfred Messerschmidt, Klaus-Dieter Müller, Christian Streit, and the relevant publications of the Office for the Study of Military History *(Militärgeschichtliches Forschungsamt)* have deprived the alleged myth of any support in current scholarship. And yet that knowledge has merely the effect of postdating the problem considered in these pages. The fact that such myth-building clearly went on for at least thirty years remains to be explained; and there is still the question of what prevented both historians and the public from accepting the documentation that had been so meticulously assembled at the time of the Nuremberg trials.[1] But the objection is also undercut from a different angle. Surprisingly, the Hamburg exhibit on the "Crimes of the Wehrmacht from 1941 to 1944," which started in 1995, provoked during the past few years a resonance in the public that was readily understood as the "breaking of a taboo" or the rejection of a "final myth." In a certain sense both designations are justified. The myth of the "unblemished" Wehrmacht had already been discredited

Notes for this section begin on page 428.

among historians, but for the general public confronting pictorial and textual materials produced by eyewitnesses still caused a sea change in its perception. Certain aspects and implications of the subject had now come to public attention, and that process alone sufficed to lend them a new quality.

But what motivations prompted the building of the myth in the postwar years, and who were the protagonists in its propagation? In discussing this second complex of issues, existing literature, including scholarly writings, mention two sources above all others. First, self-exculpatory writings emanating from the military elite have received the most attention; second, explanations have hitherto concentrated on circumstances peculiar to the Cold War. Of course, both approaches raise a host of subsequent questions. If the legend's origin was intimately and causally connected to the Cold War, why did the false perception of the "unblemished" Wehrmacht persist into the 1980s and 1990s? And if it was the military elite (or the publicity that it attracted) that promoted that perception in a (transparent) pursuit of self-justification, does not such an interpretation underestimate the complexities of the war of extermination? The "socialized violence" of total war on the German side reached beyond the commanders, and from all that is known, the extermination operations can only be interpreted as a collective phenomenon involving the "little man" no less than the military leader.

In other words, sketching out a few preliminary questions leads to the conclusion that only a social history of the myth can reveal the circumstance under which it arose and account for its durability. In any event, the Wehrmacht myth (as it might be called) confronts us with a question that challenges us both methodologically and in terms of our political memories of the Federal Republic's history: How could such an interpretation, in all its modifications, undermine opposition strategies of enlightenment, outlast its historical and political competition, survive corrections, and, last but not least, even transcend generation-specific commitments? Second, it becomes clear that this myth is not merely multifunctional, hence not merely related to various purposes, motives, and emotions, but is, as it were, protean in form. Throughout the history of the Federal Republic it has taken on various meanings. Where initially it stressed the ostensibly "apolitical and supra-political" role of the Wehrmacht (or the "old" military elite), its "clean" and "chivalrous" way of waging war, and the secondary role it played (to Hitler) in decision-making in an effort to defend its professionalism and elite standards, in later years the myth's core came to emphasize the "mistreatment" of the simple soldier and the Wehrmacht's far remove from the great crimes of the regime, especially the Holocaust. Thus, the myth was constantly modified so as to mirror current public discourse regarding the National Socialist past. Yet a turning point was reached in the myth's evolution when it became clear that questions raised in earlier versions had implications far beyond their original military and historical context.

When it became obvious that the Wehrmacht as an organization had both participated in and promoted the war of extermination, the perception of those who had been involved in the crimes of the regime underwent a change. They were no longer merely thugs in concentration camps or SS-men in Einsatzgruppen but often "quite ordinary men" (Browning) in units under arms, mass organizations, government agencies, and occupation authorities. The role of the Wehrmacht—and the myth surrounding it—thus became enmeshed in a double frame of reference: first, there was the question of how the army had conducted itself as the military arm of the regime; second, there was the fact that eighteen million Germans had served in its ranks, thus making the Wehrmacht the locus of the most intimate contacts between the German population and the aggressive criminal acts of the regime. That being the case, the problems surrounding the Wehrmacht myth have necessarily undergone a change in recent times. As now became obvious, those problems involved both professional military men and the men in the ranks and they raise the issue of how to reconcile the myth's origins with its durability.

Discerning the connections linking past and present, military elite and the proverbial "common man," requires construing the history of the Federal Republic as that of a unique "postwar society." The war as waged by the Germans had as its prerequisite and basis a "social condition" (Reemtsma); one might with no less justification also designate what is commonly referred to as the "postwar period" as a special "social condition"—specifically, the condition of a society born of extreme violence—and thus open up the question of whether or to what extent that condition still obtains.[2]

In an effort to sketch out the aspects, variations, and functions of the myth, we shall, in the following pages, trace in a thematically compressed way various explicatory formulas: the *opportunistic formula* of the Cold War period; the *exculpatory formula* of a "but weakly secularized *Volk* community"[3] of the postwar years; the *integration formula* of social consolidation; and finally the *generation formula*, which made it possible for central elements of the myth to maintain their effectiveness even beyond the community of those who had experienced the war as participants. Finally, we shall address those two formulas that touch upon issues of meaning and existential interpretations. I refer to them provisionally as the *identification formula* of those who lost their fatherland and the *shock formula* of the experience of mass death. All these formulas vary in effectiveness, articulate different aspects of the myth, and target specific groups who share common experiences. But over and above that, how the society has digested the myth through political activity relative to the past, through seeing to the needs of the victims, through legislation addressing the consequences of the war, and in other ways gave it a relevance that reaches beyond individuals who were directly affected, has found expression in institutionalized symbolism, and has thus become a part of "collective memory."

The Opportunistic Formula of the Cold War

The inception of the Cold War, which was accompanied early on by interested military speculation, naturally offered an entire reservoir of possibilities for reinterpreting an ignominious, or at least irksome, past. Set pieces were already to be found in the National Socialist ideology involving a crusade in defense of Europe, in antibolshevism, and in rhetoric about occidental culture. In that sense the Cold War—and this should not be forgotten—was always also a specifically German war and not a Western import. All at once German troops were again in demand; at the same time politicians in the Federal Republic welcomed them as props to their claims of German sovereignty. Establishing an army in the Cold War required meeting three kinds of challenges all at once: the "never again" and "Hell, no, I won't go" sentiment had to be neutralized; the need for military reform had to be taken into account (no "new Wehrmacht," no "draft"); and finally, military experts, who were considered indispensable, had to be calmed down and co-opted. This tightrope-walking was successful in a way but had unforeseen consequences for dealing with the past politically. The old military types gained the potential for exerting pressure, of which they made liberal (and successful) use. In their view rearmament was acceptable only as part of a political deal in which historical issues were addressed. The "Magna Charta" of the founding of the Wehrmacht, the memorandum that former officers prepared at Adenauer's request at Eifelkloster Himmerod[4] made that much clear. The memorandum spoke of the "rehabilitation of the German soldier," of a "vote of confidence" *(Ehrenerklärung)* by the German Bundestag, of the "release of Germans being held as war criminals" (even the chief war criminals, Dönitz and Raeder, who were serving time in Spandau, were mentioned by name). The fifteen former Wehrmacht officers went on to demand that steps be taken to "reverse public opinion at home and abroad." The politicians largely accepted all of those demands.

And yet it would be rash to trace the entire myth back to the calculations of career military men, which were completely tactically motivated, and which now seemed to be succeeding. For the strategy of self-justification pursued by the old military was complemented by an already existing popular myth that fit nicely into the political climate, which did not have to be invented but rather could claim a certain plausibility. That was the myth that, in the final battles of 1945, the German army in the east had been on a rescue mission. It became the chief source of a kind of denazified perception of an anti-bolshevist "defensive action" by the Wehrmacht, which gained for the Wehrmacht a reputation as the "defenders of the homeland" (or "heroes in defeat") that would last through the *Historikerstreit* of 1986 and the "memorial year" of 1995. The final struggle on the Eastern front was the mythically charged theater of war in which—as in a tragedy of revenge and expiation—the dirty beginnings of the war in the east seemed to have been transfigured into a purified, unblemished final act.[5]

Stated briefly, the opportunistic formula of the Cold War favored bridges of continuity and forced compromises that would be inscribed in the collective memory of the West Germans, their state, and its institutions, and would have a lasting effect beyond the era of world-political confrontation.

The Exculpatory Formula of the Federal Republic's "We" Community

Apart from opportunistic political calculations, a search for exoneration was always inherent in the war stories, war images, and corresponding myth-making. The self-serving writings of professional military men played a large, but not an exclusive, role in that process. From the end of the 1940s, but especially during the first half of the 1950s, numerous memoirs were published.[6] At the same time, discussions between the old and new military about rearmament were becoming increasingly caustic. The widespread public attention paid to the few condemned war criminals in the amnesty campaigns of those years revealed something astonishing about the public mentality. Clearly a large number of people identified with those few "war criminals" based on their own past. The Deutsche Partei representative Hans-Joachim von Merkatz graphically expressed that sentiment of solidarity during a Bundestag debate on 8 November 1950: "Men such as Manstein, Kesselring, and others serving sentences in Landsberg or Werl—these men and we are one and the same. We have suffered by proxy what has been done to them in our stead."[7]

Condemning a few high-ranking officers as war criminals along with Hitler was tantamount to condemning the German soldiers "by proxy"; to grant them amnesty—which then happened—was to exonerate the Wehrmacht of war crimes. What had been carefully negotiated politically found expression in popular literature, movies, and so-called pocket novels, as well as in the death cult of the national days of mourning and the culture of memorialization in the 1950s and 1960s. The formula of exoneration stated that German soldiers had been neither criminals nor heroes. That not only had broad social and political relevance but at the same time operated within the dynamic of the family; it meant that a zone of taboo was established in familial communication which made it possible for *both* partners to live together without raising the "ultimate questions" of each other's wartime activities. The soldiers (the men) were given the status of victims—of the war, of circumstances, of fate, etc.—and thus took their place alongside the equally victimized civil population. As Friedrich Tenbruck has observed,[8] how destiny had dealt with someone *(Schicksalskategorien)* replaced not only "social ranks" but also moral distinctions. Still to be explained is how the sovereignty of the new state was symbolically enhanced by the extensive legislation of the early 1950s dealing with the war's aftermath[9] and by the integration of the aggrieved groups into the welfare state.[10] Norbert Frei—referring to aid for the dismissed civil servants of the Reich, the so-called "131s"—speaks of how the relevant laws functioned as a "bulwark" again allied attempts at reform.[11] War veterans lost their special status in terms of both their experiences and their rights to compensation. Mindful of Weimar,[12] one may welcome such a leveling of the playing field as an act marking a return to civilized life. The price, of course, was the myth of the "unblemished" Wehrmacht.

The Integration Formula of Social Consolidation

The "communicative hushing up" (Herman Lübbe) of the past—more precisely, of certain aspects of the past—was especially effective as a means of integrating postwar German society, which found itself confronting the truly unique problem of how a mass of people including persecuted and their persecutors, mass murderers, aides and accomplices, fellow travelers and accessories, those damaged by the war, those who got away clean, and the "guiltless" could live together in the future. Exoneration and denial were two possible strategies assiduously resorted to. Another approach was required for dealing with the following problem. Although in one way or another everyone might declare himself a victim, how could a new beginning as a democracy or as a national family possibly be achieved with a population that had been deceived, defeated, exhausted, and demoralized? In addition to turning aside from old guilts and old beliefs, there had to be something with which one could connect, something that proved "valid." That did not have to be praise of the autobahns or the admissions in the early 1950s that National Socialism had really been an inherently good thing that had merely been badly put into practice. It was more (and for a longer time) a question of maintaining secondary virtues and professional standards, or of simply preserving life and survival in such a way that those virtues, once denazified, could be made part of a new framework of values, goals, and life in general.

As far as the politics of the past was concerned, this also brought risks and side-effects, as is clear from the public image of German prisoners of war (especially those who returned from the east late). In the public perception of the 1950s, these men mutated from "losers" hard to identify with and half-starved "images of misery" into robust, tough "survivors," fathers of families promising normality and restored male authority figures to whom the task of reconstruction might safely be entrusted.[13] The same, incidentally, was true of refugees and exiles who, but a few years after being completely uprooted, were permitted to attest to the strength of social integration and the will to rebuild.

Here we take note of the symbolic function of such group destinies or achievements. Certainly the war years had been "lost years," and yet they equipped survivors with an appreciation of elementary experiences and capabilities—of achievement, of doing one's "damned duty," of camaraderie, of an ability to adapt, of a willingness to sacrifice, and of flexibility.[14] This disillusioned "pathos of sobriety," which is repeatedly singled out for comment with reference to the postwar years, provided common ground for civilians, former soldiers, and probably also the younger professional officers. Nevertheless, there is—even today—something fundamentally unstable about a belief system that denies the need to reflect further on "elementary" things, on things timelessly valid, on social and political values. This attitude is reflected in that aspect of the Wehrmacht myth that stresses the ostensibly supra-historical skills and virtues of making war, which—as *basic functions*—are regarded as indispensable to, even synonymous with, the Bundeswehr. That can involve attaching primary importance to operational and technical abilities as much as enthroning the virtues of comradeship. Born of the understandable skepticism deriving from wartime experiences, this "professionalism" plays a role in present-day notions about the history of the military profession and is present in the conflicts among the military "(neo)-traditionalists," "technocrats," and "reformers"—in other words in the German military culture of today.

Generational Formulas of Rejecting War

Jan Philipp Reemtsma has pointed to surprising areas of agreement between the generations—commonalities that owe their existence to the "pacifist sentiment."[15] Shared rejection of, even emotional revulsion against, the last war, or any war, created a blind spot where denial and generalization could join hands. Both attitudes revealed an impaired capacity for moral judgment whenever they blithely equated the horrors of the war of extermination with those of any other war ("c'est la guerre")—a sweeping generalization that has the added effect of surrendering to cynicism or of consigning to the realm of illusion civilized efforts to circumscribe war with legalities and the pursuit and punishment of offenses.

One surprising aspect of "pacifist sentiment" is that it established not merely commonalities between the generations but also communicative alliances within the generation that had fought the war. For here was a major difference from World War I: in the wake of a total war, former front-line fighters could no longer claim to be special. The interpretive monopoly that politically committed former front-line soldiers managed to acquire in the 1920s was replaced in the second postwar period by an attitude of "never again" embracing both soldiers and the civilian population, which is repeatedly expressed in the literature. Thus a revival of the polarization between pacifists and the military of the Weimar years was avoided, yet the building of a new consensus contributed to an unhistorical public image of the war—an effect that impacted the perception of the Wehrmacht.

Identification Formulas of Those Who Lost Their Fatherland

The irrational thinking and emotions that attend such conflicts suggest that the Wehrmacht myth cannot be fully explained based on its political utility or as strategies of resistance and integration. And yet, if we take seriously both the war and the postwar years as unique "social conditions," it should be clear that the building of this myth and its durability also reference experiences of loss that are largely resistant to rational discourse. Various kinds of loss are involved: on the one hand, there is the loss of any promise of meaning, of something to identify with, of convictions; on the other, the sense of loss deriving from a deep, traumatizing wound. The reflexive consternation with which the Hamburg exhibit was received can be summed up in the words of a letter from Austria to the organizers: "It looks as if all the old warriors saw nothing, heard nothing, and so could say nothing. They want only peace and quiet. That is understandable from a human point of view if we fought and suffered only to have it turn out that it was all for nothing and we were deceived by a criminal regime. Then the Wehrmacht gets to wear a halo."[16]

The observation is nicely put: if it turns out "that it was all for nothing," the Wehrmacht gets a "halo." That should be noted without a hint of irony. In fact, for many in the war the Wehrmacht became a screen on which to project one's unhappy consciousness, a refuge for the most varied expectations—certainly not only expectations of an "inner emigration." In the senselessness of war, the Wehrmacht appeared to be the final authority that might guarantee that things still made "sense." It represented a source of meaning capable of providing the experience of comradeship in battle as well as an imaginary substitute for the fatherland.[17]

One might extend this line of interpretation and suppose that this has something to do with attitudes regarding life and society peculiar to postwar society. On the one hand, people learned to feel at home in rebuilding, pursuing their careers, establishing families; on the other, that large totality familiar to other societies as "the nation" was missing. The existence of the Federal Republic, which is today often described in retrospect as "postnational," was obviously experienced by many with feelings of emptiness and loss. For some it may have been satisfying;[18] others sought substitutes for the nation in something beyond "constitution patriotism."

The generalizing rhetoric adopted by the exhibit's critics[19] is perhaps a latter-day expression of this symptom. Anyone who talks about “the Wehrmacht,” it is said, in reality means something quite different and much more embracing—eighteen million soldiers, or “the Bundeswehr,” or an “entire generation,” or “the solidarity of our *Volk*.” In the Bundestag debate of 13 March 1997, Alfred Dregger, who originated the last of the foregoing formulations, expressed dramatically the dimension that is touched whenever the “Wehrmacht” complex is mentioned: “The soldiers of the Second World War are not an isolated group of our people but rather represent the entire population of that time. Almost all men were drafted. Of course, the soldiers’ mothers, sisters, daughters, girlfriends, and wives were also affected. Thus the issue here is our relationship to an entire generation of our people.”

This formulation, like the Salzburg letter cited above, must be taken at face value. It represents a straw man argument, because if talking about “the Wehrmacht” means talking about an “entire generation of our people,” “the entire population,” then it is clear that any criticism of “the” Wehrmacht or “the” German soldiers (possibly even “the Bundeswehr”)[20] simultaneously calls into question the conduct of the German population, the self-image of the broken and crushed nation. Put bluntly, the identification formula can be described as a stubborn, sometimes desperate, sometimes resentful attempt to save a shared source of meaning in the face of experienced senselessness.

Shock Formulas of Experiencing Death

Often this kind of thinking by identification is controlled by a much more elementary experience of shock and loss—the experience of death, more precisely, of mass death. Gruesome, virtually without reference in human experience, following a war of aggression and extermination, mass death became woven into guilt feelings, a loss of meaning, and experiences of impotence that contrasted sharply to the Wehrmacht soldiers’ political and habitual proximity to National Socialism, which in its time had carried the troops “from victory to victory.” Recent analyses of the letters written by soldiers show clearly racist attitudes and a propensity to violence that were often able to leap over the boundaries separating wartime “normality” from “terror.” And now it turned out that all this was not merely pointless but reprehensible (if not criminal) as well and had exacted as its price innumerable victims and casualties that could in no sense be “made right.” No wonder that postwar German societies—aside from repression and denial—had difficulty in dealing with symbols of mass death and with the rituals of grief involved in its memorializing. "The experience of mass death in the Second World War lies like a 'lava flow' (Koselleck) in all the survivors. It became an experience frozen outside of time.... There was, to be sure, a typical memorializing of the dead, and yet death lacked a public face. Trafficking with the dead was set aside, not really repressed into the unconscious, but ... haphazardly cordoned off—a half-conscious presence."[21]

The results of this practice, which, unlike in Weimar, managed to avoid the politicization of front-line fighters and their death cult, were "vagabond" experiences[22] that shunned social discourse. Suffering incurred in public life found itself consigned to the private sphere and to silence, thus playing itself out in comic, and often tragic, ways. I am arguing that clinging to the myth of an "unblemished" Wehrmacht often implies an insistence on the existential "purity" and moral "innocence" of death in war. In that sense the Federal Republic with its Wehrmacht myth is still paying a symbolic price for the (surprisingly smooth) integration of those who had participated in the war and the political neutralization of their frightening experiences with death.

Thus it is possible to recognize a bit of the Federal Republic's social history in the myth of the "unblemished" Wehrmacht—a perspective on a postwar period that has not yet ended. I shall not go so far as to call the Wehrmacht myth a component in the Federal Republic's "foundation mythology." Nevertheless, it played no small role in finding a way out of violence and in providing surrogate meaning. The fact that a society develops constructs that mock victims, exonerate perpetrators, declare many accomplices incompetent to answer for their actions, and still exerts its influence on those born after the events shows more clearly than many other things just how great the inherent self-doubt of this postwar republic must have been about whether and how a civil society could ever be possible again.[23]

—Translated by Roy Shelton

Notes

1. See Omer Bartov, "German Soldiers and the Holocaust: Historiography, Research and Implications" in *History and Memory* 9, no. 1–2 (1997): 162–188.
2. Cf. Klaus Naumann, "Nachkrieg. Vernichtungskrieg, Wehrmacht und Militär in der deutschen Wahrnehmung nach 1945" in *Mittelweg 36*, vol. 3 (1997): 11–25.
3. Norbert Frei, *Vergangenheitspolitik. Die Anfänge der Bundesrepublik und die NS-Vergangenheit* (Munich: 1996), 399.
4. Cf. Hans-Jürgen Rautenberg and Norbert Wiggershaus, "Die 'Himmeroder Denkschrift' vom Oktober 1950," in *Militärgeschichtliche Mitteilungen* 1 (1977): 135–206.
5. See Omer Bartov, *Murder in Our Midst: The Holocaust, Industrial Killing, and Representation* (Oxford, New York: 1996), esp. 71ff; Robert G. Moeller, "War Stories: The Search for a Usable Past in the Federal Republic of Germany," in *American Historical Review* (October 1996): 1008–1048; and Klaus Naumann, *Der Krieg als Text. 1945 im kulturellen Gedächtnis der Presse* (Hamburg: 1998), 124ff.
6. See Gotthard Breit, *Das Staats- und Gesellschaftsbild deutscher Generäle bei der Weltkriege im Spiegel ihrer Memoiren* (Boppard am Rhein: 1973); Rolf Düsterberg, *Soldat und Kriegserlebnis. Deutsche militärische Erinnerungsliteratur (1945–1961) zum Zweiten Weltkrieg. Motive, Begriffe, Wertungen.* Post-doctoral thesis (Osnabrück: 1998).
7. Frei, *Vergangenheitspolitik*, 202.
8. Friedrich H. Tenbruck, "Alltagsnormen und Lebensgefühle in der Bundesrepublik," in *Die zweite Republik. 25 Jahre Bundesrepublik Deutschlandeine Bilanz*, ed. Richard Löwenthal and Hans-Peter Schwarz (Stuttgart: 1974), 290.
9. See Hans Günther Hockerts, "Integration der Gesellschaft. Gründungskrise und Sozialpolitik in der frühen Bundesrepublik," in *Entscheidung für den Westen. Vom Besatzungsstatut zur Souveränität der Bundesrepublik 1949–1955*, ed. Manfred Funke (Bonn: 1988) and Lutz Wiegand, "Kriegsfolgengesetzgebung in der Bundesrepublik Deutschland" in *Archiv für Sozialgeschichte* 35 (1995): 71–90.
10. Michael L. Hughes, *Shouldering the Burdens of Defeat: West Germany and the Reconstruction of Social Justice* (Chapel Hill, London: 1999).
11. Frei, *Vergangenheitspolitik*, 79.
12. See James Diehl, *The Thanks of the Fatherland: German Veterans after the Second World War* (Chapel Hill, London: 1993).
13. See Frank Biess, "Vom 'Opfer' zum 'Überlebenden' des Totalitarismus: Westdeutsche Reaktionen auf die Rückkehr der Kriegsgefangenen aus der Sowjetunion, 1945–1955" in *Kriegsgefangenschaft im Zweiten Weltkrieg*, ed. Gunter Bischof and Rüdiger Overmans (1999).
14. See Elisabeth Domansky and Jutta de Jong, *Die langen Schatten des Krieges. Deutsche Lebens-Geschichten* (Book manuscript: 1998) for a brief treatment of this point.
15. Jan Philipp Reemtsma, "Trauma und Moral. Einige Überlegungen zum Krieg als Zustand einer kriegführenden Gesellschaft und zum pazifistischen Affekt," in idem, *Mord am Strand. Allianzen von Zivilisation und Barbarei* (Hamburg: 1998).
16. Quoted in the Salzburg program guide, 3.

17. On this point see Stephen G. Fritz, *Frontsoldaten: The German Soldier in World War II* (Kentucky: 1998), ch. 7.
18. For example, Karl Dietrich Bracher, who coined the term in *Frankfurter Allgemeine Zeitung*, 29 December 1986.
19. Hannes Heer, "Von der Schwierigkeit, einen Krieg zu beenden. Reaktionen auf die Ausstellung 'Vernichtungskrieg. Verbrechen der Wehrmacht 1941 bis 1944'" in *Mittelweg 36*, vol. 6 (1997): 65–79.
20. See Karl Feldmeyer, *Frankfurter Allgemeine Zeitung*, 29 December 1997: "Ein Mangel an Augenmaß."
21. Michael Geyer, "Das Stigma der Gewalt und das Problem der nationalen Identität in Deutschland," in *Von der Aufgabe der Freiheit. Politische Verantwortung und bürgerliche Gesellschaft im 19. und 20. Jahrhundert*, ed. Christian Jansen et al. (Berlin: 1995).
22. Klaus Latzel, *Deutsche Soldaten—nationalsozialistischer Krieg? Kriegserlebnis—Kriegserfahrung 1939–1945* (Paderborn: 1998), 370ff.
23. On the problem of an end without ending, see Klaus Naumann, "Die Frage nach dem Ende. Von der unbestimmten Dauer der Nachkriegszeit," in *Mittelweg 36*, vol. 8 (1999): 21–32.

CONTRIBUTORS

Truman Anderson is the Executive Director of the Stuart Family Foundation in Lake Forest, Illinois, and a former lecturer in history at the London School of Economics. He is currently at work on a monograph about the German occupation of Ukraine. His other publications include "A Hungarian Vernichtungskrieg? Hungarian Troops and the Partisan War in Heeresgebiet Süd, 1942," in *Militärgeschichtliche Mitteilungen* (forthcoming 2000), and "Germans, Ukrainians and Jews: Ethnic Politics in Heeresgebiet Süd," in *War in History* (forthcoming 2000).

Omer Bartov is John P. Birkelund Professor of European History at Brown University. He was a Visiting Fellow at the Davis Center, Princeton University, and a Junior Fellow at Harvard's Society of Fellows. Bartov is the author of numerous books and articles on Nazi Germany, interwar France, and the Holocaust. His works include *The Eastern Front, 1941–1945: German Troops and the Barbarisation of Warfare* (1986); *Hitler's Army* (1991); *Murder in Our Midst* (1996); and *Mirrors of Destruction: War, Genocide, and Modern Identity* (2000).

Volker R. Berghahn is the Seth Low Professor of History at Columbia University. He has written widely on German history and German-American relations. His books include *Modern Germany* (1982), *Germany and the Approach of War in 1914* (2nd edition 1993), and *Imperial Germany, 1871–1914* (1994).

Bernd Boll, historian and specialist in museum pedagogy, is a research fellow for the exhibition "Vernichtungskrieg. Verbrechen der Wehrmacht 1941 bis 1944" organized by the Hamburg Institute for Social Research. He has published "*... das wird man nie mehr los." Ausländische Zwangsarbeiter in der Offenburger Kriegswirtschaft 1939–1945* (1994).

Christian Gerlach received his Ph.D. from the Zentrum für Antisemitismusforschung at the Technische Universität Berlin. He is the author of *Krieg, Ernährung, Völkermord* (1998) and *Kalkulierte Morde. Die deutsche Wirtschafts- und Vernichtungspolitik in Weißrußland 1941* (1999).

Michael Geyer is professor of contemporary European history at the University of Chicago. He has published, inter alia, *Deutsche Rüstungspolitik, 1860–1980* (1984), "The Stigma of Violence: Nationalism and War in Twentieth Century Germany" in *German Studies Review* (Winter 1992), *Resistance Against the Third Reich* (ed. with John W. Boyer, 1994), and "Germany or: The Twentieth Century as History," in *South Atlantic Quarterly* 96 (4) (1997): 663–702.

Hannes Heer has worked as historian, film director, and research fellow at the Hamburg Institute for Social Research. His books include *Burgfrieden oder Klassenkampf* (1971); *Ernst Thälmann* (1975); *"Als ich 9 Jahre alt war, kam der Krieg"* (1983); *Tote Zonen* (1999). He was the director of the exhibition "Vernichtungskrieg. Verbrechen der Wehrmacht 1941 bis 1944."

Bernd Hüppauf is professor in the Department of German at New York University. His works include *Ansichten vom Krieg* (1984), "Kriegsfotografie an der Schwelle zum Neuen Sehen," in *Annäherungsversuche,* ed. Bedrich Loewenstein (1992); "Krieg, Gewalt und Moderne," in *Jahrbuch für Literatur und Politik in Deutschland* 1 (1994); *War, Violence, and the Modern Condition* (ed., 1997).

Walter Manoschek teaches at the Institut für Staats- und Politikwissenschaft at the University of Vienna and contributed to the exhibition "Vernichtungskrieg. Verbrechen der Wehrmacht 1941 bis 1944" organized by the Hamburg Institute for Social Research. He has published, inter alia, *"Serbien ist judenfrei." Militärische Besatzungspolitik und Judenvernichtung in Serbien 1941/42* (1993), and, in collaboration with Gabriele Anderl, *Gescheiterte Flucht. Das Schicksal des jüdischen Kladovo-Transportes auf dem Weg nach Palästina 1939–1944* (1993).

Mark Mazower is professor of history at the University of London. His works include *Greece and the Inter-War Economic Crisis* (1991); *Inside Hitler's Greece: The Experience of Occupation, 1941–1944* (1993); *Dark Continent: Europe's Twentieth Century* (1999).

Manfred Messerschmidt was research director of history at the Militärgeschichtliches Forschungsamt Freiburg from 1970 to 1988. His publications include *Die Wehrmacht im NS-Staat. Zeit der Indoktrination* (1969) and "Rassistische Motivationen bei der Bekämpfung des Widerstandes in Serbien?" in *Faschismus und Rassismus* (1992).

Klaus Naumann, historian and journalist, is a research fellow at the Hamburg Institute for Social Research. He has published articles on German postwar history and the military elite, and *Der Krieg als Text. Das jahr 1945 im kulturellen Gedächtnis der Presse* (1998).

Jan Philipp Reemtsma is professor for modern German literature at the University of Hamburg and the founder and head of the Hamburg Institute for Social Research. His works include *Folter* (ed., 1991), *More Than a Champion* (1998), *Mord am Strand. Allianzen von Zivilisation und Barbarei* (1998), and *In the Cellar* (1999).

Hans Safrian, historian, is a research fellow for the exhibition "Vernichtungskrieg. Verbrechen der Wehrmacht 1941 bis 1944" organized by the Hamburg Institute for Social Research, and Pearl Resnick Fellow at the Research Institute of the United States Holocaust Memorial Museum, Washington, D.C. He has published, inter alia, *Die Eichmann-Männer* (1993).

Theo J. Schulte is senior lecturer in European history at Anglia Polytechnic University in Cambridge. His books include *The German Army and Nazi Policies in Occupied Russia* (1989) and *War Crimes in Nazi Europe and War Crimes Trials* (forthcoming).

Christian Streit is a high school teacher. His most important publication is *Keine Kameraden. Die Wehrmacht und die sowjetischen Kriegsgefangenen* (3rd rev. ed., 1991).

Margers Vestermanis, professor of history at the University of Riga, is director of the documentation center "Die Juden in Lettland." He has published *Die Wehrmacht im Einsatz* (1973); "Der lettische Anteil an der Endlösung," in *Die Schatten der Vergangenheit,* ed. Uwe Backes et al. (1990); "Der Holocaust in-Lettland" in *Verdrängung, Vertreibung und Vernichtung der Juden unter dem Nationalsozialismus,* ed. Arno Herzig et al. (1992).

APPENDIX

Charts and Maps

Upper Command Echelon

THE FÜHRER

SUPREME COMMAND OF THE ARMED FORCES (OKW)
Armed Forces Command Staff
(Theaters of War: Norway, Finland, Africa, Western Europe, and the Balkans)

ARMY HIGH COMMAND (OKH)
(Eastern Theater)

AIR FORCE HIGH COMMAND

NAVAL HIGH COMMAND

GENERAL STAFF

General Quartermaster
Intelligence
Personnel
Operations
Organization
Other

Army Groups
Armies
Corps
Divisions

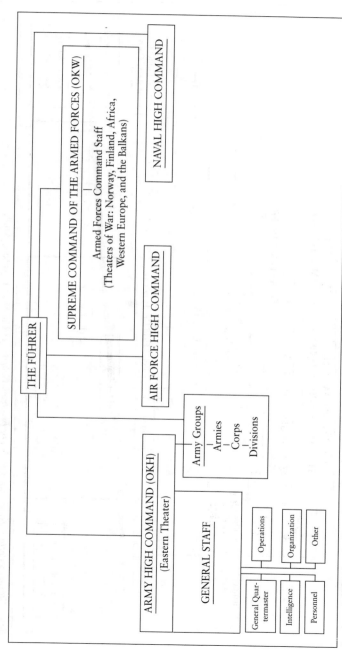

Source: Alexander Dallin, *Deutsche Herrschaft in Rußland 1941–1945* (Düsseldorf: Droste Verlag, 1958), 44.

Organization of Military Occupation Forces in 1943

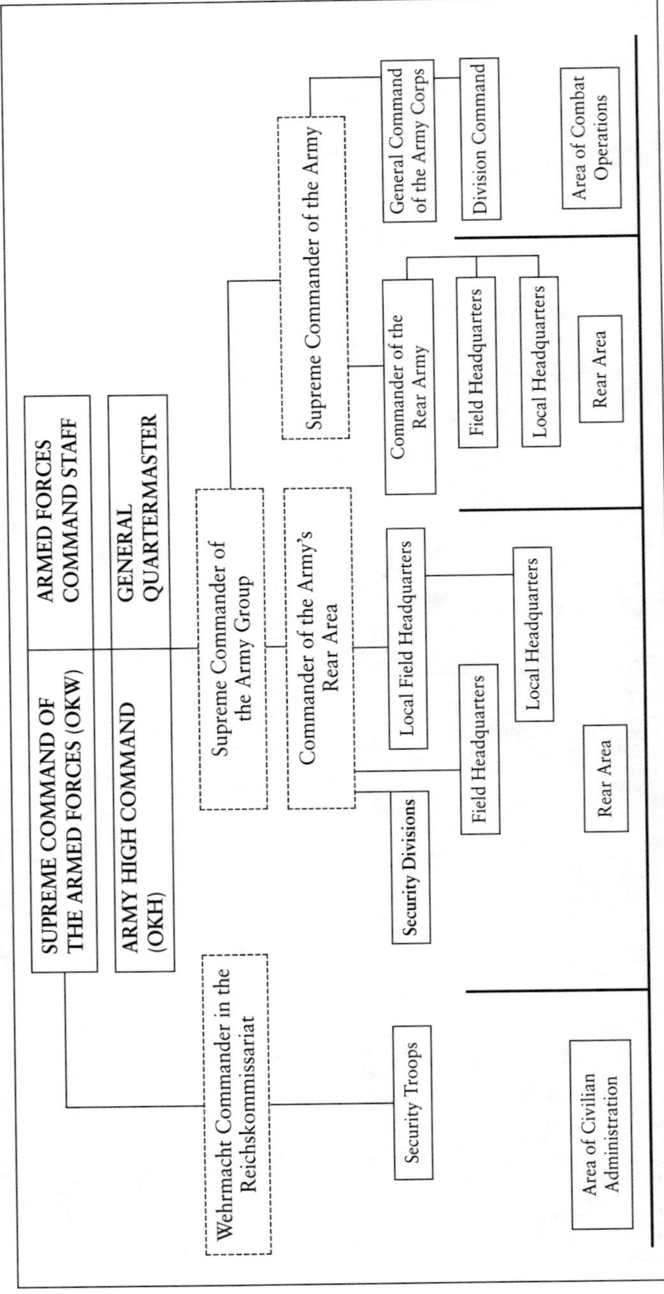

Source: *Europa unterm Hakenkreuz*, vol. 5: *Die besetzten Gebiete der UdSSR*, ed. Norbert Müller (Berlin: Deutscher Verlag der Wissenschaften, 1991), 619.

Serbia under German Military Administration, 1941–42

Ukraine: Area of Operation of the 6th Army, 1941–42

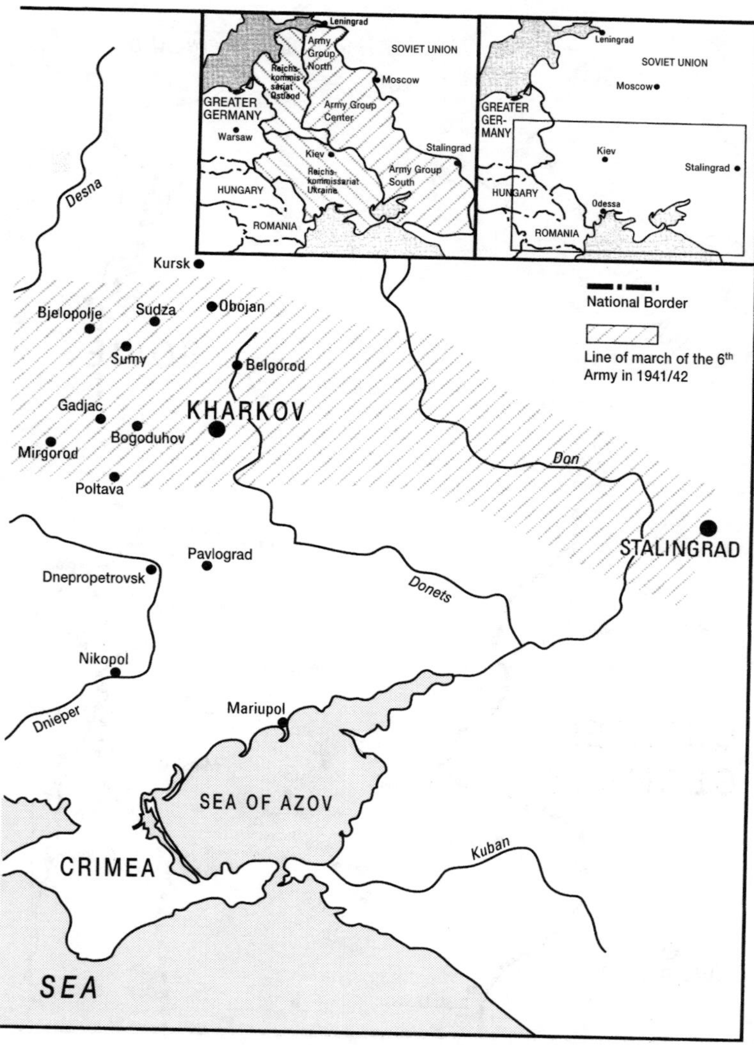
Leningrad
Army Group North
SOVIET UNION
Reichs-kommis-sariat Ostland
Moscow
GREATER GERMANY
Army Group Center
Warsaw
Stalingrad
Kiev
Reichs-kommissariat Ukraine
Army Group South
HUNGARY
ROMANIA
Leningrad
SOVIET UNION
Moscow
GREATER GER-MANY
Kiev
Stalingrad
HUNGARY
Odessa
ROMANIA
Desna
Kursk
National Border
Bjelopolje
Sudza
Obojan
Sumy
Belgorod
Line of march of the 6th Army in 1941/42
Gadjac
KHARKOV
Bogoduhov
Mirgorod
Don
Poltava
STALINGRAD
Pavlograd
Dnepropetrovsk
Donets
Nikopol
Mariupol
Dnieper
SEA OF AZOV
Kuban
CRIMEA
SEA

Soviet Union: Area of Operation of Army Group Center, 1941–44

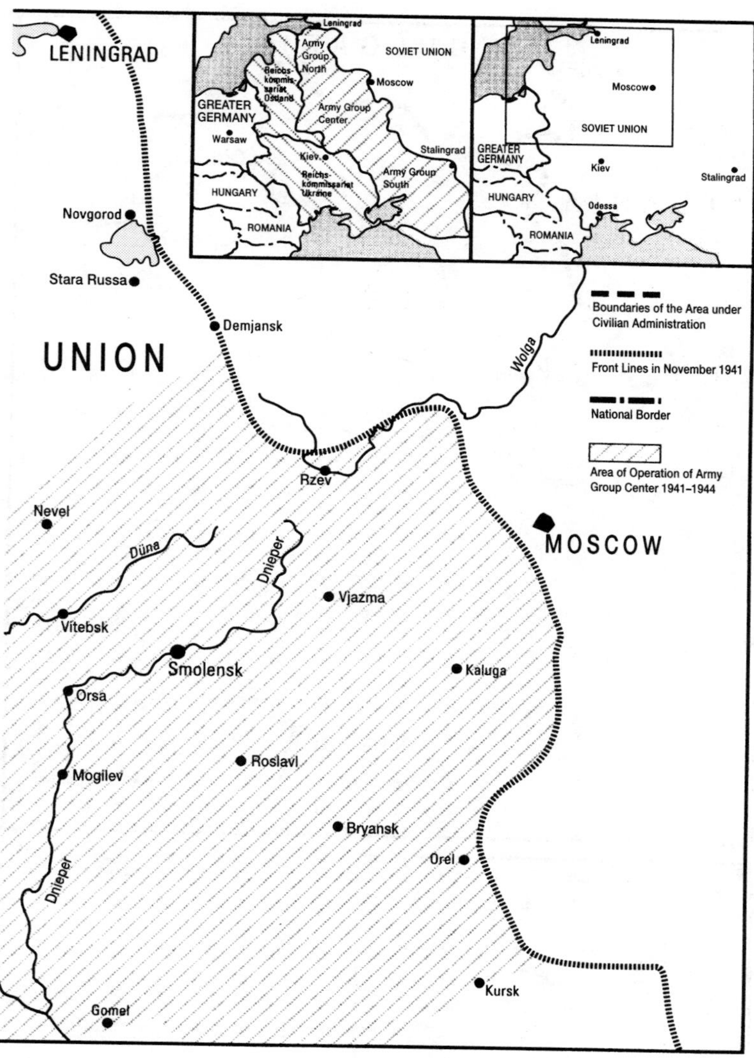
LENINGRAD
Novgorod
Stara Russa
Demjansk
UNION
Rzev
Nevel
Düna
Dnieper
Vitebsk
Smolensk
Orsa
Vjazma
Kaluga
MOSCOW
Wolga
Roslavl
Mogilev
Bryansk
Orel
Dnieper
Kursk
Gomel
Leningrad
Army Group North
SOVIET UNION
Reichs-kommis-sariat Ostland
Moscow
GREATER GERMANY
Army Group Center
Warsaw
Stalingrad
Kiev
Reichs-kommissariat Ukraine
Army Group South
HUNGARY
ROMANIA
Leningrad
Moscow
SOVIET UNION
GREATER GERMANY
Kiev
Stalingrad
HUNGARY
Odessa
ROMANIA
Boundaries of the Area under Civilian Administration
Front Lines in November 1941
National Border
Area of Operation of Army Group Center 1941–1944

Greece under German Occupation

Civitella and the Surrounding Area

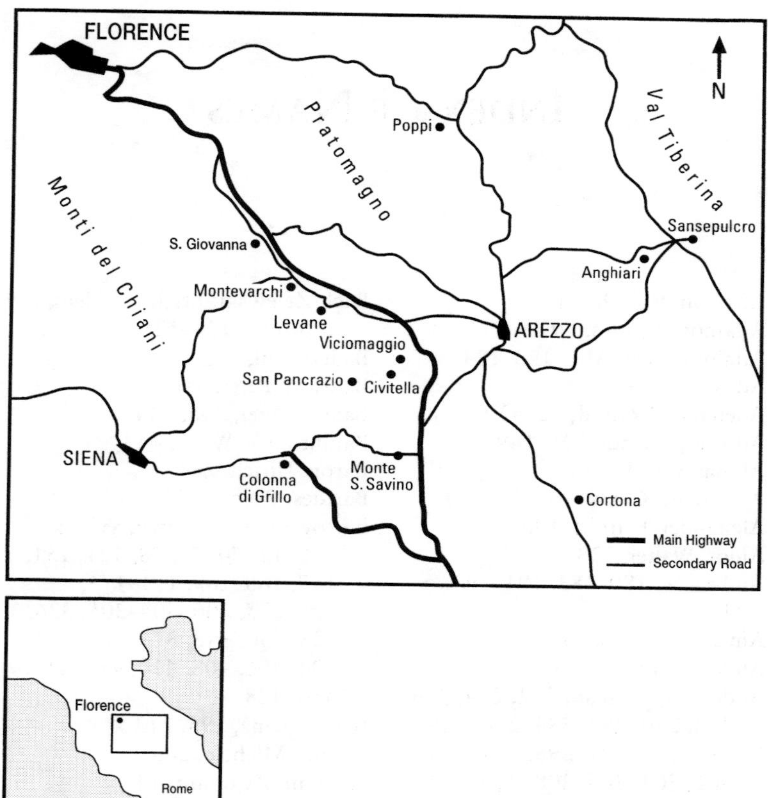

Index of Names

Index of Places